THE HISTORICAL JESUS IN CONTEXT

PRINCETON READINGS IN RELIGIONS

———

Donald S. Lopez, Jr., Editor

TITLES IN THE SERIES

———

Religions of India in Practice edited by Donald S. Lopez, Jr.

Buddhism in Practice edited by Donald S. Lopez, Jr.

Religions of China in Practice edited by Donald S. Lopez, Jr.

Religions of Tibet in Practice edited by Donald S. Lopez, Jr.

Religions of Japan in Practice edited by George J. Tanabe, Jr.

Asian Religions in Practice: An Introduction
edited by Donald S. Lopez, Jr.

Religions of Late Antiquity in Practice edited by Richard Valantasis

Tantra in Practice edited by David Gordon White

Judaism in Practice edited by Lawrence Fine

Religions of the United States in Practice: Volumes 1 and 2
edited by Colleen McDannell

Religions of Asia in Practice: An Anthology
edited by Donald S. Lopez, Jr.

The Historical Jesus in Context edited by Amy-Jill Levine,
Dale C. Allison, Jr., and John Dominic Crossan

THE HISTORICAL

JESUS

• IN CONTEXT •

Amy-Jill Levine, Dale C. Allison Jr., and

John Dominic Crossan, Editors

PRINCETON READINGS IN RELIGIONS

PRINCETON UNIVERSITY PRESS

PRINCETON AND OXFORD

Library of Congress Cataloging-in-Publication Data

The historical Jesus in context / A.J. Levine, Dale C. Allison, Jr., and John Dominic Crossan, editors.
p.   cm.   —(Princeton readings in religions)
Includes bibliographical references and index.
ISBN-13: 978-0-691-00991-9 (hardcover : alk. paper)—ISBN-13: 978-0-691-00992-6
(pbk. : alk. paper)
ISBN-10: 0-691-00991-0 (hardcover : alk. paper)—ISBN-10: 0-691-00992-9 (pbk. : alk. paper)
1. Jesus Christ—Historicity. I. Levine, Amy-Jill, 1956– II. Allison, Dale C. III. Crossan,
John Dominic. IV. Series.
BT303.2.H4845 2004
232.9'08—dc22   2006012027

British Library Cataloging-in-Publication Data is available

This book has been composed in Berkeley

Printed on acid-free paper. ∞

pup.princeton.edu

Printed in the United States of America

1 3 5 7 9 10 8 6 4 2

PRINCETON READINGS

IN RELIGIONS

Princeton Readings in Religions is a series of anthologies on the religions of the world, representing the significant advances that have been made in the study of religions in the last thirty years. The sourcebooks used by previous generations of students, whether for Judaism and Christianity or for the religions of Asia and the Middle East, placed a heavy emphasis on "canonical works." Princeton Readings in Religions provides a different configuration of texts in an attempt better to represent the range of religious practices, placing particular emphasis on the ways in which texts have been used in diverse contexts. The volumes in the series therefore include ritual manuals, hagiographical and autobiographical works, popular commentaries, and folktales, as well as some ethnographic material. Many works are drawn from vernacular sources. The readings in the series are new in two senses. First, very few of the works contained in the volumes have ever been made available in an anthology before; in the case of the volumes on Asia, few have even been translated into a Western language. Second, the readings are new in the sense that each volume provides new ways to read and understand the religions of the world, breaking down the sometimes misleading stereotypes inherited from the past in an effort to provide both more expansive and more focused perspectives on the richness and diversity of religious expressions. The series is designed for use by a wide range of readers, with key terms translated and technical notes omitted. Each volume also contains a substantial introduction by a distinguished scholar in which the histories of the traditions are outlined and the significance of each of the works is explored.

The Historical Jesus in Context is the twelfth volume in the series. It has been designed, organized, and edited by renowned New Testament scholars Amy-Jill Levine, Dale Allison, and John Dominic Crossan. The twenty-nine contributors include many of the world's leading scholars of biblical studies, Jewish studies, and classical studies. Each scholar has provided a translation of a key work or set of works, including inscriptions, myths, miracle stories, parables, and liturgical texts, which together provide a rich background for the understanding both of the enigmatic figure of Jesus and of the earliest stories told about him. Each chapter begins with a substantial introduction in which the contributor discusses the history and influence of the work or genre, identifying points of particular difficulty or interest. Amy-Jill Levine opens the book with a general introduction to the study of Jesus in his historical and cultural context.

The volumes *Zen in Practice* and *Islam in South Asia in Practice* are forthcoming in the series.

Donald S. Lopez Jr.
Series Editor

CONTENTS

Princeton Readings in Religions   v
Contributors   ix
Acknowledgments   xi

Introduction · *Amy-Jill Levine*   1

1. Archaeological Contributions to the Study of Jesus and the Gospels
· *Jonathan L. Reed*   40
2. Josephus on John the Baptist and Other Jewish Prophets of
Deliverance · *Craig A. Evans*   55
3. *Abba* and Father: Imperial Theology in the Contexts of Jesus and
the Gospels · *Mary Rose D'Angelo*   64
4. Miraculous Conceptions and Births in Mediterranean Antiquity
· *Charles H. Talbert*   79
5. *First* and *Second Enoch*: A Cry against Oppression and the Promise
of Deliverance · *George W. E. Nickelsburg*   87
6. Jesus and the Dead Sea Scrolls · *Peter Flint*   110
7. The *Chreia* · *David B. Gowler*   132
8. The Galilean Charismatic and Rabbinic Piety: The Holy Man in the
Talmudic Literature · *Alan J. Avery-Peck*   149
9. Miracle Stories: The God Asclepius, the Pythagorean Philosophers,
and the Roman Rulers · *Wendy Cotter, C.S.J.*   166
10. The Mithras Liturgy · *Marvin Meyer*   179
11. Apuleius of Madauros · *Ian H. Henderson*   193
12. The Parable in the Hebrew Bible and Rabbinic Literature
· *Gary G. Porton*   206
13. The Aesop Tradition · *Lawrence M. Wills*   222
14. Targum, Jesus, and the Gospels · *Bruce Chilton*   238
15. The *Psalms of Solomon* · *Joseph L. Trafton*   256
16. Moral and Ritual Purity · *Jonathan Klawans*   266
17. Gospel and Talmud · *Herbert W. Basser*   285
18. Philo of Alexandria · *Gregory E. Sterling*   296
19. The Law of Roman Divorce in the Time of Christ
· *Thomas A. J. McGinn*   309
20. Associations in the Ancient World · *John S. Kloppenborg*   323
21. Anointing Traditions · *Teresa J. Hornsby*   339

22. The Passover *Haggadah* · *Calum Carmichael*   343

23. *Joseph and Aseneth*: Food as an Identity Marker · *Randall D. Chesnutt*   357

24. The Pliny and Trajan Correspondence · *Bradley M. Peper and Mark DelCogliano*   366

25. Imitations of Greek Epic in the Gospels · *Dennis R. MacDonald*   372

26. Narratives of Noble Death · *Robert Doran*   385

27. Isaiah 53:1–12 (Septuagint) · *Ben Witherington III*   400

28. Thallus on the Crucifixion · *Dale C. Allison Jr.*   405

Maps   407
Glossary   409
Index of Ancient Works   417
Index of Ancient Persons   435

CONTRIBUTORS

Dale C. Allison Jr. is Errett M. Grable Professor of New Testament Exegesis and Early Christianity at Pittsburgh Theological Seminary, Pittsburgh, Pennsylvania.

Alan J. Avery-Peck is Kraft-Hiatt Professor in Judaic Studies and Chair, Department of Religious Studies, at the College of the Holy Cross, Worcester, Massachusetts.

Herbert W. Basser is Professor of Religious Studies at Queen's University, Kingston, Ontario, Canada.

Calum Carmichael is Professor of Biblical Studies and Comparative Literature in the Religious Studies Program at Cornell University, Ithaca, New York.

Randall D. Chesnutt is William S. Banowsky Chair of Religion at Pepperdine University, Malibu, California.

Bruce Chilton is Bernard Iddings Bell Professor of Religion at Bard College, Annandale-on-Hudson, New York.

Wendy Cotter, C.S.J., is Associate Professor of Theology at Loyola University Chicago, Chicago, Illinois.

John Dominic Crossan is Professor Emeritus of Religious Studies at DePaul University, Chicago, Illinois.

Mary Rose D'Angelo is Associate Professor of Theology at the University of Notre Dame, Notre Dame, Indiana.

Mark DelCogliano, Graduate Division of Religion, Emory University, Atlanta, Georgia.

Robert Doran is the Samuel Williston Professor of Greek and Hebrew in the Department of Religion at Amherst College, Amherst, Massachusetts.

Craig A. Evans is Payzant Distinguished Professor of New Testament at Acadia Divinity College, Wolfville, Nova Scotia, Canada.

Peter Flint is Canada Research Chair in Dead Sea Scrolls at Trinity Western University, Langley, British Columbia, Canada.

David B. Gowler is Pierce Professor of Religion at Oxford College, Emory University, Atlanta, Georgia.

Ian H. Henderson is Associate Professor of New Testament at McGill University, Montreal, Quebec, Canada.

Teresa J. Hornsby is Associate Professor of Religion and Director of the Women and Gender Studies Program at Drury University, Springfield, Missouri.

Jonathan Klawans is Associate Professor of Religion at Boston University, Boston, Massachusetts.

John S. Kloppenborg is Professor of Religion at the University of Toronto, Toronto, Ontario, Canada.

Amy-Jill Levine is E. Rhodes and Leona B. Carpenter Professor of New Testament Studies at the Divinity School and Graduate Department of Religion, Vanderbilt University, Nashville, Tennessee.

Dennis R. MacDonald is Professor of New Testament and Christian Origins and Director of the Institute for Antiquity and Christianity at Claremont Graduate University, Claremont School of Theology, Claremont, California.

Thomas A. J. McGinn is Professor of Classical Studies at Vanderbilt University, Nashville, Tennessee.

Marvin Meyer is Griset Professor of Bible and Christian Studies at Chapman University, Orange, California.

George W. E. Nickelsburg is Emeritus Professor of Religion at the University of Iowa, Iowa City, Iowa.

Bradley M. Peper, Graduate Department of Religion, Vanderbilt University, Nashville, Tennessee.

Gary G. Porton is Charles and Sarah Droby Professor of Talmudic Studies and Judaism at the University of Illinois at Urbana-Champaign, Urbana, Illinois.

Jonathan L. Reed is Professor of Religion at the University of La Verne, La Verne, California.

Gregory E. Sterling is Senior Associate Dean of the Faculty for the College of Arts and Letters and Professor of New Testament and Christian Origins at the University of Notre Dame, Notre Dame, Indiana.

Charles H. Talbert is Distinguished Professor of Religion at Baylor University, Waco, Texas.

Joseph L. Trafton is Distinguished University Professor of Religious Studies at Western Kentucky University, Bowling Green, Kentucky.

Lawrence M. Wills is Ethelbert Talbot Professor of Biblical Studies at Episcopal Divinity School, Cambridge, Massachusetts.

Ben Witherington III is Professor of New Testament Interpretation at Asbury Theological Seminary, Wilmore, Kentucky.

ACKNOWLEDGMENTS

———

We would like to thank Kathy Chambers and Joe Blosser for technical help with manuscript preparation, Susan Ecklund for her excellent copyediting, Heidi Geib and Abigail Redman for indexing, and Sara Lerner and Fred Appel for their patience, persistence, and good humor.

THE HISTORICAL JESUS IN CONTEXT

INTRODUCTION

Amy-Jill Levine

Interest in the "historical Jesus" has continued unabated since the Enlightenment. Each year new books and magazine articles appear, the media offer new programs, and since the 1970s, college courses on the topic have been overflowing in enrollment. No single picture of Jesus has convinced all, or even most, scholars; all methods and their combinations find their critics as well as their advocates.

This volume does not offer yet another portrait of the historical Jesus—indeed, we editors each have our own view of Jesus' agenda, of what can be considered authentic material, of how he perceived himself and how others perceived him (whether our diverse views stem from our training, our ages, our experiences, even our different religious backgrounds, cannot be determined). Rather, this volume provides information on cultural contexts within which Jesus was understood and perhaps even understood himself. This collection explores Jesus' contexts not only through presenting select primary sources (most in new translations) but also by offering commentary by experts on those sources. By looking directly at the sources from the period—Jewish and Gentile, literary and archaeological—this volume allows readers to construct the setting within which Jesus and his earliest followers lived.

The point of this search is not to find "parallels." Comparison is often an extremely subjective judgment: where one scholar finds a connection, another finds disjunction. Nor is it to suggest that Jesus simply recapitulates conventional sayings and deeds; to the contrary, had he not said or done some things that proved memorable, distinct, or arresting, it is unlikely we would have records of his teachings. Nor, however, could he have been completely anomalous; were he so, he would have made no sense either to those who chose to follow him or to those brought into the movement after his crucifixion.

All literature, be it historical report, biography, comedic anecdote, religious pronouncement, even deed of property, conforms to set patterns or what biblical scholars typically refer to as "forms." Those who recorded the stories of Jesus would have presented their materials according to the forms of their time, and in turn their readers would have understood the Gospel accounts in light of these forms. Jesus too would be familiar with both Hellenistic (Gentile) and Jewish forms: how one prayed and taught; how one was expected to act; how initiation rites such as baptism functioned; when and how one used apocalyptic language; recountings of miracles and martyrs. Further, the repertoire of stories available to Jesus' followers from both Jewish and Gentile traditions, as well as their own experiences, served as a source for adapted and even new stories of the man they considered the Messiah.

We cannot always determine which came first: a historical event or a literary creation. In some cases, Jesus may have been influenced by the scriptures of Judaism (e.g., the miracle-working prophets such as Elijah and Elisha, the suffering servant described by the prophet Isaiah, the apocalyptic "son of man" mentioned by Daniel as well as *1 Enoch*), as well as by Jewish accounts of martyrs, teachers, prophets, sages, and visionaries; yet it is equally possible that his followers, themselves steeped in these accounts, conformed their understanding of Jesus according to these narrative models. In other cases, those who told stories about him may have drawn from the rich traditions of the Greek and Roman worlds, from Homer to Aesop to Apollonius of Tyana and Apuleius of Madauros. In teaching and debating, Jesus would have used forms familiar to his audiences, such as parables and appeals to legal tradition or practice. Further, his audiences would have drawn upon this same repertoire in order to understand him.

Given its focus on an individual, or at least the records of him, this volume in the Princeton Readings in Religions series departs slightly from the focus of the earlier volumes, where the controlling factor has been a geographic region. The shift is not substantial, however. To investigate the context within which Jesus lived and his stories were told is already a focused investigation of both culture and period. The historical man from Nazareth cannot be understood fully if he is divorced from his context; the spread of the Gospel cannot be comprehended unless one appreciates its adaptations to the cultural expectations of its proselytes.

The focused approach of this collection also responds to a situation not addressed directly in the other volumes. A number of scholars working in biblical studies have insisted that we have an "ethical" responsibility to engage in historical Jesus research. Millions of people cite Gospel texts as moral guides. Consequently, it becomes imperative to determine to the best of our ability the situation in which those pronouncements were made. Do Jesus' comments on divorce or the construction of the family, for example, respond to a specific situation, perhaps one that no longer prevails, or are they universal injunctions? Are his comments on eschatology—the end of the present age—to be seen as metaphoric or literal? How are his values, or those of his followers, reflective of the Platonic dualism marking much of Hellenistic society? Did he in fact issue all the statements attributed to him, or were some added by his early followers and attributed to him, just as both Gentile and Jewish writers attributed material to prominent teachers? Are the Gospels to be assessed by criteria distinct from those applied to non-Christian material: for example, are Jesus' miracles "fact," whereas reports of the miraculous deeds of the Rabbi Honi the Circle-Drawer or the Pagan teacher Apollonius of Tyana the airy stuff of legend?

In order to locate the historical Jesus, access is needed not only to the Christian canon but also to the ancient primary sources that may confirm, complement, or complicate the canonical portraits. Today, the noncanonical Gospels and Patristic sources (writings of the Church Fathers) easily are available both in print and on-line; another volume in this series, Richard Valantasis's *Religions of Late Antiquity in Practice*, offers many of the late first-century and subsequent Christian as well as non-Christian texts. But even with the several source books available, the scholarly community still lacks a comprehensive volume that not only records the sources but also discusses their connections to the historical Jesus. This volume in the *Readings in Religion* series redresses that gap.

The History of the "Quest"

The so-called Quest for the historical Jesus seeks to understand the man from Nazareth as he was understood in his own context and as he understood himself. Its practitioners can be pictured as located on a spectrum ranging from positivism to skepticism. The positivistic side regards the Gospel accounts as accurate or at least relatively accurate reports, and the burden of proof is placed on those who would claim something attributed to Jesus was not historical (although the demand to "prove a negative" creates a logical fallacy: it is impossible, in most cases, to prove that Jesus did *not* say or do something the Gospels attribute to him). As we move toward the skeptical end, we find questors who presuppose a distinction between the "Christ of faith"—the resurrected Lord, second person of the Trinity, the divine man proclaimed in the pages of the New Testament—and the Jesus of history. The understandings of the man from Nazareth vary according to the investigator's personal interests and also vary depending on the method used, the aspects of Jesus' life highlighted, the construal of Jesus' social situation, even the investigator's theological worldview (e.g., does it accommodate miracles? does it presuppose the biblical texts are inerrant?).

Those interpreters who regard the Evangelists (the authors of the Gospels, known as Matthew, Mark, Luke, and John) as inheritors of oral tradition as well as authors in their own right seek to strip away the layers introduced by the Gospel writers as well as by Jesus' early followers to reach the pristine historical core of what he actually said and did. One conventional way of describing this distinction is to say that whereas Jesus proclaimed the kingdom of heaven, the Gospels proclaim Jesus. In this view, not every saying and deed, perhaps fewer than a half or even a quarter, the Gospels attribute to Jesus has a claim to historical authenticity. The materials are regarded as having developed among Jesus' followers, men and women who retrojected their experiences—disaffection from local synagogues, distrust by and of the Roman government, concerns over marriage, debates with other followers of Jesus as well as with both Gentiles and Jews who did not accept their claims—back to the story of Jesus himself. On this side of the spectrum, the burden of proof for claiming something historical rests with those who regard the Gospel text as reliable. But this procedure requires a skepticism that is not usually applied to comparable texts, such as Suetonius's *Lives of the Caesars* or Josephus's *Antiquities of the Jews*. Nor in either case is it clear what would constitute "proof."

There is a consensus of sorts on a basic outline of Jesus' life. Most scholars agree that Jesus was baptized by John, debated with fellow Jews on how best to live according to God's will, engaged in healings and exorcisms, taught in parables, gathered male and female followers in Galilee, went to Jerusalem, and was crucified by Roman soldiers during the governorship of Pontius Pilate (26–36 CE). But, to use the old cliché, the devil is in the details.

For centuries, there was no "quest for the historical Jesus" per se. The gospels were taken to be trustworthy historical accounts. Although the earliest versions are anonymous, and although no Gospel identifies its author, the traditional attributions of Matthew, Mark, Luke, and John were accepted as fact. Matthew (Matthew 9:9; the tax collector is called "Levi" in Mark 2:14 and Luke 5:27) was the tax collector summoned by Jesus, and "John" was considered to be the unnamed "beloved disciple" who reclined on Jesus' breast at the Last Supper (see John 13:23). Luke, who wrote both the Gospel bearing his name and the Acts of the Apostles, was considered the companion of Paul, as well as the confidant of the Virgin Mary, and Mark was the companion of Peter. Thus the testimony of the four "Evangelists" (a Greek term meaning "good news bringers"; *euaggellion*, or "good news," is the Greek term underlying the English "Gospel") was credible, resting on eyewitness testimony. The miracles happened as recorded; whereas supernatural events recorded of Pagan, Jewish, or Muslim individuals were seen as merely legends, those accorded to Jesus and his followers were seen as fact.

Discrepancies were noted: Matthew, Mark, and Luke date the Crucifixion to the first day of the Passover holiday (Matthew 26:17–19; Mark 14:12–16; Luke 22:7–13); John, who refers to Jesus as the "lamb of God" (John 1:29), dates it to the day before, when the lambs to be eaten at the festival meal were being sacrificed in the Jerusalem Temple (John 13:1; 18:28; 19:31). Mark 10:1–12 depicts Jesus as insisting there is to be no divorce; the Jesus of Matthew (5:32) states that there is to be no divorce except in cases of *porneia* (the Greek conveys the sense of "unchaste behavior" or "sexual perversion"). Even Luke remarks that whereas others had attempted to compile an orderly account of Jesus' actions, he would present the material accurately (the supposition being that the earlier materials were inaccurate [see Luke 1:1–4]). But apparent discrepancies were easily harmonized by means of allegory, or they were regarded as complementary rather than as contradictory.

Interpreters regarded stories that appeared to be variants of the same incident as accounts of separate events. Thus, Jesus was seen as having "cleansed" the Temple both at the beginning of his ministry (so John 2) and again at its end (so Matthew 21, Mark 11, and Luke 19); Jesus healed a demoniac named "Legion" at Gadara (so Mark 5) and two demoniacs named "Legion" at Gerasa (so Matthew 8). He taught "Blessed are the poor in spirit" (so Matthew's "Sermon on the

Mount," 5:3) and "Blessed are you poor" (so Luke's "Sermon on the Plain," 6:20). Even today, these matters remain debated. For some scholars, Matthew adapted Luke's "more original" Beatitude to stress personal attitude rather than economic situation; for others, Jesus spoke both Beatitudes, but on different occasions to different audiences.

The "Quest" itself formally began with the Enlightenment's questioning of both theological dogma and religious authority and in particular with the English Deists. H. S. Reimarus, a German historian whose *On the Intention of Jesus and His Disciples* (published posthumously in 1768 by the philosopher G. E. Lessing) usually is credited for starting the "Old Quest," although his arguments substantially repeat the idea of the Deists. Reimarus, who viewed the gospels as human products rather than inerrant and noncontradictory "truth," distinguished between the historical Jesus and the Christ of faith. His image of the historical Jesus was of a failed revolutionary whose disciples stole his corpse, as well as invented both the Resurrection and the Second Coming (the *parousia*) to keep their movement going.

Following Reimarus, many scholars concluded that even if the gospels did contain some eyewitness testimony, the stories had been adapted and expanded to fit the needs of Greek-speaking, increasingly Gentile churches. The task was to separate the chaff of legendary development from the wheat of historical accuracy.

Aiding in this effort was the rise of source criticism, that is, the recognition that the first three canonical gospels—Matthew, Mark, and Luke—share a common literary basis; they became known as the "Synoptic Gospels" because they "see together." But while the connection among the three was acknowledged, the specifics of that connection remained contested. The "Griesbach hypothesis"—named after its first major proponent—held that Matthew was the first Gospel, Luke followed Matthew but added material from his own sources, and Mark epitomized the two. That Luke had access to sources is indicated by the Gospel itself, for as noted earlier, Luke speaks of the "many who had attempted to compile a narrative of the events that have been accomplished among us" (Luke 1:1).

Yet Griesbach's theory had its challengers. Why, some wondered, if Mark is a summary of Matthew and Luke, are Mark's individual stories longer (e.g., Mark tells the story of the Gerasene demoniac in twenty verses [5:1–20]; Luke's version takes fourteen [8:26–39], and Matthew uses only seven [8:28–34])? Why did Mark omit such major materials as the Beatitudes and the Lord's Prayer? Why are there no nativity or resurrection accounts (Mark 16:9–20, the so-called longer ending of the Gospel, is an addition to the earliest texts)? Numerous other indicators, from grammatical infelicities to errors of fact, also contributed to the weakening of support for Griesbach.

Complicating the scholarship may well have been apologetic interests: did the church really want the first Gospel to be so "Jewish": Matthew foregrounds Jesus' Jewish ancestry by beginning with a genealogy that highlighted Abraham and David (1:1–17); Matthew depicts Jesus as insisting that he had "come not to abolish but to fulfill" the "Law and the Prophets" (5:17); Matthew has Jesus restrict his mission to "the lost sheep of the house of Israel" (10:6; 15:24). Mark, on the other hand, lacks a genealogy, depicts Jesus as declaring "all foods clean" (7:19), and indicates that Jesus engaged in a Gentile mission (7:24–8:10). By arguing for Marcan priority, scholars could also argue for a more de-Judaized Jesus.

The main alternative to the Griesbach theory, and the one held by the majority of scholars today, is known as the "four-source theory." This view argues that Mark wrote first, and that Matthew and Luke, independently, used Mark as a source. Needing to account for the material common to Matthew and Luke but absent in Mark, scholars concluded that Matthew and Luke had access to a second source, comprising mostly sayings (such as the Beatitudes, the teachings of John the Baptist, and the Lord's Prayer). This they labeled Q, which has come to be understood as related to the German *Quelle*, or "source." Completing the four sources are, along with Mark and Q, Matthew's special collection (M) and Luke's unique material (L).

In the early years of the Quest, some optimism reigned in the study of the historical Jesus. Even if Matthew and Luke were late—and John, whose relationship to the Synoptics remains even more a debatable question, was considered even later—at least Mark and Q could provide some purchase on Jesus himself. Thus, the nineteenth century's "Old Quest" produced a proliferation of Jesuses, each dependent on select citations from the gospels, and each bolstered by idiosyncratic appropriations of noncanonical sources.

Seeds of the Old Quest's demise had been planted as early as 1835, with the publication of D. F. Strauss's *Life of Jesus*. Rejecting both the supernaturalism of the literalist reader and the rationalism of the skeptic, Strauss contributed to the study of the gospels the "mythic" view, the recognition that while the gospels are based on historical fact, the facts have been so embellished by Christian teaching that a true "life of Jesus" would be impossible to write.

The optimistic bubble finally burst with the dawn of the twentieth century. Wilhelm Wrede's *Messianic Secret in the Gospels* (1901) demonstrated that Mark was no more an objective source than Matthew or Luke. Noticing that the Marcan Jesus frequently commands silence from those for whom he has performed a miracle or provided a special teaching (e.g., 1:32, 43–44; 3:12; 5:43), Wrede claimed that the injunctions to secrecy were invented by the early church and retrojected into the story of Jesus to account for why he had so few followers during his lifetime. The real reason for this lack, in Wrede's view, was that Jesus himself never claimed messianic status (a question that remains debated even today).

In the eyes of many scholars, Wrede's work fatally damaged claims that Mark provided unmediated access to Jesus, and Albert Schweitzer's *Quest of the Historical Jesus: From Reimarus to Wrede* (German 1906; English 1910) finally buried the Old Quest. Surveying the numerous "lives of Jesus" produced since Reimarus's publication, Schweitzer neatly demonstrated how each author had constructed a Jesus in his own image. His warning remains relevant for all those who seek to explain the "real" Jesus or the "historical" Jesus.

The time from the publication of Schweitzer's text until the rise of World War II is erroneously called the "No Quest" period; for the quest did continue, albeit with new interests. One stream of scholarship redirected attention away from the "life of Jesus" focus and sought to analyze individual narrative units, such as sayings, healings, controversy accounts, and parables. Influenced by folklore analysis, Martin Dibelius looked to the structure, or form, of the unit (called a *pericope*, from the Greek term for "cut out"). He observed that healings took a set form (i.e., notice of the disease; type of healing; response of healed; response of crowd), as did controversy stories, nature miracles, and so forth. Whereas scholars might not have been able to penetrate through the level of the Gospel writer or the early traditions the Evangelist received to the historical Jesus himself, they were confident that they could locate the *Sitz im Leben*, the "setting in life," of the individual forms and so come to understand the community that originally told the story. Thus, the gospels could be understood as we might, for example, understand the various versions of the story of "Cinderella" or the recountings of what have come to be known as "urban legends": we might not have access to the actual event, and there may never have been an actual event, but we do have different versions of the same story.

When faced with similar accounts or what appeared to be variants of the same story, analysts sought to determine which was earlier: did Jesus insist, "All those things which you do not want done to you, do not do to another" (the quotation is found in an early Christian source called the *Teachings of the Twelve Apostles*, or the *Didache* [1:2b]) or "do to others as you would have them do to you" (Q/Luke 6:31 [material seen as belonging originally to Q is listed according to its appearance in Luke])? Is his advice to "Be perfect, therefore, as your heavenly father is perfect" (Matthew 5:48) or is it to "Be merciful, just as your Father is merciful" (Luke 6:36)? Such concerns created an almost atomistic exegesis, wherein each word was interrogated for historical accuracy. That Jesus could have engaged in his own variations on the story rarely was acknowledged; focus was on the words themselves, with the attendant concern of retrojecting the Greek of the gospels into Jesus' native Aramaic (whether Jesus could speak Greek, or whether he taught in Greek, still remains an open question), rather than on their import.

The form-critical focus also prompted increasing recognition of how literary templates (may have) provided the origins for stories attributed to Jesus. The early church used Jesus' sayings as a lens through which to interpret their sacred texts (i.e., the Scriptures of Judaism), but they also used those texts as a resource for interpreting Jesus. These Jewish texts locate the cultural codes available to Jesus and his early followers for describing martyrs, messiahs, divinely appointed figures, heavenly mediators, and miracle workers. For example, in Mark 4:38, the disciples, fearing that they are about to drown, call to Jesus, "Teacher, do you not care that we are perishing?" Jesus rebukes the disciples, and then the storm, and so prompts the twelve to wonder, "Who is this who can stop the winds?" Perhaps, suggested the critics, the story is less a historically objective report than a meditation on Psalm 107: "They cried to the Lord in their trouble, and he brought them out of their distress. He made the storm be still, and the waves of the sea were hushed."

In like manner, Matthew 1–5 depicts Jesus as a new Moses who escapes the killing of Jewish infants ordered by Herod the Great, the new Pharaoh; like Moses, Jesus participates in a journey to and from Egypt, crosses water in a life-changing experience (the baptism recapitulates the Israelites' crossing the Red Sea), faces temptation in the wilderness for forty days as Israel was tempted to apostasy in its forty-year wilderness journey, ascends a mountain, and, like Moses again, delivers instruction (or "Torah"). John 6:25–59 makes explicit the connection between Moses who provided manna for the Israelites in the wilderness and Jesus who provided the "bread of life."

The Passion narratives (the accounts of Jesus' final week in Jerusalem) in Mark and Matthew can be read as reflections on Psalm 22, whose opening line, "My God, my God, why have you forsaken me," the Jesus of Mark and Matthew quotes from the cross (Matthew 27:46; Mark 15:34). The psalm goes on to describe the narrator's mockers and notes that "they divide my clothes among themselves, and for my clothing they cast lots." The more skeptical critic logically could conclude that for Matthew and Mark, the narrative of the Crucifixion was based not on eyewitness testimony—a conclusion bolstered by Mark's remark that Jesus' male followers "deserted him and fled" (Mark 14:50) while the women of Galilee only looked on the Crucifixion "from a distance" (Mark 15:40–41) and so perhaps were not close enough to see all the events the Evangelist reports—but on the historicizing of the psalm.

Scholars also noticed that the stories of Jesus resonated with Greek and Roman culture. The "true vine" of John's Gospel, the doer of signs who turns water into wine (John 2), is killed, and then rises, resembles Dionysius; the divine conception had numerous classical antecedents; Socrates died a heroic death as did Jesus; Apollonias of Tyana was reputed to have healed and raised the dead, taught by means of memorable short sayings, was persecuted by his enemies, was killed, and rose again.

The form-critical process did advance the Quest for the historical Jesus, but it also had, like source criticism, inherent problems. Just as source criticism could not, with complete assurance, settle on the question of which Gospel served as the source for the others, so form criticism had its own question of priority: was the *Sitz im Leben* to be understood by the analysis of the forms, or were the forms to be understood on the basis of an anterior setting in life? The argument at best risked circularity. It also left a number of people dissatisfied. The stress on the community setting of the material deflected attention from Jesus himself and onto those who received his teachings, be those first-century Galileans or early twentieth-century Central Europeans. Whereas an existential relationship with the text, as Rudolf Bultmann promulgated, held some attraction, the appeal of history had not gone away.

The Quest regressed during World War II. Some Nazi and Nazi-influenced scholars, led by Walter Grundmann, a professor of New Testament at the University of Jena, worked in the Institute for the Study and Eradication of Jewish Influence on German Religious Life. Their publications, widely disseminated in

Europe, proclaimed an Aryan Jesus fully divorced from Judaism not only in terms of practice and ideology but also by ethnicity. Whereas the various quests have never been free of bias—no historical reconstruction can be fully objective, for scholars will always need to determine what to mention, to highlight, and to ignore—the Nazi example presents the most egregious instance of such bias. Sadly, proponents of this Aryan Jesus still promulgate their hate-filled messages today; thus, they indicate yet another reason why the study of the historical Jesus includes an ethical component.

At the end of the war, spurred by both historical interest and theological need, Ernst Käsemann began the next stage—variously called the "New Quest" or the "Second Quest"—with his essay "The Problem with the Historical Jesus" (1953). Käsemann first insisted that the jettisoning of history in favor of the ahistorical folktale or a theological existentialism marked by one's personal encounter with the text (an approach resembling today's reader-response criticism) was unwarranted. The church itself was interested in history, he averred: otherwise, why write the Gospels and the Acts of the Apostles? Moreover, Christians must be concerned with some fact, for otherwise the church rests on a very poor foundation.

To provide such a foundation, Käsemann articulated what have come to be known as the "criteria of authenticity," the means by which tradition and redaction may be separated and with which scholars could penetrate behind the editorial (sometimes called the "redactional") level, behind the oral tradition (the level of form criticism's concentration), and to Jesus himself. Again, a burst of optimism was followed by sober reconsideration.

The criteria of authenticity, refined and described by various names and specifics, are basically three techniques by which the sources can be analyzed. The *criterion of multiple attestation* proffered that if a saying or action attributed to Jesus appeared in two or more independent sources, then its "authenticity" (i.e., its connection to Jesus himself) is comparably more likely. Materials that appear to fit this criterion include Jesus' institution of a memorial meal with connections drawn between bread and flesh, wine and blood; the commission is attested in the Synoptics, 1 Corinthians, the *Didache*, and probably John 6, the "bread of life discourse." Paul, Mark, and Q all attribute to Jesus a pronouncement against divorce. John and the Synoptics record Jesus' relationship with John the Baptist, gathering disciples, and feeding of the five thousand. John and Luke attest that two sisters, Mary and Martha, were Jesus' close friends.

The problem with this criterion is that we cannot with surety determine which sources are independent. Clearly the Synoptics do not fit the criterion, for they share a common source. The Synoptics and John's Gospel may be independent, but there is no scholarly consensus. Nor do we know the extent to which, if at all, Paul's letters influenced the composition of the gospels, let alone what the relationship is between the noncanonical and canonical texts. Further, conformity to the criterion cannot "prove" authenticity; it can only prove anteriority.

The second criterion, that of *dissimilarity*, claims that if a saying or deed attributed to Jesus is dissimilar to first-century Jewish thought and dissimilar or antithetical to the interests of Jesus' followers (e.g., the nascent "Church"), it has a greater claim to authenticity. Each part of the criterion has benefits and debits. Concerning the connection to Judaism, for example, Jesus' supposed preference for celibacy (e.g., Matthew 19:12) is dissimilar to the majority of Jewish thought and practice in the first century, although the Esssenes described by Josephus and the Therapeutae/Therapeutrides described by Philo show that it is not completely anomalous. The criterion works less well when we turn to Jesus' own followers. The early Christian literature shows both an ongoing interest in celibacy—such as Paul's own preference (1 Corinthians 7), the reference in Acts 21 to Philip's four virgin daughters, and the 144,000 "virgins" of Revelation 14 who "have not defiled themselves with women"—as well as strong interest in conforming to Roman family values of marriage and children (so 1 Timothy 2).

For an account dissimilar to ecclesiastical interests, the Evangelists' struggling with Jesus' baptism by John appears to fit the criterion. If John is baptizing for the remission of sins (Mark 1:4), why would the incarnate Lord proclaimed by the church need to submit himself to this ritual? Matthew (3:15) states that Jesus is baptized "to fulfill all righteousness." Luke, by providing a nativity story for John as well as making very clear that John, even in utero, recognized Jesus' superiority, avoids the impression that Jesus is subordinate to John. In John's Gospel, the Baptist never actually baptizes Jesus, but he does insist that Jesus is the "one who ranks ahead of me because he was before me" (John 1:30), a line that comports beautifully with the fourth Gospel's insistence on the preexistence of Jesus, the "Word" (*Logos*) who was "in the beginning" (1:1).

Again, the approach is compromised. Not only is our knowledge of first-century Galilean and Judean Jewish thought and practice incomplete, such that what may seem "dissimilar" is an accident of what was preserved and what was lost, but also the method risks deforming our image of Jesus by highlighting what distinguishes him from Judaism rather than what embeds him within his own religious and cultural tradition. Critics of the criterion of dissimilarity, especially in its classical focus of separating Jesus from Judaism, have also recognized the negative repercussions of this process. In light of the Shoah (the Holocaust), the Jewishness of Jesus increasingly has been highlighted (ideological pressure and historical-critical rigor need not be mutually exclusive). However, beyond recognizing that "Jesus was Jewish," rarely does the scholarship address what being "Jewish" means (aside from a connection to Mary's ethnic group—and here we might note, as well, that the entire category of ethnicity is itself fraught with difficulty). The lack is caused substantially by gaps in the training of New Testament experts: few have complete familiarity with the varied Jewish sources of the period (Pseudepigrapha, Dead Sea Scrolls, Josephus, Philo, the myriad Rabbinic texts, Targumim . . .).

A similar problem plagues the second part of the criterion. We do not know what the early followers of Jesus would have found embarrassing. Finally, it is likely that Jesus and the early church founded in his name were substantially continuous rather than distinct. Just as the criterion threatens to yank Jesus out of his Jewish context, so it threatens to sever his connection to those who followed him.

The third criterion, that of *consistency* or *coherence*, depends on the first two. If application of *multiple attestation* and *dissimilarity* assigns a saying or action to Jesus, then similar sayings or actions have, according to this criterion, greater claims to authenticity. Again, problems abound. Not only is "similarity" in the eye of the beholder, one of Jesus' followers easily could have developed a new story on the basis of the old. It is quite possible that sayings or deeds attributed in the gospels to Jesus originally were spoken or performed by another (perhaps a disciple) and only later attached to the master (a similar case can be made that King David did not kill Goliath [1 Samuel 17]; the Philistine was killed by the soldier Elkhanan [2 Samuel 21:19; cf. 1 Chronicles 20:5], but the story later became attached to the commander in chief). Attributing to religious leaders additional material is by no means uncommon.

Just as source criticism marked the Old Quest period and form criticism the No Quest phase, so redaction criticism grew in prominence in the decades following World War II. Already the form critics had noted that the Evangelists compiled individual *pericopae* into a narrative of Jesus' life. Redaction criticism turns to the Evangelist, the "redactor" (editor), first to distinguish between "redaction" (the author's contribution) and "tradition" (what the author received in either oral or written form). This approach would soon give rise to more literary forms of interpretation, wherein the Evangelists or "redactors" were acknowledged as artists and theologians rather than mere copyists. For example, Mark was seen to stress a "suffering Messiah"; Matthew presented a new Moses characterized by teaching; Luke offered the "champion of the poor"; and John's Christology, the highest of the canonical Gospels, featured a "man from heaven" and "incarnate *Logos*."

In the later decades of the twentieth century, historical Jesus studies shifted from its basis in Germany to Great Britain and then to the United States and Canada, and as it moved, so too did its sources. The Quest already had made occasional references to Philo of Alexandria and Josephus, as well as to the collection of so-called Rabbinic parallels from the somewhat tendentious *Commentary* by Hermann Strack and Paul Billerbeck (Strack was the famous scholar whose name appears first on the title page; Billerbeck was a pastor who did most of the work). From the Christian side, the Church Fathers offered a few citations of documents no longer extant, such as the *Gospel of Thomas*.

The publication of two sets of documents changed, if not the pictures of Jesus already available in the scholarly literature, at least the bibliographies of the biographies. Discovered first in 1947, with documents still continuing to surface, the Dead Sea Scrolls provided insight into an apocalyptic, eschatological Judaism disaffected from the Temple. In 1945, a cache of Coptic documents was found at Nag Hammadi in Egypt; these provided copies of many of the texts known only from Patristic citation as well as possible candidates, such as the Gospels of Thomas, Peter, and Mary, for the criterion of *multiple attestation*. For example, is the kingdom of heaven "like yeast that a woman took" (Matthew 13:33) or "like a woman who took yeast" (*Gospel of Thomas* 96)?

Lack of methodological security continued. Concerning the canon, scholars still typically privilege the Synoptics over John for historical reconstruction, but they do not explain why. Q and *Thomas*—a hypothetical document and a text that may be second-century—are sometimes seen as closer to the historical Jesus than the canonical Gospels. The less skeptical contingent finds this approach to strain credibility; the more skeptical replies that the privileging of the canon is based on religious interests, not historical evidence. Complicating any reconstruction is the lack of autographs: we have no originals of the Gospels. The earliest manuscripts of the full canonical Gospels date to the third century (ca. 200). There are approximately fifty-four hundred copies of all or parts of the Greek New Testament (copies of translations add substantially more to the total) dating from the early second century (a few fragments) to the invention of the printing press in the fifteenth century and even following that time. Moreover, save for a very few fragments, these thousands of texts are not in full agreement.

Although no new major sources have been discovered in the past quarter century, today's Quest has not failed to introduce new methods into the discussion and new categories by which to understand Jesus. The study of the historical Jesus is now accompanied by greater attention to social modeling: comparative peasant economies, scribal communities, millenarian movements, studies of shamans and folk healings, psychobiography, cultural anthropology, political theory, and the like have all been adduced to provide the context for understanding the Gospel accounts. Archaeology, especially the archaeology of the lower Galilee, also stakes a claim to direct relevance, although finding an artifact and determining its import for understanding Jesus remain quite distinct.

- Jesus has been described as a Jewish reformer seeking to prepare his people for the inbreaking of the kingdom of heaven. This is the Jesus who "makes a fence" (the expression is Rabbinic [*Pirke Avot* 1:1]) about the law to prevent transgression: rather than forbid murder, Jesus forbids hate (Matthew 5:21–22). Rather than forbid adultery, he forbids lust. This Jesus insists "not one jot or stroke of the Law will pass away" (Matthew 5:17–18).
- Conversely, there is Jesus the antinomian who "declared all foods clean" (Mark 7:18–20) and dismissed Temple and Torah as antiquated and irrelevant.
- Jesus the Cynic-like philosopher teaches a subversive wisdom and so calls into question the status quo. To those concerned with social propriety, Jesus proffers the image of the lilies of the field. To those occupied by the cares of tomorrow, he asserts, "the cares of today are sufficient" (Matthew 6:34; F. Gerald Downing's study offers numerous citations of Cynic statements with what he finds to be Gospel equivalents).
- Jesus the apocalyptic eschatological proclaimer divides the world into the saved and the damned, the "sheep and the goats" (Matthew 25), as he awaits what some Jews called "the world to come," for his "kingdom is not of this world" (John 18:36).

- Jesus the Rabbi cares about Torah, wears *tzitzit* (fringes) according to the commandment in Numbers 15:37–41, celebrates the Sabbath, and worships in synagogues as well as the Temple.
- Jesus the universalist preaches his Gospel to Samaritans (John 4) and Gentiles (the feeding of the four thousand [Mark 8, Matthew 15]).
- Jesus the nationalist restricts his mission to "the lost sheep of the house of Israel" (Matthew 10:6; 15:24).
- Jesus the charismatic wonder-worker in the mold of Elijah (see 1 Kings 17–19, 21; 2 Kings 1–2) and Elisha (see 2 Kings 2–6, 8–9, 13) and comparable to the Jewish figures Haninah ben Dosa and Honi the Circle-Maker heals and controls nature.
- Jesus the magician uses spells and incantations to facilitate cures (Mark 5:41; 7:33–34).
- Jesus the social reformer seeks to inaugurate the economic justice envisioned by the Prophets and the year of Jubilee (Leviticus 25:8–55) by teaching his followers to pray, "Forgive us our debts, as we forgive those who are indebted to us" (Matthew 6:12) and insisting, "Give when you are asked" (Matthew 5:42).
- Jesus the celibate hails those who have "made themselves eunuchs for the kingdom of heaven" (Matthew 19:10–12) and promotes a new family based on loyalty to him/to God and not on biological or marital connections. This Jesus echoes the prophet Micah (7:6) by announcing, "Do not think I have come to bring peace to the earth; I have come not to bring peace, but to bring a sword. For I have come to set a man against his father, and a daughter against her mother, and a daughter-in-law against her mother-in-law" (Matthew 10:34–35).
- Jesus the affirmer of family values reminds his followers, "For God said, 'Honor your father and mother,' and 'whoever speaks evil of father and mother must surely die'" (Matthew 15:4); he teaches, "Whoever divorces his wife and marries another commits adultery against her, and if she divorces her husband and marries another, she commits adultery" (Mark 10:11–12).
- Jesus the mystic claims esoteric knowledge (see Mark 4:11–12), sees Satan fall like lightning (Luke 10:18), and proclaims himself the "true vine" (John 15) and the "bread of life" (John 6).
- Jesus the near hedonist takes and teaches pleasure in food and companionship; this "glutton and the drunkard" (Luke 7:34) does not fast, and enjoys a woman's kiss and touch (Luke 7:36–50).
- Jesus the pacifist advises that "if someone strike you on the right cheek, turn the other also" (Matthew 5:39).
- Jesus the revolutionary has a Zealot in his entourage (Luke 6:15) and advises followers to buy swords (Luke 22:35–38).
- Jesus the nonviolent resister teaches, "If a man in authority makes you go one mile, go with him two" (Matthew 5:41; the reference is likely to the Roman custom of conscripting locals to carry their gear, but only for one mile; to carry the accoutrements of the enemy willingly signals the refusal to be victimized), and "If a man wants to sue you for your shift, let him have your coat as well" (and so literally lay bare the injustice of taking a poor person's clothing [Matthew 5:40]).

And the list goes on.

Whatever model provides the heuristic for understanding Jesus, recourse to primary sources in their historical context is essential. For all readers of the New Testament generally are aware that the texts did not take shape in a vacuum. Understanding of the history of the period is often meager at best (some New Testament textbooks dedicate a few pages in an introductory chapter to "Jewish history" and "Greco-Roman history" and then generally ignore the historical context in discussion of the canonical documents). Thus, before turning to an overview of the primary sources presented in this volume, we first explore the historical context of Jesus and that of his early followers.

The Historical Context

Judaism and Christianity (as well as Islam) are called "historical" religions because they ground their story in the manifestation of their God in time. At a particular historical moment, God appeared to Moses and through him established a covenant with the people Israel. Jesus of Nazareth, the "incarnation" (literally, "enfleshment") of divinity (so John 1), "suffered under Pontius Pilate" (the Apostles' Creed) or, as the Nicene Creed proclaims, "was crucified under Pontius Pilate." Consequently, to understand the life of the Jew Jesus and the development of accounts concerning him, one must understand the historical contexts in which he and his earliest followers lived. This context is one of cultural struggle and colonial power, regional practice and imperial standards, religious debate and cultic competition.

The background for understanding Jesus begins with what the church would eventually call the "Old Testament" and Jews the *Tanakh*, an acronym for Torah, or Pentateuch; *Nevi'im* or Prophets; and *Ketuv'im* or Writings. Jesus and his contemporaries would have been familiar with the stories of Adam and Eve, Abraham and Moses, David and Solomon. They would have known of the prophets such as Isaiah and Jeremiah, Jonah and Daniel. Moreover, these texts would not have been seen simply as records of past events; rather, the Scriptures were seen as speaking to them in their own time (as the Dead Sea Scrolls make explicit and as Luke has Jesus himself state, "'Today this Scripture has been fulfilled in your hearing'" [Luke 4:21]).

Jesus and his fellow first-century Jews were also heirs to Greek and Roman thought. Galilee and Judea, like the rest of the Middle East, became part of the empire established by Alexander the Great. In 333 BCE, Alexander defeated the Persian empire, and the lands where Jews lived, both the Diaspora (literally, "dispersion"; any place outside of the Land of Israel where Jews could be found) and Israel itself, became permeated with Greek ideas.

Through the synthesis of indigenous and Greek cultures arose "Hellenism," and it is within the matrix of Hellenism that Jewish life developed. A modern example of such penetration would be the presence of American terms (such as Coca-Cola and ATM) in the vocabularies of most languages today.

In Judea and Galilee, Aramaic remained the vernacular; Hebrew was the language of scripture and liturgy. Yet even within these regions, Greek knowledge continued to increase. By the first century CE, Justin of Tiberius and Josephus from Judea are writing in Greek. In the Diaspora, the Scriptures were translated into Greek (the translation is the Septuagint), and it would be the Greek translation that became the sacred text of the church whose own canon, the New Testament, was written entirely in Greek.

Politically, Judea (the former Persian province of Yehud) was not substantially affected by the transfer of power from Persia to Greece. Taxes continued to be paid; worship in the Jerusalem Temple continued; the sacred texts of the people continued to be copied. During the early years of this cultural synthesis, Jews also continued to produce literature. Canonical today for Roman Catholics, Anglicans, and Eastern Orthodox churches are the Deuterocanonical texts or the Old Testament Apocrypha: books preserved in and in some cases originally written in Greek.

On the international scene, following Alexander's death in 323, Judea passed from one government to another. First, it fell under the control of Alexander's general Ptolemy, who held authority over Egypt. In 190, at the Battle of Paneas, Judea passed into the control of the Seleucids, the family of another of Alexander's generals, this one whose base was in Syria. Hellenization continued, such that by the 170s, many among the upper class in Jerusalem were seeking education in Greek philosophy, participating in Greek sport, and questioning those practices and beliefs of Judaism—circumcision, condemnation of "idolatry," dietary regulations, and so forth—that made Jews a distinct nation within the wider Greek empire. By the 170s, we find high priests with such Greek names as Jason and Menelaus.

This cultural crisis came to a head when the high priests worked with the Seleucid ruler, Antiochus IV Epiphanes, to bring Judea and its Jews fully into imperial culture. The events, recorded by Josephus as well as in the Deuterocanonical volumes of 1 and 2 Maccabees and hinted at in several of the documents associated with the community at Qumran, attest to religious and cultural as well as political struggle. Antiochus arranged for the succession of one of the assimilationists, Jason, to the high priesthood and so replaced the legitimate priest, Onias III.

Meanwhile, in Jerusalem, Antiochus and his local affiliates banned circumcision and sacrificed a pig on the altar of the Jerusalem Temple. According to 1 Maccabees 1:60–61, babies found to have been circumcised were killed and then tied to the necks of their mothers as a sign to all of the fate of those who insisted on practicing their tradition. Leading the revolt against this system was a family from Modein: a local priest named Eliezar, son of Hasmon, and his sons. Under the leadership of one son, Judah, called "Maccabee" or "Hammerer," these Hasmoneans or Maccabees through guerrilla warfare in 165 defeated the Syrian army, rededicated the Temple ("rededication" is, in Hebrew, "Hannukah," and hence the origin of the holiday mentioned in John 5 and still celebrated by Jews today), and took over the government. Shortly thereafter, they also took over the priesthood, a move that caused additional disaffection among several Jewish groups. Likely at this point, a group of Jews led by the "Teacher of Righteousness" (or Righteous Teacher) rejected both the Temple and Jerusalem. Eventually settling at Qumran, by the Dead Sea, they produced their own scriptures as they waited for the redemption of Israel.

The Hasmoneans reigned for the next one hundred years. Consolidating their power, they engaged in expansionist practices that included the annexation of territories both north and south of Jerusalem. By the end of the reign of Alexander Jannaeus (107–76), the borders of Israel were more-or-less equivalent to the territories associated with King David: from Dan (upper Galilee) in the north to Beersheva (the Negev) in the south. Local populations were given the choice: circumcision or death; most chose the former option, including the Idumaeans and Ituraeans. Relations with the Samaritan population to the north, which were never smooth, worsened when Alexander Jannaeus burned their temple on Mount Gerizim (see John 4).

Josephus, our first-century historian, locates during the Hasmonean period the origin of the three major Jewish groups (he calls them *haireseis*, meaning "parties" or "sects") often mentioned in New Testament introductions. In the context of the high priesthoood of Jonathan, circa 145, he notes that there arose three groups "which held different opinions concerning human affairs; the first being that of the Pharisees, the second that of the Sadducees, and the third that of the Essenes. As for the Pharisees, they say that certain events are the work of fate, but not all; as to other events it depends upon ourselves whether they shall take place or not. The sect of Essenes, however, declares that Fate is the mistress of all things, and that nothing befalls people unless in accordance with her decree. But the Sadducees do away with Fate, holding that there is no such thing and that human actions are not achieved in accordance with her decree, but that all things lie within our own power" (*Ant.* 13.171–73). The impact of Hellenism is epitomized by the descriptions, for Josephus has presented the Jewish groups as philosophical schools; he will later compare Pharisees to Stoics (*Life* 12), Essenes to Pythagoreans (*Ant.* 13.171–73), and (implicitly) Sadducees to Epicureans.

The New Testament does not mention the Essenes; whether this group should be associated with the Dead Sea Scrolls and so the group that followed the Righteous Teacher remains, although usually accepted, still not demonstrated by the scrolls themselves. The scrolls do mention a "wicked priest" (1QpHab), an illegitimate figure presiding in the Temple: Jonathan (ca. 152 BCE) as well as his brother Simon (ca. 143/142 BCE) are both plausible candidates. Whereas Josephus indicates that the Essenes lived in groups throughout Judea, Pliny the Elder and Dio Crysostom locate their community by the Dead Sea. Both views may be correct. The document known as the Rule of the Community (1QS; the number indicates which of the fourteen caves in which the scroll was found; Q stands for Qumran, and the S stands for *Serek ha-yachad*, Hebrew for "Rule of the Community") notes that the community was composed of celibate men, but the Cairo-Damascus Document (CD), a text that surfaced earlier than the finds at the Dead Sea but that is clearly associated with the people who composed the scrolls (as we see with the 4QDamascus Document Fragments and other remains), mentions married members with children. Archaeological investigation indicates that the Qumran community itself was inhabited from approximately 140 BCE until 68 CE, when it was overrun by the Roman Legion 10 Fratensis and turned into army barracks.

The Gospels mention the Sadducees in the context of the Passion narrative, and Sadducees are oddly grouped with Pharisees as coming to John the Baptist. The Gospels as well as Acts confirm the Sadducees' lack of belief in the Resurrection.

Jesus is more often portrayed as in confrontation with the Pharisees. Josephus, the Gospels, Paul (see Philippians 3), and the Rabbinic sources can be correlated to provide at least a partial reconstruction of Pharisaic beliefs, such as their "handing down to the people certain regulations from the ancestral succession and not recorded in the Laws of Moses" (*Ant.* 13; cf. *Pirke Avot* 1; Mark 7/Matthew 15). Although never explicitly identified as "Pharisees" in the early Rabbinic documents, Hillel and Shammai are typically seen as representing diverse forms of Pharisaic thought. It is Hillel who is recorded as responding, when asked to summarize the Law while standing on one foot, "What is hateful to you, to not do to others. This is the whole Torah; the rest is commentary. Now go and learn" (*b. Shabbat* 31a). (Given the difficulties of using the various tendentious sources for reconstructing Pharisaic views, a "quest for the historical Pharisees" would be well in order.)

Hasmonean power began to crumble within a generation. Jannaeus was succeeded by his wife, Queen Salome Alexandra (Shlomzion or Shalom-Zion), who according to Josephus reigned with the support of the Pharisees. Her rule would mark the last independent Jewish state until 1948. Under her direction, the Sanhedrin shifted from being an entirely aristocratic organization to a more representative juridical body.

Upon the queen's death in 67 BCE, her two sons, Aristobulus and Hyrcanus II, vied for power. Aristobulus garnered Sadducaic support and so returned to power the group that previously held influence in the court of Jannaeus. Meanwhile, his older brother, Hyrcanus II, not only the heir apparent but also the high priest, attempted to consolidate his own support base. Following a battle between the two forces, Hyrcanus eventually surrendered, and Aristobulus took the throne as well as, likely, the high priesthood.

Aided by, indeed, prompted by, several allies, including Antipater, the son of the Idumean governor appointed by Jannaeus, Hyrcanus made a second attempt at the throne. Both brothers, recognizing that support from outside was required for securing power, turned to Rome. And Rome was more than happy to gain one more holding in the Middle East. In 64 BCE, Pompey brought the former Seleucid territories, including Judea and Galilee, into Roman control. Solicited by both brothers, in 63 Pompey also was petitioned by representatives from the population of Jerusalem, who rather than being ruled by either Aristobulus or Hyrcanus, actually requested direct Roman rule. When Pompey delayed his decision in order to resolve a crisis concerning neighboring Nabatea, Aristobulus attempted to seize power yet again, this time by occupying the fortress of Alexandrium. Pompey then invaded Jerusalem, where Hyrcanus welcomed him by opening the city gates. Aristobulus held the Temple grounds for three months until Pompey finally defeated his forces. The Roman general himself secured the Temple and entered the inner sanctum, the Holy of Holies. The *Psalms of Solomon*, expressing one form of Jewish messianic hope, were written in the wake of Pompey's incursions.

Pompey took formal control over the remaining Hasmonean territories: Judea, Galilee, Idumea, and Perea. He did return Hyrcanus II to his high priestly duties, but the office was stripped of much of its political power. Local power was put instead into the hands of Hyrcanus's Idumean adviser, Antipater. During the war of the First Triumvirate, in 48, Hyrcanus sent troops to support Julius Caesar in Egypt. As a reward, Caesar appointed Hyrcanus "Ethnarch of the Jews," but the position was more symbolic than authoritative.

Antipater appointed his son Herod the governor of Jerusalem in 47, and Rome expanded Herod's rule to include Coele-Syria and Samaria. In 42, Marc Antony, who along with Octavian and Lapidus defeated Brutus and Cassius and so ended the old Republican system, appointed Herod tetrarch of Judea. In 40, Antigonus, the son of Aristobulus II, allied with the Parthians, attacked Judea, captured Hyrcanus (and, by cutting off his ears, prevented him from continuing to serve as high priest; cf. Leviticus 21:17), and gained the throne. The Roman Senate then appointed Herod king of Judea; Herod, with full Roman support, regained complete power in 37 and held it until his death, decades later, in 4 BCE. It was during the latter years of this reign that, according to Matthew's Gospel, Jesus was born.

This combination of local Herodian rule and imperial Roman control provides the context for Jesus' life. The instability in local politics that created shifts in power between Pharisees and Sadducees, the founding of the Qumran community, and the replacement of Hasmonean with Herodian control was mirrored on the international scene. In 36, Herod's patron Antony left his wife, Octavian's sister, and married Cleopatra of Egypt. Five years later, Octavian avenged his sister and gained his own complete power over Rome with his defeat of Antony at the Battle of Actium. Octavian gained the title "Augustus" ("exalted one"; see Luke 2:1) and during his rule (27 BCE–14 CE) presented himself as the people's savior who established (by military means) the Pax Romana, the "peace of Rome," upon all his territories. From 31 on, Herod securely held Judea and Galilee, and Augustus held the throne in Rome. The empire was at peace, and Herod turned his attention to domestic matters.

Herod's building projects changed the face of his territories. He rebuilt Samaria (called "Sebaste" in honor of Augustus), built the port of Caesarea, reinforced the Hasmonean building complex on Masada, and began renovations of the Jerusalem Temple, a project that was not completed until 64 CE during the reign of his great-grandson, Agrippa II. The Temple, whose importance to Judaism has been noted already in connection with the Maccabean revolt, remained central in Jewish thought. For some it was a site of pilgrimage (see Luke 2) and worship (see Acts

1); for others it was a corrupt institution that would eventually be replaced (so from the Dead Sea Scrolls, 11QTemple). Religiously, it was the point of contact between heaven and earth, the dwelling place of the universal God. Economically, it was the national bank. Politically, it represented the relationship between Rome and the Jews, for the high priest could serve only with Rome's approval, and from 6 CE on, following the exile of Herod's son Archelaus from Judea, Rome kept control of the high priestly vestments. The Temple served as the basis of power for the party of the Sadducees; the Pharisees adapted the holiness signified by the Temple altar to the domestic sphere, such that the home became also a locus of sanctity. Jesus' followers continued to worship there (so Acts), a point that complicates any understanding of his "cleansing" of the Temple (John 2, Mark 11, Luke 19, Matthew 21). Did he mean to renew it? Reform it? Predict its destruction? Proclaim its illegitimacy? Did he even engage in an action in the Temple, or did his condemnation of certain Temple practices metastacize through legendary development into a full-blown scene of disrupting Temple activities?

Upon Herod's death, his territory was divided among his three surviving sons; he had executed his others, along with his Hasmonean mother-in-law, her daughter and his beloved wife, Mariamme, and a good many other rivals, both actual and imagined. (Matthew's account of the "Slaughter of the Innocents" [Matthew 2:16–18], although not elsewhere attested and certainly following the story of Moses, is not inconsistent with Herod's increasingly erratic behavior.) One son, Archelaus, ruled Judea from 4 BCE until 6 CE, when he was replaced by direct Roman rule. At this point, Judea and Samaria fell under the jurisdiction of a series of prefects; notable among these is Pontius Pilate, who ruled from 26 to 36 CE.

Another son, Herod Antipas, ruled Galilee from 4 BCE until he was exiled by Caligula in 39 CE. Antipas continued such large-scale construction with the rebuilding of Sepphoris, just a few miles from Nazareth, and the establishment of the new capital city of Tiberias. These two cities—the largest centers of Galilee—are not mentioned in the pages of the New Testament, although their connection to Jesus remains a matter of much speculation. Perhaps Jesus, identified in Mark's Gospel (Mark 6:3; cf. Matthew 13:55) as a "builder" (*tektōn*, sometimes translated "carpenter"), found work in Sepphoris; perhaps he found in Galilee's growing urbanization a depletion of peasant resources and the consequent increase in the disparity between rich and poor, or perhaps the new cities created an economic boom for the local population. Antipas is mentioned in the Gospels for his execution of John the Baptist (Mark 6, Matthew 14, Luke 9; cf. Luke 3). Whether the execution was prompted by John's condemnation of Antipas's incestuous marriage to Herodias (so the Gospels), or whether Antipas had engaged in a preemptive strike against the popular teacher (so Josephus, *Ant.* 18:118–19), the execution does indicate that gathering crowds in Galilee, or speaking of alternative rules to that of Rome and its local representatives, was a very dangerous enterprise. The fates of other "prophets of deliverance" such as the Samaritan prophet who led a crowd to Mount Gerizim (he and his followers were massacred by Pontius Pilate) confirm this point. The Gospel of Luke mentions that Pilate, learning that Jesus was a Galilean, sent him to Antipas, who had come to Jerusalem for the Passover festival. Finding him innocent, Antipas returns him to Pilate (Luke 23).

In discussing the tenure of Pontius Pilate, Josephus records in *Ant.* 18:

> About this time there appeared Jesus, a wise man, if one should even call him a man. For he was a doer of striking deeds and as a teacher of such people as accept the truth gladly. He gained a following both among many Jews and among many of the Greeks. He was the Messiah [Greek: *Christ*]. When Pilate, upon hearing him accused by leading men among us, had condemned him to be crucified, those who had in the first place come to love him did not give up their affection for him. On the third day he appeared to them, living again, for the prophets of God had prophesied these and countless other marvelous things about him. And the tribe of Christians, so called after him, still to this day has not disappeared.

The passage remains controversial for several reasons, including the following: all extant Greek manuscripts are preserved by the church, and the earliest dates to the eleventh century (did pious monks add to a less "Christian" original?); Arabic versions lack this passage (did pious Muslim scribes remove it?); although Josephus sometimes is cited by Patristic writers, this particular passage is not attested in the Patristic corpus prior to the fourth century; Josephus does not in any other writing, including his autobiography, attest to Christian belief himself; his accounting of the death of James, whom he describes as "the brother of Jesus, the so-called Christ" (*Ant.* 20.9.1), still does not indicate that Josephus had become a member of the movement.

Although Josephus typically is regarded as offering the only secure non-Christian testimony to Jesus, the Pagan (or possibly Samaritan) historian Thallus may be not only another source but an earlier one. His account of an eclipse at the time of Jesus' Crucifixion, an account Dale Allison translated for this volume, may even provide evidence of a pre-Marcan Passion story.

Similarly controversial is the Babylonian Talmud's account of Jesus' death (to the extant that some Rabbinic experts do not think the reference is to the Jesus of the New Testament!). Tractate *Sanhedrin* (43a) records: "On the eve of Passover they hanged Yeshu of Nazareth. And the herald went before him forty days, saying, 'Yeshu of Nazareth is going forth to be stoned, since he has practiced sorcery and cheated, and led people astray. Let everyone knowing anything in his defense come and plead for him.' But they found no one in his defense, and they hanged him on the eve of Passover." This very confused statement, with its combination of hanging (i.e., on the cross) and stoning (the prescribed penalty for blasphemy [Leviticus 24:14]), reflects Jewish reaction to Christian claims. Accepting the New Testament's story and so the standard Christian teaching that the Sanhedrin condemned Jesus (there is no Sanhedrin trial in John's Gospel, but it is mentioned in the Synoptics), the Rabbis provided their own interpretation: Jesus was provided every opportunity for release; the legal process was followed.

The New Testament, as we have suggested, has its own agenda. Jesus' followers recorded what they recalled of his teachings, whether in direct citation (translated from the Aramaic or even originally in Greek) or in idea if not exact word-ing. They recounted those teachings and events that would have had special meaning to them and their communities, and they adapted this material to the needs of their communities (hence, four canonical Gospels rather than just one). As the followers of Jesus spread their message beyond Jerusalem, to Diaspora Jews, Samaritans, and Gentiles, again, the message was adapted to changing needs and circumstances. Christian teachers needed to show how Jesus fulfilled Jewish prophecy, but they also needed to be sure that they would not be en-trapped by sporadic Gentile hostilities against Jews, such as the social intolerance that marked Alexandria and Antioch and Rome between 38 and 41 CE.

From Philo, the Jewish philosopher from Alexandria, comes additional indica-tion of how diverse, and how precarious, Jewish life was. Philo is today best known for clothing the stories of Jewish scriptures in Platonic terms and speak-ing of the *Logos*, the "Word," as the mediating principle between divine transcen-dence and materiality (cf. John 1:1). He mentions with great approbation a group of celibate Jews, men (Therapeutae) and women (Therapeutrides), who gather for common meals and worship and who dedicate their lives to philosophical study. Conversely, he condemns the "extreme allegorists" who take the biblical materials only as symbolic and therefore dismiss circumcision, dietary practices, and other activities that mark Judaism's distinction. Ironically, Philo's works were preserved not by Jews but by Christians who found his allegorical readings of scripture compelling. Philo's comments on Jewish orthodoxy and orthopraxy, in-cluding his teaching that "what someone hates to experience, he should not do" (*Hypothetica* 8), and his reflections on eschatological hope help to locate Jesus within his broader Jewish context.

Philo is also one source (Josephus is the other) for the events in the 40s that again brought Jewish sensibilities and the Roman state into conflict. In 37 CE, Caligula became emperor and almost immediately began to involve himself in Is-rael's politics. A friend of Herod Agrippa I (the grandson of Herod the Great and his Hasmonean wife, Mariamne), Caligula exiled Antipas and Herodias (Agrippa's sister) from Galilee. He gave to Agrippa not only the tetrarchy held by Herod's other son, Philip (including Caesara Philippi), but also Antipas's Galilee. The population of Alexandria mocked Agrippa I when he visited in 38; Philo's de-scription of this event bears striking similarity to the mocking of Jesus (Matthew 27:27–31; Mark 15:16–20; John 19:2–3). Similarly, Philo's description of the scourging of Jewish leaders by Flaccus provides detail on the type of torture Jesus likely endured (Matthew 27:26; Mark 15:15).

But this favorable attitude toward Agrippa, the new "King of the Jews," shifted in 40/41, when Caligula determined to have his statue placed in the Jerusalem Temple. The Judean population threatened revolt; Josephus recounts, "Many tens of thousands of Jews with their wives and children came" to the Syrian governor "with petitions not to use force to make them transgress and violate their ances-tral code"; they state, "on no account would we fight . . . but we will sooner die than violate our laws" (*Ant.* 18; *War* 2; we might compare Jesus' comments about nonviolent resistance). Philo's treatment of this same incident offers a detailed description of Pontius Pilate; whether exaggerated or not, this view of Pilate contrasts with the Gospels' more benign presentations. Agrippa did his best to keep the people calm during the crisis. Before his order could be enacted, Caligula was assassinated; he was succeeded by Claudius, who rewarded Agrippa also with Judea and Samaria. Agrippa ruled until 44 (his death is recorded in both *Ant.* 19 and Acts 12). His rule was marked, inter alia, by persecution of Jesus' followers (see Acts 12:1–19).

During the early 40s, as the proclamation that Jesus of Nazareth was the Christ began to spread, controversy accompanied the message. The proclamation did not convince the majority of Jews: those who did have messianic expectations expected the messianic age to come with the Messiah (hence Paul's statement that Jesus is the "first fruits of the resurrection" [1 Corinthians 15:20]; the agricultural metaphor indicates that Paul expected the final harvest during the same season). Some Jews found the proclamation not only unbelievable but dangerous: to announce that one followed a new "king" was politically perilous in the Roman Empire. The problem was especially acute in the Diaspora, where relations between Jews—granted special privileges by the Roman government, such as exemption from participating in sacrifices to the gods and serving in the army (a problem for those who insisted on kosher food and who would not march on the Sabbath)—and the local populations were not without difficulties. We already have noted the hatred of Jews manifested by the Alexandrians' mocking of Agrippa I. It may be the struggles between Jews who accepted the Christian proclamation and those who did not that prompted the expulsion of the Jews from Rome. Suetonius (*Life of Claudius* 25.4) reports, "Since the Jews were constantly causing disturbances at the instigation of Chrestus, Claudius expelled them from Rome." Or, the otherwise unknown "Chrestus" could have been a local agitator.

In 44, Agrippa I died. Because his son and heir, Agrippa II, was only seventeen at the time, Claudius annexed his territory and appointed over it a series of governors (first "prefects" and then "procurators"). Fadus (44–46) ruled when the charismatic leader Theudas attempted to part the Jordan; his successor, Tiberius Julius Alexander—Philo's nephew—ruled from 46 to 48, the period that witnessed the revolts of the sons of Judas the Galilean. Cumanus (48–52) allowed tensions between Galilee and Samaria to worsen until Judea became involved; only when Agrippa II urged Claudius to take action was Cumanus removed. Felix (52–60), whose personal involvement with Agrippa II's sister Drusilla is noted both by Acts 24:24 and by Josephus (*Ant.* 18–20; *War* 2), put down several inchoate revolts; he also dispersed the followers of another charismatic leader, called by Josephus "the Egyptian," who attempted to set himself up as king. His successor, Festus (60–62; see Acts 25:12), exacerbated local tensions by threatening to raze a wall that blocked the Temple from his view. During this period, persecution of Jesus' followers was sporadic. In 62, between the departure of Festus and the arrival of Albinus (62–64), the high priest ordered the execution of James, the leader of the Jerusalem church. Josephus records, "Ananus called the

Sanhedrin together, brought before it James, the brother of Jesus who was called the Christ, and certain others . . . and he caused them to be stoned" (*Ant.* 20). Josephus does not indicate that James's messianic views prompted his execution; the context of the passage suggests instead that James and the "others" may have protested the high priest's greed in withholding tithes from the Levites.

Meanwhile, Agrippa II, finally coming of age, began his own political career. In 49, Claudius granted him control of the Temple, including the power to appoint the high priest. Indeed, upon receiving complaints by Pharisees against Ananus's execution of James, Agrippa removed the high priest from office. As Rome continued to add more territory to his control, Agrippa continued his fidelity to the emperor. When hostilities against Rome broke out in 66 during the governorship of Florus (64–66), he counseled peace.

Numerous factors prompted the revolt, including inept and voracious procurators, growing nationalism fanned by religious fervor, strife between Jews and Gentiles, economic disasters caused by drought and famine and exacerbated by high taxes, unemployment in Jerusalem created by the completion of the Temple's renovations, and banditry. Several groups promoted the rebellion, including the Zealots (whom Josephus calls the "Fourth Philosophy" [*Ant.* 18], and the *Sicarii*, "dagger men" whose practice was to assassinate Roman officials and their collaborators). Within a year, the rebels took the Temple, and the daily offerings to the emperor were stopped. Although along with Agrippa II others counseled peace, including the scholar Yochanan ben Zakkai, other Jews in Galilee and Judea as well as Samaritans took up arms.

Nero sent Vespasian to quell the revolt. In 67, Vespasian entered Galilee, where the rebel general, our historian Josephus, not only surrendered but also predicted Vespasian's success. Joining the Roman camp, Josephus took the commander's family name, Flavius. By 68, Vespasian reached Qumran. The covenanters, who had expected the "War of the Sons of Light against the Sons of Darkness" (1QM), met the might of Rome instead.

In Jerusalem, Jewish factions vied for power. Simon bar Giora, John of Gischala, and the priest Eliezer ben Simeon each controlled portions of the Temple Mount. Burning the city's store of grain, the groups sacrificed Jerusalem's security in favor of temporary military advantage. Letting the Jews in Jerusalem kill each other, Vespasian secured the rest of the country by 69. During this time, the Pharisaic leader Yochanan ben Zakkai escaped Jerusalem. Late Rabbinic accounts (*b. Gittin* 56b; *Avot de Rabbi Natan* version A ch. 4) suggest that he received Vespasian's permission to establish a school in Jamnia (also called Yavneh); alternatively, Yavneh could have been a Roman prison camp.

In July 69, following Nero's suicide, Rome's armies in the eastern part of the empire declared Vespasian emperor. Vespasian appointed his son Titus to lead the troops in Jerusalem and returned, with Josephus, to Rome. In August 70, the Temple burned, whether by the Roman troops or the local Zealots or by accident remains unknown. Only the western wall (the "Wailing Wall"; the *Kotel*), constructed of Herodian stone, remains. Titus took seven hundred prisoners to

Rome for his victory parade; his commemorative arch depicts the Temple's major symbols, including the seven-branched candelabrum (*menorah*) and the altar table. Rome transformed the two-drachma (half-shekel) Temple tax into the *Fiscus Judaicus*, the "Jew tax," now to be paid by all Jewish men for the upkeep of the temple of Jupiter in Rome. Coins inscribed with "Judea Capta" and depicting a weeping woman celebrated Rome's victory.

The Flavians—Vespasian, Titus, and the younger son Domitian—would rule Rome for the next several decades. Judaism would turn to the successors of the Pharisees and the scribes, the group soon to be known as the "Rabbis" (the term comes from the Aramaic word for "teacher"; see John 1:38) or "Tannaim." Following their time at Jamnia, first under the leadership of ben Zakkai and then Gamaliel II (ca. 80–120), the group would relocate to Galilee. In Caesarea, their successors would codify the oral law in the Mishnah (ca. 200). Christianity would turn increasingly toward the Gentile world, and worship of Jesus would come to the attention of the state.

It is within this fascinating and complex historical setting that Jesus was born, engaged in what would become a world-transforming ministry, was executed on a Roman cross, and was proclaimed the Resurrected Lord by his followers. What he actually said and did, however, remain, as we have seen, open questions for many students of the Gospels. The sources translated and discussed in this volume will allow these students to locate Jesus within history and, perhaps, to find his history as well.

Sources

Jonathan L. Reed's selection of archaeological evidence of the emperor cult in the eastern Mediterranean, urbanization in first-century Palestine, and domestic space in Galilean village life establishes the major parameters by which we can contextualize the world of Jesus and his followers. In the public areas of Rome's cities, the emperor advertised his power and that of the state through temples and statues, sacrifices and games. Titles such as "Lord," "Savior," and "Son of God," as well as use of the term "good news" or "good tidings" (Greek: *euaggelion*; English: Gospel) for his acts of public beneficence, show the inextricability of what we today would call "religious" and "political" discourse. There was no "separation of church and state" in the Roman Empire, and that a human being could be seen as "divine" and could be hailed as bringing "Gospel" was by no means anomalous. This imperial cult penetrated even into Jesus' Galilee: the fragmentary Latin inscription that records the name of Pontius Pilate comes from the Tiberium, a structure erected for the worship of the emperor Tiberius, in Caesarea.

However, there was no Roman legionary presence in Galilee at the time of Jesus, and the tetrarch Herod Antipas (who ruled from 4 BCE to 39 CE) erected no Pagan temples and minted no coins depicting human faces. Nor, as Reed observes, were the new cities of Sepphoris and Tiberias "Pagan centers of Hellenization or Romanization." We might therefore conclude that Jesus' concerns, at least while he remained in Galilee, focused less on the wider Roman world than on local economic practices, for those new cities certainly would have affected village life.

People residing by the Sea of Galilee lived modestly (at best) in homes of unhewn basalt fieldstone, with walls smeared with mud, straw, and even dung, beaten-earth floors, and thatched straw and mud roofs; in contrast, houses in Sepphoris had mosaic floors, tiled roofs, and walls decorated with frescoes. Reed suggests that to "feed these cities and to pay for their construction, Antipas needed to increase agricultural production across the Galilean valleys, and in the process some farmers would have been moved off their land or become tenants on what was once their land. The Gospel traditions seem to be well aware of such phenomena, which represent the darker side of urbanization." On the other hand, tenant farmers and peasants are staple figures in preindustrial agricultural contexts; the extent to which the economic demographics in, for example, the environs of Nazareth, Capernaum, or Bethsaida changed in the 20s and 30s remains debated.

Jerusalem was another story. Like Caesarea, Jerusalem witnessed massive amounts of Hellenistic and Roman influence, in particular through Herod the Great's rebuilding of the Temple. This institution, which functioned as the center of Jewish sacrificial worship as well as the national bank and a tourist attraction, drew visitors from throughout the empire, Jewish as well as Gentile. Further, Roman soldiers were a presence in Judea, and Pilate's entourage would accompany him to Jerusalem at the pilgrimage festivals such as Passover. Thus, it is possible that Jesus' message changed as he moved from the villages of Galilee to Jerusalem of Judea.

The entire area was thoroughly marked by Jewish concerns. Throughout Galilee and Judea, in strata dated to the late Second Temple period, archaeologists have located numerous stone vessels (used because they were not susceptible to ritual impurity; see John 2), miqva'ot (stepped plastered pools for ritual immersion), and, here a negative example, the absence of pork bones, for pork was considered "unclean" (see Leviticus 11).

Within the rapidly changing cultural setting, as Roman architecture began to mark the landscape and Roman coins to proclaim the power of the empire, Jewish "Prophets of Deliverance," as Craig Evans labels them, began to appear. Josephus (37–100 CE), whose four extant works provide our most detailed information about Jewish life in the first century CE, records, along with commentary on Pharisees, Sadducees, Essenes, and Zealots, information about public figures who attracted crowds of Jews and who paid for that popularity with their lives. As Evans demonstrates, "Review of the activities of these figures helps us understand better the political tensions and religious hopes of the Jewish people in late antiquity, again clarifying the context in which Christianity emerged."

Josephus offers a detailed account of John the Baptist that differs somewhat from the portrait painted by the canonical Gospels. Whereas the Baptist in the Gospels is an eschatologically oriented prophet anticipating the messianic king, Josephus emphasizes John's interest in purity and his popularity with the crowds (according to Josephus, it was John's popularity, not his condemnation of Antipas's marriage to Herodias, that prompted his arrest and execution). The Evangelists may have sought to harmonize John's role with that of Jesus and so mitigate any sense of rivalry between the two; Josephus, who had his own agenda, may have omitted John's eschatological interests lest he offend the sensibilities of his Roman audience.

Next, Josephus mentions "a certain Samaritan" who led a group of followers to Mount Gerizim (see John 4), likely in the hopes of the appearance of the *Taheb*, the "restorer" who would fulfill the promises of Deuteronomy 18. Following them came Pilate's troops and, because of the ensuing massacre, Pilate was recalled (finally) by Rome. Other such figures—Theudas, "the Egyptian," Jonathan—all suffered similar fates, as Luke also remarks (Acts 5:36–37 mentions both Theudas and Judas the Galilean). That Jesus believed he would suffer and die in Jerusalem would not be unexpected, given the fate of both the prophets according to some Jewish traditions (see Matthew 23 as well as the Pseudepigraphon *Lives of the Prophets*) and the popular leaders such as John the Baptist in his own time.

Jesus' own teachings can even be seen as having a distinct political edge. Mary Rose D'Angelo details how the reference to God as "father" (Aramaic: *Abba*), famous from the Lord's Prayer—"Our Father [who is] in heaven" (Matthew 6:9)—presents a challenge to Rome, for the emperor Augustus and his successors had appropriated from pre-Roman Platonic and Stoic thought the title "Father" (*pater patriae*, "Father of the Fatherland"). Given the recent swing in historical Jesus studies toward a focus on Roman colonialism, the chapters by Reed, Evans, and D'Angelo helpfully provide the sometimes overlooked details concerning both prevailing imperial authority and various reactions to it.

D'Angelo's contribution also helpfully discusses the tendency in earlier "historical Jesus" research to insist upon a distinction between Jesus and "Judaism" (itself tendentiously defined), an insistence supported by the criterion of dissimilarity. "Abba," addressed by Jesus only in Mark 14:36 and cited twice by Paul (Galatians 4:6; Romans 8:15), had been, incorrectly as well as apologetically, deemed "an absolutely new and unique relationship with the deity." Instead, the reference to the Deity as "father" appears in the Dead Sea Scrolls as well as other Jewish texts from the Second Temple period, and it attested to the people's belief in divine providence, power, and justice. To call the Deity one's father was thus both theological affirmation and statement of hope.

To call a god one's father was also a familiar motif in the Greco-Roman world, as Charles Talbert demonstrates in his contribution on "miraculous conceptions and births." "Divine births" fill Greek and Roman mythologies: Achilles is the son of Thetis, and his rival Aeneas the son of Aphrodite; Zeus fathered Hercules and Dionysus; Apollo was the father of Asclepius and Aristaeus; Romulus, the founder of Rome, was the son of Mars. . . . Divine paternity also was accorded to historical figures: Plato was deemed the son of Apollo, and Alexander the Great the son of Zeus. Seutonius speaks of Augustus Caesar as Apollo's offspring; Apollonius of Tyana was, according to his biographer Philostratus, fathered by Proteus, an Egyptian god, and the list continues. Nor was Plutarch alone in recording accounts of virgins impregnated by a god (his skepticism is palpable). Given these narratives, Talbert summarizes what the Evangelists' first readers would have gathered: "The Greco-Roman conviction that a human's superiority can be explained only by a divine creative act is used to establish the prevenience of divine grace in the divine-human relation."

The "miraculous birth" form also was familiar to Jews. Scripture recounts numerous special conceptions, including those of Isaac (Genesis 18, 21), Samson (Judges 13), and Samuel (1 Samuel 1–2) to women considered infertile, and by the Hellenistic period, Jewish tradition conceived new and even more miraculous tales of special births. George Nickelsburg discusses *1 Enoch* and Qumran's *Genesis Apocryphon's* recordings of the miraculous circumstances surrounding Noah's birth, as well as *2 Enoch's* narrative of the birth of Melchizedek (see Genesis 14; Psalm 110), a figure identified with Jesus in the Epistle to the Hebrews (6:19–7:10). Peter Flint's translation of the Qumran text 11QMelchizedek indicates the association of this priestly figure with forgiveness of sins, the announcement of salvation, acts of final judgment, the defeat of Satan (here called Belial), and the year of Jubilee when debts are forgiven, even as it seems to understand Melchizedek himself as divine.

When we turn from accounts of Jesus' birth to the teachings attributed to him, again we find numerous connections to forms well known among both Jews and Gentiles. However, before the formal contextualization can be discussed, we begin with information on how stories were composed and transmitted. David Gowler's contribution on the composition of a *chreia*—"a remembrance of some saying or action or a manifestation of both that has a concise resolution for the purpose of something useful" (Hermogenes 3–4) demonstrates the freedom rhetoricians had in conveying information and thus the potential that any search for the "exact words" or "exact deeds" of Jesus may be thwarted by the Evangelists' rhetorical skills. Gowler explains how ancient authors had "the freedom to change, adapt, and expand" materials.

Among the changes were adaptations from earlier accounts. Stories of Jesus' healings, exorcisms, and control over nature find biblical antecedents in Elisha (2 Kings 4, 5) and Isaiah (Isaiah 38). By late antiquity, as Alan J. Avery-Peck demonstrates in his chapter "The Galilean Charismatic and Rabbinic Piety: The Holy Man in the Talmudic Literature," Jewish sources had fully developed views about disease as well as the ability of select pious individuals to effect cures through exorcism, prayer, or ritual. Yet with the destruction of the Jerusalem Temple in 70 and then the disaster of the Bar Kokhba revolt against Rome (132–35), the Rabbis recognized the dangers of claiming direct heavenly commission or revelation. In their view, the age of prophecy was over: knowledge of the divine will would come from study of the Written and Oral Torahs, not visionary experience and not charismatic claims. Consequently, Rabbinic holy men and miracle workers such as Honi the Circle-Drawer and Hanina ben Dosa are domesticated from charismatic prophets to faithful scholars.

The Gentile world also had its healers and teachers, although their prevalence in the first century CE is a matter of some debate. Whereas Wendy Cotter argues in her contribution on the god Asclepius, the Pythagorean philosophers, and the Roman rulers that stories of "healings, raisings from the dead, exorcisms, and nature miracles" were plentiful in both Jewish and Gentile settings, she also notes that Gerd Theissen claims instead that it was Christianity that created widespread interest in such accounts.

As Cotter demonstrates, Asclepius—child of a divine father, rescued from death, a healer who surpassed his teachers, able to restore life to the dead, and killed himself by the order of Zeus—was the focus of popular devotion from at least the third century BCE onward. Known for his compassion, lack of regard for the social status of his supplicants, and the "absence of any myths of selfishness around him," he was one model of an early savior figure. The Pythagorean philosophers were seen as having intimate knowledge of and contact with the divine, which enabled them to perform nature miracles such as stilling storms. The first-century CE holy man Apollonius of Tyana was a Pythagorean philosopher known for healings and raising the dead; his biographer Philostratus wrote in order to exculpate him from charges of sorcery. Finally, Cotter adduces accounts of imperial propaganda, such as Julius Caesar's stilling of a storm and Vespasian's curing of the blind and the lame.

This world of healers and miracle workers is marked not only by attention to piety but also by a pervasive attention to magic (what one witness would label as "miracle" another might call "magic" and still a third "medicine": the distinction often had more to do with the forces invoked in the cure as well as its cost than with the process itself). Such interest in accessing the spiritual or supernatural world is epitomized by the Mithras Liturgy, translated by Marvin Meyer. The text speaks of the "ecstatic ascent of the soul" and the opportunity to be "born again," of purification rituals (baptisms) and sacred meals of bread and cup that symbolize body and blood (of a bull, a "divine sacrifice"), of a god who dies and rises and who, as one inscription reads, "saved us after having shed the eternal blood." As Meyer trenchantly notes, the resemblance of Mithraism to early Christianity is so extensive that it makes "Christian apologists scramble to invent creative theological explanations to account for the similarities."

Also demonstrating the pervasive influence of magic is the early second-century CE *Metamorphoses* (also called the Book of Transformations or the *Golden Ass*) of Apuleius. The *Metamorphoses*, as Ian H. Henderson explains, helps "modern readers to imagine historically what Greco-Roman polytheist religion might have been like" and, specifically, how a "magician" would have been perceived. Replete with prayers to the goddess Isis and visionary dreams (cf. Matthew 1–2; Acts 10), purification rituals involving immersion and diet, miraculous healings, and even a trial before a provincial Roman court, the text relies upon its readers' cultural knowledge to recognize where *realia* cedes to artificiality and history gives way to farce.

Such distinction between history and farce, as well as between the literal and allegorical, leads directly to Gary Porton's detailed study of the parable (Hebrew: *mashal*) in both the Tanakh/Old Testament and Rabbinic literature. Porton begins with a wise caution: "Although the Synoptic Gospels and the Rabbinic collections share the phenomenon of the parable featuring human characters, it is extremely difficult to determine how the parables and the parable form in the Synoptic Gospels related to the Rabbinic corpus." Then follows an extremely helpful overview not only of the Rabbinic corpus but of why such comparisons between the Gospels and Rabbinic literature must be undertaken with enormous care.

Regarding the parables, Porton finds a number of connections in terms of form, but also a number of strong distinctions between those attributed to Jesus and those attributed to the Rabbis. For example, Rabbinic parables often begin with a scriptural prompt and function as biblical intepretation, while those attributed to Jesus do not. This distinction may come from the different settings of the speakers: the Rabbis are scholars who directly engage Judaism's scriptures; Jesus is not operating in the atmosphere of a "school" wherein study of the Law is paramount.

It would be insufficient to see Jesus' parables only in the context of Rabbinic teachings, for the Gentile world made, most famously in Aesop's fables, its own contributions to the genre. Further, Jesus and Aesop share some remarkable connections, including what might be called the "quest for the historical Aesop"; as Lawrence Wills remarks in the opening to his fascinating study, "It is not clear that there ever was a historical Aesop." Aesop's story, as it was recounted, is a "Gospel" of sorts. Wills summarizes: Aesop has a lowly beginning but receives divine favor, he engages in a soteriologically motivated ministry and is despised by many as a result, he faces trumped-up charges of blasphemy, and, after he is executed, a cult dedicated to him begins. However, whereas the stories told about Jesus are generally serious, the *Life of Aesop* is marked by whimsy and satire as well as, occasionally, scatology. In the traditions concerning Jesus, it is in his parables where the whimsy and satire are found, not in the story of his Passion. Nevertheless, perhaps given Aesop's "life" as an intertext, readers may find a bit more humor and satire in the depictions of Jesus in the Galilee.

The Targumim (from the Aramaic for "translation"), Aramaic paraphrases of scripture that combine scholarly exegesis with folktale interests, provide yet another window into early Jewish understandings of their sacred texts. After succinctly detailing the problems of using these texts to recover first-century views, let alone gain access to first-century Galilean Aramaic—indeed, while the Targumim may have influenced Jesus, it is also possible that the teachings of Jesus and his followers influenced the Targumim—Bruce Chilton cautiously explains how, nevertheless, "one may discern in them the survival of materials which did circulate in the time of Jesus, influencing his teaching and/or the memory of that teaching among his disciples."

Chilton categorizes four types of comparison between the Targumim and the Gospels: comparable material with cognate wording and based on the same scriptural passage; comparable understanding but without the linguistic connections; the appearance of Targumic phrases in the New Testament; and a shared thematic emphasis. To give but one example, Chilton demonstrates that the influence of Targumic usage on Jesus would help to account for one of the most striking features of his theology: his insistence that the kingdom is a dynamic, even violent, intervention within human affairs.

Some scholars would debate the claim that "kingdom of God" has, at least on the lips of Jesus, an eschatological flavor; similarly in question is Jesus' use of apocalyptic and eschatological language (e.g., Mark 13:24–27, "But in those days, after that suffering, the sun will be darkened, and the moon will not give its light; and the starts will be falling from the heavens, and the powers in the heavens will be shaken. Then they will see the Son of Man coming in clouds with great power and glory; then he will send out the angels, and gather his elect from the ends of earth to the ends of the heavens"). According to George Nickelsburg, who provides for this volume selections from the Enochic corpus, "The sense that one was living in the end-time was the air that was breathed by the members of the early Christian communities," although "to what extent Jesus himself subscribed to an eschatological worldview that was apocalyptically oriented is a much debated topic."

Of particular import to the study of the historical Jesus in the Enochic corpus is its use of "Son of Man," a title that appears to be Jesus' preferred self-designation and that appears in all the Gospel strata (Mark, Q, M, L, and John). Again, scholars debate both what Jesus said and what he meant: Did "Son of Man" suggest a heavenly figure such as found in Daniel 7 or 1 Enoch's "Parables"? Did he speak of a coming "Son of Man" other than himself? Given the diverse descriptions of the "Son of Man" in early Jewish literature as well as Second Temple Judaism's diverse messianic speculation, "it is not surprising," as Nickelsburg observes, "that many Jews did not subscribe to the early church's proclamation when it applied this Enochic tradition to Jesus."

Not only Nickelsburg's study of 1 Enoch but also Peter Flint's contributions on the Dead Sea Scrolls and Joseph Trafton's study of Psalms of Solomon dismantle the stereotype held by many today that "the Jews" were all expecting a warrior-Messiah and so did not flock to Jesus' message of peace. Qumran's Rule of the Community anticipates the advent of three eschatological figures—a prophet, a priestly Messiah, and a kingly Messiah—even as it speaks of the "Messiah of Israel" presiding over an eschatological banquet (see Matthew 8:11; Luke 22; Revelation 19). It is even possible that this text speaks of God "fathering" the Messiah of Israel. The Apocryphon of Daniel (sometimes called the Aramaic Apocalypse or 4Q246) references a coming "Son of God" who "will be called great" and "Son of the Most High" (see Luke 1:32–35). Another scroll, 4Q521 (the Messianic Apocalypse), offers a list of messianic characteristics, including the ability to raise the dead. Finally, while the Pesher on Nahum (4Q169) does contain a reference to crucifixion, contrary to some popular reports, 4Q285 (a version of the Book of War) does not depict the execution of a messiah.

Reacting to the capture of Jerusalem in 63 BCE by the Roman general Pompey and then to Pompey's death in Egypt in 48, the *Psalms of Solomon* anticipate the arrival of an eschatological "Son of David" who will purify the nation. As Trafton notes, "The lengthy description of the anticipated Messiah in *PssSol* 17 (cf. *PssSol* 18) provides the longest such passages in all of Second Temple Judaism." The psalmist also condemns many of his fellow Jews as "sinners" and "hypocrites" (see especially Matthew 23; for the frequent use of this term as well as a discussion of stock invectives, see Johnson's "The New Testament's Anti-Jewish Slander"), accuses them of defiling the Temple (see Matthew 21; Mark 11; Luke 19; John 2), and descries their establishing a non-Davidic king. For the psalmist, however, the expected "Son of David" does not engage a militaristic response to his enemies both local and in Rome. His trust is in God rather than in weaponry, and his roles are king, judge, and shepherd rather than warrior.

This same concern for peace marks Philo's own messianic understanding, as Gregory Sterling notes: following Isaiah 11, Philo offers a vision of universal peace, harmony between humanity and the animals, and—citing Numbers 24:7—the coming of a man. Yet avoiding any hint of this figure's royalty or even connection to David, Philo emphasizes the man's courage, virtue, and strength.

Perhaps the best-known biblical statements concerning peace are Jesus' Beatitudes found in the Sermon on the Mount (Matthew 5:1–12)//Sermon on the Plain (Luke 6:20–49). The beatitude itself is not, however, original to Jesus: it is a well-recognized literary form, familiar from Wisdom literature and, as translated in this volume by Peter Flint, also the Qumran scrolls (4Q525). As Flint explains, the Beatitudes attributed to Jesus follow the same structure and show some similarities in subject to those from Qumran (e.g., a concern for humility and distress).

Jesus shares with Qumran as well a concern for "purity," a category that, like "magic," permeated antiquity. As Jonathan Klawans demonstrates, the topic of "purity" creates difficulties that range from distinguishing between its forms (ritual impurity, such as that created by contact with a corpse; moral impurity, such as that caused by idolatry or incest), to understanding the esoteric sources, to correcting the modern West's frequent lack of familiarity and resultant dismissal of purity regulations as ridiculously quaint, mere superstitions, or even signs of neuroses. Additionally complicating the discussion is a popular view that Jesus sought to replace the Jewish purity system—seen as creating class-based distinctions, filtering funds to the Temple (itself seen as a corrupt institution), marginalizing women (who would be in states of impurity because of menstruation and parturition), and concentrating piety and so power in the hands of the Pharisees—with a system of compassion. This false distinction (the opposite of purity is impurity, and of compassion, lack of compassion) is based on a variety of factors: the equally false distinction sometimes drawn between Law and Grace, the reductive equation of ritual impurity with sin, a presumption that first-century Jews followed the Mosaic Torah fully, literally, and uniformly, ignorance of purity's import to Gentiles, the false assumption that men were not concerned with and subject to ritual impurity, the equating of purity and class (the high priest can become ritually impure; a peasant or a widow can be in a state of purity), basic misunderstandings of the ancient sources (with materials sometimes taken out of context both historical and literary), and, occasionally, Christian apologetic.

Whereas the Rabbis tended to separate ritual and moral defilement, the Qumran scrolls attest an overlap. Klawans comments: "For the Hebrew Bible and Rabbinic Judaism, the sources of ritual impurity were considered natural, unavoidable, even obligatory, and therefore not sinful. These substances could hardly be less natural for the Dead Sea sectarians, but the sectarians seem to have considered them sinful nonetheless." As for Jesus, Klawans demonstrates how his discussions about purity are not about rejection (Mark 7:19b—"thus he declared all foods clean"—is the Evangelist's editorial comment, not a statement from Jesus). What Jesus did do (if the general discussion about the Law in Mark 7 is authentic, and there are good reasons to believe that the entire scene is a Marcan composition) is merge matters of moral and ritual defilement, as did the Qumran covenanters. But Jesus differed from the Qumran texts as well, for he did not appear to have regarded sin as ritually defiling.

Broadening the discussion from "purity" to the Mosaic Torah, Herbert W. Basser addresses one of the most controversial questions concerning Jesus' teaching. While some scholars regard Jesus as stretching the Torah beyond any other Jew's view of acceptable interpretation (e.g., by dismissing purity regulations and even preaching an incipient antinomianism), others see him as engaging his Pharisaic interlocutors according to the terms of Rabbinic exegesis. Basser argues in his "Gospel and Talmud" not only that Jesus' rhetoric in his approach to Torah conformed to the general standards of first-century Jewish interpretation but also that, according to Rabbinic commentary, his exegetical points were "so good the Rabbis feared they could attract too much appreciation." Basser further argues that Jesus possessed knowledge not only of Torah but also of the means by which it was interpreted, for "had it been otherwise, why would anyone have bothered to pay close attention?" Thus, Jesus was by no means an antinomian and by no means functioned outside the rubrics of Rabbinic thought.

Both the Jesus of the Gospels and the Rabbis of Mishnah and Talmud follow the approach of what Basser terms "literal unacceptable: stretch apt"; this reshaping of a verse's words or structure typically served to alleviate any hardship created by following the more literal sense. Exemplifying this process in the Gospels are the "Antitheses" of Matthew 5 that follow the formulaic structure, "You have heard that it was said . . . But I tell you. . . ." While the interpretation of Matthew 5:44, "But I tell you, love your enemies and pray for those who persecute you," is novel (although Proverbs does insist "Do not rejoice when your enemies fall" [24:17] and "If your enemies are hungry, give them bread to eat; if they are thirsty, give them water to drink" [25:21]), the means by which the Gospel derives this interpretation are not: as Basser observes, the word "neighbor" can be stretched to include "enemy" because the terms in Hebrew share the same consonants; only the pronunciation differs. To this we also might add that Epictetus voiced a similar point: "[The Cynic] must be flogged like an ass, and while he is being flogged he must love the man who flogs him, as though he were the father or brother of them all" (*Discourses* 3).

Basser next turns to John's use of another technique: "rational arguments based on legal exegesis" of "redundant letters and phrases." This model underlies John 7, Jesus' arguments concerning healing on the Sabbath. The third model, one of "debate forms," appears in the Synoptic Sabbath healings (Matthew 12:10–12; Mark 2:23–28; Luke 13:14–16). Complementing these observations is Gregory Sterling's contribution on Philo of Alexandria, a Jewish philosopher roughly contemporary with Jesus. Like the Synoptic Jesus (Matthew 22:34–40; Mark 12:28–34; Luke 10:25–28), Philo summarized Torah, engaged in discussion of the Sabbath, and even addressed the *Corban* sacrifice (see Mark 7; Matthew 15).

A fourth approach to Jesus and the Law is through the subject of one specific injunction, that of divorce. Most if not all scholars of the historical Jesus agree that Jesus forbade divorce. Some argue that Matthew's exception clause—divorce is forbidden except in cases of *porneia* (Matthew 5:31–32; 19:7–9)—is an addition designed to provide an escape mechanism required by the delay of the *parousia* (Jesus' return), but the majority accept that the absolute prohibition found in Mark 10:2–12 and echoed in 1 Corinthians 7:10–16 is authentic: divorce is forbidden, and those who marry divorced individuals are guilty of adultery. What Jesus said, and meant, are urgent issues for people today who seek to remain biblically faithful but who also are entrapped in loveless or abusive relationships.

On the question of divorce, Jesus' exhortations stand out from their cultural context. According to Thomas McGinn, Roman citizens would have found, from a legal standpoint, no difficulty in divorcing; all that was needed was the wish of either husband or wife to dissolve the relationship. The only problem: disposition of the dowry, which typically was returned to the woman. Conversely, a freedwoman married to her former owner required his consent to a divorce. But despite Rome's comparably lax attitude, we cannot conclude that divorce was rampant (let alone conclude that Jesus forbade divorce because he disapproved of Roman social policy). McGinn notes, first, that Roman culture placed a high valuation on marriage and found divorce at best a "regrettable necessity." Second, with the exception of the freedwoman, the question of the frequency of divorce can be applied only to the upper classes. In the data available, only the "most successful politicians of the late Republic and early Empire" approached the two-to-one divorce rate of the United States in the early twenty-first century.

Jewish and Roman views of marital legalities were distinct: Jews practiced polygamy; Romans did not; Jews contracted marriages via the *Ketubah*, a legal writ, and obtained divorce via the *Get*, another legal writ; laws differed on permitted consanguinity. On the Jewish side, whether one could divorce was usually not the question: Deuteronomy 24:1–4 instructs that if a husband found in his wife something "obnoxious" or "unclean" (the specifics, as with the Greek *porneia*, remain unstated), he is to give her a "bill of divorce." Although the Rabbis conclude therefore that only the man can initiate divorce (*Gittin* 20a), Jewish women, at least in the Herodian household, did obtain divorces, and Mark's version of Jesus' injunctions presupposes that women also could obtain divorce.

Guidelines for social relations in antiquity extended well beyond divorce to other forms of associations. According to Matthew 18:15–17 (see also Luke 17:3–4), Jesus establishes a set of guidelines for rebuking a member of the "church" (Greek: *Ekklesia*; in the canonical Gospels, the term is unique to Matthew). Thus, as John Kloppenborg reveals, the church structure is comparable to that of ancient voluntary societies, those "more or less permanent associations or clubs, organized around an extended family, a specific cult, an ethnic group, or a common profession" that often both "had religious dimensions" and served "social goals." These organizations, unlike the civic assemblies, were open to women, noncitizens, slaves, and freed slaves. Perhaps Jesus himself was familiar with associations of individuals involved in the fishing industry around the Sea of Galilee. Stronger, however, is the thesis that early Christians, especially in the Diaspora, would have seen themselves and have been seen by others as forming a type of voluntary society or domestic association dedicated to an Eastern deity.

One marker of such groups was the language of "fictive kinship." Greeting each other as "brother" and "sister," association members created new social units that complemented, or served as a replacement for, the extended household (Greek: *oikos*) or the biological family. Kloppenborg notes that "for the Jesus groups to extend kinship language to themselves implied sharply heightened social obligation," an ethos that likely attracted potential proselytes. According to the Gospels, Jesus himself used kinship language: in his new family of faith, his "brother and sister and mother" is the one who "does the will of God" (Mark 3:35).

Whether Jesus sought to establish a permanent or semipermanent community, or whether he anticipated that there would be "some standing here who would not taste death until they see that the kingdom of God has come with power" (Mark 9:1) is yet another debated question. It is also possible that Jesus held to both views: prepare for the future, but expect the eschaton.

Although discussions of the "anointed one" most often address Jesus' messianic self-consciousness or diverse definitions of "Messiah," the New Testament prompts another discussion of Jesus as anointed. According to Matthew 26:6–13 and Mark 14:3–9, an unknown woman anoints Jesus' head; according to John 12, this woman is Mary, the sister of Martha and Lazarus, and she anoints not Jesus' head but his feet and dries them with her hair. Luke 7:36–50 recounts a related story, set not at the outset of the Passion but at the beginning of the ministry, wherein an unnamed "woman who was a sinner" anoints Jesus' feet, bathes them with her tears, and wipes them with her hair. The anointing of an individual was a common practice in antiquity, but the wiping of expensive oil off someone's feet by means of one's hair was by no means a quotidian occurrence.

Teresa Hornsby surveys numerous types of anointings—"ritual anointings, baths, grooming, gestures of hospitality, and the preparations of corpses"—but finds scant connection to the Gospel accounts. Following the work of Dennis R. MacDonald and so complementing his contribution to this volume, "Imitations of Greek Epic in the Gospels," she does find in the *Odyssey* a woman anointing someone whom she recognizes to be a king. The only other text wherein hair is used as part of the service derives from a homoerotic banquet in Petronius's *Satyricon*.

Differing in the chronology of the anointing, all four Gospels do situate Jesus' Passion at the Passover. As noted earlier, according to Matthew, Mark, and Luke, the Last Supper is a Passover meal, a seder (Hebrew for "order," here as in "order of service"); according to John, Jesus dies on the Day of Preparation, at the time the Paschal lambs are being sacrificed in the Temple. To understand both the rituals known to Jesus for the celebration of the Passover and the details of the seder meal adopted and adapted by his followers, Calum Carmichael reconstructs the Passover *Haggadah* (Hebrew for "story" or "narrative"), the script for the seder.

Carmichael's study shows both how Jewish tradition influenced the Last Supper and how, possibly, the developing Christian church influenced the *Haggadah*. Further, it offers numerous plausible insights into other Gospel scenes, from traditions concerning Moses' nativity to an explication for why Jesus refuses the drink extended to him on the cross. Concerning the multiply attested statement in which Jesus equates his body with bread and his blood with wine, Carmichael suggests that the original import of the word *Aphikoman* and its use in the ritual point to the means by which the celebrant, consuming the *Aphikoman*, unites with his mystical redeemer. The one new thing Jesus does is to claim that the Messiah is no longer a hidden, mystical figure, but himself in his own person.

A second text depicting a meal replete with symbolism is the Pseudepigraphon *Joseph and Aseneth*. This story of the conversion of the Egyptian Aseneth and her subsequent marriage to Joseph contains, in Randall Chesnutt's terms, "formulaic references to the bread of life, cup of immortality, and ointment of incorruption." Yet Chesnutt disagrees with scholars who see in these passages a "sacred meal" such as those shared by the Qumran community or Philo's Therapeutae; he finds a reference not "to a special ritual meal but to Jewish scruples about food in general and, by metonymy, to the entire Jewish way of life." This symbolism could be expected, given the emphasis on meals not only in the Gospels and by Paul (1 Corinthians), but also by the Dead Sea Scrolls, *Havurah* groups, and the voluntary societies. Nevertheless, the expression "bread of life" appears only in one other early Jewish (using the term broadly) text aside from *Joseph and Aseneth*, namely, John 6, and both Pseudepigraphon and Gospel display a realized eschatology.

Several sources provide information on the Roman governor during that fateful Passover. Sterling presents Philo's brief portrait of Pontius Pilate, an account similar to that offered by Josephus (*War* 2; *Ant.* 18; see also Luke 13:1–2), which describes the governor's complete lack of consideration for the sensibilities of his subject population. Whether the Gospels improve Pilate's profile to make him less a villain, or whether Philo exacerbated Pilate's evil for his own political reasons, or whether both theories have a bit of truth, remains debated.

The correspondence between Pliny the Younger, governor of Bythynia-Pontus circa 110 CE, and the emperor Trajan concerning Christian liturgical assemblies may grant some access to Pilate's legal parameters. Pliny, who interrogated those participating in what he termed a "depraved and fanatical superstition," had the prerogative, as did Pilate before him, to pronounce sentence on members of the local population. Bradley M. Peper and Mark DelCogliano state, "While legal actions were chiefly instigated by the public, the provincial governor alone performed the actual trials (*cognitio extra ordinem*)."

The Pliny-Trajan correspondence raises a second question about the relation of Christians to the state. According to Matthew 10:17–20; Mark 13:9–11; Luke 12:10–11; and John 15:18–27, Jesus predicts that his followers would face persecution from governing authorities; Acts 16, 18, and 21–26 shows Silas and Paul undergoing such persecution (composed at the end of the first century or, more likely, at the beginning of the second, Acts may be contemporaneous with the Pliny-Trajan correspondence). In Rome, Jewish-Christians were caught up in the expulsion of the Jews from Rome by Claudius (49–54 CE), and Christians were persecuted by Nero in 54. Did Jesus predict that his followers would face the empire's representatives, or are Mark 13 et alia, as Peper and DelConigliano suggest, "later retrojections inserted into the Jesus tradition by the Evangelists, who sought to bolster the resolve of their Christian communities when faced with the persecution of individual Christians"?

Included in his contribution on Philo, Gregory Sterling remarks that the Jewish philosopher's description of the mocking of an insane man named Karabas by Alexandrian Gentiles in order to show their hatred of the visiting Jewish king, Agrippa I, in 38 CE is "strikingly similar" to the mocking of Jesus recorded in Matthew 27:27–31; Mark 15:16–20; and John 19:2–3. Such mocking scenes are another well-attested form: Sterling notes examples from Plutarch and Dio Cassius. Philo also provides a description of scourging, the whipping Jesus is described as enduring (Matthew 27:26; Mark 15:15).

Like the miraculous birth, the tradition of the "noble death" was well known in both Jewish and Gentile Greco-Roman contexts, as Dennis R. MacDonald's contribution, "Imitations of Greek Epic in the Gospels," demonstrates. Homeric imitations in the Gospels raise the inevitable question of the extent to which the Gospels report "what happened," and the extent to which they reflect what anyone familiar with Homeric models—MacDonald observes that "narrative poetry" was "the oxygen of Greco-Roman culture" for literate and illiterate alike—presumed happened. According to MacDonald, the Evangelists did not merely imitate; rather, they drew upon earlier stories to show how the Christian message superseded them.

Robert Doran's "Narratives of Noble Death" expands MacDonald's study. Under the rubric "Better to have one man die for the people" (Caiaphas's response in John 11:50 to Jesus' popularity and possible Roman reprisal), Doran offers passages from Pompeius Trogus, Livy, and 2 Maccabees. Under the rubric "Philosophic deaths," he translates excerpts from Plutarch, Diogenes Laertius, Philostratus, and 4 Maccabees. From these extensive selections, readers can find numerous connections to the Passion narratives, including "a leader offering himself to death for the salvation of the fatherland" (Pompeius Trogus); the offering of sacrifices and invocations for divine help (Livy); the accepting by "free choice" to die rather than submit to the demands of the Gentile king, and the hope for "resurrection into life" (2 Maccabees).

Along with classical templates, the Evangelists drew upon biblical precedents, especially the Psalms (22 and 69), along with echoes Amos 8:9, Zechariah 9–14, and Wisdom 2, to recount Jesus' suffering and death. Also influencing the Gospel writers and, quite likely, Jesus himself, were Isaiah's Suffering Servant songs, particularly Isaiah 53. Ben Witherington translates for this volume both the Hebrew and the Septuagintal renditions of this chapter, and the distinctions are substantial. For example, Witherington notes that whereas the Greek focuses on the "sufferer being justified as a righteous person," the Hebrew speaks of "him making many righteous"; the Gospels, as opposed to Acts 8, draw primarily upon the Hebrew rather than the Greek, and thus the case that Jesus himself spoke in Isaianic terms becomes stronger. Finally, as Witherington observes, "The historical likelihood that Jesus spoke of shedding his blood in the place of many seems high, not least because Maccabean martyrs [see Doran's contribution] had conceptualized their roles like this before Jesus."

Concluding this section on the noble death, Dale C. Allison Jr. provides the report from Thallus, the first-century CE Pagan (or possibly Samaritan) historian who may be the earliest non-Christian witness to Jesus. Thallus mentions an earthquake (see Matthew 27:51) and attendant darkness (see Mark 15:33) at the time of Passover; he also dates the Crucifixion to the day before Passover. Unfortunately, Thallus's extensive history of the Mediterranean world is no longer extant, and neither is the work by the third-century Christian Julius Sextus Africanus that quotes him. We have only a citation of Africanus by the ninth-century Byzantine historian George Syncellus.

Such source-critical jumps from Thallus to Julius Africaus to George Syncellus may make the idea of understanding Jesus of Nazareth seem much simpler. We do not have to traverse several centuries to move from the Evangelists to Jesus himself. Yet as the movements within the Quest, the history of the period, and the numerous texts that contribute to the cultural makeup of Jesus and his early followers demonstrate, the doing of history necessarily requires not only rigorous investigation, careful translation, and cultural sensitivity but also hope, luck, and imagination.

Understanding Jesus and the Gospels requires appreciation of Judaism and the Pagan world: their history, literature, ethics, and practices. For the first time, this volume presents these variegated sources, almost all in original translations. Some of the contents will prompt readers to a new view of the historical Jesus; perhaps what previously had been seen as authentic will come to be seen as derivative of a

Pagan or Jewish model. Other readers will appreciate the cultural embeddedness of the Christian tradition, how it told its stories and conveyed its teachings in the idiom of the people. And still other readers will come to see how the teachings of and about Jesus would have sounded to those who first heard them, and perhaps, through that echo, come to a new understanding for themselves.

Bibliography

In addition to the bibliography supplied here, each contribution offers its own set of additional sources, both primary and secondary, and many of these scholars have authored more than one work on the historical Jesus. Readers are encouraged to consult their other publications as well as the myriad (not an exaggerated term) of other books and articles on this ever-fascinating, and perhaps ever-elusive, topic.

Allen, Charlotte. *The Human Christ: The Search for the Historical Jesus*. New York: Free Press, 1998.

Allison, Dale C. *Jesus of Nazareth Millenarian Prophet*. Minneapolis, MN: Fortress Press, 1998.

Becker, Jürgen. *Jesus of Nazareth*. Translated by James E. Crouch. New York: Walter de Gruyter, 1998.

Boers, Hendrikus. *Who Was Jesus: The Historical Jesus and the Synoptic Gospels*. San Francisco: Harper and Row, 1989.

Borg, Marcus. *Jesus: A New Vision*. San Francisco: Harper and Row, 1987.

Boring, M. Eugene, Klaus Berger, and Carsten Colpe. *Hellenistic Commentary to the New Testament*. Nashville, TN: Abington Press, 1995.

Brandon, S.G.F. *Jesus and the Zealots: A Study of the Political Factor in Primitive Christianity*. Manchester: Manchester University Press, 1967.

Charlesworth, James H., ed. *Jesus and the Dead Sea Scrolls*. Anchor Bible Reference Library. New York: Doubleday, 1992.

Chilton, Bruce. *Rabbi Jesus: An Intimate Biography*. New York: Doubleday, 2000.

Copan, Paul, and Craig Evans, eds. *Who Was Jesus? A Jewish-Christian Dialogue*. Louisville, KY: Westminster John Knox, 2001.

Corley, Kathleen E. *Women and the Historical Jesus: Feminist Myths of Christian Origins*. Santa Rosa, CA: Polebridge Press, 2002.

Crossan, John Dominic. *The Historical Jesus: The Life of a Mediterranean Jewish Peasant*. San Francisco: HarperSanFrancisco, 1991.

Downing, F. Gerald. *Christ and the Cynics: Jesus and Other Radical Preachers in First-Century Tradition*. Sheffield, England: JSOT Press, 1988.

Dunn, James D. G. *Jesus Remembered*. Grand Rapids, MI: Eerdmans, 2003.

Ehrman, Bart D. *Jesus: Apocalyptic Prophet of the New Millennium*. Oxford: Oxford University Press, 1999.

Fiorenza, Elisabeth Schüssler. *Jesus and the Politics of Interpretation*. New York: Continuum, 2000.

Fredrickson, Paula. *Jesus of Nazareth: King of the Jews*. New York: Knopf, 1999.

Funk, Robert Walter. *Honest to Jesus: Jesus for a New Millennium*. San Francisco: HarperSan-Francisco, 1996.

Hanson, K. C., and Douglas E. Oakman. *Palestine in the Time of Jesus: Social Structures and Social Conflicts*. Minneapolis, MN: Fortress Press, 1998.

Hoover, Roy W., ed. *Profiles of Jesus*. Santa Rosa, CA: Polebridge Press, 2002.

Horsley, Richard A. *Jesus and the Spiral of Violence: Popular Jewish Resistance in Roman Palestine*. San Francisco: Harper and Row, 1987.

Johnson, Luke Timothy. "The New Testament's Anti-Jewish Slander and the Conventions of Ancient Polemic." *Journal of Biblical Literature* 108 (Fall 1989): 419–41.

Journal for the Study of the Historical Jesus. January 2003–.

Keck, Leander E. *Who Is Jesus: History in Perfect Tense*. Columbia: University of South Carolina Press, 2000.

Lüdemann, Gerd. *The Great Deception: What Jesus Really Said and Did*. London: SCM, 1998.

Mack, Burton L. *The Lost Gospel: The Book of Q and Christian Origins*. New York: HarperCollins, 1993.

Mason, Steve. *Josephus and the New Testament*. Peabody, MA: Hendrickson Publishers, 1992.

Meier, John. *A Marginal Jew: Rethinking the Historical Jesus*. 3 vols. Anchor Bible Reference Library. New York: Doubleday, 1991–2001.

Miller, Robert Joseph, ed. *The Complete Gospels: Annotated Scholars Version*. Revised and expanded ed. Sonoma, CA: Polebridge Press, 1994.

Powell, Mark Allan. *Jesus as a Figure in History*. Louisville, KY: Westminster John Knox Press, 1998.

Reed, Jonathan L. *Archaeology and the Galilean Jesus: A Re-examination of the Evidence*. Harrisburg, PA: Trinity Press International, 2000.

Sanders, E. P. *The Historical Figure of Jesus*. London: Allen Lane/Penguin Books, 1993.

Schweitzer, Albert. *The Quest of the Historical Jesus*. First complete edition. Edited by John Bowden. Minneapolis, MN: Fortress Press, 2001.

Tabor, James D. *The Jesus Dynasty: The Hidden History of Jesus, His Royal Family, and the Birth of Christianity*. New York: Simon and Schuster, 2006.

Theissen, Gerd, and Annette Merz. *The Historical Jesus: A Comprehensive Guide*. Translated by John Bowden. Philadelphia: Fortress Press, 1987.

Theissen, Gerd, and Dagmar Winter. *The Quest for the Plausible Jesus: The Question of Criteria*. Translated by M. Eugene Boring. Louisville, KY: Westminster John Knox Press, 2002.

Vermes, Geza. *Jesus the Jew: A Historian's Reading of the Gospels*. Philadelphia: Fortress Press, 1973.

Witherington, Ben, III. *The Jesus Quest: The Third Search for the Jew from Nazareth*. San Francisco: InterVarsity, 1995.

Wright, N. T. *Who Was Jesus?* Grand Rapids, MI: Eerdmans, 1992.

—1—

Archaeological Contributions to the Study
of Jesus and the Gospels

Jonathan L. Reed

Archaeology's contributions to the study of the Gospels and the historical Jesus cannot be overestimated. At the same time, it is difficult to overcome the caricature of biblical archaeologists seeking relics or sinking their spades in the ground to find sites listed in the Bible or artifacts mentioned in the New Testament. They have been caricatured at worst as Indiana Jones–like relic hunters chasing down objects like the Holy Grail or scanning the (illegal and immoral) antiquities markets and turning up forgeries like the bone box inscribed with "James, son of Joseph, brother of Jesus." Or, at best, they are seen as having a myopic preoccupation with finds like Saint Peter's House, the Jesus Boat, the Pilate Inscription, or the Caiaphas Ossuary.

Even though these latter discoveries are of importance for studying Jesus and the Gospels, modern-day archaeologists do not go into the field to locate where Jesus walked or find what he might have touched; instead, they conduct scientifically rigorous excavations and analyze patterns among sites and artifacts that can be used to reconstruct the world in which Jesus and the Gospels existed. Hence archaeology makes its contribution by helping assess where Jesus walked and why the Gospels depict him as they did, as it sketches their world from the available archaeological evidence. This body of evidence is ever-growing as excavations continue, and as we will see, it includes sites and artifacts never mentioned in the New Testament but which are nevertheless important for understanding their world.

Archaeological evidence is particularly valuable for two reasons. First, it is independent from the literary texts typically used to reconstruct the historical Jesus or the world of the Gospels. Those texts often have a deeply religious bias, are mostly written much later than the events they describe, and are usually written by upper-class males. In contrast, archaeology is in a sense more democratic: it uncovers the stuff of everyday life from all classes and groups. Archaeologists deal with quotidian paraphernalia, with items that have been unintentionally preserved, like pots, lamps, walls, and floors; these artifacts help reconstruct, inter alia, demographic configurations, socioeconomic differences, and trade patterns. Second, archaeology uncovers monumental structures like temples, civic buildings, public inscriptions, and the works of art sponsored by rulers and elites, items that often go unmentioned but are assumed rather than articulated in literary texts; without these materials the texts cannot be understood. Indeed, such public artifacts formed the stage on which civic life took place and to a great degree shaped it.

An exhaustive treatment of all of archaeology's contributions to the study of the Gospels is impossible in such a short space, but a few select topics will illustrate the ways in which sites and artifacts illuminate the study of early Christianity. Moving from the Gospels' broader first-century Mediterranean context to Jesus' immediate Galilean context, we examine (1) the importance and pervasiveness of the emperor cult in the eastern Mediterranean; (2) the impact of city-building and urbanization on Palestine around Jesus' lifetime; and (3) the distinctively Jewish character of the domestic space of Jesus' Galilee. As we move geographically from the Roman-controlled Pagan world to the Jewish world of Jesus, and from aspects of public, visible space to the private, domestic sphere, we will gain a sense of the contrast between these two worlds and so come to understand their eventual clash.

The Archaeology of Public Space in the Eastern Mediterranean

The most dominant figure in the Roman Empire was the emperor, and the most pervasive phenomenon in the eastern Mediterranean city was the imperial cult. The various efforts designed by locals to honor him included sacrifices at altars, the placement of his statues in temples, the establishment of priesthoods devoted to him, and the distribution of gifts, sponsoring of games, or sharing of communal meals in his name. Consequently, the surface of the erstwhile Roman Empire remains littered to this day with faces of dead emperors on coin, and the ruined cities are filled with their heads in statue and their names inscribed on stone. Artifacts ranging from small coins to large temples to whole cities give a clear picture of Caesar's centrality to the empire's inhabitants.

The first emperor was Augustus (31 BCE–14 CE), whose political and cultural revolution shaped the Roman world far more than any of his successors, whether Tiberius (14–37 CE) under whom Jesus lived, the other Julio-Claudians dynastic heirs, or the later Flavians (69–98 CE) under whom the Gospels were probably written. But anyone who claimed that Jesus was the expected "anointed one," whether *Messiah* (Hebrew) or *Christ* (Greek), had to compete with the widespread claim that Caesar was "Lord," "Lord of the World," "Savior," "Deliverer," "God," "Son of God," or "God made Manifest," to use just a few of the titles gleaned from inscriptions. Such claims are known from literary texts, but only archaeology reveals how pervasive they were across the empire and especially in the eastern Mediterranean, whether Greece, Turkey, or Syria, the very centers of early Christianity where the Gospels enjoyed circulation at an early time.

Coins

The eighteen-year-old Octavian, soon to become Augustus and emperor of Rome, was the adopted son of the assassinated Julius Caesar. After this murder in the Senate on the Ides of March in 44 BCE, the young Octavian set out against his father's assassins; his arms included not only legions raised at his own expense but also an even more powerful mythology that allowed him later to rule Rome. When a comet appeared shortly after Julius Caesar's murder, Octavian urgently promoted and the people willingly accepted it as his father's apotheosis, his divine spirit ascending to take his place among the heavenly gods. Octavian ubiquitously displayed that star as consolidating his power. It was engraved on ring gemstones, pressed into clay seal impressions and cheap glass beads, and minted especially on coins whose legends drew the logical conclusion that, if the father was now divine, the adopted son was therefore "Son of a Divine One" or "Son of God." That Latin title DIVI FILIUS is on most of his coins and is variously abbreviated as DI FI, DIVI F, or DIVI FI.

Roman sacred law officially deified Julius Caesar in 42 BCE, and Octavian later was renamed Augustus by the Senate (Greek *Sebastos*), the multivalent term that can be variously translated as "the revered one," "the holy one," or "one who causes to grow." But Augustus was only the first in a series of new gods, as divine status and the accompanying title were passed on to subsequent emperors with greater and greater ease. Their deification continued in abbreviated form on coins with DI FI and was symbolized by pointy solar rays emanating from the emperor's head. Coinage was one of the earliest means of mass propaganda, and the message of the emperor as God was thus placed, literally, into the hands of all Caesar's subjects.

These coins help make sense of Mark 12:13–17, in which Jesus was asked about paying taxes to Caesar. After they brought him a coin he asked first, "Whose portrait is this? And whose inscription?" and then advised to "Give to Caesar what is Caesar's and to God what is God's." The answer becomes much more subversive when one knows that Roman coinage proclaimed Caesar to be God.

Inscriptions

Numismatic legends and depictions of solar rays were not the only forms of propaganda to declare the emperor's divinity and cosmic significance; inscriptions throughout the empire served the same function. The most astonishing for the study of the Gospels is a Greek inscription from Priene, a city just south of Ephesus on the western coast of what is now Turkey. The two-part inscription, copied and distributed across what was then called Asia Minor, contains the earliest and most striking instance of the term "Gospel" or "good tidings" (plural: *euaggelia*), not to describe Jesus' message of the kingdom of God but to proclaim Caesar's Roman imperial theology. Part one records how the Roman governor of Asia, Paulus Fabius Maximus, proposed to the Asian cities that they change their calendar so that Augustus's birthday would be henceforth New Year's Day. It reads in part:

> [It is a question whether] the birthday of the most divine Caesar is more pleasant or more advantageous, the day which we might justly set on a par with the beginning of everything, in practical terms at least, in that he restored order when everything was disintegrating and falling into chaos and gave a new look to the whole world, a world which would have met destruction with the utmost pleasure if Caesar had not been born as a common blessing to all. For that reason one might justly take this to be the beginning of life and living, the end of regret at one's birth. . . . It is my view that all the communities should have one and the same New Year's Day, the birthday of the most divine Caesar, and that on that day, 23rd September, all should enter their term of office.

Part two records the enthusiastic response and official decree by local magistrates, which both established that calendrical change and inaugurated a series of competitive public celebrations among the cities of Asia Minor. Some key lines read:

> Since the providence that has divinely ordered our existence has applied her energy and zeal and has brought to life the most perfect good in Augustus, whom she filled with virtues for the benefit of mankind, bestowing him upon us and our descendants as a savior—he who put an end to war and will order peace, Caesar, who by his epiphany exceeded the hopes of those who prophesied good tidings (*euaggelia*), not only outdoing benefactors of the past, but also allowing no hope of greater benefactions in the future; and since the birthday of the god first brought to the world the good tidings (*euaggelia*) residing in him. . . . For that reason, with good fortune and safety, the Greeks of Asia have decided that the New Year in all the cities should begin on 23rd September, the birthday of Augustus . . . and that the letter of the proconsul and the decree of Asia should be inscribed on a pillar of white marble, which is to be placed in the sacred precinct of Rome and Augustus. (*Supplementum Epigraphicum Graecum* 4.490)

As early as 29 BCE, immediately after Augustus became the sole ruler of the Roman Empire, a golden crown had been decreed in the Roman province of Asia for whoever best honored Augustus, "our god"; twenty years later, that diadem was given to the governor Paulus Fabius Maximus, who had "discovered a way to honor Augustus that was hitherto unknown among the Greeks, namely to reckon time from the date of his nativity."

Such adulation continued throughout the first century. Even the loony emperor Caligula, who ruled only four short years (37–41 CE) before being killed by the Legions, was honored similarly with an oath of loyalty, preserved in an inscription from the city of Assos in northeastern Turkey. Sworn by both the

Romans and Greeks, it is rife with cosmic or what we might even consider messianic imagery:

> Since the announcement of the coronation of Gaius Caesar Germanicus Augustus
> [Caligula], which all mankind had hoped and prayed for, the world has found no
> measure for its joy, but every city and people has eagerly hastened to view the god as
> if the happiest age for mankind had now arrived: It seemed good to the council and to
> the Roman businessmen here among us, and to the people of Assos, to appoint a del-
> egation made up of the noblest and most eminent of the Romans and also of the
> Greeks, to visit him and offer their best wishes and to implore him to remember the
> city and take care of it, even as he promised our city upon his first visit to the province
> in the company of his father Germanicus. (*Sylloge Inscripionum Graecarum* 3.797)

These and other inscriptions contain imagery and words, whether stars and calendar, nativity and visitations, hope and joy, good tidings and good news, or Savior and Son of God, that surely merit consideration when reading either Matthew's or Luke's story of Jesus' birth.

In Statue

It has been estimated that there were between twenty-five and fifty thousand portraits or sculptures of Augustus alone across the empire; those of his successors push the numbers even higher. Their programmatically copied facial features and hair locks made whichever Caesar in power the most recognizable person in the world. His statue stood in temples that were dedicated to him and to Roman power, or it stood alongside local gods in a way that fused Roman power with local civic religion. As the Priene inscription suggests, those statues were accompanied by a programmatic cosmology or theology.

A good example comes from the city of Aphrodisias in inland Turkey, the city of Aphrodite (the Roman Venus), who was the mythological progenitor of the Julio-Claudian dynasty. In the city center, a three-hundred-foot-long plaza was flanked on both sides by three-story-high galleries with sculptural panels; at the far end of the plaza was a temple dedicated to the worship of the emperors. An inscription states that the complex was built for Aphrodite, the *Theoi Sebastoi*, and the People; the *Theoi Sebastoi* are literally the "divine revered ones," that is, the divine family of the Julio-Claudian rulers. Along the gallery, a series of five-foot panels sculpted in high relief combined Hellenistic allegories like Day and Night or Land and Sea, along with traditional Greek deities like Zeus, Poseidon, Asclepius, and of course Aphrodite. Accompanying them were a series of statues that personified the peoples conquered by Rome, including the Jews, all imaged as females in elegant and native dress. The personifications came from all across the Roman world and so emphasized the many victories of divine Julio-Claudian emperors up to and including Nero.

Two panels are of particular note. The first depicts Augustus, naked except for a back cloak and spear scepter in his right hand, with a Jupiter eagle at his right foot, a barbarian prisoner with hands tied behind his back at his left, and the winged female figure of Nike or Victory holding out a crown. The second is of Claudius, similarly nude, striding forward with his cloak billowing in a wide semicircle above his head. On his left a female earth figure gives him a cornucopia, symbol of control over earth's fertility, and on his right a female sea figure gives him an oar rudder, symbol of control over ocean's safety. That panel points to divine control over both land and sea, and both panels' nudity, so common in all Caesar's statues, was the Greek and Hellenistic iconographic indication of divinity: imperial nudity meant imperial divinity.

Still more can be gained from the Aphrodisias Sebasteion. It fused Roman and Greek elements and styles, and even though the emperor's portraits—whether Augustus, Claudius, or Nero—closely copied imperial models distributed by Rome, their bodies and scenes were local creations and represented Greek interpretation of Roman imperial rule. The local civic council not only endorsed the Sebasteion's construction; an inscription records that it was financed by two wealthy Aphrodisian families attracted to the imperial favors or blessings that would inevitably follow. Those imperial blessings extended to the city's masons, craftsmen, sculptors, and workshops who received commissions for the construction. The many panels prompted a sudden demand for skilled labor and led to the hasty promotion of marble cutters to figural sculptors; many a new apprentice took up mallet and chisel for on-the-job training, as is apparent from the uneven quality of carving. But the imbalance in workmanship was cleverly disguised by having novices cut the panels' less visible lower portions and having experts prepare the upper portions more visible from the plaza, especially the imperial portraits.

Roman imperial rule brought peace, the Pax Romana, to the eastern Mediterranean; it energized places like Aphrodisias's workshops; it was a boon to the local economy. Any potential criticism of the elite's attraction to the Roman imperial family would be muted by those many prospering shops and increased incomes, and the construction of a Sebasteion with a temple for the Roman imperial cult was a seductive proposition for any city; it was Good News for many in that city's economy.

In Cities

Excavations and surveys across areas conquered or controlled by Rome in the first century reveal how its subjects were integrated and acculturated into the empire. Three waves of building activity are discernible in the collective archaeological record from sites across the Roman East. That threefold sequence, a general pattern for Roman urbanization, repeats across all newly acquired areas and focuses on cities or urbanization. The first wave, begun well before the first century in many areas, was to secure a travel network at whose core were new Roman roads. These well-made routes facilitated trade and travel by linking inland areas with ports on the Mediterranean's sea lanes; more important, they provided an efficient means to move Legions throughout the empire to ensure the Pax Romana.

The second wave discernible in the archaeological record is the erection of imperial monuments and temples, always conspicuously located in the heart of the city. Ports and roads funneled local, regional, and imperial travelers to city centers where the emperor's statue or temple was located, be it called a Sebasteion as at Aphrodisias, and Augusteium or Tiberium as elsewhere. At these sites, local elites sponsored festivals, games, and sacrifices to honor Caesar. The emperor cult is so pervasive in the archaeological record because it was the physical and visible expression of local gratitude for the blessings of the Pax Romana, or alternatively, the demand for imperial allegiance.

A third wave, not prevalent at the time of Jesus but rapidly growing in the latter half of the first century when the Gospels were written, was the spread of urban amenities for leisure activities. This included the creation of theaters, amphitheaters, or hippodromes as venues for spectacles, and most notably, the construction of large-scale public bathhouses as well as the Roman-engineered aqueducts that fed them. New Roman technology that used mortar, domed roofs, and hypocaust tiles enabled underground heating systems with circulation through clay pipes in the walls. For centuries, the Greek world had attached tub-and-basin baths to the gymnasium where wealthy male youths competed in athletics as part of a broad education. But under Rome, the elite gymnasium's athletic aspect became a mere appendage to the centrality of public bathing that was opened to broader segments of the population.

Baths were affordable and served public hygiene. Further, their warm pools and hot and cold tubs, which could be accompanied by libraries, lecture halls, massage parlors, weight rooms, barbers and body-hair pluckers, became the urban area's most treasured institution. Daily, men would congregate in the afternoon, and some would stay late into the evening; women eagerly awaited their allotted times, though some places permitted mixed bathing. Closure of the public baths was a feared censure that kept communities in line. The imperial cult may have been more visible, but bathing made the cult of luxury the most seductive aspect of Romanization. It was one of the blessings of Roman rule.

Access through roads, allegiance through the emperor cult, and the amenities of urban life helped Rome transform the conquered world into the Roman world. And Rome tied urbanization to its emperors, as so many inscriptions, temples, or names of cities indicate. For some examples of the latter, one can turn to the Anatolian province of Galatia, where in the middle of the first century a series of cities were founded by Rome or renamed by local civic councils to honor the emperor Claudius. Its map thus includes Neoclaudiopolis, Claudiopolis, Claudioderbe, Claudioconium, Claudiolaodicea, Claudiocaesarea Mistae, and Claudioseleuceia.

The Archaeology of Cities in Palestine

To what extent did Roman urbanization penetrate the Jewish homelands? In the earlier Hellenistic period, Alexander the Great's successors built Greco-Roman-style cities (the *polis*) in places like Egyptian Alexandria and Syrian Antioch, and others along the coast as well as inland in the Transjordan in the loose confederation of cities later known as the Decapolis. But these all were on the periphery of Jewish homelands and had less of an immediate impact on Jews living in Palestine. There, elements of Hellenistic or Roman cities already had been selectively adopted when Rome granted Herod control of the Jewish homeland and the title of King of the Jews. But even a master builder like Herod was exceptionally cautious. By uncovering much of his building program, archaeology underscores his somewhat contradictory nature as both Friend of Rome and King of the Jews. On the one hand, he could construct the Pagan and Roman-style city of Caesarea on the coast, but at the same time and on the other hand, rebuild and expand the Jewish Temple Mount in Jerusalem. He built and sponsored Pagan temples to honor Roman power while adhering to the strict laws avoiding idols or imagery in the holy city of Jerusalem. Incidentally, he totally neglected Galilee in his building projects during his reign (40–4 BCE).

Caesarea

After Herod secured his rule, he set about building an enormous city and harbor on the coast. Literary sources tell us that he named the city Caesarea after his patron Augustus and that he placed in its center a temple dedicated to the divine Augustus and the goddess Roma; the archaeological evidence shows how heavily he borrowed (as well as modified) Roman materials, elements, and styles. To open his kingdom to Rome and the West, he built a harbor of some forty acres with breakwater piers extending nearly eight hundred feet into the open sea. The project set hydraulic concrete in casings with a mix containing *pozzolana*, volcanic sand shipped from the Bay of Naples, then floated them out to sea, where they were sunk section by section for the pier's foundations. Likely accomplished with the aid of Roman architects and know-how, the harbor was named Sebaste to honor Augustus.

Ships entering that protected harbor would have to turn inland through an opening where they would face the massive temple that dominated the landscape and also sat at the intersection of the major north-south and east-west streets. Although badly damaged over time, a life-size torso of the emperor Trajan (98–117 CE) and a headless seated Hadrian (117–38 CE) offer concrete evidence of the imperial cult in Caesarea.

The cult provides the context for understanding the famous Pontius Pilate inscription. Found flipped upside down and reused in the seating of the theater, the fragmentary Latin inscription reads ". . . this Tiberium, Pontius Pilate, prefect of Judea, erected. . . ." While many think that the inscription's importance lies in proving that Pilate existed (and, by extension, that the Gospels are historically reliable), the inscription's significance lies in showing that during Jesus' lifetime a Tiberium, a structure dedicated to the worship of Tiberius, existed at Caesarea, and that the Latin text along with the building clearly communicated the fact that Rome ruled.

Along with the emperor cult, Herod also introduced into his kingdom a few items of the Roman cult of luxury. A large theater and an amphitheater created a vast entertainment complex in Caesarea's southern part, and a high-level aqueduct brought water to the city from miles away, but to date no bath has been found from the first century, only from later periods.

Significantly, no Roman-style roads extending into inland areas like Galilee were built in the first century. Only after Rome's two wars against the Jews (66–70, 132–35) were Roman Legions permanently stationed in Palestine and an artery-like system of roads constructed to facilitate immediate military intervention in the interior. Until those wars, there was only a nominal Roman Legionary presence in Judea, and none in Galilee at the time of Jesus.

Jerusalem

The archaeological excavations in Jerusalem reveal Herod's caution in introducing any Pagan influences. His building energies there concentrated on beautifying and expanding the Jewish Temple in such a way that did not violate biblical tradition. For example, Herod decorated the entire complex on the outside in a simple stone aesthetic; the Temple Mount's facade was made with what has come to be called a "Herodian boss-and-margin style" in which each stone's face had an outer frame of some three to six inches chiseled deeper than the roughly cut internal area. Instead of presenting a monolithic whitewashed facade, this technique allowed individual stones to stand out; in the course of the day, the sun's rays would shift shadows off the boss and into the margins, creating a rich texture that captured a pinkish hue on the sandy-yellow stones at sunrise and sunset, but that shone like marble in the heat of the day. Inside the Temple Mount, like the stairway underneath the so-called Royal Stoa that led up to the plaza facing the sanctuary, Herod built variously colored and fantastically ornate round-domed chambers that combined geometric patterns with floral rosettes resembling chrysanthemums, crowfoot, and other local flowers, with vines and grape clusters featured prominently. But no human images have been found in obedience to the second Mosaic commandment.

Herod did not have carte blanche in rebuilding the sanctuary—its basic arrangement had to remain true to the Solomonic Temple (1 Kings 6–7) and he had to accommodate the biblical prescriptions for the priestly sacrifices and Levitical chores—so he spent most of his energies on encasing the sanctuary in a splendid and massive setting by doubling the platform or Temple Mount on which it stood. To do so he cut into slopes, filled in valleys, and built the foundations on a series of underground vaults with massive retaining walls unprecedented in the history of architecture. The colossal lower courses include stones that measure a full forty feet in length, are more than ten feet high, and perhaps fifteen feet thick, which would weigh in at more than five hundred tons and dwarf the megaliths at Britain's Stonehenge. Thus the disciples' comment in Mark

13:1, "Look, Teacher! What massive stones! What magnificent buildings!" conforms perfectly to the archaeological evidence.

The retaining wall was made of stones so evenly cut and smoothly chiseled that no mortar of any kind was necessary, and they fit so tightly even to this day that neither a knife can be wedged nor a piece of paper slid between them. But despite its massive size and solid construction, the Mount and its Temple were destroyed by Roman Legions in 70 CE at the end of the First Jewish Revolt, along with the rest of the city. Massive stones and enormous columns from the Royal Stoa were thrown down and scattered on the broken pavement below; a cracked Hebrew inscription announcing "for the place of trumpeting" that once capped the pinnacle of the wall also had been cast down, as were two Greek inscriptions threatening any Gentile or Pagan with capital punishment from entering the Court of the Jews.

Galilee

Herod the Great totally neglected Galilee in his building programs; his son Herod Antipas—appointed by Augustus as tetrarch of Galilee (along with Perea)—set about a process of urbanizing it when he took rule. He constructed what were at the time the first cities in Galilee, rebuilding and expanding Sepphoris in the center of Galilee after 4 BCE (four miles from Jesus' hometown Nazareth) and later in 19 CE founding Tiberias (not far from Capernaum, where Jesus spent much of his ministry), named in honor of the then-emperor Tiberius. He coated each of his cities with a Roman architectural veneer, with materials and styles similar to urban sites across the eastern Mediterranean. Both cities were built with orthogonal grids in which major thoroughfares intersected at the center; in both, Antipas used columns and even some marble; the facades of white-plastered walls, frescoes, mosaics, and red roof tiles made the two cities stand out from other towns and villages in Galilee.

But Antipas, like his father, was cautious of introducing Pagan elements that could upset his Jewish subjects. From the time of his rule (4 BCE–39 CE), we find no Pagan temples, no evidence of the imperial cult, no statues; he also avoided putting his face on his coins in keeping with Jewish sensibilities but instead placed symbols like palms, palm branches, or reeds (the latter is of note for Luke 7:24, since it suggests Jesus was contrasting Antipas as a "reed shaking in the wind" with John the Baptist). Though in each city theaters have been found, archaeologists still debate whether they date to Jesus' lifetime or decades later, and as yet no public bathhouses have been found from the first century.

Sepphoris and Tiberias were not Pagan centers of Hellenization or Romanization, and apparently Jesus visited neither during his ministry: the Gospels do not even mention Sepphoris, and Tiberias is mentioned only incidentally in John (as the "Sea of Tiberias" instead of Sea of Galilee in 6:1 and 21:1, and as the place from where some boats came in 6:23). But that does not mean that they are unimportant for understanding Jesus, since they certainly had a demographic and socioeconomic impact on Galilee. On the one hand, their construction fueled the local economy and would have been a boon to some segments of the population, similar to what we saw at Aphrodisias's Sebasteion. In fact, some scholars have suggested that since Nazareth was so close to Sepphoris, Joseph and maybe even Jesus might have worked on its construction projects; their occupations are traditionally translated as "carpenters," but the Greek word *tektōn* more broadly refers to one who works with his hands and includes stone masons and the like (Matthew 13:55 and Mark 6:3).

Many Galileans would have been attracted to life in these cities, but others might have been coerced into living there, if Josephus's account of the founding of Tiberias can be trusted (*Ant.* 18:36–37). In either case, the two cities concentrated many people into two centers that in the new economy fostered a population growth apparent in the increase of sites and their size in the first century. This, in turn, increased the demand on local agriculture. To feed these cities and to pay for their construction, Antipas needed to increase agricultural production across the Galilean valleys, and in the process some farmers would have been moved off their land or become tenants on what was once their land.

The Gospel traditions seem to be well aware of such phenomena, which represent the darker side of urbanization: the Lord's Prayer asks for the repeal of debts (Luke 11:4), the courts are viewed as offering no recourse for indebtedness (Luke 12:58–59), the accountability of the tenants to their owners is well known (Mark 12:1–11), as is the practice of seasonal day laborers looking for work (Matthew 20:1–15) and the abusive steward (Matthew 24:47–51). Antipas began the urbanization of Galilee right at the time of Jesus' life and ministry; he thought those two cities were Good News to some in Galilee, but they certainly were not Good News to all.

The Archaeology of Private Space in Jesus' Galilee

Excavations at the two Galilean cities and many of its villages have concentrated to a considerable degree on domestic houses, which illustrate the socioeconomic distinctions both within sites and between city and country generally. This difference should not be characterized as crass luxury opposed to abject poverty, but social differences among Galileans did appear to have been accentuated in the first century. For example, the majority of houses on the acropolis at Sepphoris were made with evenly cut stones laid out in header-and-stretcher technique, floors were plastered or even covered with mosaics, roofs were tiled, and walls were painted with frescoes. Inside, a certain amount of imported or luxury items were common, like molded glass, lamps from abroad, and ivory makeup applicators. These urban houses of the affluent, along with a few others like them in the towns of Jodefat and Gamla, contrast to a considerable degree with what were the more common houses of Galilean villages, such as those found at Capernaum.

Among those houses at Capernaum is one which had a commemorative octagonal shrine built atop it during the fifth century CE and which later pilgrim reports describe as the house of the "prince of the apostles"; today it is simply called Saint Peter's House. As early as the second century, its floors and walls were plastered and replastered and inscribed with Christian graffiti in Aramaic, Hebrew, Syriac, Greek, and Latin. But whether it actually marks the spot of one of Jesus' miracles or was in fact Peter's house is perhaps less important than its characterizing the context of Jesus' first followers: a house in a simple fishing village that contrasted with those excavated at Sepphoris. In its first-century phase it was like other houses around it, a modest set of rooms surrounding a courtyard; the construction is mostly of unhewn basalt fieldstones; walls were smeared with mud, straw, and even dung; floors were of beaten earth; and roofs were thatched with straw and mud as no roof tiles were found. This, by the way, is why Mark 2:4 says that the friends of the paralytic "dug through the roof" to lower him to Jesus, a phrase that Luke 5:19 changes to lower "through the tiles," which was probably the kind of house with which the author of that Gospel was more familiar.

The houses that have been excavated in Capernaum were similar to most others excavated in Galilean villages, and they show that neither farming nor fishing put people in the higher tiers of the social pyramid. Along these lines, the fishing boat discovered in 1986 and hailed as the "Jesus Boat" is less important because Jesus might have embarked on it than for what it reveals about fishing on the lake. It had to be patched, pegged, and glued together of various kinds of inferior wood and scraps from previous boats, and when it finally gave out, nails and any sturdy wood were removed to use in a subsequent boat. Thus, even though according to Mark 1:19–20 James and John's father had hired men to help with fishing, from what we can tell from the boat and the houses excavated along the lake, that enterprise did not guarantee a life of affluence. Galilean villagers eked out a living that was modest at best.

In addition to these socioeconomic considerations, archaeology helps us understand the ethnic and religious identity of the Galileans. For some time archaeologists sought to settle this issue based on the presence of synagogues in Galilee, but all that have been excavated date to much later periods. As yet no first-century synagogues have been found in Galilee, which suggests that the "synagogues" of the Gospels might refer more to the gatherings than to recognizable structures. Alternatively, the issue of ethnicity has been addressed by looking at the language of inscriptions and assessing the relative proportions of Greek, Hebrew, Aramaic, or Latin. But again, there is a dearth of first-century inscriptions in Galilee, a fact that might suggest lower literacy rates than elsewhere or may simply be due to a lack of interest on the part of local elites in promoting themselves with stone inscriptions.

Be that as it may, such public architecture and visible inscriptions, along with coins and statues, were built either by political rulers or by local elites. Instead of looking to such public and visible space, there are artifacts found inside domestic space or controlled by private initiative that provide better evidence for the broader populace's identity, and which are beginning to be examined for what they can tell us about gender roles, an approach that is promising but still in its infancy. But a set of artifacts from Galilean private space does provide clear data on the population's ethnicity and religion. Four kinds of artifacts, widespread in Galilee and also in Judea and Jerusalem, are associated with Jewish identity: (1) stone vessels, (2) stepped plastered pools for ritual immersion, (3) secondary burial in shaft tombs, and (4) absence of pork in the diet.

Stone vessels are ubiquitous in the first-century layers of excavations in the Jewish homelands. They come in the form of bowls, cups, mugs, lids, and even large jars made of soft white or slightly grayish limestone like those "used for Jewish rites of purification," according to John 2. They appear in Judea and Galilee during the reign of Herod the Great in the late first century BCE but disappear quickly after the destruction of the Temple in 70 CE, going out of use entirely in the beginning of the second century. They appear in the archaeological record just when the great Rabbis Hillel and Shammai were debating such matters as hand washing and purity (e.g., *b. Shabbat* 14b), along with later Rabbinic passages that praise stone's imperviousness to ritual impurity transmitted by liquids (e.g., *m. Oholoth* 5:5, c.f. *m. Parah* 8:5–7). Some scholars suggest they were used for priestly purity rituals; others connect them to Pharisee-inspired purity practices like the washing of hands and eating meals in purity at Pharisaic households (see Mark 6). But they are so pervasive in the archaeological record, not just at every site but in every single house in well-excavated sites like both Capernaum and Sepphoris, that they point to widespread purity concerns among the population who wished to live in such a way that acknowledged God.

More than three hundred stepped, plastered pools, which most people take to be *miqva'ot* (singular *miqvah*), or ritual baths, have been discovered in Galilee and Judea, and they are numerous at the site of Qumran, where the Dead Sea Scrolls were found. Like stone vessels, they are sparse along the coast and in Samaria or in the Transjordan. They are cut into the ground and heavily plastered, and many have some kind of channel to collect rainwater; their descending steps distinguish them from reservoirs or cisterns, since such steps would otherwise subtract from the volume of water being stored. Like stone vessels, *miqva'ot* flourished from the time of Herod the Great through the first century CE, and an entire tractate of the Mishnah (*miqva'ot*) is dedicated to their use, which provides the Rabbis' rulings on their uses for the common Jewish concerns for ritual purity. It was through immersion in "living water" (that is to say, rainwater, spring water, or a lake) that Jews could become ritually pure. Probably since the lake was so close by and provided ample opportunities for immersion, none has been found in Capernaum, but in inland Galilee they are found inside private homes at Sepphoris and at Jodefat as was common in the upper city of Jerusalem, where presumably the more well-to-do could afford this kind of plastered construction. Elsewhere in the north they are at times shared facilities, like at Gamla where one is near an agricultural installation and another next to the synagogue. Ritual baths, so common in Galilee, Judea, and Jerusalem, are never mentioned in the Gospels, even though John is called the baptizer and baptism later became a key ritual of the church. One would presume, then, that Jesus simply had no criticism to offer of their use and the practices associated with them.

Burial practices are one of the most enduring and stable traditions of ethnic and religious groups, and the close parallels between Judean and Galilean burial practices in the first century confirm that Galilee was essentially Jewish. In the Jewish tradition of secondary burial, the deceased were laid out in *kokhim*, body-length shafts cut at right angles into the walls of an underground tomb chamber, or on so-called *arcosolia*, shelves cut into the walls of burial chambers. Once the flesh had decayed (after approximately one year), the bones were gathered together and placed alongside those of other deceased relatives in the shaft, in a hollowed-out repository, or more rarely in Galilee, in a bone box or ossuary. Ossuaries were more common in Jerusalem. One, discovered in a tomb on the ancient city's outskirts and dating to the middle of the first century, was decorated ornately with intricate rosettes and was inscribed on the side with "Joseph son of Caiaphas"; this ossuary is very likely that of the high priest involved in the trial of Jesus (Matthew 26:3, 57). But the recent and highly publicized ossuary that was turned up by a private collector claiming to have bought it from an antiquities dealer, and which allegedly belonged to the pillar of the early Jerusalem church James, brother of Jesus, is a fake. Careful scientific examination by the Israel Antiquities Authority determined that the phrase "James, the son of Joseph, the brother of Jesus," was inscribed in the modern period: it cut through the ancient patina and showed other signs of tampering. Nevertheless, the stories of Jesus' death and resurrection conform to what archaeology tells us about Jewish burial practices of the time, with the body laid out in an underground tomb whose entrance was covered by a rolled stone. Perhaps most important, that reminds us, even in death as much as his life, Jesus must be placed within a Jewish context.

Although not always collected and examined in older excavations, wherever Galilean bone profiles have been analyzed, they reveal a pork-free diet in the first century. Among many scraps of discarded bones or larger faunal remains from butchering, pig is absent in the time of Jesus in Galilee, unlike the rest of the Mediterranean world, where pork was consumed widely and was one of the frequent offerings at Pagan altars. Avoidance of pork was a long-standing Jewish tradition, and there is no evidence of the raising or herding of swine in Galilee; the story in Mark 5 of Jesus' casting the demons into the herd of swine is set on the other side of the Sea of Galilee, that is, in Gentile territory.

All this evidence serves as a reminder that Jesus and his message of the kingdom of God must be understood within a Jewish environment. That environment, to be sure, was not too far from Gentile areas, but it was perhaps because of that very proximity that the Jews in Galilee left an archaeological profile that distinguished them so clearly from their neighbors.

Summary

Archaeology shows rather clearly that the Galilean world of Jesus was Jewish, and while not completely isolated, relatively sheltered from the overt Pagan aspects of urbanization, the Roman emperor cult, and a Legionary presence, all of which came to Galilee only in the second century after the Second Jewish Revolt against Rome. Nevertheless, Galilee was urbanized at the time, and the socioeconomic impact of Antipas's two new cities hit Galilee right at the time of Jesus, which is bound to have had an impact on his formulation of what the kingdom of God meant. But as that message of the kingdom of God spread from Galilee into the wider Mediterranean world, archaeology signals the extent to which the writers of the Gospels would have to contend with the widespread emperor cult and the proclamation of the divine Caesar. Thus the contribution of archaeology to the study of Jesus and the Gospels is not to act as an arbiter of faith and confirm or deny his message or its historicity but to provide concrete aspects of its context, whether demographics, economics, politics, or religion.

Bibliography

Crossan, John Dominic, and Jonathan L. Reed. *Excavating Jesus: Beneath the Stones, behind the Texts.* Rev. ed. San Francisco: HarperSanFrancisco, 2003.

Deissmann, Adolf. *Light from the Ancient East.* London: Hodder and Stoughton, 1910.

Freyne, Sean. "The Geography, Politics, and Economics of Galilee and the Quest for the Historical Jesus." Pages 75–121 In *Studying the Historical Jesus: Evaluations of the State of Current Research.* Edited by Bruce Chilton and Craig Evans. Leiden: Brill, 1994.

Horsley, Richard. *Archaeology, History, and Society in Galilee: The Social Context of Jesus and the Rabbis.* Valley Forge, PA: Trinity Press International, 1996.

Meyers, Eric. "Aspects of Everyday Life in Roman Palestine with Special Reference to Private Domiciles and Ritual Baths." Pages 193–220 In *Jews in the Hellenistic and Roman Cities.* Edited by J. R. Bartlett. London: Routledge, 2002.

Price, S.R.F. *Rituals and Power: The Roman Imperial Cult in Asia Minor.* Cambridge: Cambridge University Press, 1984.

Reed, Jonathan L. *Archaeology and the Galilean Jesus: A Re-examination of the Evidence.* Harrisburg, PA: Trinity Press International, 2000.

Sawicki, Marianne. *Crossing Galilee: Architectures of Contact in the Occupied Land of Jesus.* Harrisburg, PA: Trinity Press International, 2000.

Stern, Ephraim, ed. *The New Encyclopedia of Archaeological Excavations in the Holy Land.* New York: Simon and Schuster, 1993.

Zanker, Paul. *The Power of Images in the Age of Augustus.* Translated by A. Shapiro. Ann Arbor: University of Michigan Press, 1990.

2

Josephus on John the Baptist and

Other Jewish Prophets

of Deliverance

Craig A. Evans

The writings of Josephus (ca. 37–100? CE) are probably the most important writings outside of the Bible itself for understanding the world of early Christianity. Four of his works survive: *Jewish War* (seven volumes), *Antiquities of the Jews* (twenty volumes), *Against Apion* (two volumes), and *Life* (one volume). In these works we hear of Pharisees and Sadducees, of scribes and priests (including Annas and Caiaphas), of familiar rulers and political figures, such as Herod, Pontius Pilate, and Agrippa. Many of the very places mentioned in the New Testament are found in the narratives of Josephus, including Galilee, Caesarea, Jericho, the Mount of Olives, and, of course, Jerusalem. Josephus has much to say about the Temple, about Israel's biblical and postbiblical history, and about various nationalities and ethnic groups, such as Greeks, Romans, Nabateans, and Samaritans. In a few places, Josephus actually mentions figures who play an important role in the founding of the Christian movement. These include Jesus, his brother James, and John the Baptist.

Although scholars from time to time have expressed doubts about the authenticity of Josephus's accounts of Jesus (*Ant.* 18.63–64) and James (*Ant.* 20. 200–201), his account of the preaching and death of John the Baptist is widely accepted as authentic. Most scholars believe that this account is independent of the tradition found in the New Testament Gospels. What Josephus says about John is important not only because it offers us an independent perspective but also because it places John into a broader political and historical context. Part of this broader context involves other public figures who attracted crowds and ran afoul of the authorities. Review of the activities of these figures helps us understand better the political tensions and religious hopes of the Jewish people in late antiquity, again clarifying the context in which Jews lived and Christianity emerged.

John the Baptist is familiar to readers of the New Testament Gospels. The public ministry of Jesus begins with the Baptist, who calls on the Jewish people to repent and be baptized (i.e., immersed) in the Jordan River (Mark 1:4–5), and, according to material found only in Luke (3:10–14), the Baptist urges people to be honest and generous. In the Gospels the message of John is given a distinctly eschatological orientation. The prophecy of Isaiah 40:3 ("Prepare the way of the Lord") is linked to his ministry. Moreover, he warns of coming judgment, and he predicts the coming of one "mightier" than himself, who will baptize the people in spirit and fire (Mark 1:7–8).

The New Testament Gospels go on to say that John criticized Herod Antipas, the tetrarch of Galilee (r. 4 BCE–39 CE), for divorcing his wife (the daughter of Aretas IV, the king of Nabatea to the east) and marrying Herodias, the wife of his half brother Philip (Mark 6:18). Incensed, Herod imprisoned John (Mark 6:17). Later, to make good on a boast before distinguished guests, Herod has John beheaded (Mark 6:16, 27–28).

Some of this story appears in Josephus's account, though the emphasis is different. The Jewish historian and apologist focuses on the tensions between Galilee and Nabatea, which reached a crisis when the Nabatean king, in response to Herod's treatment of the king's daughter, attacked and destroyed Herod's army. The destruction of Herod's army, it was widely believed among the Jewish people, was divine retribution upon Herod for putting John to death. A few paragraphs later, Josephus refers to Herodias leaving her husband and—in violation of Jewish custom—marrying his half brother Herod (*Ant.* 18.5.4 §136); thus, at a very important point, the account in Josephus coincides with the account in the New Testament Gospels.

Where the respective accounts differ is in the description of John's message. The New Testament Gospels emphasize John's fiery call for repentance and warning of coming judgment. Josephus, who says none of this, emphasizes instead John's ministry of purification for those committed to righteousness. As the numbers drawn to John swelled, Herod became alarmed and eventually imprisoned the Baptist.

Josephus's portrait of John as ethicist probably is colored by a desire to portray the Baptist in Greco-Roman philosophical dress. But the portrait may not be wholly fictional, for in Luke's Gospel (3:10–14) we are told that John urged people to live just lives.

What prompted Josephus to mention John at all was the widespread opinion among Jews that the catastrophe that overtook Herod (and contributed to Rome's eventual removal of him from office) came about because of his treatment of the Baptist. Evidently Josephus agrees with this assessment and so portrays John as a "good man" who urged righteous Jews to join him in baptism. But Josephus must be careful in what he says about John's message. Any hint of an agenda of reform or restoration would create in Roman minds sympathy for Herod, whose actions would then seem appropriate.

Whether Josephus knew more about John's preaching and suppressed it out of his reluctance to divulge to the Roman public Jewish interest in eschatology and messianism is difficult to say. But what Josephus tells us does complement in important ways the portrait in the New Testament Gospels, especially when viewed in the context of the activities and promises made by other men of this time.

According to tradition shared by Matthew and Luke (in what usually is identified as the Q source), the Baptist warns the Jewish people not to presume upon God's grace by saying, "We have Abraham as our father." No Jew can say this, John asserts, because "God is able from these stones to raise up children to Abraham" (Matthew 3:9; cf. Luke 3:8). Reference to "these stones" in the context of the Jordan River may well have alluded to the story of Joshua building a monument of twelve stones when the twelve tribes of Israel crossed the Jordan to enter the promised land. On this occasion Joshua says to the people: "When your children ask their fathers in time to come, 'What do *these stones* mean?' then you shall let your children know, 'Israel passed over this Jordan (River) on dry ground'" (Joshua 4:21–22 [emphasis added]; cf. Deuteronomy 27:4; Joshua 4:2–23). The symbolism of twelve stones also appears in the story of Elijah, who led the struggle in Israel against the adoption of foreign gods (see 1 Kings 18:31: "Elijah took twelve stones, according to the number of the tribes of Jacob"), who for a time lived near the Jordan River (see 1 Kings 17:3–5) and even parted its waters (see 2 Kings 2:8), and whose disciple Elisha also parted the water (see 2 Kings 2:14) as well as later ordered the Syrian captain to be immersed in the Jordan River (see 2 Kings 5:10–14). This is significant, for the clothing of John the Baptist resembles that of Elijah (Mark 1:6; cf. 2 Kings 1:8), and Jesus himself identifies John as the famous prophet of old (Mark 9:11–13).

It seems clear that John's preaching and activities were informed significantly by biblical symbolism, especially the symbolism of the Jordan River and, by inference, the tradition of the twelve stones. Jesus' appointment of twelve disciples (see Mark 3:14–19; 6:7) provides significant support for this line of interpretation. Most commentators rightly recognize that the number twelve was intended to symbolize the twelve tribes of Israel, implying that the goal of the ministry of Jesus was the restoration of the whole of the nation. Other prophetic figures mentioned in Josephus, invariably in highly negative, prejudicial language, had similar goals and in some instances utilized similar biblical symbolism. We may survey these figures in chronological sequence.

What brought the administrations of Pontius Pilate, governor of Judea and Samaria, and Caiaphas, high priest of the Jewish Temple in Jerusalem, to an end was their mishandling of the Samaritan affair in late 36 CE. According to Josephus, a certain Samaritan convinced many of his people to follow him to Mount Gerizim, where he would show them the place where their sacred Temple vessels were buried. (The Samaritan temple on Mount Gerizim had been destroyed by John Hyrcanus in 128 BCE; cf. Josephus, *Ant.* 13.256.) Pilate sent a detachment of troops, which routed the pilgrims before they could ascend the mountain (*Ant.* 18.85–87). This episode, although not a Jewish affair, parallels the type of thinking found in Jewish regions (i.e., Galilee and Judea). This Samaritan "uprising" probably had to do with the Samaritan hope for the appearance of the *Taheb*, the "restorer," whose coming was expected in keeping with the promise of Deuteronomy 18:15–18 ("I will raise up for them a prophet like you [Moses] from among their brethren"; cf. *Memar Marqah* 4:12; John 4:20, 25: "Our [Samaritan] fathers worshipped on this mountain [i.e., Mount Gerizim]. . . . I know that Messiah is coming . . . when he comes, he will show us all things"). As such, it is another example of the messianic fervor and unrest of the region in this period.

During the administration of Cuspius Fadus (44–46 CE), Josephus tells us of a man named Theudas who urged the people to take up their possessions and meet him at the Jordan River, where at his command the waters would be parted (*Ant.* 20.97–98). The Roman governor dispatched the cavalry, which scattered Theudas's following. The would-be prophet was himself decapitated and his head put on display in Jerusalem. Acts 5:36 tells us that he had a following of about four hundred men. Although he regarded himself as a "prophet [*prophetes*]," Josephus calls Theudas an "impostor [*goes*]" who "deceived many." (Note the similar description in 2 Timothy 3:13: "Evil men and impostors will go from bad to worse, deceivers and deceived." Judging by Philo's usage [*On Special Laws* 1.315], a *goes* was the precise opposite of the genuine *prophetes*.) Theudas's claim to be able to part the Jordan River is an unmistakable allusion either to the crossing of the Red Sea (Exodus 14:21–22) or, more likely, to the crossing of the Jordan River (Joshua 3:14–17), part of the imagery associated with Israel's redemption (see Isaiah 11:15; 43:16; 51:10; 63:11). In either case, it is probable that Theudas was claiming to be the prophet "like Moses" (Deuteronomy 18:15–19; cf. 1 Maccabees 4:45–46; 14:41; 9:27), who could perform signs like those of Moses' original successor, Joshua.

During the administration of Antonius Felix (52–60 CE), a Jewish man from Egypt made an appearance in Jerusalem. He stationed himself on the Mount of Olives, which overlooks the Temple Mount, and summoned people to himself, claiming that at his command the walls of the city will fall down, permitting him and his following to enter the city and, presumably, to take control of it. Governor Felix promptly dispatched the cavalry, which routed and dispersed the following. However, the Egyptian himself escaped. In the parallel account in *Jewish War*, Josephus calls the Egyptian a "false prophet" and "impostor" who, with a following of thirty thousand, "proposed to force an entrance into Jerusalem and, after overpowering the Roman garrison, to set himself up as tyrant over the people" (*War* 2.261–63). The hoped-for sign of the walls falling down probably was inspired by the story of Israel's conquest of Jericho, led by Joshua the successor of Moses (Joshua 6:20). This Egyptian is mentioned in other sources as well. According to Acts 21:38, a Roman tribune asked the Apostle Paul: "Are you not the Egyptian, then, who recently stirred up a revolt and led the four thousand men of the Assassins out into the wilderness?" Further, according to the accounts in Acts and *Jewish War*, the Egyptian summoned people "out into the wilderness." This wilderness summons, as well as the Joshua-like sign of the walls falling down, is very likely part of the prophet-like-Moses theme, or some variation of it, that evidently lay behind much of the messianic speculation of the first century. Moreover, the fact that this Jewish man was known as the man from Egypt also might have had to do with some sort of association with Moses, who also came out of Egypt, to begin his preparation for the deliverance of Israel.

Similar confrontations took place during the administration of Porcius Festus (60–62 CE). In a context in which he described the troubles brought on by the *Sicarii*, Josephus reports that Festus sent armed forces against a throng of people deceived by an impostor who had promised salvation and "rest" if they followed him out into the wilderness (*Ant.* 20.188). It is likely that this "impostor" was another messianic prophet, probably in keeping with the prophet-like-Moses theme (as the wilderness summons would seem to indicate). The impostor's promise of rest, moreover, may have had something to do with Psalm 95:7b–11, a passage warning Israelites not to put God to the test, as they did at Meribah and Massah "in the wilderness," and consequently fail to enter God's "rest" (cf. Exodus 17: 1–7; Numbers 20:1–13). Although the parallel is not precise, it is worth noting that this passage is cited and commented upon in Hebrews (3:7–4:13), a writing in which Jewish Christians are exhorted not to neglect their "salvation" (2:3) but to "strive to enter that rest" (4:11).

Finally, Josephus tells us of one Jonathan, who, following the Roman victory over Israel and the capture of Jerusalem (70 CE), fled to Cyrene (North Africa). According to Josephus, this man, by trade a weaver, was one of the *Sicarii*. He persuaded many of the poorer Jews to follow him out into the desert, "promising to show signs and apparitions" (*War* 7.437–38; *Life* 424–25). Catullus the Roman governor dispatched troops who routed Jonathan's following and eventually captured the leader himself (*War* 1.439–42). Although Josephus does not describe Jonathan as a (false) prophet, it is likely that this is how the man viewed himself, as the desert summons would imply.

The activities of the several men who have been considered clarify and place in context the preaching and activities of John the Baptist. The Baptist's ministry at the Jordan River, reference to "these stones," and the promise of one to come who will be far mightier than the Baptist himself and who will immerse the people with spirit and fire—not water—strongly suggest that John was one of several men who anticipated the restoration of Israel and imagined it in terms of past acts of salvation. The Baptist was guided not only by a Jordan typology (especially as seen in the stories of Joshua and Elijah) but also probably by the language and imagery of some of the classical prophets, such as Malachi, who inveighed against divorce and adultery (see Malachi 2:16; 3:5) and foretold the day of the Lord (see Malachi 3:1), coming fiery judgment (see Malachi 3:2–3; 4:1–2 [Hebrew 3:19–20]), and the return of Elijah the prophet (cf. Malachi 4:5–6 [Hebrew 3:23–24]). The prophet Isaiah also contributed to John's language, as seen in the quotation of Isaiah 40:3 and in other allusions (e.g., Isaiah 30:27–28, which speaks of fire, wrath, coming, spirit, and water).

In the translations that follow, we have Josephus's versions of the teachings and activities of John the Baptist and other prophetic figures that appeared after him. One must remember that these accounts are hardly unbiased. Josephus has little sympathy for eschatology and messianism. Although his portrait of John is some-what sympathetic, the eschatological element is carefully expunged. As for the other would-be prophets of deliverance, Josephus is harsh in his criticism, re-garding them and others like them as ultimately responsible for the rebellion against Rome and its catastrophic results.

JOHN THE BAPTIST (ANT. 18.116–19, 136)

Now it seemed to some of the Jews that the destruction of Herod's army was by God, and was certainly well deserved, on account of what he did to John, called the Baptist. For Herod had executed him, though he was a good man and had urged the Jews—if inclined to exercise virtue, to practice justice to-ward one another and piety toward God—to join in baptism. For baptizing was acceptable to him [God], not for pardon of whatever sins they may have committed, but in purifying the body, as though the soul had beforehand been cleansed in righteousness. And when others gathered (for they were greatly moved by his words), Herod, fearing that John's great influence over the peo-ple might result in some form of insurrection (for it seemed that they did everything by his counsel), thought it much better to put him to death before his work led to an uprising than to await a disturbance, become involved in a problem, and have second thoughts. So the prisoner, because of Herod's suspi-cion, was sent to Machaerus, the stronghold previously mentioned, and there was executed. But to the Jews it seemed a vindication of John that God willed to do Herod an evil, in the destruction of the army.

. . .

But Herodias, their sister, was married to Herod [Philip], the son of Herod the Great, a child of Mariamme, daughter of Simon the high priest; and to them was born Salome. After her birth Herodias, thinking to violate the ways of the fathers, abandoned a living husband and married Herod [Antipas]—who was tetrarch of Galilee—her husband's brother by the same father.

THE SAMARITAN (ANT. 18.85–87)

Now the Samaritan people did not escape upheaval. For a man who thought nothing of lying rallied them, contriving everything according to the pleasure of the multitude, commanding them to gather to him at Mount Gerizim, which is to them the holiest of mountains. He assured that when they arrived there he would reveal the sacred vessels that were buried there, where Moses had set them down. So they, regarding the word as plausible, came in arms. Taking up position at a certain village, which was called Tirathana, they wel-comed those who arrived, as they planned the ascent up the mountain. But Pi-late prevented their ascent by sending cavalry and heavily armed infantry, who engaging the first arrivals in the village killed some and put others to flight. They led many away as prisoners. The leaders of these and the most influential of those that fled Pilate executed.

THEUDAS (*ANT*. 20.97–98)

Now when Fadus was procurator of Judea, a certain pretender named Theudas persuaded the greater part of the mob to take up their possessions and follow him to the Jordan River. For he told them that he was a prophet and that at his command he could divide the river, providing them with easy passage. Saying these things, he deceived many. Fadus, however, did not permit them to take advantage of the madness, but sent a squadron of cavalry against them, which falling upon them unexpectedly killed many and took many alive. Capturing Theudas, they cut off his head and conveyed it to Jerusalem.

THE EGYPTIAN JEW (*WAR* 2.259–60, 261–63; *ANT*. 20.167–68, 169–70)

For deceivers and impostors, pretending to be under divine inspiration and fomenting upheavals, persuaded the multitude to madness and led them out into the desert, as if there God would show them signs of liberation. Against these Felix—for he supposed it to be the foundation of insurrection—having sent cavalry and armed infantry, destroyed a great multitude.

But the Egyptian false prophet dealt a more evil blow to the Judeans. For this man, appearing in the country, was a pretender. Having gained for himself a reputation of prophet, he collected about thirty thousand that had been beguiled and led them about from the wilderness to the mountain called Of Olives. From there he was to force entry into Jerusalem and, overpowering the Roman garrison, become tyrant of the people, putting to work as bodyguards those who poured in with him. But Felix prevented his attempt, meeting him with heavily armed Roman infantry, and all the people joined in the defense. In the resulting engagement, the Egyptian fled with a few; most of those with him were killed or captured, and the remainder dispersed, sneaking away to their homes.

. . .

And now pretenders and deceivers persuaded the mob to follow them into the wilderness. For they said that they would show them visible wonders and signs in keeping with God's plan. And many, persuaded, suffered the consequences of their folly. For having returned them Felix punished them. But at this time a certain person from Egypt came to Jerusalem, saying that he was a prophet and counseling the general population to go out with him to the Mount of Olives, which lies opposite the city at a distance of five furlongs. For he said he wished to show them from there that at his command the walls of

Jerusalem would fall down, through which he promised to provide entrance for them. When Felix learned these things, he ordered the soldiers to take up arms. With many cavalry men and foot soldiers, he set out from Jerusalem and fell upon those around the Egyptian and killed four hundred of them and took two hundred alive. But the Egyptian himself, escaping from the battle, disappeared.

ANOTHER ANONYMOUS "IMPOSTOR" (ANT. 20.188)

Festus sent a force of cavalry and infantry against those who had been deceived by a certain pretender who had promised them salvation and rest from hard times, if they decided to follow him into the wilderness. Those who were sent destroyed both that one himself and those who had followed him.

JONATHAN THE REFUGEE (WAR 7.437–40; LIFE 424–25)

But also the madness of the Sicarii, like a disease, reached as far as the cities of Cyrene. For Jonathan, a most wicked person and weaver by trade, having escaped into Cyrene, persuaded not a few to heed him and follow him into the wilderness, promising to show signs and apparitions. He concealed these things from others, but worthy persons among the Jews of Cyrene reported his exodus and preparation to Catullus the governor of the Libyan Pentapolis. Having sent forth cavalry and infantry he easily overpowered the unarmed crowd, most of whom perished in the encounter, but some taken alive were brought up to Catullus.

. . .

A certain Judean, Jonathan by name, having raised an insurrection in Cyrene and having persuaded two thousand of the natives to take part, became a cause of destruction for them. He was put in chains by the one governing the country and then, when he was sent to the emperor, he alleged that I [Josephus] had sent him weapons and money. Not being deceived, Vespasian condemned him to death; and, handed over, he died.

Bibliography

Chilton, Bruce D. "John the Baptist: His Immersion and His Death." Pages 25–42 in *Dimensions of Baptism: Biblical and Theological Studies*. Edited by Stanley E. Porter and Anthony R. Cross. *Journal for the Study of the New Testament*, Supplements 234. London: Sheffield Academic Press, 2002.

———. "Yohanan the Purifier and His Immersion." *Toronto Journal of Theology* 14.2 (1998): 197–212.

Dunn, James D. G. "John the Baptist's Use of Scripture." Pages 42–54 in *The Gospels and the Scriptures of Israel*. Edited by Craig A. Evans and W. Richard Stegner. *Journal for the*

Study of the New Testament, Supplements 104. Studies in Early Judaism and Christianity 3. Sheffield: Sheffield Academic Press, 1994.

Evans, Craig A. "The Baptism of John in a Typological Context." Pages 43–71 in *Dimensions of Baptism: Biblical and Theological Studies*. Edited by Stanley E. Porter and Anthony R. Cross. *Journal for the Study of the New Testament*, Supplements 234. London: Sheffield Academic Press, 2002.

Hoehner, Harold W. *Herod Antipas: A Contemporary of Jesus Christ*. Society for New Testament Studies Monograph Series 17. Cambridge: Cambridge University Press, 1972.

Horsley, Richard A. "Popular Prophetic Movements at the Time of Jesus: Their Principal Features and Social Origins." *Journal for the Study of the New Testament*, Supplements 26 (1986): 3–27.

Horsley, Richard A., and John S. Hanson. *Bandits, Prophets, and Messiahs: Popular Movements at the Time of Jesus*. San Francisco: Harper & Row, 1998.

Meier, John P. "John the Baptist in Josephus: Philology and Exegesis." *Journal of Biblical Literature* 111 (1992): 225–37.

Saulnier, Christiane. "Herode Antipas et Jean le baptiste: Quelques remarques sur les confusions chronologiques de Flavius Josephe." *Revue Biblique* 91 (1984): 362–76.

Taylor, Joan. *The Immerser: John the Baptist within Second Temple Judaism*. Studying the Historical Jesus. Grand Rapids, MI: Eerdmans, 1997.

Trumbower, Jeffrey A. "The Role of Malachi in the Career of John the Baptist." Pages 28–41 in *The Gospels and the Scriptures of Israel*. Edited by Craig A. Evans and W. Richard Stegner. *Journal for the Study of the New Testament*, Supplements 104. Studies in Early Judaism and Christianity 3. Sheffield: Sheffield Academic Press, 1994.

Webb, Robert L. *John the Baptizer and Prophet: A Socio-historical Study. Journal for the Study of the New Testament*, Supplements 62. Sheffield: Sheffield Academic Press, 1991.

———. "John the Baptist and His Relationship to Jesus." Pages 179–229 in *Studying the Historical Jesus: Evaluations of the State of Current Research*. Edited by Bruce D. Chilton and Craig A. Evans. New Testament Tools and Studies 19. Leiden: Brill, 1994.

———. "John's Baptizing Activity in the Context of First-Century Judaism." *Forum*, n.s., 2.1 (1999): 99–123.

———. "Josephus on John the Baptist: *Jewish Antiquities* 18.116–119." *Forum* n.s., 2.1 (1999): 141–68.

3

Abba and Father: Imperial Theology
in the Contexts of Jesus
and the Gospels

Mary Rose D'Angelo

One of the most widely held but problematic ideas about the historical Jesus is the claim that Jesus had an absolutely new and unique relationship with the Deity that he expressed by addressing God with the Aramaic word *abba*. This argument was laid out in an article in the *Theological Dictionary of the New Testament* (*TDNT*) by Gerhard Kittel, who interpreted the word *abba* as a form of baby talk and concluded that "Jewish usage shows how this Father-child relationship to God far surpasses any possibilities of intimacy assumed in Judaism, introducing indeed something which is wholly new." Kittel was not only editor of the *TDNT* but also the author of *Die Judenfrage* (1933) and of contributions to the Nazi publication *Forschungen zur Judenfrage*. His arguments were expanded, supplemented, and popularized after the war by Joachim Jeremias's influential essay "Abba" and were revived against feminist calls to avoid masculine theological imagery.

In fact, the evidence that the word *abba* was important to or even used by Jesus is, at best, extremely slender. This word occurs only once in the Gospels, in a scene for which the Evangelist provides no witnesses (Mark 14:35–36). Mark presents Jesus at prayer in Gethsemane in terms and circumstances that recall the prayer of Joseph (see below): "And going ahead a little way he fell upon the earth and began to pray that the hour might pass from him, and he was saying, Abba! Father! (Greek: *Abba ho pater*) all things are possible to you. Take this cup away from me. But not what I will, but what you do." The scene reflects the theology of the Evangelist, writing sometime between the late 60s and early 80s (probably after the fall of Jerusalem in 70) rather than a historical event.

Evidence from early Judaism and Christianity begins in the second half of the first century (i.e., slightly later than Jesus) and shows that it was used by adults, both for their natural fathers and as a title honoring teachers. Paul twice attributes *abba* to the Holy Spirit in the community (Galatians 4:6; Romans 8:15). In Galatians, *abba* functions not as baby talk or an expression of childlike trust and intimacy but as a sign that women and men believers have become God's fully mature "sons."

Jeremias's case rested especially on the claim that "for Jesus to address God as 'my Father' is therefore something new. . . . We can say quite definitely that there is no analogy at all in the whole literature of Jewish prayer for God being addressed as *Abba*. . . . there is as yet no evidence in the literature of ancient Palestinian Judaism that 'my Father' is used as a personal address to God" (57). His case was undergirded by the assumption that texts written in Greek were of no relevance to interpreting the context of Jesus, who was assumed to have been, and probably was, a speaker of Aramaic.

But both the claim and the assumption are problematic. Jesus can be reached only through the Gospels, texts written in Greek and closely related to Greek-speaking Jewish texts. Further, since Jeremias, two texts have been found from Qumran which demonstrate that "Palestinian" Jews of and before Jesus' time could and did address God as "my father." There is no way of knowing whether Jesus was familiar with these texts, or indeed whether he was literate. But the texts show that individual Jews of his milieu addressed God as father. Read in the context of other Hebrew prayers, as well as Greek prayers by Jews that refer to or address God as father, the texts from Qumran make clear that Jewish prayer to God as father was of real significance in the period of Jesus and the Gospels. It was particularly important in prayers that sought God as the refuge of the afflicted and persecuted, especially those persecuted by the unbelieving and in petitions for or assurances of forgiveness. Both petitions for rescue and prayers for forgiveness rely on the way that "father" evoked the power and providence that govern the world.

The bifurcation of Jesus and the Gospels' context into Palestinian/Aramaic-speaking Judaism and Greek-speaking Judaism is itself problematic, for it obscures a feature of their context that exerted considerable, indeed extreme, pressure on all groups, first of Jews, including Jesus and his companions, then of early Christians: the overarching rule of Rome.

It cannot be shown with certainty that Jesus used the address "father" for God; "father" appears as a designation for the Deity far less frequently in the earliest sources, Mark (4 uses) and Q (9 uses in three or four passages), than in their revisers (about 42 uses in Matthew and about 19 in Luke) or in John (about 109). While it is probable that the Gospels, especially Matthew and John, reflect the theological thinking of their time and authors, the appearance of the address in the two texts from Qumran and in Jewish texts in Greek from the period enhances the evidence of the Gospels and increases the likelihood that Jesus and his companions might have drawn upon this practice in their preaching of God's reign. If they used "father" as an address to God, they must have done so not because it was novel and revelatory but because it spoke to the deepest convictions and aspirations of their (Jewish) audience. Chief among these was the conviction that God alone was the true ruler of the world and the aspiration to serve and worship the creator in "holiness and justice," free from Rome's idolatrous domination.

Among Rome's idolatrous claims was the emperor's appropriation of the title "father." Roman tradition was hostile to the title king (Latin, *rex*); when Octavian consolidated imperial power in his own person, he needed other titles that could enhance his authority without offending this sensibility. Shortly after defeating Antony and Cleopatra (31 BCE), he acquired the appellation "Augustus," which suggested both sacrality and piety: it implied his devotion to the gods while simultaneously assimilating him to their status. His admirers also began to call him *pater patriae*, "father of the fatherland," a title that originated for military heroes whose deeds were thought to have saved the Roman state, although he officially accepted the title only in 2 BCE. In Augustus's program, the title was allied to his moral legislation and accompanied by a sort of "family values" campaign; it asserted a personal oversight and providence toward his fellow citizens and subjects. Both "Augustus" and *pater patriae* continued to function as imperial titles throughout the first and second centuries CE and were disseminated on coins and inscriptions. The Greek-speaking parts of the empire felt no discomfort with the title "king" (Greek, *basileus*), and there thinking of the emperor as king and father further assimilated him to Zeus.

Jews of the time, including Jesus, and the early Christians who cherished his memory found in their God a father and king immeasurably greater than Rome's ruler of the world. To announce God's kingdom, God's reign, was to remind oneself and one's fellow Jews that it is God and not the emperor who truly reigns; to call upon the divine Father is to place oneself under a protection far greater than the reach of Rome. This is not to say that Jewish understandings of God as father originated under Roman influence; it is quite clear that the divine Father appears in much earlier texts (see, e.g., Schuller, *Post-exilic Prophets*). Rather, the resistance inspired by Roman rule and the accommodations it required enhanced the urgency of calls upon the father and maker of all.

The selection of texts here is far from exhaustive; it does not attempt to represent the use of "father" in pre-Roman Platonic and Stoic theology. Nor does it include all Jewish and Roman texts from the period of Rome's domination of the Mediterranean (mid–second century BCE through the sixth century CE). These selections are intended to illustrate the functions of an appeal to God as father in the political and religious context in which Jesus and his companions preached God's reign, and the Gospels were written. The Jewish texts in particular use the title to invoke the divine power and providence that reign over the world (including those human powers who reign over the Jews), to seek divine forgiveness or to celebrate it, and to call upon the Deity to rescue righteous Jews from the Gentiles who threaten them and their devotion to their "father in heaven."

There is every reason to sustain George Foote Moore's early judgment: "That God is so often called our Father who is in heaven, or invoked in prayer, O our Father! does not indicate that the age had a new conception of God, or put a new emphasis on one element of the conception. What these phrases express is not an idea of God, but a characteristic attitude of piety in which Jesus and his immediate disciples were brought up" (211). The Roman texts expose one of the pressures against which Jesus and other Jews of his time marshaled their courage by an appeal to their father and king. Together these texts suggest that approaches to the historical

Jesus that seek to contrast him with "the Judaism of his time" or that ignore the Roman imperial context of his death and life distort the origins of Christianity.

1QHODAYOTH: HYMNS COLS. 15 (FORMERLY 7), 20–24 AND 17 (FORMERLY 9), 29–36

The Hymns found among the Dead Sea Scrolls generally are understood as an expression of the spirituality of the sectarian community located at Qumran. The section from which these selections are taken appears to have been composed late in the second century BCE, and it is sometimes attributed to the Teacher of Righteousness. During this period, the Romans were active in the region, but the text predates any direct dominion by Rome. Brackets indicate points at which the manuscript is incomplete or unreadable.

In 15 (Sukenik 7), 20–24, the sage speaks of himself as father and wet nurse to the community while expressing both his own sense of being under siege and his confidence that God's power will rescue him: "You have made me a father for the sons of kindness, like a wet-nurse to the men of portent; they open their mouth like a chi[ld on the breast of its mother,] like a suckling child in the lap of its wet-nurse" (translated by García Martinez and Tigchelaar, vol. 1, 179).

In 17 (Sukenik 9), 29–36, we find a selection that communicates a relationship with the deity characterized by profound intimacy and tenderness. Its relation with the wisdom tradition is suggested by the way the imagery that applied to the teacher in the preceding selection applies here to the Deity:

For you have known me since my father, from the womb [. . . , . . . of] my mother you have rendered good to me from the breasts of her who conceived me your compassion has been upon me, on the lap of the wet-nurse [. . .] from my youth you have shown yourself to me in the intelligence of your judgment and with certain truth you have supported me. . . . For my father did not know me and my mother abandoned me to you. Because you are a father to all the [son]s of your truth. You rejoice in them and like her who loves her child, and like a wet-nurse you take care of all your creatures on (your) lap. (Translated by García Martinez and Tigchelaar, vol. 1, 185)

4Q372: 4QAPOCRYPHON OF JOSEPH 1, 14–25

The manuscript of this Hebrew text about Joseph was found in Cave 4 at Qumran; it was copied in the late Hasmonean to early Herodian period—that is, at some point from the time Pompey arrived in Jerusalem (63 BCE) to the first years of Augustus's reign. But the text does not mention the special concerns of the sectarians and so is probably somewhat older than the manuscript. In it Joseph calls for help against the persecuting foreigners; he addresses God as "my father" and promises to do God's will:

And while all this happened, Joseph [was delivered] into the hand of foreigners who consumed his strength and broke all his bones up by the time of his end. And he became wear[y . . .] and he summoned the powerful God to save him from their hands. And he said, "My father and my God, do not abandon me to the hands of the Gentiles [. . .] do me justice, so that the poor and afflicted do not perish. You have no need of any people or nation for any help. [Your] fing[er] is bigger and stronger than any there are in the world. For you choose truth and in your hand there is no violence at all. And your mercies are great and great is your compassion for all who seek you; [. . .] they are greater than me and my brothers who are associated with me. An enemy people lives in it [. . .] and opens its mouth against all the sons of your beloved Jacob with insults for [. . .] the moment of their annihilation from the whole world and they shall be delivered [. . .] I shall arise to do right and just[ice . . .] the will of my creator, to offer sacrifices [of thanksgiving . . .] to my God. (Translated by García Martinez and Tigchelaar, vol. 2, 737)

4Q460 FRAG. 5 COL. 1, 1–5

This very fragmentary Hebrew manuscript from Qumran Cave 4 also appears to have been a prayer embedded in a narrative. The speaker likewise invokes God as father in face of persecution from enemies who appear to be idolaters:

[. . .] you, and before you I am in dread, for like the dread of God, they plan evil [. . .] for confusion in Israel, and for something horrible in Ephraim. [. . . from the l]and of guilty deeds to the height of the Most High, from generation [to generation . . . f]or you have not forsaken your servant [. . .] my father and my lord. (Translated by García Martinez and Tigchelaar, vol. 2 [4Q274–11Q31], 1998, 937, 39)

3 MACCABEES 6:2–3

Third Maccabees, a novel written by a Greek-speaking Jew, depicts the miraculous aversion of a violent persecution planned by Ptolemy against the Jews of Egypt. Likely written during the first century BCE, it reflects attitudes toward Roman treatment of the Jews in Alexandria; the Ptolemy in the narrative plays the role of the governor of Egypt and, behind him, the emperor. The narrator closes and introduces communal prayer with references to the Deity as "God the surveyor and founding father of all, holy among the holy" (2:21) and as "the all-ruling lord, who is lord over every power, their (the Jews') merciful God and father" (5:7). In the opening of a lengthy prayer for the aversion of the calamitous persecution that threatens the Jews of Egypt, the elderly priest Eliezer invokes the Deity as "father" as well as king, laying stress on the divine power:

Almighty king, God most high, all-ruler, guiding all the creation with mercy, look upon the seed of Abraham, upon the children of the sanctified Jacob, the people of your sanctified portion, perishing as strangers in a strange land—father!

PHILO, *LEGATION TO GAIUS* 114–15, 292–93

Philo, a Greek-speaking Jewish philosopher and exegete who lived in Alexandria (see Gregory Sterling's contribution in this volume) was a member of a delegation of Alexandrian Jews sent by their community to the emperor Gaius (Caligula) to argue that the Jews ought to be citizens of Alexandria of same status as Greeks. During Philo's stay in Rome, Gaius announced his intention of erecting a colossal statue of himself in the Temple in Jerusalem. *Legation to Gaius* (written ca. 41–50 CE) recounts the attempts of the delegation to dissuade him from an enterprise that the Jews could not but regard as catastrophically blasphemous. Philo often refers to God as Father and Maker, a phrase that derives in part from his Platonism and is frequent throughout his works. Here it asserts Jewish monotheism against Gaius's imperial demands:

Have we not already learned from (what I have described) that Gaius ought be likened to none of the gods or demigods, being of neither the same nature, nor substance, nor inclination? But desire is blind, as it seems, especially when it combines empty pride and quarrelsomeness with the ultimate power, by which we, once so fortunate, were being destroyed. For he looked with suspicion upon the Jews alone, since they alone chose the opposite opinions, having been taught from, in a sense, their swaddling clothes by parents and pedagogues and teachers and, much more, by the holy laws and even by the unwritten customs to honor one Father and Maker of all.

. . .

No one, neither Greek, nor barbarian, neither satrap nor king, no implacable enemy, neither riot nor war, neither siege nor sack, nor any other thing of any sort, ever committed so gross an innovation as to set up an image or statue or any piece of handiwork. For even if as enemies they were hostile to the inhabitants of the land, still a certain shame and reverence intervened against breaking any of the things prescribed from the beginning for the honor of the Maker of the universe and its Father.

THE *ROMANCE OF [JOSEPH AND] ASENETH* 12:8–11

The date of this ancient Greek novel that relates the conversion of the Egyptian Aseneth and her marriage to Joseph is much disputed and ranges from the late second century BCE to the fourth century CE (see Randall Chesnutt's chapter in this volume). Although it is usually identified as a Jewish text, it was preserved by Christians, and the rites at its center cannot readily be identified with Jewish forms of initiation. The prayer of Aseneth cited below pleads for rescue from Gentile persecution in terms that are strikingly reminiscent of the much earlier and Hebrew *Hodayoth* from Qumran (see the first two selections as well as Peter Flint's contribution):

> [8]For as a frightened young child flees to his father,
> and the father reaches out his hands and picks him up off the ground
> and embraces him against his chest,
> and the child clasps his hands around his father's neck
> and sighs relief from his fear
> and rests upon his father's chest,
> while the father smiles at his childish alarm,
> so you also, Lord, reach out your hands to me as a father who loves his
>   child,
> and pick me up off the ground.
> [9]For, behold, the wild old lion pursues me,
> because he is the father of the gods of the Egyptians,
> and his children are the gods of those obsessed with idols.
> And I have come to hate them
> because they are the lion's children,
> and I threw all of them away from me and destroyed them.
> [10]And their father the lion fiercely pursues me.
> [11]But you, Lord, rescue me from his hands,
> and deliver me from his mouth,
> lest he carry me away like a lion and tear me to pieces,
> and throw me into the flaming fire,
> and the fire throw me into the tempest,
> and the tempest enshroud me in darkness
> and throw me out into the depths of the sea,
> and the great eternal sea monster swallow me
> and I perish forever.
> (Translated by Randall Chesnutt)

MISHNAH, *YOMA* 8.9

Even the earliest Rabbinic literature is significantly later than the career of Jesus and the works of the New Testament and cannot be used as direct evidence for the Judaism of the earlier period. Jeremias recognized that Rabbis did use "father" as an address to God and wrongly interpreted the fairly widespread occurrence of "father" as the introduction of a new vocabulary beginning from the time of Rabban Yochanan ben Zakkai (*Prayers*, 16–17). Many illustrations of Rabbinic use could be adduced here, but for the purposes at hand, it is also noteworthy that a number of the instances in early Rabbinic literature are either associated with martyrdom or attributed to the Rabbis who suffered through the wars with Rome. Rabbi Aqiba in particular supported the Bar Kochba revolt and died as a martyr. Attributing an appeal to God as father to Aqiba may reflect memories that it could proclaim God's reign over against that of the emperor.

The Mishnah was codified in the early part of the third century CE; in this text from the treatise on the Day of Atonement, Akiba is made to voice the conviction that the Deity supplies directly for the lost purificatory rites of the temple:

R. Aqiba said: Blessed are you, O Israel. Before whom are you made clean? Who makes you clean? Your father in heaven as it is written, "And I will sprinkle clean water upon you and you shall be clean."

BABYLONIAN TALMUD, *TA'ANITH* 25B

The Babylonian Talmud (largely in Aramaic) appears to have been collected during the sixth century CE; in the context of a long list of miraculous rain in response to prayer, the following brief litany is attributed to Akiba. It appears to have become the basis of a much longer litany that forms part of the New Year liturgy:

Our father, our king, we have no king but you;
Our father, our king, for your own sake have mercy on us.

MEKILTA DE-RABBI ISHMAEL, BAHODESH 6, 136–43

Mekilta is a commentary on parts of the text of Exodus. Although it cannot be dated with certainty, it appears to be one of the earliest of the Midrashim, perhaps as early as the second half of the third century CE (see Alan Avery-Peck's chapter in this volume). The Rabbi Nathan cited here is a figure of the mid–second century. The text highlights the role of the father in heaven as the refuge of martyrs:

R. Nathan says: "Of them that love Me and keep My commandments," refers to those who dwell in the Land of Israel and risk their lives for the sake of the commandments. "Why are you being led out to be decapitated?" "Because I circumcised my son to be an Israelite." "Why are you being led out to be burned?" "Because I read the Torah." "Why are you being led out to be crucified?" "Because I ate unleavened bread." "Why are you getting a hundred lashes?" "Because I performed the ceremony of the Lulab." And it says: "Those with which I was wounded in the house of my friend" (Zechariah 13.6). These wounds caused me to be beloved of my father in heaven. (Lauterbach, *Mekilta de-Rabbi Ishmael*, 247)

LETTER TO THE GALATIANS 3:26–4:6 (CA. 55 CE)

In this famous passage, Paul attempts to dissuade his communities in Galatia (central Turkey) from being circumcised in order to attain the status of "seed of Abraham." Here "*abba*! father!" is a charismatic, spirit-driven invocation attesting the privilege of men and women believers as God's adult sons and heirs, whether circumcised or not:

All you are sons of God through faith in Christ Jesus, for as many of you as have been baptized into Christ have put on Christ. There is among you neither Jew nor Greek, neither slave nor free, no "male and female," for you are all one in Christ Jesus. If you are Christ's, then you are seed of Abraham, heirs according to the promise.

But I say, as long as the heir is a child, he differs in no way from a slave, though he is master of all, but is under overseers and stewards until the time the father has set. So also we, when we were children, were enslaved under the elements of the cosmos. But when the fullness of time came, God sent his son, born of a woman, born under the law, to redeem those under the law, so that we might receive adoption as sons. Because you are sons, God has sent the spirit of his son into our hearts, crying out abba! father! (Greek: *abba ho pater*) So you are no longer a slave but a son, and if a son, also an heir through God.

LETTER TO THE ROMANS 8:12–15 (EARLY 60S CE)

Romans, probably written a few years later than Galatians, also presents "abba! father!" as the cry of spirit in the community:

Therefore, brothers and sisters, we are debtors, not to the flesh, to live by the flesh, for if you live by the flesh you will die. But if by the spirit you kill the works of the flesh, you will live. For as many as are led by the spirit of God, these are God's sons. For you did not receive a spirit of slavery again for fear, but you received a spirit of adoption, by which we cry out, abba! father! (Greek: *abba ho pater*). The spirit itself attests with our spirit that we are children of God.

CICERO, *DE RES PUBLICA* 1. 36. 56, 39.64 (CA. 55 BCE)

Marcus Tullius Cicero (106–43 BCE) was among the last generation of Roman consuls who governed the city and empire of Rome before all power resided in the emperor. He himself bore the title *pater patriae* as an acknowledgment that he had saved his country from the plot of Catiline. In his dialogue called the *Repub-*

lic (actually *Res Publica*, the common or public matter), he uses Scipio Africanus to articulate the connotations the title carries:

rightly we begin our discussion from him whom the learned and unlearned alike agree is the one king of gods and human beings. . . . Perhaps the foremost public men have established for its usefulness for life this, that there be thought to be one king in heaven who by a nod, as Homer says, should reverse all Olympus and that he be held both king and father of all. . . .

. . . they (the generation of Romulus) called neither "masters" nor "lords" nor finally "kings" those to whom they were justly subject, rather "guardians of the fatherland," rather "fathers," rather, "gods."

HORACE

Quintus Horatius Flaccus (65–8 BCE) ranks with Virgil as representative of Augustan literature. His work includes a number of celebrations of Augustus's reign, frequently emphasizing Augustus's claim to have rescued Rome from the horrors of civil war.

The opening and closing stanzas of *Odes* 1.2 (ca. 27 BCE) see the strife following the assassination of Julius Caesar as the result (and manifestation) of Roman moral corruption; fearing its return, Horace entreats Augustus to stay in Rome and maintain his control of the city. Written long before Augustus officially accepted the title *pater patriae* in 2 BCE, the poem shows that it was used for him and acceptable to him much earlier than that date:

> Now the divine Father has sent
> enough snow and dreadful hail upon the lands,
> and with red right hand striking the sacred hilltops
> has terrified the city,
>
> whom shall the people call
> from among the gods to help the falling rule?
> With what pleading chant shall the holy virgins
> weary Vesta, who little hears?
> To whom shall Jupiter give the task
> of expiating guilt?
>
> . . . Be here to love being called "father" and "princeps"
> and do not let the Medes ride unpunished,
> while, Caesar, you lead.

A second selection, similarly from the early part of Augustus's career (*Odes* 3.24.26–30), also shows that the title implied a father's responsibility for *mores* and also may imply the emperor's paternity toward the whole empire, not simply the city of Rome:

whoever would remove impious slaughter
and civic strife
if he seeks to have "father of cities"
written on his statues, let him dare
bridle unbroken license,
   and be famed
to future generations.

PUBLIUS OVIDIUS NASO, *FASTI* 2.127–33

Ovid's relationship with Augustus was more strained than that of Horace; in fact, he ended his days in exile on the Black Sea. His poetry also includes many pieces honoring Augustus, as well as an entire work endeavoring to get himself recalled from exile (*Tristia*) and a collection of epistolary poems dedicated to the same end (*Ex Ponto*). *Fasti* was a book of poems for the days of the Roman calendar partially composed before his exile (between 2 BCE and about 8 CE) and apparently revised during it. This extract is from the lines celebrating the anniversary of the day on which Augustus received the title *pater patriae*. Ovid extends its meaning to "father of the world":

> Holy father of the fatherland, to you the people, to you the senate
> gave this name; we the equites gave it.
> Reality beforehand had given it. Though late, you have borne
> true titles: long you have been the father of the world.
> Throughout the lands you have that name that Jupiter holds
> in high heaven: you are father of human beings, he of gods.

AUGUSTUS, *RES GESTAE* 34–35

According to Suetonius, Augustus composed an account of his accomplishments shortly before his death in 14 CE and deposited it with his will in the repository of wills kept by the vestal virgins (*Augustus* 101). It survived, in both the original Latin and a Greek paraphrase, in three inscriptions from Galatia (Turkey). These last two paragraphs celebrate the honors bestowed on him, demonstrating that he considered the title *pater patriae* the apex of his career:

In my sixth and seventh consulships, after I had extinguished civil war and was through universal consent empowered over all (public) matters, I transferred the government (*rem publicam*) from my power to the control of the senate and the Roman people. For this benefaction of mine, I was named Augustus, the door-posts of my house were clothed with laurel by public decision, and a civic crown was placed above my door and a golden shield was placed in the Julian Senate House. The inscription of the shield attested that it had been given to me by the senate and the people of Rome because of my fortitude and clemency, justice and piety. After this time I have exceeded all in authority, although I have possessed no more power than others who were my colleagues in office.

While I was conducting my thirteenth consulship, the senate, the equestrian order and the entire Roman people named me father of the country, and decided that it should be inscribed in the vestibule of my residence, in the Julian Senate House, and in the Forum of Augustus, under the chariot which was placed there in my honor by senatorial decree. As I write I am passing my seventy-sixth year.

DIO CHRYSOSTOM, *DISCOURSES* 1.22–25, 39–40

Dio Chrysostom (died after 112 CE) was a Greek orator and philosopher. Among his many discourses are four speeches on kingly rule or empire (*basileia*) which he is thought to have delivered before the emperor Trajan. These two short extracts from the first discourse on kingly rule illustrate both the way "father" assimilated the emperor to the divine father and ruler, Zeus, and the continued use of the title *pater patriae* to make moral appeals to later emperors like Trajan:

[The true king] thinks that on account of his rule, he has more not of money or of pleasures, but of care and concerns, so he is labor-loving more than others are money-loving or pleasure-loving . . . thus he alone is able . . . not only to be called father of his citizens and subjects but to be shown so in deeds. . . . Those who have seen and been with him do not wish to leave him; those who hear of him yearn to see him more than children yearn to discover their unknown fathers.

After the topic I have just completed I wished to discourse on the greatest and first king and ruler, whom those who direct mortals and mortal affairs ought always to imitate, directing and likening their own approach to him as far as is possible.

. . .

For Zeus alone of gods is named the father and king, and *Polieus* (Civic) and *Philios* (of friends) and *Hetaireios* (of comrades) and *Homognios* (connatural) and further *Hikesios* (of suppliants) and *Phuxios* (of refuge) and Xenios (of strangers) and having ten thousand other titles all good and the causes of good things. He is named "king" because of his rule and power, but "father," I think, because of his clemency and mildness. . . . (Parentheses supplied by translator)

EPICTETUS, *DISCOURSES* 1.9.4–7

Epictetus (died around 135 CE) was once a slave to Epaphroditus, the freedperson-secretary of Nero and patron of Josephus. Once freed, he became a student of Musonius Rufus, and when the philosophers were banished by Domitian, set up a school in Nicopolis. Like Dio Chrysostom, he treats the divine rule of the universe as analogous to the empire as a household headed by the emperor, but his philosophical counsel reflects a very different social location and experience than that of Dio Chrysostom. Epictetus advises the one who has absorbed the teaching that human beings are kin to God to follow Socrates' practice of never saying "I am an Athenian" but "I am a world citizen" (*kosmikos*):

One, then, who has become a student of the governance of the world and learned that: "what is greatest and most legitimate and most inclusive of all, this is the commonwealth of human beings and of God, whose seeds, then, have descended not to my father only, nor my grandfather, but to all things that have been born and grow upon the earth, but especially to those with reason, since these alone by nature commune with God, entwined in his companionship through reason"—why should such a one not call himself a son of God? and why fear anything that happens among human beings? But kinship with Caesar or some other of the mighty at Rome is enough to enable people to live in safety and without contempt and fearing nothing. To have God as our maker and father and guardian—will this not deliver from pains and fears?

CASSIUS DIO, *ROMAN HISTORY* 53.16.6–8, 18.2–3

Cassius Dio was a Greek senator of the late second and early third century CE; he is thought to have begun the *Roman History* around the year 202. The selections below come from a section describing the powers and honors Augustus used to create the office of emperor as it continued to be exercised in Dio's day:

When he had achieved them (the powers and honors described earlier) in actuality, the name of Augustus was added both from the senate and from the people. While they wished to address him with something distinctive, and some were proposing and choosing this and others that, Caesar (Octavian) fiercely desired to be called Romulus, but recognizing that he was being suspected on this account of desiring a kingship (*basileias*), he laid no claim to it, but took the cognomen "Augustus," implying that he was something more than human. For all the most valued and holy things are called augusta. Hence in Greek also they addressed him as Sebastos, from *sebazesthai* (to worship), as someone holy. . . .

And in this way, from all these democratic names, (the emperors) have clothed themselves in all the power of the government, so that they possess all the appurtenances of the kings except the crass one of their title. For the designation of "Caesar" or of "Augustus" adds no inherent power to them, but only makes clear in the first case their succession in their family, in the second the splendor of their status.

The appellation of "father" perhaps gives them, with regard to us all, a certain authority which fathers once had over their children, not, indeed originally for this, but as an honor and as an admonition that they should love those be-ing ruled as children and that they in turn should revere them also as fathers. (Parentheses mine)

Bibliography

Barr, James. "'Abba and the Familiarity of Jesus' Speech." *Theology* 91 (1988): 173–79.

―――. "Abba Isn't Daddy." *Journal of Theological Studies*, n.s., 39 (1988): 28–47.

D'Angelo, Mary Rose. "Abba and 'Father': Imperial Theology and the Traditions about Je-sus." *Journal of Biblical Literature* 111 (1992): 611–30.

―――. "Theology in Mark and Q: Abba and 'Father' in Context." *Harvard Theological Review* 85 (1992): 149–74.

Fitzmyer, Joseph. "Abba and Jesus' Relation to God." Pages 1–38 in *A Cause de l'Evangile: Études sur les Synoptiques et Actes offertes a Jacques Dupont O.S.B. a l'occasion de son 70e anniversaire*. Lectio Divina 123. Publications de Saint-André. Paris: Cerf, 1985.

García Martinez, Florentino, and Eibert J. C. Tigchelaar, trans. *The Dead Sea Scrolls Study Edition*. 2 vols. Leiden: Brill; Grand Rapids, MI: Eerdmans, 1997, 1998.

Gnadt, Martina. "'Abba Isn't daddy': Aspekte einer feministisch-befrieungstheolgische Re-vision des 'Abba Jesu.'" Pages 115–31 in *Von der Wurzel getragen: Christlich-femistische Exegese in Auseinandersetzung mit Antijudaismus*. Edited by Luise Schotroff and Marie-Theres Wacker. Biblical Interpretation 17. Leiden: Brill, 1996.

Hamerton-Kelly, Robert. *God the Father: Theology and Patriarchy in the Teaching of Jesus*. Overtures to Biblical Theology, 4. Philadelphia: Fortress Press, 1979.

―――. "God the Father in the Bible." In *God as Father?* Edited by Johannes-Baptist Metz and Edward Schillebeeckx. English language editor Marcus Lefébure. *Concilium* 143: Dogma. Edinburgh: T and T Clark; New York: Seabury Press, 1981.

Jeremias, Joachim. "Abba." Pages 11–65 in *The Prayers of Jesus*. Translated by John Bow-den. London: SCM, 1967.

―――. *Abba: Studien zur neutestamentlichen Theologie und Zeitgeschichte*. Göttingen: Van-denhoeck & Ruprecht, 1966.

Karris, Robert J. *Prayer and the New Testament: Jesus and His Communities at Worship*. Com-panions to the New Testament. New York: Herder and Herder/Crossroad, 2000.

Lauterbach, Jacob Z. *Mekilta de-Rabbi Ishmael*. Vol. 2. Philadelphia: Jewish Publication So-ciety of America, 1933.

Marchel, W. *Abba Pere! La priere du Christ et des Chrétiens*. Analecta Biblica 19. Rome: Pon-tifical Biblical Intsitute, 1963.

Moore, George Foote. "The Father in Heaven." Pages 201–11 in vol. 2 of *Judaism in the First Centuries of the Christian Era: The Age of the Tannaim*. 1927. Repr., New York: Schocken, 1971.

Schelbert. G. "Sprachgeschichtliches zu 'Abba.'" Pages 395–447 in *Mélanges Domini que Barthélemy: Études bibliques offertes a l'occasion de son 60e anniversaire*. Edited by P. Casetti et al. Orbis biblicus et orientalis 38. Fribourg: Editions Universaires; Göttingen: Vandenhoeck & Ruprecht, 1981.

Schrenk, Gottlob, and Gottfried Quell. "πατήρ, πατρός, πατρία, πάτωρ, πατρικός." *Theologisches Wörterbuch zum Neuen Testament* 5 (1954). Translated by Geoffrey W. Bromily. *Theological Dictionary of the New Testament* 5 (1964): 945–1022.

Schuller, Eileen. "4Q372 1: A Text about Joseph." *Revue de Qumran* 14 (1990): 343–70.

————. *Post-exilic Prophets*. Message of Biblical Spirituality 4. Wilmington, DE: Glazier, 1988.

————. "The Psalm of Joseph (4Q372 1) within the Context of Second Temple Prayer." *Catholic Biblical Quarterly* 54 (1992): 67–79.

Strotmann, Angelika. *"Mein Vater Bist Du!" (Sir 51,10): Zur Bedeutung der Vaterschaft Gottes in kanonischen und nichtkanonishcen frujudischen Schriften*. Frankfurt am Main: Verlag J. Knecht, 1991.

Thompson, Marianne Meye. *The Promise of the Father: Jesus and God in the New Testament*. Lousiville, KY: Westminster/John Knox Press, 2000.

4

Miraculous Conceptions and Births
in Mediterranean Antiquity

Charles H. Talbert

Two canonical gospels, Matthew and Luke, contain infancy narratives. Matthew's narrative compares Jesus with the traditions about Moses' early life (e.g., Magi speak of the birth of a Jewish king; the current ruler attempts to kill all the Jewish male babies; the key baby is saved so he can be the future savior of the people; there is a flight from or to Egypt; after the ruler's death there is a message to return from whence the child had fled). This typology (i.e., viewing the earlier material as the prototype or foreshadowing of the latter) functions as part of Matthew's Christology (Jesus is the new Moses of Deuteronomy 18:15–18), and it adds authority to what Jesus will say in five teaching sections (chaps. 5–7; 10; 13; 18; 24–25). Luke's material about the birth and early life of Jesus functions within the ancient genre of prophecies of future greatness. Prophecies, portents, and other material foreshadow the future greatness of the child.

The two infancy narratives share a tradition that says Jesus was miraculously conceived by the Spirit. According to Matthew 1:20, the angel says to Joseph: "Joseph, son of David, do not be afraid to take Mary as your wife, for the child conceived in her is from the Holy Spirit." Luke 1:34 has Mary ask the angel who has told her she will bear the Son of the Most High: "How can this be, since I am a virgin?" The angel answers in 1:35: "The Holy Spirit will come upon you, and the power of the Most High will overshadow you; therefore the child to be born will be holy; he will be called Son of God."

The question to be asked is: How would the authorial audience have heard this material in Matthew and Luke? What cultural assumptions did auditors bring?

Ancient Mediterranean peoples did tell stories of miraculous conceptions and births. There were accounts, set in the mythic past, of individuals born to a divine mother and a human father, for example, Achilles (son of the divine Thetis and the human Peleus—*Iliad* 20.206–7; 24.59), Aeneas (son of Aphrodite and the mortal Anchises—*Iliad* 2.819–22; 5.247–48; see also the late first-century BCE through early first-century CE Ovid, *Metamorphoses* 14.588), and Persephone (daughter of of Demeter and Iasion—*Odyssey* 5.116–28).

In the *Iliad* 20.199–209, Aeneas and Achilles meet in battle. As custom dictated, they taunted one another before fighting:

> Aeneas said: "Son of Peleus, do not try to frighten me with words, as if I were a child, since I too know how to taunt. We know each other's parents and lineage for we have heard the ancient stories. . . . They say that you [Achilles] are the son of Peleus and that your mother was Thetis, a daughter of the sea. I am the son of Anchises and my mother is Aphrodite."

Those believed to be the offspring of a god and a human mother included Asclepius (son of Apollo and the mortal Coronis—so the first-century BCE Diodorus of Sicily 4.71.1); Hercules (son of Zeus and the human Alcmene—*Iliad* 14.315–28; Diodorus of Sicily 4.9.1, 3); Dionysus (son of Zeus and Semele—*Iliad* 14.315–28); Perseus (son of Zeus and Danae—*Iliad* 14.315–28); Aristaeus (son of Apollo and Cyrene—Diodorus of Sicily 4.81.1–3); Romulus (son of Mars and the mortal Ilia, or Rhea, or Silvia—so the first-century BCE Cicero, *Republic* 1.41; 2.2; Plutarch, *Parallel Lives*, "Romulus," 2.3–6).

Diodorus of Sicily 4.2.1–4 relates what the Greeks say about Dionysus. Cadmus was sent from Phoenicia to search for the maiden Europa. During his travels, in obedience to an oracle, he founded the city of Thebes and settled there. He married Harmonia and had a number of offspring, one of whom was Semele:

> Now with Semele, because of her beauty, Zeus had intercourse, doing it without speaking. . . . Whereupon she asked him to treat her as he did Hera. Zeus, therefore, encountered her as a god with thunder and lightning, making himself manifest as they came together. Semele, who was pregnant, was not able to bear the god's power. So she gave birth prematurely and was herself killed by the fire.

Zeus then had Hermes take the child to the Nymphs to raise. As a result of his upbringing, Dionysus discovered wine and taught humans how to cultivate the vines.

Diodorus of Sicily says: "Aristaeus was the son of Apollo and Cyrene, the daughter of Hypseus, son of Peneius" (4.81.1). According to myth, Apollo was attracted to a maiden named Cyrene. He carried her off to Libya, where he later founded a city named after her. In 4:81.2–3 Diodorus says:

> Apollo begat of Cyrene a son, Aristaeus, in that land. He gave the baby to the Nymphs to raise. . . . The boy learned from the Nymphs how to make cheese, how to make beehives, and how to cultivate olives. He was the first to teach these things to humans. . . . those who received the benefits gave Aristaeus honors like those given to gods, as had been done for Dionysus.

The first-century BCE historian Dionysius of Halicarnassus, *Roman Antiquities*, tells of a vestal virgin, Ilia or Rhea (1.76.3–4), who went to a grove consecrated to

Mars to fetch pure water for use in the sacrifices and was "ravished by someone in the sacred area" (1.77.1):

> Most relate a myth of the divinity of that place . . . whose appearance was much more marvelous than the size and beauty of humans. They say the ravisher . . . told her not to grieve. For the marriage had been with the divinity of that place. Out of her being ravished, she would give birth to two sons whose deeds would excel all others [i.e., Romulus and Remus]. (1.77.2)

Sometimes ancient authors would give two traditions: one miraculous and the other nonmiraculous. Plutarch's *Parallel Lives*, "Romulus," from the end of the first to the beginning of the second century CE, offers an example. One story, according to Promathion in his history of Italy, runs:

> Tarchetius, king of the Albans, . . . encountered a strange phantom at home. A phallus rising up out of the hearth remained for many days. An oracle of Tethys was in Tuscany. From it an interpretation of the phenomenon was brought to Tarchetius. A virgin should mate with the phantom. From her a son would be born who would have great valor, good fortune, and great strength. Tarchetius, therefore, told the prophecy to one of his daughters and instructed her to mate with the phantom. She resisted and sent a handmaid instead. . . . When the handmaid bore twins by the phantom, Tarchetius gave them to Teratius to destroy. He carried them to the riverside. There a she-wolf came to them and nursed them. Birds brought bits of food to them. A cowherd found the twins and took them home with him. In this way they were saved. (2.3–6)

In 3.1–3, Plutarch says the story that has the greatest credence is the one given by Diocles of Peparethus and Fabius Pictor. It focuses on a vestal virgin, Ilia, or Rhea, or Silvia who was found to be pregnant, contrary to the law for vestals. She was saved from death by the intercession of the king's daughter, Antho. The vestal virgin gave birth to two boys, large and beautiful. Plutarch (4.2) says it was the boys' mother who claimed that Mars was the father. It was said by others, however, that the girl was deceived into doing this by Amulius, who came to her dressed in armor.

Stories of miraculous conceptions and births were also told about rulers and philosophers in historical time. Among the philosophers, Pythagoras was said to be the offspring of Apollo and the human Pythais, the most beautiful of the Samians (Porphyry, *Life of Pythagoras* 2); Plato was believed to have been the son of Apollo and Amphictione (Diogenes Laertius, *Lives of Eminent Philosophers* 3.1–2; 3.45); Apollonius of Tyana was thought to be the son of Proteus, a divinity of Egypt, or Zeus (Philostratus, *Life of Apollonius of Tyana* 1.4.5–9; 1.6).

Diogenes Laertius, in the third century CE but citing early sources, says of Plato (*Lives of Eminent Philosophers* 3:1–2):

> Plato was the son of Ariston and Perictione. . . . Speusippus in the work titled *Plato's Funeral Feast*, Clearchus in the *Encomium on Plato*, and Anaxilaides in the second book *Concerning Philosophers*, tell how at Athens there was a story . . . that Apollo appeared to Ariston in a dream; whereupon he did not touch Perictione until the child's birth.

The early third-century church father Origen, *Against Celsus* 1.37, offers a supplement to Laertius's account:

> It is not absurd to employ Greek stories to talk with Greeks, to show we Christians are not the only people who use a miraculous story like this one [i.e., about Jesus' conception]. For some (Greeks) think it proper . . . to relate even of recent events that Plato was the son of Amphictione, while Ariston was prevented from having sexual intercourse with his wife until she gave birth to the one sired by Apollo.

Philostratus, in his third-century CE *Life of Apollonius of Tyana*, says of Apollonius (1.4.5–9):

> To his mother, before his birth, came a divinity of Egypt, Proteus. . . . She was not frightened but asked him: "What will I bear?" He said: "Me!" She asked: "Who are you?" He said: "Proteus, the god of Egypt."

The narrator then explains that Proteus excelled in wisdom, knowing past and future. He promises that as the story progresses, Apollonius will be seen to excel even Proteus!

Among the rulers spoken of in terms of a miraculous conception and birth, Alexander the Great and Augustus Caesar stand out. At the end of the first or the beginning of the second century CE, Plutarch's "Alexander" contains this account:

> Philip, after the vision [in a dream, he saw himself putting a lion-shaped seal on his wife's womb—2.4], sent Chavion of Megalopolis to Delphi. Chavion then brought Philip a word from the god [Apollo], telling him to sacrifice to Ammon and to reverence this god greatly. He also told Philip that he would lose his sight in the eye with which he had spied on the god, who in the form of a snake, had shared the bed of his wife. Also Olympias, as Eratostheues says, when Alexander was sent upon his expedition, told him alone the secret about his begetting. She challenged him to behave worthily of his origins. Others, however, say she rejected the idea and said: "Alexander must stop slandering me to Hera." (3:1–4)

In the second century CE, Aulus Gellius, *Attic Nights* 13.4.1–2, has this to say about Alexander's origins:

> Olympias, wife of Philip, sent a witty response to her son, Alexander, when he wrote to her: "King Alexander, son of Jupiter Hammon, to his mother Olympias, sends greeting."
>
> Olympias responded in this manner: "Please, my son, be quiet, neither slandering nor accusing me before Juno. She will be vengeful toward me if you say in your letters that I am her husband's lover."

Gellius comments that in this way Olympias urged Alexander to give up the foolish idea he had formed from his incredible success, namely, that he was the son of Jupiter (13.4.3).

In the early second-century CE, Suetonius, *Lives of the Twelve Caesars*, "Augustus," 94.4, wrote:

> In the books of Asclepias of Mendes, Theologumena, I read: Atia came to the solemn service of Apollo in the middle of the night. Her litter was set down in the temple and she went to sleep. A snake crawled up to her, then went away. Upon awakening she purified herself as she would after sexual relations with her husband. There then appeared on her body a mark colored like a snake. She could not rid herself of it, so she stopped going to public baths. Augustus was born ten months after and therefore was thought to be the son of Apollo.

In most of these stories the liaisons between gods and humans involved sexual relations, either with the deity's identity known (as with Zeus and Semele [Diodorus of Sicily 4.2.1–4] or Proteus and the mother of Apollonius of Tyana [Philostratus, *Life of Apollonius* 1.4.5–9]) or with the deity taking another form (e.g., when Zeus could not overcome Alcmene's chastity, he assumed the form of her husband [Diodorus of Sicily 4.9.3], or in a number of cases the deity took the form of a snake [Plutarch, "Alexander," 3.1–4; Suetonius, "Augustus," 94.4]).

There was, however, another tradition that was averse to thinking of physical sexual contact between deity and humanity; consequently, a begetting that did not involve physical sexual contact was sought. Aeschylus is an early example. In "Suppliants" 17–19, Io is said to be impregnated by Zeus in the form of "the on-breathing of his love." "Prometheus" 848–52 states that at Canobus near the mouth of the Nile, Io will be restored to her senses by Zeus through "the touch of his unterrifying hand." The offspring will be Epaphus (= touch-born, named from the touch [*ephapsis*] of the hand of Zeus).

Plutarch gives fullest exposition of this point of view. The first is in "Table Talk" VIII, Question 1.2 (*Moralia* IX, 114–19). The first speaker, Florus, refers to those who attribute Plato's parentage to Apollo and claim that Ariston, Plato's father, had a vision in his sleep, which forbade him to have intercourse with his wife for ten months. The second speaker, Tyndares, replies that it is fitting to celebrate Plato with the line: "He seemed the child not of a mortal man but of a god." When, however, Plato himself speaks of the uncreated and eternal god as father and maker of the cosmos, "it happened not through semen but by another power of God (*dunamei tou theou*) that God begot in matter the principle of generation, under whose influence it became receptive and was changed." So, Tyndares says he does not think it strange if "it is not by a physical approach, like a man's, but by some other kind of contact or touch that a god alters mortal nature and makes it pregnant with a more divine offspring." Tyndares continues: "The Egyptians say that Apis (= the sacred bull, the incarnation of Osiris) is begotten by the touch (*epaphe*) of the moon."

In "Numa" 4.1–4, Plutarch begins by speaking of the story that Numa forsook city life to live in the country because, it was said, he had a marriage with a goddess, Egeria. Such a tale, Plutarch states, is like stories from the Phrygians, Bithynians, and Arcadians. He concludes that it is not impossible to think that the

Deity should be willing to consort with men of superlative goodness, wisdom, and holiness. In 4.3, however, he says: "It is difficult to believe that a god or phantom would take carnal pleasure in a human body and its beauty." In 4.4 he continues: "Nevertheless the Egyptians make a plausible distinction in such a matter. A woman can be made pregnant by a spirit (*pneuma*) of a god, but for a human there is no physical intercourse with a god." This trajectory shows that it was possible in Mediterranean antiquity to think of a miraculous conception without understanding it in terms of sexual intercourse between a deity and a human. It would be no surprise, then, for ancient auditors to hear that Jesus' conception was via "spirit," "power," and involved "overshadowing" (touch).

There were two main reasons the ancients spoke of miraculous conceptions and divine descent. The first was an attempt to explain an individual's superiority to other mortals. Generally Mediterranean peoples looked at one's birth or parentage to explain one's character and behavior. In Plutarch's "Romulus," 7.3– 4, Remus has been brought before Numitor for punishment. When Numitor sees Remus, he is "amazed at the youth's surpassing greatness of body and strength, and noting from his face the unsubdued boldness and vitality of his psyche despite the present circumstances, and hearing that his works and acts were like his appearance, . . . he asked who he was and what were the circumstances of his birth." Birth explains later deeds and character!

If the possibility of miraculous conception or birth was believed to be true in general, then a truly superior person could only be explained by a divine origin. Several examples make the point. Dionysius of Halicarnassus, *Roman Antiquities* 1.77.2, in his account of the vestal virgin Ilia's being ravished in the grove consecrated to Mars, has the ravisher say to the maiden after the event that she should not grieve because "out of her being ravished, she would give birth to two sons whose deeds would excel all others." A divine begetting results in superior deeds!

The first-century BCE Diodorus of Sicily, *Library of History* 4.9.2, says: "When Zeus had sexual relations with Alcmene he made the night three times longer than usual and by the length of time given to making the child he foreshadowed the superior nature of the one begotten."

The second-century CE Arrian, *Anabasis* 7.30, says of Alexander the Great: "And so not even I can suppose that a man quite beyond all other men was born without some divine influence." Aulus Gellius, in *Attic Nights* 13.4.3 (second century CE), says that Olympias attempted to get Alexander to give up the idea he had formed from his incredible success, namely, that he was the son of Jupiter. Here great success implies a divine origin! The third-century CE Philostratus, *Life of Apollonius of Tyana* 1.4.5–9, has the narrator explain that Apollonius would excel in wisdom because he had been begotten by the deity Proteus, who also excelled in wisdom. The early third-century CE Church Father Origen, *Against Celsus* 1.37, says that Greek stories like that of Apollo's begetting Plato

are really fables. They have been invented about a man they think has greater wisdom and power than others. Their claim, then, is that he received the beginning of his physical existence from a better, diviner sperm, something that is fitting for persons who are greater than ordinary humans.

Diogenes Laertius, *Lives of Eminent Philosophers* 3.45, quotes an epitaph:

And how, if Phoebus [Apollo] did not cause Plato to be born in Greece, did he [Plato] heal human minds with letters? For even as the divinely begotten Asclepius is a healer of the body, so Plato is of the immortal soul.

One could not do what Plato did had he not been the offspring of a god! One reason the ancients used stories of miraculous conceptions and births was as an explanation of the superiority of the individual.

The second function of such stories of miraculous conceptions in antiquity was the veneration of a benefactor. For example, Cicero, *The Republic* 1.41 (first century BCE), gives a quote from Ennius regarding Romulus: "O father, O sire, O one whose blood comes from gods." In 2.2 Cicero says concerning Romulus that he was one

who was born of father Mars (we concede this to the popular tradition, preserved from ancient times, handed down by our ancestors who thought that those who merited good from the community should be regarded as descendants of the gods and endowed with divine qualities).

Here the tradition of Romulus's supernatural conception is part of the ancient Roman veneration of benefactors.

Ovid, *Metamorphoses* 14.581–608, tells of Venus approaching Jupiter with a request on behalf of Aeneas, her son and Jupiter's grandson. Based on Aeneas's worthiness, Jupiter grants Venus's wish. So Aeneas, the legendary ancestor of the Romans, is honored by the Roman populace with temple and sacrifice. It was part of the Roman mentality to venerate benefactors by ascribing divinity to them. This often included stories of their miraculous conception and birth.

Early Christian auditors of Matthew and Luke would have assumed that the stories of Jesus' divine begetting were certainly needed to explain his marvelous life. A divine origin was appropriate for their chief benefactor and founder. This much the Greco-Roman materials make clear. These auditors, however, were heir not only to the Greco-Roman traditions but also to the Christian traditions before and contemporary with them. Two aspects of this Christian tradition call for attention.

First, the Gospel of Mark, which most scholars think was earlier than Matthew and Luke, lacks a birth narrative. It begins with John the Baptist and with Jesus as an adult. Second, some Christians believed that their relation with God depended on their taking the initiative and performing acceptably so that God would respond approvingly (e.g., Galatians 2:15–16; 3:1–5). The late second-century Church Father Irenaeus, *Against Heresies* 1.26, speaks of one Cerinthus (late first century) who believed

Jesus was not born of a virgin, but was the son of Joseph and Mary according to the usual manner of begetting. Because he was more righteous, more prudent, and wiser than other humans, after his baptism the Christ descended upon him in the form of a dove. Then he preached the unknown Father and performed miracles.

The Gospel of Mark, without a miraculous birth narrative, was susceptible to such an interpretation of a meritorious Jesus who is rewarded by God. If Jesus is the model for Christians, then they too must be meritorious. Ever since Paul, at least, this was not what mainstream Christians believed. The relation with God was based on God's gracious initiative to which humans responded in trust and obedience (i.e., faith).

When Matthew and Luke added birth narratives with a miraculous conception as part of their rewriting of Mark, they were saying that this type of life can be produced only by God's prior gracious, creative act. If it is so for Jesus, then it is likewise true for his followers. The tradition of miraculous conceptions and births is thereby refined in its Christian-Jewish context. The Greco-Roman conviction that a human's superiority can be explained only by a divine creative act is used to establish the prevenience of divine grace in the divine-human relation. This is what an ancient auditor would have heard.

Bibliography

Note: The translations are made from Greek and Latin texts found in the Loeb Classical Library and Migne's *Patrologia*. Quotations from the Bible are from the NRSV.

Box, G. H. "The Gospel Narratives of the Nativity and the Alleged Influence of Heathen Ideas." *Zeitschrift für neutestamentliche Wissenschaft* 6 (1905): 80–101.

Brown, Raymond E. *The Birth of the Messiah: A Commentary on the Infancy Narratives in Matthew and Luke.* Garden City, NY: Doubleday, 1977.

Cartlidge, David R., and David L. Dungan. *Documents for the Study of the Gospels.* Cleveland, OH: Collins, 1980.

Fitzmyer, Joseph A. "The Virginal Conception of Jesus in the New Testament." Pages 41–78 in *To Advance the Gospel: New Testament Studies.* New York: Crossroads, 1981.

Talbert, Charles H. "Jesus' Birth in Luke and the Nature of Religious Language." *Heythrop Journal* 35 (1994): 391–400.

——. "Prophecies of Future Greatness: The Contribution of Greco-Roman Biographies to an Understanding of Luke 1:5–4:15." Pages 129–42 of *The Divine Helmsman: Studies on God's Control of Human Events, Presented to Lou H. Silberman.* Edited by James L. Crenshaw and Samuel Sandmel. New York: KTAV, 1980.

—5—

First and Second Enoch:

A Cry against Oppression and the

Promise of Deliverance

George W. E. Nickelsburg

The *Book of Enoch*, or *1 Enoch*, is a collection of apocalyptic (revelatory) texts that were composed between roughly 350 BCE and 50 CE in the name of the patriarch mentioned in Genesis 5:18–24. The collection as a whole is extant only in an Ethiopic translation of a Greek translation of Aramaic origins, eleven fragmentary manuscripts of which were found among the Dead Sea Scrolls (Nickelsburg, *1 Enoch 1*, 9–20). The literary form of apocalyptic revelations is usually a first-person account of a vision or audition that one has received in a dream or in an ascent to heaven that might have occurred in a dream. The revelations themselves pertain to the hidden things of the cosmos and/or to God's adjudication of the evils and injustices experienced by the authors and their communities. Other examples include Daniel 7–12, 2 and 3 *Baruch*, 4 *Ezra*, and the *Apocalypse of Abraham* (see Collins, 78–92, 155–204).

1 Enoch 92–105

1 Enoch 92–105 differs in its literary form from other apocalyptic revelations in that it does not recount a vision or audition but purports to be an Epistle that is based on Enoch's visions, which are recounted in *1 Enoch* 1–36 and 81:1–4. In the Epistle, the ancient patriarch addresses his children and his spiritual descendants, "the righteous, the pious, and the chosen," who will live in "the last generations." The perspective is "eschatological," that is, related to the end-time (Greek *eschaton*). In a series of "woes" that imitate biblical oracles (e.g., Isaiah 5:8–25; Jeremiah 22:13–19), the author predicts in detail how the end-time will be marked by false religious teachings that pervert divine Law and by the unjust oppression of the righteous and lowly by the rich and powerful (*1 Enoch* 94:6–100:9). The revelations promise, however, that God will intervene in history by righting the present wrong state of affairs. God will compensate the righteous for their piety and punish the false teachers and the oppressors for their evil deeds. The Epistle's portrayal of events, in fact, reflects both the real author's understanding of events in his own time and his conviction that divine justice must prevail. Thus the Epistle serves both as religious and social criticism and as comfort for those whose world is a constant source of physical and emotional distress, anxiety about the future, and perhaps disintegrating trust in God's ability to order creation.

The text was composed, partly of traditional material, sometime in the second century BCE. The author and his associates or community believed that they were God's chosen people and that their understanding of divine Law excluded contrary interpretations by other Jews (Nickelsburg, *1 Enoch* 1, 423–24). Paradoxically, however, like the authors of other parts of *1 Enoch*, they expected that some of "the children of the whole earth" (i.e., non-Jews) would eventually accept their teachings and receive divine blessing (Nickelsburg, *Ancient Judaism*, 85–87).

The passage below and its context (102:4–103:8; 104:7–8) form the climax of the Epistle. The selected part divides into two subsections. The first (103:9–15) poignantly expresses the despair of those who understand themselves to be the righteous, but who are experiencing the curses with which God had threatened those who disobeyed the covenant (Deuteronomy 28:15–68). They are helpless before those who oppress them, confiscate their crops, and treat them as beasts of burden. While they have turned for help to their rulers, who are responsible for keeping order and maintaining justice, they have not been given a hearing, much less the justice that they deserve. Although the complaints voiced in the Epistle are colored by authorial bias, their specificity would be pointless were it not based on real experience. These are the words of a battered people in a state of religious despair.

In the second section, the author offers the revealed solution to the present calamity. Enoch has ascended to the heavenly throne room, where he has witnessed the intercession of the angelic patrons of the righteous. These patrons read aloud the names of their human clients, which are inscribed in books that stand on the shelves in the presence of the glorious, enthroned Deity, and they recount their oppressors' evil deeds. Judgment and the execution of justice are imminent. The evils that the righteous have unjustly experienced will become the lot of their enemies, and the righteous, like Enoch, will ascend to heaven to enjoy all the blessings that they deserved but did not receive on earth. There, along with their dead friends whose spirits now languish in the underworld (102:4–103:4), they will have the companionship and the glorified status of the angels (cf. Daniel 12:3; *2 Baruch* 49–51).

The worldview expressed by this author is typical of Jewish apocalyptic literature of the Greco-Roman period. A polarity exists between an earth that is the place of evil and injustice and heaven where God's will is done, and between the present evil age and the new age to come. This polarity will be overcome when a final divine judgment of cosmic proportions eliminates evil and injustice. The apocalypticist's claim to revelation is the guarantee that makes present life bearable.

The sense that one was living in the end-time was the air that was breathed by the members of the early Christian communities. They believed that in Jesus' death and resurrection, God had intervened in history and initiated the new age. Through his resurrection, Jesus was exalted to heaven, whence he would soon return as Judge. His resurrection was the guarantee that Christians who had died in the meantime also would be raised from the dead. According to Paul (1 Corinthians 15:42–54; Philippians 3:20–21), this resurrection would result in the Christians' glorification into the likeness of the exalted Christ rather than to an angelic status as in *1 Enoch*. Different from the saying attributed to Jesus in Matthew 22:30//Mark12:25//Luke 20:36, Paul transforms Jewish tradition to fit the Christological orientation of his theology.

In some cases, as in the Book of Revelation, Christians expressed their eschatological consciousness in the literary form of an apocalypse. In most of the New Testament, authors adopted other literary forms, such as Gospels and Epistles. In all cases, however, the Christian message was presented as divine revelation, and this guaranteed its veracity. Ultimately this revelation seems to have been based on claims to have had a vision of the glorified, risen Christ.

To what extent Jesus himself subscribed to an eschatological worldview that was apocalyptically oriented is a much-debated topic. The Gospel of Mark ascribes to him apocalyptic sayings, such as "In those days, after that tribulation, the sun will be darkened and the moon will not give its light; the stars of heaven will fall, and the powers in the heaven will be shaken. Then they will see the Son of Man coming in the clouds with great power and glory. And then he will send his angels and gather together his elect from the farthest part of earth to the farthest part of heaven" (Mark 13:24–27). Luke 10:18 depicts Jesus saying, "I saw Satan fall like lightning from heaven." However, some scholars view these and other apocalyptic sayings as deriving not from Jesus himself but from his followers.

1 Enoch 46–49, 51, 62–63

Different from the Epistle, chapters 37–71 of *1 Enoch* take the form of an apocalypse, purporting to be an account of Enoch's visions as he toured the cosmos and viewed the places of the luminaries and the meteorological elements, the sites of eternal punishment, the resting places of the righteous, and the heavenly throne room itself. The text divides into three major sections called "parables," a term used also in *1 Enoch* 1:2–3 and 93:1, 3, to denote revelatory discourses.

Of central importance for this author is a sequence of vignettes that depict the great judgment and the events leading up to it. The principal figure in these vignettes is a transcendent heavenly being who is called variously "the Son of

Man," "the Chosen One," "the Righteous One," and "the Anointed One." He is the agent of God's great judgment—who vindicates "the righteous and chosen" and condemns "the kings and the mighty" who persecute them and rule the earth, denying and defying God's power and worshiping idols. These titles and the manner in which the author depicts this figure indicate that this heavenly being is the embodiment of four characters in biblical literature: the "one like a son of man" in Daniel 7:13–14; the Servant of the Lord in Second Isaiah (Isaiah 42:1–4; 49:1–6; 51:4–8; and 52:13–53:12); the Anointed One of the Lord (usually called "the Messiah") in the royal oracles of the Psalms and the Prophets; and heavenly Wisdom in Proverbs 8 and Sirach 24, who existed before creation.

The passages reproduced below depict the principal events relating to the judgment and indicate how the author has employed and revised these received traditions. Chapters 46–47 draw principally on Daniel 7:10–14. The Deity—in Daniel "the Ancient of Days" with a head of white hair—is here "the Head of Days." Daniel's "one like a son of man"—an angelic figure who looks like a human being—is called "this Son of Man" or "that Son of Man" and is here explicitly one who looks like a human being but is also glorious like an angel. Anticipating later scenes, he is said to be the one who will pass judgment on kings and the mighty who deny God and persecute the righteous. In this capacity, the Enochic Son of Man differs from his prototype in Daniel 7, who is enthroned only after the judgment has taken place. The motifs of human prayer and angelic intercession (47:1–2), also missing in Daniel 7, are drawn from an earlier part of 1 Enoch (chap. 9).

Chapters 48–49, which recount the naming of the Son of Man, reflect the author's other sources. The first of these is the account of the commissioning of the Servant of the Lord in Isaiah 49:1–6 (cf. 48:2//Isaiah 49:1; 48:4//Isaiah 49:6; 48:6//Isaiah 49:2). The title "the Chosen One," which runs through much of chapters 48–49, corresponds to the same title in Second Isaiah. That the Son of Man was named before the creation of the universe and the present age (48:3, 6) parallels the characteristic attributed to heavenly Wisdom in Proverbs 8:22–31 (cf. Sirach 24:3), a connection that is strengthened by the ascription of "wisdom" to the Son of Man (1 Enoch 48:1; 49:1–2). The author's final source is evident in 48:8, 10, and 49:3, which paraphrase verses in the royal oracles in Psalm 2 (v. 2) and Isaiah 11:1–5 (v. 2), respectively. The title "the Anointed One" (48:10) appears also in 1 Enoch 52:4. The wording of 49:4bc corresponds to Second Isaiah's first Servant poem (cf. Isaiah 42:1).

In chapter 51 the author of the Parables describes the initial event of the judgment, the resurrection of the dead, from among whom the Chosen One will choose the righteous. Different from the Epistle, earth rather than heaven is singled out here as the place of salvation for the righteous and chosen (vv. 4–5).

Chapters 62–63 form the climax of the events related to the Chosen One. He sits on God's glorious throne and presides over the judgment; he confronts and condemns the kings and the mighty, and he brings deliverance to the chosen and righteous whom they have persecuted. This scene of judgment, with the exaltation of the Chosen One and the confession of the kings and the mighty, reflects the climactic scene of the exaltation of the Servant and the confession of the kings and the nations in Isaiah 52:13–53:12 (Nickelsburg, *Resurrection*, 70–74).

The Book of Parables (chaps. 37–71) appears to have been composed some time in the last decades BCE or the early decades CE (Nickelsburg, *Jewish Literature* 254–56). "The kings and the mighty" are the Roman emperors and triumvirs. Concerning the author and his audience, we can say only that they were people familiar with earlier Enochic traditions who saw themselves as God's righteous and chosen. Some of their number eventually joined the early Christian movement and applied these traditions to Jesus (see below).

The conflation of biblical material in these chapters indicates the remarkable flexibility with which Jews interpreted their sacred traditions. The Davidic king, a human being who was responsible for administering justice, is here identified with "the one like a son of man," a angelic figure who in Daniel's vision is enthroned as God's viceroy after the judgment has been completed. Second Isaiah's Servant of the Lord, a human figure who suffers and is exalted, is here a heavenly figure who vindicates the suffering of God's people.

The traditions about the Chosen One/Son of Man in *1 Enoch* are critical for an understanding of early Christian speculation about Jesus. The title "Son of Man" is ascribed to him in all strata of the Gospel tradition (Mark, Q, Matthew's and Luke's special material, and John; for the passages, see Nickelsburg, "Son of Man," 142–47). Often he is seen as a future figure who is the agent of the great judgment (Q: Matthew 10:32–33//Luke 12:8–9; cf. Mark 8:38; Matthew 12:38–42//Luke 11:29–32; Matthew 19:28//Luke 22:28–30; Matthew 24:26–27, 37–39//Luke 17:22–37; Matthew 24:43–44//Luke 12:39–40; Mark: 13:26–27; 14:62; Matthew's special source: Matthew 13:24–30, 36–43; 25:31–46 [cf. especially *1 Enoch* 62–63]; Luke's special source or emphasis: 6:22; 17:22–18:8; John 5:25–29). This particular interpretation of Daniel 7 parallels its interpretation in the Parables of Enoch. The tradition appears also in the Book of Revelation (Nickelsburg, "Son of Man," 148) and appears to have been known by the apostle Paul (147–48). Whether Jesus himself spoke about a coming Son of Man is a hotly debated subject, not least because the Gospels apply these traditions to the resurrected Christ. Passages like Mark 8:38 ("For whoever is ashamed of me and my words [or "and of mine"] in this adulterous and sinful generation, of them the Son of Man also will be ashamed when he comes in the glory of his Father with the holy angels") and Luke 12:8 ("everyone who acknowledges me before others, the Son of Man also will acknowledge before the angels of God"), which do not expressly identify the Son of Man with Jesus, as the church did, might suggest that Jesus himself spoke of a coming Son of Man who was a figure distinct from himself.

Thus the Parables of Enoch shed important light on the New Testament. In literary form, the Parables are the closest parallel to the Book of Revelation, which also pits the glorified Christ against the kings of the earth who persecute God's people. Since the Parables attest a Jewish interpretation of Daniel 7 that the early church applies to the resurrection and glorified Jesus, some early Christians may well have applied the title "the Anointed One" to Jesus in his role as the heavenly, exalted one rather than as the son of David. More generally, the Parables reveal the richness and diversity of Jewish biblical interpretation, and in this respect the early Christians followed suit. This Jewish diversity meant, however, that many Jews who believed in a "Messiah" who was, for example, the son of David, would not have accepted this author's particular interpretation of messianic tradition. Thus it is not surprising that many Jews did not subscribe to the early church's proclamation when it applied this Enochic tradition to Jesus (Nickelsburg, *Ancient Judaism*, 89–117).

1 Enoch 106–7; 2 Enoch 71–72

People in the ancient Near East and the Greco-Roman world often celebrated the importance of figures in their religious and national traditions through claims and stories about the special circumstance of their conception and birth (see Charles Talbert's contribution in this volume). Greeks and Romans told tales about the copulation of gods or goddesses and human beings. Some of the successors of Alexander the Great (the so-called Diadochi) claimed divine parentage (Nickelsburg, *1 Enoch* 1, 170). Biblical figures like Isaac, Samuel, and Samson were conceived when God intervened to "open the womb" of their barren mothers.

The present two texts offer a special twist on the tradition. Most of *1 Enoch* focuses on the great judgment, and some parts of the corpus see the Flood in Genesis 6–9 as a prototype of this judgment. Thus, the corpus concludes with a story about the birth of Noah, the central figure in the Flood story and the one who foreshadows the righteous who will survive the great judgment. The story presupposes a tradition in *1 Enoch* 6–11 that describes how rebel angels took human wives and begat giants who ravaged the earth (cf. Genesis 6:1–4). Noah's glorious appearance terrifies his father, Lamech, who thinks that his wife has had intercourse with an angel. Methuselah runs to Enoch the revealer (as throughout *1 Enoch*) and learns that Noah's glorious appearance is related not to an angelic conception but to his status as the righteous one who will survive the judgment and revive the human race. A more developed form of this story in the "Genesis Apocryphon," a text, perhaps from the first century BCE, found among the Dead Sea Scrolls, recounts an emotional conversation in which Lamech and his wife, Bitenosh ("daughter of man"; cf. Genesis 6:1–2), exchange suspicious accusations and vehement denials.

These two stories and their antecedents in the Hebrew Bible will have a familiar ring for persons cognizant of the accounts of Jesus' conception and birth in Matthew 1–2 and Luke 1–2. Specifically, the Lucan accounts of Jesus' conception and youth are reminiscent of the story of Samuel (1 Samuel 1:1–2:26), while Matthean versions bear some resemblance to the story of Samson (cf. Matthew 1:21; 2:23 with Judges 13:5). The primary difference is that in both Matthew and Luke, Jesus' conception is effected through the agency of the Holy Spirit, and his mother is a virgin, whereas Samson and Samuel are born to mothers who have been barren, and their fathers appear to have been the husbands of their mothers.

The stories about Noah relate best to Matthew, not least because they are all told from the point of view of the father (Luke's story is told from Mary's viewpoint). Moreover, Matthew's story is paralleled best in the Genesis Apocryphon; in both, the narrator emphasizes the husband's suspicion about the circumstances of the conception. There is, however, an inverse relationship between Matthew and its Jewish prototypes. In *1 Enoch* and the Genesis Apocryphon, the husband suspects that a supernatural agent (an angel) has catalyzed the conception, and this turns out not to be true. In Matthew, Joseph suspects that Mary has been unfaithful to him (with another man), and he learns that a supernatural agent (the Holy Spirit) has begotten the child. How exactly the Gospel stories relate to these Jewish parallels is unclear. They seem to indicate a move away from their biblical prototypes in which divine agency in conception involves more than the removal of the impediment of barrenness. In this respect they are reminiscent of some Greek and Roman stories about divinely initiated conceptions.

The story of Melchizedek's conception and birth is baffling when compared with the aforementioned Jewish and Christian texts. *Second Enoch* is a Jewish text, perhaps from the first century CE, that was preserved by Christians in a Slavonic translation of the Greek original. It appears to be based on something very close to *1 Enoch*, and like *1 Enoch*, it concludes with the story of a miraculous birth (Nickelsburg, *Jewish Literature* 221–25; translation here from F. I. Anderson, *Old Testament Pseudepigrapha* [used by permission]). In this case, it is the birth of the mysterious priestly figure mentioned in Genesis 14:18–20. According to this account, Melchizedek was the son of Sopanim, the wife of Nir, the brother of Noah. He was conceived without benefit of a human father. Here the story differs from *1 Enoch* 106–7 and the Genesis Apocryphon, as well as from all its parallels in the Hebrew scriptures. Its placement at the end of *2 Enoch* corresponds precisely with the placement of the story of Noah's birth in *1 Enoch*. However, the angry exchange between Nir and his wife is paralleled not in *1 Enoch* 106–7 but in the Genesis Apocryphon. To compound the problem, the fact that Melchizedek has no human father is paralleled in Matthew 1 (and Hebrews 7:1–3) and not in the Jewish stories. We may ask: Is this story a Christian creation that reflects knowledge of Matthew and Hebrews, or has a Jewish author concerned about priestly succession and authority, who knows the Noachic stories, speculated about the possibility of a divine conception? As in the case of the Parables of Enoch, noncanonical texts enlighten the New Testament material. At the same time, they warn us against simple answers and straightforward solutions.

1 ENOCH 103:9–104:6

103⁹ Do not say, you who are righteous and pious in life:
"In the days of our tribulation, we toiled laboriously;
and every tribulation we saw, and many evils we found.
We were consumed and became few, and our spirits, small;

10   and we were destroyed and there was no one to help us with
          word and deed;
      we were powerless and found nothing.
      We were crushed and destroyed,
          and we gave up hope any more to know safety from day to day;
11   we had hoped to be the head and became the tail.
      We toiled and labored and were not masters of our labor;
          we became the food of the sinners.
      The lawless weighed down their yoke upon us;
12   our enemies were our masters;
      they goaded us on and penned us in,
          and to our enemies we bowed our necks,
          and they had no mercy on us.
13 We sought to get away from them,
          so that we might escape and be refreshed;
          but we found no place to flee and be safe from them.
14 We complained to the rulers in our tribulation,
          and cried out against those who struck us down and
              oppressed us;
      but our complaints they did not receive,
          nor did they wish to give a hearing to our voice.
15 They did not help us,
          they did not find (anything) against those who oppressed us
              and devoured us;
      But they strengthened against us
          them who killed us and made us few.
      They did not disclose their iniquities,
          nor did they remove from us the yoke of them who
              devoured us and dispersed us and murdered us.
      They did not disclose concerning those who murdered us,
          nor did they make mention that they raised their hands
              against us."
104¹ I swear to you that the angels in heaven make mention of you for
          good before the glory of the Great One,
          and your names are written before the glory of the Great One,
2   Take courage, then;
          for formerly you were worn out by evils and tribulations,
          but now you will shine like the luminaries of heaven,
          you will shine and appear,
          and the portals of heaven will be opened for you.
3   And your cry will be heard,
          and the judgment for which you cry will also appear to you.
      For from the rulers inquiry will be made concerning your
          tribulation,

and from all who helped them who oppressed you and
    devoured you, (inquiry will be made) regarding your evils.
4   Take courage, and do not abandon your hope,
    for you will have great joy like the angels of heaven.
5   And what will you have to do?
  You will not have to hide on the day of the great judgment,
    and you will not be found as the sinners,
    and the great judgment will be (far) from you for all the
    generations of eternity.
6   Fear not, O righteous, when you see the sinners growing strong
  and prospering,
    and do not be their companions;
  but stay far from all their iniquities,
    for you will be companions of the host of heaven.

1 ENOCH 46–49, 51, 62–63

ENOCH SEES THE HEAD OF DAYS AND THE SON OF MAN

46¹ There I saw one who had a head of days;
    and his head was like white wool.
  And with him was another, whose face was like the appearance
  of a man;
    and his face was full of graciousness like one of the holy
    angels.
2   And I asked the angel of peace, who went with me and
    showed me all the hidden things, about that son of man—who he
    was and whence he was (and) why he went with the Head of Days.
3   And he answered me and said to me,
  "This is the son of man who has righteousness,
    and righteousness dwells with him.
  And all the treasuries of what is hidden he will reveal;
    for the Lord of Spirits has chosen him,
    and his lot has prevailed through truth in the presence of
    the Lord of Spirits forever.
4   And this son of man whom you have seen—
    he will raise the kings and the mighty from their
    couches,
    and the strong from their thrones.
  He will loosen the reins of the strong,
    and he will crush the teeth of the sinners.
5   He will overturn the kings from their thrones and their kingdoms,
    because they do not exalt him or praise him,

or humbly acknowledge whence the kingdom was given to
them.
6 The face of the strong he will turn aside,
and he will fill them with shame.
Darkness will be their dwelling,
and worms will be their couch.
And they will have no hope to rise from their couches,
because they do not exalt the name of the Lord of Spirits.

7 And these are they who †judge† the stars of heaven,
and raise their hands toward the Most High,
and tread upon the earth and dwell on it.
All their deeds manifest unrighteousness,
and their power (rests) upon their wealth.
Their faith is in the gods that they have made with their hands,
and they deny the name of the Lord of Spirits.
8 And they persecute the houses of his congregation,
and the faithful who depend on the name of the Lord of Spirits."

THE PRAYER OF THE RIGHTEOUS AND THE INTERCESSION OF THE HOLY ONES

47¹ And in those days, there had arisen prayer of the righteous,
and the blood of the righteous one, from the earth, into the
presence of the Lord of Spirits.
2 In these days, the holy ones who dwell in the heights of heaven were
uniting with one voice,
2c and they were glorifying and praising and blessing the name of the
Lord of Spirits,
2bd and were interceding and praying on behalf of the blood of the
righteous that had been shed,
and the prayer of the righteous, that it might not be in vain in
the presence of the Lord of Spirits;
that judgment might be executed for them,
and endurance might not be their (lot) forever.

3 In those days, I saw the Head of Days when he took his seat on the
throne of his glory;
and the books of the living were opened in his presence;
and all his host, which was in the heights of heaven, and his
court, were standing in his presence.
4 And the hearts of the holy ones were filled with joy,
for the number of <the righteous> was at hand;
and the prayer of the righteous had been heard,
and the blood of the righteous one had been required in the
presence of the Lord of Spirits.

THE SON OF MAN IS NAMED

48¹   In that place, I saw the spring of righteousness, and it was
          inexhaustible;
             and many springs of wisdom surrounded it.
          And all the thirsty drank from them and were filled with wisdom;
             and their dwelling places were with the righteous and the
                holy and the chosen.
   ²   And in that hour, that son of man was named in the presence of
          the Lord of Spirits;
             and his name, before the Head of Days.
   ³   Even before the sun and the constellations were created,
             before the stars of heaven were made,
             his name was named before the Lord of Spirits.

   ⁴   He will be a staff for the righteous,
             that they may lean on him and not fall;
          And he will be the light of the nations,
             and he will be a hope for those who grieve in their hearts.
   ⁵   All who dwell on the earth will fall down and worship before him,
             and they will glorify and bless and sing hymns to the name the
                Lord of Spirits.

   ⁶   Because of this (reason) he was chosen and hidden in his presence,
             before the age was created and forever.
   ⁷   And the wisdom of the Lord of Spirits has revealed him to the holy
          and the righteous;
             for he has preserved the portion of the righteous.
          For they have hated and despised this age of unrighteousness;
             yea, all its deeds and its ways they have hated in the name
                of the Lord of Spirits.

          For in his name they are saved,
             and he is the vindicator of their lives.
   ⁸   In those days, downcast will be the faces of the kings of the earth,
             and the strong who possess the earth, because of the deeds
                of their hands.
          For on the day of their tribulation and distress they will
             not save themselves;
   ⁹   and into the hand of my chosen ones I shall cast them.
          As straw in the fire and as lead in the water,
             thus they will burn before the face of the holy,
          and they will sink before the face of the righteous;
             and no trace of them will be found.

10   And on the day of their distress there will be rest upon the earth,
            and before them they will fall and not rise,
            and there will be no one to take them with his hand and raise
               them.
      For they have denied the Lord of Spirits and his Anointed One.
         Blessed be the name of the Lord of Spirits.

49¹   For wisdom has been poured out like water,
            and glory will not fail in his presence forever and ever.
   2 For he is mighty in all the secrets of righteousness;
            and unrighteousness will vanish like a shadow,
            and will have no place to stand.
      For the Chosen One has taken his stand in the presence of the
         Lord of Spirits;
            and his glory is forever and ever,
            and his might, to all generations.

   3 And in him dwell the spirit of wisdom and the spirit of insight,
            and the spirit of instruction and might,
            and the spirit of those who have fallen asleep in righteousness.
   4 And he will judge the things that are secret,
            and a lying word none will be able to speak in his presence;
      For he is the Chosen One in the presence of the Lord of Spirits
            according to his good pleasure.

RESURRECTION, JUDGMENT, LIFE ON A RENEWED EARTH

51¹   And in those days, the earth will restore what has been entrusted
            to it,
            and Sheol will restore what it has received,
            and destruction will restore what it owes.

   5a For in those days, my Chosen One will arise,
   2   and choose the righteous and holy from among them,
            for the day on which they will be saved has drawn near.
   3 And the Chosen One, in those days, will sit upon my throne,
            and all the secrets of wisdom will go forth from the counsel
               of his mouth
            for the Lord of Spirits has given (them) to him and glorified
               him.
   4 In those days the mountains will leap like rams,
            and the hills will skip like lambs satisfied with milk;
      and the faces of all the angels in heaven will be radiant
            with joy,

^{5b}   and the earth will rejoice,
    and the righteous will dwell on it
      and the chosen will walk on it.

THE CHOSEN ONE PRESIDES OVER THE GREAT JUDGMENT

The Confrontation

62¹   And thus the Lord commanded the kings and the mighty and the
     exalted and those who possess the earth, and he said,
       "Open your eyes and lift up your horns,
       if you are able to recognize the Chosen One."
  ² And the Lord of Spirits <seated him> upon the throne of his glory;
     and the spirit of righteousness was poured upon him.
  And the word of his mouth will slay all the sinners,
     and all the unrighteous will perish from his presence.

  ³ And there will stand up on that day all the kings and the mighty
     and the exalted and those who possess the earth.
  And they will see and recognize that he sits on the throne of
   his glory;
     and righteousness is judged in his presence,
     and no lying word is spoken in his presence.
  ⁴ And pain will come upon them as (upon) a woman in labor,
     when the child enters the mouth of the womb,
     and she has difficulty in giving birth.
  ⁵ And one group of them will look at the other;
     and they will be terrified and will cast down their faces,
     and pain will seize them when they see that son of man sitting
      on the throne of glory.
  ⁶ And the kings and the mighty and all who possess the earth
     will bless and glorify and exalt him who rules over all, who
      was hidden.
  ⁷ For from the beginning the son of man was hidden,
     and the Most High preserved him the presence of his might,
     and he revealed him to the chosen.
  ⁸ And the congregation of the chosen and the holy will be sown;
     and all the chosen will stand in his presence on that day.

The Condemnation of the Kings and the Mighty

  ⁹ And all the kings and the mighty and the exalted and those who
     rule the earth will fall on their faces in his presence;
     and they will worship and set their hope on that son of man,
     and they will supplicate and petition for mercy from him.

10   But the Lord of Spirits himself will press them,
  so that they will hasten to depart from his presence;
  and their faces will be filled with shame,
  and the darkness will grow deeper on their faces.
11   And he will deliver them to the angels for punishment,
  so that they may exact retribution from them
  for the iniquity that they did to his children and his chosen
   ones.
12   And they will be a spectacle for the righteous and for his chosen
  ones;
  and they will rejoice over them,
because the wrath of the Lord of Spirits rests upon them,
  and his sword is drunk with them.

The Salvation of the Righteous and Chosen

13   And the righteous and the chosen will be saved on that day;
  and the faces of the sinners and the unrighteous they will
   henceforth not see.
14   And the Lord of Spirits will abide over them,
  and with that son of man they will eat,
  and they will lie down and rise up forever and ever.

15   And the righteous and the chosen will have arisen from the earth,
  and have ceased to cast down their faces,
  and have put on the garment of glory.
16   And this will be your garment, the garment of life from the Lord of
  Spirits;
  and your garments will not wear out,
  and your glory will not fade in the presence of the Lord of
   Spirits.

The Confession of the Kings and the Mighty

63[1]   In those days, the mighty and the kings, who possess the earth,
  will beseech (him)
that from the angels of his punishment, to whom they have
  been delivered,
  he might give them a little respite,
that they might fall down and worship in the presence of the
  Lord of Spirits,
  and that they might confess their sins in his presence.

2   They will bless and glorify the Lord of Spirits and say,
"Blessed is the Lord of Spirits and the Lord of kings,

and the Lord of the mighty and the Lord of the rich,
and the Lord of glory and the Lord of wisdom.

3 Your power is splendid in every secret thing for all generations,
and your glory forever and ever.
Deep are all your secrets and without number,
and your righteousness is beyond reckoning.

4 Now we know that we should glorify and bless the Lord of the kings,
and him who reigns over all kings."

5 And they will say,
"Would that we might be given respite,
that we might glorify and praise
and make confession in the presence of your glory.

6 And now we desire a little respite and do not find it;
we pursue it and do not lay hold of it.
And light has vanished from our presence,
and darkness is our dwelling forever and ever.

7 For in his presence we did not made confession,
nor did we glorify the name of the Lord of the kings;
And our hope was upon the scepter of our kingdom
and <throne of> our glory.

8 And on the day of our affliction and tribulation it does not
save us,
nor do we find respite to make confession,
that our Lord is faithful in all his deeds and his judgment
and his justice,
and his judgments have no respect for persons.

9 And we vanish from his presence because of our deeds,
and all our sins are reckoned in righteousness."

10 Now they will say to themselves,
"Our souls are full of ill-gotten wealth,
but it does not prevent our descending into the flame of the
torture of Sheol."

11 And after that their faces will be filled with darkness and shame
in the presence of that son of man;
and from his presence they will be driven,
and a sword will abide before him in their midst.

12 Thus says the Lord of Spirits,
"This is the law and the judgment of the mighty and the kings
and the exalted and those who possess the earth,
in the presence of the Lord of Spirits."

MIRACULOUS BIRTHS

1 ENOCH 106–107

The Birth of Noah

106¹   After a time, I took a wife for Methuselah my son, and she bore a
son and called his name Lamech. Righteousness was brought
low until that day.

And when (Lamech) had come of age, he took for himself a wife,
and she conceived from him and bore a child.² And when the
child was born, his body was whiter than snow and redder than
a rose, his hair was all white and like white wool and curly.
Glorious <was his face>. When he opened his eyes, the house
shone like the sun.³ And he stood up from the hands of the
midwife, and he opened his mouth and praised the Lord of
eternity.

⁴   And Lamech was afraid of him, and he fled and came to
Methuselah his father.⁵ And he said to him, "A strange child
has been born to me. He is not like men, but (like) the sons of
the angels of heaven. His form is strange, not like us. His eyes
are like the rays of the sun, and glorious is his face.⁶ I think
that he is not from me, but from the angels. And I fear him, lest
something happen in his days on the earth.⁷ I beg you, father,
and beseech you, go to Enoch our father and learn the truth
from him, for his dwelling is with the angels."

⁸   When Methuselah heard the word of his son, he came to me at the
ends of the earth, where he heard I was then. And he said to me,
"My father, hear my voice and come to me."

And I heard his voice and came to him and said, "Behold, here
I am, child. Why have you come to me, child?"

⁹   He answered and said,
"Because of great distress have I come to you,
and because of a stern vision have I approached here, father.

¹⁰   And now, my father, hear me,
for a child has been born to Lamech my son,
and his form and appearance are not like the form of men.
And his color is whiter than snow and redder than a rose,
and the hair of his head is whiter than white wool.
And his eyes are like the rays of the sun,
and he opened his eyes and made the whole house bright.

¹¹   And he stood up from the hands of the midwife,
and he opened his mouth and praised the Lord of eternity.

12 And Lamech my son was afraid
>and he fled to me.
>He does not believe that (the child) is his son,
>>but that (he is) from the angels of heaven.
>And, behold, I have come to you,
>>because from the angels you have the exact facts and the truth."
13 Then I, Enoch, answered and said,
>"The Lord will renew his commandment upon the earth,
>>Just as, child, I have seen and told you.
>That in the generation of Jared, my father, †they transgressed the
>word of the Lord/the covenant of heaven,†
14 and behold, they went on sinning and transgressing the custom.
>With women they were mingling,
>>and with them they were sinning.
>They married some of them,
>>and they went on begetting (children), not like spirits, but
>>fleshly.
15 And there will be great wrath upon the earth and a flood,
>and there will be great destruction for a year.
16 And this child that was born to you will be left upon the earth,
>and his three children will be saved with him,
>when all men on the earth die.
17 And he will cleanse the earth from the corruption that is on it.
18 And now tell Lamech,
>'He is your child in truth,
>>and <this child will be righteous and> blameless;
>And Noah> call his name,
>>for he will be your remnant,
>>from whom you will find rest.'
>He and his sons will be saved from the corruption of the earth
>>and from all sins and from all iniquities that are consummated
>>upon the earth in his days.
19 And after this there will be stronger iniquity than that which was
>formerly consummated upon the earth. (For I know the
>mysteries <of the Lord> which the holy ones have revealed
>and shown to me, and which I have read in the tablets
>of heaven.
107¹ And I have seen written in them that generation upon generation
>will do evil in this way,
>>and the evil will be until there arise generations of
>>righteousness.)
>And evil and wickedness will end,
>>and violence will cease from the earth;
>>and good things will come upon the earth to them.

2   And now go, child, and tell Lamech your son that this child that
    has been born is his child, truly and without deception."
3   And when Methuselah heard the words of Enoch his father—for
    (Enoch) revealed them to him secretly—(Methuselah)
    returned and revealed everything to (Lamech).
    And his name was called Noah—
        he who gladdens the earth from destruction.

2 ENOCH 71–72

The Birth of Melchizedek

71¹   Behold the wife of Nir, (whose) name was Sopanim, being sterile
       and never having at any time given birth to a child by Nir—
2   And Sopanim was in the time of her old age, and in the day of her
    death. She conceived in her womb, but Nir the priest had not
    slept with her, nor had he touched her, from the day that the
    LORD had appointed him to conduct the liturgy in front of the
    face of the people.
3   And when Sopanim saw her pregnancy, she was ashamed and
    embarrassed, and she hid herself during all the days until she
    gave birth. And not one of the people knew about it.
4   And when 282 days had been completed, and the day of birth had
    begun to approach, and Nir remembered his wife, and he called
    her to himself in his house, so that he might converse with her.
5   (And) Sopanim came to Nir, her husband; and, behold, she was
    pregnant, and the day appointed for giving birth was drawing
    near.
6   And Nir saw her, and he became very ashamed. And he said to her,
    "What is this that you have done, O wife? And (why) have
    you disgraced me in front of the face of these people? And
    now, depart from me; and go where you began the disgrace of
    your womb, so that I might not defile my hand on account of
    you, and sin in front of the face of the LORD.
7   And Sopanim spoke to Nir, her husband, saying, "O my Lord!
    Behold, it is the time of my old age, and the day of my death has
    arrived.
    I do not understand how my menopause and the barrenness of
    my womb have been reversed."
8   And Nir did not believe his wife, and for the second time he said
    to her, "Depart from me, or else I might assault you, and
    commit a sin in front of the face of the LORD."
9   And it came to pass, when Nir had spoken to his wife, Sopanim,
    that Sopanim fell down at Nir's feet and died.

10   Nir was extremely distressed; and he said in his heart, "Could this
      have happened because of my word, since by word and
      thought a person can sin in front of the face of the LORD?

11   Now may God have mercy upon me! I know in truth in my heart
      that my hand was not upon her. And so I say, 'Glory to you,
      O LORD, because no one among mankind knows about this
      deed which the LORD has done.'"

12   And Nir hurried, and he shut the door of his house, and he went
      to Noe his brother, and he reported to him everything that
      had happened in connection with his wife.

13   And Noe hurried. He came with Nir his brother; he came into Nir's
      house, because of the death of Sopanim, and they discussed
      between themselves how her womb was at the time of giving birth.

14   And Noe said to Nir, "Don't let yourself be sorrowful, Nir, my
      brother! For the LORD today has covered up our scandal, in
      that nobody from the people knows this.

15   Now, let us go quickly and let us bury her secretly, and the LORD
      will cover up the scandal of our shame."

16   And they placed Sopanim on the bed, and they wrapped her
      around with black garments, and shut her in the house,
      prepared for burial. They dug a grave in secret.

17   And a child came out from the dead Sopanim. And he sat on the
      bed at her side. And Noe and Nir came in to bury Sopanim,
      and they saw the child sitting beside the dead Sopanim, and
      wiping his clothing.

18   And Noe and Nir were very terrified with a great fear, because the
      child was fully developed physically, like a three-year-old.
      And he spoke with his lips, and he blessed the LORD.

19   And Noe and Nir looked at him and behold, the badge of
      priesthood was on his chest, and it was glorious in
      appearance.

20   And Noe and Nir said, "Behold God is renewing the priesthood
      from blood related to us, just as he pleases."

21   And Noe and Nir hurried, and they washed the child, and they
      dressed him in the garments of priesthood, and they gave him
      the holy bread and he ate it. And they called his name
      Melkisedek.

22   And Noe and Nir lifted up the body of Sopanim, and divested her
      of the black garments, and they washed her, and they clothed
      her in exceptionally bright garments, and they built a shrine
      for her.

23   Noe and Nir and Melkisedek came, and they buried her publicly.
      And Noe said to his brother Nir, "Look after this child in
      secret until the time, because people will become treacherous

in all the earth, and they will begin to turn away from God,
and having become totally ignorant, they will put him to death."
And then Noe went away to his own place.

24   And great lawlessness began to become abundant over all the earth
in the days of Nir.

25   And Nir began to worry excessively, especially about the child,
saying, "How miserable it is for me, eternal LORD, that in my
days all lawlessness has begun to become abundant over the
earth. And I realize how much nearer our end is, {and} over
all the earth, on account of the lawlessness of the people.

26   And now, LORD, what is the vision about this child, and what is his
destiny, and what will I do for him? Is it possible that he too
will be joined with us in the destruction?

27   And the LORD heeded Nir, and appeared to him in a night vision.
He said to him, "Nir, the great lawlessness, which has come
about on the earth among the multitude {which} I shall not
tolerate.
And behold, I desire now to send out a great destruction onto
the earth, and everything that stands on the earth shall perish.

28   But, concerning the child, don't be anxious, Nir; because in a short
while I shall send my archistratig, Michael. And he will take
the child, and put him in the paradise of Edem, in the
Paradise where Adam was formerly for seven years, having
heaven open all the time up until he sinned.

29   And this child will not perish along with those who are perishing
in this generation, as I have revealed it, so that Melkisedek
will be the priest to all holy priests, and I will establish him
so that he will be the head of the priests of the future."

30   And Nir arose from his sleep and blessed the LORD who had
appeared to him, saying,
"Blessed be the LORD, the God of my fathers,
who has told me how he has made a great priest in my day,
in the womb of Sopanim, my wife.

31   Because I had no child in this tribe who might become the great
priest,
but this is my son and your servant, and you are the great God.

32   Therefore honor him together with your servants and great priests,
with Sir, and Enos, and Rusi, and Amilam, and Prasidom, and
Maleleil, and Serokh, and Arusan, and Aleem, and Enoch, and
Methusalam, and me, your servant Nir.

33   And behold, Melkisedek will be the head of the thirteen priests
who existed before.

34   And afterward, in the last generation, there will be another
Melkisedek, the first of twelve priests. And the last will be the

head of all, a great archpriest, the Word and Power of God, who will perform miracles, greater and more glorious than all the previous ones.

35 He, Melkisedek, will be priest and king in the place Akkuzan, that is to say, in the center of the earth, where Adam was created, and there will be his final grave.

36 And in connection with that archpriest it is written how he also will be buried there, where the center of the earth is, just as Adam also buried his own son there—Abel, whom his brother Cain murdered; for he lay for three years unburied, until he saw a bird called Jackdaw, how it buried its own young.

37 I know that great confusion has come and in confusion this generation will come to an end; and everyone will perish, except that Noe, your brother, will be preserved. And afterward there will be a planting from his tribe, and there will be another people, and there will be another Melkisedek, the head of priests reigning over the people, and performing the liturgy for the LORD."

72¹ And when the child had been forty days in Nir's tent, the LORD said to Michael, "Go down onto the earth to Nir the priest, and take my child Melkisedek, who is with him, and place him in the paradise of Edem for preservation. For the time is approaching, and I will pour out all the water onto the earth, and everything that is on the earth will perish."

3 Michael hurried, and he came down when it was night, and Nir was sleeping on his bed. And Michael appeared to him, and said to him, "Thus says the LORD: 'Nir! Send the child to me whom I entrusted to you.'"

4 And Nir did not realize who was speaking to him, and his heart was confused. And he said, "When the people find out about the child, then they will seize him and kill him, because the heart of these people is deceitful in front of the face of the LORD." Nir said to the one who was speaking, "The child is not with me, and I don't know who you are."

5 And he who was speaking to me answered, "Don't be frightened, Nir! I am the LORD's archistratig. The LORD has sent me, and behold, I shall take your child today. I will go with him and I will place him in the paradise of Edem, and there he will be forever.

6 And when the twelfth generation shall come into being, and there will be one thousand and seventy years, and there will be born in that generation a righteous man. And the LORD will tell him that he should go out of that mountain where stands the ark of Noe, your brother. And he will find there another Melkisedek, who has been living there for seven years, hiding himself from

the people who sacrifice to idols, so that they might not kill him. And he will bring him out, and he will be the first priest and king in the city Salim in the style of this Melkisedek, the originator of the priests. The years will be completed up to that time—3432—from the beginning and the creation of Adam.

7 And from that Melkisedek the priests will be twelve in number until the great Igumen, that is to say, Leader, will bring out everything visible and invisible."

8 And Nir understood the first dream, and believed it. And having answered Michael he said, "Blessed be the LORD who has glorified you today for me! And now, bless your servant Nir! For we are coming close to departure from this world. And take this child, and do to him just as the LORD said to you."

9 And Michael took the child on the same night on which he had come down; and he took him on his wings, and he placed him in the paradise of Edem.

10 And Nir got up in the morning. He went into his tent and he did not find the child. And there was instead of joy very great grief, because he had no other son except this one.

11 Thus Nir ended his life. And after him there was no priest among the people. And from that time great confusion arose on the earth.

Bibliography

Andersen, F. I. "2 (Slavonic Apocalypse of) Enoch." Pages 91–212 in *Old Testament Pseudepigrapha*. Edited by James H. Charlesworth. Garden City, NY: Doubleday, 1983.

Bow, Beverly A. "The Birth of Jesus: A Jewish and Pagan Affair." Ph.D. diss., University of Iowa, 1995.

———. "Melchizedek's Birth Narrative in 2 Enoch 68–73: Christian Correlations." Pages 33–41 in *For a Later Generation: The Transformation of Tradition in Israel, Early Judaism, and Early Christianity*. Edited by Randall A. Argall, Beverly A. Bow, and Rodney A. Werline. Harrisville, PA: Trinity Press International, 2000.

Brown, Raymond E. *The Birth of the Messiah*. Garden City, NY: Doubleday, 1977.

Collins, John J. *The Apocalyptic Imagination: An Introduction to the Jewish Matrix of Christianity*. New York: Crossroads, 1984.

Higgins, J. B. *The Son of Man in the Teaching of Jesus*. Society for New Testament Studies Monograph Series 39. Cambridge: Cambridge University Press, 1980.

Nickelsburg, George W. E. *Ancient Judaism and Christian Origins: Diversity, Continuity, and Transformation*. Minneapolis, MN: Fortress Press, 2003.

———. *1 Enoch 1: A Critical Commentary on the Book of 1 Enoch Chapters 1–36; 81–108*. Hermeneia. Minneapolis, MN: Fortress Press, 2001.

———. *Jewish Literature between the Bible and the Mishnah: A Historical and Literary Introduction* 2nd ed. with CD-Rom. Minneapolis, MN: Fortress Press, 2005.

————. *Resurrection, Immortality, and Eternal Life in Intertestamental Judaism.* Harvard Theological Studies 26. Cambridge, MA: Harvard University Press, 1972.

————. "Son of Man." Pages 137–50 in vol. 6 of *Anchor Bible Dictionary.* Edited by David Noel Freedman. 6 vols. New York: Doubleday, 1992.

Nickelsburg, George W. E., and James C. VanderKam, eds. *The Book of Enoch or 1 Enoch Translated from the Ethiopic Version, the Greek Texts and the Aramaic Dead Sea Fragments.* Minneapolis, MN: Fortress Press, 2004.

Orlov, Andrei. "Melchizedek Legend of 2 (Slavonic) Enoch." *Journal for the Study of Judaism in the Persian, Hellenistic, and Roman Periods* 31 (2000): 23–38.

————. "Noah's Younger Brother: The Anti-Noachic Polemics in 2 Enoch." *Henoch* 22 (2002): 207–21.

Theisohn, Johannes. *Der auserwählte Richter: Untersuchungen zum traditionngeschtlichen Ort der Menschensohngestalt der Bilderreden des Äthiopischen Henoch.* Studien zur Umwelt des Neuen Testaments 12. Göttingen: Vandenhoeck & Ruprecht, 1975.

Tödt, Heinz Eduard. *The Son of Man in the Synoptic Tradition.* Philadelphia: Westminster, 1965.

Vermes, Geza. "A Genesis Apocryphon." Pages 292–99 in *The Dead Sea Scrolls in English.* Edited by Geza Vermes. 4th ed. London: Penguin, 1995.

—— 6 ——

Jesus and the Dead Sea Scrolls

Peter Flint

The "Dead Sea Scrolls" denotes ancient manuscripts that were discovered at various sites along the western shore of the Dead Sea between 1947 (or perhaps 1946) and 1965. The most important site is at Wadi Qumran, where eleven caves containing some 870 Scrolls were found between 1946/47 and 1956. A nearby settlement also was discovered and was excavated in the 1950s. Almost all scholars now agree that the community that wrote and stored the Scrolls were Essenes, and pottery analysis conducted in the late 1990s confirms that those living at the site deposited jars containing Scrolls in at least some of the caves. Paleographic analysis and carbon 14 tests show that the earliest manuscripts were copied about 250 BCE or a little earlier, and the latest shortly before the destruction of the Qumran site by the Romans in 68 CE.

In addition to the finds at Qumran, dozens more Scrolls were discovered at other locations, including Wadi Murabbaât (1951–52), Nahal Hever (1951–61), and Masada (1963–65).

Approximately 220 Scrolls at Qumran are classified as "biblical." Every book of the Old Testament is represented, with the exception of Esther, Nehemiah, and 1 Chronicles. These manuscripts constitute our earliest witnesses to the text of Scripture, and they offer important evidence for the closing stages of the Hebrew Bible.

Many of the other (almost) 800 Qumran documents—the "nonbiblical" Scrolls—are of direct relevance to early Judaism and emerging Christianity. They provide information about Judaism in the late Second Temple period, anticipate some teachings found in later Rabbinic writings, and illuminate many passages and ideas found in the New Testament.

The Scrolls, Jesus, and Early Christianity

Early Speculations

Long before the discovery of the Dead Sea Scrolls, several links were alleged between the Essenes—as described by Josephus, Philo, and Pliny the Elder—and Jesus. In

1790, Karl Bahrdt tried to account for the mysteries in Jesus' life by suggesting he was a "secret agent" of the Essenes. In 1863, the biblical scholar Ernest Renan proposed that Jesus had been trained by the Essenes. Such speculation was given added impetus when the Scrolls were found. Many scholars recognized that these ancient documents are relevant for our understanding of Jesus and his ministry, as well as for several other aspects of New Testament studies. This is not surprising, since most of the Scrolls were written during the latter stages of the Second Temple period, a time that includes the life of Jesus and the growth of the early church.

Soon after the discovery, several writers sought to make connections between Jesus and the Essene movement. The journalist Edmund Wilson, for example, published several articles in the *New Yorker* on the Dead Sea Scrolls which maintained—among other things—that Jesus had spent his childhood years with the Essenes. These pieces were collected in a 1955 volume entitled *The Scrolls from the Dead Sea* and expanded in 1969 as *The Dead Sea Scrolls: 1947–1969*. In 1962, Charles Francis Potter proposed that Jesus was a mere human whose teachings about God and his messianic ideas were shaped by the Essenes.

Perhaps the most brilliant early insights were offered by the French scholar André Dupont-Sommer. In 1950, when the contents of only a few Scrolls were known, he argued that Jesus appeared to be an "astonishing reincarnation" of the Teacher of Righteousness (whom he called the "Master of Justice"):

> Everything in the Jewish New Covenant heralds and prepares the way for the Christian New Covenant. The Galilean Master, as He is presented in the writings of the New Testament, appears in many respects as an astonishing reincarnation of the Master of Justice. Like the latter He preached penitence, poverty, humility, love of one's neighbor, chastity. Like him, He prescribed the observance of the Law of Moses, the whole Law, but the Law finished and perfected, thanks to His own revelations. Like him He was the Elect and the Messiah of God, the Messiah redeemer of the world. Like him He was the object of the hostility of the priests, the party of the Sadducees. Like him He was condemned and put to death. Like him He pronounced judgment on Jerusalem, which was taken and destroyed by the Romans for having put Him to death. Like him, at the end of time he will be the supreme judge. (*Dead Sea Scrolls*, 99)

Although such lofty language gives the impression that Dupont-Sommer saw real connections between the Essenes of Qumran and early Christianity, this is not the case. He continues:

> The Master of Justice died about 65–63 BCE; Jesus the Nazarene died about 30 CE. In every case where the resemblance compels or invites us to think of a borrowing, this was on the part of Christianity. But on the other hand, the appearance of faith in Jesus—the foundation of the New Church—can scarcely be explained without the real historic activity of a new Prophet, a new Messiah, who rekindled the flame and concentrated on Himself the adoration of men. (*Dead Sea Scrolls*, 99–100)

Several other early authors—whose writings are less dramatic or speculative than those mentioned so far, and thus received less attention—also discussed the similarities and differences between the Scrolls and various aspects of the New Testament writings. For example, William LaSor compared Jesus with the Teacher of Righteousness as part of a larger book on the contribution of the Scrolls for understanding Christian faith (see especially 166–68).

Arriving at a Balanced View

In the closing decades of the twentieth century and beyond, studies of relations between the Scrolls and Jesus, or between the people of the Scrolls and the first Christians, have offered a range of views. A decided minority claim that the Scrolls are Christian texts or that several of these documents contain specific references to Jesus and new revelations about his life. A second decided minority claim that the Scrolls are of very little value for understanding Jesus, the early Christians, or the New Testament. Both views are extreme.

The Dead Sea Scrolls were not written by Christian authors, and they never mention any Christian individuals by name. However, as the translated passages and accompanying comments will show, some manuscripts are important for understanding Jesus' life and teaching, and others anticipate several New Testament doctrines. Specifically, these ancient documents throw welcome light on the Gospels by

1. Providing helpful information about Jewish society, groups, practices, and beliefs at the time of Jesus and the early Christians.
2. Increasing our knowledge about early Judaism, which makes it clear that many aspects of the Gospel message are indebted to the mother religion.
3. Helping us see in sharper outline some of the basic differences between the message of Jesus and those of other Jewish groups.
4. Providing new texts with similarities to certain Gospel passages, which shows that a good deal of Jesus' teaching was anticipated in earlier texts rather than being the product of the later church. A few documents contain wording that is very close or identical to passages found in the Gospels, which means that this material was known to some or many Jews in the first century BCE. Such key texts confirm the authenticity of certain New Testament passages by showing it credible or likely that Jesus would have spoken the words attributed to him by the Gospel writers.

The texts translated below are grouped in five sections: the Messiah and messianism; John the Baptist or baptism; the person of Jesus; the teaching of Jesus; and crucifixion and the suffering Messiah.

A Note on the Translations

The new translations presented here are fairly literal. For material that came to light relatively recently and is often ambiguous or difficult to understand, free renderings may be misleading or may include words that were not in the original

Hebrew or Aramaic. For the same reasons, inclusive language has been used only to a limited extent. Finally, some words or phrases are reconstructed in order to avoid broken sentences, but only where these reconstructions seem certain or plausible. In such cases the supplied letters are enclosed in square brackets. In 11QMelchizedek, for example, line 13 of col. 2 reads as follows:

> [13]And Melchizedek will carry out the vengeance of Go[d]'s judgments. [And on that day he will de]li[ver them from the hand of] Belial, and from the power of all the sp[irits of his lot].

TEXTS RELATING TO THE MESSIAH AND MESSIANISM

The four passages below fall into two categories for our purposes. The first two (from the Rule of the Community and the Rule of the Congregation) speak of two Messiahs: a priestly one (Messiah of Aaron) and a kingly or military one (Messiah of Israel). However, the other two texts—both from the Damascus Document—speak of "the Messiah of Aaron and of Israel" or "the Messiah from Aaron and from Israel." The question of the priestly and kingly offices being found in one or two Messiahs is of relevance to studies on Jesus *the Christ*.

As for the apparent discrepancy with respect to the Messiah or Messiahs, Martin Abegg (325–58, esp. 334–35) sees the phrase in the Damascus Document as a "distributive construct," in which the first singular noun is in the construct, followed by a compound genitive. In other words, "the Messiah of Aaron and of Israel" means "the Messiah of Aaron and (the Messiah) of Israel." Two biblical examples of this rare construction are "the heads of Oreb and Zeeb" (Judges 7:25) and probably "the kings of Sodom and Gomorrah" (Genesis 14:10).

However, in the B Version (for this term, see below) of the Damascus Document, the phrase "the Messiah from Aaron and from Israel" presents a problem, since both words, "Aaron" and "Israel," are preceded by "from."

"THE PROPHET" AND "THE MESSIAHS OF AARON AND ISRAEL" IN THE RULE OF THE COMMUNITY

The passage is from one of the Qumranites' most prized compositions, the Rule of the Community, written in the first century BCE. This portion of col. 11 discusses the purpose of the Community. Following details of a House of Holiness and provisions regarding justice and property, the section ends—a blank interval follows—by looking forward to the arrival of three figures. The first is "the Prophet," which recalls the prophet like Moses predicted in Deuteronomy 18:17–19, or John the Baptist in the New Testament. The other figures are not one but two Messiahs: of Aaron (a priestly Messiah) and of Israel (presumably of David, and thus a kingly Messiah).

RULE OF THE COMMUNITY (1QS) COL. 11:5–11

(Trever, 74)

At that time the men ⁶of the Community shall set apart a House of Holiness for Aaron, so that it may be united as a Holy of Holies, and a House of Community for Israel, those who walk blamelessly. ⁷The sons of Aaron alone shall have authority with respect to justice and property. They shall decide on the lot for every provision concerning the men of the Community ⁸and on property matters of the holy men who walk blamelessly.

Their property shall not to be merged with the property of the men of deceit, who ⁹have not cleansed their path by separating from wickedness and walking in a blameless manner. They shall not deviate from any counsel of the Law to walk ¹⁰in all the stubbornness of their hearts, but they shall be governed by the original precepts in which the men of the Community started out being instructed, ¹¹until there shall come the Prophet and the Messiahs of Aaron and Israel.

THE PRIESTLY MESSIAH AND THE MESSIAH OF ISRAEL
AT THE MESSIANIC BANQUET

The Rule of the Congregation (1QSa) is another of the Qumranites' own compositions; it was composed as an appendix to the Cave 1 copy of the Community Rule. The single surviving copy dates from the first century BCE.

The translated portion below is particularly interesting for four reasons. First, one coming figure is called the "Messiah of Israel" (lines 14, 20); this conquering leader would arise from the line of David. Another messianic figure is "the Priest" (lines 12 [not preserved], 19), who clearly has priority over the Messiah of Israel. Second, 1QSa describes a banquet or feast, associated with the arrival of the Messiah, in which all Israel will take part in the Last Days. The connection of this meal with the Messiah's coming recalls references to the eschatological banquet in the Gospels (e.g., Luke 22:29–30, where at the Last Supper Jesus tells his disciples, "I confer on you, just as my Father has conferred on me, a kingdom, so that you may eat and drink at my table in my kingdom, and you will sit on thrones judging the twelve tribes of Israel"; see also Luke 22:16, 18), and the "marriage supper of the Lamb" in the Book of Revelation (19:6–9).

Third, the church historian Hippolytus mentions a comparable feast that was held by the early Christians, the Agape, or "love feast," which was associated with—but distinct from—the sacrament of communion. The New Testament (e.g., 1 Corinthians 11:17–22) and other early Christian literature refer to disorderly behavior that was sometimes associated with these meals. Finally, the probable reference in col. 2:11–12 to God "fathering" the Messiah of Israel seems to describe a messianic figure who is a special "son of God." Such a Messiah has much in common with several New Testament references to Jesus. For another relevant text on this theme, see the translation under "Son of God" and "Son of the Most High" below.

RULE OF THE CONGREGATION (1QSA OR 1Q28A) COL. 2:11–22

DJD 1. 110–11

[11]This is the [seat]ing plan of the men of renown [called] to the meeting of the Community Council, when [God] has fathered [12]th[e] Messiah with them: [the Priest] shall enter [at] the head of the whole congregation of Israel, and all [13][his] bro[thers, the sons of] Aaron the priests [those called] to the meeting, the men of renown. And they shall sit [14]be[fore him, each man] according to his distinction. And then the [Mess]iah of Israel shall en[ter], and the heads [15]of the th[ousands of Israel] shall sit before him, [each] man according to his distinction, according to [his func]tion in their camps and according to their marches. And all [16]the heads of fa[mily of the congre]gation, together with the wis[e men of the holy congregation(?)], shall sit before them, each one according to [17]his distinction.

And [when they] gather [for the] communal [tab]le [or to drink ne]w wine and the communal table is set [18][and the ne]w wine [is poured] for drinking, let no one [stretch out] his hand on the first portion (or: first fruits) [19]of the bread or [of the new wine] before the Priest. For it is [he who] shall [bl]ess the first portion (or: first fruits) of the bread [20]and of the new wi[ne, and he shall stretch out] his hand on the bread first. Thereaf[ter], the Messiah of Israel [shall str]etch out his hands [21]on the bread. [Finally], all the congregation of the Community, each [one according to] his distinction [shall say a bl]essing. In accordance with this statute [they] shall proceed [22]at every me[al], when at least ten me[n are ga]thered together.

REFERENCES TO "THE MESSIAH OF AARON AND ISRAEL"
IN THE DAMASCUS DOCUMENT

In 1896 Solomon Schechter of Cambridge University was working with texts from a *geniza*—a storage room for worn-out or damaged manuscripts—in Cairo, when he identified a full copy and a smaller one of a mysterious document that he called *Fragments of a Zadokite Work*. The standard abbreviation CD for this work stands for Cairo Damascus (the text mentions Damascus several times as a place where a covenant was made). In the 1950s, fragmentary remains of the same composition were found at Qumran, ten copies in all. How this work reached the Cairo Geniza is a complicated topic, but the presence of so many copies at Qumran shows that the Damascus Document was important to the group associated with the site. Scholars also believe the Damascus Document was specific to Qumran—in other words, it was composed by a member or members of the community.

The two copies from the Cairo Geniza are known as the "A Version" and the "B

Version," and they are quite distinct. The first passage below, from the A Version, provides rules for those living in camps. Note especially the reference to "the Messiah of Aaron and of Israel" (cols. 12:23–13:1).

Another relevant passage from the A Version is col. 14:18–19, which includes the phrase "[until the Messi]ah of Aaron and of Israel [takes his stand]."

DAMASCUS DOCUMENT (GENIZA A) COLS. 12:22–13:7

(Broshi, 32–35)

And this is the rule for the assembly of [23]the ca[mp]s. Those who walk to and fro by them (i.e., these statutes) in the time of wickedness, until the Messiah of Aaron 13 [1]and of Israel takes his stand: (groups of) up to ten men at least, by thousands, hundreds, fifties, [2]and tens (cf. Exodus 18:25). And in a place where ten are, a priest learned in the *Book of Hagy* should not be absent; by [3]his command he shall govern them all.

But if he is not experienced in all these (matters), and one of the Levites is experienced in [4]them, then the decision (lit. "lot") about going out and coming in falls upon him, (with respect to) all the members of the camp.

But if [5]it is a case of the law of skin diseases against someone, then the Priest shall come and stand in the camp, and the Overseer [6]shall instruct him in the exact interpretation of the Law.

Even if he (i.e., the Priest) is naive, it is he who shall confine him (i.e., the one suffering from skin disease), because that decision [7]is for them (i.e., the priests).

The B Version of the Damascus Document was a later copy that was revised to reflect the outlook of the Qumran Community. The passage below, from this version, lays greater stress than the A Version on the fulfillment of prophecy. Of particular interest here is the reference to "the Messiah from Aaron and from Israel" (col. 20:1).

DAMASCUS DOCUMENT (GENIZA B) COLS. 19:7–13, 33–35; 20:1–3

(Broshi, 43–47)

19 [7]When the word that is written by the hand of the Prophet Zechariah comes true, *"Awake, O sword, against [8]my shepherd, against the man who is my companion," says God. "Strike down the shepherd, and the sheep will be scattered; [9]and I will turn my hand against the little ones"* (so Zechariah 13:7).

But those who pay heed to him (i.e., God) are the poor ones of the flock (so Zechariah 11:11). [10]They will escape in the time of punishment, but those who remain will be delivered up to the sword when the Messiah of [11]Aaron and of Israel comes, as happened at the time of the first punishment, as he said by the hand of [12]Ezekiel, *To put his mark on the foreheads of those who sigh and groan* (so Ezekiel 9:4), [13]but those who remain were delivered up to the sword that carries out the vengeance of the covenant. . . .

[33]Thus all the men who entered the new covenant [34]in the land of Damascus, but then turned back, and acted treacherously, and departed from the well of living waters, [35]shall not be counted among the council of the people, and they shall not be written in their register from the day of 20[1] the Unique Teacher's gathering (i.e., death), until the Messiah from Aaron and from Israel takes his stand.

And this is the decision for all [2]who enter the congregation of the men of perfect holiness and then become sick of carrying out the instructions of the upright. [3]This is the type of person who is melted in the furnace (cf. Ezekiel 22:21).

TEXTS RELATING TO JOHN THE BAPTIST OR BAPTISM

INTERPRETATION OF SCRIPTURE BY JOHN THE BAPTIST
AND THE QUMRAN COMMUNITY

The significance of John's ministry is expressed in all four Gospels through the words of Isaiah 40:3; he was "the voice of one crying out in the wilderness: 'Prepare the way of the Lord, make his paths straight'" (Mark 1:3; Matthew 3:3; Luke 3:4; cf. John 1:23). In the Rule of the Community (1QS) the Qumran covenanters use the same passage to explain their presence in the wilderness: to prepare for the Lord's coming through the study of the Torah.

RULE OF THE COMMUNITY (1QS) COL. 8:12–16

(Trever, 71)

Col. 8 [12] . . . And when these have become a community in Israel [13]according to these rules, they shall be separated from the dwelling-place of perverse men to go to the wilderness, in order to prepare there the way of him, [14]just as it is written: "In the wilderness prepare the way of the Lord, make straight in the desert a highway for our God" (so Isaiah 40:3). [15]This is the expounding of the Law wh[i]ch (God) commanded by the hand of Moses, in order to act according to all that has been revealed in every each age, [16]and according to what the prophets have revealed by his holy spirit.

BAPTISM OR RITUAL WASHING AND THE FORGIVENESS OF SINS

While there is no firm evidence linking John the Baptist with the Qumran community, several scholars believe he had contact or links with them during his ministry, since they have features in common. For example, John's urgent message that the time was at hand, that the axe was poised to strike the root (Luke 3:9), is reminiscent of the Qumran belief that the final conflict would come soon and the last days were nearly here. Moreover, the prominent place of baptism or washings with water in John's ministry and in the life of the Qumranites (Luke's Gospel states that John "went into all the region around the Jordan, proclaiming a baptism of repentance for the forgiveness of sins" [Luke 3:3]) has some resemblance to several passages from the community's Scrolls that indicate that baptism or ritual immersion—sometimes associated with forgiveness of sins—was a prominent feature of life at Qumran.

John, however, probably understood the baptisms he administered in a different way than the people of Qumran conceived of theirs. First, he himself administered the baptisms. At the Qumran site, in contrast, the pools used for such a purpose had steps allowing the ritually impure person to walk down, enter the water himself, and come up from the pool cleansed—all apparently without assistance from others. Second, the washings at Qumran were a daily feature, whereas the baptisms administered by John were onetime ceremonies.

RULE OF THE COMMUNITY (1QS) COLS. 2:25–3:9

(Trever, 65–66)

Col. 2 [25] . . . Anyone who refuses to enter [26][the Covenant of G]od in order to walk in the stubbornness of his heart, shall not [enter the Com]munity of his truth, because his soul
Col. 3 [1]has detested the disciplines fundamental to knowledge (lit. "disciplines of knowledge"): the laws of righteousness. He lacks the endurance to convert his life, and shall not be counted among the upright. [2]His knowledge, his powers, and his possessions shall not enter the council of the Community, since he plows in the mire of wickedness, and there are stains [3]on his conversion. He shall not be justified while he defends the stubbornness of his heart; he looks on darkness as the ways of light. In the sight (lit. "eye") of the blameless [4]he shall not be counted. He shall not become clean by acts of atonement, nor purified by cleansing waters (lit. "waters of impurity"), nor be sanctified by seas [5]and rivers, nor purified by any ablution. Unclean, unclean shall he be. All the days that he despises the laws [6]of God he shall receive no instruction in the Community of his counsel.
For only through the spirit of God's true counsel are the ways of man atoned for, all [7]his transgressions, so that he can look on the light of life and be joined to his truth by his (i.e., God's) holy spirit; he will be purified from all [8]his transgressions. Through an upright and humble spirit his sin will be covered, and by the humble submission of his soul to all the statutes of God his flesh [9]shall be made pure, through sprinkling with purifying waters and being made holy by cleansing waters.

TEXTS RELATING TO THE PERSON OF JESUS

THE COMING OF THE MESSIAH AND THE RESURRECTION OF THE DEAD

One of the most important Qumran texts of relevance to Jesus and his ministry is 4Q521 (the Messianic Apocalypse). There is no evidence to identify this text—

which was copied in the first century BCE—as specifically Qumranian (sectarian), which means that the ideas it contains were more widespread among Jews by the first century CE.

In the main preserved section, 4Q521 describes the expected activity of a prophetic Messiah with a "recipe" or list of characteristics that some or many Jews expected would take place with the Messiah's coming. This reveals much about Jewish messianism at the time and contains fascinating parallels to Luke 4:16–21 (Jesus' sermon in Nazareth in which he quotes Isaiah 58:6 and 61:1–2) and 7:20–22 (see also Matthew 11:2–5). Most significantly, 4Q521 shows that (1) in the Gospel passages mentioned, Jesus claimed to be the Messiah by referring to a recipe that already existed, and (2) the reference to the raising of the dead as one sign that the Messiah has come (Luke 7:22) was known in Judaism in the first century BCE. Since this sign is not yet included in Hebrew Bible prophecies, 4Q521 may be described as a missing link (although not a direct one) between the Hebrew Scriptures and the Gospels.

MESSIANIC APOCALYPSE (4Q521) COL. 2:1–13

DJD 25.10

Col. 2 [1][. . . For the hea]vens and the earth will listen to his Messiah (or, anointed one) [2][and all t]hat is in them shall not stray from the commandments of the holy ones.
[3]Strengthen yourselves, you seekers of the Lord, in his service!
[4]Will you not discover the Lord in this, all you who hope in their heart?
[5]For the Lord will bestow care on the pious, and he will call the righteous by name;
[6]and over the poor his spirit will hover, and he will renew the faithful with his strength.
[7]For he will honor the pious upon the throne of an (or: the) eternal kingdom, [8]setting captives free, opening the eyes of the blind, lifting up those who are bo[wed down] (cf. especially Psalms 146:7–8; also Isaiah 58:6; 61:1).
[9]And for [ev]er I shall cling [to] those who [ho]pe, and in his mercy [. . .];
[10]and the fru[it of . . .] will not be delayed for anyone;
[11]And the Lord will perform glorious things which have not existed, just as he s[aid].
[12]For he will heal the wounded (lit. "pierced"), he will make the dead live, he will bring good news to the poor (cf. Isaiah 61:1);
[13]and he will [. . . the . . .]. He will lead with care the uprooted ones, and he will make the hungry rich.

"SON OF GOD" AND "SON OF THE MOST HIGH"

Sometimes referred to as the *Son of God Text* or the Aramaic Apocalypse, 4Q246 is now officially called the Apocryphon of Daniel. There are no sectarian markers to identify this document as having been composed at Qumran. The surviving text—written in Aramaic and copied in the late first century BCE—consists of two nine-line columns, the first of which is mostly missing.

Several terms or phrases in 4Q246 are reminiscent of sections of Daniel, but there is disagreement among scholars as to whom the passage describes. Some regard the titles in the first part as attributed to an oppressive ruler during a time of suffering and war, a period followed by victory for God's people who establish an eternal kingdom of peace under divine rule. Suggested identifications are a historical king, the Antichrist, an angelic figure such as Melchizedek, Michael, or the Prince of Light, or the Jewish people collectively. Other scholars, however, understand the titles as being attributed to a messianic figure at the end-times.

Whatever the identity of this ruler, there are interesting parallels with the Annunciation account in Luke 1:30–35: the coming figure "will be called great" (cf. col. 1:9 with Luke 1:32); "'Son of God' he shall be called" (cf. col. 2:1 with Luke 1:35); and "they will name him 'Son of the Most High'" (cf. col. 2:1 with Luke 1:32). It seems reasonable to see connections, whether direct or indirect, between 4Q246 and the Lukan passages.

Two different translations of this important text are provided, the first describing an oppressive ruler followed by the victory of God's people, and the second describing a messianic figure at the end-times. Differences are indicated by the use of italics.

APOCRYPHON OF DANIEL (4Q246) COLS. 1:9–2:9

DJD 22.167–68
VERSION A (*OPPRESSIVE RULER AND THE VICTORY OF GOD'S PEOPLE*)

[9][. . . gr]eat he will *call himself*, and by his name he will *designate himself*. Col. 2 [1]"Son of God" he will *proclaim himself*, and "Son of the Most High" they will call him. Like the sparks [2]of the vision (or: that you saw), so will their kingdom be. For year[s] they will rule over [3]the earth, and they will trample all. People will trample on people (cf. Daniel 7:23) and *province on province*, [4]until the *people of God arises* and *all will rest* from the sword.
[5]*Their* [lit. "its" (i.e., the people of God's)] kingdom will be an everlasting kingdom (cf. Daniel 7:27) and all *their* way will be in truth. *They* will judge [6]the earth in truth and all will make peace. The sword will cease from the earth, [7]and *all the provinces* will pay homage to *them*. The great God (cf. Daniel 2:45) will be *their* strength. [8]He will wage war on *their* behalf; he will give nations into *their* hand, [9]and he will cast them all away before *them*. *Their* dominion will be an everlasting dominion (cf. Daniel 7:14), and all the depths of . . .

VERSION B (*MESSIANIC FIGURE AT END TIMES*)

[9][. . . gr]eat he will *be called*, and by his name he will *be designated*. Col. 2 [1]"Son of God" he will *be proclaimed*, and "Son of the Most High" they will call

him. Like the sparks [2]of the vision (or: that you saw), so will their kingdom be. For year[s] they will rule over [3]the earth, and they will trample all. People will trample on people (cf. Daniel 7:23) and *city on city*, [4]until *he raises up the people of God* and *makes everyone* rest from the sword.

[5]*His* kingdom will be an everlasting kingdom (cf. Daniel 7:27) and all *his* way will be in truth. *He* will judge [6]the earth in truth and all will make peace. The sword will cease from the earth, [7]and *all the cities* will pay homage to *him*. The great God (cf. Daniel 2:45) will be *his* strength. [8]He will wage war on *his* behalf; he will give nations into *his* hand, [9]and he will cast them all away before *him*. *His* dominion will be an everlasting dominion (cf. Daniel 7:14), and all the depths of . . .

MELCHIZEDEK IN HEBREWS AND IN THE DEAD SEA SCROLLS

One fascinating portrait of Jesus Christ is found in Hebrews 6:19–7:10, where he is compared with Melchizedek, a rather obscure figure in the Hebrew Bible (especially Genesis 14:18–20). Melchizedek, king of Salem and priest of God Most High, met Abram, who was returning from his victory over Chedorlaomer (former overlord of the country between Dan and Elath) and his allies. He brought out bread and wine and blessed Abram. Then "Abram gave him a tenth of everything" (Genesis 14:20), which shows that the patriarch acknowledged his authority.

Psalm 110:4 then tells us that Melchizedek belongs to an eternal priesthood of Yahweh. One commentator reconstructs the preceding verse (3) to suggest that Melchizedek was a supernatural being engendered by Yahweh: "With thee is the dignity in the day of thy power. In the holy mountains, from the womb of Dawn, like the Day Star I have begotten thee" (Astour, p. 685).

The Letter to the Hebrews quite likely was written to a group of Judeo-Christians of Essene background who believed that the Levitical priesthood was still necessary for Christians. Through insightful and brilliant argumentation, the author urges them to recognize that Jesus was a legitimate and superior priest, despite not being of the tribe of Levi. The author argues for the eternal nature of Christ's priesthood:

[Melchizedek] is first, by translation of his name, king of righteousness, and then he is also king of Salem, that is, king of peace. He is without father or mother or genealogy, and has neither beginning of days nor end of life, but resembling the Son of God he continues a priest forever. (Hebrews 7:2b–3)

The letter also demonstrates the superiority of Christ's priesthood over the human priesthood of Levi and his sons by saying that Abraham, on his return from the slaughter of the kings, gave a tenth of everything to Melchizedek (Hebrews 7:1–2a). This shows that Melchizedek was superior to Abraham and to Abraham's descendant Levi, who was indirectly paying tithes through Abraham:

[7]It is beyond dispute that the inferior is blessed by the superior. [8]Here tithes are received by mortal men; there, by one of whom it is testified that he lives. [9]One might even say that Levi himself, who receives tithes, paid tithes through Abraham, [10]for he was still in the loins of his ancestor when Melchizedek met him. (Hebrews 7:4–10)

The notion of Melchizedek as a primeval, immortal being, coeternal with the Son of God, gave rise to speculations in the early Christian church, to the extent that there arose a sect of Melchizedekians who regarded Melchizedek as equal or superior to Christ. Such speculations lasted until the fifth century CE, when the church ceased to focus on the mysterious figure of Melchizedek.

MELCHIZEDEK IN QUMRAN LITERATURE

The Book of Leviticus (25:8–55) describes the year of Jubilee, in which all land alienated from its original owners was to be returned, and all Israelites who had become enslaved for debt were to be set free. It began on the Day of Atonement, and was signaled by the blowing of trumpets throughout the land and the proclamation of release. 11QMelchizedek must be understood in the context of the Jubilee year, with the remission of debts involving not only land, money, and slaves but also the forgiveness of sin. The agent of this salvation is to be Melchizedek, who is an exalted divine being. The author even applies to Melchizedek Hebrew names that are generally used for God alone: *El* and *Elohim*, both usually translated as "God."

In citing Isaiah 61:2, which mentions the year of the Lord's favor, the author substitutes Melchizedek for God's most holy name (Yahweh, line 9). This makes it possible to understand him (line 10) as a god or an angel (*Elohim*), who holds judgment in the midst of the gods (*Elohim*). Melchizedek also is said to atone for the sins of the Sons of Light (line 8), and to carry out judgment upon Belial and the spirits of his lot (line 12)—actions that usually are associated with God himself.

It has been suggested that the Qumran group identified Melchizedek with the archangel Michael. However, although there is some similarity between the roles of Melchizedek in the text below and of Michael in the *War Scroll* (1QM 17:5–8) and in Daniel, Melchizedek is not identified specifically with Michael in the Qumran texts.

11QMELCHIZEDEK (11Q13) COL. 2, LINES 2–25

DJD 23.224–26

Col. 2 [2][. . .] And concerning what he said, "*In [this] year of jubilee [you shall return, every one, to his property*" (so Leviticus 25:13) and concerning it he said, "*And th]is *[3]*is the [ma]nner of [the remission]: every creditor shall remit the*

loan he has lent [to his neighbor; he shall not exact it of his neighbor, his brother,
because it has been proclaimed] a remission for G[od]" (so Deuteronomy 15:2).
[4][Its interpretation] is for the Last Days concerning the captives, as [he said:
"To proclaim release to the captives" (so Isaiah 61:1). . . . just] as [5]their teachers . . .] and from the inheritance of Melchizedek, f[or . . .] the inheritan[ce of
Melchize]dek, who [6]will make them return to what is theirs. And he will proclaim to them release, to set them free [from the burden of] all their iniquities.
And this thing [will happ]en [7]in the first week of the Jubilee that follows [the]
nine Jubilees. And the D[a]y of [Atone]ment i[s] the e[nd of] the tenth
[Ju]bilee, [8]when he shall atone for all the Sons of L[ight a]nd the men [of]
Mel[chi]zedek's lot. [. . .] upo[n the]m [. . .] accor[ding to] a[ll] their [wo]rks.
For [9]it is the final time of *the year of Melchizedek's favor* (so Isaiah 61:2, modified), and for [his] armi[es, the peo]ple of God's holy ones, and for a just dominion, as it is written [10]concerning him in the Songs of David, who said: *Elo-*
him has [ta]ken his place in the coun[cil of God]; in the midst of the gods (elohim)
he holds judgment (so Psalm 82:1). *And concerning him he sai[d, "And] over [it]*
[11]*return on high; El will judge the peoples"* (so Psalm 7:7b–8a).
And as for what he s[aid, *How long will y]ou[11] judge unjustly, and sh[ow par]tial-*
ity to the wick[e]d? [S]elah" (so Psalm 82:2), [12]its interpretation concerns Belial
and the spirits of his lot, wh[o rebe]lled by turn[ing asi]de from God's statutes
to [become wicked]. [13]And Melchizedek will carry out the vengeance of
Go[d]'s judgments. [And on that day he will de]li[ver them from the hand of]
Belial, and from the power of all the sp[irits of his lot]. [14]To his aid will be all
the "gods of justice," and he is the one wh[o . . .] all the sons of God.
This vi[sitation] [15]is the Day of [Salvation (or: Peace)] about which he spoke
[through Isai]ah the Prophet who said: *[How] beautiful [16]upon the mountains*
are the feet of the one who brings good ne[ws, who] announces peace, who brings
n[ews of good, who announces salvat]ion, who [s]ays to Zion, "Your Elohim
[reigns]" (so Isaiah 52:7).
[17]Its interpretation: *the mountains* [are] the prophet[s]; they [. . .] to all
I[srael]. [18]*The one who brings good news* i[s] the Anointed of the spir[it], just as
Dan[iel] spoke [concerning him: *Until an anointed one, a leader, there shall be*
seven weeks (so Daniel 9:25; cf. 9:26).
The one who brings news of] [19]*good, who announc[es salvation]* is the one about
whom it is wri[tt]en, *[to proclaim the year of the Lord's favor, and the day of*
vengeance of our God]; [20]*to comfo[rt] th[ose who mourn* (so Isaiah 61:2).
Its interpretation]: to gi[ve] them insight into all the ages of ti[me . . .] [21]in
truth. [. . . It is] he w[ho . . . [22]. . .] who has been turned away from Belial and
has ret[urned to . . . [23]. . .] by the judgment[s of] God, just as it is written concerning him, *[who says to Zi]on "Your Elohim reigns"* (so Isaiah 52:7). [Z]ion
i[s [24]the Community of all the sons of righteousness, those who] uphol[d] the
Covenant, who turn from walking [in the w]ay of the people. And *your*
El[o]him is [25][Melchizedek, who will del]iv[er them from the ha]nd of Belial.

TEXTS RELATING TO THE TEACHING OF JESUS

A LIST OF BEATITUDES FOUND AT QUMRAN

An interesting example of wisdom literature at Qumran is 4Q525 (Beatitudes), which was copied in the first century BCE. One section contains a list of beatitudes similar to those found in the Sermon on the Mount (Matthew 5:1–12) and in the Sermon on the Plain (Luke 6:20–23). Although much of the relevant passage is not preserved, the original text seems to have contained eight short beatitudes followed by a longer one. Since the list in Matthew contains the same structure (8 short and 1 long), 4Q525 suggests that this Gospel preserves an ancient listing because it corresponds to a standard literary form found elsewhere. One contribution of 4Q525 is not to confirm the actual words of Jesus but to show that the structure of the Beatitudes in Matthew 5 most likely was familiar to many Jews in the first century BCE.

4Q525 sheds light on the Gospel Beatitudes from a second angle. When we compare the wording of the Qumran document with the Beatitudes in Matthew 5, we find several parallels:

Matthew 5	4Q525
*Blessed are the pure in heart (v. 8).	* [Blessed is the one who . . .] Frgs. 2 ii + 3 with a pure heart.
*Blessed are you when men revile you . . . rejoice and be glad (vv. 11–12).	* Bles[sed] are those who rejoice in her (2 ii + 3, line 2).
*Blessed are the meek (v. 5).	* and in the humility (or: affliction) of his soul he does not loath[e her]. (2 ii + 3, line 6).

There is no direct relationship between the two texts; moreover, the Beatitudes in Matthew 5 (and Luke 6) are eschatological, whereas those in 4Q525 are sapiential. Yet the structure and parallels suggest that both the content and the style of Jesus' teaching are at home in Jewish wisdom tradition.

In the translation below, the intervals found in the original Hebrew text are important for determining where each beatitude ends. The first four short beatitudes are not preserved, but content and spacing suggest that they were once present. The second four are preserved; they are followed by a long ninth beatitude (note the "ands," which show that this beatitude continued on to the interval in line 6). The words that follow to the end of line 7 are clearly prose; a few more very fragmentary lines are preserved but are not translated here.

4QBEATITUDES (4Q525) FRGS. 1, 2 II AND 3

DJD 25.120, 122

Frg. 1 [1][The words of . . . that he spok]e in the wisdom that God gave to him
[. . .] [2][. . . in order to kno]w wisdom and disc[ipline], in order to understand
[. . .] [3][. . .] in order to increase kn[owledge . . .]

> [Blessed . . . .]
> [Blessed . . . .]
> [Blessed . . . .]
> [Blessed . . . .]
> [Blessed is the one who . . .] Frgs. 2 ii + 3 [1]with a pure heart
>> and does not slander with his tongue. [*interval*]
>
> Blessed are those who hold fast to her (i.e., Wisdom's) statutes
>> and do not hold [2]to the ways of injustice. [*interval*]
>
> Bles[sed] are those who rejoice in her,
>> and do not burst forth on paths of folly. [*interval*]
>
> Blessed are those who search for her [3]with pure hands,
>> and do not look for her with a deceitful he[art]. [*interval*]
>
> Blessed is the man who has attained Wisdom, [*interval*]
>> and walks [4]in the Law of the Most High,
>> and directs his heart to her ways, [*interval*]
>> and controls himself by her corrections,
>> and is al[w]ays pleased with her punishments,
>> [5]and does not forsake her in the face (lit. eyes) of [his] hardships,
>> and at the time of distress does not abandon her,
>> nor forgets her [on the day of] dread,
>> [6]and in the humility (or: affliction) of his soul he does not loath[e her].
>> [*interval*]

For he continually meditates on her, and in his anguish he concentrates [on
her, and in al]l [7]his life [he thinks] on her; [and he places her] before his eyes
so not to walk in the ways [of injustice, and . . . [8]. . .]

REBUKING A FELLOW MEMBER

One practice attested in both the Gospels and Qumran literature is rebuking a
fellow member of the group when one has been offended or wronged by another.
Both the Qumran community and the early Christians had rules about this matter, since it is based on teachings in Leviticus 19. Each group, however, developed the teachings of Leviticus in parallel ways.

In Matthew 18:15–17, Jesus offers a set of guidelines for rebuking a member
of the church or fellowship (cf. Luke 17:3–4). The Qumran covenanters' approach
to such matters is outlined in cols. 5:24–6:1 of the Community Rule (1QS). The

same three successive stages are evident here as in Matthew: personal confrontation, confrontation before witnesses, and bringing the matter before the entire group. A similar approach is found in col. 9:2–8 of the Damascus Document (CD), which quotes Leviticus 19:18, one of the scriptural bases of the practice.

One more interesting text—which is very fragmentary and so is not translated here—is 4Q477 (*Rebukes Reported by the Overseer*). This document seems to contain a list of members of the community who were rebuked, and records some of their transgressions.

RULE OF THE COMMUNITY (1QS) COLS. 5:24–6:1

(Trever, 68–69)

24. . . Each man is to rebuke 25his fellow in tr[u]th, humility and compassionate love for another.
He shall not speak to him in anger, or ill-temper, 26or with a [stiff] neck, [or with the env]y of a wicked spirit. He shall not hate him because of his own [uncircum]ci[sed] heart, but he shall rebuke him on that (same) day so that he does not 6 1incur guilt because of him. Moreover, no man shall bring a charge against his fellow before the Many (i.e., the Community) without reproof in the presence of witnesses.

DAMASCUS DOCUMENT (CD) COL. 9:2–8

(Broshi, 26–27)

2And as for the passage that says, *You shall not take vengeance nor bear a grudge against the children of your people* (so Leviticus 19:18), any of those brought into 3the covenant who brings against his fellow an accusation without reproaching him before witnesses, 4or who brings an accusation in the heat of anger, or who tells it to his elders so that they despise him, he is a vengeance-taker and a grudge-bearer.
5Is it not written that only *he* (i.e., the Lord) *takes vengeance on his enemies, and he bears a grudge against his foes*" (so Nahum 1:2). 6If he has kept silent toward him from one day to another, and then in the heat of his anger against him spoke against him in a capital matter, 7he has testified against himself because he did not carry out the commandments of God who said to him, *You* 8*shall reprove your companion, and you shall not incur sin because of him* (so Leviticus 19:17).

TEXTS RELATING TO CRUCIFIXION AND THE SUFFERING MESSIAH

One major difference between Judaism and Christianity is the latter's central belief in a Messiah who would suffer and die for the sins of his people and the sins of the world. The Gospels and several additional New Testament books contain many statements by Jesus and others indicating that he would be put to death as an atoning sacrifice. This outlook is very evident in Philip's meeting with the Ethiopian official (Acts 8:26–40), where Jesus is identified with the Suffering Servant of Isaiah 53:

[30]So Philip ran up to it and heard him reading the prophet Isaiah. He asked, "Do you understand what you are reading?" [31]He replied, "How can I, unless someone guides me?" And he invited Philip to get in and sit beside him. [32]Now the passage of the Scripture that he was reading was this:
"Like a sheep he was led to the slaughter, and like a lamb silent before its shearer, so he does not open his mouth. [33]In his humiliation justice was denied him. Who can describe his generation? For his life is taken away from the earth" (Isaiah 53:7–8).
[34]The eunuch asked Philip, "About whom, may I ask you, does the prophet say this, about himself or about someone else?" [35]Then Philip began to speak, and starting with this Scripture, he proclaimed to him the good news about Jesus.

The question of whether the Dead Sea Scrolls contain evidence of a suffering or dying Messiah is a difficult one, and it centers on a few key texts.

A REFERENCE TO CRUCIFIXION IN THE SCROLLS

The translation below is from the Pesher on Nahum (4Q169), which was copied in the late first century BCE. (The *pesher* [plural, *pesharim*] is a type of commentary on Scripture that presents a contemporizing biblical exegesis and was specific to the Qumran Community.) It refers to Alexander Jannaeus, the "Angry Lion" who ruled over Judaea as king and high priest from 103 to 76 BCE. Many Jews resented him for being lax in religious observance, and he took harsh measures to suppress dissent. Josephus tells us that the Pharisees were opponents of Jannaeus, who was allied with the Sadducees and priestly groups. (The passage from 4Q169 refers to the Pharisees as "those who seek smooth things," in other words, those who look for easy interpretations.) Jannaeus's enemies formed an alliance with Demetrius III of Syria and invited him to invade their country and depose the king. Demetrius accepted, putting Jannaeus to flight in a battle near Shechem, but many of the king's allies—fearing Gentile dominance—went over to his side. Demetrius then withdrew his forces. The Jewish king took harsh revenge against those he considered traitors, banishing many of the rebels and executing others. According to Josephus, his most notable act of revenge was the crucifixion of eight hundred rebel leaders. As they looked down from their crosses, Jannaeus also strangled the rebels' wives and children.

The passage became widely known in 1956, when John Allegro announced on a BBC program that he had found a text at Qumran that described the community as worshiping a crucified Messiah, whom they believed would return in glory. According to Allegro, this passage teaches that the "Angry Lion" or Wicked Priest crucified the "seekers of smoothness" as well as the Teacher of Righteousness, who would rise again:

[Jannaeus, that is, the Angry Lion] descended on Qumran and arrested its leader, the mysterious "Teacher of Righteousness," whom he turned over to his mercenaries to be crucified. . . . When the Jewish king had left, [the Qumran sectarians] took down the broken body of their Master to stand guard over it until Judgment Day. . . . They believed their Master would rise again and lead his faithful flock (the people of the new testament, as they called themselves) to a new and purified Jerusalem. . . . What is clear is that there was a well-defined Essenic pattern into which Jesus of Nazareth fits. (*Time*, 6 February, 1956, quoted in Fitzmyer, *Responses*, 164)

For Allegro, these words summarize a common first-century Judean superstition, of which belief in the death, resurrection, and return of Jesus was but another example. Such views—and his claim that the Scrolls provided concrete evidence for them—caused several other members of the official editorial team (R. de Vaux, J. T. Milik, P. Skehan, J. Starcky, and J. Strugnell) to write to the London *Times*, denying that there was any "close connection between the supposed crucifixion of the 'teacher of righteousness' of the Essene sect and the crucifixion and resurrection of Jesus Christ" (see Silberman, 133–34). According to these scholars, Allegro had "misread the texts, or he has built up a chain of conjectures which the materials do not support" (Silberman, 134).

In a new century, scholars are agreed that the reference to crucifixion in 4Q169 is likely, but that Allegro's comments on the Teacher of Righteousness and on "a well-defined Essenic pattern into which Jesus of Nazareth fits" are incorrect.

PESHER ON NAHUM (4Q169) COLS. 1:5–9

DJD 5.38

The lion tears enough for his cubs, and strangles prey for his lionesses (Nahum 2:13a [Heb 2:12a]). [5][Its interpretation] concerns the Angry Young Lion who strikes by means of (or: strikes) his nobles and by means of (or: and) the men of his counsel.
[6][. . . *And he fills] his cave [with prey], and his den with torn game* (so Nahum 2:13b [Heb 2:13b]). Its interpretation concerns the Angry Young Lion [7][who . . . takes ven]geance against those who seek smooth things, the one who hangs men alive. [8][This has not been done(?)] in Israel since ancient times; for of anyone hanged alive on the tree (cf. Deuteronomy 21:23), [he pro]claims: *Behold, I am against [you],* [9]*say[s the Lord of Hosts]* (so Nahum 2:14a).

A DYING OR CONQUERING MESSIAH IN 4Q285?

A fascinating document that was composed at Qumran is the Book of War, which may be described as an independent composition related to the War Scroll. This text is represented by two Scrolls (4Q285 and 11Q14), which were copied in the first century BCE. In the early 1990s, heated discussion centered on one tiny piece (frg. 5) of 4Q285, which according to one scholar (Robert Eisenman) referred to the killing or execution of the Messiah. Most scholars, however, now believe that in 4Q285 the Messiah—here called the Branch of David—is not being slain but does the killing himself.

The two contrasting interpretations mostly are dependent on a single Hebrew word in line 4 (*whmytw*). Depending on the vocalization (i.e., vowels that are used), this word can mean that the Messiah is being killed: "*and they put to death* the Leader of the Community, the Branch of David." Alternatively, it can mean that the Messiah is putting someone else to death: "and the leader of the Community, the Branch of David, *will have him put to death*." Compare the two translations in the following:

A Dying Messiah (Eisenman)	A Conquering Messiah (Vermes)
1.]Isaiah the prophet[	1.]Isaiah the prophet, And [they] shall cut down
2.]the staff shall go forth from the	2. will f]all, and a shoot shall spring root of Jesse from the stump of Jesse
3.]Branch of David and they shall be judged	3.]Branch of David. And they shall be judged
4.]and they put to death the leader of the community, the B[ranch of David	4.]and the Leader of the Community—the Bran[ch of David] will have him put to death,
5.]with wounds, and the [High] Priest shall order	5. tambourine]s and dancers, and the [High] Priest shall order
	6. the c]orpse[s of] the Kitti[m].

When the fragment is studied in context, it becomes clear that the second interpretation (a conquering Messiah) is the correct one. The piece begins with a quotation from Isaiah 11:1, which just a few verses later refers to the slaying of the wicked: "He shall strike the earth with the rod of his mouth, and with the breath of his lips he shall kill the wicked" (Isaiah 11:4b). Also, in other Scrolls the Leader of the Community is portrayed as a victorious son of David who leads Israel to victory over the nations.

Following the discussion that took place in the 1990s, scholars now broadly agree on several features of frg. 5 of 4Q285: (1) the text refers to Isaiah 10:34–11:1, which says that the forces of evil will be cut down by the messianic "shoot from the stump of Jesse"; (2) the branch that will grow out of his roots is the Branch of David (the Messiah); (3) someone—most likely the enemy leader—will be brought before the Leader of the Community (cf. line 4 and frgs. 6 + 4, line 10), and he will be executed; (4) all Israel will rejoice with tambourines and dancers (line 5). There also is reference to the corpses of the Kittim (line 6).

We must conclude, then, that this brave attempt to identify a dying Messiah in the Dead Sea Scrolls has not proved successful.

BOOK OF WAR (4Q285) FRG. 7, LINES 1–6

DJD 36.238

> [1][. . . just as it is written in the book of] Isaiah the Prophet,

> "And [they] will hack down [the thickets of the forest] [2][with an ax,
> and Lebanon by a mighty one will f]all.
> And a shoot shall come up from the stump of Jesse,
> [3][and a branch shall bear fruit from his roots." (so Isaiah 10:34–11:1).

This is the] Branch of David. Then they will enter into judgment with [. . . , [4]. . .] and the Leader of the Community—the Bran[ch of David]—will have him put to death. [5][Then . . . with tambourine]s and dancers, and the [High] Priest shall order [6][them to . . . the s]lai[n of] the Kitti[m].

Bibliography

Almost all the Dead Sea Scrolls are published in the series Discoveries in the Judean Desert (DJD) by Oxford University Press; in two of the earlier volumes (4 and 5), the series was called Discoveries in the Judean Desert of Jordan (DJDJ). Above most translations, the number of the DJD volume containing the official edition is given, together with the relevant page numbers.

English Translations of the Dead Sea Scrolls

THE BIBLICAL SCROLLS

Abegg, M. G., P. W. Flint, and E. Ulrich. *The Dead Sea Scrolls Bible*. San Francisco: Harper-SanFrancisco, 1999.

THE NONBIBLICAL SCROLLS

Broshi, M., ed. *The Damascus Document Reconsidered*. Jerusalem: The Israel Exploration Society/shrine of the Book, Israel Museum, 1992.
García Martínez, F. *The Dead Sea Scrolls Translated: The Qumran Texts in English*. 2nd ed. Leiden: Brill; Grand Rapids, MI: Eerdmans, 1996.
Gaster, T. H. *The Dead Sea Scriptures*. 3rd ed. New York: Doubleday, 1976.
Schechter, Solomon. *Fragments of a Zadokite Work*. Documents of Jewish Sectaries 1. Cambridge: Cambridge University Press, 1910.
Trever, J. C. *Scrolls from Qumran Cave I*. Jerusalem: The Albright Institute of Archaeological Research and the Shrine of the Book, 1974.

Vermes, G. *The Complete Dead Sea Scrolls in English*. London: Penguin, 1997.

Wise, M. O., M. G. Abegg, and E. C. Cook. *The Dead Sea Scrolls—Revised Edition. A New Translation*. San Francisco: HarperSanFrancisco, 2005.

Secondary Literature

Abegg, Martin. "The Hebrew of the Dead Sea Scrolls." Pages 325–58, esp. 334–35, in *The Dead Sea Scrolls after Fifty Years: A Comprehensive Assessment*. Edited by P. W. Flint and J. C. VanderKam. 2 vols. Leiden: Brill, 1998–99.

Astour, Michael C. "Melchizedek (Person)." Pages 684–86 in vol. 4 of *The Anchor Bible Dictionary*. Edited by David Noel Freedman. 6 vols. New York: Doubleday, 1992.

Charlesworth, James H., ed. *Jesus and the Dead Sea Scrolls*. Anchor Bible Reference Library 4. New York: Doubleday, 1992.

Collins, J. J. *The Scepter and the Star: The Messiahs of the Dead Sea Scrolls and Other Ancient Literature*. Anchor Bible Reference Library 10. New York: Doubleday, 1995.

Cook, E. *Solving the Mysteries of the Dead Sea Scrolls*. Grand Rapids, MI: Zondervan, 1994.

Dupont-Sommer, A. *The Dead Sea Scrolls: A Preliminary Survey*. Translated from the French edition 1950. Oxford: Blackwell, 1952.

Evans, Craig A. "Jesus and the Dead Sea Scrolls from Qumran Cave 4." Pages 91–100 in *Eschatology, Messianism, and the Dead Sea Scrolls*. Edited by Craig A. Evans and Peter W. Flint. Studies in the Dead Sea Scrolls and Related Literature. Grand Rapids, MI: Eerdmans, 1997.

———. "Jesus and the Messianic Texts from Qumran." Pages 83–154 in *Jesus and His Contemporaries: Comparative Studies*. Edited by Craig. A. Evans. Arbeiten zur Geschichte des antiken Judentums und des Urchristentums 25. Leiden: Brill, 1995.

Fitzmyer, Joseph A. *The Dead Sea Scrolls and Christian Origins*. Studies in the Dead Sea Scrolls and Related Literature. Grand Rapids, MI: Eerdmans, 2000.

———. *Responses to 101 Questions on the Dead Sea Scrolls*. New York: Paulist Press, 1992.

Flint, P. W., and J. C. VanderKam, eds. *The Dead Sea Scrolls after Fifty Years: A Comprehensive Assessment*. 2 vols. Leiden: Brill, 1998–99.

García Martínez, F. *Qumran and Apocalyptic: Studies on the Aramaic Texts from Qumran*. Studies on the Texts of the Desert of Judah 9. Leiden: Brill, 1992.

LaSor, W. *Amazing Dead Sea Scrolls*. Chicago: Moody Press, 1956. Reprinted as *The Dead Sea Scrolls and the Christian Faith*, Chicago: Moody Press, 1962.

Murphy-O'Connor, J. "Qumran and the New Testament." Pages 55–71 in *The New Testament and Its Modern Interpreters*. Edited by E. J. Epp and G. W. MacRae. Atlanta: Scholars Press, 1989.

Potter, Charles. *The Lost Years of Jesus Revealed*. Greenwich, CT: Fawcett, 1958.

Schiffman, L., and J. C. VanderKam, eds. *Encyclopedia of the Dead Sea Scrolls*. 2 vols. New York: Oxford University Press, 2000.

Shanks, H. "The 'Pierced Messiah' Text—An Interpretation Evaporates." *Biblical Archaeology Review* 18/4 (1992): 80–82.

Silberman, N. A. *The Hidden Scrolls: Christianity, Judaism, and the War for the Dead Sea Scrolls*. New York: Putnam, 1994.

VanderKam. J. C., and P. W. Flint. *The Meaning of the Dead Sea Scrolls*. San Francisco: HarperSanFrancisco, 2002.

Wilson, Edmund. *The Scrolls from the Dead Sea*. New York: Oxford University Press, 1955.

—— 7 ——

The *Chreia*

David B. Gowler

Because Hellenistic culture influenced both Diaspora and Palestinian Judaism to varying extents, the New Testament Gospels cannot be understood in some pristine "Jewish" manner divorced from the wider culture. A careful reading of the Gospels, in fact, makes clear that they are multicultural; they merge biblical patterns with Hellenistic patterns and conventions.

This multicultural context is essential for understanding the words and actions of Jesus as portrayed in the Gospels and, therefore, for the study of the historical Jesus himself. The recognition of the *chreia* form, for example, has significant implications for the study of the New Testament in general and the Synoptic Gospels in particular. In brief, the composition of the stories in the Synoptic Gospels is very similar to such exercises as the expansion and elaboration of *chreiai* found in other ancient literature and delineated in ancient rhetorical handbooks.

Definitions

The best definitions of *chreia* appear within the compositional textbooks that eventually came to be known as *Progymnasmata*. The *Progymnasmata*, or "preliminary exercises," were written for the purpose of instilling the fundamental skills necessary for students to progress into the more complex forms of composing longer speeches and narratives.

The two handbooks most important for the study of the Gospels are the ones by Aelius Theon of Alexandria (middle to late first century CE) and Hermogenes of Tarsus (second century CE). Although the fourth-century CE textbook by Apthonius came to be the standard by which other *Progymnasmata* were judged, it is too late to give us firm information about first-century practices. It does, however, provide valuable information about the *chreia*, when its definition is evaluated in light of the ones given by Theon and Hermogenes:

> A *chreia* is a brief statement or action that is aptly attributed to some person or something analogous to a person (Theon 3–4).

A *chreia* is a remembrance of some saying or action or a manifestation of both that has a concise resolution for the purpose of something useful (Hermogenes 3–4).

A *chreia* is a concise remembrance aptly attributed to some person. Since it is useful, it is called a *chreia* (Apthonius 2–4).

These slightly different definitions reveal four essential elements of a *chreia* (Hock and O'Neil 1986: 23–27). First, the term *remembrance* (or "reminiscence") formally denotes a saying, an action, or a combination of both, an aspect made partially in Theon's definition and more completely in Hermogenes' definition. Second, a *chreia* is brief or concise. There is an economy of words, and the point is made forcefully through a succinct recounting of a person's words and/or deeds. Third, a *chreia* must be "aptly attributed." On one hand, the *chreia* needed to suit the character of the person who spoke or acted it. The correspondence between the point of *chreia* and the person to whom it was attributed was critical. On the other hand, the *chreia* needed to be "well aimed" in the sense that it was appropriate to the situation that it addressed. Fourth, the *chreia* was not used merely as an anecdote. Often, as Hermogenes notes, the words and deeds in a *chreia* reinforce each other to make a specific "useful" point, and Apthonius states that the *chreia* must be "useful." Another quotation from Theon makes this point explicit as well: "It has the name *chreia* because of its excellence, for more than other exercises it is useful in many ways for life" (Theon 25–26). The *chreia* thus was used not only to capture the character and the quick wit of the person who spoke or acted; it also was used (but not always) as an example to hearers/readers for how they should—or should not—act or behave.

Theon also explains how the *chreia* is different from the proverb (*gnōmē*). A proverb is never attributed to a person. Once a proverb is attributed to a person, however, it becomes a *chreia*. A proverb also makes only a general statement, whereas a *chreia* could make either a general or a specific statement. In addition, a proverb almost always concerned something useful in life or had some sort of moral. A *chreia*, on the other hand, sometimes did not. Finally, the proverb is always only a saying, but a *chreia* could be a saying, an action, or a combination of both (Theon 5–18). The difference between the two forms can be seen by comparing the proverb "God helps those who help themselves" with the following *chreia*:

Seeing someone perform rites of purification, [Diogenes] said, "Unhappy person, do you not know that you cannot get rid of errors of conduct by sprinklings any more than you can errors in grammar?" (Diogenes Laertius, *Lives of Eminent Philosophers* 6:42; third century CE)

Implications for the Study of the New Testament and the Historical Jesus

An exploration of *chreiai* in ancient literature, including the exercises and elaborations found in the *Progymnasmata*, gives us significant comparative data that provide insights into how the *chreiai* in the Synoptic Gospels were created, transmitted, and reworked. Versions of *chreiai* in the Synoptics demonstrate the same types of similarities and differences as do those in other ancient literature. The skills learned through these exercises also influence or even determine how *chreiai* are manipulated in literary compositions, such as we find in the Synoptic Gospels. Thus the level of rhetorical composition in the Synoptics is quite similar to the progymnastic tradition of secondary Hellenistic-Roman education.

Progymnasmata were a standard part of the first-century CE educational curriculum, and the exercises found in them represent widespread educational practices from the early first century BCE. The work performed in these texts prepared students to use *chreiai* rhetorically within extended prose composition (Bonner 1977: 250, 276; Hock and O'Neil 2002: 81–83). These exercises took youths one step at a time through the skills required to construct more complex rhetorical compositions. The basic emphasis was to develop students' abilities to say and write the same thing—or variations of the same thing—in different ways. These exercises thus also greatly influenced students' skills of oral argumentation.

The rhetorical handbooks and other *chreia* elaborations in ancient literature demonstrate that speakers/authors were free to vary the wording, details, and dynamics of *chreiai* according to their ideological and rhetorical interests. Speakers/authors were taught and encouraged to make minor and/or major changes to bring clarity and persuasiveness to the point they wanted to make with a *chreia* in specific contexts.

This rhetorical exercise necessarily influenced the Synoptics, although only recently has its impact been acknowledged. Most New Testament scholarship has been dominated by a literary paradigm that focused on the written word. Source criticism, for example, attempted to identify the earliest written materials (e.g., the Q "document") and how Gospel authors incorporated those texts into their Gospels. Form criticism focused on small units of oral tradition, tried to classify them according to literary forms or types (e.g., pronouncement story), and examined the stages of development. Even when scholars gave lip service to the period of "oral tradition," they often implicitly still used a literary paradigm (e.g., an approach that assumed one pristine "original" version of a saying or action of Jesus) when discussing that oral period. Redaction criticism also concentrated on written texts and sources and primarily examined how authors redacted their (written) sources. More recent forms of literary criticism, such as reader-response criticism, also operate within the assumptions of a literary paradigm.

Today, some scholars correctly reject the dominance of the literary paradigm for the study of the Gospels. These scholars investigate how different an "oral culture" is from modern society's focus on the written word. For example, they readily admit that no single, pristine "original form" of a saying ever existed; there were most likely several versions of a tradition from the very beginning. What we have are oral performances in a group setting, and these performances varied according to memory, context, and group interactions.

The critical flaw in all the above approaches, however, is that the Synoptic Gospels were not created/written in a "literary culture" or an "oral culture." The Synoptic Gospels were instead created in a *rhetorical* environment where oral and written speech interacted closely with one another. In the type of environment evidenced by the *Progymnasmata*, for example, writing/speaking and rewriting/retelling *chreiai* were preparatory exercises for adapting a unit for a larger rhetorical/literary persuasive setting. The written exercises within the *Progymnasmata*, therefore, also greatly influenced the oral skills of argumentation, since students were required to express them orally as well (cf. Robbins 1991; Bonner 1977: 250–76). This interaction of oral and written speech characterizes the type of rhetorical composition we see in the Synoptic Gospels in particular.

More conservative interpreters defend the basic authenticity of the traditions of/about Jesus by focusing on the "reliable" transmission of oral traditions. Some note that the words and deeds of Jesus must have had a significant impact and made a lasting memory on those first followers of Jesus who formed the nucleus of the post-Easter movement. Some even claim that the tradition reached a fairly fixed form during Jesus' public activity in Galilee. These interpreters also argue that the "accuracy" of those traditions as they were being remembered, interpreted, and transmitted would have been guaranteed by eyewitnesses.

A study of *chreiai*, the *Progymnasmata*, and the Gospels, however, belies these claims. The Gospels give decisive evidence that they were created using the basic rhetorical exercises of the *Progymnasmata*, such as the techniques for expanding or condensing *chreiai*. The issue is not whether some sort of "corporate memory" was there to impose standards of accuracy on oral traditions that varied from the very beginning. The critical issue is that changes in the tradition by the Gospel authors were *deliberate*, and that such changes were standard rhetorical exercises used to teach students how to read/write/speak Greek. This standard rhetorical practice meant that changes could be slight or substantial. The type and amount of expansion, elaboration, or other changes in the *chreiai* found in the Synoptics are generated by the author's rhetorical interests and perspective.

By demonstrating the importance of the *chreia* for a study of the Synoptics, I am not arguing that complex "formal" rhetoric was used to create them. The preliminary rhetorical exercises found in the *Progymnasmata* represent widespread educational practice, and examples of these exercises permeate the Synoptics. A focus on the *chreia* also demonstrates that "rhetoric" is not merely stylistic; it is social discourse and encompasses societal formation, and therefore interpreters should focus also on the social and cultural contexts of the speaker/writer and audience, not just on the elaboration or expansion of *chreiai*. Explorations of *chreiai* move beyond focusing on either the sayings *or* deeds of Jesus. They lead into a productive examination of the dialogic interaction of the words and deeds in the *chreia*, and interdisciplinary investigations of the impact of those *chreiai* (cf. Gowler 1993; 2003).

Types of *Chreiai*

Theon categorizes three main types of *chreiai*: sayings-*chreiai*, action-*chreiai*, and mixed-*chreiai*. Sayings-*chreiai* make their primary point in words, not action: for example, Diogenes the philosopher, on being asked by someone how he could become famous, responded: "By worrying as little as possible about fame" (Theon 31–35). To this we might compare Luke 21:1–4, "[Jesus] looked up and saw rich people putting their gifts into the treasury; he also saw a poor widow put in two small copper coins. He said, 'Truly I tell you, this poor widow has put in more than all of them; for all of them have contributed out of their abundance, but she out of her poverty has put in all she had to live on.'"

Sayings can be further categorized, because the saying could either be an unprompted statement or a reaction to a specific situation. An example of an unprompted saying-*chreia* from Theon (39–40) is: "Isocrates the sophist used to say that gifted students are children of the Gods." Similarly, Matthew 6:19–20 reads: "[Jesus began to speak and taught them, saying,] 'Do not store up for yourselves treasures on earth, where moth and rust consume and where thieves break in and steal; but store up for yourselves treasures in heaven, where neither moth nor rust consumes and where thieves do not break in and steal.'"

The other type of sayings-*chreiai* includes a response to a specific circumstance, often taking the form of a response to a question or as a witty riposte to a specific situation: "When someone praised an orator for his ability in making much of small matters, Agesilaus said that a shoemaker is not a good craftsman who puts big shoes on small feet" (Plutarch, *Moralia*, III:208C; 100–125 CE). The same form appears in the *Gospel of Thomas* (100): "They showed Jesus a gold coin and said to him, 'Caesar's people demand taxes from us.' He said to them, 'Give Caesar the things that are Caesar's, give God the things that are God's, and give me what is mine.'"

Action-*chreiai*, on the other hand, reveal some thought or message through an action unaccompanied by a saying: "Crates, when he saw an uneducated youth, struck his teacher" (Greek: *pedagogue*; Quintillian 26–27; first century CE). Theon (100–102) offers the following example: "Diogenes the Cynic philosopher, on seeing a boy who was a gourmand, struck the teacher with his staff"; Hermogenes (10–11) gives the variant: "Diogenes, on seeing a youth misbehaving, beat the teacher." From the *Infancy Gospel of Thomas* (2:1), we find another action-*chreia*: "When this boy Jesus was five years old he was playing at the ford of a brook, and he gathered together into pools the water that flowed by, and made it at once clean, and commanded it by his word alone."

Finally, the third type of *chreia*, the mixed-*chreia*, shares characteristics of both the saying-*chreia* and the action-*chreia*. Some differences in formulation occur in the *Progymnasmata*. Theon argues that the primary point of the mixed-*chreia* is made through the action, and he gives the following example: "Pythagoras the philosopher, on being asked how long human life is, went up to his bedroom and peeked in for a short time, showing thereby its brevity" (Theon 111–13). Mark 1:29–31 presents the same form: "As soon as they left the synagogue, they entered the house of Simon and Andrew, with James and John. Now Simon's mother-in-law was in bed with a fever, and they told [Jesus] about her at once. He came and took her by the hand and lifted her up. Then the fever left her, and she began to serve them."

The problem with the focus on action, however, means that sometimes the point of the *chreia* can be unclear. Note how Theon's example above has to include an explanatory elaboration about life's brevity. In contrast to Theon, Hermogenes correctly recognizes that the focus of the mixed *chreia* could also be made (more clearly) through the final comment or riposte. This focus allows a final comment by the main character in the *chreia* to elucidate the main point. For example, "One day [Diogenes] shouted out for men, and when people gathered, hit out at them with his stick, saying, 'I called for men, not scoundrels'" (Diogenes Laertius, *Lives of Eminent Philosophers* 6:32; third century CE). Another example would be: "Diogenes, on seeing a youth misbehaving, beat the teacher and said, 'Why were you teaching such things?'" (Hermogenes 6:13–15; second century CE).

John 2:14–16 offers a focus on action with the final comment by the main character elucidating the point: "In the temple [Jesus] found people selling cattle, sheep, and doves, and the money changers seated at their tables. Making a whip out of cords, he drove all of them out of the temple, both the sheep and the cattle. He also poured out the coins of the money changers and overturned their tables. He told those who were selling doves, 'Take these things out of here! Stop making my Father's house a marketplace!'"

These *chreiai* were more than anecdotes or reminiscences. In the ancient world, people's actions and words were seen as revelatory of their innate character. From at least the fifth century BCE, *chreiai* and collections of *chreiai* thus served a fundamental biographical function. Ancient biographies drew upon such collections of *chreiai*, and this practice was not limited to Hellenistic-Roman literature. For example, the first-century CE Jewish text *Lives of the Prophets* incorporates many *chreiai* in its twenty-three thumbnail sketches of Israelite prophets (Aune 34–35, 41):

> [When Jonah] had been cast forth by the sea monster and had gone away to Nineveh and had returned, he did not remain in his district, but taking his mother along he sojourned in Sour, a territory (inhabited by) foreign nations; for he said, "So shall I remove my reproach, for I spoke falsely in prophesying against the great city of Nineveh" (*Lives of the Prophets* 10:2–4).

It is not surprising, then, to discover that the early Christian authors utilize *chreiai* in their compositions in a similar way—to display the character (*ēthos*) of Jesus, and, to a lesser extent, that of his followers and opponents. We can clearly see this and other similarities by comparing the Gospels to other ancient works and noting how they follow the exercises within the *Progymnasmata*. We also have external evidence such as comments from other Christian authors. One example is the following quotation from Eusebius (late third/early fourth century), who quotes Papias (second century), who quotes the "Presbyter" (perhaps the presbyter John, who was mentioned in the verse just previous to this selection):

> Mark, who was the interpreter of Peter, wrote down accurately, though not in order, what he remembered of the things said or done by the Lord. For he had not heard the Lord or followed him, but afterward, as I said, he had followed Peter, who formulated his teaching in the form of *chreiai*, but not as a finished composition of the Lord's sayings, so that Mark made no error when he wrote things down individually as he remembered them. (Eusebius, *Church History* III.39.15)

The *Chreia*: Classroom Exercises

In antiquity, education took place at three levels or stages: primary/elementary, secondary, and higher/tertiary. *Chreiai* were used for instruction at all three levels. At the primary level, students learned their letters and progressed on to read proverbs, *chreiai*, and Homer. *Chreiai* at this level were used to teach reading of short passages, and students also practiced writing and copying them. The *chreiai* at this primary level were often quite simple, such as this one found on a second-century CE ostracon discovered in Elephantine, Egypt: "Euripides, the writer of tragedies, said: 'Chance, not good counsel, directs human affairs'" (Hock and O'Neil 2002: 3–4, 37).

After students learned basic reading, writing, and arithmetic skills, they moved to the secondary level to learn grammar and to read and interpret longer literary works. Finally, on the tertiary level, students engaged in specialized study of either philosophy or rhetoric. The *Progymnasmata* and their "pre-rhetorical compositions" came into play primarily at the secondary level: students began their study with shorter, simpler compositions in order to learn the rudiments of rhetorical argumentation and style. They then worked progressively through stages of composition to reading/speaking/writing longer and more complex compositions (Hock and O'Neil 2002: 81–83).

A brief look at the exercises offered by Theon and Hermogenes demonstrates the types of work that students performed. The approaches of these two textbooks toward *chreia* exercises in some ways differ significantly. Theon has eight different exercises, each of which builds upon the other, so that students can continually increase their dexterity and improve their general compositional skills (Hock and O'Neil 1986: 35). Examples of almost all types of these exercises are found in the Gospels' manipulation of *chreiai* about Jesus.

1. *Recitation*—Reciting or reporting the *chreia* very clearly in very similar words.
2. *Inflection*—The inflecting or declining of a *chreia* throughout the singular, plural, and dual numbers, as well as through the five cases: nominative, genitive, dative, accusative, and vocative.

3. *Commentary*—Commenting on a *chreia* as to whether it is true, noble, advantageous, or has appealed to people of distinction.

4. *Objection*—Objecting to a *chreia* that has qualities opposite of those listed in number 3 above.

5. *Expansion*—Expanding a *chreia* by reciting or writing it at greater length and enlarging on the questions and responses expressed in it.

6. *Condensation*—Condensing a *chreia* by making an expanded version more concise.

7. *Refutation*—Refuting a *chreia* on the basis that it is obscure, pleonastic, elliptical, impossible, implausible, false, unsuitable, useless, or shameful.

8. *Confirmation*—Confirming a *chreia* with a short essay, including an introduction, narration, arguments and elaboration, digressions, and character delineation, where there are opportunities for them. (Theon 190–400)

Hermogenes does not offer separate exercises; instead he presents an integrated approach of one "exercise" in a sequential order of argumentation, and he creates a process by which students learn to construct a persuasive argument. This process includes eight different types of *chreia* elaborations as the focus of the exercises, and all eight types of these elaborations are found in the Synoptics.

Hermogenes illustrates these eight elaborations by starting with the following concise *chreia* about Isocrates—"Isocrates said that education's root is bitter, its fruit is sweet"—and then giving descriptions and examples of those elaborations (*ergasia*):

1. *Praise*—Students present the subject. Theon begins with: "Isocrates was wise," which establishes his virtue, authority, and reason for heeding the advice given in the *chreia*.

2. *Paraphrase*—Students amplify the *chreia* by embellishing or amplifying it.

3. *Rationale*—Students explain the *chreia*: "For the most important affairs generally succeed because of hard work, and once they have succeeded, they bring pleasure." The heart of the student's argument is found in the *chreia* and its rationale.

4. *Statement to the contrary*—Students buttress the argument with arguments from the "opposite." In this case, the "root is bitter but its fruit is sweet" *chreia* is elaborated with: "For ordinary affairs do not need hard work, and they have an outcome that is totally without pleasure, but serious affairs have the opposite outcome."

5. *Analogy*—Students offer an analogous situation to put forward their arguments: "For just as it is the lot of farmers to reap their fruits who work with the soil, so also is it for those who work with words."

6. *Example*—Students give a concrete example for the truth of the *chreia*: "Demosthenes, after locking himself in a room and working a long time, later reaped the rewards: wreaths and public acclamations" (Demosthenes was famous for both his work ethic and his resulting successes).

7. *Citation of an authority*—Students back up their case with a concurring judgment from an authoritative figure: "For example, Hesiod said, 'In front of virtue, gods ordained sweat.' Another poet says, 'At the price of hard work do the gods sell every good to us.'"

8. *Exhortation*—Students conclude with an exhortation that encourages others to heed the advice given by the main actor and/or speaker in the *chreia*. (Hermogenes 30–64)

CHREIAI AND THEIR ELABORATION IN THE SYNOPTIC GOSPELS

A version of Tertullian's classic complaint—"What does Athens have to do with Jerusalem?"—is often the initial response of New Testament scholars when discussing the composition of the Synoptic Gospels. When we look carefully, however, we discover that the rhetorical composition of the Synoptics is extremely close to the *progymnastic* exercises and composition in secondary Hellenistic-Roman education.

A straightforward way to discover these similarities is simply to catalog the persuasive strategies in various Synoptic pericopae. Two examples will suffice (cf. Robbins 1988: 20–21):

LUKE 6:1–5

1. *Chreia* setting (6:1–2)
One Sabbath while Jesus was going through the grainfields, his disciples plucked some heads of grain, rubbed them in their hands, and ate them. But some of the Pharisees said, "Why are you doing what is not lawful on the Sabbath?"
2. Example (6:3–4)
Jesus answered, "Have you not read what David did when he and his companions were hungry? He entered the house of God and took and ate the bread of the Presence, which it is not lawful for any but the priests to eat, and gave some to his companions?"
3. Rationale (6:5)
Then he said to them, "The Son of Man is lord of the Sabbath."

Luke's unexpanded chreia has a simple example and rationale. Matthew's version, however, demonstrates significant elaboration in the forms that Hermogenes delineates in his textbook. Almost all the elements in Hermogenes' sequence of argumentation are found:

MATTHEW 12:1–8

1. *Chreia* setting (12:1–2)
At that time Jesus went through the grainfields on the Sabbath; his disciples were hungry, and they began to pluck heads of grain and to eat. When the

Pharisees saw it, they said to him, "Look, your disciples are doing what is not lawful to do on the Sabbath."

2. Example (12:3–4)

He said to them, "Have you not read what David did when he and his companions were hungry? He entered the house of God and ate the bread of the Presence, which it was not lawful for him or his companions to eat, but only for the priests."

3. Analogy (12:5)

"Or have you not read in the law that on the Sabbath the priests in the temple break the Sabbath and yet are guiltless?"

4. Comparison (12:6)

"I tell you, something greater than the temple is here."

5. Statement to the contrary and citation of authority (12:7)

"But if you had known what this means, 'I desire mercy and not sacrifice,' you would not have condemned the guiltless."

6. Rationale (12:8)

"For the Son of Man is lord of the Sabbath."

The exercises in the *Progymnasmata* gave students the facility to vary the content and phrasing of *chreiai*, because authors/speakers were not constrained to a rigid recitation. The freedom to change, adapt, and expand were vital aspects of one's educational abilities, rhetorical interests, ideological point of view, and ability to persuade hearers/readers.

Sometimes the changes in a *chreia* in different settings were minimal. Theon's first exercise, *recitation*, involved reciting the *chreia* very clearly in very similar words. An example of such recitation appears in Plutarch's three versions of Lysander's words and actions during a dispute over territorial boundaries (Robbins 1991).

Plutarch, Lysander 22.1	Plutarch, Moralia 190E	Plutarch, Moralia 229C
For instance, when the Argives were arguing	To the Argives when they seemed to state a better case than the Spartans	To the Argives, who were disputing with the Spartans
about boundaries of land,	about the disputed territory,	about boundaries
and thought they stated a better case than the Spartans,		and said they stated the better case than them,
[Lysander] pointed to his sword,	[Lysander] drew his sword,	[Lysander] drew his sword
and said, "He who is master of this discourses best about boundaries of land."	and said, "He who is master of this discourses best about boundaries of land."	and said, "He who is master of this discourses best about boundaries of land."

Compare the similarities and differences in those three versions of the *chreia*—all by the same author—with the three Synoptic versions of Jesus' authority being challenged in the temple. These versions also demonstrate "recitation" of a *chreia*.

Matthew 21:23–27	*Mark 11:27–33*	*Luke 20:1–8*
When he entered the temple,	Again they came to Jerusalem. As he was walking in the temple,	One day, as he was teaching the people in the temple and telling the good news,
the chief priests and the elders of the people came to him as he was teaching, and said, "By what authority are you doing these things, and who gave you this authority?" Jesus said to them, "I will also ask you one question; if you tell me the answer, then I will also tell you by what authority I do these things. Did the baptism of John come from heaven, or was it of human origin?" And they argued with one another, "If we say 'From heaven,' he will say to us, 'Why then did you not believe him?' But if we say, 'From human origin,' we are afraid of the crowd; for all regard John as a prophet." So they answered Jesus, "We do not know." And he said to them, "Neither will I tell you by what authority I am doing these things."	the chief priests, the scribes, and the elders came to him and said, "By what authority are you doing these things? Who gave you this authority to do them?" Jesus said to them, "I will ask you one question; answer me, and I will tell you by what authority I do these things. Did the baptism of John come from heaven, or was it of human origin? Answer me." They argued with one another, "If we say, 'From heaven,' he will say, 'Why then did you not believe him?' But shall we say, 'Of human origin'?"—they were afraid of the crowd, for all regarded John as truly a prophet. So they answered Jesus, "We do not know." And Jesus said to them, "Neither will I tell you by what authority I am doing these things."	the chief priests and the scribes came with the elders and said to him, "Tell us, by what authority are you doing these things? Who is it who gave you this authority?" He answered them, "I will also ask you a question, and you tell me: Did the baptism of John come from heaven, or was it of human origin?" They discussed it with one another, saying, "If we say, 'From heaven,' he will say, 'Why did you not believe him?' But if we say, 'Of human origin,' all the people will stone us; for they are convinced that John was a prophet." So they answered that they did not know where it came from. Then Jesus said to them, "Neither will I tell you by what authority I am doing these things."

Although the subjects are vastly different, the mode of (slight) variations among the three versions of the Lysander *chreia* is very similar to the type of variations found in the *chreia* of Jesus in the temple. These similarities in patterns multiply as we work through other *chreiai* in the Synoptics. Recitation of a *chreia* combines variations with significant verbatim repetitions, both of which are subject to the speaker/author's rhetorical inclinations. In recitation composition, the variations among versions of the *chreia* are primarily (1) variations in wording or (2) adding or omitting details (e.g., Luke's addition of "telling of good news" in 20:1).

This freedom to be flexible sometimes extends to the same author utilizing the same basic *chreia* to illustrate the character of a different person.

Again, when a corrupt and extravagant man was expatiating in the senate on frugality and self-restraint, Amnaeus sprang to his feet and said: "Who can endure it, my man, when you sup like Lucullus, build like Crassus, and yet harangue us like Cato?" (Plutarch, *Cato the Younger* 19.5; 100–125 CE)

Once when a youthful senator had delivered a tedious and lengthy discourse, all out of season, on frugality and temperance, Cato rose and said: "Stop there! You get wealth like Crassus, you live like Lucullus, but you talk like Cato" (Plutarch, *Lucullus* 40.3; 100–125 CE).

Recitation of a *chreia* in very similar language is one of the more basic exercises in the *Progymnasmata*. Once students became proficient in these foundational exercises, such as the recitation or declension/inflection of *chreiai*, they moved on to more complex exercises: expansion, condensation, refutation, and confirmation of *chreiai*.

Theon, for example, offers a "concise" *chreia* and then gives a possible expansion, one that primarily offers an explanation of the concise version:

Epameinondas, as he was dying childless, said to his friends: "I have left two daughters—the victory at Leuctra and the one at Mantineia." (314–17)

Epameinondas the Theban general was, of course, a good man in time of peace, and when war against the Lacedaemonians came to his country, he displayed many outstanding deeds of great courage. As a Boeotarch at Leuctra, he triumphed over the enemy, and while campaigning and fighting for his country, he died at Mantineia. While he was dying of his wounds and his friends were lamenting, among other things, that he was dying childless, he smiled and said, "Stop weeping, friends, for I have left you two immortal daughters: two victories of our country over the Lacedaemonians, the one at Leuctra, who is the older, and the younger, who is just now being born at Mantineia." (318–33)

These more complex variations of *progymnastic* exercises can not only reflect the speakers/authors' rhetorical interests but also begin to demonstrate their ideological and persuasive interests. For example, Seneca offers the following *chreia* about Diogenes and his slave Manes:

Diogenes's only slave ran away, but he did not even think it worthwhile to take him back home when he was pointed out to him. Rather, he said: "It is a disgrace if Manes can live without Diogenes, but Diogenes cannot live without Manes." (Seneca; Hock and O'Neill 1986: 39; first century CE)

Diogenes Laertius recites this *chreia* in a slightly different way:

Diogenes said to those who were advising him to look for his runaway slave: "It is ridiculous if Manes is living without Diogenes, but Diogenes will not be able to live without Manes." (Diogenes Laertius; Hock and O'Neill 1986: 39)

The recitation by Diogenes Laertius shows some variations from Seneca's *chreia* (e.g., in Seneca's version, Manes is pointed out, whereas in Diogenes Laertius, Diogenes refuses even to look). These minor differences exhibit only variations in recitation. The following version of this *chreia* offered by Aelian, however, is significantly different:

When Diogenes left his homeland, one of his household slaves, Manes by name, tried to follow him, but could not endure his manner of life and so ran away. When some people advised Diogenes to seek after him, he said, "Is it not shameful that Manes has no need of Diogenes, but that Diogenes should have of Manes?" Now this slave was caught at Delphi and torn to pieces by dogs—a just punishment, in light of his master's name, for having run away. (Aelian; Hock and O'Neill 1986: 39; ca. 220 CE)

Aelian's version of the *chreia* still reflects the main point, the Cynic's independence from the alleged "necessities" of life as envisioned by society, but his version is a significant expansion that includes even a final judgment about the appropriateness of Manes's punishment. Since Diogenes the *Cynic* (*kynikos*) means that Diogenes is "doglike" in his behavior, it is fitting that Manes was torn to pieces by dogs.

The Synoptic authors also expanded or condensed *chreiai*, depending on their perceived rhetorical/ideological needs. The "cleansing" of the Temple shows such significant differences (as does John's version). The first column below shows the *chreia* in its most condensed form (Luke's version). Mark's version in the center is a moderately expanded version of the *chreia*. Matthew's version, however, is significantly expanded:

Luke 19:45–46	*Mark 11:15–17*	*Matthew 21:12–16*
Then he entered the temple and began to drive out those who were selling things there, and he said, "It is written, 'My house shall be a house of prayer'; but you have made it a den of robbers."	Then they came to Jerusalem. And he entered the temple and began to drive out those who were selling and those who were buying in the temple, and he overturned the tables of the money changers and the seats of those who sold doves; and he would not allow anyone to carry anything through the temple. He was teaching and saying, "Is it not	Then Jesus entered the temple and drove out all who were selling and buying in the temple, and he overturned the tables of the money changers and the seats of those who sold doves. He said to them, "It is written, 'My house shall be called a house of prayer'; but you are making it a den of robbers." The blind and the lame came to him in the temple, and he

Luke 19:45–46	Mark 11:15–17	Matthew 21:12–16
	written, 'My house shall be called a house of prayer for all the nations'? But you have made it a den of robbers."	cured them. But when the chief priests and the scribes saw the amazing things that he did, and heard the children crying out in the temple, "Hosanna to the Son of David," they became angry and said to him, "Do you hear what these are saying?" Jesus said to them, "Yes; have you never read, 'Out of the mouth of infants and nursing babies you have prepared praise for yourself'?"

The various exercises that students completed on *chreiai* resulted in a great variety in versions of the stories, even when the versions were created by the same speaker/author. Plutarch's three versions of Alexander's refusal to run in the Olympic footrace is a prime example:

Plutarch, Moralia 179D	Plutarch, Alexander 4.10	Plutarch, Moralia 331B
Being nimble and swiftfooted,	In contrast,	Since he was the swiftest of foot of the young men of his age,
when he was appealed to	when those around him inquired whether he would be willing	and his comrades urged him to enter
by his father to run at the Olympic footrace,	to compete in the Olympic footrace, for he was swiftfooted,	at Olympia,
he said: "Indeed, if I were to have kings as competitors."	he said: "Indeed, if I were to have kings as competitors."	he asked if kings were competing. And when they replied in the negative, he said that the contest was unfair in which victory would be over commoners, but a defeat would be the defeat of a king.

As Vernon Robbins notes (1991: 155–60), the greater degree of variations in this *chreia* is similar to many versions of *chreiai* in the Synoptic Gospels. In all three of Plutarch's versions, Alexander responds that he would run if he had kings for competitors. The first version portrays Alexander's father (Philip II) making the request that Alexander run the race. In the verse just previous to this *chreia*, Plutarch reported all of Philip's successes. In this context, Alexander's response indicates that he will not be distracted by exploits that are less prestigious than his father's and suggests an implicit competition between Alexander and his father.

The second version, found in *Life of Alexander* 4:10, has "those around" Alexander inquiring whether he would compete. This version contains significantly different words, although Alexander's final riposte includes the same words (albeit with two of the Greek words interposed). Despite this (almost) verbatim agreement, the import and rhetorical effect of the second version is quite different. The thrust of the passage is that this footrace is an opportunity for Alexander to display his excellence, his fleetness of foot. This story is not about Alexander's competition with his father or resentment at his father's successes that may diminish his own later ones. Instead, it is meant to demonstrate Alexander's "self-restraint and maturity," because, unlike his father, Alexander did not court "every kind of fame from every source . . . as Philip did" (*Life of Alexander* 4:9). So, by beginning the *chreia* in 4:10 with "in contrast," Plutarch distinguishes Alexander's actions in 4:10 with Philip's actions in 4:9. Plutarch thus manipulates the *chreia* to make a significantly different point in this version than in the first: Alexander did not flaunt his successes, unlike his father.

The third version is also significantly different (*Moralia* 331B). Only here does Plutarch inform us that Alexander was not just swiftfooted; he was the "swiftest of foot of the young men of his age." Alexander converses with his "comrades," and Plutarch further expands the *chreia*: Alexander asks his friends if kings are competing. An additional unique element of this version is that Alexander gives a closing rationale for his refusal to run. This rationale, in fact, implies that Alexander already considers himself a king: "a defeat would be the defeat of a king." Alexander's reasoning involves the fairness or injustice of a race between "commoners" and a king. A king, in other words, must protect his honor.

As Robbins also points out, a similar process of elaboration, albeit by different authors, is found in the Synoptic accounts of the woman who touched Jesus' cloak. There obviously is some sort of dependence among the three versions, but their significant differences indicate different rhetorical interests. Matthew's version of the *chreia* is its most concise form. Mark expands the *chreia* to include a discussion with his disciples, Jesus' perceiving that healing power had gone forth from him, and a concluding statement by Jesus to the woman to "go in peace." Unlike Matthew's version, however, the statement by Jesus does not produce the miracle; the fact that the woman touched him (in faith) produces the miracle. In Luke's version, the woman does not speak, although Peter does, in contrast to "his disciples" in Mark (Robbins 1987: 502–15; 1991: 160–67):

Matthew 9:20–22	Mark 5:25–34	Luke 8:43–48
Then suddenly a woman who had been suffering from hemorrhages for twelve years	Now there was a woman who had been suffering from hemorrhages for twelve years. She had endured much under many physicians, and had spent all that she had; and she was no better, but rather grew worse. She had heard about Jesus,	Now there was a woman who had been suffering from hemorrhages for twelve years; [and though she had spent all she had on physicians] no one could cure her.
came up behind him	and came up behind him in the crowd	She came up behind him,
and touched the fringe of his cloak, for she said to herself, "If I only touch his cloak, I will be made well."	and touched his cloak, for she said, "If I but touch his clothes, I will be made well."	and touched the fringe of his clothes,
	Immediately her hemorrhage stopped; and she felt in her body that she was healed of her disease. Immediately aware that power had gone forth from him,	and immediately her hemorrhage stopped.
Jesus turned	Jesus turned about in the crowd and said, "Who touched my clothes?" And his disciples said to him, "You see the crowd pressing in on you; how can you say, 'Who touched me?'" He looked all around to see who had done it. But	Then Jesus asked "Who touched me?" When all denied it, Peter said, "Master, the crowds surround you and press in on you!" But Jesus said, "Someone touched me; for I noticed that power had gone out from me." When the woman
and seeing her	the woman, knowing what had happened to her, came in fear and trembling, fell down before him, and told him the whole truth.	saw that she could not remain hidden, she came trembling; and falling down before him, she declared in the presence of all the people why she had touched him, and how she had been immediately healed.

Matthew 9:20–22	*Mark 5:25–34*	*Luke 8:43–48*
he said, "Take heart, daughter; your faith has made you well."	He said to her, "Daughter, your faith has made you well; go in peace,	He said to her, "Daughter, your faith has made you well; go in peace."
And instantly the woman was made well.	and be healed of your disease."	

Bibliography

Aune, David E. *The New Testament in Its Literary Environment.* Philadelphia: Westminster John Knox, 1987.

Bonner, Stanley F. *Education in Ancient Rome: From the Elder Cato to the Younger Pliny.* Berkeley: University of California Press, 1977.

Gowler, David B. "Hospitality and Characterization in Luke 11:37–54: A Socio-narratological Approach." *Semeia* 64 (1993): 213–51.

———. "Text, Culture, and Ideology in Luke 7:1–10: A Dialogic Reading." Pages 89–125 in *Fabrics of Discourse: Culture, Ideology, and Religion.* Harrisburg, PA: Trinity Press International, 2003.

Hock, Ronald F., and Edward N. O'Neill. *The Chreia and Ancient Rhetoric: Classroom Exercises.* Leiden: Brill, 2002.

———. *The Chreia in Ancient Rhetoric: The Progymnasmata.* Atlanta: Scholars Press, 1986.

Mack, Burton L. *Anecdotes and Arguments: The Chreia in Antiquity and Early Christianity.* Claremont, CA: Institute for Antiquity and Christianity, 1987.

Mack, Burton L., and Vernon K. Robbins. *Patterns of Persuasion in the Gospels.* Sonoma, CA: Polebridge Press, 1989.

Porter, Stanley F., ed. *Handbook of Classical Rhetoric in the Hellenistic Period, 330 BC–AD 400.* Leiden: Brill, 1997.

Robbins, Vernon K. *Ancient Quotes and Anecdotes: From Crib to Crypt.* Sonoma, CA: Polebridge Press, 1989.

———. "The Chreia." Pages 1–23 in *Greco-Roman Literature and the New Testament.* Edited by David E. Aune. Atlanta: Scholars Press, 1988.

———. "The Woman Who Touched Jesus' Garment: Socio-rhetorical Analysis of the Synoptic Accounts." *New Testament Studies* 33 (1987): 502–15.

———. "Writing as a Rhetorical Act in Plutarch and the Gospels." Pages 157–86 in *Persuasive Artistry: Studies in New Testament Rhetoric in Honor of George A. Kennedy.* Edited by Duane F. Watson. Sheffield: JSOT, 1991.

8

The Galilean Charismatic and Rabbinic Piety:

The Holy Man in the Talmudic Literature

Alan J. Avery-Peck

Israelite religion from its beginnings recognized the existence and power of charismatic miracle workers and faith healers. In scripture, the power to heal and to affect natural phenomena primarily was associated with the priesthood and prophets who magically restored life (e.g., the story of Elisha and the son of the Shunammite women [2 Kings 4:19–37]) or prescribed other effective means of healing (e.g., bathing in the Jordan, proposed by Elisha to cure Naaman from leprosy [2 Kings 5], or the fig plaster used by Isaiah to restore health to Hezekiah [Isaiah 38:21]).

By late antiquity, Jewish sources reveal a fully articulated theory both of disease and of its cure alongside a broader perspective on the ability of holy men to manipulate the invisible forces at work throughout the human world. As Geza Vermes describes in *Jesus the Jew*, by the first centuries, Jews imagined a world populated by a vast array of demons that were responsible for evil and illness. These demons were overcome, and humans were healed of disease or spared other evils, through the intervention of charismatic miracle workers and faith healers, whose distinctive piety and closeness to God empowered them to defeat the forces of evil, whether through exorcism, prayer, or other ritual or magical methods. Vermes describes these individuals, frequently depicted as born or active in Galilee, and their power in the same terms he understands the special gifts of Jesus, "a man whose supernatural abilities derived, not from secret powers, but from immediate contact with God, [which] prove[d] him to be a genuine charismatic, the true heir of an age-old prophetic religious line" (69).

Strikingly, the Rabbinic Judaism that emerges in the first centuries CE largely rejects the model of prophet and charismatic leader prominent in Judaic writings from scripture through the literature of Qumran, the Apocrypha/Deuterocanonical literature, and Hellenistic authors such as Josephus. Rather than on models of a personal piety that might provide an individual with special access to God and God's blessings, the Rabbis focus on the activities of the schoolhouse, seeing in the intellectual pursuit of the true meaning of the Torah the key to reinvigorating Judaism in the face of the loss of the sacrificial cult, which ended with the destruction of the Jerusalem Temple in 70 CE. This meant downplaying, or completely rejecting, other images of how one might know God. In line with this, the Rabbis were clear, for instance, that the age of prophecy, and so of direct revelation from God, had ended. All knowledge of God and God's will would now come as a result of the Rabbis' own study of the legacy of the Sinai revelation, the written and oral Torahs.

Rabbinic Judaism thus depicted the holy man as an individual skilled in the manipulation of the law. This is an image quite different from that which had existed in Judaism up to the Rabbis' day. This shift away from the ideal of the charismatic prophet, miracle worker, or healer with a special status in the eyes of God reflects the Rabbis' distinctive understanding of the history of the Jewish people in their own day. The destruction of the Temple in 70 CE and the failed revolt under Simeon bar Kokhba in 133–35 CE had resulted from an overtly messianic ideology, in which prophets and charismatics asserted that, if the people of Israel rose up in rebellion against Rome, God would be compelled to fight on behalf of his beleaguered nation. Charismatic leaders, especially the pseudo-messiah Bar Kokhba, had led the nation into terrible danger and, in so doing, had significantly worsened the community's political, economic, and ritual circumstance. The Rabbis—with their notion that the age of prophecy had ended—proposed an entirely different model of leadership, one that rejected the charismatic holy man as a model of community leadership.

But despite this overall perspective, which focused on the intellectual activities of the study house rather than on miracles done in the streets, Rabbinic literature of the first centuries neither ignores nor maligns charismatic holy men. Such individuals clearly had a significant place within Jewish life in the first centuries and so find a place within the Rabbinic texts that emerged from that period. For our purposes, however, the important point is to recognize the ways in which the Rabbis subsume these individuals within the Rabbis' own system of Judaic belief. Even as the Rabbis depict the special powers that derive from charismatic holy men's distinctive status before God, they also show these individuals to have essentially the same defining trait as the greatest Rabbis: knowledge of the proper interpretation of Torah. In the Rabbinic literature, this is to say, the principal charismatic holy men of the first centuries are, first and foremost, Rabbis, that is, expert teachers and practitioners of the Rabbinic reading of the law. Similarly, even as these texts depict the miracles worked by these holy men, they portray the Rabbis' ambivalent attitude toward such miracles and toward those who work them. The Rabbis thus make the powerful point that, even as they count charismatic holy men among their numbers, the distinctively Rabbinic method of bringing God's blessings upon the community, the accurate delineation and practice of the law, is the preferred path for the nation as a whole.

In the following, we examine Rabbinic traditions concerning two charismatic healers and miracle workers, the first-century BCE Honi the Circle-Drawer and the first-century CE Hanina ben Dosa ("ben" means "son of," so that, as is the norm throughout the Rabbinic literature, Hanina is referred to by his own name and that of his father; in the following "ben" is abbreviated "b."). Both Honi and Hanina are recalled for their special piety and for the miracles this piety allows them to perform: healing the sick, successfully praying for rain, and the like. In light of their closeness to God and the miracles they can bring about, both are viewed as exemplary models of holiness and piety. And yet, in neither case is the Rabbinic literature unequivocally positive in its attitudes toward these figures' use of their power to induce God to act on their behalf.

Before we turn to the stories themselves, let us understand the specific documents in which they appear: the Mishnah, Tosefta, and Babylonian Talmud. The Mishnah was redacted in the early third century CE but contains material that dates over the preceding three hundred years. It records disputes among Rabbinic authorities over matters of ritual, civil, and criminal law. Only in a few cases, the stories of Honi the Circle-Drawer and Hanina b. Dosa among them, are anecdotal tales regarding the lives and actions of specific Rabbis reported. Rather, the Mishnah primarily presents short legal statements, sometimes anonymously and sometimes attributed to named authorities. It generally does not provide supporting details indicating the foundation of any statement of law, whether that foundation is scripture, traditional practice, a logical assessment of the law as a whole, or simply the stature of the one who states it. Personality or individual charisma or piety thus does not generally validate the laws in the Mishnah. Where stories of individuals occur, rather, they generally are used to illustrate the application of a specific law or legal principle.

Completed approximately one generation after the Mishnah, in the fourth century, the Tosefta, like the Mishnah, contains materials that may go back hundreds of years to the inception of Rabbinism. Overall, the Tosefta's legal statements amplify the Mishnah's topics and laws, which the Tosefta cites and glosses with additional rules. Using the Mishnah's same literary conventions and quoting its same authorities, the Tosefta depends on the Mishnah for its rhetoric and topical program. Like the Mishnah, it typically does not focus on traits of personality. When it does, the stories generally illustrate points of Rabbinic law rather than indicate how, by virtue of his charismatic personality or status before God, any particular individual has the authority to set the law one way or another.

Stylistically and formally distinct from the Mishnah and Tosefta, the Babylonian Talmud, deriving from the sixth century CE, is a vast commentary on the Mishnah. It contains sustained and systematic analyses of the Mishnah, which is commented on in a law-by-law and, often, word-by-word analysis. The Talmud is relevant to our discussion because, in the course of its treatment of the Mishnah (and, at times, the Tosefta), it cites and analyzes teachings attributed to the same authorities cited in the earlier documents but not found in them. While the Talmud derives from the sixth century, it thus is a source for laws and other materials that, if they are authentic representations of what the Mishnaic authorities did or said, derive from the same period as the earlier documents. Although unknown from earlier documents, these statements appear in the same literary style as materials found in the Mishnah and Tosefta themselves.

This being the case, the question of the authenticity of statements and actions attributed to earlier authorities but found only in later documents brings us to the heart of an issue we must briefly consider before we turn to the specific texts on Honi and Hanina. The problem is that, even if the materials to be discussed represent what actually was said or done by those individuals, they were collected and redacted many years after those events by people who had their own theological and social agendas. In establishing the literary framework within which those earlier traditions would appear, these authorships shaped them to serve their own ideational purposes. This they did by supplying the specific contexts within which the stories would take place, by determining what details would be included or omitted, and, insofar as Rabbinic documents reveal internally consistent literary styles—with a small number of literary forms expressing all the document's substance—by imposing on earlier materials the literary forms in which they would be preserved. Consequently, we must understand the stories reviewed here about charismatic holy men who lived at the turn of the millennia to reflect more about the attitudes and theologies of the third through sixth centuries, when the documents in which they are contained were edited, than about these individuals and their own historical periods.

Even if the Rabbinic literature accurately portrays the salient personality traits of Honi and Hanina—and we have no way of knowing whether or not it does—we must be clear that these stories have been formulated and placed in their documentary contexts in order to make points in line with the interests of later Rabbinic authorships. We can know about the early figures only what those authorships want us to know. Similarly, the way in which the stories are told necessarily instructs us regarding the later Rabbis' own social and theological programs. What did those later Rabbis think about the charismatic healer or pious wonder worker who represented such a powerful figure within Judaism up into the first centuries? As we discuss the pertinent passages, we must be clear as much about what they teach about the interests of the later Rabbis as they teach about the holy men themselves.

Turning to the case of Honi the Circle-Drawer, we shall see the extent to which stories about him illustrate both the traits of the Galilean miracle worker and the way in which later Rabbinic masters used stories of such individuals to advance their own perspective on community leadership and appropriate modes of addressing God. Honi lived in the first century BCE and, alongside references in the Rabbinic literature, is known from Josephus (*Ant.* 14.22–30) as a righteous miracle worker, particularly effective in prayer. Josephus—who writes for a Roman audience and treats Honi as an unequivocally positive model of Jewish piety—reports that Honi died a martyr, probably in April of 65 BCE. As we shall see, the Rabbis have a different tradition. We begin with Mishnah, *Taanit* 3:8, which reports the power of Honi's prayers (adapted from Jacob Neusner, *The Mishnah: A New Translation*):

A. On account of every sort of trouble that affects the public (May it not happen!) they sound the shofar,

B. except for too much rain.

C. [There was] an incident (*ma'aseh*): They said to Honi the Circle-Drawer, "Pray that rain will fall."

D. He said to them, "Go and bring in the clay ovens used for Passover, so that they do not soften [in the rain that will result from my prayer]."

E. He prayed, but it did not rain.

F. What did he do?

G. He drew a circle and stood in the middle and said, "Lord of the world! Your children have turned to me, for before you I am like a member of the family. I swear by your great name that I will not move from here until you take pity on your children!"

H. It began to rain drop-by-drop.

I. [Honi] said, "This is not what I wanted, but rain for [filling up] cisterns, pits, and caverns."

J. Rain fell violently.

K. He said, "This is not what I requested, but rain of good will, blessing, and graciousness."

L. It [now] rained the right way, until Israelites had to flee from Jerusalem up to the Temple Mount because of the amount of rain.

M. They came and said to him, "Just as you prayed for rain to fall, now pray for it to go away."

N. [Honi] said to them, "Go and see whether the Stone of the Strayers has disappeared [under the rising water]."

O. Simeon b. Shatah said to him, "If you were not Honi, I should decree a ban of excommunication against you. But what can I do with you? For you importune before the Omnipresent like a son who importunes his father, so he does what he wants.

P. "Concerning you, Scripture says, 'Let your father and your mother be glad, and let her that bore you rejoice' (Proverbs 23:25)."

The incident involving Honi illustrates the law stated at A–B: in times of trouble, the community cries out (through the sounding of the ram's horn, the shofar) to God for help. But in the case of a surfeit of rain, such action is not deemed appropriate; excess rain, even if it is an inconvenience, represents no real danger and therefore does not warrant God's intercession. In line with this rule, Honi intercedes with God to bring rain, C–K, but will not pray to end the rain, N, unless it has reached truly destructive levels. We return to this point in a moment. But first let us examine what the story reveals about the Rabbinic attitude toward miracle-working holy men such as Honi.

Honi is called upon—it is not clear whether by Rabbis or by the common people—because his prayers are known to be effective. Indeed, he is so certain of himself that he announces his success before he even begins to pray (D). Then the sequence at G–L depicts the extent of Honi's power, which is such that God responds to each of his specific demands until exactly the right sort of rain is achieved, L.

Since Honi's personality is depicted clearly at G–L, it hardly takes Simeon b. Shatah's assessment, O, for us to see that at the heart of the story is the Rabbis' discomfort with Honi. Rather than focusing on Honi's miracle and the extent of his power, the passage wishes clearly to demarcate the limits of what Honi can accomplish. As the Rabbis tell the story, Honi's power to supplicate God brings what the people need, which is rain. But Honi's actions also entail a significant level of risk. Honi cannot guarantee that God's response to him will be the desired one: not only the right kind of rain but also the right amount. Asking for too much, asking at the wrong time, or asking for something like the cessation of rain, which can have horrible results, is dangerous and therefore prohibited except in the most dire circumstances. Even Honi will take no additional action—he will not ask that the rain stop—so long as the Stone of the Strayers (presumably a tall landmark in Jerusalem) is above water. This rock's being submerged would signify a flood so severe that it is necessary to petition God to stop the rain. Prior to that point, God should be left to his own plan. Honi resorts to ultimatums such as at G only when it is absolutely necessary to save the people from imminent danger.

An implication of the Mishnah's depiction of Honi's power, and its limits, is that even a charismatic holy man becomes subsumed within the Rabbis' own system of piety. Honi knows and abides by the Rabbis' rules. Though he lived prior to the beginning of the Rabbinic period and is not himself designated by the title "Rabbi," he is rabbinized, shown to know and follow the the Rabbis' way of doing things. Alongside his personal piety that gives him special power with God, Honi's greatest trait—one played upon in the passage we discuss next—is that he is also a good Rabbi.

Simeon b. Shatah's response to Honi, O–P, makes the point explicit. Honi, we saw at D, is brash and overconfident, qualities that Rabbinic Judaism denigrates. Making demands of God and expecting immediate results are dangerous—as the example of this story proves—and strongly discouraged. And yet, through Honi's example, God is seen to be present and with the people, responding to the nation's needs and saving his people from distress. By subsuming Honi within the Rabbinic system, by turning him into a Rabbi, the Mishnah's authorship surely increases its own authority and standing among people who would have seen pious miracle workers such as Honi as natural community leaders. The special piety and power of individuals such as Honi thus are described as reasons for joy, P. But Honi is an appropriate model for community leadership only because, as A+M–N suggests, he knows and follows the Rabbis' rules. People should emulate not his special powers with God but his knowledge and observance of the law.

In this context, one final aspect of the story deserves note, namely, its failure to reflect any level of awe or wonderment at Honi's success in bringing rain—an act that is nothing short of a miracle. Those who called upon Honi initially are not heard from again, and the people who do respond react not to the miracle of the rain but only to the flooding Honi has caused. For reasons to which we will return below, the Rabbis focus negatively on miracles that break the flow of nature, and one reason for that attitude is reflected here when the miracle goes awry. Miracles, in the Rabbinic view, are neither to be depended upon nor to be extolled as the greatest proof of God's existence and power. Just as God's failure to produce a miracle does not signify the cessation of his providential concern for the people of Israel, so the occasion of a miracle cannot be depended upon to prove divine concern. Miracles simply stand outside of the system of study and observance of the Torah through which the Rabbis discern God's presence and power.

This aspect of the Rabbis' attitude toward the charismatic miracle worker is revealed in a second tale about Honi, this one found in the Talmud (Babylonian Talmud, *Taanit* 23a; translation adapted from *The Soncino Talmud*):

A. R. Yochanan said, "Throughout the whole of his life, this righteous man [Honi] was troubled about the meaning of the verse, 'A Song of Ascents, When the Lord brought back those that returned to Zion, we were like unto them that dream' (Psalm 126:1). Is it possible for a man to dream continuously for seventy years?"

B. One day [Honi] was journeying on the road and he saw a man planting a carob tree; he asked him, "How long does it take [for this tree] to bear fruit?" The man replied, "Seventy years." [Honi] then further asked him, "Are you certain that you will live another seventy years?" The man replied, "I found [ready grown] carob trees in the world; as my forefathers planted these for me, so I too plant these for my children."

C. Honi sat down to have a meal and sleep overcame him. As he slept, a rocky formation enclosed him, which hid him from sight, and he continued to sleep for seventy years. When he awoke he saw a man gathering the fruit of the carob tree, and he asked him, "Are you the man who planted the tree?" The man replied, "I am his grandson." Thereupon [Honi] exclaimed, "It is clear that I slept for seventy years."

D. He then caught sight of his ass who had given birth to several generations of mules; and he returned home. He there enquired, "Is the son of Honi the Circle-Drawer still alive?" The people answered him, "His son is no more, but his grandson is still living." Thereupon he said to them, "I am Honi the Circle-Drawer," but no one would believe him.

E. He then repaired to the schoolhouse, and there he overheard the scholars say, "The law is as clear to us as in the days of Honi the Circle-Drawer, for whenever he came to the schoolhouse he would settle for the scholars any difficulty that they had."

F. Then he called out, "I am he"; but the scholars would not believe him nor did they give him the honor due to him. This hurt him greatly, and he prayed [for death] and he died.

G. Raba said, "Hence the saying, 'Either companionship or death.'"

As in our first story, the point of this pericope in context is not simply or primarily to preserve memory of or to extol Honi as a model of righteousness. While the Babylonian Talmud, *Taanit* 23a, preserves a number of stories concerning Honi and his grandsons, within the Rabbinic literature in general such stories have not been gathered so as to create large compendiums about charismatic leaders. Even as the Rabbis report on figures such as Honi, they present no accounts of their lives and deeds similar to what is found, for instance, in the Gospels. Rather, dispersed throughout the Rabbis' legal materials and exegetical discussions, these stories always are made to delineate points of biblical exegesis or Rabbinic law. However the common people might have reacted to these tales, or whatever the reasons for their original composition, the Rabbis thus rendered them subservient to the same issues that pervade their discourse in general. Thus, in the first story, the tale of Honi's prayer for rain illustrates the application of the law regarding the public sounding of the shofar in times of communal distress. In this Talmudic passage, the question is the accuracy of a verse of Scripture: Can a person really dream for seventy years, as the Rabbinic reading of Psalm 126:1, based upon Jeremiah 25:11 and 29:10, suggests the Israelites in exile did? Honi's experience proves that one can. That is the initial point of the story. Only alongside that point do we, in the Rabbinic retelling of Honi's experience, additionally learn about Honi's piety and special stature before God and, finally, about the Rabbinic attitude toward miracles and those who experience them.

As Galit Hasan-Rokem points out, the tale's underlying folk motif—the importance of planting for the future—is ignored. The focus, rather, is the miracle done for the righteous Honi. He is perplexed by Psalm 126:1, understood to mean that the Israelites were in a dream state during the entirety of the Babylonian captivity. Honi wonders whether such a sleep in fact is possible, and God responds by proving that it is by causing Honi himself to fall into just such a seventy-year sleep. While we might anticipate a reflection on how wondrous are God's miracles or even on the fact that God proves to the pious the truth of Scripture, the opposite occurs. The story's details are carefully set out to show that Honi has good reason to be exceedingly honored by the miracle done as a result of his righteousness. He learns, D, that his son produced children, and, E, that his teaching has survived and is held in the highest regard. Perhaps the passage's redactor intends by D to reflect the pericope at the Babylonian Talmud, *Ketubot* 50a, which interprets Psalm 128:6 ("May you see your children's children! Peace be upon Israel!") to mean that the birth of grandchildren guarantees that the people of Israel will enjoy communal harmony. Honi now is assured of this blessing. And the incident of Honi in the schoolhouse, E, is reminiscent of the image of Moses, who, according to the Rabbis, similarly was allowed by God to visit a study hall that existed long after his life span, but who, unlike Honi, found great reassurance in learning of his legacy within the legal tradition (Babylonian Talmud, *Menahot* 29b).

Especially in light of these connections, it is particularly striking that Honi does not experience God's miracle as a great thing at all. The point of the story is that what really matters is the respect one experiences in the give-and-take of the schoolhouse. Absent the ability to engage in study with his colleagues and without the honor that comes from one's place in the community of scholars, life itself, however miraculous, is not worth living. Oddly, the final prayer that God grants Honi is for Honi's own death. The Rabbis depict Honi's charismatic piety and ability to work miracles as coming to this sad ending. Better he had not found out the truth of scripture through a miracle at all. That way of finding out God's truth, unlike the Rabbinic method of scholarly debate, leads only to suffering such as Honi experienced.

As in the previous Mishnaic story, the Rabbis recognize the power an individual such as Honi has before God. But, again as in the preceding story, the Talmud's authorship is at best ambivalent about the miracles such stature can produce. Just as his insistence that God bring rain creates a significant problem for the community, so the piety that leads God to work a miracle for Honi leads not to awe at God's greatness but to death. We are left in high regard of Honi's special piety. But we also are left to recognize that both the community and the individual are better off if God is not induced to intervene within the natural order of things. The people are better left to their everyday, sometimes successful, sometimes unsuccessful, prayers, and the scholars to the daily discussion of the study house that requires them—without God's intervention—to determine what is or is not an accurate interpretation.

As we turn to our second set of stories, concerning Hanina b. Dosa, we must be conscious of the fact that the Rabbinic documents we are addressing were not created as works of systematic theology. They do not present monolithic and cogent perspectives on the issues facing Jews and Judaism in the first centuries. This means that this next set of stories does not make exactly the same points, in exactly the same ways, as emerge in the stories of Honi. And yet the themes are similar, and the overall picture is consistent. The Rabbinic texts laud this individual's piety and knowledge of and adherence to Rabbinic law. Nevertheless, the texts consistently make the point that what distinguishes these figures from common Israelites and even from Rabbis, their ability to use their closeness to God to work miracles, is an at best ambivalent gift. God's breaking into the natural order does not, in the end, accomplish what the miracle worker truly desires.

Hanina b. Dosa was a student of Yochanan b. Zakkai, who, in the period of the destruction of the Jerusalem Temple in 70 CE, founded the Rabbinic academy at Yavneh. Unlike Honi, Hanina thus is a product of Rabbinism proper. He is titled "Rabbi" and counted among the Tannaim, the authoritative teachers of the period of the Mishnah itself. But while Hanina brings us directly into the period of the Rabbis, still, like Honi, he is known not for the laws cited in his name but for his power as a healer and for the other miracles done for him by God. Indeed, in some of the few statements attributed to him (rather than the stories told about him), Hanina presents not laws but wisdom statements. These are appropriate to the context of Mishnah Tractate *Avot* in which they appear, since this section of the Mishnah contains wise sayings concerning right conduct with God, society, and self. Hanina speaks of the nature of piety (*Pirke Avot* 3:9–10):

3:9

    A. R. Hanina b. Dosa says, "For anyone whose fear of sin takes precedence over his wisdom, his wisdom will endure."

    B. "And for anyone whose wisdom takes precedence over his fear of sin, his wisdom will not endure."

    C. He would say, "Anyone whose deeds are more than his wisdom—his wisdom will endure."

    D. "And anyone whose wisdom is more than his deeds—his wisdom will not endure."

3:10

    A. He would say, "Anyone from whom people take pleasure, the Omnipresent takes pleasure."

    B. "And anyone from whom people do not take pleasure, the Omnipresent does not take pleasure."

As Jacob Neusner comments in *Torah from Our Sages*, at issue is the balance between learning and doing, and Hanina's point is that to have value ("endure"), learning must lead to proper action. In Neusner's words, "You cannot separate your learning of Torah from the life you lead. The one is the foundation of the other" (107). In particular, Hanina sees the value of learning in its forming of a person who acts for the benefit of others ("from whom people take pleasure"). As Neusner additionally points out, Torah accordingly is about the creation of a community that can transcend the reality of everyday Jewish life under Roman rule in the first centuries. It is about deeds of love and compassion for others, about wisdom in the service of the community as a whole, not used for the self or in response to an abstract concept of knowledge of God.

This principle is illustrated in the stories regarding Hanina's piety and the miracles done for him as a result of that piety. At the foundation of the Rabbinic depiction of Hanina is the idea that his stature and special power derive from his adherence to the principles the Rabbinic movement endorses and desires to inculcate into the nation as a whole: the people of Israel are responsible for each other, and the life of Torah is a source of power before God. In a moment we shall see how Hanina uses his powers for the benefit of others, a central theme of the Talmudic stories about him. But the earliest depictions of him, first, portray his distinctive fervor and concentration in prayer. Like the stories of Honi, these materials illustrate a specific Mishnaic principle, in this case regarding the correct state of mind for prayer. The principle is expressed at Mishnah Tractate *Berakhot* 5:1:

    A. One may stand to pray only in a solemn frame of mind.

    B. The early pious ones used to tarry one hour [before they would] pray,

    C. so that they could direct their hearts to the Omnipresent.

    D. [While one is praying] even if the king greets him, he may not respond.

    E. And even if a serpent is entwined around his heel, he may not interrupt [his prayer].

This point, regarding the seriousness with which one should focus upon prayer, is developed at Mishnah *Berakhot* 5:5A–C and then illustrated by an anecdote about Hanina, D–G:

A. One who prays and errs—it is a bad sign for him.

B. And if he is a communal agent, [who prays on behalf of the whole congregation], it is a bad sign for them that appointed him.

C. [This is on the principle that] a man's agent is like [the man] himself.

D. They said concerning R. Hanina b. Dosa, "When he would pray for the sick he would say 'This one shall live' or 'This one shall die.'"

E. They said to him, "How do you know?"

F. He said to them, "If my prayer is fluent, then I know that it is accepted [and the person will live]."

G. "But if not, I know that it is rejected [and the person will die]."

As he prays for the sick, Hanina is able immediately to recognize whether or not his prayer has been efficacious. Hanina's power with God thus is expressed quite differently from Honi's, the latter being able to impose his will on God, whereas Hanina seems simply to accept what he perceives God's will to be. The story of Hanina appears here to illustrate the Mishnaic principle that fluency in prayer is a gift from God and errors in prayer are a sign that God has rejected the prayer.

Tosefta *Berakhot* 3:20 develops Mishnah *Berakhot* 5:1's principle that one must not interrupt his prayer for any reason, even if a serpent is entwined around his heel. After other examples of cases in which prayer may not be interrupted, an incident involving Hanina illustrates Mishnah *Berakhot* 5:1E:

A. One who was standing and reciting the Prayer [of Eighteen Benedictions, the central prayer of the obligatory liturgy] in a camp or in a wide highway—

B. lo, he may move aside to allow an ass, an ass-driver or a wagon-driver pass in front of him, but he may not interrupt [his recitation of the Prayer].

C. They related about R. Hanina b. Dosa that once while he was reciting the Prayer, a poisonous lizard bit him, but he did not interrupt [his recitation].

D. His students went and found it [the lizard] dead at the entrance to its hole.

E. They said, "Woe to the man who is bitten by a lizard. Woe to the lizard that bit Ben Dosa."

Hanina b. Dosa's absolute focus in prayer protects him from the venomous lizard. In context, this is presented not in praise of a distinctive trait of a charismatic holy man but, rather, as an example of the importance of adherence to the Rabbinic precept regarding concentration in prayer. The Talmud presents a more developed version of the same story, in which Hanina makes a point regarding the association between sin and death (Babylonian Talmud, *Berakhot* 33a):

A. Our Rabbis have taught on Tannaitic authority:

B. There was the case concerning a certain place in which a lizard was going around and biting people. They came and told R. Hanina b. Dosa.

C. He said to them, "Show me its hole."

D. They showed him its hole. He put his heel over the mouth of the hole. The lizard came out and bit him and died.

E. He took it on his shoulder and brought it to the school house. He said to them, "See, my sons, it is not the lizard that kills but sin that kills."

F. At that moment they said, "Woe to the man who meets a lizard, and woe to the lizard that meets up with R. Hanina b. Dosa."

The Talmud's version turns the incident of the lizard into an opportunity for Hanina to underscore an additional principle idea of Rabbinic Judaism, that piety, represented in adherence to the law, protects from danger. Again, the focus here is not simply or primarily a distinctive trait of a holy man (though F certainly focuses on Hanina's particular piety). Rather, this story of a holy man becomes a setting in which the Talmudic authors can emphasize the importance of the central Rabbinic value, avoidance of sin through observance of the law.

The Babylonian Talmud, at Tractate *Berakhot* 34b, also develops the Mishnah's account of the meaning to Hanina of fluency in prayer:

A. Our Rabbis have taught on Tannaite authority:

B. There was the case in which the son of Rabban Gamaliel fell ill. He sent two disciples of sages to R. Hanina b. Dosa to pray for mercy for him. When he saw them, he went up to his upper room and prayed for mercy for him.

C. When he came down, he said to them, "Go, for his fever has left him."

D. They said to him, "Are you a prophet?"

E. He said to them, "I am not a prophet nor a disciple of a prophet, but this is what I have received as a tradition: *"If my prayer is fluent, then I know that he [for whom I pray] is accepted, and if not, then I know that he is rejected"* [citing Mishnah *Berakhot* 5:5, F–G].

F. They sat down and wrote down the hour, and when they came back to Rabban Gamaliel, he said to them, "By the Temple service! You were neither early nor late, but that is just how it happened. At that very moment, his fever left him and he asked us for water to drink."

G. There was the further case involving R. Hanina b. Dosa. He went to study Torah with R. Yochanan b. Zakkai, and the son of R. Yochanan b. Zakkai fell ill.

H. He said to him, "Hanina, my son, pray for mercy for him so that he will live."

I. He put his head between his knees and prayed for mercy for him, and he lived.

J. Said R. Yochanan b. Zakkai, "If Ben Zakkai [that is, I] had put his head between his knees all day long, they would not pay attention to him [in Heaven]."

K. Said his wife to him, "And is Hanina greater than you?"

L. He said to her, "No. But he is like a slave before the king, and I am like a prince before the king."

The Mishnah's story of Hanina's praying is expanded. This example highlights the extent to which stories of holy men emerge out of the thought world of Rabbinism and do not simply portray the lives and actions of individuals who lived hundreds of years before the Talmud was completed. The present instance highlights this fact by its focus on the point raised at L: Hanina's power derives not from his princely stature before God but from his total subservience. This message is particularly pertinent in the period of the formation of the Talmud, in which, under Roman and then Christian dominion, the people of Israel lived much more as slaves than as princes.

One of the central points that emerged in the stories about Honi the Circle-Drawer concerns the way in which miracles do not necessarily produce the desired results. Here, at Babylonian Talmud, *Taanit* 24b, a comparable point is made. Hanina has the power to start and stop rain. But he cannot use that power indiscriminately:

- A. R. Hanina b. Dosa was journeying on the road when it began to rain. He exclaimed, "Master of the Universe, the whole world is at ease, but Hanina is in distress." The rain then ceased.
- B. When he reached home, he exclaimed, "Master of the Universe, the whole world is in distress and Hanina is at ease," whereupon rain fell. . . .

Hanina, like Honi, can cause rain to start or stop. But when a miracle provides Hanina what he wants, other people suffer. For the world to be set right, the miracle must be undone. While addressing the issue in different terms, the continuation of the series of stories about Hanina found at Babylonian Talmud *Taanit* 25a reflects a similar point. Hanina suffers in terrible poverty, a condition that seems incommensurate with his ability to accomplish miracles. But his prayer for wealth teaches that miracles in fact cannot solve the problem:

- A. Once his wife said to him: "How long shall we go on suffering so much?"
- B. He replied, "What shall we do?"
- C. [She said], "Pray that something may be given to you."
- D. He prayed and there emerged the figure of a hand reaching out to him a leg of a golden table. Thereupon he saw in a dream that the pious would one day eat at a three-legged golden table, but he would eat at a two-legged table.
- E. Her husband said to her, "Are you content that everybody shall eat at a perfect table, but we at an imperfect table?"
- F. She replied: "What then shall we do? Pray that the leg should be taken away from you."
- G. He prayed and it was taken away.
- H. A Tanna taught: The latter miracle was greater than the former; for there is a tradition that a thing may be given but once; it is never taken away again.

Compensation in this world for one's piety proportionally reduces one's reward in the world to come. This suggests, on the one hand, that people should not look too much to miracles (or miracle workers) to improve their current circumstance. But it also means, on the other hand, that suffering in this world is not necessarily a sign of sin and abandonment by God. Consistent with the common Rabbinic perspective, suffering in this world means, rather, that the individual—or the nation as a whole—can experience a greater divine reward in the coming world. While an exemplar of piety and closeness to God, Hanina illustrates what the people of Israel experience: suffering in this world as a prelude to a perfect reward in the world to come. The postscript at H makes an additional point in line with what we already have seen. The undoing of a miracle, or the fact that a miracle is not completed, may be the greatest miracle of all. This suggests that people indeed should not turn to charismatic miracle workers in their quest to find divine presence and power.

When we view the stories regarding Honi the Circle-Drawer and Hanina b. Dosa together, we gain an overall perspective on Rabbinic literature's portrayal of the charismatic holy man. Most important, we see how this portrayal highlights the Rabbis' own characteristic way of looking at their world. These stories portray learning of Torah in the service of the community to be of the greatest value. Knowledge of Torah and observance of the law define one as pious and give one the ability to perform miracles. But, as the stories about both figures make clear, miracles, even though they can be accomplished, cannot be counted on to solve an individual's or the nation's problems. Miracles do not always achieve the desired results, and they may even be dangerous. Even if they appear to give a person what he or she wants, for example, added wealth, the fact is that using miracles to increase one's reward in this, temporary world diminishes it in the coming, eternal one.

By using the figures of Honi and Hanina to project these ideas, the Talmudic literature makes a point pertinent to the era in which the Rabbinic movement emerged and then flourished: the first through third centuries, when the Mishnah and Tosefta were compiled, witnessed two failed Jewish attempts to wrest the land of Israel from Rome's political control; the third through sixth centuries, when the Talmud was created, witnessed Christianity's rise to world dominance. Especially the failed revolts inculcated in Judaism's earliest Rabbinic leadership the view that an actualized messianism—the idea that God is immediately present and ready to respond to the needs of his suffering nation—is an unworkable, indeed, a dangerous, approach to seeking fulfillment of God's covenantal promises. In the wars with Rome, the Jews' use of their own military might to force God miraculously to intervene on the side of his people had led to the Temple's destruction, to the end of the sacrificial cult, to untold Jewish deaths, and, ultimately, to the loss of access to the Temple Mount and to Jerusalem itself. In these wars, particularly in 132–35 under the pseudo-messiah Simeon bar Kokhba, the kind of charismatic leadership that depended on and promised divine miracles had provoked not salvation but catastrophe.

In this setting, figures such as Honi and Hanina—not pseudo-messiahs by any means, but individuals whose miraculous powers suggested that God could be called upon to act as and when the people needed—were portrayed ambiguously. Their piety, a consequence of their knowledge of Rabbinic law, is a model to which all Israelites can aspire. But while the miracles that derive from that piety are lauded, they also are ambivalent, beyond the control even of the holy men themselves and not always producing the desired results. The point made by Simeon b. Shatah regarding Honi—"If you were not Honi, I should decree a ban of excommunication against you"—stands tacitly behind the entire grouping of tales: to importune God as does the charismatic holy man is inappropriate and dangerous. Indeed, as the story of Hanina and the golden table leg indicates, any benefit achieved in this way in this world surely will reduce one's reward in the world to come.

While a distinction must be made between the individuals discussed here and messianic pretenders such as Bar Kokhba, still, these figures all share the trait of claiming to be able to call God to immediate action. Understanding the Rabbinic literature's attitude toward Bar Kokhba and the messianic hopes he inspired thus takes us a long way toward comprehending the Rabbis' approach to charismatic holy men. The central point is that the Rabbis rejected such messianic figures and looked down on anyone who would imagine that the Messiah was destined soon to arrive. This is the point made in *Lamentations Rabbah* 2:4, a midrashic compilation of the sixth century CE (translation adapted from the Soncino edition):

> R. Yochanan said: "Rabbi [Judah the Patriarch] used to expound [the verse at Numbers 24:17], 'There shall step forth a star (*kokab*) out of Jacob,' thus: Read not '*kokab*' but '*kozab*' [that is, 'lie']." When R. Aqiba beheld Bar Koziba [that is, Kokhba, but with the name read to signify "lie" instead of "star"], he exclaimed, "This is the King Messiah!" R. Yochanan b. Torta retorted: "Aqiba, grass will grow in your cheeks, and he [that is, the Messiah] will still not have come!"

Bar Kokhba was a liar, not a Messiah, and the real Messiah can be expected no time soon. Thus the Rabbis directed that people should take with a grain of salt any claim that messianic events were beginning to occur or could be made to commence. Neither of the individuals whose stories we have reviewed presented even vaguely messianic claims. But the Rabbis' dicta would have urged the people to ignore the actions or claims of charismatic holy men who purported that the miracles they brought about had any deep significance. *Avot deRabbi Natan* B, 31 (Schechter, 66–67), produced in the fifth or sixth century, makes this clear:

> Yochanan b. Zakkai says, "If a plant is in your hand [ready to be planted], and [people] say to you, 'Behold the Messiah [has arrived]!'—go and plant the planting, and after that go out to receive him."

People are not to be anxious to investigate, let alone to be drawn in by, messianic claims.

The preceding investigation has implications both for our understanding of Rabbinic Judaism and for study of the historical Jesus. Regarding Judaism, we see clearly that the early Rabbinic movement was familiar with and in many regards honored the figure of the charismatic holy man. The Rabbis accepted the idea that special piety gives an individual the power to intercede directly with God and, as a result, to perform miracles: to bring rain, to heal the sick, and the like. At the same time, the Rabbinic view of such individuals and their actions was ambivalent. Rather than praising charismatic holy men's special powers, the Rabbinic stories highlight the danger of demanding that God work miracles. What the Rabbis see as most important about charismatic figures, rather, is that they—like Rabbis— know Torah and engage in the intellectual work of the study house. Honi's greatest joy is, and his power comes from, knowledge of the Torah, studied as the Rabbis study it and observed in its details as the Rabbis insist it be observed.

Charismatic holy men's ability to produce miracles is not condemned. It is a source of gladness for the community and a sign that God remains with the peo- ple of Israel. Still the use of miracles is always secondary to the life of Torah. This view made sense within the first-century Jewish community, which had been all but destroyed by those who were certain that God could be importuned to act on their behalf. These claims had proved wrong and dangerous. As Rabbinic Ju- daism embarked on a new and distinctive path, in which the presence of God would be evidenced not in miracles but in the power of the human intellect, fig- ures such as Honi and Hanina became memories of a type of charismatic piety that typified an earlier age that had ceased to exist.

Implications of this Rabbinic material for understanding the historical Jesus are more complex. On the one hand, the evidence suggests that, as scholars from Geza Vermes on have argued, the model of the charismatic holy man existed within the Judaism of Jesus' day. The sources discussed here depict holy men similar to the Gospel's Jesus, "whose supernatural abilities derived, not from se- cret powers, but from immediate contact with God" (Vermes, *Jesus the Jew*, 69). The problem is that, beyond this general fact, supported by evidence from Jose- phus, the Dead Sea Scrolls, and other Second Temple documents in addition to the later Rabbinic literature, none of the specific actions assigned to Honi or Han- ina, and certainly not the traits of their personalities, can be firmly assigned to the period of Jesus' ministry. The Rabbinic accounts are centuries later than the period they claim to describe. We have no way of ascertaining what aspects of the Rab- binic accounts did or did not circulate centuries before the completion of the com- pilations in which they are now found.

A single example makes the point. The Rabbinic story of Honi's miraculous seventy-year sleep and death, which differs completely from the account found in Josephus, comprises a miraculous folktale, important not as evidence for what actually happened but as a means of access to the thought-world of the time. But to what period does this story give access? It certainly reflects the ideas of the Tal- mudic authorship that, in the fifth or sixth century, determined to include it in Tractate *Taanit*. It is associated with Yochanan, a third-century master, and so fur- ther may reflect his view of charismatic miracle workers. But we have no knowl- edge of the form in which the story was known—if it was known at all—prior to Yochanan's day. The story's details make sense within the structure of the Rab- binic Judaism emergent in Yochanan's time. But are these details creations of this period, or do they go back to, and so teach us about, the Judaism of Jesus' day? Insofar as the depictions we have analyzed are shaped by and serve the purposes of the later Rabbinic authorities, their use to portray specific details of Jewish life or attitudes in the late Second Temple period must remain conjectural.

Much evidence suggests the model of the charismatic holy man existed in late Second Temple Judaism. The Rabbinic literature contributes to this picture. But the specific details it provides, and the examples of particular individuals it offers, cannot be accepted uncritically as representative of the religious world of Jesus.

Bibliography

Charlesworth, James. "Honi." Page 282 in vol. 3 of *The Anchor Bible Dictionary*. Edited by David Noel Freedman. 6 vols. New York: Doubleday, 1992.

Hasan-Rokem, Galit. *Tales of the Neighborhood: Jewish Narrative Dialogues in Late Antiquity*, pp. 86ff., esp. 109–10. Berkeley: University of California Press, 2003.

Neusner, Jacob. *Development of a Legend: Studies on the Traditions Concerning Yohanan ben Zakkai*, p. 28. Leiden: Brill, 1970.

———. *The Mishnah: A New Translation*. New Haven, CT: Yale University Press, 1987.

———. *Torah from Our Sages: Pirke Avot*. Dallas, TX: Rossel Books, 1984.

The Soncino Talmud. New York: Judaica Press, 1973.

Vermes, Geza. *Jesus the Jew: A Historian's Reading of the Gospels*. London: Collins, 1973.

9

Miracle Stories: The God Asclepius,
the Pythagorean Philosophers,
and the Roman Rulers

Wendy Cotter, C.S.J.

The Jesus miracles, like all first-century material, require a full cultural contextualization within the Greco-Roman world, the only world available to the author and the audience for whom the stories were written. Assiduous and constant reference to that culture, its values, presuppositions, and favorite icons must establish the controls for the responsible evaluation and elucidation of each story's most probable messages. Two elements combine in the Jesus miracles—the work of power and the particular circumstances of encounter between Jesus and the petitioner/s—which help communicate the significance of his power and the revelation of his character.

Most studies focus on the first of these elements, striving to set up a backdrop for Jesus' miraculous works; several important scholars have contributed invaluably to the endeavor, such as Barry Blackburn, Howard Kee, Harold Remus, and Graham Twelftree. Gerd Theissen has focused special attention on the classification of the Jesus miracles, but he differs from the aforementioned scholars in arguing that it was Christianity that made the miracle story plentiful and popular rather than that the Jesus stories shared the same world stage with well-known accounts of other heroes and gods.

All Christians participated in the Mediterranean Greco-Roman world, including the Jews. Nevertheless, scholarship does not always reflect this fact. Most scholars confine their study of Jesus' miracles to Old Testament allusions or to subsequent stories in late Rabbinic traditions. It certainly is true that several of the Jesus miracles do indeed show that the author intended a reference to a Septuagintal story, or hero. But unless the general stories known throughout the Mediterranean world by both Jews and non-Jews are studied, any intended allusions to them will be completely ignored, and a statement made about Jesus' person, power, and message will be lost. And this has happened.

Scholars who focus solely on specifically Jewish texts justify their controls on the sources by claiming that since Jewish religious sensibilities governed early Christianity, writers and teachers would have looked to the Jewish scriptures alone. However, we have to understand that when a Jewish Christian did choose an Old Testament story for an allusion, it was always because it made sense to him or her, as he or she looked at that story through a first-century Greco-Roman lens

A very good example of this broader Mediterranean context is found in the Jewish scholar Josephus's efforts to justify the miracle of Moses at the Red Sea. He makes a comparison with a well-known story about Alexander the Great, when the sea, recognizing Alexander's power, curled its waves over in a bow to him and facilitated his crossing the waters:

> Nor let anyone marvel at the astonishing nature of the narrative [of the sea parting when Moses lifted his rod] or doubt that it was given to men of old, innocent of crime, to find a road of salvation through the sea itself, whether by the will of God or maybe by accident, seeing that the hosts of Alexander King of Macedon, men but born the other day, beheld the Pamphylian Sea retire before them and when there was none, offer a passage through itself, what time it pleased God to overthrow the Persian empire; and on that all are agreed who have recorded Alexander's exploits. (Josephus, Ant. 2.347–48)

Here we see that Josephus's interpretation of the Exodus story demonstrates a strong awareness of the popular legends of his day. But something more is evident here. Josephus shows that he shares the Hellenistic philosophical stance that the elements of earth are intelligent and recognize those designated by God for world leadership. Josephus understands the Exodus miracle in a way influenced by his Hellenistic world and by the Hellenistic philosophy that he had studied. He understood, and wanted his audience to understand, that the miracle of the sea's parting at Moses' command has the same dignity and message as the sea's bowing to Alexander: the sea "recognized its Lord."

This example alerts us to the importance of being familiar with all the most well-known miracles attributed to heroes and gods for the populace of the first-century Mediterranean world. In my source book, The Miracles in Greco-Roman Antiquity, I used Rudolf Bultmann's classification of dividing the examples into four groups: healings, raisings from the dead, exorcisms, and nature miracles. It was during the preparation of that book that I became impressed by three categories of gods and heroes that kept presenting themselves: the god Asclepius, Pythagoras and his disciples, and certain of the Roman emperors. In the material that follows, each of these categories is examined and several stories from each category presented, so that we might say something about the source of the power and the significance of the miracles attributed to them.

The God Asclepius: The Doctor with Divine Paternity

Of these [good *daimones*] they deem gods only those who having guided the chariot
of their lives wisely and justly and having been endowed afterward by men as divini-
ties with shrines and religious ceremonies are commonly worshiped as Amphiarus in
Boetia Mopsus in Africa, Osiris in Egypt, one in one part of the world and another in
another part, Asclepius everywhere. (Apuleius, *De Deo Socratis* 15.153)

The god with the greatest reputation for healing was Asclepius (whom the Romans called Asculapius). He was born of a human mother, Coronis, who had
been impregnated by Apollo. Thus, Asclepius was certainly the son of a god and,
indeed by the first century, his devotion was so strong that his statue was to be
found in the temple of Apollo. Rescued as a newborn from death by his father,
Asclepius was placed in the care of the healer Chiron who taught him all his
skills. But Asclepius soon surpassed Chiron and his powers were so great that he
was said to return people from death (text 1.1). He was to pay for this with his
life because Hades complained to his brother Zeus that the population of his
realm was being reduced by a mortal's *hubris*. Zeus then ordered the Cyclops to
create a thunderbolt with which he slayed Asclepius. But as Apuleius states above,
popular devotion made Asclepius a deity known "everywhere."

Texts 1.2–5 are third-century BCE testimonies recording a variety of miracles
performed by the god. At Asclepius's temple in Epidaurus, petitioners spent the
night in a type of dormitory and awaited a dream in which the god would reveal
to them the secret to their healing, or heal them outright. Texts 1.6–7 are second-
century CE inscriptions that attest to the continued devotion to the doctor-deity.
However, the role of the god differs from the third-century BCE texts in that Asclepius reveals the necessary combination of healing medical aids rather than a direct healing in sleep or request for symbolic acts.

Clearly, Asclepius's power for miracles relies on his being the son of the god of
wholeness, Apollo. But the devotion to Asclepius warmed due to his great humanity, his compassionate concern for continued life and health for all devotees
no matter what their social stratum, and the absence of any myths of selfishness
around him. He served no particular throne, represented no one's army, nor was a
featured member of any princely family. Thus Asclepius was international, so to
speak, and carried the single valence of savior-doctor-deity.

Human Heroes

In a second category, and substantially less plentiful, are stories that attribute to
heroes the power to perform a miracle. These heroes are to be distinguished from
those whose role is to pray for the intervention of a god, or whose actions are dictated by a god, for in these cases it is clearly the god who performs the miracle.

Rather, this category focuses on heroes who are claimed to cause miracles, by their own authority. Here we briefly review two seemingly incompatible categories of powerful miracle workers: Pythagorean philosophers and Roman rulers.

The Pythagorean Philosophers

Pythagoras's myth credits him with having been the first philosopher to discover the new cosmology and to probe physics, the mathematics of the cosmos. Pythagoras was a fifth-century BCE philosopher from Samos and supposedly he formed an order of scholars devoted to uncovering the patterns of cosmic order. The rigorous virtuousness of Pythagoras and his followers was necessary, since they saw their life as a probing of the divine's most sacred truths. According to tradition, this constant contact with the divine forces, the entities of the cosmic order, made Pythgoras and his disciples known to these powers and entities. As a result of this intimacy, Nature's powers and entities would give way to the desires of the Pythagoreans in what amounted to miracles, especially "nature miracles." Note text 2.1, where the stream returns Pythagoras's greeting, and text 2.2, where Pythagoras stills a storm to save his disciples from an unhappy crossing. Text 2.3 lists the special Pythagoreans who explicitly demonstrated miraculous powers over Nature; text 2.4 singles out Empedocles as especially powerful in miracle working; text 2.5 represents his conveying this conviction about the power over Nature to his disciple.

So in this tradition preserved by third-century CE authors (the Neo-Pythagoreans Porphyry and Iamblichus as well as the historian Diogenes Laertius), miraculous power also can be explained as Nature's concession to one who is both known by Nature's elements and personally respected by them as worthy.

A Special Case: Apollonius of Tyana

Apollonius of Tyana, a first-century CE holy man, was styled as a Pythagorean philosopher. When later in the third century his miracles were being rejected as sorcery, the empress Domna Julia prevailed on a Neo-Pythagorean, Philostratus, to write a biography of Apollonius that would set matters right and free him from such charges. The miracles of Apollonius are thus supposedly in the same category as those of the Pythagoreans. However, Philostratus does not take the opportunity to remind his audience of Pythagoras's miracles. He rather creates a kind of distance between Apollonius and his supposed father of philosophical thought. Texts 2.6–8 offer examples of his healing, while text 2.9 features a raising from the dead. Apollonius is able to perform these miracles on the basis of his great wisdom and virtue. Nature's forces, like servants, seem to obey his every whim.

The Roman Rulers

This last section presents texts that illustrate a hero's miraculous power because Nature's forces know that he has been empowered with authority to govern the earth. For this reason, the hero's desires and plans may not be obstructed, and Nature must give way. There are very few specific miracle stories attributed to Roman emperors, but those we have illustrate the propaganda that justifies complete obedience to them. Even the elements obey him. Text 3.1 illustrates this attitude in the case of Julius Caesar's efforts to cross the Adriatic Sea. He is convinced that the storm cannot submerge him, since Nature knows that he is designated ruler from heaven. Text 3.2 illustrates the same notion in the sycophantic poetry of Calpurnius Siculus. These are precisely the ideas that operate in Jesus' "Stilling of the Storm." Healings usually are seen as more local and specific. Suetonius explains how Vespasian, the newly named emperor, cured the blind and healed the lame (text 3.4). Notably, these healings are seen to be needed to bolster the new emperor's sense of "authority." But note that ideas of cosmic or global healing as a miracle are accorded to Augustus Caesar by Philo in his interpretation of the Great Peace that Augustus gave to the whole world (text 3.5).

These texts help us to assess at least three ways in which a miracle could be understood. A miracle can be the direct intervention of a heavenly deity (Asclepius), or it can reveal Nature bending to the wishes of an exceptional holy man (Pythagoras and his followers), or it can demonstrate Nature's obedience to a divinely empowered hero, entrusted with the earth by Zeus/Jupiter, whom it must aid and never obstruct (Roman rulers). All these ideas, separate and combined, are to be allowed as well known to Jesus' earliest followers who heard his miracle stories.

ASCLEPIUS

TEXT 1.1 RAISING THE DEAD (FIRST CENTURY CE)

I [Apollodorus] found some who are reported to have been raised by him, to wit, Capaneus and Lycurgus, as Stesichorus [645–555 BCE] says in the *Eriphyle*, Hippolytus, as the author of the *Naupatica* [sixth century BCE] reports; Tyndareus, as Panyasis [ca. 500 BCE] says; Hymenaeus, as the Orphics report; and Glaucus, son of Minos, as Melasagoras [fifth century BCE] relates. But Zeus, fearing that men might acquire the healing art from him and so come to the rescue of each other, smote him with a thunderbolt.

TEXT 1.2 CURING BLINDNESS, *INSCRIPTIONES GRAECAE*, 4.1.121–22.18 (THIRD CENTURY BCE), ALCETAS OF HALLEIS

The blind man saw a dream. It seemed to him that the god [Asclepius] came up to him and with his fingers opened his eyes, and that he first saw the trees in the sanctuary. At daybreak he walked out sound.

TEXT 1.3 CURING A MUTE BOY, *INSCRIPTIONES GRAECAE*, 4. 1.121–22.5
(THIRD CENTURY BCE),A VOICELESS BOY

He came as a suppliant to the temple for his voice. When he had performed the preliminary sacrifices and fulfilled the usual rites, thereupon the temple servant who brings in the fire for the god, looking at the boy's father, demanded he should promise to bring within a year the thank-offering for the cure if he obtained that for which he had come. But the boy suddenly said, "I promise." His father was startled at this and asked him to repeat it. The boy repeated the words and after that became well.

TEXT 1.4 CURING A CHEST ABSCESS AND PARALYSIS OF THE HANDS, *INSCRIPTIONES GRAECAE*, 4.1.125 (THIRD CENTURY BCE)

As an example of your power, Asclepius, I have put this rock that I had lifted up, manifest for all to see, an evidence of your art. For before coming under your hands and those of your children I was stricken by wretched illness, having an abscess in my chest and being paralyzed in my hands. But you, Paean, by ordering me to lift up this rock made me live free from disease.

TEXT 1.5 CURING A LAME FOOT, *INSCRIPTIONES GRAECAE*, 4. 1.121–22.36
(THIRD CENTURY BCE)

Cephisias . . . with the foot. He laughed at the cures of Asclepius and said: "If the god says he has healed lame people he is lying; for, if he had the power to do so, why has he not healed Hephaestus?" But the god did not conceal that he was inflicting penalty for the insolence. For Cephisias, when riding, was stricken by his bullheaded horse that had been tickled in the seat, so that instantly his foot was crippled and on a stretcher he was carried into the temple. Later on, after he had entreated him earnestly, the god made him well.

TEXT 1.6 CURING BLINDNESS, *INSCRIPTIONES GRAECAE*, 14.966
(SECOND CENTURY CE)

Valerius Aper, a blind soldier, the god revealed that he should go and take blood of a white cock along with honey and compound an eye salve and for three days should apply it to his eyes. And he could see again and went and publicly offered thanks to the god.

TEXT 1.7 CURING SICKNESS OF STOMACH AND THROAT,
INSCRIPTIONES GRAECAE, 4 SYLL. 3.11170 (CA. 160 CE)

I, M. Julius Apellas, was sent forth by the god, since I fell sick often and was stricken with indigestion. On the journey to Aegina, not much happened to me.

When I arrived at the sanctuary, it happened that my head was covered for two days during which there were torrents of rain. Cheese and bread were brought to me, celery and lettuce. I bathed alone without help; was forced to run; lemon rinds to take; soaked in water; at the *akoai* in the bath I rubbed myself on the wall; went for a stroll on the high road; swinging; smeared myself with dust; went walking barefoot; at the bath, poured wine over myself before entering the hot water; bathed alone and gave the bath-master an Attic drachma; made common offering to Asklepius, to Epion [his wife], to the Eleusinian goddess; took milk with honey. I used the oil and the headache was gone. I gargled with cold water against a sore throat, since this was another reason that I had turned to the god. The same remedy for swollen tonsils. I had occasion to write this out. With grateful heart and having become well, I took leave.

PYTHAGORAS

TEXT 2.1 PORPHYRY (232–305 CE), *LIFE OF PYTHAGORAS*, 27

It is said that while he with many companions was crossing the Caucas river, he addressed it, and the river calling out, piercingly clearly, in everyone's hearing, solemnly pronounced, "Greetings Pythagoras."

TEXT 2.2 IAMBLICHUS (250–325 CE), *LIFE OF PYTHAGORAS*, 28

Myriads of most divine and most amazing things, without deviation and agreed upon by all, are related of the man, such as the foretelling of inescapable earthquakes, and swiftly averting plagues and violent winds, hailstorms, indeed the flooding waters lulled, both swollen rivers and seas bound fast that companions might cross them with ease.

TEXT 2.3 PYTHAGORAS'S DISCIPLES: IAMBLICHUS (250–325 CE), *LIFE OF PYTHAGORAS*, 28

Taking advantage of these often [foretelling inescapable earthquakes, swiftly averting plagues and violent winds, hailstorms, flooding waters lulled, both swollen rivers and seas bound fast] Empedocles of Agrigentum, Epimenes the Cretan and Abaris the Hyperborean also accomplished things like this themselves. But their deeds were conspicuous, so that also "Wind-Preventer" was being [given as] the surname [epithet] of Empedocles, "Purifier [from Defilement/Guilt]" of Epimenes, and "Air-Treader" of Abaris.

TEXT 2.4 EMPEDOCLES (492–432 BCE), PYTHAGORAS'S DISCIPLE DIOGENES LAERTIUS (THIRD CENTURY CE), "EMPEDOCLES," *LIVES OF EMINENT PHILOSOPHERS* 8.60–62

Heraclides in his book *On Diseases* says that he [Empedocles] furnished Pausanias with the facts about the woman in a trance. This Pausanias, according to Aristippus and Satyrus, was his [Empedocles's] bosom-friend, to whom he dedicated his poem "On Nature". . . . At all events, Heraclides testifies that the case of the woman in a trance was such that for thirty days he [Empedocles] kept her body without pulsation although she never breathed; and for that reason Heraclides called him not merely a physician but a diviner as well, deriving titles from the following lines also: My friends, who dwell in the great city sloping down to yellow Acragas, hard by the citadel, busied with goodly works, all hail! I [Empedocles] go about among you an immortal god, no more a mortal, so honored of all, as is meet, crowned with fillets and flowery garlands. Straightway as soon as I enter with these, men and women, into flourishing towns, I am reverenced and tens of thousands follow, to learn where is the path which leads to welfare, some desirous of oracles, others suffering from all kinds of diseases, desiring to hear a message of healing.

TEXT 2.5 EMPEDOCLES'S DISCIPLES: DIOGENES LAERTIUS, *LIVES OF EMINENT PHILOSOPHERS* 8.59

[Empedocles taught his disciples] Thou shalt arrest the violence of the unwearied winds that arise and sweep the earth, laying waste the cornfields with their blasts, and again, if thou so will, thou shall call back winds in requital. Thou shalt make after the dark rain a seasonable drought for men, and again for the summer drought thou shalt cause tree-nourishing streams to pour from the sky. Thou shalt bring back from Hades a dead man's strength.

APOLLONIUS THE "PYTHAGOREAN"

TEXT 2.6 EXORCISES A YOUTH, PHILOSTRATUS (171?–247? CE), *THE LIFE OF APOLLONIUS OF TYANA* 4.20

Now while he was discussing the question of libations, there chanced to be present in his audience a young dandy who bore so evil a reputation for licentiousness, that his conduct had long been the subject of coarse street-corner songs. His home was Corcyra, and he traced his pedigree to Alcinous the Phaecian who entertained Odysseus. Apollonius then was talking about libations, and was urging them not to drink out of a particular cup, but to reserve it for the gods, without ever touching it or drinking out of it. But when he also urged them to have handles on the cup, and to pour the libation over the handle, because that is the part of the cup at which men are least likely to drink, the youth burst out into loud and coarse laughter, and quite drowned his voice. Then Apollonius looked up at him and said: "It is not yourself that perpetrates this insult, but the demon, who drives you on without your knowing it." And in fact the youth was, without knowing it, possessed by a devil; for he would laugh at things that no one else laughed at, and then he would fall to weeping for no reason at all, and he would talk and sing to himself. Now most people thought that it was the boisterous humor of youth which led him into such excesses; but he was really the mouthpiece of the devil, though it only seemed a drunken frolic in which on that occasion he was indulging. Now when Apollonius gazed on him, the ghost in him began to utter cries of fear and rage, such as one hears from people who are being branded or racked; and the ghost swore that he would leave the young man alone and never take possession of any man again. But Apollonius addressed him with anger, as a master might a shifty, rascally, and shameless slave and so on, and he ordered him to quit the young man and show by a visible sign that he had done so. "I will throw down yonder statue," said the devil, and pointed to one of the images that were in the king's portico, for there it was that the scene took place. But when the statue began moving gently, and then fell down, it would defy anyone to describe the hubbub which arose thereat and the way they clapped their hands with wonder. But the young man rubbed his eyes as if he had just woke up, and he looked towards the rays of the sun and assumed a modest aspect, as all had their attention concentrated on him; for he no longer showed himself licentious, nor did he stare madly about, but he had returned to his own self, as thoroughly as if he had been treated with drugs; and he gave up his dainty dress and summery garments and the rest of his sybaritic way of life, and he fell in love with the austerity of philosophers, and donned their cloak, and stripping off his old self modeled his life in future upon that of Apollonius.

TEXT 2.7 VARIOUS HEALINGS, PHILOSTRATUS, *THE LIFE OF APOLLONIUS OF TYANA* 3.39.1–10

There also arrived a man who was lame. He was already thirty years old and was a keen hunter of lions; but a lion had sprung upon him and dislocated his hip so that he limped with one leg. However, when they massaged his hip with their hands, the youth immediately recovered his upright gait. And another man had had his eyes put out, and he went away having recovered the sight of both of them. Yet another man had his hand paralyzed, but left their presence in full possession of the limb.

TEXT 2.8 HEALING A BOY BITTEN BY A MAD DOG, PHILOSTRATUS, *THE LIFE OF APOLLONIUS OF TYANA* 6.43

Here too is a story that they tell of him in Tarsus. A mad dog had attacked a lad, and as a result of the bite the lad behaved exactly like a dog, for he barked and howled and went on all four feet using his hands as such, and ran about in that manner. And he had been ill in this way for thirty days when Apollonius, who had recently come to Tarsus, met him and ordered a search to be made for the dog that had done the harm. But they said that the dog had not been found, because the youth had been attacked outside the wall when he was practicing with javelins, nor could they learn from the patient what the dog was like, for he did not even know himself any more. Then, Apollonius reflected a moment and said: "O Damis, the dog is a white shaggy sheep-dog, as big as an Amphilochian hound, and he is standing at a certain fountain trembling all over, for he is longing to drink the water, but at the same time is afraid of it. Bring him to me to the bank of the river, where there are wrestling grounds, merely telling him that it is I who call him." So Damis dragged the dog along, and it crouched at the feet of Apollonius, crying out as a suppliant might do before an altar. But he quite tamed it by stroking it with his hand, and then he stood the lad close by, holding him with his hand; and in order that the multitude might be cognizant of so great a mystery, he said: "The soul of Telephus of Mysia has been transferred into this boy, and the Fates impose the same things upon him as upon Telephus." And with these words he bade the dog lick the wound all round where he had bitten the boy, so that the agent of the wound might in turn be its physician and healer. After that the boy returned to his father and recognized his mother, and saluted his comrades as before, and drank of the waters of the Cyndnus. Nor did the sage neglect the dog either, but after offering a prayer to the river he sent the dog across it; and when the dog had crossed the river, he took his stand on the opposite bank, and began to bark, a thing which mad dogs rarely do, and he folded back his ears and wagged his tail, because he knew that he was all right again, for a draught of water cures a mad dog, if he has only the courage to take it.

TEXT 2.9 RAISING FROM THE DEAD, PHILOSTRATUS, *THE LIFE OF APOLLONIUS OF TYANA* 4.45

A girl had died just in the hour of her marriage, and the bridegroom was following her bier lamenting as was natural, his marriage left unfulfilled, and the whole of Rome was mourning with him, for the maiden belonged to a consular family. Apollonius then, witnessing their grief, said, "Put down the bier, for I will stay the tears that you are shedding for this maiden." And withal he asked what was her name. The crowd accordingly thought that he was about to deliver such an oration as is commonly delivered as much to grace the funeral as to stir up lamentation; but he did nothing of the kind, but merely touching her and whispering in secret some spell over her, at once woke up the maiden from her seeming death; and the girl spoke out loud, and returned to her father's house, just as Alcestis did when she was brought back to life by Hercules. And the relations of the maiden wanted to present him with the sum of 150,000 sesterces, but he said that he would freely present the money to the young lady by way of a dowry.

ROMAN RULERS

TEXT 3.1 JULIUS CAESAR, LUCAN (39–65 CE), *PHARSALIA* 5.591–93

Caesar, in disguise, commands the owner of a boat to take him back across the sea to Brindisium where troops await, but as they set out a storm arises and the owner now pleads that they return. But Caesar was confident that all dangers would make way for him. "Despise the angry sea," he cried [to the boat owner], "and spread your sail to the raging wind. If you refuse to make for Italy when Heaven forbids, then make for it when I command. One cause alone justifies your fear, that you know not whom you carry. He is a man whom the gods never desert, whom Fortune treats scurvily when she comes merely in answer to his prayer. Burst through the heart of the storm, relying on my protection. Yonder trouble concerns the sky and sea, but not our bark, for Caesar treads the deck, and her freight shall insure her against the waves. . . . Fortune is seeking to confer a boon on me."

[Although Caesar did have to return to shore, the fact that he was not drowned by the waves was a sign that he was right. The gods would not allow the elements to destroy him. Fortune was protecting him so that she could confer a boon on him. This is a sign of Caesar's empowerment from Heaven.]

TEXT 3.2 NERO, CALPURNIUS SICULUS (FIRST CENTURY CE), *ECOLOGUE* IV 97–100

Do you see how the green woods are hushed at the sound of Caesar's [Nero] name? I remember how, despite the swoop of a storm, the grove, even as now, sank into peace with boughs at rest. And I said, "A god, surely a god, has driven the east winds hence."

TEXT 3.3 VESPASIAN, TACITUS (56–115 CE), *THE HISTORIES* 4.81

During the months while Vespasian was waiting at Alexandria for the regular season of the summer winds and a settled sea, many marvels occurred to mark the favor of heaven and a certain partiality of the gods toward him. One of the common people of Alexandria, well known for his loss of sight, threw himself before Vespasian's knees, praying him with groans to cure his blindness, being so directed by the god Serapis, whom this most superstitious of nations worships before all others; and he besought the Emperor to deign to moisten his cheeks and eyes with his spittle. Another, whose hand was useless, prompted by the same god, begged Caesar to step and trample on it. Vespasian at first ridiculed these appeals and treated them with scorn; then, when the men persisted, he began at one moment to fear the discredit of failure, at another to be inspired with hopes of success by the appeals of the suppliants and the flattery of his courtiers; finally he directed the physicians to give their opinion whether such blindness and infirmity could be overcome by human aid. Their reply treated the two cases differently: they said that in the first [the case of the blind man] the power of sight had not been completely eaten away and it would return if the obstacles were removed; in the other [the useless hand], the joints had slipped and become displaced, but they could be restored if a healing pressure were applied to them. Such perhaps was the wish of the gods, and it might be that the Emperor had been chosen for this divine service; in any case, if a cure were obtained, the glory would be Caesar's, but in the event of failure, ridicule would fall only on the poor suppliants. So Vespasian, believing that his good fortune was capable of anything and that nothing was any longer incredible, with a smiling countenance, and amid intense excitement on the part of the bystanders, did as he was asked to do. The hand was instantly restored to use, and the day again shone for the blind man. Both facts are told by eye-witnesses even now when falsehood brings no reward.

TEXT 3.4 AUGUSTUS CAESAR, PHILO, *LEGATION TO GAIUS* 144–45

The whole human race exhausted by mutual slaughter was on the verge of utter destruction, had it not been for one man and leader, Augustus, whom men fitly call the averter of evil. This is the Caesar who calmed the torrential storms on every side, who healed pestilences common to Greeks and Barbarians, pestilences that descending from the south and east coursed to the west and north sowing seeds of calamity over the places and waters which lay between them.

Bibliography

Ancient Authors in Greek/English

Calpurnius Siculus. *Ecologue IV*. Translated by James Duff. London: Heinemann, 1961.

Diogenes Laertius. "Empedocles." In vol. 2 of *Lives of Eminent Philosophers*. Translated by R. D. Hicks. 2 vols. London: Heinemann, 1925.

Lucan. *Pharsalia*. Translated by James Duff. London: Heinemann, 1962.

Philo. "To Gaius." In *Philo*. Translated by F. H. Colson and G. H. Whitaker. 10 vols. London: Heinemann, 1962.

Philostratus. *The Life of Apollonius of Tyana*. Edited and Translated by F. C. Conybeare. 2 vols. Cambridge, MA: Harvard University Press; London: Heinemann, 1969.

Tacitus. *The Histories*. Translated by Clifford Moore. 4 vols. Cambridge, MA: Harvard University Press; London: Heinemann, 1962.

Collections in Translation

Cotter, Wendy. *The Miracles in Greco-Roman Antiquity*. London: Routledge, 1999.

Edelstein, Emma J., and Ludwig Edelstein. *Asclepius*. 2 vols. Baltimore: Johns Hopkins University Press, 1945.

Guthrie, Kenneth. *The Pythagorean Sourcebook and Library*. Grand Rapids, MI: Phanes, 1987.

Books and Articles

Achtemeier, Paul J. "Gospel Traditions and the Divine Man." *Interpretation* 26 (1972): 174–97.

Blackburn, Barry. *Theios Aner and the Markan Miracle Traditions*. Wissenschaftliche Untersuchungen zum Neun Testament 2/40. Tübingen: Mohr, 1991.

Farnell, Lewis R. *Greek Hero Cults and Ideas of Immortality*. Oxford: Clarendon Press, 1921.

Flinterman, Jaap-Jan. *Power, Paideia and Pythagoreanism: Greek Identity, Conceptions of the Relationships between Philosophers and Monarchs and Political Ideas in Philostratus' Life of Apollonius*. Amsterdam: J. C. Geiben, 1995.

Kee, Howard Clark. *Medicine, Miracle and Magic in New Testament Times*. Cambridge: Cambridge University Press, 1986.

———. *Miracle in the Early Christian World: A Study in Sociohistorical Method*. New Haven, CT: Yale University Press, 1983.

Pepin, Jean. "Cosmic Piety." Pages 408–35 in *Classical Mediterranean Spirituality*. Edited by A. H. Armstrong. New York: Crossroads, 1986.

Remus, Harold. *Pagan-Christian Conflict over Miracle in the Second Century*. Patristic Monograph Series 10. Cambridge, MA: Philadelphia Patristic Foundation, 1983.

Smith, Jonathan Z. "Towards Interpreting Demonic Powers in Hellenistic and Roman Antiquity." *Aufstieg und Niedergang der römischen Welt*, 2nd ser., 17/1 (1978): 425–39.

Theissen, Gerd. *The Miracle Stories of the Early Christian Tradition*. Philadelphia: Fortress Press, 1983.

Twelftree, Graham H. *Jesus the Exorcist: A Contribution to the Study of the Historical Jesus*. Wissenschaftliche Untersuchungen zum Neun Testament 54. Tübingen: J.C.B. Mohr (Paul Siebeck), 1993.

—10—

The Mithras Liturgy

Marvin Meyer

The Mithras Liturgy, as the present text usually is entitled, is one of the most significant and fascinating of the texts of the ancient mystery religions. For students of Mediterranean religions, including Judaism and Christianity, the Mithras Liturgy sheds important light on Mithraism, magic, and religion in Greco-Roman antiquity and late antiquity, and its syncretistic liturgy for the ecstatic ascent of the soul may be compared with descriptions of spiritual ascent in apocalyptic, gnostic, and mystical texts. The Mithras Liturgy promises that an encounter with the divine will result in divine revelation, and it offers the initiate the opportunity to be "born again" (*metagennasthai, palinginesthai*) and experience immortalization (*apathanatismos*).

As a Mithraic text, the Mithras Liturgy is of value for the study of early Christianity, which in general resembles Mithraism in a number of respects—enough to make Christian apologists scramble to invent creative theological explanations to account for the similarities. Devotees of Mithras typically enter sanctuaries of Mithras, called *Mithraea* and designed as caves, and participate in various purifications, initiatory rites, and sacred meals. According to Tertullian (*On the Crown* 15; *On Baptism* 5; *Prescription against Heretics* 40), Mithraic initiates experience ordeals and tests of valor, are washed or baptized with water, and are sealed on their foreheads. According to Justin Martyr (*First Apology* 66.4), Mithraic initiates join in a sacred meal in which they take bread and a cup of water (or a mixed cup of wine and water; the bread and the cup apparently are symbolic of the body and blood of a sacrificed bull) and utter appropriate formulas. Justin adds that through this sacred meal the Mithraic initiates are simply imitating the Christian Eucharist, and the devil, that diabolical counterfeiter, along with his demons, is making them do it. Justin seemingly can find no other way that is theologically acceptable to him to explain the clear similarities between Mithraism and early Christianity.

The Mithras Liturgy reflects the world of Mithraism, but precisely how it relates to other expressions of the mysteries of Mithras is unclear. Apparent Mithraic motifs are abundant in the Mithras Liturgy, and they may include the reference to "the great god Helios Mithras" (line 482), the mention of the eagle (line 484), the invocation of the elements (lines 487–537), the depiction of fire-breathing Aion (lines 587–616), and the portraits of Helios the sun god (lines 635–37) and the highest god (lines 693–704). In particular, the representation of the highest god recalls typical portraits of Mithras from Mithraic monuments. He is presented as youthful, crowned with a golden crown, wearing trousers (*anaxyrides*), holding a bull's shoulder in his right hand, and projecting astral power: lightning comes from his eyes and stars from his body. With the leg of the bull, interpreted astronomically, the Mithraic god, or Mithras, turns the sphere of heaven around, and if the text suggests that Mithras "moves heaven and turns it back (*antistrephousa*)," Mithras may be responsible for the astronomical preces-sion of the equinoxes, the progressive change in the earth's orientation in space caused by a wobble in the earth's rotation (so Ulansey). This cosmological role of Mithras in the Mithras Liturgy corresponds well with recent scholarly interpreta-tions of Mithras as a cosmic savior, with astronomical abilities and powers (Beck, Ulansey).

Mithras's cosmic role also calls to mind the Child of Humanity (or, the "Son of Man") coming with the clouds of heaven in apocalyptic literature (Daniel 7:13–14; 2 *Esdras* 13:1–3; Revelation 1:7) and the Synoptic Gospels (Mark 13:26; 14:62; Matthew 24:30; 26:64; Luke 21:27). Likewise, Mithras endowed with astral power is reminiscent of the Child of Humanity in Revelation 1: the Child of Humanity is brilliant to look at, his face is like the sun and his eyes are like flames of fire, and he has stars in his hand and a double-edged sword in his mouth.

Although Mithras holds the leg of the bull in the Mithras Liturgy, there is no scene of *Mithras tauroktonos*, Mithras slaying the bull, in the text. Elsewhere such a scene (along with the scene of the sacred meal shared by Mithras and Helios or Sol) is central to Mithraic iconography and theology. Like other expressions of the ancient mystery religions, such manifestations of Mithraism proclaim salvific interest in the dying—and rising—of the divine. In Mithraism the death of the bull is a divine sacrifice, and archaeological monuments show heads of grain growing from the dying bull as an anticipation of new life. These themes also are found in the Latin inscriptions from the Mithraeum of Santa Prisca in Rome. One inscription refers to "one that is piously reborn (*renatum*) and created (*creatum*) by sweet things," and another reads, "And you saved us after having shed the eternal blood." These inscriptions resemble passages in the Gospel of John and other early Christian texts. In early Christianity, particularly in the New Testa-ment Gospels and the Letters of Paul, there is a similar preoccupation with Jesus dying and rising, and the proclamation of the crucified and risen savior has dom-inated much of Christian theological thinking over the centuries. Furthermore, in early Christianity and the mystery religions, these interests in dying and rising also are applied to human life; it is said that the dying and rising of the savior fig-ures may be realized in the lives of the people who die and rise with them.

Such a comparison of Jesus dying and rising in Christian texts with dying and rising gods and goddesses in the mystery religions has been debated among scholars for a long time. Some scholars are willing to admit that the story of the death of Jesus may resemble the stories of the deaths of savior figures in the mystery religions, but they also may insist that the deities in the mysteries do not rise as Jesus is said to have risen. Like Jesus, the deities in the mysteries indeed die, but after death they stay where they belong, that is, dead. Such an argument may well be motivated by Christian apologetic concerns designed to affirm the uniqueness of Christianity and the place of the resurrection of Christ and Christians within Christianity.

In fact, the mystery religions and their deities and initiates provide ample evidence for the proclamation of life and the rising of new life in the mysteries. Besides what has already been cited from Mithraism, a few additional examples may be noted. In the Eleusinian mysteries, Kore, daughter of Demeter, returns mythically from her yearly sojourn in Hades to the land of the living, after the manner of the grain in the field (cf. John 12:24–25; 1 Corinthians 15:36–37). In the mysteries of Isis and Osiris, Osiris lives on in the realm of death as the ruler of the underworld, and the "grain Osiris" demonstrates the growth or rebirth of grain and of Osiris. When Lucius is initiated into the mysteries of Isis, according to the *Metamorphoses* of Apuleius of Madauros, he undergoes a nocturnal death experience by passing through the realm of Osiris and appearing the next morning, dressed like the rising sun, to celebrate his initiation as a birthday (see Henderson's contribution on Apuleius in this volume). Elsewhere Apuleius also refers to the initiate as one reborn (*renatus*), as in the case of Lucius, who is brought back to human life from his asinine condition through the power of the goddess. Similarly, a late inscription (376 CE) states that a person who experiences the bath of blood in the *taurobolium* (ritual slaughter of a bull) or *criobolium* (ritual slaughter of a ram), sometimes a practice in the mysteries of the great mother Kybele and Attis, is "reborn for eternity" (*in aeternum renatus*). Attis himself provides at least an intimation of life after death, since his body does not decay, his hair keeps on growing, and his little finger continues to move. During a spring festival, the death of Attis is observed on the Day of Blood in a way that may be comparable to Good Friday observance in Christianity, and thereafter new life for Attis, and for the initiate, may be celebrated in the Hilaria, in a way that may be comparable to Easter celebrations.

Here in the Mithras Liturgy are echoes of these same concerns. At the conclusion of the liturgy for the ascent of the soul, the initiate professes (lines 718–23):

> O lord, though born again, I am passing away,
> though growing and having grown, I am dying,
> though born from a life-generating birth, I am passing on,
> released to death,
> as you have founded,
> as you have decreed
> and have established the mystery.

It is no wonder that Clement of Alexandria, in his *Exhortation to the Greeks* 12.120, proclaims that Christianity may be properly understood to be a mystery religion. He writes, "O truly sacred mysteries! O pure light! In the blaze of torches I have a vision of heaven and of God. I become holy by initiation. The Lord reveals the mysteries." These are true mysteries, Clement maintains; these are Christian mysteries.

The Mithras Liturgy occupies lines 475–834 (or 820) of the *Great Magical Papyrus of Paris* (Bibliothèque Nationale, Supplément grec 574) and hence assumes a prominent place as a magical text or text of ritual power. As such, the Mithras Liturgy contributes a great deal to the study of magic, miracle, and ritual in religions in antiquity and late antiquity, including Christianity, and the stories of miracles attributed to Jesus and others may profitably be studied with texts like the Mithras Liturgy at hand. In the Mithras Liturgy, the magical features include descriptions of breathing techniques, recipes, rituals, amulets, and words of ritual power (*voces magicae*). The words of ritual power can be onomatopoetic (PPP, making a popping sound, perhaps like thunder, and SSS, making a hissing sound), symbolic (AEĒIOYŌ, reciting or chanting the seven Greek vowels in a series), or glossolalic (speaking in tongues, uttering the sounds of vowels or other combinations of letters in ecstasy). In magical texts like the Mithras Liturgy, commonly there is a fascination with spells in other languages (cf. Mark 5:41). Some names and words of power in the Mithras Liturgy derive from languages that can be identified, for instance, Greek (PROPROPHEGGĒ, perhaps "primal brightener," and PSYCHŌ[N] DEMOU PROCHŌ PRŌA—perhaps restore MACHARPH[Ō]N in line 536 on the basis of the previous line); Egyptian (ARARMACHĒS, "Horus of the horizon," and PHRĒ, "Re," the sun god—perhaps restore PHR[Ē] in line 488); and Hebrew or another Semitic language (SEMESILAM, "eternal sun," and IAŌ, a version of the tetragrammaton, the ineffable name of the Jewish God, which played a large role in a variety of magical texts and traditions). Sometimes the very letters of the words may be manipulated for the sake of power (PSINŌTHER NŌPSITHER THERNŌPSI, permutations of the phrase "the son of god" in Egyptian, and IAŌ ŌAI AIŌ, permutations of the ineffable name of God). It is even possible that the last four letters of the name of power PEPPER PREPEMPIPI attempt to reproduce, visually, the four letters of the tetragrammaton in Hebrew.

The Paris magical codex, part of the papyrological collection of Giovanni Anastasi, was acquired by the Bibliothèque Nationale in 1857. According to reports, it may have come from Thebes in southern Egypt. The codex has been dated to the early fourth century CE, and Albrecht Dieterich has proposed that the Mithras Liturgy itself may originally have been composed in about 100–150 CE. The exact parameters of the text of the Mithras Liturgy remain somewhat uncertain, especially for the conclusion. Hans Dieter Betz has suggested that line 820, *kai to hypomnēma echei*, translated here as "And it has this text," should be understood as the conclusion of the Mithras Liturgy and translated as follows: "[With this] the memorandum has [finally] reached its completion." The translation given below is adapted from Marvin Meyer, *The "Mithras Liturgy,"* and is used with the permission of the Society of Biblical Literature. The translation is revised for the present publication, and insights from Hans Dieter Betz, *The "Mithras Liturgy,"* are incorporated. Explanatory headings are added as an aid to understanding the text and its structure, and line numbers for every fifth line in the manuscript are included for ease of reference.

THE MITHRAS LITURGY

Be gracious to me, O Providence and Psyche, as I write these mysteries handed down, but <not> for profit. I request immortality for an only child, for an initiate of this our power. Moreover, O daughter, you must take [480] the juices of herbs and spices, which will <be made known> to you at the end of my holy treatise. The great god Helios Mithras ordered this to be revealed to me by his archangel, so that I alone may ascend to heaven as an eagle [485] and behold the universe.

LITURGICAL MYSTERY FOR THE ASCENT OF THE SOUL: STAGES OF ASCENT

1. The Four Elements

This is the invocation of the ceremony:
First origin of my origin, AEĒIOYŌ,
first beginning of my beginning, PPP SSS PHR[.],
spirit of spirit, first of the spirit [490] in me, MMM,
fire given by god to my mixture of the mixtures in me,
first of the fire in me, ĒU ĒIA EĒ,
water of water, first of the water in me, ŌŌŌ AAA EEE,
earthy substance, first of the earthy substance in me, [495] YĒ YŌĒ,
the complete body of me, NN child of mother NN,
formed by a noble arm and an incorruptible right hand
in a world without light and radiant,
soulless and soulful, YĒI, AUI EUŌIE.

If it be your will, METERTA [500] PHŌTH—
METHARTHA PHĒRIĒ, elsewhere—
IEREZATH,
give me over to immortal birth
and then to my underlying nature,
so that, after the present need which is pressing me sorely,
I may gaze upon the immortal [505] beginning with the immortal spirit,
ANCHREPHRENESOUPHIRIGCH,
with the immortal water,
ERONOUI PARAKOUNĒTH,

with the most steadfast air,
EIOAĒ PSENABŌTH,
that I may be born again in thought,
KRAOCHRAX R OIM ENARCHOMAI, [510]
and the sacred spirit may breathe in me,
NECHTHEN APOTOU NECHTHIN ARPI ĒTH,
that I may wonder at the sacred fire,
KYPHE,
that I may gaze upon the unfathomable, awesome water of the dawn,
NYŌ THESŌ ECHŌ OUCHIECHŌA,
and the vivifying [515] and encircling ether may hear me,
ARNOMĒTHPH.

For today I am about to behold,
with immortal eyes,
I, born mortal from mortal womb,
transformed by tremendous power and an incorruptible right hand, [520]
and with immortal spirit,
the immortal Aion and master of the fiery diadems,
I, sanctified through holy consecrations,
while there subsists within me, holy, for a short time,
my human soul power,
which I shall receive again [525]
after the present bitter and relentless necessity
pressing down upon me,
me, NN child of mother NN,
according to the immutable decree of god,
EUĒ YIA EĒI AŌ EIAU IYA IEŌ.

Since I, born mortal, [530] cannot rise
with the golden brightnesses of the immortal brilliance,
ŌĒY AEŌ ĒYA EŌĒ YAE ŌIAE,
stand, O perishable nature of mortals,
and at once <receive> me safe and sound
after the inexorable and pressing [535] need.
For I am the son PSYCHŌ[N] DEMOU PROCHŌ PRŌA,
I am MACHARPH[.]N MOU PRŌPSYCHŌN PRŌE.

2. The Lower Powers of the Air

Draw in breath from the rays, drawing up three times as much as you can, and you will see yourself being lifted up and [540] ascending to the height, so that you seem to be in midair. You will hear nothing either of humanity or of any other living thing, nor in that hour will you see anything of mortal affairs on earth, but rather you will see all immortal things. For in that day [545] and hour you will see the divine order of the skies: the presiding gods rising into heaven, and others setting. The course of the visible gods will appear through the disk of god, my father, and in similar fashion the so-called pipe, [550] the origin of the ministering wind. For you will see it hanging from the sun's disk like a pipe. You will see the outflow of this object toward the regions westward, boundless as an east wind, if it is assigned to the regions of the east, and the other (the west wind), similarly, toward its own [555] regions. And you will see the gods staring intently at you and rushing at you.

So at once put your right finger on your mouth and say,

Silence! Silence! Silence!
Symbol of the living, incorruptible god! [560]
Guard me, silence, NECHTHEIR THANMELOU.

Then make a long hissing sound, next make a popping sound, and say,

PROPROPHEGGĒ MORIOS PROPHYR PROPHEGGĒ
NEMETHIRE ARPSENTEN PITĒTMI MEŌY ENARTH PHYRKECHŌ
PSYRIDARIŌ [565] TYRĒ PHILBA.

Then you will see the gods looking graciously upon you and no longer rushing at you, but instead going about in their own order of affairs.

When you see that the world above is clear [570] and circling, and that none of the gods or angels is threatening you, expect to hear a great crash of thunder, so as to shock you. Then say again,

Silence! Silence!—the prayer.
I am a star, wandering about with you,
shining from [575] the deep, OXY OXERTHEUTH.

Immediately after you have said this, the sun's disk will expand. After you have said the second prayer, where there is "Silence! Silence!" and what follows, make a hissing sound twice and a popping sound twice, and immediately you will see [580] many five-pronged stars coming from the disk and filling all the air. Then say again,

Silence! Silence!

When the disk is open, you will see the fireless circle, and the fiery doors shut tight. [585]

3. Aion and His Powers

At once close your eyes and recite the following prayer. The third prayer:

Give ear to me,
hearken to me, NN child of mother NN,
O lord, you who have bound together with your breath
the fiery bars of the fourfold [590] root,
O fire-walker, PENTITEROUNI,
light-maker—others: encloser—
SEMESILAM,

fire-breather, PSYRINPHEU,
fire-feeler, IAŌ,
light-breather, ŌAI,
fire-pleaser, ELOUR,
beautiful light, AZAI,
Aion, ACHBA, [595]
light-master, PEPPER PREPEMPIPI,
fire-body, PHNOUĒNIOCH,
light-giver,
fire-sower, AREI EIKITA,
fire-driver, GALLABALBA,
light-forcer, AIŌ,
fire-whirler, PYRICHIBOOSĒIA,
light-mover, SANCHERŌB,
thunder-shaker, [600] IĒ ŌĒ IŌĒIŌ,
glory-light, BEEGENĒTE,
light-increaser, SOUSINEPHI,
fire-light-keeper,
SOUSINEPHI ARENBARAZEI MARMARENTEU,
star-tamer:
open for me,
PROPROPHEGGĒ EMETHEIRE
MORIOMOTYRĒPHILBA.

Because, [605] on account of the pressing, bitter, inexorable necessity,
I invoke the immortal names, living and honored,
which never pass into mortal nature
and are not declared in articulate speech
by human tongue or mortal speech [610] or mortal sound:
ĒEŌ OĒEŌ IŌŌ OĒ ĒEŌ ĒEŌ OĒ EŌ IŌŌ OĒĒE ŌĒE
ŌOĒ IĒ ĒŌ OŌ OĒ IEŌ OĒ ŌOĒ IEŌ OĒ IEEŌ EĒ IŌ
OĒ IOĒ ŌĒŌ EOĒ OEŌ ŌIĒ ŌIĒ EŌ OI III ĒOĒ ŌYĒ
ĒŌOĒE EŌ ĒIA AĒA EĒA [615] ĒEEĒ EEĒ EEĒ IEŌ ĒEŌ
OĒEEOĒ ĒEŌ ĒYŌ OĒ EIŌ ĒŌ ŌĒ ŌĒ EE OOO YIŌĒ.

Say all these things with fire and spirit, until completing the first utterance.
Then, similarly, begin the second, until you complete the [620] seven immortal
gods of the universe. When you have said these things, you will hear thunder-
ing and shaking in the surrounding realm, and you likewise will feel yourself
being agitated. Say again,

Silence!—the prayer.

Then open your eyes, and you will see the doors [625] open and the world of the
gods within the doors, so that from the pleasure and joy of the sight your spirit
runs ahead and ascends.

4. Helios, the Sun

Stand still and at once draw breath from the divine into yourself, while you look intently. When [630] your soul is restored, say,

> Come, lord,
> ARCHANDARA PHŌTAZA PYRIPHŌTA ZABYTHIX
> ETIMENMERO PHORATHĒN ERIĒ PROTHRI PHORATHI.

When you have said this, the rays will turn toward you. Look into the center of them. When [635] you have done this, you will see a youthful god, beautiful in appearance, with fiery hair, in a white tunic and a scarlet cloak, and wearing a fiery crown. At once greet him with the fire greeting:

> Greetings, O lord,
> great power, great might, [640] king, greatest of gods,
> Helios, lord of heaven and earth, god of gods.
> Mighty is your breath,
> mighty is your strength, O lord.

> If it be your will,
> announce me to the supreme god,
> the one who has conceived and made you:
> that a person,
> I, NN child of mother NN, [645]
> who was born from the mortal womb of NN and from semen,
> who, since he has been born again from you today,
> has become immortal out of so many myriads in this hour
> according to the wish of god the exceedingly good,
> resolves to worship [650] you,
> and prays with all human power,
> that you may take along with you
> the horoscope of the day and hour today,
> which has the name THRAPSIARI MORIROK,
> that he may appear and give revelation during the good hours,
> EŌRŌ RŌRE ŌRRI ŌRIŌR RŌR RŌI [655] ŌR REŌRŌRI
> EŌR EŌR EŌR EŌRE.

After you have said these things, he will come to the celestial pole, and you will see him walking as if on a road.

5. The Seven Fates

Look intently and make a long bellowing sound, like a horn, releasing all your breath and straining your sides. Kiss [660] the amulets and say, first to the right,

> Protect me, PROSYMĒRI.

After saying this, you will see the doors thrown open and seven virgins coming from deep within, dressed in linen garments and with the faces of asps. They are called the fates [665] of heaven, and they wield golden wands. When you see them, greet them in this manner:

> Greetings, O seven fates of heaven, noble and good virgins,
> sacred ones and companions of MINIMIRROPHOR,
> most holy guardians of the four pillars.[670]

> Greetings to you, the first, CHREPSENTHAĒS.
> Greetings to you, the second, MENESCHEĒS.
> Greetings to you, the third, MECHRAN.
> Greetings to you, the fourth, ARARMACHĒS.
> Greetings to you, the fifth, ECHOMMIĒ.
> Greetings to you, the sixth, TICHNONDAĒS.
> Greetings to you, the seventh, EROU ROMBRIĒS.

6. The Seven Pole Lords

Another seven gods also come forward, gods who have the faces of black bulls, in linen [675] loincloths, and holding seven golden diadems. They are the so-called pole lords of heaven, whom you must greet in the same manner, each of them with his own name:

> Greetings, O guardians of the pivot of the heavenly sphere,
> sacred and brave youths,
> who turn [680] at one command
> the revolving axis of the vault of heaven,
> who send out thunder and lightning
> and jolts of earthquakes and thunderbolts
> against the nations of impious people,
> but to me, who am pious and god-fearing,
> you send health and soundness of body [685]
> and acuteness of hearing and seeing
> and calmness in the present good hours of this day,
> O my lords and powerfully ruling gods!

> Greetings to you, the first, AIERŌNTHI.
> Greetings to you, the second, MERCHEIMEROS.
> Greetings to you, the third, ACHRICHIOUR. [690]
> Greetings to you, the fourth, MESARGILTŌ.
> Greetings to you, the fifth, CHICHRŌALITHŌ.
> Greetings to you, the sixth, ERMICHTHATHŌPS.
> Greetings to you, the seventh, EORASICHĒ.

7. The Highest God, Mithras

Now when they take their place, here and there, in order, look in the air and you will see lightning bolts going down, lights flashing, [695] the earth shaking, and a god descending, a god immensely great, with a bright appearance, youthful, golden-haired, wearing a white tunic, a golden crown, and trousers, and holding in his right hand a golden [700] shoulder of a young bull. This is the Bear that moves heaven and turns it around, moving upward and downward in accordance with the hour. Then you will see lightning bolts leaping from his eyes and stars from his body.

At once [705] make a long bellowing sound, straining your belly, that you may excite the five senses. Bellow long until the conclusion, kiss the amulets again, and say,

MOKRIMO PHERIMO PHERERI,
life of me, NN:
Stay.
Dwell in [710] my soul.
Do not abandon me, for one entreats you,
ENTHO PHENEN THROPIŌTH.

Gaze upon god while bellowing long, and greet him in this manner:

Greetings, O lord, master of the water.
Greetings, O founder of the earth.
Greetings, O ruler of the wind.
O bright lightener, [715]
PROPROPHEGGĒ EMETHIRI ARTENTEPI
THĒTH MIMEŌ YENARŌ PHYRCHECHŌ PSĒRI DARIŌ
PHRĒ PHRĒLBA.

Give revelation, lord, concerning the matter of NN.
O lord, though born again, I am passing away,
though growing and having grown, [720] I am dying,
though born from a life-generating birth, I am passing on,
released to death,
as you have founded,
as you have decreed
and have established the mystery.
I am PHEROURA MIOURI.

INSTRUCTIONS FOR THE USE OF THE MYSTERY

After you have said these things, he will immediately respond with a revelation. [725] You will grow weak in soul and will not be in yourself when he answers you. He speaks the oracle to you in verse, and after speaking he will depart. You remain silent, since you will be able to comprehend all these matters by yourself, for at a later time [730] you will remember infallibly the things spoken by the great god, even if the oracle contained myriads of verses.

If you also wish to use a fellow initiate, so that he alone may hear with you the things spoken, let him remain pure together with you for <seven> [735] days and abstain from meat and the bath. Even if you are alone, and you undertake the things communicated by the god, you speak as though prophesying in ecstasy. And if you also wish to show him, judge whether he is completely worthy as a person. [740] Treat him as if in his place you were being judged in the matter of immortalization, and whisper to him the first prayer, the beginning of which is "First origin of my origin, AEĒIOYŌ." Say the successive things as an initiate, over his [745] head, in a soft voice, so that he may not hear, as you are anointing his face with the mystery. This immortalization takes place three times a year. If anyone, O child, after the teaching, wishes to disobey, then for him it will no longer [750] be in effect.

INSTRUCTION FOR THE RITUAL

[Scarab]

Take a sun scarab that has twelve rays, and make it fall into a deep, turquoise cup, at the time when the moon is invisible. Put in together with it the seed of the fruit pulp of the lotus, [755] and after grinding it with honey, prepare a cake. At once you will see the scarab moving forward and eating, and when it has consumed the cake, it immediately dies. Pick it up and throw it into a glass vessel of excellent rose oil, as much as you wish. [760] Spread sacred sand in a pure manner and set the vessel on it, and say the formula over the vessel for seven days, while the sun is in midheaven:

> I have consecrated you,
> that your essence may be useful to me, NN alone,
> IE IA Ē EĒ OU EIA,
> that you may prove useful to me [765] alone.
> For I am PHŌR PHORA PHŌS PHOTIZAAS—
> others: PHŌR PHŌR OPHOTHEIXAAS.

On the seventh day pick up the scarab and bury it with myrrh and Mendesian wine and fine linen, and put it away in a flourishing bean field. [770] Then, after you have entertained and feasted together, put away, in a pure manner, the ointment for the immortalization.

[Herbs]

If you want to show this to someone else, take the juice of the herb called Kentritis, and smear it, along with rose oil, around the eyes of the one you wish, [775] and he will see so clearly that it will amaze you. I have not found a greater spell than this in the world. Ask the god for what you want, and he will give it to you.

Presentation before the great god is like this. Obtain the above-mentioned herb [780] Kentritis, at the conjunction (of the sun and the moon) occurring in the Lion. Take the juice, mix it with honey and myrrh, and write on a leaf of the persea tree the eight-letter formula, mentioned below. Keep yourself pure for three days before. Set out early in the morning toward the east, [785] lick off the leaf while you show it to the sun, and then the sun god will listen attentively to you. Begin to consecrate this at the divine new moon, in the Lion. This is the formula:

I EE OO IAI.

Lick it up so that you may be protected, and roll up the leaf [790] and throw it into the rose oil. Many times have I used the spell, and I have been truly amazed.

The god said to me,

Use the ointment no longer,
but after casting it into the river,
<you must> consult while wearing the great mystery [795] of the scarab
revitalized through the twenty-five living birds,
and consult once a month, at full moon, instead of three times a year.

The Kentritis plant grows from the month of Pauni, in the regions of the [800] black earth, and is similar to the erect verbena. This is how to recognize it: When an ibis wing is dipped at its black tip and smeared with the juice, the feathers fall off when touched. After the lord [805] pointed this out, it was found in the Menelaitis region near Phalagry, at the river banks, near the Besas plant. It is of a single stem and reddish down to the root, and the leaves are rather crinkled and have fruit [810] like the tip of wild asparagus. It is similar to the so-called Talapes, like the wild beet.

[Amulets]

The amulets require this procedure: Copy the right one onto the skin [815] of a black sheep, with myrrh ink, and after tying it with the sinews of the same animal, put it on. Copy the left one onto the skin of a white sheep, and use the same procedure. The left one is very full of "PROSTHYMĒRI." [820] And it has this text:

"So speaking, he drove through the trench the single-hoofed horses" (*Iliad* 10.564).
"And men gasping among grievous slaughters" (*Iliad* 10.521).
"And they washed off their profuse sweat in the sea" (*Iliad* 10.572).
"You will dare to lift up your mighty spear against Zeus" (*Iliad* 8.424). [825]

Zeus went up to the mountain with a golden bullock and a silver dagger. Upon all he bestowed a share, only to Amara did he not give, but he said,

Let go of what you have,
and then you will receive,
PSINŌTHER NŌPSITHER THERNŌPSI,
and so on, as you like.[830]

"So Ares suffered, when Otos and mighty Epialtes . . . him" (*Iliad* 5.385).

Spells

Spell for restraining anger: "You will dare to lift up your mighty spear against Zeus" (*Iliad* 8.424).

For friends: "Let . . . seize . . . , lest we become a source of joy for our enemies" (*Iliad* 10.193).

Bibliography

Beck, Roger. *Planetary Gods and Planetary Orders in the Mysteries of Mithras*. Études Préliminaires aux Religions Orientales dans l'Empire Romain (Religions in the Graeco-Roman World) 109. Leiden: Brill, 1988.

Betz, Hans Dieter. *The "Mithras Liturgy": Text, Translation, and Commentary*. Studien und Texte zu Antike und Christentum 18. Tübingen: J.C.B. Mohr (Paul Siebeck), 2003.

Burkert, Walter. *Ancient Mystery Cults*. Carl Newell Jackson Lectures. Cambridge, MA: Harvard University Press, 1987.

Clauss, Manfred. *The Roman Cult of Mithras: The God and His Mysteries*. Translated by Richard Gordon. New York: Routledge, 2000.

Dieterich, Albrecht. *Eine Mithrasliturgie*. Leipzig, Germany: Teubner, 1903. 2nd ed. Edited by Richard Wünsch. 1910. 3rd ed. Edited by Otto Weinreich. 1923. Reprint, Darmstadt: Wissenschaftliche Buchgesellschaft, 1966.

Merkelbach, Reinhold, and Maria Totti, eds. *Abrasax: Ausgewählte Papyri religiösen und magischen Inhalts*. Abhandlungen der Rheinisch-Westfälischen Akademie der Wissenschaften, Sonderreihe Papyrologica Coloniensia 17.1–4. 4 vols. Opladen: Westdeutscher Verlag, 1990–96, particularly Band 3, *Zwei griechisch-ägyptische Weihezeremonien* (*Die Leidener Weltschöpfung; Die Pschai-Aion-Liturgie*).

Metzger, Bruce M. "A Classified Bibliography of the Graeco-Roman Mystery Religions, 1924–1973, with a Supplement, 1974–77." Pages 1259–1423 in *Aufstieg und Niedergang der römischen Welt*. Edited by Hildegard Temporini and Wolfgang Haase. Band II.17.3. Berlin: Walter de Gruyter, 1984.

Meyer, Marvin. *The Ancient Mysteries: A Sourcebook of Sacred Texts*. Philadelphia: University of Pennsylvania Press, 1999.

———. *The "Mithras Liturgy."* Society of Biblical Literature Texts and Translations 10. Missoula, MT: Scholars Press, 1976.

———. "*PGM* IV.475–829." Pages 48–54 in *The Greek Magical Papyri in Translation, Including the Demotic Spells*. 2nd ed. Edited by Hans Dieter Betz. Chicago: University of Chicago Press, 1992.

Smith, Jonathan Z. *Drudgery Divine: On the Comparison of Early Christianities and the Religions of Late Antiquity*. Jordan Lectures in Comparative Religion 14. Chicago: University of Chicago Press, 1990.

Ulansey, David. *The Origins of the Mithraic Mysteries: Cosmology and Salvation in the Ancient World*. New York: Oxford University Press, 1989.

— 11 —

Apuleius of Madauros

Ian H. Henderson

Apuleius of Madauros was born in North Africa around 125 CE. His importance for understanding Jesus and his world is twofold. Generally, the writings of Apuleius are among the most powerful tools available to help modern readers to imagine historically what Greco-Roman polytheist religion might have been like, from the viewpoint of a deeply engaged and articulate participant. Writing to his converts in Corinth, Paul of Tarsus took for granted that while they were "still Gentiles," they experienced powerful attraction "toward mute idols" (1 Corinthians 12:2). Apuleius's most important books are invaluable to understanding how such an attraction might work at several levels of seriousness and sophistication.

Apuleius's most famous and influential work is a sprawling fictional narrative of magical and religious transformation, the *Metamorphoses* (the Book of Transformations) or the *Golden Ass*. No narrative summary could possibly do justice to this extraordinarily complex composition, but the central plot concerns the young Lucius, whose interest in magic leads him, like many a sorcerer's apprentice, into adventures beyond his control. Turned by hasty incantation into a donkey, Lucius witnesses an entertaining sample of the absurdities of human life. Over and over again, the progress of donkey-Lucius's adventure is interrupted or diverted by side narratives, magical, amusing, erotic, and mythical (the famous myth of Cupid "Desire" and Psyche "Soul" [4.28–6.24]). Eventually, Lucius is saved from his bewitchment and restored to humanity by the intervention of the Egyptian goddess Isis—like the God of Jerusalem, a successful religious export from the magical, prophetic East throughout the Greco-Roman world.

The last book of the *Metamorphoses*, in which Lucius is saved by Isis and sings her praises, adopts a tone of religious seriousness which it is hard for modern Western readers to reconcile with the witty, sexy, magical low-life atmosphere of the bulk of the work. The passage convincingly imagines a fanciful experience of personal deliverance through prayer, visionary dreams, miracles, personal dedication, and public, congregational, and personal rituals. Lucius's encounter with Isis provides the reader with a rich vocabulary for comparative imagination of religious experiences and movements in antiquity. Moreover, the Lucius of the last, eleventh book is stunningly identified (by divine revelation in a dream) with Apuleius himself as a native of Madauros (11.27).

The *Metamorphoses* is not a work for the fastidious: it revels in startling turns and deliberate incongruities of style and content. It describes itself from the beginning as a hybrid text, marked by a leapfrogging style (*desultoria scientia* [1.1]) and contents to match. It constantly advertises its own artificiality. Written, no doubt, as a deliberate tour de force, the *Metamorphoses*, precisely because it is an unabashed exaggeration, must build upon basically shared cultural perceptions in its intended readers. This curiously postmodern creation is thus an apt evocation of the imaginative world of Greco-Roman religions, for which "Pagan" is a completely inadequate denominator. The long selection from the climactic, but therefore atypical, book 11, is therefore chosen here as an instance of Greco-Roman religious discourse utterly unlike that of parable and gospel yet comparably exotic, inviting, and forceful as a promise of personal transformation.

More specifically, Apuleius himself is cited often in historical Jesus research to give flesh to an ideal type of "magician." Both in the essentially fictional *Metamorphoses* and in the, on balance, nonfictional *Apologia pro se de Magia* ("Self-Defense on a Charge of Magic"), Apuleius shows his main character engaged in activities which his contemporaries would call "magic." Like Jesus of Nazareth in the Gospels (Mark 3:22), Apuleius in his *Apologia* was plausibly represented by his enemies as an agent of black magic. In later Talmudic tradition, Jesus is tried and executed on a Jewish charge of misleading Israel into sorcery (*b. Sanhedrin* 43a). Indeed, Apuleius actually was brought to trial on a potentially capital charge of using magic to seduce a wealthy widow into marriage without her family's consent.

We cannot know to what extent Apuleius's *Apologia* accurately records his self-defense on those charges. Where should we situate the *Apologia* along the spectrum from declamation to verbatim transcript, from literary-rhetorical exhibition piece to documentary source? The *Apologia* is in fact a uniquely clear instance of the invalidity of such dichotomies in certain social contexts, specifically in relation to the socially most mobile speakers in the Greco-Roman world. The *Defense* is surely a "masterpiece" of highly cultivated, artificial Greco-Roman rhetoric (Helm 1955) and was quite likely revised for circulation. None of this, however, logically or even probably requires that the speech is fictional and not essentially the representation of an actual performance. Details aside, there is every reason to suppose that a professional like Apuleius could actually talk like this, both in quantity and in quality—and that a cultured Roman judge might find the effect flattering and impressive.

Magic or witchcraft was condemned both in Judaism and in Greco-Roman law. Paradoxically, magic and witchcraft were practiced widely, and no one in Greco-Roman society was above employing their practitioners on occasion. Ambivalence about magic only exceptionally resulted in clear distinctions between "good" and "bad" varieties or between "magic" and "religion," though the more gruesome practices were feared more widely. Jews and Christians, like other exotic ethnic and religious groups but more than most, were stereotyped as likely to be involved in such arts. Magic practices, rituals, and spooky, powerful names moved freely among religious traditions. Greco-Roman public religion was cosmopolitan; Greco-Roman magic was exuberantly eclectic. Few indeed (Epicureans and Cynics) doubted the influence for good and evil of intermediate semidivine powers and of humans gifted by nature or trained to work with them. Apuleius gives this worldview his most solemn affirmation (43). It is entirely in keeping that Apuleius includes "Moses," perhaps even "John," within his list of notorious or, rather, celebrity (*celebratus*) magicians (90).

Again, we cannot know exactly how the charge of magic was formulated against Apuleius, since what we do know comes in terms of his naturally biased and fragmentary references. Apuleius himself refers only to the archaic Twelve Tables (47.3; 82.6), but this is typical of his own affected old-fashionedness. The charge before the court was, however, almost certainly couched in the legal formulas of *maleficia magica* (magic harm) and *venena et carmina* (potions and incantations), formulas that more or less invoke the old *Lex Cornelia de sicariis et veneficiis* of 81 BCE. The legal situation is clarified a little by a fictional declamation written by Apuleius's contemporary, Hadrian of Tyre. Like Apuleius, Hadrian was a professional public speaker and, like Apuleius, was in his lifetime accused of magic (Philostratus, *Vitae Sophistarum* 590) and of murder (587). In the extant exhibition piece, Hadrian attacks a hypothetical witch not for any harmful practice but merely for being a witch (in Polemon, *Declamationes* [ed. Hinck, 44–45], Ogden, 284; Dickie, 148). In principle under Roman law one did not need actually to have injured anyone to be liable to prosecution and execution as a witch or magician: one only needed to know how to cause harm (*maleficium*).

It is hard to avoid a certain analogy between the legal framework under which someone could be accused of magic, as in Apuleius's case by relatives in a dispute over marriage and property rights, and that under which someone might be accused of being Christian, also typically by neighbors and kin. In his famous letter to the emperor Trajan, Pliny as proconsul of Pontus and Bithynia asks whether Christians brought before him were liable to punishment for "the name itself" or only if associated criminal acts (*flagitia*) could be proved (*Ep.* 10.96–7). Punishment for a name alone would become a key topic in Christian apologetics (see Bradley Peper and Mark DelCogliano's contribution in this volume on the correspondence between Pliny and Trajan). In law the charge of being a sorcerer, like that of being a Christian, did not technically require the accuser to prove that any harm actually had been done, though a few juicy allegations could help. There is thus a noteworthy overlap among the slanders lodged against exotic religious interests in the Greco-Roman world, whether Christians or devotees of Bacchus or Isis or, eventually, Christian heretics, and those associated with attacks on individuals as magicians: sexual license, abuse of children, seduction of women, nocturnal conspiracy, ritual murder, and cannibalism (Beard, North, and Price 1.149–56, 228–44; 2.260–87).

It is remarkable, then, that prosecutions and executions for magic are not attested more widely in Greco-Roman antiquity. Until quite late in antiquity neither type of prosecution (against magicians or against *superstitio*) was brought by the state. If the charge could include a hint of antistate magic—for example, if the alleged magician was seeking a new sovereign *basileus*—an element of lèse-majesté might give state officials an interest in police action. It is just barely possible that this was an element in the Romans' perception of Jesus of Nazareth. Otherwise, bringing a private accusation against a local witch doctor may well have been riskier than bringing such a prosecution against a Christian sectarian. Apuleius suggests that anyone who really believes that his neighbor is a powerful witch doctor ought to be too afraid to make a public accusation of magic (26). In fact, in the course of his defense, Apuleius offers several moments when he seems to be boldly performing ritual incantations right in the middle of the trial, evoking in hymnic tones the presence of his mysterious patron god only a few lines after pronouncing an intimidating curse on his opponents (64).

The whole of Apuleius's defense is remarkable, largely for its sheer audacity. Apuleius shows himself quite conscious of the distinction between being a magus and actually hurting anybody by magic. As often as possible, he represents the charge as that of being a magus and not only that of having performed magic rites. In fact, he systematically subordinates the question of fact ("Did I use potentially dangerous potions and incantations?") to the questions of definition ("Am I really a magus?" and "Is being a magus necessarily/always against the law?"). Yet he does so, amazingly, by virtually granting all issues of fact, as though to say, "So what if I did do this or that? Does that make me a magus?" (9.3; 13. 5–6; 28.2; 30.1; 55.2–4).

It is hard to imagine two defendants coming before provincial Roman courts who are more different than Jesus of Nazareth and Apuleius of Madauros. Jesus is represented as having very little to say to his Roman judge (Mark 14:61; John 18:33–37). Apuleius boasts at the outset that he never had a thought he could not proclaim (5), and he quickly looks determined to prove it. In fact, however, religious silence and reticence at several levels of discourse turn out to be strangely central to the professionally loquacious defendant. Apuleius makes a show of denying almost none of the facts that are alleged against him. Thus he does not contest charges of performing occult ceremonies (57–60), of enchanting an epileptic boy with song, and of examining a freeborn woman suffering from the same disorder (42–48). He admits to owning various mysterious cult objects, such as a statuette of Mercury, patron god of magic (63), and a ritual bundle associated with his initiation into many divine cults (he mentions specifically the mysteries of the gods Liber and Asclepius, both popular in North Africa) (55).

The statuette in particular is interesting as reflecting Apuleius's personal devotional practices: it is alleged against him as a symptom of his magicianship that he secretly worshiped this object and addressed it as "king" (*basileus*). Although he identifies the statuette as of Mercury (*Mercuriolus*, his little Mercury [63]), Apuleius confirms his habit of addressing it with a royal title. He then goes further by dramatically refusing to divulge his patron god's real, ineffable name in a bold mixture of Platonic, philosophical reticence and Hermetic, magical taboo

(64). Two of Jesus' best-attested speech habits, addressing God by a private address ("*Abba*") and speaking of his God's "kingship," are no doubt grounded in Jewish covenantal piety—but they also are recognizable beyond their Jewish context as the habits of a charismatic individual claiming peculiar intimacy with the divine (see Mary Rose D'Angelo's chapter in this volume).

Personally, Jesus of Nazareth and Apuleius of Madauros represent polar opposites within the world of Mediterranean antiquity. Their opposition may usefully define for us one essential axis through the religious world, that is, the axis of magic. Their differences also point to another key axis: social class. Ultimately, Apuleius's defense against the capital charge of magic rests on an extraordinarily clear distinction, which is not the widespread distinction between good, white magic and bad, black magic. Instead, Apuleius constructs a distinction between his own scholarly, bookish magic and the vulgar magic of the ordinary folk, and he does so by offering a strikingly lucid description of what in vulgar parlance a magus would be and do (26). Apuleius admits throughout to behavior that, if any definition of magic were ever to be legally tenable, would surely identify him as a magician. Yet he holds himself to be innocent of illegal magic because he learned his magic from Plato. The vulgar enchanter and common shaman, though equally capable of "communing with the immortal gods" (26) and not necessarily evil in his actions, is left by Apuleius without imaginable defense before his cultured Roman judge.

There are fine modern translations of Apuleius's works available: Harrison, Hilton, and Hunink for Apuleius's rhetorical works, and Hanson for the *Metamorphoses*. The selections and translation below seek to highlight the ritual and experiential aspects of Apuleius's language. No English translation can do justice to his jumpy, fascinating Latin style, but I have tried to suggest the poetized, incantatory effect of at least certain passages of speech.

THE REVELATION OF ISIS

APULEIUS, *METAMORPHOSES* 11

[5–6] "Now here I am, Lucius, moved by your prayers,
I, parent of the nature of things,
mistress of all the elements,
initial progeny of the ages,
sum of divine powers,
queen of the ghosts of the dead,
first of heavenly beings,
the uniform face of gods and goddesses.
I control by my nod the bright heights of heaven,
the wholesome breezes of the sea,
the lamented silences of the underworld.

My divine power is unique,
worshiped by the whole world in diverse style,
with different rites and manifold names.
Here the primal Phrygians call me Mother of the Gods at Pessinus;
there the first people of Attica call me Minerva, daughter of Cecrops;
the maritime Cypriots, Venus of Paphos;
the archers of Crete, Dictynna Diana;
the trilingual Sicilians, Stygian Proserpina;
the Eleusinians, Attic Ceres;
some call me Juno, some Bellona, others Hecate, still others Rhamnusia.
Those illumined by the first rays of the rising Sun-god, both kinds of
    Ethiopian,
and the Egyptians, strong in ancient learning,
worship me with my proper ceremonies
and call me by my real name: Queen Isis.
I am here moved by your misfortunes,
I am here favorable and propitious.
Stop your tears and cease grieving now.
Dispel your bitterness.
Now by my providence the day of salvation is dawning for you.

So, then, give careful attention to these my commands: The day, the day
born from this night, has been named an eternal observance for me. Now that
the winter storms have subsided and the sea's storm-tossed waves are calmed,
my priests by dedicating to the navigable sea a hitherto unused vessel consecrate the first-fruits of the shipping season. You must wait for this ritual with a
mind neither anxious nor profane. For at my order a priest will bear in his
right hand a rose crown joined to a sistrum [an Egyptian ritual-musical instru-
ment] as part of his provision for the parade. Therefore supported by my wish
in the confusion of the crowds unhesitatingly follow my parade and from close
up softly, as though about to kiss the priest's hand, snatch the roses and forth-
with strip yourself of the skin of that miserable and to me long since detested
beast. And do not recoil from anything to do with me as though it were hard.
For at this very moment as I am coming to you, I am present there too and am
instructing my priest through a dream as to what steps must be followed. At
my order the thick crowds of people will yield to you. No one, with all the
happy ceremonies and festive spectacle, will be shocked at that deformed appearance which you bear, nor will anyone ill-interpret your suddenly transformed face and meanly bring charges against you.

You shall remember distinctly and ever hold established in your inner mind,
the remaining course of your life as bound over to me right to the last moments of your last gasp. Nor is it unfair that you should owe to her, by whose
benefice you return to humankind, everything you live. Yet you shall live as
one of the blessed, you shall live glorious in my patronage. And when you

have measured the span of your time and descended to the dead, there too in that underworld vault you will be able to worship me regularly, whom you see before you now, only then shining among the shadows of Acheron and reigning in the Stygian hiding places, while you dwell in the Elysian fields, favored by me. But if by consistent devotion and regular worship and firm chastity you earn my divine approval, you shall know that it is permitted to me to extend life for you beyond the span laid down by your fate."

Lucius attends the goddess's sacred procession and is transformed back into human form (7–14). The priest of the goddess then addresses Lucius:

[15] "After enduring many and varied labors, driven by great tempests and hurricanes of Destiny, you, Lucius, have at last come to the haven of Quiet and altar of Mercy. For neither birth nor social standing nor even that learning in which you excel has done you any good at all. Instead, slidden in the slippery season of green youth into slavish lusts, you reaped the sinister reward of ill-advised curiosity. But even Destiny's blindness, while she crossed you with the worst dangers, still brought you by her unseeing malice to this divine blessedness. Let her go now and rage in all her cruelty and search out some other matter for her pitilessness. For rotten luck has no place in those whose lives the majesty of our goddess has claimed for her enslavement. How have thieves, beasts, enslavement, roundabout detours of bitterest journeys, fear of daily death done any good with malicious Destiny? Now, however, you are in the care of a Destiny who is not blind, who by the splendor of her light enlightens even the other gods. Now put on a happier face to go with that bright garb of yours. Follow the procession of the salvific goddess with a renewing step. Let the impious look, let them look and recognize their error. See! With his former calamities ended by the providence of great Isis, Lucius joyfully triumphs at his Destiny. In order, however, that you may be safer and better armed, put your name in for this holy militia; not long ago you were invited to its "oath of allegiance" (sacramentum). Dedicate yourself now to the observance of our way of life and accept the free yoke of her service. For once you begin to serve the goddess, then you will appreciate more the fruit of your freedom."

Lucius takes up residence in the precinct of Isis's sanctuary, experiencing constant dream-apparitions of the goddess and considering entering her (celibate) priesthood:

[21] In fact day by day, more and more my desire grew to be admitted into the sacred rites, and I often would approach the head priest with the most earnest prayers, begging him finally to initiate me into the secrets of the sacred night. But he, a man rather grave and known for his observance of a strict rule of life, put off my insistence gently and kindly—as parents do, when they restrain the impetuous impulses of children. And he used to calm my rather anxious mind

with the solace of hope for something better: For even the date when any person could be initiated was determined by the will of the goddess, and also the priest who should perform the ritual was chosen by her providence. Even the costs necessary for the ceremonies were destined by a similar instruction. And he used to advise me to bear with all these things with proper endurance, since I ought to beware particularly of over-eagerness and obstinacy, and shun either fault—of hesitating once called or of rushing unbidden. Nor indeed, he said, was there anyone from his priesthood of such a twisted mind or, indeed, so damned to death, as to dare carrying out a casual and sacrilegious service and to commit a deadly offense, unless his lady distinctly ordered him. For both the gates of hell and life's safekeeping are in the hands of the goddess, and the initiation itself is celebrated as if it were a voluntary death and prayed-for salvation. In fact the approval of the goddess often leads on those who, their life's days already done, have arrived at the very threshold of extinguished light, to whom, however, the great mysteries of our order could be safely entrusted. By her providence they were in some sense born again, restored once more to the course of a new well-being. I too, therefore, ought to uphold the heavenly precept, although a clear and particular mark of great divine approval had long ago appointed me and destined me for a blessed service. No different from other worshipers, I should abstain from unholy and forbidden food, so that I might arrive more directly at the arcane secrets of the purest order.

The priest leads Lucius through ten days of purificatory rites of bathing and fasting:

[23] . . . you may perhaps, attentive reader, wonder anxiously what then was said, what done. I would speak if speaking were allowed; you would find out if hearing were allowed. But ears and tongue alike would be punished, the one for impious loquacity, the other for casual curiosity. Nonetheless, I will not torture you with prolonged constriction as you are hanging on a devout longing. So listen, but believe, this is the truth.

> I approached the confine of death
> and having stood on the threshold of Proserpina,
> and borne through all the elements
> I returned.
> At midnight I saw the sun vibrating with a brilliant light.
> I approached the gods below
> and the gods above
> and adored them from nearby.

See, I have reported to you things which even when you have heard them, you must still fail to understand. So I shall report only what can be told without punishment to the minds of the uninitiated. . . .

Lucius celebrates his initiation with several days of feasting:

[24] . . . But at last on the command of the goddess, once my thanks had been paid, of course not fully, yet to the best of my modest means, I get ready for my delayed homecoming, though the chains of my burning desire are hardly broken. So then, prostrate in the presence of the goddess, her feet washed for a long time with my face, tears welling, mixing speech with sobbing and choking on my words, I manage to say:

[25] "You, holy and perpetual savior of humankind,
ever generous in nourishing mortals,
you bestow a mother's sweet love on the situations of the distressed.
No day nor any repose nor even an instant goes by empty of your benefits:
you protect people by land and sea,
scattering the storms of life
you stretch out your saving right hand.
With it you unravel the hopelessly tangled knots of the Fates,
you ease Fortune's tempests
and you prevent dangerous movements of the stars.
Those above honor you,
those below respect you.
You turn the globe,
light the sun,
rule the earth,
and trample Tartarus.
The stars answer to you,
the seasons return,
the divine powers rejoice,
the elements submit.
At your nod the winds blow,
the clouds nourish,
seeds sprout, buds grow.
The birds of the sky tremble at your majesty,
the wild beasts wandering the mountains,
the snakes skulking on the ground,
the monsters swimming the deep.
But I am feeble in wit for offering you praises,
And weak in wealth for providing sacrifices.
The fertility of my speech is not enough for saying what I feel about your
    majesty,
not even a thousand mouths and tongues,
nor an eternal sequence of unwearying speech.
So whatever an observant, but poor person can do,
I shall make sure to do:
Forever guarding your divine looks and holiest presence
stored in the depths of my heart,
I shall contemplate."

THE PUBLIC SPEAKER ON TRIAL FOR MAGIC

APULEIUS, *APOLOGIA*

Stereotypes of vulgar magic and Apuleius's cultured, literary practices:

[25] The whole accusation was anchored by Aemilianus on this one thing, that I am a "magician." And so, I would like to ask his learned counsel what actually a "magician" is. For, if what I read in many authorities is correct, that in the language of the Persians "magician" is what "priest" is in ours, what crime is there in it? Can it be wrong to be a priest, to know properly and to understand, and to be experienced with the laws of ceremonies, the duties of sacred rituals, and religious order? At any rate if "magic" means what Plato means, when he examines the branches of study in which, among the Persians, a young heir to the throne is educated. . . .

Apuleius quotes Plato, *Alcibiades*, 121e–122a in Greek:

[26] Do you hear, you who casually accuse it, that magic is an art accepted by the immortal gods? It is expert about their worship and veneration, truly pious and knowledgeable about the divine, already ennobled by its founders Zoroaster and Oromazes, heavenly high priest! It is taught among the first skills of royalty among the Persians: it is not permitted to become a magician casually any more than to become a king. . . .

If, indeed, they reckon in the vulgar fashion that someone is a "magician" who by communion of speech with immortal gods, is powerful with the incredible strength of incantations for everything he wants, then I am really amazed: why weren't they afraid to accuse someone whom they declare has such power? . . . this is not the kind of accusation anyone makes, if they believe it.

[42] Thus on the model of common opinion and rumor, they came up with the story of some boy. Enchanted by a spell, spectators far away, at a secret place, with a small altar and a lamp, and just a few accomplices as witnesses, he is supposed to have collapsed where he was enchanted, then later came to knowing nothing—yet they did not dare to push their lie further. For in order to complete the fable, it would be necessary to add something like this: that this boy foretold many things with prophecy. For as we learn, this is the great benefit of spells: prophecy and divination—not just in popular opinion, but also on the authority of learned men this marvel is attested with reference to boys.

Apuleius gives examples from classical Latin authors:

[43] . . . these and other things about magic arts and boys I read in many authors, but I am of doubtful mind whether I should say they are possible or deny

it. In fact I do believe Plato, that certain intermediate powers of deities, by nature and location somewhere between gods and people, control all divinations
and magicians' miracles. Anyway, for myself I tend to think this: it is possible
for a human soul, especially a boyish and simple soul, to be put to sleep either
by evocation through spells or by allurement through smells and be moved outside itself into forgetfulness of present things. It can then briefly direct the
memory released from the body and return to its nature, which of course is immortal and divine. And so in a sort of sleep it can foretell the future of things.

Apuleius and "King" Mercury, unmentionable patron god of magic and curses:
the accuser, Aemilianus, claimed that Apuleius in secret had a spooky statuette
made for himself from choice wood for magical rites and that Apuleius revered
this object suspiciously with the Greek name for "King." Apuleius produces a
statuette in court—presumably the right one:

[64] Yet, Aemilianus, for that lie [that the statuette looks skeletal] may that
god [Mercury], the messenger between the upper world and the nether, reward you with the bad grace of the gods of both! And may he ever bring the
faces of the dead before your very eyes,

> and whatever shades there are,
> whatever specters,
> whatever ghosts,
> whatever goblins,
> all apparitions of the night,
> all frights of the grave,
> all terrors of the tombs—from which you by age and justice are not far!

On the other hand, we of the Platonic family know nothing but what is festal and joyful and solemn and sublime and heavenly! Indeed, this school in its
devotion to what is highest has tracked things more sublime than heaven itself, and has taken its stand on the outer surface of the world. Maximus (the
judge) knows that I am speaking the truth, for he has diligently read in the
Phaedrus about [Apuleius quotes *Phaedrus* 247b–d in Greek] "the superceles-
tial place" and the "outer surface of heaven."

This same Maximus also understands very well—so that I can answer you
about the name [of my patron god]—who it is who, not by me, but by Plato,
was first called *"Basileus"*: "everything surrounds this king [*basileus*] of all,
and everything is for his sake." [*Epist.* 2.312e]—

> who this "King" is,
> of the whole nature of things
> cause and reason and initial origin,
> ultimate begetter of the soul,
> eternal sustainer of living things,

continuous artisan of his world,
yet artisan without effort,
sustainer without care,
begetter without procreation.
Defined neither by place,
nor by time,
nor by any motion,
therefore comprehensible to few,
nameable by none.

What is more, I am going to add to the suspicion of magic:
I am not going to answer you, Aemilianus, what *"Basileus"* I worship.
Even if the proconsul himself were to ask me what my god is, I remain silent.

Apuleius promises that if his accusers can show a motive for his alleged seduction of Pudentilla, he will list himself among the world's most famous magicians:

[90] If there were one reason discovered, even a tiny one, why I would have wanted to get married with Pudentilla for the sake of my own advantage, if you could prove any profit at all, then let me be Carmendas or Damigeron or that Moses or John [perhaps Jannes, Moses' opponent? (Hunink, 2, 223)] or Apollobex or Dardanus himself or someone else after Zoroaster and Ostaenes, someone famous among magicians.

Bibliography

Apuleius. *Metamorphoses*. Translated by J. Arthur Hanson. Vol. 1, books I–VI; Vol. 2, books VII–XI. Loeb Classical Library. Cambridge, MA: Harvard University Press, 1989.
————. *Rhetorical Works*. Translated by Stephen J. Harrison, John Hilton, and Vincent Hunink. Oxford: Oxford University Press, 1999.
Beard, Mary, John North, and Simon Price. *Religions of Rome*. Vol. 1, *A History*. Vol. 2, *A Sourcebook*. Cambridge: Cambridge University Press, 1998.
Dickie, Matthew W. *Magic and Magicians in the Greco-Roman World*. London: Routledge, 2001.
Gordon, Richard. "Imagining Greek and Roman Magic." Pages 159–275 in *Witchcraft and Magic in Europe: Ancient Greece and Rome*. Edited by B. Ankarloo and S. Clark. London: Athlone, 1999.
Harrison, Stephen J. *Apuleius: A Latin Sophist*. Oxford: Oxford University Press, 1999.
Helm, R. "Apuleius' Apologie: Ein Meisterwerk der zweiten Sophistik." *Altertum* 1 (1955): 86–108.
Hunink, Vincent, ed. *Apuleius of Madauros*. Pro Se De Magia (Apologia). Vol. 1, *Text*. Vol. 2, *Commentary*. Amsterdam: Gieben, 1997.
Kippenberg, Hans. "Magic in Roman Civil Discourse: Why Rituals Could Be Illegal." Pages 137–64 in *Envisioning Magic: A Princeton Seminar and Symposium*. Studies in the History of Religions 75. Edited by P. Schäfer and H. G. Kippenberg. Leiden: Brill, 1997.

Ogden, Daniel. *Magic, Witchcraft, and Ghosts in the Greek and Roman Worlds: A Sourcebook.* Oxford: Oxford University Press, 1999.

Rives, James B. "Magic in Roman Law: The Reconstruction of a Crime." *Classical Antiquity* 22 (2003): 313–39.

Sandy, Gerald. *The Greek World of Apuleius: Apuleius and the Second Sophistic.* Leiden: Brill, 1997.

— 12 —

The Parable in the Hebrew Bible
and Rabbinic Literature

Gary G. Porton

The Greek word *parable* means comparison, juxtaposition, or analogy, and the Septuagint—the Greek translation of the Hebrew Bible completed in Alexandria, Egypt, in the third to the first centuries BCE—chose this word to translate the Hebrew word *mashal* (*meshalim* in the plural). The Hebrew texts do not distinguish among a fable, allegory, simile, metaphor, or parable. They all appear in the Rabbinic documents in similar literary formulations, and the Hebrew word *mashal* can refer to any one of them. Many who have studied the parables in the Synoptic Gospels have drawn distinctions among these categories; however, those who have dealt with parables within the Hebrew texts have not been engaged in dividing the *meshalim* into similar categories.

There are a limited number of parables in the Hebrew Bible in the form of stories that make a single point. Scholars seem to agree that Judges 9:7–15; 2 Samuel 12:1–14; 2 Samuel 14:1–20; 1 Kings 20:35–43; and Isaiah 5:1–7 are the only examples of developed story parables in the Hebrew Scriptures. Some writers have suggested that the entire biblical books of Ruth and Jonah are merely extended parables, but the majority of biblical exegetes do not accept this reading of these stories. Other biblical scholars have argued that Ezekiel 17:3–10; 19:2–9; 19:10–14; 23:2–21; and 24:3–5 are allegories and that Judges 14:14 is a riddle, which is another meaning of the Greek term *parable*. Some have suggested that the metaphors in the prophetic oracles, such as Isaiah 1:5–6 and Hosea 2:2–15, are also types of parables.

These biblical examples often are placed within the context of other Near Eastern wisdom traditions. For example, the Sumerian and Akkadian collections contain several examples of highly articulate plants and animals engaging in debates concerning their relative virtues and strengths, and some authorities have argued that these can be compared to many Greek and later Hebrew fables. However, within the context of the ancient Near East, the Hebrew Bible appears to be the first document that contains parables in which humans are the main characters.

There are a few animal fables in the Apocrypha and Pseudepigrapha, but these texts lack parables that center on humans or human activity. The Synoptic Gospels are the first texts after the Hebrew Bible that depict a Jew, Jesus, recounting parables wherein humans are the primary actors. This type of parable also appears in the full range of Rabbinic documents—from the Mishnah through the Babylonian Talmud, the Talmud of the Land of Israel, and the Midrashim.

Although the Synoptic Gospels and the Rabbinic collections share the phenomenon of the parable featuring human characters, it is extremely difficult to determine how the parables and the parable form in the Synoptic Gospels related to the Rabbinic corpus. First, the Mishnah, the earliest Rabbinic text, by most scholarly opinions, was edited about 220 CE, perhaps a century or more after the Gospel of Luke. The Talmud of the Land of Israel dates from the fifth century CE, and the Babylonian Talmud from the seventh–eighth century CE. Similarly, the collections of Rabbinic biblical interpretations and comments are dated from the third century through the eighth century CE. Thus, all the Rabbinic documents are considerably later than the Synoptic Gospels. This means that even if we find common images within the Gospels and the Rabbinic documents, the Rabbinic collections come from a later time than the New Testament texts. Second, all the Rabbinic texts are collections edited over many decades in the case of Mishnah and the earliest midrashim, and over centuries in the case of the two Talmuds. They contain materials that have been gathered over many more years than the Gospels, and they have passed through many more editorial stages than the earliest accounts of Jesus' ministry. Exactly at which stage in the editing process the parables entered the Rabbinic documents is virtually impossible to determine.

Third, while tradition may claim that one person edited a Rabbinic collection, such as Judah ha-Nasi's (Rabbi Judah the Prince) editing of Mishnah, the tradition does not claim that anyone wrote them in the same sense that "Mark" wrote his Gospel or "John" composed his (despite the original anonymity of the Gospels, they present themselves as the work of a single author). The Rabbinic collections are just that—a collection of materials from a variety of sources from many geographic locations edited in various stages over a period of time. We do not know who the editors were, what the process was, or even what the editors were trying to accomplish as they collected some materials and rejected others. Some of the midrashim are organized as a running commentary on the biblical text, but even here we find many digressions that easily could stand independently of the biblical verses. Even though the two Talmuds are organized as if they were commentaries to the Mishnah, this description hardly does justice to the complexity of the Talmudic page or the documents as a whole. While the Synoptic Gospels focus on one person and his ministry in one geographic area, the Rabbinic texts are much more diverse.

Fourth, the Gospels focus on one figure, Jesus—his life and his teaching. The Rabbinic documents do not center on any person but are complex anthologies of attributed and anonymous sayings, stories, myths, biblical comments, and the like by generations of sages, most often presented without any narrative context that might help us unpack the significance of the statement to the sage or the setting in which it allegedly was proclaimed. And no one within the Rabbinic tradition would claim that the parables are the words of a divine being.

Although parables appear in all the Rabbinic documents, we find most of them in the midrashic texts. These are collections of comments organized around a biblical verse. Most of the Rabbinic parables are constructed to explain a particular biblical verse, and most have two parts: the *mashal* itself and the *nimshal*, the occasion or text that generated the parable. The term *mashal* indicates that a simple simile, a narrative, or a developed metaphor will follow. Usually both the *mashal* proper and the *nimshal* begin with "it is like/it is comparable to" (*mashal le*) and "similarly" (*kakh*). In the midrashic collections, the *nimshal* usually concludes by citing a verse. In the Rabbinic collections, the parable (*mashal*), unlike the precedent (*ma'aseh*), is abstract and requires the reader/hearer to use his or her imagination. Whereas the *ma'aseh* refers to an event or a particular occasion, the *mashal* is not located in a specific time or place. In addition, the *mashal* usually can stand independently of its literary context, but the *ma'aseh* generally makes little sense when it is removed from its redactional setting. The *mashal* is an effective teaching tool both because it demands that its audience actively participate in its interpretation and because it presents its message in two parts—the *mashal* and the *nimshal*.

The relationship of the *nimshal* to the *mashal* has been the subject of a good deal of study, with most scholars arguing that the *mashal* is primary and the *nimshal* secondary. However, Stern and Neusner have presented totally new understandings of the relationship between these two parts of the Rabbinic parable. Stern concentrated on the parable in midrashic texts, especially within *Lamentations Rabbah*, a collection of Rabbinic comments to the Book of Lamentations usually dated to the fifth century CE. He concluded that the *nimshal* provided the missing narrative context in which the *mashal* was stated. This means that by citing the biblical verse, the *nimshal* provides the reason for the parable. Neusner examined the parable in the total range of Rabbinic documents, midrashic and nonmidrashic. He also concluded that the *nimshal* was primary and the *mashal* secondary. The primary task of the *mashal* is set forth in the *nimshal*. Furthermore, Neusner has shown that each parable conforms to the programmatic task of the document in which it occurs, so that the same parable will appear differently as we examine it by moving from document to document. Just as the exact wording of each parable in the New Testament reflects the agenda of the Gospel in which it is found, so each Rabbinic *mashal* serves the agenda of the Rabbinic document in which it appears. In the case of the Rabbinic documents, however, we are not necessarily talking about slight variations of wording. We may be dealing with totally different patterns of construction.

Below we have several examples of Jewish parables drawn from the Hebrew Bible, as well as from the full range of Rabbinic documents. I have tried to set each text into some time frame. I also have indicated the relative lifetimes of the sages to whom the parables are attributed. A Tanna is a sage who lived before 250

CE in Palestine, and an Amora is a sage who lived from the middle of the third century through the seventh century CE in either Palestine or Babylonia, modern-day Iraq. Hebrew is a laconic language, and the Rabbinic documents exhibit this trait more than any other Hebrew literature. I have placed in brackets words that do not appear in the original Hebrew/Aramaic text but that are necessary for understanding the flow of the story.

The sample is small and was chosen to reflect not only the biblical material but also the full range of Rabbinic collections and to show some similarities and differences with the parables in the Gospels. There are hundreds of parables in the Jewish collections; it was a popular literary creation, and likely just as popular in the oral culture. This fact means that the appearance of parables attributed to Jesus in the Synoptic Gospels is what we would expect from a Jewish teacher/scholar/sage/preacher in Galilee in the first century CE.

While parables appear in Greek, Roman, and Hellenistic documents, the parables attributed to Jesus in the Gospels and those assigned to Rabbis in the Rabbinic texts share some commonalities, such as their form, their images, their themes, and in fact their abundance. The gospel as a literary form does not have parallels within the Jewish documents, and the so-called pronouncement story—another literary form in which Jesus' sayings are recorded in the Gospels—finds extremely few parallels in the Rabbinic collections. The explanation for these distinctions is rather simple. The Gospels focus on an individual, Jesus. The Rabbinic collections primarily focus more on what the sages said/taught, their Torah, than on their personalities; therefore, we do not find "biographies" or even collections of statements by one sage until the third or fourth century CE. The thrust of the pronouncement story is the individual as a spokesperson in a particular setting. Again, the Rabbinic documents are less concerned with narrative setting than the Gospels probably because the statements in the Rabbinic texts are part of the Oral Torah, part of the timeless revelation from Sinai, in which both setting and sage are much less important than content. However, the parable is a teaching technique that focuses on content, not context and not personality, at least in the Rabbinic documents. Furthermore, the vast majority of Rabbinic parables occur as interpretations of the Bible, so that their narrative setting is the biblical text and not the plains of Galilee or the cities of Judah. Thus, Jesus' teaching through parables is a more or less "Jewish" thing for him to have done. The parables abound in the Rabbinic documents from Palestine and Babylonia, so that given the Palestinian setting and the Jewish culture in which Jesus was raised, one would expect the "historical" Jesus to have taught throughout his life by means of parables.

For centuries scholars have assumed that we can get close to Jesus' personality, and perhaps his own words, through the parables, and as noted, Jesus most likely would have used parables as a form for teaching his message to his fellow Jews. However, moving back from the material we now find in the Gospels to Jesus' actual words is a perilous journey. Frequently the parables that occur in more than one Synoptic exhibit differences, and the *Gospel of Thomas* offers additonal variations on some of the parables; while some parables are grouped together in the

Gospels, those same parables often are scattered throughout *Thomas*. Further, some of the details of the parables attributed to Jesus reflect the realities of Roman practice in Palestine and not the Jewish ways of doing things. Finally, the Gospels were collected and edited several decades after Jesus' death, and many scholars have argued that in their current form, they often reflect the concerns of the nascent church in addition to or instead of what Jesus meant while he was alive. Thus, although the parables may accurately reflect one of Jesus' teaching methods, one cannot be certain that they retain his exact words (see also David Gowler's contribution on *chreia* in this volume).

Scholars have disagreed, and likely will continue to disagree, about how we should interpret Jesus' parables. For the first centuries after Jesus' death, the parables were read as allegories, sometimes with complex hidden messages and agendas. Since the end of the nineteenth century, however, scholars have moved away from the allegorical interpretation to viewing the parables as relatively self-explanatory teaching tools. Even though many scholars today argue that some of the parables are allegories, virtually all emphasize that one should read the parables in their real-life settings because they each arose at a particular time, in a unique place, and to address specific situations in the lives of the people to whom Jesus was speaking. When the parables are placed within the context of their Jewish environment, some scholars point to Jesus' (or his followers') apocalyptic frame of reference as a key to unpacking their meaning. The parables thus may be seen as one way in which Jesus explained some of the details of the New Era, the kingdom of God on earth. In the biblical and Rabbinic texts, the parables often serve as means for humans to understand God, the King of Kings, the Holy One, blessed be He, apart from eschatological speculation. Jesus' parables can, and perhaps do, attend to this focus as well.

BIBLICAL PARABLES

We begin our examination of Jewish parables by looking at the parable from 2 Samuel and its interpretation. David has just sent Uriah the Hittite to die in battle, so that he could take his wife (Bathsheba) for himself. Nathan then appears before David and tells him the parable of the rich man and the poor man. David responds to the parable, and Nathan tells David that it is really about him and what he has done to Uriah. The story continues with God's delineating David's punishment.

The next parable is from the Book of Isaiah. Isaiah's main activity occurred at the end of the eighth century and beginning of the seventh century BCE. The image of the vineyard is central to this parable, and it plays an important role in many of the parables in the Synoptic Gospels. Wine was one of the most important agricultural products of the Land of Israel, so the use of this image is natural. The parable is rather straightforward, especially after its key, the identification of the vineyard and its owner, appears at its end.

2 SAMUEL 12:1–14

And the Lord sent Nathan to David, and he came to him and said to him: "There were two men in one city. One was rich, and one was poor. The rich one had very many sheep and cattle. The poor one had only one small lamb that he had purchased. He tended her, and she grew up with him and his children. She ate from his bread, drank from his cup, and would lie in his bosom like his own daughter. One day a traveler came to the rich man, but he lacked the compassion to take from his own flock or herd to give to the traveler who had come to him, so he took the lamb belonging to the poor man and gave it to the one who had come to him."

David became very angry with the man, and said to Nathan, "As the Lord lives, the one who did this deserves death. And the worth of the lamb he should repay four times over because he did this thing and showed no pity."

Then Nathan said to David, "You are the man. Thus said the Lord, the God of Israel, 'I anointed you king over Israel, and I saved you from Saul's hand. I gave you your lord's house, and your lord's wives I placed into your bosom. And I gave you the House of Israel and Judah. And if that were not enough, I would have added more and more. Why did you spurn the word of the Lord to do this evil thing in His eyes? You smote Uriah the Hittite with a sword. You took his wife to yourself as a wife and had him killed by the sword of the Ammonites. Therefore, the sword will never depart from your household— because you spurned me and took the wife of Uriah the Hittite to be your wife.'

Thus said the Lord, 'Behold, I will cause evil from within your house to rise against you. And I will take your wives from before your very eyes and give them to your neighbor. He shall sleep with your wives under this very sun. You have acted in secret, but I will do this thing before all Israel and in broad daylight.'"

Then David said to Nathan, "I have sinned before the Lord." Then Nathan said to David, "The Lord has removed your sin. You shall not die. However, because you have indeed deeply offended the Lord with this thing, the son which has been born to you shall indeed die."

ISAIAH 5:1–7

Let me sing for my beloved, a song about my beloved's vineyard.
My beloved had a vineyard on a very fruitful hill.
He broke up the ground, cleared the stones from it, and planted it with
   vines.
He built a watchtower in it, and he also hewed out a wine press in it,
For he hoped it would yield grapes. However, it produced wild grapes.
But now dwellers of Jerusalem, and men of Judah,
Judge between me and my vineyard:

What more can you do to my vineyard that I have not done in it?
Why, when I hoped it would yield grapes, it produced wild grapes?
But, now, I will let you know what I will do to my vineyard.
I will remove its hedge so that it may be ravaged.
I will break down its wall, so that it may be trampled.
I will make it a desolation;
It shall not be pruned or hoed, and thorns and thistles shall overgrow it.
I shall command the clouds from dropping rain upon it.
For the House of Israel is the vineyard of the Lord of Hosts
And the men of Judah are the seedlings He lovingly tended.

RABBINIC PARABLES

MISHNAH

The Mishnah is the earliest collection of Rabbinic sayings we possess. The text, edited about 220 CE in Palestine, was used by later generations as a law code. The context in which the parable appears provides its *nimshal*, the occasion for the parable. The Mishnah asks: If one must consider the *sukkah* (i.e., the booth) as his primary residence during the holiday of Tabernacles (Booths), when is it permissible to get out of the rain? The Mishnah states that one may leave the *sukkah* if it is raining hard enough to spoil or dilute a thick bowl of porridge. However, we do not know why this is so. The parable tells us that it is like a slave who comes to serve his master, but his master rejects him. Although we do not know what the slave did that caused his master to throw the wine in his face, we do know that the master was upset with his slave. From this we learn that when it rains on a person in a *sukkah*, it is a sign that God is upset with that individual.

All seven days that a person observes [the holiday of Sukkot/Tabernacles], his *sukkah* is [his] permanent [residence], and his house is [his] secondary [residence. If] it rains, when is [he] permitted to vacate [his *sukkah*]? From [the time that] the porridge spoils. They created a parable. To what is the thing comparable? [It is comparable] to a slave who comes to mix his master's cup [of wine, and his master] emptied the flask on his face. (*Sukkot* 2:9)

SIFRA

Our second example is from *Sifra*, a collection of exegetical comments on the Book of Leviticus, probably edited in the middle of the third century in Palestine. In this case the parable could stand on its own, for the *nimshal*, the full quotation of verse from Leviticus, sets the stage for the parable.

The following parable, also from *Sifra*, draws a clear parallel between the righteous ones and God. In the messianic future, God will walk along with the righteous ones through the Garden of Eden. Although the righteous ones will tremble in God's presence, he will rebuke them, claiming that they and he are just the same. For that reason, they should not tremble in God's presence but should enjoy strolling with him through the garden.

So that the land will not vomit you forth for defiling it [as it vomited forth the nation that was before you] (Leviticus 18:28). The Land of Israel is not like any [other] land. It does not support those who engage in transgressions. They created a parable. To what is the thing comparable? [It is comparable] to a prince to whom they fed something that did not sit well in his stomach, so that he vomited it out. Thus, the Land of Israel does not support those who engage in transgression; therefore, it is said [in Scripture]: So that the Land will not vomit you forth for defiling her as it vomited forth the nation that was before you. (*Sifra Qedoshim* 11:14)

And I will walk among you (Leviticus 26:12). They recited a parable. To what can this thing be compared? [It can be compared] to a king who went out to stroll in the orchard with his tenant farmer. And it happened that the tenant farmer hid from him. The king asked the tenant farmer, "Why have you hidden from me? Behold, I am just like you." And [likewise] the Holy One, blessed be He, inquired of the righteous ones, "Why are you trembling before me?" Thus, in the future, the Holy One, blessed be He, will stroll with the righteous ones in the Garden of Eden in the future to come. But the righteous ones will see him and tremble before him. [He will inquire of them, "why are you trembling before me?] Behold, I am just like you." (*Sifra BeHuqotai* pereq 3:3)

MEKHILTA

Mekhilta is a collection of exegetical comments on major portions of the Book of Exodus. This document probably also was compiled in the third century in Palestine. The first parable below is included in a collection of comments on Exodus 14:15. The Israelites are faced with the Egyptians behind them and the Sea of Reeds before them. They complain to Moses: were there not graves in Egypt that you took us out to die in the desert? Moses asks God what he should do, and the Lord said to Moses, "Why do you cry out to me? Tell the Israelites that they should travel forward. Just as the father had forgiven his son, so God has forgiven Israel; therefore, they should stop complaining, have faith and move forward into the sea." Some have compared this parable to the Parable of the Prodigal Son in Luke (15:11–32), because the point of both stories seems to be that the father forgives the son unconditionally. However, the differences between the two parables are significant.

The second parable again illustrates a biblical verse that describes the situation immediately before the Israelites are about to enter the Sea of Reeds. At this point, God assures them that he will take the angel and the pillar of fire that have been leading them through the desert and place them behind the Israelite camp to protect the Israelites from the Egyptians as they cross through the sea. Just as the father keeps moving his son to protect him and provides for his needs as they travel along the road, so God continually acts to protect the Israelites and to provide them with their needs as they travel through the desert on their way to the promised land.

The third section from *Mekhilta* comments on Exodus 14:22, "then the children of Israel went into the midst of the sea." The point of the parable is that God will reward those who act with the intent of glorifying him, even if their actions are not always exactly what he may have stated or what others may do. Different people have different roles in life and different ways they are to honor God, just like the king who gives different instructions to his two sons.

Rabbi Avtolas the Elder says: "It is a parable. To what is the thing comparable? [It is comparable] to a man who is angry with his son and banished him from his house. His [son's] friend entered to ask on the [son's] behalf [permission] to return to his house. [The father] said to him: 'You seek nothing from me, because, my child, I have already reconciled [myself] with my son.' Thus the Omnipresent One said: 'Why do you cry out to me? (Exodus 14:15), I have already reconciled myself to them.'" (*Mekhilta Beshalah* 3)

And the angel of God who is walking before the Israelite camp will walk behind them (Exodus 14:19). R. Judah says: "Behold this verse is rich [in meaning, and its importance is reflected] in many places. It is a parable. To what is the thing comparable? [It is comparable] to one who was walking on the road and leading his son in front of him. [If] robbers [were to] come to capture him from the front, [the father] takes him from in front of him and places him behind him. [If] a wolf [were to] come and snatch him from the rear, [his father would] take him from the rear and place him in front of him. [If] robbers come from the front and wolves from behind, [his father would] take him and put him in his arms. [If] the child began to suffer from the [heat of] the sun, his father would spread his cloak over him. [If] he became hungry, [his father would] feed him. [If] he became thirsty, [his father would] give him [something to] drink. Thus did the Holy One, blessed be He, [for Israel]; for it is said, 'I taught Ephraim to walk. He took them into his arms, but they did not know that I healed them' (Hosea 11:3). [If] the child began to suffer from the [heat of] the sun, his father would spread his cloak over him, for it is said, 'he spread a cloud for a cover, and fire to illumine the night' (Psalm 105:39). [If] he became hungry, [his father would] feed him bread, for it is said, 'Behold, I will rain down for you bread from heaven' (Exodus 16:4). [If] he became thirsty, [his father would] give him water to drink, for it is said, 'and he brought forth streams from the rock' (Psalm 78:15). But [the word for streams really] refers to running water, for it is said, 'A fountain of gardens, a well of running water, and streams' (Canticles 4:15). And it says, 'Drink water from your own cistern and running water from your own well' (Proverbs 5:14)." (*Mekhilta Beshalah* 4)

[There is the younger one Benjamin who rules them] the princes of Judah who command them (Psalm 68.28). It is a parable. To what can the thing be compared? [It can be compared] to a king of flesh and blood who had two sons—

one older and one younger. He entered the younger one's room at night and told him to wake him at the first light of the sun. He told the elder [son] to wake him at the third hour. [In the morning], the younger one came to wake him with the first light of the sun, but the older one wouldn't allow him [to wake their father]. The elder said to him, "He told me [to wake him] at the third hour of the day." But, the younger one said to him, "He told me [to wake him] at the first light of the sun." While they were standing [and] arguing, their father woke up. He said to them, "My sons, both of you [acted only with] the intention of honoring me; therefore, I will not withhold your rewards [from either of you, even though you didn't wake me]." Thus, the Holy One, blessed be He, said, "What reward shall be given to the Benjaminites who entered the Sea [of Reeds] first? The Holy Presence shall dwell on their portion, for it is said, 'Benjamin is a ravishing wolf'" (Genesis 49:27). And it says, "Of Benjamin he [Moses] said, 'The beloved of the Lord shall dwell in safety by Him' (Deuteronomy 33:12). And what reward shall be given to the tribe of Judah, who threw stones [at the people so they would run into the Sea of Reeds]? They are worthy to receive the kingship, for it is said, 'the princes of Judah who command them' (Psalm 68:28). Command refers only to kingship, for it is said, 'Then, at Belshazzar's command, they dressed Daniel in purple, placed a golden chain around his neck, and declared that he should rule as one of the three in the kingdom' (Daniel 5:29)." (*Mekhilta Beshalah* 5)

SIFRE

Sifre is a collection of exegetical comments on the biblical Book of Numbers. Most scholars date the collection to the middle of the third century CE. The following is an interesting parable because in it not only does Israel complain to God about their wandering through the desert, but also God expresses his displeasure with Israel's complaining. The parable is curious, for the Israelites wandered through the desert because of their insubordination against God and Moses. The parable depicts Israel as never being satisfied with what God has done for them. This point is implied in the verse, for the ark's leading the Israelites through the desert was a visible sign that God was with them and would protect them.

And whenever the ark set out (Numbers 10:29). It is a parable. To what can the thing be compared? [It can be compared] to people who said to the king, "We shall see if you will travel with us to the ruler of Akko." By the time [they] arrived at Akko, he had gone to Tyre. By the time [they] arrived at Tyre, he had gone to Sidon. By the time they reached Sidon, he had gone to Biri. By the time they reached Biri, he had gone to Antioch. When the people reached Antioch they began to complain to the king that they had been wandering from place to place on the road. But the king expressed his discontent to them, for because of them he had wandered along the road from place to place. Thus, the Divine Presence traveled thirty-six miles in one day, so that Israel might enter the Land [of Canaan. At that point] Israel began to complain before the Omnipresent

One, "We have wandered on this road [through the desert from place to place for forty years]." But, the Omnipresent one expressed his discontent with them, because for their sake the Holy Presence had traveled thirty-six miles in one day, so that Israel might enter the Land [of Canaan]. (*Sifre Numbers* 84)

GENESIS RABBAH

A midrashic collection on the Book of Genesis, *Genesis Rabbah* was probably compiled in Palestine in the fifth century CE. The first parable below introduces Rabbi Hoshiya. There were two sages with this name. One was a first-generation Palestinian Amora, and the other was a third-generation Palestinian Amora. This parable, which is part of a collection of comments on Genesis 1:26: "And God said, 'Let us make Adam in our image . . . ,'" makes several points. First in terms of their appearance, it was extremely difficult to distinguish between the first human and God. It was so difficult that even the angels who had served God for all time could not tell them apart. However, God made it clear that Adam was not a divine being, for unlike God, Adam needed to sleep. The parable also tells us a lot about the similarity between God and the first human. Finally, it makes one of the central points of this section of the Midrash: even though humans share in some divine attributes, they are not divine.

The next parable is attributed to Rabbi Yudan, a fourth-generation Palestinian Amora. It explains why God was with Joseph, and thus it implies in its literal sense that God was not with Joseph's eleven brothers. Underlying the parable is the Jewish concern about wine. By the fourth century, Jewish law prohibited Jews from using wine with which a Gentile had come into contact. The Jews believed that the first thing Gentiles would do with wine was pour some out as a libation to their deities. Once the wine was used in the honor of a foreign divine being, Jews could not use it. In the parable, the herder is concerned that the Gentile owner of the store will take the wine off the animal and offer some of it to his deity. If that happens, the Jewish herder cannot sell the wine to Jews. The Jew is not concerned about the animals on the road because they are out in the open on public property, and if people see non-Jews tampering with the wine, they can stop them. Behind the doors of one's own shop, however, one is free to do as he wishes. Like the animals on the public road who are protected, Joseph's eleven brothers were protected by their father. Joseph, however, like the beast of burden in the Gentile's shop, was unprotected by someone else and left to his own devices. Thus, just as the herder went after the lone animal, God went down to Egypt to protect Joseph. This parable has some external similarities with the Parable of the Good Shepherd (or Parable of the Lost Sheep) in Matthew 18:10–14 (see also Luke 15:3–7), for in both a herder leaves his herd to go after one animal that has gone astray; however, the points of the two stories are quite different.

Said Rabbi Hoshiya: "When the Holy One, blessed be He, created the first human, the ministering angels erred with regard to him, and they sought to declare 'Holy' before [the human, thinking that he was divine]. To what may this thing be compared? [It may be compared] to a king and a governor who were placed in a chariot, and the people of the province sought to declare 'Sovereign' before the king; however, they did not know which one he was. What did the king do? He pushed out [the governor] and threw him [out of the] chariot. Then [the people] knew [which one] was the king. Thus, when the Holy One, blessed be He, created the first human and the angels erred, what did the Holy One, blessed be He do? He caused sleep to fall upon [Adam], then all knew that he was a mere mortal. Thus it is written, 'Turn away from Adam' (Isaiah 2:22)." (*Genesis Rabbah* 8:27)

And the Lord was with Joseph (Genesis 39:4). Said Rabbi Yudan, "[To what can this matter be compared? It can be compared] to an animal driver who had twelve beasts of burden before him carrying wine. One of them [left the herd] and entered a Gentile's shop. [The herder] left the [other] eleven and went after [the one who had entered the shop]. They said to him, 'Why did you leave the eleven and go after the one?' He said to them, 'These [were standing] in a public domain, and I was not concerned that the wine would be made unfit [for consumption by a Jew].' But this one entered a Gentile's shop, and I was concerned that the wine would be made unfit [for consumption by a Jew]. Thus, these [eleven brothers of Joseph] grew up under their father's authority; but this one was young and by himself; therefore, 'the Lord was with Joseph.'" (*Genesis Rabbah* 86:2)

BABYLONIAN TALMUD

The Babylonian Talmud is a massive collection of Rabbinic statements, stories, exegetical comments, legal decisions, and the like. It was edited sometime between the sixth and eighth centuries CE. Although the first parable below is attributed to Yochanan ben Zakkai, a sage who lived in the first century CE, it is impossible to ascertain whether he actually told it. The parable has some parallels with the Parable of the (Wedding) Feast in Matthew (22:1–14) and Luke (14:15–24). However, in the Gospels, those who are not prepared for the feast are bound and cast out into the outer darkness. The moral of the Christian parable is "many are called, but few are chosen." The parable in the Talmud has a different point, for those who were not prepared got to stand at the side and watch. Although they did not get to enjoy the feast, they were not "bound and cast into outer darkness."

In the second parable, the name Eleazar could refer to any number of sages who lived from the second through the fifth centuries CE. In this parable, the king's guests refuse to help the beggar; therefore; he approaches the king directly, as Hannah (1 Samuel 1) did. The guests ignored the poor man's needs, but he knew the king would not ignore him.

The third parable depicts Meir, a late second-century sage, quoting a parable attributed to Rabban Gamliel, a first-century patriarch of the Palestinian Jewish community. The point of the parable is that the one who invited all of the city's citizens, except for the king's family, deliberately insulted the king. The other individual invited guests from a totally different population; therefore, he did not insult the king.

Let your clothes always be white and may you never lack ointment on your head (Ecclesiastes 9:8). Said Rabban Yochanan ben Zakkai: "It is a parable. [It is comparable] to a king who invited his servants to a feast, but he didn't set a time for them [for the feast]. [The] shrewd ones among them adorned themselves and sat by the door of the king's residence. They said [to themselves], 'Does the king's residence lack anything?' The foolish ones among them went about their daily tasks. They said [to themselves], 'Would there be a feast without [the king taking time to] prepare [for it]?' Suddenly, the king sought out his servants [for the feast]. The shrewd ones among them entered before [the king's] presence properly adorned. But the foolish ones entered [the king's] presence soiled and smelly. The king was happy to greet the shrewd ones, but angry greeting the foolish ones. [The king] said: 'Those who have prepared themselves for the feast may sit, eat, and drink. Those who have not prepared themselves for the feast must stand [to the side] and watch.'" (Shabbat 153a)

Then [Hannah] vowed a vow saying, "Lord of Hosts [. . .]" (1 Samuel 1:11). Said Rabbi Eleazar: "From the day that the Holy One, blessed be He, created his universe, no person called the Holy One, blessed be He, [Lord of] Hosts until Hannah came and called him [Lord of] Hosts. Hannah said before the Holy One, blessed be He, 'Master of the universe, from all the array of hosts that you have created in your universe, is it difficult in your eyes for you to give me one son?' It is a parable. To what is the thing comparable? [It is comparable] to a king of flesh and blood who made a feast for his servants. One poor person came and stood by the door. He said to [the guests], 'Give me one morsel.' But they did not heed him. He pushed [through the crowd of guests] and entered [the room] near the king. He said to him, 'My lord, the king, from all [the things] you have prepared [for the] feast, is it difficult in your eyes to give me one morsel?' [For it is said: Then Hannah vowed a vow saying, 'Lord of Hosts], if indeed you will look upon [the affliction of your maidservant, and remember me and not forget your maidservant, and if you will give your maidservant a male child . . .].'" (Berakhot 31b)

For they said: "The Lord has forsaken the land, and the Lord does not see" (Ezekiel 9:9). Said R. Meir: "They recited a parable in the name of Rabban Gamliel. To what is the thing comparable? [It is comparable] to two people who were in a city, and they [each] made a feast. One invited the city's citizens, but not the king's family. And [the other] one did not invite [either] the city's citizens [or] the king's family. Which one of them [deserves] the greater punishment? You must say, 'the one who invited the city's citizens, but not the king's family.'" (Baba Qama 79b)

ECCLESIASTES RABBAH

Ecclesiastes Rabbah is a midrashic collection that probably comes from eighth-century Palestine. Phineas is a fifth-generation Palestinian Amora, and Reuben is a second-generation Palestinian Amora. The point of the parable seems evident. In the "world to come," a Rabbinic phrase for the messianic era, people will suffer the consequences of the life they have lived. Those who have lived lives of strife, contentiousness, and evil will suffer in Gehenna and observe the reward those who lived just lives receive from God.

But the righteous man is rewarded with life (Habakkuk 2:4). Rabbi Phineas in the name of Rabbi Reuben [said]: "It is a parable. To what is the thing comparable? [It is comparable] to a king who made a banquet. [When] he invited [the] guests the king issued a decree, saying that each person should bring for himself what he intended to recline upon [during the feast]. Some brought [soft, fine] cloth, some brought mats, some brought mattresses for a couch, some brought [soft] cloth covers [for their couches], some brought upholstered chairs, some brought wood, and some brought stones. The king [observed the situation], became annoyed, and said, 'Each one [of you] must recline on what he has brought with him.' Those who were sitting on the wood and the stones became annoyed with the king, and said, 'Does this [properly reflect on] the king's glory that we should be sitting on wood and stones?' When the king heard them, he said to them, 'Isn't it enough for you that you disgraced with stones and wood the palace that was erected for me at great cost! But you [also] act disrespectfully, level accusations, and join together against me. But, [in truth], you have done this to yourselves.' Similarly, in the future [world] to come, the evil ones will be judged [and sent down] to Gehenna, and they will be annoyed with the Holy One, blessed be He. [They will say], 'We see the salvation of the Holy One, blessed be He, and similarly we want it for ourselves.' The Holy One, blessed be He, says to them, 'In the world in which you lived, were you not contentious, were you not rumor mongers, were you not totally evil, were you not constantly in strife with others, were you not violent creatures? Thus it is written, Behold, all of you who kindle a fire, who gird yourselves with firebrands. Therefore, you shall walk into the flame of your fire, and among the brands that you have kindled. And perhaps you will say, "This has come to you from My hand" (Isaiah 50:11). But, no! You have brought this upon yourselves; therefore, you shall lie down in pain (Isaiah 50:11).'" (*Ecclesiastes Rabbah* 3:11)

PALESTINIAN TALMUD

The Palestinian Talmud probably was compiled in the late fifth or early sixth century CE. Rabbi Bun bar Hiyya was a third-generation Palestinian Amora. The point of the parable is that one is not judged by how long one labors; rather, one is judged by what one can accomplish in the time one has to labor. This parable has some similarities with the parable in Matthew 20:1–16 about the house-holder who hired workers throughout the day but paid them all the same wage. However, the meanings of the two parables differ substantially.

When Rabbi Bun bar Rabbi Hiyya died, Rabbi Zeira applied [Ecclesiastes 5:11] to him: " 'Sweet is the worker's sleep.' The word sleep is written here only to in-dicate that whether he has much or little to eat [it is appropriate for him]. To whom can Rabbi Bun bar Rabbi Hiyya be compared? [He can be compared] to a king who hired many workers. But there was one worker more efficient in his work than the others. What did the king do? [After he had quickly finished his work], the king took him and gave him long and short beds to rest on. Evening arrived, and those workers came to collect their pay. [The king] gave [the more efficient worker] the same wage as he gave them. The [other] workers became boisterous and said, 'We worked all day, but this one worked only two hours, but you gave him the same wage!' The king said to them, 'This one did more in two hours than [the rest of] you did working all day long.' Thus, Rabbi Bun who labored [as a student] of Torah for [only] twenty-eight years became as re-markable as a sage who had studied for one hundred years." (*Berakhot* 2:8 [5c])

DEUTERONOMY RABBAH

Probably compiled in Palestine, *Deuteronomy Rabbah* has the most complex textual history of any of the midrashic collections we are discussing. Different scholars date the collection anywhere from the fifth to the ninth century. We do not know any-thing about Samuel Pargarita; this is the only place his name appears in the entire Rabbinic corpus. Meir is a second-century Palestinian Tanna. The point of the para-ble is that a father will always welcome his child back, no matter what the child has done. The parable is similar to Luke's Parable of the Prodigal Son (15:11–32).

Another matter: [when you are in distress because all these things have befallen you and, in the end,] return to the Lord your God [and obey him] (Deuteron-omy 4:30). Said Rabbi Samuel Pargarita in the name of Rabbi Meir: "To what can this thing be compared? [It can be compared] to a king's son who set out on a path of depravity. The king sent his tutor after him. 'Return my son with you.' But the son sent him [back], and he said to his father, 'Can I return to you like this? I would be embarrassed in your presence.' But his father sent him [back to his son] and said to him, 'My son, should a son ever be embarrassed to return to his father? And if you return, are you not returning to your father?' Thus, the Holy One, blessed be He, sent Jeremiah to Israel in the hour of their sinning, and he said to him, 'Go, tell my children, you must return.' From where [do we learn this? We learn it from Jeremiah 3:12], for it is said, 'Go and proclaim these words. . . .' But Israel said to Jeremiah, 'Can we return to the Holy One, blessed be He, like this?' From where [in Scripture do we learn this? We learn it from Jeremiah 3:25], for it is said, 'Let us lie down in our shame, let our disgrace cover us. . . .' But the Holy One, blessed be He, sent and said to them, 'My children, if you return, are you not returning to your father?' And from where [in Scripture do we learn this? We learn it from Jeremiah 31:9], for 'I am always a father to Israel. . . . ' " (*Deuteronomy Rabbah* 2:24)

AVOT DE-RABBI NATHAN, *VERSION A*

The *Avot de-Rabbi Nathan*, version A, probably dates from the third century. Elisha ben Abuya is a second-century Tanna. The point of the parable is simple: a person strengthens himself through his good deeds and his study of Torah. The parable makes sense if we remember that bricks, unlike rocks, could be porous and not impervious to water lapping against them. The images in this parable are similar to those in Matthew 7:24–27; however, again the points of the two parables are quite different.

Elisha ben Abuyah says: "A man who has [to] his [credit] multiple good deeds and much Torah study, to what can he be compared? [He can be compared to] a man who builds [a building by placing] rocks first and after that bricks [on top of the rocks]. Even if much water comes and stands [against] their side, it will not destroy them from their place. But a man who does not have [to] his [credit] multiple good deeds and Torah study, to what can he be compared? [He can be compared to] a man who builds [a building by placing] the bricks first and afterwards the stones [on top of them]. Even if a little water comes, immediately it destroys them." (*Avot de-Rabbi Nathan* A 24)

Bibliography

Dodd, Charles H. *The Parables of the Kingdom*. Rev. ed. New York: Scribner's, 1961.

Jeremias, Joachim. *The Parables of Jesus*. Translated by S. H. Hook. 3rd rev. ed. London: SCM Press, 1972.

Kissinger, Warren S. *The Parables of Jesus: A History of Interpretation and Bibliography*. Metuchen, NJ: American Theological Library Association, 1979.

Neusner, Jacob. "Parable." Pages 612–29 in *Encyclopaedia of Midrash: Biblical Interpretation in Formative Judaism*. Vol. 2. Edited by Jacob Neusner and Alan J. Avery-Peck. Leiden: Brill, 2005.

Rabinowitz, Louis Isaac. "Parable in Talmud and Midrash." Pages 72–77 in vol. 13 of *Encyclopedia Judaica*. 17 vols. Jerusalem: Encyclopedia Judaica; New York: Macmillan, 1972–82.

Scott, Robert B. Y. "Parable." Pages 74–75 in vol. 13 of *Encyclopaedia Judaica*. Edited by Cecil Roth and Geoffrey Wigoder. 17 vols. Jerusalem: Keter Publishing, 1972.

Stern, David. *Parables in Midrash: Narrative and Exegesis in Rabbinic Literature*. Cambridge, MA: Harvard University Press, 1991.

Strack, Herman L., and Gunter Stemberger. *Introduction to the Talmud and Midrash*. Translated by Markus Bockmuehl. Edinburgh: T & T Clark, 1991.

Vermes, Geza. *The Religion of Jesus the Jew*. Minneapolis, MN: Fortress Press, 1993.

Young, Bradford H. *Jesus and His Jewish Parables*. New York: Gospel Research Foundation, 1989.

13

The Aesop Tradition

Lawrence M. Wills

It is not clear that there ever was a historical Aesop, but he was a revered figure in the Greek and Roman tradition from early times. Considered one of the "seven sages" of the Greek world, unlike the others he was an outsider. He was a misshapen slave who advanced through cleverness and a sharp tongue. His memory is preserved in three ways. References to him as a purveyor of fables can be found in several classical authors (Herodotus 2.134; Plato, *Phaedo* 60d). Later, fables attributed to him were collected into example books for use in rhetoric (according to Diogenes Laertius 5.80, Demetrius of Phalerum made such a collection in the fourth century BCE). Third, there was a prose version of the *Life of Aesop* that may have arisen before the Common Era, but it certainly existed by the first or second century CE. In addition, there was likely in ancient times a cult of Aesop, as there were for other poets, heroes, and philosophers. Thus Aesop was a well-known personage in the Greco-Roman world who bore some resemblance to the figure of Jesus: he had a distinctive means of imparting his teachings—animal fables—just as Jesus used a distinctive kind of parable that utilized social scenes from everyday life (cooking, farming, fishing, being a slave or commanding slaves, and so on), and as in the case of Jesus, so also for Aesop there was a "gospel" of his life, death, and subsequent cult.

Aesop is thus an important figure in Greek and Roman culture, a sharp-tongued social critic who, because of his ugly appearance, is sometimes compared with Socrates. In terms of his philosophy, however, Aesop is less like Plato's version of Socrates than he is the Cynic version. Aesop the slave peels back the layers of social convention and pretension. Whether the tales attributed to him were intended as subversive criticism of the power structure or were more an opportunity for comic release of class tension is not clear. At any rate, the type of the "grotesque outsider" is known in ancient mimes, in art, and in the figure of Socrates himself; it might be compared to the role of the fool in some of Shakespeare's plays.

Aesop's fables, and ancient fables in general, are stories, often with animal characters, that are extended metaphors for human relations. They are usually cynical and biting, even cruel, and in the Aesop collections, they combine humor and satire of human foibles with a healthy respect for worldly wisdom and cunning. The characters are generally trying to get ahead by connivance; some succeed, and some get caught in their own devices. The underlying lesson is: be clever, but not too clever. The only morality seems to be: don't get caught. This may seem somewhat amoral—and indeed this tone is found in fables in other ancient cultures as well—but the reason the fables are cruel is that they are example stories for rhetorical speeches, and no one is likely to be convinced by a mild example. (Note how Aesop uses the fables in his trial scene below, and compare Jesus' Parable of the Wicked Tenants in Mark 12:1–9.) At some point the fables acquired concluding applications (not included in this collection) to instruct the budding rhetorician in how best to utilize them in order to persuade.

The Aesop tradition is important for the study of the Gospels for two reasons. First, Aesop's fables can be formally compared to Jesus' parables. Readers will recognize in some of the fables below individual motifs that are also found in the Gospel parables, as well as the use of ideal scenes that provoke reflection, even if the point to be taken from them is quite different. Second, the *Life of Aesop* is roughly contemporary with the Gospels and bears some remarkable similarities. These similarities may derive from the fact that the *Life* and the Gospels both dramatize the life and death of the ostracized hero, told in an age of prose novels and novelistic histories. (Later Christian tradition [*Acts of Peter* 24; Clement of Alexandria, *The Instructor* 3.1] even adds that Jesus was ugly, based on a reading of Isaiah 53:2.) The *Life* is about the same length as the Gospels, written in a relatively low style. Like the Gospels, it gives the sense of being a longer text composed of many originally independent episodes. If Jesus in the Gospels is more prophet than sage, and Aesop is more sage than prophet, the difference is minor compared with the overall similarity in structure:

1. The protagonist has lowly beginnings but experiences a deity's favor.
2. The protagonist has a period of ministry with a salvific message.
3. The protagonist is despised as a result of the message.
4. Trumped-up charges involving blasphemy of the deity are brought forward.
5. The protagonist is executed as a result.
6. A cult of the protagonist is instituted.

Within some of these general similarities, we can perceive even closer parallels in the details. The *Life of Aesop* begins with a visitation by the goddess Isis and the bestowal of powers on Aesop, not unlike the scene of Jesus' baptism at the beginning of the Gospels with the voice from heaven. At the end of the *Life* there is a geographic shift from Samos to Delphi, that is, from the periphery to the center of the worship of Apollo, just as there is a shift in the Gospels from the periphery of Galilee to the center at Jerusalem. Finally, at the transition at the end of these texts from ministry to a trial and passion, the process by which this shift occurs is also similar. In both groups of texts, conflicts that are punctuated by the use of a special kind of discourse arise, and this leads directly to the trial and execution of the protagonist:

Aesop 125–26	Mark 12	John 8
Fable that describes Delphians as descended from slaves	Parable of Wicked Tenants re: Jerusalem authorities	Dialogue: Jews are offspring of the devil

In addition, in all three texts the charge of "blasphemy" figures heavily in the conspiracy to execute the protagonist (*Life of Aesop* 132; Mark 14:64; John 10:33). This is true even though the charges of blasphemy in the three cases are not clearly stated and may be quite different. In *Aesop*, the protagonist is accused of being a temple robber; in Mark, blasphemy is often discussed by scholars in terms of Jewish law on this subject (Leviticus 24:16), but the charge seems to focus instead on Jesus' implication that he himself is the coming Son of Man; in John the Jewish authorities tell Jesus that the charge of blasphemy arises because "you are making yourself God." Blasphemy should thus be seen in its literary context as the "standard" false charge that separates the wise hero from his people. It is also roughly equivalent to the false charge of impiety leveled against Socrates. In Socrates' case the charges were corrupting the young, neglecting the gods, and introducing new ideas (Plato, *Apology*).

The difference in tone between the Gospels and the *Life of Aesop*—urgent and demanding in the case of the Gospels, broadly satirical in the case of the *Life of Aesop*—can be attributed to the difference in the protagonists' messages. Jesus brings the good news of God's plan of salvation at the end of time, while Aesop the Cynic sage preaches a gospel of liberation from human convention and complacency and an awareness of the true nature of things. (Some scholars would argue that this places the *Life of Aesop* closer in religious outlook to the sayings source Q or the *Gospel of Thomas*. If that is the case, then the *Life of Aesop* is structurally closer to one part of the Gospel tradition, and thematically closer to another.) This overall literary similarity between the *Life of Aesop* and the Gospels indicates that the genre "gospel" was not as unique as some have thought, and the particular motifs of the Gospels may owe more to the general background of reverence for philosophers than has been previously acknowledged.

The *Life of Aesop* is entertaining and whimsical, and was not likely considered historical in its details. But even within Aesop's humorous adventures, he often sounds a much loftier note. This ugly and misshapen slave transcends his bodily limitations through his surprising wisdom and way with words: "My worthless body," he says, "is my instrument by which I utter wise sayings to benefit the lives of mortals."

Because the *Life of Aesop* is sometimes bawdy and scatological, it may seem to modern readers to be a dubious comparison to the Gospels. However, its satirical perspective is similar to other texts of the time, such as Plautus's comedies, Petronius's *Satyricon*, and Apuleius's *Golden Ass* (see Teresa Hornsby's and Ian Henderson's contributions in this collection); like them it provides a comic release from social convention. It has also been likened by scholars to George Bernard Shaw's *Pygmalion* in its reflection on Aesop as a beast or an inanimate object who, through the power of speech alone, rises to the level of true philosopher in a world of pretenders. The *Life of Aesop* and the Gospels also share similarities with the large body of popular novelistic writing that arose at the turn of the era in the ancient Mediterranean. Jewish novels such as Esther, Judith, Tobit, and *Joseph and Aseneth* (although the latter may be later than the Gospels and written by a Christian author [see Randall Chesnutt's chapter in this volume]) arose at about the same time as the international novelistic histories of Ahikar, the Alexander romance, and the Ninus romance. The later Christian Apocryphal Acts and the Hellenistic romances followed in this same literary genre. Thus despite the great individual differences among these texts, during this period various peoples were composing novelistic works of about the same length to give expression to religious and philosophical themes.

Although the Gospels are usually considered more like ancient biographies than ancient novels, there is an overlap in style and theme. Even the *Life of Aesop* is part novel, part biography. The Aesop tradition thus sheds light on the literary context of the Gospels and on what options were available to the authors. Popular treatments of revered figures became something of a stock item (for instance, biographies of poets and philosophers such as Homer and Hesiod, and Jewish accounts of Abraham, Joseph, and Moses by Artapanus and Philo); the Gospel authors were not creating in a vacuum.

Was Jesus himself aware of this similarity? Probably not, but those who wrote the Gospels were likely influenced by the same literary model that gave rise to the *Life of Aesop*. The Gospel authors were not simply creating a life of Jesus out of thin air to match a popular literary form; rather, they placed the teachings and actions of Jesus in narrative form according to an already existing pattern.

SELECTED FABLES OF AESOP

11 THE PIPING FISHERMAN

A fisherman who knew how to play the pipes once took his pipes and his nets and went down to the sea. At first he stood upon a promontory and played his pipes, thinking that the fish would hear the sweet sound and come up out of the water on their own. When he had played for a while, however, and not attained his goal, he put his pipes aside, took up his net, and casting it into the water caught a large number of fish. He took them out of his net and dumped them on the shore, and when he saw them wriggling said, "You worthless creatures! When I piped to you, you did not dance, but now that I have stopped, you do!"

21 THE FISHERMEN AND THE TUNA

Some fishermen had set out for a catch, and after struggling for a long time and catching nothing, sat dejectedly in their boat. At that point a tuna, swimming along briskly, leapt out of the water and accidentally landed in their boat. The fishermen grabbed the fish, rowed back to the city, and sold it.

40 THE ASTRONOMER

An astronomer would go out each evening to look at the stars. Once as he was walking through the outskirts of the city, his mind was wholly occupied with the heavens, and he accidentally fell into a well. He began to shout and cry out, and a man passing by heard his moans. When he learned what had happened to him, he said, "My good man, while you are trying to see the things in heaven, do you not see the things on earth?"

70 THE OAK AND A REED

An oak and a reed were arguing over who was stronger. When a strong wind arose, the reed bent and swayed in the gusts of wind and thus avoided being uprooted, but the oak stood rigid and was pulled out by the roots.

77 THE DOE AND THE GRAPEVINE

A doe being pursued by hunters hid under the leaves of a grapevine. When the hunters had passed, the deer began to eat the leaves of the vine. One of the hunters, however, turned back, saw her, and struck her with his spear. As she lay dying, she groaned and said to herself, "It is right that I should suffer, for I harmed the grapevine that saved me."

82 THE ASS, THE ROOSTER, AND THE LION

On a certain farm there was an ass and a rooster. A hungry lion saw the ass and got into the fold. He was about to devour him, but at the sound of the rooster crowing he cowered in fear—for they say that lions are afraid of the crowing of roosters—and he ran away. When the ass saw that the lion was afraid of a rooster, he went out to pursue him, but when they got away from the farm, the lion devoured him.

149 THE LION, THE ASS, AND THE FOX

A lion, an ass, and a fox entered into an agreement and went out to hunt. When they had made a large catch, the lion commanded the ass to divide it up for them. The ass divided it into three equal parts and told him to take his pick. The lion, however, became angry, jumped on the ass and devoured him. He then turned to the fox and commanded him to divide the catch. Leaving only a small portion for himself, the fox gathered the rest of it into one pile and bade the lion take it. When the lion then asked the fox who had taught him to divide things in that way, the fox replied, "The experience of the ass."

LIFE OF AESOP

[1]Aesop, the storyteller and composer of fables and great benefactor of humanity, was born in Amorium of Phrygia, as fate would have it, a slave. He was truly horrible to behold: worthless, pot-bellied, slant-headed, snub-nosed, hunchbacked, leather-skinned, club-footed, knock-kneed, short-armed, sleepy-eyed, bushy-lipped—in short, an absolute monstrosity. But even worse than all this, he had one other defect even greater than the overall disharmony of his bodily appearance: he was dumb and could not utter a word.

[4]As Aesop was digging in the field, a priestess of Isis happened to wander away from the road and into the field where he was working. She saw him working away in his drudgery, and unaware of the circumstances of his condition, said to him, "Good man, if you have any pity for another human being, show me the way back to the road that leads to the city."

Aesop turned and saw her, dressed in the clothes of a goddess. Being a pious man, he bowed down to her. He then motioned to her, as if to ask, "Why did you leave the main road and wander out into the field?"

She realized that he could hear but could not speak, but all the same began to gesture as she spoke, "I am a stranger to these parts, and as you can see, a priestess of Isis. Since I have wandered from the road, would you please show me the way back?" Aesop picked up his mattock, took her by the hand, and led her to a grove of trees. There he placed before her bread and olives, and cut wild greens and brought them to her. He urged her to partake of his food, which she did. Then he led her to a spring, and offered her a drink. She shared both his food and water, and then prayed that Aesop should receive the greatest possible blessings. She then asked by signs that he bestow one final gift, and show her the way back to the road. He led her to the main road, and when he had pointed it out to her, returned to his labors. [5]The priestess of Isis, however, on her way again, did not forget Aesop's kindness. She raised her hands to heaven and said, "Many-named Isis, Diadem of the whole world, have mercy on this poor worker, who suffers and is yet pious. He has exhibited this piety not to me, O Mistress, but to your image. And if it is not your will to reward this man with great wealth, recompensing him for what the other gods have taken away, at least grant him the power of speech, for you can bring into the light those things that have fallen into darkness." When the priestess of Isis finished her prayer, the heavenly mistress consented, for any report of piety quickly makes its way to the ears of the gods.

[6]Since it was very hot, Aesop said to himself, "I am allowed two hours rest by my overseer. I'll take my rest now and sleep while it's hot." He chose a pleasant spot, green and secluded, a shaded grove of trees surrounding a blanket of green grass and all sorts of flowers, encompassed by a brook. Aesop threw his bag down beside his mattock, and using his sheepskin for a pillow, stretched out on

the grass and took his rest. The brook echoed the rustling of the branches of the trees round about. As a sweet, gentle wind began to blow, the verdant limbs were gently moved and wafted over him a cool breeze, creating in the many-blossomed wood a fresh and restful spot. The hum of cicadas in the branches filled the air, and the chorus of many different kinds of birds could be heard. While a nightingale lamented, the olive branches sang back in sympathy, and the slenderest branches of the pine trees fluttered in the wind, mimicking the black-bird. And Echo, the imitator of voices, uttered her responsive sounds in harmony. All of these voices conspired to lull Aesop into a deep and blissful sleep.

[7]Our lady, the goddess Isis, then made her appearance, together with the nine Muses, and said, "You see here, my daughters, the very image of true piety, a man who may be ill-proportioned on the outside, but is above all reproach in regard to his inner spirit. He once gave guidance to my servant when she had lost her way, and now in your presence I shall reward him. I myself shall restore his voice, while you bestow upon that voice the most noble ability in speaking." When she had said this, Isis removed from Aesop's tongue the impediment that had prevented him from speaking, and gave him back his voice. She also persuaded each of the Muses in turn to grant Aesop something of her own gifts. They bestowed upon him the power to compose and elaborate Greek tales. The goddess prayed further that Aesop might achieve fame, and then she withdrew. The Muses each in turn then conferred upon him her own gift, and ascended to Mount Helicon.

[8]When Aesop had finished the dream that had been planted by Isis, he awoke and said, "What a pleasant rest!" He then began to name each item he saw—mattock, pouch, sheepskin, ox, ass, sheep—and said, "By the Muses, I am speaking! Where did I get the power of speech? It must have come to me because I helped the priestess of Isis. Surely it is a good thing to be pious. No doubt I can expect to receive even more rewards from the gods!"

[Aesop is purchased by the philospher Xanthos, and is presented to the household.]
[33]"Aesop," said Xanthos's wife, "from what you have said, it is obvious that you are astute, but I was misled by my dream. I thought I was to receive a good-looking slave, but you are loathsome."

"Do not be surprised," said Aesop, "that you were tripped up by a dream, for not all dreams are true. At the request of Apollo, the head of the Muses, Zeus granted him the gift of prophecy, so that he excelled everyone in divining oracles. Since Apollo was marveled at by all people, he thought himself superior and became boastful in other ways as well, both because his prophecies were accurate and because they gave him such authority. This angered Zeus, who did not want him to possess this much power over people. Zeus then created dreams, which accurately told people during their sleep what was about to happen. When Apollo realized that people would no longer have any need of his prophecy, he asked Zeus to forgive him and not undermine his oracles. Zeus relented, and so created other dreams for people that were not true, and the human race, once thus deceived, would again be forced to rely on Apollo's prophecy. And so for this reason, the false dreams, when they come, appear like the true ones. Don't be surprised, therefore, when many things appear one way in your dreams, but turn out another way. It was not the first kind of dream you saw, but one of the lying ones, which has come to deceive you with false visions."

[34]Xanthos praised Aesop, noting how intelligent and articulate he was. He said to him, "Aesop, bring a carrying bag and come with me. We will buy some vegetables from the gardener for dinner." So Aesop threw the bag over his shoulder and followed along. When they came to the garden and found the proprietor, Xanthos said, "Give me some cooking vegetables." The gardener took his knife and cut some stalks of kale, beets, asparagus tips, and other savory vegetables, tied them in a neat bundle and handed them to Aesop.

Xanthos opened his moneybag and was about to pay the man, [35]when the gardener said, "What's that for, Professor?"

Xanthos replied, "I'm paying you for the vegetables."

"Why bother?" said the gardener. "As far as the garden and the produce are concerned, you can have this garbage. Just tell me one thing."

"Well, by the Muses," said Xanthos, "I won't take the money or the vegetables unless you explain to me first how anything I can tell you would be of value to a gardener. I'm not a handyman or a smith to make you a hoe or a leek slicer. I am a philosopher."

"But sir," said the gardener, "that is very useful for me. There's a small matter that has been bothering me so much I can't sleep at night. I have been pondering and pondering why it is that I put seeds into the ground, hoe them and water them, give them the best of attention, and yet the weeds still come up faster than what I planted."

Xanthos listened to this philosophical question, but when he could not answer it on the spot, said, "All things come to pass through divine providence." [36]Aesop, standing behind Xanthos, began to laugh. "Are you laughing with me or at me?" asked Xanthos.

"Oh, not at you," replied Aesop.

"At whom, then?"

"At the professor you studied under."

"You abominable wretch, you are uttering blasphemy against the entire Greek world! I studied in Athens, under philosophers, rhetoricians, learned professors. Are you able to ascend Mount Helicon, where the Muses hold forth?"

"If you speak gibberish, you can expect to be ridiculed."

"Does this problem he posed have some other solution? Things that happen by divine providence cannot be investigated by philosophers. Do you think that you are capable of solving it?"

Aesop said, "Agree to do it, and I will solve it for you."

37Xanthos was embarrassed and said, "It would be highly irregular for me—a philosopher who has debated in the greatest lecture halls—to engage in debate here in a garden. But so be it." He turned to the gardener and said, "My slave-boy here is very worldly. Put the question to him and he will solve it."

"Where is he?" asked the gardener.

"Here he is," said Xanthos.

"This worthless slave has learning?" asked the gardener.

Aesop laughed and said to him, "You should talk, you miserable wretch!"

"I'm a miserable wretch?" exclaimed the gardener.

"You're a gardener, aren't you?"

"Yes."

"How can you object to being called a miserable wretch if you are a gardener? But do you want to know why you plant seeds in the ground, you hoe them, water them, tend them with loving care, and yet you say the untended weeds come up quicker than your vegetables? Listen carefully to what I say. It's like what happens when a woman is married a second time, and has children from her first marriage, but also finds that her new husband has children from his first wife. She is now mother of those children she bore, but stepmother of her husband's children. The difference between them is great. She lavishes great care and affection on those whom she bore, but she is jealous of those who were brought into this world through another woman's labors, and hates them, cutting back on their food and provisions to give more to her own children. It is only natural that she loves her own children and hates her husband's, and treats them as strangers. In the same way, the earth is the mother of the plants that come up on their own, but stepmother of those planted by others; nourishing her own, she causes them to grow faster than the orphans which you plant."

Upon hearing all this, the gardener said, "You have taken a load off my shoulders. Here, take the vegetables as a gift, and if you ever need any more, come and treat the garden as your own."

51On the next day, Xanthos invited his students to dinner, and said to Aesop, "I have invited my friends to dinner. Go and buy the best thing in the whole world."

He went to the butcher's shop and bought pigs' tongues, then returned home and began to prepare them: some he boiled, some he roasted, some he spiced.

Xanthos said, "Aesop, give us something to eat." Aesop brought each of them a boiled tongue, served with spicy sauce.

The students said, "Indeed, even your dinner expresses your philosophy! You never do anything that isn't carefully thought out, for at the very beginning of the dinner, tongues are served."

52And after two or three drinks, Xanthos said, "Aesop, give us something else to eat."

Aesop again gave each a tongue, this time roasted, served with salt and pepper. The students exclaimed, "Inspired, Professor! By the Muses, this is excellent! Every tongue is sharpened by fire, and even better, by salt and pepper, for the salt is mixed with the sharpness of the tongue to bring out a razor-sharp wit."

After they had drunk again, Xanthos said for the third time, "Bring us something else to eat."

Aesop brought each a spiced tongue.

"Democritus!" said one of the students to another, "I have worn out my tongue eating tongues."

"Is there anything else to eat?" asked another. "Wherever Aesop labors, nothing good can come of it."

When the students tasted the spiced tongues, they became nauseous. Xanthos said, "Aesop, bring us each a bowl of soup."

Aesop served them tongue soup. The students did not even touch this, but said, "This is Aesop's final blow. We have been beaten by tongues."

"Aesop, do we have anything else?" asked Xanthos.

"No, nothing else," he replied.

[53]"Nothing else, you wretched slave? Did I not tell you to buy 'the best thing in the whole world'?"

"I'm glad that you find fault with me in the presence of so many learned men," responded Aesop. "You told me to buy 'the best thing in the whole world.' Well, what is better or finer than the tongue? You will note that all philosophy and all education depend on the tongue. Without the tongue, nothing could happen—no giving, no receiving, no enterprise. Through the tongue cities are constituted and ordinances and laws are established. If, therefore, all living depends upon the tongue, nothing could be greater."

The students said, "By the Muses, he speaks well! You were mistaken, Professor!" The students then got up and went home, but all night long they suffered from bouts of diarrhea.

[54]On the next day, the students complained to Xanthos, but he said, "Gentlemen and scholars, it was not my fault, but the fault of that worthless slave Aesop. But tomorrow I'll make good on my dinner, and I'll give him his instructions in your presence." So calling Aesop, he said to him, "Since you seem determined to turn my words upside down, go into the marketplace and buy the worst, the vilest thing in the whole world." Aesop readily agreed and went to the butcher, and again he purchased pigs' tongues. He then brought them home and prepared them for dinner. When Xanthos arrived with his students, they all took their places at the table. After their first drink, Xanthos said, "Aesop, bring us something to eat." Aesop served each of them a pickled tongue with hot sauce.

The students said, "What is this? Tongue again?" Xanthos blanched. The students continued, "Maybe he wants the vinegar to soothe our stomachs from yesterday's diarrhea." After they had a second round of drinking, Xanthos said, "Bring us something to eat."

Aesop served each of them a roast tongue. "Oh no, what's this?" said the students. "That idiot from yesterday is trying to make us sick again with tongues!"

[55]Xanthos said, "Not again, you scum! Why did you buy these? Didn't I tell you to buy 'the worst, the vilest thing in the world'?"

Aesop replied, "And what bad thing does not come about through the tongue? On account of the tongue there are enemies, plots, conflicts, battles, jealousy, strife, wars. Surely there is nothing worse than this most abominable tongue."

"Professor," said one of the students, "if you pay attention to him, he will soon drive you crazy. Like body, like mind. This slave is abusive and mischievous, and isn't worth a copper!"

[Aesop eventually obtains his freedom and travels on his own.]

[101]After spending many years in Samos and receiving numerous honors, Aesop decided to tour the world. He procured a large income through his lecturing, and in his travels came ultimately to Babylon, ruled over by Lycurgos. Aesop exhibited his philosophy there, and as a result was proclaimed a great man. Because of his intelligence even the king became enamored of his teaching and made him chief counselor. [102]In those days the kings had a practice of receiving tribute by means of contests of valor, but rather than engage in wars and battles, they would send letters containing philosophical conundrums, and the one who could not discover the solution would send tribute to the one who sent it. Aesop solved many of the problems sent to Lycurgos, acquiring great honors for the king. He also sent many problems to other kings in the name of Lycurgos, forcing them to send tribute when they could not solve them. Thus the kingdom of the Babylonians expanded, so that it included not only the barbarian peoples, but most of the lands up to Greece.

[121]On the next day, King Nectanebo of Egypt met privately with his advisers, and said, "As I see it, on account of this unsightly and accursed fellow, I am going to have to send tribute to King Lycurgos of Babylon."

But one of his advisers said, "Let us pose to him the following problem: What is there that we have neither seen nor heard of? Whatever answer he proposes, we shall say that we have seen it or heard of it. He will not be able to contradict us and will admit defeat."

The king was very pleased with this plan, supposing that by this device he would finally attain victory. When Aesop arrived, King Nectanebo said to him, "Solve just one more problem, and I will pay tribute to Lycurgos. Tell us something we have neither seen nor heard of."

Aesop answered, "Give me three days, and I will answer you." He departed from the king, and began to turn the problem over in his mind: "Whatever I say, they will say that they are familiar with it." [122]But Aesop, always very clever in such matters, sat down and wrote a record of a loan that read, "Loaned to Nectanebo by Lycurgos, a thousand talents of gold." He then included the date on which it was due. After three days, Aesop returned to King Nectanebo and found him with his advisers, awaiting Aesop's concession of defeat. Aesop, however, brought forth the false note and said, "Read this record of an agreement."

The advisers of King Nectanebo lied and said, "We have seen this and heard of it many times."

"I am glad that you will testify to its authenticity," said Aesop. "Let King Nectanebo pay it back immediately, for it is overdue."

When King Nectanebo heard this, he said, "How can you testify to the authenticity of a loan I never received?"

The advisers said, "We have never seen or heard of this."

"If that is your conclusion," said Aesop, "then the problem you posed to me has been solved."

[123]Nectanebo said, "Lycurgos is truly blessed to have procured such wisdom for his kingdom." Handing over to Aesop ten years' worth of tribute, Nectanebo sent him back to Lycurgos with a letter bearing greetings of peace. When Aesop arrived in Babylon, he recounted to Lycurgos everything that had happened in Egypt, and presented him with the money. Lycurgos then commanded that a golden statue be erected of Aesop with the Muses, and held a great festival in honor of Aesop's wisdom.

[124]Aesop decided that it was time to go to Delphi, so he said good-bye to the king, but promised that he would return to him again and reside in Babylon for his remaining days. He traveled by way of many other cities, demonstrating his wisdom and learning, and finally came to Delphi and began to exhibit his wisdom there as well. Although the crowds enjoyed his presentations at first, they gave him nothing. [125]Deliberately trying to offend them, he said, "O Delphians, you are like driftwood afloat on the sea. Seeing it from afar, bobbing about on the waves, we think it is something valuable, but as we approach it we find that it is an insignificant thing, worth nothing. Similarly, while I was living at a distance from your city, I was quite impressed with your wealth and magnanimity, but now that I see how inferior you are to other people, both in your leading families and in the constitution of your city, I realize that I erred in holding a positive opinion of you. Indeed, you act in a way not unworthy of your ancestors."

[126]"And who are our ancestors?" asked the Delphians.

"Freed slaves," replied Aesop. "And if you are unaware of this, then listen carefully. There was a law among the Greeks in ancient times that when they captured a city, they would send a tenth part of the spoils to Apollo, so that out of a hundred oxen, they would send ten, and similarly with goats and with everything else—money, male slaves, female slaves. It was from these slaves that you are descended, and you are thus like bondsmen and women, slaves of all Greeks."

When he had said this, he prepared to depart, [127]but the city officials, smarting at his abuse, reasoned among themselves: "If we allow him to depart, he will make a round of the other cities saying even worse things about us." They decided, therefore, to kill him through deceit. Apollo was also angry, because Aesop had slighted him in Samos by not including him with the statues of the nine Muses.

Since the Delphians had no legitimate charge against Aesop, they devised a cunning plan, so that visitors to their city could not help him. They kept a close watch on Aesop's slave resting at the city gate, and when he fell asleep, they took a golden cup from the temple, and hid it in Aesop's baggage. The next day, Aesop set out for Phocis, unaware of what he was carrying. [128]Some of the Delphians caught up with him, bound him, and dragged him back to the city. He called out, "Why are you hauling me away in bonds?"

They answered him, "You have stolen vessels from the temple."

"Let me die if I am found guilty of any such charge!" said Aesop, whose conscience was clear.

The Delphians searched through his bags and found the cup, then showed it to the city as they dragged Aesop about for all to see. Aesop realized that the cup must have been planted among his belongings as part of a plot, and pleaded with the Delphians to release him, but they would not listen. Aesop said, "Since you are but mortals, do not consider yourselves higher than gods!" But they locked him in jail to await punishment. Aesop found himself unable to devise any means of escape, and said, "If I am but a mortal man, how shall I be able to escape what is about to happen?" Aesop cried to himself and said,

'Do not despair, my heart, if you are too weak to flee.
My eyes beheld beforehand what is in my soul,
That the Delphians would act without just cause.'

[129]A friend of his came to the jail, and obtaining permission from the guards, entered into the place where Aesop was kept. When he saw Aesop crying, he said, "How did this happen, my miserable friend?"

Aesop told him a fable: "A woman who had buried her husband was sitting at his tomb, weeping and overcome with grief. A plowman saw her and began to desire her, so he left his oxen standing with the plow and came over to her, pretending to weep. She paused and asked, 'Why are you crying?' The plowman answered, 'I have just buried a good and wise wife, and when I cry, I find it makes my grief easier to bear.' The woman said, 'I have also lost a good husband, and when I do as you do, I also find it takes away some of the grief.' So he said to her, 'If we have suffered the same fate, why don't we get to know each other better? I shall love you as I did her, and you will love me as you did your husband.' He thus persuaded the woman, but while he was lying with her, someone untied his oxen and led them away. When the plowman got up and discovered that his oxen were gone, he began to wail in genuine grief. The woman asked, 'Why are you crying again?' And he replied, 'Woman, now I really do have something to mourn!' So you ask me why I am grieving when you see my great misfortune?"

[130]The friend, saddened by Aesop's predicament, said, "Why did you get it into your mind to insult them in their own country and city, while you were under their authority? Where is your training? Where is your learning? You have advised cities and entire peoples, but when it comes to yourself, you are a fool. . . ."

Aesop replied, "I have lost even the little sense I already had in coming to Delphi." Aesop's friend shed many tears for him, and then left.

[132]Afterward, the Delphians came in and said to Aesop, "By a vote of the city, today you will be executed by being thrown off a cliff, as is fitting for a temple-robber, a huckster, and a blasphemer. You won't even be deemed worthy of a burial. Prepare to meet your end."

When Aesop saw that they were now ready to kill him, he said, "Just hear one fable." They allowed him to proceed. Aesop said, [133]"When animals all spoke the same language, a mouse became friends with a frog and invited him to dinner. He brought him into a very rich storeroom, in which there were bread, meat, cheese, olives, and figs, and said, 'Eat!' The frog indulged himself gladly, and then said, 'Now you must also come to my house for dinner, and I shall receive you well.' He took the mouse to his pond and said, 'Dive in!' The mouse said, 'I don't know how to dive.' The frog said, 'I'll teach you,' and tying the mouse's foot to his own with a string, he jumped into the pond, pulling the mouse with him. As the mouse was drowning he said, 'Although I am dead, I will take my revenge on the living.' When he had said this, the frog dove down and finished off the mouse. But as the dead mouse lay floating on the water, a raven seized it and carried it away, with the frog still tied to it. The bird devoured the mouse, then turned and tore the frog apart as well. Thus the mouse got his revenge on the frog. So also, men of Delphi, although I die, I shall be the death of you as well. Indeed, Lydians, Babylonians and practically all of Greece will reap the fruits of my death."

[134]All his words failed to persuade the Delphians, but as they were leading him away to the cliff, he took refuge in the temple of the Muses. They had no mercy on him, however, but dragged him away against his will. He said to them, "Men of Delphi, do not scorn this temple! At the right time it will proclaim my innocence! Listen to this fable: [135]The rabbit, pursued by an eagle, took refuge with a dung-beetle and begged him to save him. The dung-beetle pleaded with the eagle not to disregard the rabbit's request, adjuring her in the name of Zeus not to scorn him because of his small size, but the eagle knocked over the beetle with her wing, grasped the rabbit in her claws, and tore him apart and ate him. [136]The beetle became angry and flew off after the eagle, observing the location of the nest where the eagle safeguarded her eggs. The beetle returned later and smashed the eggs. When the eagle arrived back at the nest, she moaned and wailed, and set out to find the one who did this in order

to tear him apart. When it was nesting season again, the eagle laid an egg in an even higher nest, but the dung beetle returned again, did as before, and departed. The eagle mourned the loss of her egg, saying that this bitterness was ordained by Zeus in order to make eagles an even rarer species. [137]When the nesting season again returned, the eagle was so despondent that she did not even place the eggs in the nest, but instead flew up to Mount Olympus and dropped them in the lap of Zeus, saying, 'Twice now my eggs have been broken, so now I am depositing them with you to safeguard them for me.' The dung-beetle found this out, and covering himself with dung flew up to Zeus and circled around his head. Zeus was so startled by this filthy bug that he jumped up, forgetting the eagle eggs in his lap, and broke them. [138]Zeus later learned that the dung-beetle had been wronged, so when the eagle returned, Zeus said to her, 'You deserved to lose your eggs, for you have wronged the dung-beetle.' The beetle added, 'Not only has she wronged me, but she has been very impious toward you as well. I had adjured her in your name, but she was unconcerned and killed the one who sought my protection. I will never stop until I have punished her to the fullest extent.' [139]Zeus did not want the species of eagles to die out entirely, and tried to persuade the dung-beetle to be reconciled, but the beetle would not listen. Therefore, Zeus altered the laying season of eagles to the time when the dung-beetles do not appear on the earth. In the same way, men of Delphi, you should not despise this temple where I have taken refuge, even though it is a small shrine, but remember the dung-beetle and revere Zeus, god of strangers and Olympos."

[140]The Delphians once again were unmoved, but led Aesop to the edge of the cliff. When Aesop saw that his end was near, he said, "Since I have addressed you in many different ways and not convinced you, hear just one more fable: A farmer who had grown old in the country, but had never seen the city, asked his children to let him go away to see the city before he died. So his children hitched up the wagon to the donkeys for him, and said, 'Just drive the donkeys, and they will take you to the city,' But when a storm came up and it became dark, the donkeys went astray and took him to a place surrounded by cliffs. When the man saw the danger, he said, 'O Zeus, how have I wronged you so that I should die? And I am not being killed by horses, but by these wretched donkeys!' Just so, I am upset that I shall die, not at the hands of reputable men, but at the hands of these wretched slaves!"

[141]And just as Aesop was about to be thrown from the cliff, he told them yet another fable: "A certain man fell in love with his own daughter, and was so consumed with passion that he sent his wife to the country and forced himself upon his daughter. She said to him, 'Father, this is an unholy thing you have done! I would rather have submitted to a hundred men than to you.' That is how I feel toward you, men of Delphi—I would rather wander through Syria, Phoenicia, and Judea than be killed by you here, where one would least expect it."

[142]Aesop cursed them, called upon Apollo, the head of the Muses, to bear witness that he was dying unjustly, and threw himself off the cliff. In this way

he ended his life. But when the Delphians were afflicted with a plague, they consulted an oracle from Zeus, which stated that they should expiate the death of Aesop. And when the Greeks, Babylonians, and Samians heard of Aesop's execution, they avenged his death.

Bibliography

Compton, Todd. "The Trial of the Satirist: Poetic *Vitae* (Aesop, Archilochus, Homer) as Background for Plato's Apology." *American Journal of Philology* 111 (1990): 330–47.

Daly, Lloyd W. *Aesop without Morals*. New York: Thomas Yoseloff, 1961.

Holzberg, Niklas. *The Ancient Novel: An Introduction*. London: Routledge, 1995.

———, ed. *Der Äsop-Roman: Motivgeschichte und Erzählstruktur*. Tübingen: Gunter Narr Verlag, 1992.

Hopkins, Keith. "Novel Evidence for Roman Slavery." *Past and Present* 138 (1993): 3–27.

Morgan, J. R., and Richard Stoneman, eds. *Greek Fiction: The Greek Novel in Context*. London: Routledge, 1994.

Nagy, Gregory. *The Best of the Achaeans: Concepts of the Hero in Ancient Greek Poetry*. Baltimore: Johns Hopkins University Press, 1979.

Perry, Ben Edwin. *Aesopica*. New York: Arno Press, 1980.

Wills, Lawrence M. *The Jewish Novel in the Ancient World*, pp. 1–39, 245–56. Ithaca, NY: Cornell University Press, 1995.

———. *The Quest of the Historical Gospel: Mark, John and the Origin of the Gospel Genre*, pp. 23–50, 180–215. London: Routledge, 1997.

Winkler, John J. *Auctor & Actor: A Narratological Reading of Apuleius' Golden Ass*. Berkeley: University of California Press, 1985.

—14—

Targum, Jesus, and the Gospels

Bruce Chilton

The Aramaic word *targum* by itself denotes "translation" in Aramaic, yet the type and purpose of the rendering involved in Judaism means the term also refers to a type of literature. We need to appreciate the general phenomenon of targum, and the specific documents called Targumim, before we can take up the question of Targumic influence on Jesus and the Gospels.

Aramaic survived the demise of the Persian Empire as a lingua franca in the Near East. It had been embraced enthusiastically by Jews (as by other peoples, such as Nabateans and Palmyrenes); the Aramaic portions of the Hebrew Bible (in Ezra and Daniel) attest a significant change in the linguistic constitution of Judaism. Even before Hebrew emerged as a distinct language, Abraham had been an Aramaean, although the variants of the Aramaic language during its extensive history are stunning. Conceivably, one reason for Jewish enthusiasm in embracing Aramaic during the Persian period was a distant memory of its affiliation with Hebrew, but it should always be borne in mind that Hebrew is quite a different language. By the time of Jesus, Aramaic had become the common language of Judea, Samaria, and Galilee (although distinctive dialects were spoken); Hebrew was understood by an educated (and/or nationalistic) stratum of the population, and some familiarity with Greek was a cultural necessity, especially in commercial and bureaucratic contexts.

The linguistic situation in Judea and Galilee demanded translation of the Hebrew Bible into Aramaic, for purposes of popular use and worship among the majority of Jews. Although fragments of Leviticus and Job in Aramaic, which have been discovered at Qumran, are technically targumim, they are unrepresentative of the genre targum in literary terms. They are reasonably "literal" renderings; that is, there is a formal correspondence between the Hebrew rendered and the Aramaic that is presented. The Targumim that Rabbinic Judaism produced are of a different character.

The aim of Targumic production was to give the sense of the Hebrew Scriptures, not just their wording, so paraphrase is characteristic of the Targumim. Theoretically, a passage of Scripture was to be rendered orally and from memory in the synagogue by an interpreter (a *meturgeman*) after the reading in Hebrew from a scroll; the *meturgeman* was not to be confused with the reader, lest the congregation mistake the Aramaic interpretation with the original text (see *m. Megillah* 4:4–10 and *b. Megillah* 23b–25b). (Regulations that specify the precise number of verses that may be read prior to the delivery of a Targum probably date from centuries after the period of the New Testament. The same may be said of cycles of specified lectionary readings.) Although the renderings so delivered were oral in principle, over the course of time, traditions in important centers of learning became fixed, and coalescence became possible.

The emergence of the Rabbis as the dominant leaders within Judaism after 70 CE provided a centralizing tendency without which literary Targumim could never have been produced. Yet it is quite clear that the Rabbis never exerted complete control over Targumic production. The Targumim preserved by the Rabbis are paraphrases, yet the theological ideas conveyed are not always consistent, even within a given Targum. Although the Rabbis attempted to regulate Targumic activity, the extant Targumim sometimes even contradict Rabbinic rules directly. For example, *m. Megillah* 4:9 insists that Leviticus 18:21 ("You must not give of your seed, to deliver it to Moloch") should not be interpreted in respect of sexual intercourse with Gentiles; the Targum Pseudo-Jonathan—a late work, produced well after Rabbinic authority had been established—takes just that line.

The Targumim evince such oddities because they are the products of a dialectical interaction between folk practice and Rabbinic supervision—sometimes mediated through a love of dramatic and inventive speculation, and this dynamic tension continued over centuries. Each of the extant Targumim crystallizes that complex relationship at a given moment.

The Documents Called Targumim

The Targumim divide themselves up among those of the Torah (the Pentateuch), those of the Prophets (both "Former Prophets," or the so-called historical works in the English Bible, and the "Latter Prophets," or the Prophets as commonly designated in English), and those of the Writings (or Hagiographa), following the conventional designations of the Hebrew Bible in Judaism. The fact needs to be stressed at the outset, however, that although the Hebrew Bible is almost entirely rendered by the Targumim in aggregate, there was no single moment, and no particular movement, that produced a comprehensive Bible in Aramaic. The Targumim are irreducibly complex in dates, origins, purposes, and dialects of Aramaic. They cannot be assigned to a single epoch of ancient Rabbinic Judaism. This makes arguments based on the assumption that the Targumim as a whole predate the New Testament untenable; those that assume they are all post-Christian are equally spurious.

Among the Targumim to the Pentateuch, Targum Onqelos is a suitable point of departure because it corresponds best of all the Targumim to Rabbinic ideals of

translation. Although paraphrase is evident, especially to describe God and his
revelation in suitably reverent terms, the high degree of correspondence with the
Hebrew of the Masoretic Text (and evidently with the Hebrew text current in antiquity) is striking. The dialect of Onqelos is commonly called "Middle Aramaic,"
which would place the Targum between the first century BCE and 200 CE. A better
designation, however, would be "Transitional Aramaic" (200 BCE–200 CE), embracing the various dialects (Hasmonaean, Nabataean, Palmyrene, Arsacid, Essene, as well as Targumic) that came to be used during the period, since what followed was a strong regionalization in dialects of Aramaic, which we can logically
refer to as "Regional Aramaic" (200 CE–700 CE). Because the dialect of 200 BCE–200
CE was transitional between earlier Persian forms and later regionalization, various Targumim were produced in Transitional Aramaic even after its demise as a
common language. For that reason, the year 200 CE is not a firm date, after which
a Targum in Transitional Aramaic cannot have been composed. Onqelos should
probably be dated toward the end of the third century, in the wake of similar efforts to produce a literal Greek rendering, and well after any strict construal of
the principle that Targumim were to be oral. By contrast with the later Rabbinic
ethos, which permitted the creation and preservation of Onqelos in writing, one
might recall the story of Rabbi Gamaliel, who is said during the first century to
have immured a Targum of Job in a wall of the Temple (Talmud *Shabbath* 115a),
scarcely a gesture of approval.

The Targum Neophyti I was discovered in 1949 by Alejandro Díez Macho in
the Library of the Neophytes in Rome. Neophyti paraphrases more substantially
than Onqelos. Entire paragraphs are added, as when Cain and Abel argue in the
field prior to the first case of murder (Genesis 4:8):

> Cain answered and said to Abel,
> I know the world is not created with mercies,
> and it is not led in respect of fruits of good deeds,
> and there is accepting of persons in judgment:
> for what reason
> was your offering received with favor
> and my offering was not received from me with favor?
> Abel answered and said to Cain,
> I know the world is created with mercies,
> and in respect of fruits of good deeds it is led:
> and because my good deeds surpassed yours
> my offering was received from me with favor
> while your offering was not received from you with favor.
> Cain answered and said to Abel,
> there is no judgment and there is no judge,
> and there is no other world,
> there is no giving good reward to the righteous
> and there is no repaying from the wicked.

> Abel answered and said to Cain,
> there is judgment and there is a judge,
> and there is another world,
> and there is giving good reward to the righteous
> and there is repaying from the wicked in the world to come.

This is no "rendering" as we understand translation, but a substantial theodicy. Abel is right, according to the Targum: in this world, God's favor is a matter of justice and mercy, because it hangs on good deeds. In the world to come, all wrongs are to be righted. When the remarkable freedom to introduce a theology of this kind prevails over the text, it is impossible to predict the outcome in purely literary terms.

The dialect of Neophyti is often known as "Palestinian Aramaic," although "Tiberian" (or Galilean) is a better designation, because the Rabbis did not establish permanent academies in Jerusalem or Judea after 70 CE. In any case, the dialect is a form of Regional Aramaic (200 CE–700 CE), distinct from what used to be called the "Babylonian Aramaic" of Onqelos. The distinction between "Tiberian" and "Babylonian" manifests the nascent regionalization in the Aramaic language to which we have referred. But Neophyti is produced in a frankly Regional Aramaic, whereas Onqelos appears in a Transitional Aramaic that is on the way to becoming Regional. Yet the chronology of the two Targumim is about the same, although Neophyti appears somewhat later; the differences between them are more a function of interpretative program than of dating. The Rabbis of Babylonia, who called Onqelos "our Targum," exerted greater influence over the Rabbinic movement as a whole than did their colleagues in the west, as the normative status of the Talmud of Babylonia (the *Bavli*) attests.

The latest representative of the type of expansive rendering found in Neophyti is Targum Pseudo-Jonathan. Its reference to the names of Muhammad's wife and daughter in Genesis 21:21 put its final composition sometime after the seventh century CE. This oddly designated Targum is so called because the name "Jonathan" was attributed to it during the Middle Ages, when reference to the document was abbreviated with the letter *yod*. The letter probably had stood for "Jerusalem," although that designation is also not provably original. The title "Pseudo-Jonathan" is therefore an admission of uncertainty. Neophyti and Pseudo-Jonathan are together known as "Palestinian Targums," to distinguish their dialects and their style of interpretation from those of Onqelos. In fact, however, Pseudo-Jonathan was produced at the dawn of the period of Academic Aramaic (700–1500 CE), during which Rabbinic usage continued to develop the language in a literary idiom after it has been supplanted by Arabic as a lingua franca in the Near East.

Neophyti and Pseudo-Jonathan are associated with two other Targumim, or, to be more precise, Targumic groups. The first group, in chronological order, consists of the fragments from the Cairo Geniza. They were originally part of more complete works, dating between the seventh and the eleventh centuries, which were deposited in the Geniza of the Old Synagogue in Cairo. In the type and substance of its interpretation, these fragments are comparable to Neophyti and

Pseudo-Jonathan. The same may be said of the Fragments Targum, which was collected as a miscellany of Targumic readings during the Middle Ages. An interesting feature of the Targumim of this type is that their relationship might be described as a synoptic one, in some ways comparable to the relationship among the Gospels. All four of the paraphrastic Targumim, for example, convey a debate between Cain and Abel comparable to what has been cited from Neophyti, and they do so with those variations of order and wording which are well known to students of the Synoptic Gospels.

Both the Former and the Latter Prophets are extant in Aramaic in a single collection, although the date and character of each Targum within the collection needs to be studied individually. The entire corpus is ascribed by Rabbinic tradition (b. Megillah 3a) to Jonathan ben Uzziel, a disciple of Hillel, the older contemporary of Jesus. On the other hand, there are passages of the Prophets' Targumim that accord precisely with renderings given in the name of Joseph bar Chiyya, a Rabbi of the fourth century (see, e.g., Isaiah Targum 5:17b and Talmud Pesaḥim 68a). As it happens, the Isaiah Targum (which has been subjected to more study than any of the Prophets' Targumim) shows signs of a nationalistic eschatology that was current just after the destruction of the Temple in 70 CE, and also of the more settled perspective of the Rabbis in Babylon some three hundred years later. It appears that Targum Jonathan as a whole is the result of two major periods of collecting and editing interpretations by the Rabbis, the first period being Tannaitic, and the second Amoraic.

Long after Targum Jonathan was composed, probably around the same time the Fragments Targum (to the Pentateuch) was assembled, targumic addenda were appended in certain of its manuscripts; they are represented in the Codex Reuchlinianus and in a manuscript in the Bibliothèque Nationale (mis)labed Hébreu 75. These represent the phenomenon of Targum upon Targum: a further interpretative extension of the Aramaic wording, not just the Hebrew original in the Bible.

Of the three categories of Targumim, that of the Writings is without question the most diverse. Although the Targum to Psalms is formally a translation, substantially it is better described as a midrash, while the Targum to Proverbs appears to be a fairly straightforward rendition of the Peshitta, and the Targum(im) to Esther seems designed for use within a celebration of the liturgy of Purim. The Targumim to the Writings are the most problematic within modern study, but they are also of the least interest of the three general categories of Targumim from the point of view of understanding the New Testament, in view of their late (in several cases, medieval) dates.

Uses of Targumim in the Study of Jesus and the Gospels

The significance of the Targumim for appreciating Jesus and the Gospels follows naturally from assessing their purpose and provenience. Fundamentally, the Targumim constitute evidence of the way in which the congregations for whom the

Targumim were intended understood the Hebrew Scriptures—at issue is not merely Rabbis' exegesis but common interpretation. Insofar as what is reflected in a Targum is representative of the reception of Scripture in the first century, that Targumic material is of importance for any student of the New Testament. But care needs to be taken, so the perspectives of later Targumic materials are not accepted uncritically as representative of an earlier period: that would result in anachronistic reading.

There are clearly readings in the Targumim that presuppose events subsequent to the death of Jesus. One example of such a reading is Targum Isaiah 53:3–9. In the translation here, as is customary, I italicize evident departures of the Aramaic text from the Hebrew original. Still, only comparison with an English translation of Isaiah (if memory does not serve in this case) will reveal what a militantly messianic teaching this Targum conveys, even as it laments the departure of the divine presence ("the Shekhinah") from Mount Zion as the result of the Roman arson of 70 CE:

> Then the glory of all the kingdoms will be for contempt and cease; they will be faint and mournful, behold, as a man of sorrows and appointed for sicknesses; and as when the face of the Shekhinah was taken up from us, they are despised and not esteemed. Then he will beseech concerning our sins and our iniquities for his sake will be forgiven; yet we were esteemed wounded, smitten before the LORD and afflicted. And he will build the sanctuary which was profaned for our sins, handed over for our iniquities; and by his teaching his peace will increase upon us, and in that we attach ourselves to his words our sins will be forgiven us. All we like sheep have been scattered; we have gone into exile, every one his own way; and before the LORD it was a pleasure to forgive the sins of us all for his sake. He beseeches, and he is answered, and before he opens his mouth he is accepted; the strong ones of the peoples he will hand over like a lamb to the sacrifice, and like a ewe which before its shearers is dumb, so there is not before him one who opens his mouth or speaks a saying. From bonds and retribution he will bring our exiles near; the wonders which will be done for us in his days, who will be able to recount? For he will take away the rule of the Gentiles from the land of Israel; the sins which my people sinned he will cast on to them. And he will hand over the wicked to Gehenna and those rich in possessions which they robbed to the death of the corruption, lest those who commit sin be established, and speak of possessions with their mouth.

This text clearly anticipates that the reader takes the destruction of the Temple as given. But commentators have frequently made that same observation in regard to the way the Parable of the Vineyard is handled in the Synoptic Gospels (see Matthew 21:33–46 with 22:7; Mark 12:1–12; Luke 20:9–19). Here it is of special interest that Isaiah's image of the vineyard in 5:1–7 is specifically related to the sanctuary and the altar on Mount Zion in the Targum. Modern students of the New Testament have sometimes become so obsessed with the issue of whether Targumim predate Jesus in particular, they appear to have forgotten that Targumic influence on the Gospels does not require that chronology at all. In this case, ignoring the Targum means overlooking a source that attests the catastrophe the destruction of the Temple represented, deep antipathy to the Romans and to the wealthy in general, and a remarkably clear articulation of messianic hope in the period after 70 CE. This passage is an example of the Tannaitic level of the Isaiah Targum, which was composed during the same period that much of the New Testament was.

A particular problem is posed for modern study by the persistent notion that there is somewhere extant today a "Palestinian Targum" that substantially represents the understanding of the Hebrew Bible in the time of Jesus and in exactly his language. There was a time when that was a comprehensible position, because documents in what was called "Palestinian Aramaic" were thought to be more ancient than those in "Babylonian Aramaic." That is one good reason for speaking more accurately of "Tiberian" or "Galilean" Aramaic, rather than of "Palestinian" Aramaic: people do tend to conflate any reference to what is ancient and Palestinian to what must have existed in the period of Jesus. But the old position also runs up against the current understanding of how the Aramaic language developed: the discoveries at Qumran have cast new light on Onqelos and Jonathan, which makes them appear more ancient than was supposed some sixty years ago, and more similar to Aramaic as spoken in Palestine. Onqelos and Jonathan, insofar as they represent Transitional Aramaic, convey an earlier form of the language than what we find in the Cairo Geniza, the Pseudo-Jonathan, and the Fragments Targumim. To the same extent that the last three Targumim are Tiberian in language, they also represent the later, Regional dialect of Aramaic. Moreover, the present understanding of early Judaism is that it was too variegated to allow of the formation of a single, authoritative tradition of rendering, such as the designation "Palestinian Targum" would suggest. Pseudo-Jonathan appears to represent a more recent tendency not only in language but also in its historical allusions and its form.

The difficulty of assessing the precise form of Targumic tradition(s) within the first century should also make us wary of any claim that we know the precise dialect(s) of Aramaic current in that period. The literary remains of the language are sporadic, dialectical variation was great, and sometimes there may have been a significant difference between the language as spoken and the language as written. For all those reasons, attempts to "retranslate" the Greek Gospels into Jesus' own language are extremely speculative; when the Targumim are appealed to by way of antecedent, speculation is piled upon speculation. In purely linguistic terms, it is obvious that the Aramaic of Qumran (account being taken of their provenience from Judea), more than that of any of the Targumim, offers a useful guide in the exercise of retroversion.

The composite nature of the Targumim is nonetheless such that on occasion one may discern in them the survival of materials that did circulate in the time of Jesus, influencing his teaching and/or the memory of that teaching among his disciples. Whatever Qumran may tell us of the language of Jesus, his thought and its environment are often better represented by the Targumim. An example of such a survival is Leviticus 22:28 in Pseudo-Jonathan, "My people, children of Israel, since our father is merciful in heaven, so should you be merciful upon the earth." The expansion in the Targum is unquestionably innovative, as compared with what may be read in the Masoretic Text, so that there is a possible echo in Luke 6:36, within the address known conventionally as "the sermon on the plain": "Become merciful, just as your Father is also merciful." Since the comparison is with the Targum, and no other source so far identified, the possibility should logically be entertained that the Targumic tradition was current during the first century, and that it influenced Jesus. It is, of course, theoretically possible that the saying originated with Jesus and was then anonymously taken up within the Targum. Without doubt, the statement is rhetorically more at home within Luke than in Pseudo-Jonathan, where it appears unmotivated. But it seems inherently unlikely that Pseudo-Jonathan, which of all the Pentateuch Targumim is perhaps the most influenced by a concern to guard and articulate Judaic integrity, would inadvertently convey a saying of Jesus. More probably, Pseudo-Jonathan and Luke's Jesus independently pass on wisdom of a proverbial nature: both sources convey material from the stock of folk culture. After all, the same Targum twice explains love of another person (whether an Israelite or a stranger) with the maxim "that which is hateful to you, do not do" (Leviticus 19:18, 34 in Pseudo-Jonathan, cf. Luke 6:31; Matthew 7:12). Luke shows that the stock goes back to the first century, and Pseudo-Jonathan shows that it continued to be replenished until the seventh century. The Targumic echo is therefore most certainly not immediately the source of Jesus' statement, but it may help us to describe the nature, general type, and origin of Jesus' statement.

Examples such as Leviticus 22:28 in Pseudo-Jonathan demonstrate that the Targumim might have a heuristic value in illustrating the sort of Judaism that Jesus and his followers took for granted. The example cited is a case in which a Targum just happens to be a good resource for understanding Judaism in the first century, and therefore Jesus. Targumim may therefore enable us to find materials that are useful in comparison with the Gospels and the rest of the New Testament. Recent study has greatly increased the catalog of such instances.

But it is possible now to go beyond heuristic comparisons and to specify four ways in which Targumic texts can be used to enhance our understanding of Jesus and the Gospels. Only a few examples may be given here within each category, but they will establish the viability of these comparisons and illustrate the issues involved in research.

Category 1: Jesus (According to the Gospels) Citing a Targumic Rendering

Sometimes the Gospels as they stand (despite the fact they are written in Greek and usually refer to the Hebrew Scriptures in the Greek version called the Septuagint) have Jesus cite a form of Scripture that is closer to the Targum than to any other extant source. In these cases, an awareness of the fact helps us better to understand his preaching in a much more specific way than the general similarity between Luke and Pseudo-Jonathan illustrates. Targum Isaiah 6:9, 10 is an especially famous example, and it helps to explain Mark 4:11, 12. The statement in Mark could be taken to mean that Jesus told parables with the express purpose that (*hina*) people might see and not perceive, hear and not understand, lest they turn and be forgiven:

> And he was saying to them, To you the mystery has been given of the kingdom of God, but to those outside, everything comes in parables, so that (*hina*) while seeing they see and do not perceive, and while hearing they hear and do not understand, lest they repent and it be forgiven them.

The Targum also (unlike the Masoretic Text and the Septuagint) refers to people not being "forgiven" (rather than not being "healed"), which suggests that the Targum may give the key to the meaning supposed in Mark. The relevant clause in the Targum refers to people who behave *in such a way* "so that" (*d* in Aramaic) they see and do not perceive, hear and do not understand, lest they repent and they be forgiven. It appears that Jesus was characterizing people in the Targumic manner, as he characterizes his own fate similarly in Mark with a clause employing *hina* (cf. 9:12); he was not acting in order to be misunderstood.

In this famous case from Mark, then, the underlying Aramaism of using the clause with *d* produced the saying of Jesus with the term *hina* in Greek, which may mean "in order that" or "so that." If the former meaning obtains, Mark's Jesus speaks so as not to be understood, and deliberately to preclude the forgiveness of those who do not understand. If the latter meaning obtains, then Jesus referred to Isaiah in its Targumic form in order to characterize the kind of people who do not respond to his message, and what happens to them. The fact of the similarity in wording with the Targum shows us that the second meaning is preferable, as does the fact that Jesus elsewhere in Mark refers to *his own followers* as being hard-hearted, with unseeing eyes and unseeing ears (Mark 8:17–18). His point in alluding once again to Isaiah 6 is given at the end of the rebuke "Do you not yet understand?" (Mark 8:21). Jesus' citation of Isaiah 6 in its Targumic form was intended to rouse hearers to understanding, not to make their misunderstanding into his own program.

"All those who grasp a sword will perish by a sword" (Matthew 26:52): the sword, like the measure (see below under category 3) seems to have been a proverbial figure. The Isaiah Targum 50:11 applies it graphically:

> Behold, all you who kindle a fire, *who grasp a sword!* Go, *fall* in *the* fire *which you kin-dled* and on the *sword which you grasped!*

The link to the passage in Isaiah (or any passage of Scripture) cannot be demonstrated in the case of Jesus' saying, so that the correspondence seems to be of the proverbial type of the saying about the measure. Nonetheless, the close agreement in wording and imagery makes this a comparison of the first type.

The final verse of the Book of Isaiah in the Targum identifies who will suffer—and specifies where they will suffer—at the end of time, when it says "*the wicked shall be judged in Gehenna until the righteous will say concerning them, We have seen enough*" (66:24). "Gehenna" is just what Jesus associates with the statement that "their worm will not die and their fire will not be quenched" (Mark 9:48, and see vv. 44, 46 in many manuscripts), which is taken from the same verse of Isaiah. In the Targum, the first part of the phrase reads, "their *breaths* will not die." The term "Gehenna" refers in a literal sense to the Valley of Hinnom in the Kidron Valley, just across from the Temple in Jerusalem. But because that had been a place where idolatrous human sacrifice by fire had taken place (see 2 Kings 16:3; 21:6), the site was deliberately destroyed and desecrated by King Josiah as part of his cultic reform during the seventh century BCE (see 2 Kings 23:10). As a result, Gehenna came to be known as the place of the definitive punishment of the wicked.

Apart from James 3:6, the term "Gehenna" appears exclusively in sayings of Jesus in the New Testament; otherwise, only the Pseudepigrapha (especially the *Book of Enoch*) and Rabbinic literature provide us with examples of the usage from the same period or near the same period that enable us to see what the term means. Gehenna is the place of fiery torment for the wicked. But it is not known as such in the Septuagint, Josephus, or even Philo: evidently, the usage is at home in an Aramaic environment. Rabbi Aqiba also is said to have associated Gehenna with the end of the Book of Isaiah (in the Mishnah, see *Eduyoth* 2:10):

> The judgment of the wicked in Gehinnom lasts twelve months, as it is said (Isaiah 66:23), And it shall be from new moon to new moon . . .

Aqiba, however, refers to punishment in Gehenna having a limit of twelve months; for Jesus, as in the Isaiah Targum, part of the threat of Gehenna was that its limit could not be determined in advance. Targumic Gehinnam and New Testament Gehenna correspond well.

Category 2: Jesus (According to the Gospels) Sharing an Interpretation with a Targum

The second type of affinity does not involve the sharing of explicit wording, but it does presuppose a comparable understanding of the same biblical passage in the Targumim and the New Testament. An example is Jesus' Parable of the Vineyard in Matthew 21:33–46; Mark 12:1–12; and Luke 20:9–19. After he has told his story of the abuse suffered by those the owner sends to acquire his share of the vintage, the Synoptic Gospels agree that the opposition to Jesus among the Jewish authorities hardened to the point that they wanted to seize him. When the symbolism of the vineyard in the Isaiah Targum 5:1–7 is considered, the opposition to Jesus becomes easily explicable. There, the vine is a primary symbol of the Temple, so that the tenants of Jesus' parable are readily identified with the leadership of the Temple. They knew he was telling the parable against them. Both Matthew (21:33) and Mark (12:1) allude to Isaiah 5:2, when they refer to a hedge set around the vineyard. Their allusion is to the Septuagintal version of Isaiah 5:2, so that any conscious awareness of the Targum at the point of the composition of those Gospels cannot be claimed. The point is rather that the memory of allusion to Isaiah 5 is preserved; what the Targumic version of Isaiah explains, while other versions do not, is why the priestly opposition to Jesus would feel particularly engaged by his parable.

Category 3: Jesus' Usage (According to the Gospels)
of a Phrase Characteristic of a Targum

The third type of affinity concerns characteristically Targumic phrases appearing within the New Testament. The best example is the central category of Jesus' theology: the kingdom of God, which also appears in the form "kingdom of the LORD" in the Targumim (see Targum Onqelos, Exodus 15:18; Targum Jonathan, Isaiah 24:23; 31:4; 40:9; 52:7; Ezekiel 7:7; Obadiah 21; Zechariah 14:9). The first usage in the Isaiah Targum (24:23) associates the theologoumenon of the kingdom of God with God's self-revelation on Mount Zion, where his appearing is to occasion a feast for all nations (see 25:6–8). The association of the kingdom with a festal image is comparable to Jesus' promise in Matthew 8:11 and Luke 13:28–29, that many will come from the ends of the earth to feast with Abraham, Isaac, and Jacob in the kingdom of God.

The influence of Targumic usage on Jesus would help to account for one of the most striking features of his theology: his insistence that the kingdom is a dynamic, even violent, intervention with human affairs. The Isaiah Targum provides a theological precedent for the sort of usage that Jesus developed further. The Masoretic Text offers a picture of the Lord descending upon Mount Zion as a lion, which is not afraid of the shepherds who attempt to protect the prey. That arresting image is referred explicitly to the kingdom in the Isaiah Targum (31:4):

> As *a* lion, *a* young lion *roars* over its prey, and, when a band of shepherds *are appointed* against it, it is not *broken up* at their shouting or *checked* at their *tumult, so the kingdom of* the LORD of hosts will *be revealed to settle* upon *the* Mount *of* Zion and upon its hill.

This passage simply refutes the outworn generalization that the kingdom within Judaic usage was static, and that the dynamic aspect was Jesus' innovation. The kingdom's dynamism was not original with Jesus; his particular contribution was in his portrayal of how the kingdom comes.

The Job Targum speaks of God making the righteous sit "upon the throne *of his kingdom with established* kings" (36:7) in a way that invites comparison with Luke 22:28–30, and Matthew 19:28. Here, the motif of entry into the kingdom and joint reign with the just is clearly articulated. Stress upon the ethical conditions that make entry into the kingdom possible was characteristic of Jesus' message (see Matthew 19:16–30 as a whole, with its parallels).

"With *the* measure you *were measuring with they will measure you*," appears in the Isaiah Targum 27:8, and, of course, a saying of Jesus' is strikingly similar (Matthew 7:2; Mark 4:24):

> In the measure you measure it shall be measured you.

The fact is, however, that the measure in the Isaiah Targum is applied to a single figure, the oppressor of Jacob, rather than to a general group, as in Jesus' saying. A similar aphorism, crafted in the third person, was common in Rabbinic literature (see, e.g., *Sotah* 8b and Genesis 38:25 in Pseudo-Jonathan), so it should be taken that we have here a proverb in Aramaic that Jesus and a *meturgeman* of Isaiah both just happened to use. This is an instance in which, despite close verbal agreement, no case for dependence can be made one way or the other.

Other usages from the Isaiah Targum may be mentioned under the category of comparisons of the third type. The phrase "mammon of deceit" in the Isaiah Targum is certainly not unique within Rabbinic or Judaic usage, but 1 Samuel Targum 8:3; 12:3; 2 Samuel Targum 14:14; Isaiah Targum 5:23; 33:15 provide an analogy with Jesus' usage in the Parable of the Unjust Steward (Luke 16:9), because in all those cases bribery is at issue. In any case, "mammon" is a shared usage between Jesus and the Targumim. "*The people inquire of their idols*, the living *from* the dead," is a turn of phrase that is an obvious rebuke in the Targum (8:19), but its concluding expression may be echoed in the pointed question to the women at the tomb of Jesus (Luke 24:5). Obviously, these are matters of turns of phrase rather than content, but they remain striking.

Also in Luke, Jesus cites what appears to be a passage from Isaiah 61 in a synagogue (Luke 4:18–19), but it turns out to be a mixture of several passages or themes from the Book of Isaiah. Among them is Isaiah 42, which in the Targum (42:3, 7) especially refers to the poor, the blind, and prisoners, who are pointedly mentioned in Jesus' "citation." At the time of Jesus' baptism, a voice is said to attest that God "is well pleased" with him (so Matthew 3:17; Mark 1:11; Luke 3:22); in the Isaiah Targum, God is said to be well pleased with Israel or Jacob (41:8–9; see also 43:20; 44:1) and the Messiah (43:10), when the Masoretic Text speaks only of God's choice of such figures. Similarly, the idiom that there is (or is not) "pleasure before" God is shared by the Gospels (Matthew 18:14) and the Targumim (Zephaniah Targum 1:12).

The Gospel according to John has not featured prominently in discussion of possible affinity with the Targumim, yet Martin McNamara has called attention to a notable convergence. The phrasing of Jesus' promise in John 14:2, that he goes "to prepare a place" for his followers, is similar to the theme expressed in the Pentateuchal Targumim generally that God or his Shekhinah prepares for Israel a place of encampment or rest. As McNamara points out, the usage renders a variety of Hebrew terms in the Masoretic Text and should therefore be seen as characteristically Targumic. The usage in John is not sufficiently specific to make the Targumic connection more than possible, but the convergence remains notable.

Category 4: Thematic Agreement between Jesus (According to the Gospels) and a Targum

The theme of the consequences of not attending to the voice of the prophets was shared by Jesus with Judaic tradition, including the Isaiah Targum, but Jesus also formulated a demand based on the unique experience of his followers (Matthew 13:17; cf. Luke 10:24):

Amen I say to you that many prophets and just people wished to see what you see and did not see, and hear what you hear and did not hear.

This conviction that a fresh experience of God brings with it new requirements of response is also reflected in the Isaiah Targum (48:6a):

> You have heard: *has what is revealed to you been revealed to* any *other people;* and will you not declare it?

Obviously, no case for dependence can be made here, but the thematic coherence is nonetheless worthy of note.

The Isaiah Targum speaks of "*the righteous, who desire teaching as a* hungry *person desires bread, and the words of the law, which they desire as a* thirsty *person desires water*" (32:6). That interpretation of hunger and thirst is reminiscent of the Matthean Jesus, who blesses those who hunger and thirst after righteousness (see Matthew 5:6). This comparison does not extend to the Lukan Jesus (cf. Luke 6:21), which raises the possibility that the present wording in Matthew was shaped during the course of transmission along the lines of Targumic interpretation. Similarly, The Targum's association of the image of those who are lame with sinners and exiles might illuminate Matthew 21:14–15 (see 2 Samuel 5:8; Zephaniah 3:19; Isaiah 35:6; Micah 4:6–8, all in Targum Jonathan, and the article by Craig Evans). The statement "Blessed are you, the righteous" in Targum Jonathan at 2 Samuel 23:4 might also be mentioned, together with a striking comparison in the Jeremiah Targum (23:28b) that Robert Hayward has called attention to:

> Behold, just as one separates the straw from the grain, so one separates the wicked from the righteous, says the LORD.

The image appears both in the preaching of John the Baptist (Matthew 3:12) and in a parable of Jesus' (Matthew 13:30). (For the related motif of the handling of chaff, see Matthew 3:12; 13:30; Luke 3:17; Hosea Targum 13:3; Zephaniah Targum 2:2). Perhaps even more striking is the phrase "*doers of* the truth," which appears in the Jeremiah Targum 2:2 and in Johannine literature (John 3:32; 1 John 1:6). A more general, but less exact, analogy exists between Jesus' complaint about the "adulterous and sinful generation" he found himself in (see Matthew 12:39; 16:4; Mark 8:38) and the cognate characterization in the Isaiah Targum 57:3. Jesus' reference to sin as "debt" (see Matthew 6:12; 18:23–35) appears to be an idiom shared with the Targumim.

In contrast to cases where the Targumim instance usages that influenced the Gospels, Hayward suggests that the statement in the Jeremiah Targum 33:25 contradicts Christian belief that God would cause the present heaven and earth to pass away. Similar cases include the rendering of the Hosea Targum 11:1, "Out of Egypt I have called *them* sons." That corrects the passage away from the singular application of "Out of Egypt I have called to my son," which had long been used as a Christian testimonium (see Matthew 2:15). It obviously cannot be demonstrated that the Targum here responds to the testimonial usage; but that it removes the possibility of such an interpretation is notable. Perhaps for a similar reason, the Zechariah Targum omits the reference to thirty pieces of silver at 11:12, the reference to "the potter" at 11:13 (cf. Matthew 27:3–10), and the reference to "him whom they have pierced" at 12:10 (cf. John 19:37; Revelation 1:7). On the other hand, Zechariah 14:21 in the Targum refers to the time when there will be no "trader," rather than Canaanite, in the Temple, and that may be an antecedent of Jesus' complaint in John 2:16. It has also been suggested that the surprising rendering of Malachi, "But *if you* hate *her, divorce her*," which contradicts the straightforward meaning of the Hebrew ("But he hates *divorce*"), is designed to militate against the stricter Christian teaching (see Matthew 5:31–32; 19:3–9; Mark 10:2–12; Luke 16:18; Romans 7:2–3; 1 Corinthians 7:10–11).

Conclusion

Our initial finding must be categorical and negative. The comparison of the second type, where the New Testament and the Targumim share a common, literary understanding of the same biblical passage, resulted in the smallest harvest of cases of all the categories of comparison we have considered. That underscores what has emerged as a theme in this discussion as a whole: in their literary form, the Targumim had not fully emerged by the first century. Had that been the case, the literary category of comparison would have been much more strongly represented.

It may seem paradoxical, but the fact is that comparison of the first type, where actual wording is involved (in the interpretation of the same scriptural passage or in a more general assertion) represents a stronger relationship between the New Testament and the Targumim. Why should that be the case? In each instance, a saying of Jesus was involved, and a saying of Jesus in regard to a key concept within his teaching (forgiveness, violence, and Gehenna). Evidently, the Targumim represent traditions that were a formative influence on the tradition of the Gospels at an early stage. Once the Gospels emerged in their Greek form, however, Targumic influence all but disappeared. That is why the second, literary type of comparison yielded so few results.

That complex relationship, in which the Targumim do represent traditions from the formative period of Judaism in texts that are relatively late in their literary forms, is best attested in the third type of comparison. Here, many of Jesus' most famous sayings find their echoes: the kingdom of God and thrones set for the righteous, the measure by which one is measured, mammon, the citation of Isaiah 61, the expression "preparing a place." But this comparison (unlike the comparison of the first type) is not limited to sayings of Jesus. Characteristic expressions of God being well pleased and of people seeking the living among the dead also find their place here. That raises interesting questions in regard to actual contacts which may be posited between the Targumim and the communities that produced the Gospels.

Finally, the fourth type of comparison includes more passages than may be repeated here individually, but it is instructive in its range. It includes Jesus' statements about the revelation of what was hidden from the prophets to Jesus' own followers and those who hunger and thirst after righteousness, divine judgment as the separation of straw and grain, various characterizations of the righteous and sinners, the present generation as adulterous and sinful, and the understanding of sin as a form of debt. Although it should be borne in mind that comparisons of the fourth type do not concern typically Targumic expressions, the very fact of this overlap means they are of value in an understanding of the New Testament. For all the variety of the dates, involving different degrees of distance from the first century, the Targumim include material that is resonant with some of the most primitive materials in the New Testament.

In all such inquiry, it needs to be kept in mind that the written composition of Rabbinic literature generally postdates the time of Jesus by several centuries. That fact has been used among some scholars of the New Testament to claim that Rabbinic sources should not be used in exegesis at all. I have to say I find that an odd argument. Exegetes routinely refer to later Roman historians, such as Tacitus and Dio Cassius, to later Hellenistic authors, such as Philostratus and Athanaeus, to later Christian writers, such as Justin Martyr and Eusebius, and to later Gnostic sources, such as the the *Trimorphic Protennoia* and *On the Origin of the World*, all in order to understand the New Testament better. (I choose those examples, by the way, because they are widely cited and involve a time lag after Jesus that is comparable to the delay in the production of the Mishnah, the Talmud, and the Targumim.) In cases other than Rabbinic Judaism, the technique of extrapolating backward from literary evidence is accepted. Once, Jewish sources were excluded from consideration for doctrinal reasons, and now it seems a kind of chronological fundamentalism is being applied to them alone.

In any case, no one would seriously argue that Rabbinic sources were simply made up by authors on the spot at the time of written composition. By means of both oral and written transmission, their heritage reaches back behind the period of the New Testament. Naturally, critical care is necessary to sort out earlier and later material in all ancient literature, but that is a normal task of scholarship.

On the evidence of the Gospels, Jesus seems never to have cited Targumic wording exactly. Even when he quotes the Book of Isaiah and the connection with the Targum is evident (Mark 4:11–12) the deviation from any known textual form is striking. The reference to Isaiah 66:24 in Mark 9:48 constitutes a usage of Targumic tradition that is similarly free. The abbreviation—relative to Isaiah Targum 50:11—in Matthew 26:52 manifests the same phenomenon in respect of Jesus' usage of proverbial material, and that observation also applies to Matthew 7:2 and Mark 4:24. Usage of the idiom "mammon of deceit" at Luke 16:9 seems to be a bold application of language normally associated with biblical interpretation. For that matter, the fact that Jesus used the phrase "the kingdom of God" in the context of experience, not of exegesis, shows that an innovative tendency is characteristic of his style of teaching.

This aspect of Jesus' character as a teacher illuminates a famous passage (Luke 4:16–30) that concerns his near stoning after he spoke on the basis of Scripture at the synagogue in Nazareth. Luke's Gospel smoothes out the narrative of the service to accord with a Hellenistic notion of what worship in a synagogue entails. This Gospel does not, for example, mention the translation of the Hebrew Scriptures into Aramaic, but assumes everything happened in Greek.

Because Luke presents the setting as routine, the congregation's response to Jesus seems completely irrational. That feeds another pet theme of Luke's: the senseless rejection of Jesus by the Jewish people (see also Acts 13:13–52). By the same token, the reference at the close of Luke's passage to the healing of the non-Jew Naaman by Elisha tells us more about the church of Luke than about the thinking of Jesus. Here the Hellenistic, non-Jewish idiom is as obvious as it often is in John's Gospel.

Still, it is also evident that who Jesus was and what he said brought about an effort to stone him in Nazareth. Luke misses the dynamics of the synagogue's rejection of Jesus for cultural reasons.

The citation Jesus uses from Isaiah begins, "The Lord's spirit is upon me, forasmuch as he anointed me." Jesus told the congregation that God's Spirit had been with him since his mastery of John's teaching, signaled by the descent of the dove as he was immersed in the Jordan in the story of Jesus' baptism. Jesus claimed that he fulfilled Isaiah's prophecy of someone who would be born into Israel, anointed by the Spirit, and, therefore, able to speak on God's behalf. In Greek, as in Hebrew and Aramaic, the term "messiah" basically means "anointed one." This etymology is of more than academic interest because the very verb used here (*khrio* in Greek, *mashach* in Hebrew and Aramaic) associated itself in the ear with the term "messiah" (*meshiach*) or "christ" (*khristos*). In Nazareth of all places, where stories of his irregular birth must have circulated, Jesus entered the solemn congregation to insist that he was God's anointed, the bearer of his father's Spirit. Jesus is messiah because that Spirit is upon him, and he made the text from Isaiah into a description of his own action.

The synagogue's violent response to Jesus was not only to his messianic claim; he also manipulated Isaiah's words. Jesus' "citation" is no citation at all but a free paraphrase of the biblical book, different from any ancient version (Greek, Hebrew, or Aramaic). This dissonance is not a Lukan creation because the governing pattern of that Gospel is to make the correspondence to the Greek version of the Bible (the Septuagint) in biblical citations as close as possible.

Fortunately, the wording of this speech in the Old Syriac Gospels (in a language closely related to Jesus' indigenous Aramaic) provides an even more radical paraphrase of Isaiah, closer to what Jesus actually said:

> The spirit of the Lord is upon *you*, on account of which
> > he has anointed *you* to message triumph to the poor;
> > And he has delegated me to proclaim to the captives release,
> and to the blind sight
> —and *I* will free the broken with release—
> and to proclaim the acceptable year of the Lord.

Luke's Greek irons out a vital part of Jesus' originality for the benefit of Hellenistic readers accustomed to the Septuagint: the crucial change in pronouns (here italicized). By speaking these words, Jesus portrays himself as responding to a divine charge: "The spirit of the Lord is upon *you*, on account of which he has anointed *you* to message triumph to the poor." Then he emphatically accepts that charge: "And he has sent me to preach to the captives release, and to the blind sight—and *I* will free the broken with release—and to preach the acceptable year of the Lord." Both the charge and the emphatic acceptance are produced by the signal changes in pronouns, attested only in Syriac, and changing the wording of Scripture to reflect the sense of purpose that his immersions with John had given him. (Both on the bank of the Jordan and here, Jesus was addressed directly, as the "you" whom divine spirit inspired.) Those changes are part and parcel of Jesus' conscious alteration of the language taken from the book of Isaiah.

The alteration is typical of his style of employing Scripture, especially the Book of Isaiah and especially in a Targumic form. He paraphrased and changed the Scripture to explain his experience of God, and how God was active in what he said and did. Jesus' prophetic claims were sufficient to startle any congregation; making them in a messianic context invited outrage. Because the term "messiah" could be defined in different ways in ancient Judaism, he set in motion a controversy that has never ceased. Messiah could refer—for example—to one "anointed" to make war, or "anointed" to offer sacrifice, or "anointed" to prophesy, or "anointed" to rule as king. To which category of messiah did he belong? The words from Luke discussed above, especially in their Syriac form, make it clear he referred to himself as anointed to prophesy. But "messiah," the chosen of God from the house of David, had for centuries been at the center of expectations of the removal of foreign dominion. Through Joseph, Jesus claimed Davidic descent, even though the circumstances of his birth were disputed. That raised the specter that Herod Antipas and the Romans might respond violently to the news that a disciple of John the Baptist's was using messianic terms to refer to himself.

Despite the legitimate fear of official sanctions, Jesus said in public that he preached and healed on the basis of his access to God's Spirit, which spoke to him of his anointing. The distinctive usage of Scripture that made Jesus both an appealing teacher and a controversial teacher comes to light by means of an understanding of his relationship to the Targumic traditions of his time.

Bibliography

Ådna, Jostein. "Der Gottesknecht als triumphierender und interzessorischer Messias. Die Rezeption von Jes 53 im Targum Jonathan untersucht mit besonderer Berücksichtigung des Messiasbildes." Pages 129–58 in *Die leidende Gottesknecht. Jesaja 53 und sine Wirkungsgeschichte.* Forschungen zum Alten Testament 14. Edited by Bernd Janowski and Peter Stuhlmacher. Tübingen: Mohr, 1996.

Beyer, Klaus. *Die Aramäische Texte vom Toten Meer samt den Inschriften aus Palästina, dem Testament Lev is und der Kairoer Geniza, der Fastenrolle und den alten talmudischen Zitaten.* Göttingen: Vandenhoeck and Ruprecht, 1984.

Bowker, John W. *The Targums and Rabbinic Literature: An Introduction to Jewish Interpretation of Scripture.* Cambridge: Cambridge University Press, 1969.

Chilton, B. D. *A Galilean Rabbi and His Bible: Jesus' Use of the Interpreted Scripture of His Time.* Good News Studies 8. Wilmington, DE: Glazier, 1986.

———. *The Glory of Israel: The Theology and Provenience of the Isaiah Targum.* Journal for the Study of the Old Testament Supplements 23. Sheffield: JSOT, 1982.

———. *The Isaiah Targum: Introduction, Translation, Apparatus, and Notes.* The Aramaic Bible 11. Wilmington, DE: Glazier; Edinburgh: Clark, 1987.

———. *Profiles of a Rabbi: Synoptic Opportunities in Reading about Jesus.* Brown Judaic Studies 177. Atlanta: Scholars Press, 1989.

———. *Rabbi Jesus: An Intimate Biography.* New York: Doubleday, 2000.

———. *Targumic Approaches to the Gospels: Essays in the Mutual Definition of Judaism and Christianity.* Studies in Judaism. Lanham, MD: University Press of America, 1986.

Evans, C. A. "A Note on 2 Samuel 5:8 and Jesus' Ministry to the 'Maimed, Halt, and Blind.'" *Journal for the Study of the Pseudepigrapha* 15 (1997): 79–82.

———. *To See and Not Perceive: Isaiah 6.9–10 in Early Jewish and Christian Interpretation.* Journal for the Study of the Old Testament Supplement Series 64. Sheffield: Sheffield Academic Press, 1989.

Hayward, Robert. *The Targum of Jeremiah.* The Aramaic Bible 12. Wilmington, DE: Glazier, 1987.

McNamara, Martin. *The New Testament and the Palestinian Targum to the Pentateuch.* Analecta Biblica 27. Rome: Pontifical Biblical Institute, 1966.

———. *Targum and Testament. Aramaic Paraphrases of the Hebrew Bible: A Light on the New Testament.* Grand Rapids, MI: Eerdmans, 1972.

———. "'To Prepare a Resting-Place for You': A Targumic Expression and John 14:2f." *Milltown Studies* 3 (1979): 100–108.

York, A. D. "The Dating of Targumic Literature." *Journal for the Study of Judaism* 5 (1974): 49–62.

———. "The Targum in the Synagogue and the School." *Journal for the Study of Judaism* 10 (1979): 74–86.

—15—

The *Psalms of Solomon*

Joseph L. Trafton

A few years before the birth of Jesus, a group of Jews struggled to reconcile a debacle at the hands of a foreign conqueror with the belief that Israel was God's chosen people. The result was a collection of eighteen psalms that eventually—and for reasons that are not altogether clear—was given the title *Psalms of Solomon* (here abbreviated as *PssSol*). These psalms provide insight into both intra-Jewish quarrels of this period and the hope of at least one Jewish group for the coming of a Messiah.

The author (or authors) of the *PssSol* write with two distinct opponents in mind. The first is the foreign conqueror from the West, mentioned in *PssSol* 2, 8, and 17, who captured Jerusalem and defiled the Temple. Although a few scholars have argued that the psalmist was referring to Herod the Great, most agree that the allusions fit the Roman general Pompey, who captured Jerusalem in 63 BCE and was slain in Egypt in 48 BCE. This dates the *PssSol* to the last half of the first century BCE.

The second is a particular group of Jews. In a general sense, the psalmist divides Jews into two camps. He identifies himself with those whom he calls the righteous, the holy ones, the poor, the innocent, and those who fear the Lord; on the other side are the wicked, the lawless, the sinners, the deceitful, and the hypocrites. But he also provides more specific criticisms: his opponents have defiled the Temple and its sacrifices and have set up a non-Davidic monarchy. Such charges suggest that the Jewish opponents in view are the Hasmoneans—the dynasty that was descended from the leaders of the Maccabean Revolt against the Greeks in the second century BCE and took over both the high priesthood and the kingship before giving way to the Romans in the first century BCE.

Faced with the calamities that these two opponents brought upon the nation, the psalmist looks forward to the day when the Messiah, the Son of David, will purify the nation of its enemies and restore Jerusalem to its proper place. Yet the psalmist does not see the Messiah as a military figure. His trust will be in God, not in horse or rider or bow. Building upon such traditional texts as Psalm 2 and Isaiah 11, the psalmist develops his vision of the Messiah in terms of the roles of king, judge, and shepherd.

Many scholars have argued that the *PssSol* are Pharisaic, others that they are the product of a group of Essenes. While there are some strong parallels between the *PssSol* and the Dead Sea Scrolls, it is noteworthy that no manuscript of the *PssSol* has been identified among the scrolls. Given our growing awareness of the diversity within Judaism in this period, it is probably unwise to move beyond the affirmation that the *PssSol* were written by a group of Jews that opposed the Hasmonean dynasty. What is especially important about the *PssSol* for the study of Jesus is precisely the intra-Jewish critique that they exhibit.

The selections translated here place three areas of the Jesus tradition into their Jewish context. First, the criticism of Jews who defile the Temple in *PssSol* 1, 2, and 8 recalls Jesus' "cleansing" of the Temple (Matthew 21:12–14; Mark 11:15–17; Luke 19:45–46; John 2:13–16). Second, the severe denunciation of "hypocrites" in *PssSol* 4 recalls Jesus' woes to the scribes and the Pharisees (Matthew 23; cf. Mark 7:1–13; Luke 13:10–17). Whether the specific offenses that elicited these criticisms are the same in each case is not the issue; notable is that Jews could—and did—criticize the Temple leadership and brand other Jews as hypocrites. Finally, the lengthy description of the anticipated Messiah in *PssSol* 17 (cf. *PssSol* 18) provides the longest such passage in all of Second Temple Judaism. The significance of this passage for understanding Jewish messianic expectation at the time of Jesus and the early church can scarcely be overestimated.

Originally composed in Hebrew, the *PssSol* now exist only in two versions— the Greek and the Syriac. The translation that follows is based on both. Robert B. Wright has graciously provided me with a proof copy of the critical edition of the Greek that he is preparing for Sheffield Academic Press. The standard edition of the Syriac is that of W. Baars in *The Old Testament in Syriac according to the Peshitta Version*, part IV, fascicle 6 (Leiden: Brill, 1972). I have undertaken a thorough comparison of the two versions in *The Syriac Version of the Psalms of Solomon: A Critical Evaluation*.

PSSSOL 1:1–8

[1]I called out to the Lord when I was severely distressed,
   To God when sinners attacked me.
[2]Suddenly the noise of war was heard before me;
   He will hear me because I have been filled with righteousness.
[3]I thought in my heart that I have been filled with righteousness,
   When I was rich and had grown large with many children.
[4]For their wealth extended to all the earth,
   And their glory to the end of the earth.
[5]They were raised up to the stars,
   And they said they would not fall.
[6]And they acted insolently in their prosperity,
   And they did not understand.

⁷For their sins were in secret,
  And I did not understand.
⁸And their lawlessness was greater than that of the nations before them.
And they defiled the Temple of the Lord with defilement.

PSSSOL 2:1–13

¹In arrogance the lawless one cast down strong walls with a battering
  ram,
  And you did not restrain him.
²Foreign nations went up against your altar,
  And they trampled it with their shoes in arrogance,
³Because the sons of Jerusalem defiled the sanctuary of the Lord,
  And they defiled the offerings of God in lawlessness.
⁴Therefore he said, "Remove them and cast them away from me!"
⁵And the beauty of her glory did not prosper them.
  It was despised before the Lord,
  And it was utterly disgraced.
⁶Her sons and daughters were in bitter captivity,
  And upon their neck was placed the sealed yoke of the nations.
⁷And according to her sins he did to them,
  Because he abandoned them into the hand of one who was stronger.
⁸For he turned his face from mercy upon them,
  Young and old and their children together,
  Because they did evil together, that they might not hear.
⁹And heaven was angered greatly,
  And the earth despised them,
  Because no one did upon it as they did,
¹⁰So that the earth might know all your righteous judgments, O God.
¹¹They set up the sons of Jerusalem as objects of ridicule in the place of
  the harlots in her.
  And everyone who transgressed did so before the sun,
¹²They mocked their lawlessness, as they also were doing;
  They exposed their lawlessness before the sun.
¹³And the daughters of Jerusalem were defiled according to your
  judgments,
  Because they defiled themselves with unrestrained intercourse.

PSSSOL 4

¹Why do you sit, O wicked man, in the synagogue of the righteous,
  With your heart far from God,
  And in your lawlessness provoking the God of Israel?

²Abounding more than everyone in your words and in your signs
 Is the one who is harsh in his words to condemn sinners in
  judgment.
³And his hand is first upon him as in zeal,
 And he is guilty of a multitude of sins and self-indulgence.
⁴His eyes look without modesty upon every woman,
 And his tongue lies when making agreements with an oath.
⁵In the night and in secret places, as if unseen,
 He speaks with his eyes to every woman in an evil scheme,
 And he is quick to enter every house joyfully as one who is
  innocent.
⁶May God remove those who judge in hypocrisy,
 Who live with the holy ones in the corruption of their body and
  the poverty of their flesh.
⁷May God reveal the works of those who please people;
 May he reveal their works with ridicule and scorn.
⁸The holy ones will justify the judgment of their God
 When the wicked are removed from before the righteous,
 The hypocrite who speaks the law deceitfully.
⁹His eyes look calmly upon a house, like a snake,
 To destroy the wisdom of each with words of lawlessness;
¹⁰His words are deceptive for the practice of lawless desire.
 And he did not cease to scatter them in bereavement,
¹¹And he devastated the house because of his lawless desire,
 And he considered with words that there is no one who sees or
  judges.
¹²And he was filled with this lawlessness,
 And his eyes looked upon another house to destroy it with words
  that put to flight,
¹³And his soul, like Sheol, is not satisfied in all these things.
¹⁴May his portion, O Lord, be in disgrace before you;
 May his going out be with groans and his coming in with curses.
¹⁵May his life, O Lord, be in pains and in poverty and in want,
 His sleep in sorrows and his waking in anxieties.
¹⁶May sleep be removed from his temples during the night;
 May he fall in disgrace by every work of his hands.
¹⁷May he enter his house empty-handed,
 And may his house be lacking in everything that satisfies the
  soul.
¹⁸And may each of his offspring make war against him.
¹⁹May the flesh of the hypocrites be scattered by beasts,
 And the bones of the lawless before the sun in disgrace.
²⁰May the ravens pluck out the eyes of the hypocrites,
 Because they devastated many peoples' houses in disgrace,
 And they scattered them in desire.

²¹And they did not remember God,
>   And they did not fear God in all these things.
>   But they provoked God and he was angered
²²So that he will destroy them from the earth,
>   Because they deceived innocent souls with deception.
²³Blessed are those who fear the Lord in their innocence.
>   The Lord will save them from deceitful and lawless people,
>   And he will save us from every stumbling block of the lawless.
²⁴May God destroy those who commit every injustice with pride,
>   Because the Lord our God is a powerful judge.
²⁵May your mercy, O Lord, be in righteousness upon all those who love
you.

PSSSOL 8:1–13

¹My ears heard tribulation and the sound of war,
>   The trumpet of war announcing slaughter and destruction,
²The sound of a great people like a strong and great wind,
>   Like a whirlwind of fire that comes upon the desert.
³And I said to my heart, "Where will God judge?"
⁴I heard a sound in Jerusalem the holy city,
>   And the joints of my back were loosened at what I heard,
⁵And my knees shook, and my bones trembled like linen.
⁶And I said, "They will make their ways straight in righteousness."
⁷And I remembered the judgments of the Lord from the creation of
heaven and earth,
>   And I justified God in all his judgments from eternity.
⁸God revealed their sins before the sun,
>   And all the earth came to know the righteous judgments of the
>   Lord.
⁹They committed lawlessness in the underground hiding places,
>   The son united with his mother, and the father with his daughter,
¹⁰Each of them committed adultery with the wife of his neighbor,
>   And they made covenants among themselves concerning these
>   things.
¹¹They plundered the sanctuary of God
>   As if there were not one who inherits and saves.
¹²And they trampled the Temple in all their defilement,
>   And they defiled the sacrifices with menstrual blood like defiled
>   meat.
¹³And there was no sin greater even than those of the nations that they
did not commit.

PSSSOL 17

¹O Lord, you are our King now and forever
    Because in you, O God, our soul will glory.
²And what is the life of a man upon the earth?
    According to his time, so also is his hope.
³But we hope in God our Savior
    Because the power of our God is merciful forever,
    And the kingdom of our God is over the nations in judgment forever.
⁴You, O Lord, chose David to be king over Israel,
    And you swore to him concerning his descendants
    That his kingdom would not be blotted out from before you.
⁵But sinners rose up against us in our sins,
    And they came upon us and took us away.
With force they took the things you did not give them charge over,
    And they did not praise your precious name with praise.
⁶They set up a kingdom in place of their exalted position;
    They devastated the throne of David in the pride of change.
⁷But you, O God, will overthrow them,
    And you will remove their descendants from the earth.
And when a man foreign to our race rises up against them,
⁸You will repay them according to their sins, O God,
    And it will be found to them according to their works.
⁹Do not have mercy on them, O God;
    Visit their descendants and do not leave even one of them.
¹⁰Faithful is the Lord in all his judgments that he does upon the
    earth.
¹¹The lawless one devastated our land so that no one lived in it;
    He destroyed the young and the old and their children together.
¹²In the anger of his wrath he sent them away to the west,
    And he also did not spare the rulers of the land from scorn.
¹³The enemy boasted in a foreign manner,
    And his heart was foreign from our God.
¹⁴And he did everything in Jerusalem
    That the nations do in their cities to their gods.
¹⁵And the sons of the covenant practiced these things;
    They were promiscuous among the nations,
    And no one among them did mercy and truth in Jerusalem.
¹⁶Those who loved the synagogue of the holy ones fled from them;
    They flew like sparrows who fly from their nests,
¹⁷And they wandered in the desert in order to save their soul from evil,
And precious in their eyes was the wandering of the soul that was saved
    from them;

[18]Their dispersion by the lawless was into all the earth.
Therefore, the heaven was held back lest it send down rain upon the earth,
[19]And eternal springs were held back from the abysses and the high mountains,
Because no one in them did righteousness and judgment.
[20]From the great to their least they were in all sins:
The king was in lawlessness, the judge in godlessness, and the nation in sin.
[21]Look, O Lord, and raise up for them their king the son of David
In the time that you see, O God,
That he might rule over Israel your servant.
[22]And provide him with strength
That he might humble the rulers of lawlessness,
That he might purify Jerusalem from the nations that trample her to destruction,
[23]To cast out the lawless from your inheritance,
To shatter the pride of the sinner like a potter's vessel,
[24]To shatter their whole essence with a rod of iron,
To destroy the lawless nations with the word of his mouth—
[25]At his rebuke the nations will flee from his face—
And to correct sinners with the word of their heart;
[26]That he might gather a holy nation that he will lead in righteousness.
And he will judge the tribes of the nation
That will be made holy by the Lord his God.
[27]And never again will he allow sin to lodge among them,
And never again will a man who knows evil dwell among them.
For he will know them that they are all sons of their God,
[28]And he will divide them into their tribes in the land,
And no wanderer or foreigner will dwell with them any more.
[29]He will judge peoples and nations in the wisdom of his righteousness.
Selah.
[30]And he will possess a nation from the nations to serve him under his yoke,
And they will glorify the Lord openly in all the land.
And he will purify Jerusalem in holiness as of old
[31]That the nations might come from the ends of the earth to see his glory.
When they bring gifts to her sons who were scattered from her,
And to see the glory of the Lord with which God glorified her.
[32]And he will be a righteous king over them, taught by God.
And there will be no lawlessness among them in his days
Because all of them will be holy.
And their king will be the Lord Messiah.

³³For he will trust in neither horse nor rider nor bow;
>He will not amass for himself gold and silver for war,
>And he will not trust in many on the day of war.
³⁴For the Lord himself is his king;
>His hope for power rests upon his hope in his God,
>And he will have compassion on all of the nations before him in fear,
³⁵For he will strike the earth with the word of his mouth forever,
>And he will bless the nation of the Lord with wisdom and with gladness.
³⁶And he will be pure from sin, the ruler of a great nation,
>To rebuke rulers and to destroy sinners with his word.
³⁷And his days will not be shortened by his God,
>Because God will make him powerful by the holy spirit,
>And wise by the counsel of understanding with strength and righteousness.
³⁸And the blessing of the Lord will be with him in power,
>And he will not grow weak.
³⁹His hope is in the Lord,
>And who will stand against him?
⁴⁰For he will be powerful in his works and strong in the fear of his God,
>Tending the flock of the Lord in righteousness and in faithfulness,
>And he will not allow any among his flock to grow weak.
⁴¹He will lead all of them in serenity,
>And pride will not be found among them that any might be oppressed.
⁴²This is the beauty of the king of Israel, which God knew,
>To raise him up over the house of Israel to discipline it.
⁴³His words will be proven more than precious gold
>To separate in the synagogues the tribes of the holy nation;
>His words are like the words of holy ones among the holy nation.
⁴⁴Blessed are those who live in those days
>To see the good things of Israel in the synagogue of the tribes.
⁴⁵May God hasten his mercy upon Israel,
>That he might deliver us from the defilement of impure nations.
⁴⁶For the Lord is our King now and forever.

PSSSOL 18:1–9

¹O Lord, your mercy is upon the works of your hands forever;
>Your goodness is upon Israel with a rich gift.
²Your eyes see everything,
>And there is nothing that hides from them.
>And your ears hear the prayer of the poor in hope.

[3]Your judgments are upon all the earth in mercy,
  And your love is upon the descendants of Israel, the son of Abraham.
[4]Your discipline is upon us as an only, first-born son,
  To return the obedient soul from unlearnedness and ignorance,
[5]To purify Israel for the day of mercy in blessing,
  For the day of election in the raising up of his Messiah.
[6]Blessed are those who live in those days,
  To see the good things of God that he will do in the coming
    generation,
[7]Under the rod of discipline of the Lord Messiah in the fear of his God,
  In the wisdom of the spirit and in righteousness and strength,
[8]To lead people in righteous works by the fear of God,
  To establish all of them before the Lord,
[9]A good generation living in the fear of God in days of mercy. *Selah.*

Bibliography

Atkinson, Kenneth. *I Cried to the Lord: A Study of the Psalms of Solomon's Historical Background and Social Setting.* Supplements to the *Journal for the Study of Judaism* 84. Leiden: Brill, 2004.

———. *An Intertextual Study of the Psalms of Solomon.* Studies in the Bible and Early Christianity, vol. 49. Lewiston, NY: Edwin Mellen Press, 2001.

Charlesworth, James H. "The Concept of the Messiah in the Pseudepigrapha." Pages 188–218 in *Aufstieg und Niedergang der romischen Welt: Geschichte und Kultur Roms im Spiegel der Neueren Forfchung, II.* Edited by W. Haase. Principat: Neunzehnter Band (1. Halbband): Berlin: Walter de Gruyter, 1979.

———. "From Jewish Messianology to Christian Christology: Some Caveats and Perspectives." Pages 225–64 in *Judaisms and Their Messiahs at the Turn of the Christian Era.* Edited by J. Neusner, W. S. Green, and E. S. Frerichs. Cambridge: Cambridge University Press, 1987.

Collins, John J. *The Scepter and the Star: The Messiahs of the Dead Sea Scrolls and Other Ancient Literature.* Anchor Bible Reference Library. New York: Doubleday, 1995.

Davenport, Gene. "The 'Anointed of the Lord' in *Psalms of Solomon* 17." Pages 67–92 in *Ideal Figures in Ancient Judaism.* Edited by J. Collins and George Nickelsburg. Chico, CA: Scholars Press, 1980.

Jonge, M. de. "The Expectation of the Future in the Psalms of Solomon." Pages 3–17 in *Jewish Eschatology, Early Christian Christology and the Testaments of the Twelve Patriarchs.* Supplements to Novum Testamentum 63. Edited by M. de Jonge. Leiden: Brill, 1991.

Trafton, Joseph L. "The Bible, The Psalms of Solomon, and the Dead Sea Scrolls." In *The Bible and the Dead Sea Scrolls: The Jubilee Publication: The Second Princeton Symposium on Judaism and Christian Origins.* Vol. 2. *The Dead Sea Scrolls and the Christian Community.* Edited by James H. Charlesworth. Waco, TX: Baylor Press, 2006.

———. "Research on the Psalms of Solomon since 1977." *Journal for the Study of the Pseudepigrapha* 12 (1994): 3–19.

———. "Solomon, Psalms of." Pages 115–17 in vol. 5 of *The Anchor Bible Dictionary.* Edited by David Noel Freedman. 6 vols. New York: Doubleday, 1992.

————. *The Syriac Version of the Psalms of Solomon. A Critical Evaluation.* Society of Biblical Literature Septuagint and Cognate Studies Series. Vol. 11. Atlanta, GA: Scholars Press, 1985.

Wright, R. B. "Psalms of Solomon." Pages 639–57 in vol. 2 of *The Old Testament Pseudepigrapha.* Edited by James H. Charlesworth. 2 vols. Garden City, NY: Anchor Bible, 1985.

—16—

Moral and Ritual Purity

Jonathan Klawans

Like many religious traditions past and present, early Judaism categorized persons, places, and other things as "pure" or "impure." Indeed, early Jews used these terms in a variety of ways. One notion of impurity (ritual impurity) concerned contact with various natural substances relating to birth, death, and genital discharge. Direct or even indirect contact with the sources of ritual defilement rendered one temporarily unfit to enter the Temple or to encounter sacred objects. Another notion of defilement (moral impurity) concerned the dangers of defilement associated with grave sins such as idolatry, incest, and murder. While this sort of defilement was less contagious, its effects were ultimately more severe. An accurate understanding of these matters, including the distinction between ritual and moral defilement, is essential for fully understanding the New Testament. Various sayings attributed to Jesus use the terms "pure" and "impure," and the sources we survey below provide some of the background for understanding these statements.

Our topic is both complicated and controversial. The complications arise from the difficult nature of the primary sources that treat these matters: the biblical and interpretive texts are often dryly legal, highly technical, and conceptually obscure. The situation is hardly helped by the fact that ancient conceptions of purity seem very different from our own: the modern reader is culturally programmed to scoff at seemingly irrational ritual avoidances, especially when they pertain to death and sex. Too many modern readers—scholars included—have been reluctant to give these texts the time it takes to understand their meaning and message.

The controversies surrounding the understanding of purity arise in part from the difficult nature of the texts. It is to be expected that scholars have disagreed on how certain complicated parts of the biblical Book of Leviticus are to be understood. The controversies also arise, however, from ancient and modern religious disputes regarding the place of law in general (and purity practices in particular) in Christianity and Judaism. Purity has become both a buzzword and a battleground for disputes concerning, for instance, the historical Jesus' place in his early Jewish or Hellenistic context. Jesus is seen by some as a religious radical who raged against the oppressive priestly and Pharisaic purity regulations of his time (see Borg). Others see Jesus as articulating purity ideas that are hardly Jewish, and thoroughly Hellenized (see Booth). In too many cases, the terms "purity" and "impurity" are bandied about in ways that are imprecise or even inaccurate, and so the misunderstandings and the controversies continue.

The academic foundation for the study of purity was set in the 1960s with the publication of *Purity and Danger*, by the well-known anthropologist Mary Douglas. The book changed forever the way scholars looked on ancient and modern notions of defilement and taboo. Before Douglas, purity laws such as those found in Leviticus were dismissed as meaningless taboos, hardly worthy of scholarly interest, let alone detailed investigation. Douglas demonstrated that purity rules, when interpreted properly, express fundamental societal ideologies.

While the book remains a classic, it is also a problematic one, for *Purity and Danger* is no less complicated than its stated topic. While it should still be read, it needs to be read slowly, and carefully (Klawans 2003a). It too often seems that scholars base their understandings of early Judaism's purity laws highly or even entirely on *Purity and Danger* (e.g., Borg, Malina). Yet Douglas's surprising interpretations of Jewish purity laws generated many important responses (Eilberg-Schwartz), and Douglas herself no longer thinks she was right about biblical Israel in *Purity and Danger* (Douglas 1999). The lasting significance of her book is not so much the interpretations of Jewish purity laws laid out there, but her insistence that the Jewish purity laws are a topic worthy of scholarly analysis. Modern analysis of purity owes a great debt to Mary Douglas, and such study begins with her work. But it cannot end there.

Three principle errors seem to predominate over much of the discussion on purity in New Testament scholarship, and these misunderstandings can be traced back, in part, to readings or misreadings of *Purity and Danger*. One frequent error is the blind identification of impurity with sin: it is frequently assumed that sinners were considered defiling and were therefore excluded from the Temple and other social gatherings. Another frequent error is blind identification of purity with status: it is assumed that not just sinners but others of low social or religious rank (such as women or Gentiles) also would have been considered ritually impure as a matter of course. A third frequent error is based on the previous misunderstandings: it often is supposed that the purity system was the tool by which the socially dominant Pharisees, or the priests who ran the Temple, asserted their power over those elements of society that they despised and wished to lord over. As we will see below, a careful review of the evidence puts the lie to all three of these common assumptions.

To understand purity in the New Testament, one must begin by better understanding purity in the Hebrew Bible. With some careful reading and precise definitions, much light can be shed on this confusing topic. But one cannot then simply jump from the Hebrew Bible to the New Testament. When one looks beyond the Bible—in the Dead Sea Scrolls and in Rabbinic literature—one finds strong evidence not only that early Jews cared deeply about purity issues but also that they debated rather vigorously about their religious meaning and social consequences. Once one understands these disputes, the actual meaning and the greater context of Jesus' statements about the purity of the body and the community become much more clear.

What follows presents an overview of the steps required to understand purity in the New Testament. First, we present a thumbnail sketch of the purity regulations as laid out in the Hebrew Bible. In the second and third sections, we survey the different approaches to these matters taken in the Dead Sea Scrolls and Rabbinic literature. Finally, we indicate some of the ramifications these texts may have for understanding the "historical Jesus."

Ritual and Moral Purity in the Hebrew Bible

In recent years, an increasing number of scholars have come to recognize that the Hebrew Bible knows not just of one, but two distinct concepts of defilement and purification, referred to here as "ritual" and "moral." While this kind of approach has gained ground recently, it is not new, and goes back well over one hundred years (Klawans 2000, 2003a; Büchler). Some scholars draw this distinction in different terms, speaking of "permitted" (ritual) and "prohibited" (moral) impurities (Wright).

As commonly understood, ritual impurity refers to the sort of defilement described in Leviticus 11–15 and Numbers 19. This defilement results from direct or indirect contact with any one of a number of natural processes, including childbirth (Leviticus 12:1–8), certain skin diseases (13:1–46; 14:1–32), funguses in clothes (13:47–59) and houses (14:33–53), genital discharges (15:1–33), the carcasses of certain impure animals (11:1–47), and human corpses (Numbers 19:1–22). Paradoxically, ritual impurity also comes about as a by-product of some sacrificial procedures, including the production of the "purifying water" that decontaminates corpse impurity (Numbers 19:7–8; cf. Leviticus 16:28). To generalize, these impurities are natural, more or less unavoidable, typically impermanent, and generally not sinful.

That the sources of ritual impurity are natural is quite clear. Birth, death, sex, disease, and discharge are part of life, normally so lived. Ritual impurity is also generally part of life. While certain defiling substances are relatively avoidable (e.g., touching carcasses), discharge, disease, and death are inescapable. Some ritual impurities are not just inevitable but obligatory. All Israelites (priests included) are obligated to reproduce (Genesis 1:28, 9:7). All Israelites (except the high priest) are required to bury their deceased relatives (Leviticus 21:10–15; cf. 21:1–4). Priests also are obligated to perform cultic procedures that leave them defiled as a result (Leviticus 16:28; Numbers 19:8).

It is not a sin to contract these ritual impurities. This idea proceeds logically from the observations drawn above. While priests must limit their contact with corpse impurity (Leviticus 21:1–4), it is not prohibited for them to contract other impurities (22:3–7). To be sure, priests are sternly warned against eating sacred food or entering sacred precincts when in a state of ritual impurity (Leviticus 7:19–21; 22:3–7). Yet the primary concern incumbent upon the priests is not to avoid ritual impurity at all times but to safeguard the separation between ritual impurity and purity (Leviticus 10:10; cf. Ezekiel 44:23). By extension, Israelites are obliged to remain aware of their ritual status, lest they accidentally come into contact with the sacred while in a state of ritual impurity (Leviticus 15:31). Whereas refusal to purify oneself would constitute a transgression (Numbers 19:20), this does not make being ritually impure sinful in and of itself. As long as Israelites remain aware of their status—and do what is necessary to ameliorate the situation—there is little chance of danger or transgression. "Leprosy" could come about as a punishment for sin (Numbers 12:10), but Leviticus itself does not assume that lepers are sinners.

Moral impurity, by contrast, is inherently sinful and results from committing certain acts so heinous that they are considered defiling. Such behaviors include sexual sins (e.g., Leviticus 18:24–30), idolatry (e.g., 19:31; 20:1–3), and bloodshed (e.g., Numbers 35:33–34). These acts are specifically referred to as "abominations," and they bring about an impurity that morally—but not ritually—defiles the sinner (Leviticus 18:24), the Land of Israel (Leviticus 18:25; Ezekiel 36:17), and the sanctuary of God (Leviticus 20:3; Ezekiel 5:11). The defilement of the sanctuary renders it unfit for the divine presence that dwells there (Numbers 35:34; Ezekiel 8:1–11:25). This in turn leads to the expulsion of the people from the Land of Israel (Leviticus 18:28; Ezekiel 36:19). The bulk of the references to these ideas can be found in priestly traditions (especially the Holiness Code) and in the most priestly of prophetic books, Ezekiel. Additional articulations of the notion or echoes of it can be found in various strands of biblical tradition, including Genesis 34:5; Deuteronomy 24:1–4; 1 Kings 14:24; Jeremiah 2:7, 23; 3:1; Hosea 5:6; 6:10; and Psalms 106:34–40.

There are a number of important differences between moral and ritual impurity. First, although ritual impurity is generally not sinful, moral impurity is a direct consequence of grave sin. Second, a characteristic feature of moral impurity is its deleterious effect on the Land of Israel. Ritual impurity, in contrast, poses no threat to the land. Third, whereas ritual impurity often results in a contagious defilement, there is no personal contact-contagion associated with moral impurity. Moral impurity does defile the sinners themselves (Leviticus 18:24; 19:31; cf. Genesis 34:5; Deuteronomy 24:1–4). But one need not bathe subsequent to direct or indirect contact with an idolater, a murderer, or an individual who committed a sexual sin. Fourth, whereas ritual impurity results in an impermanent defilement, moral impurity leads to a long-lasting, if not permanent, degradation of the sinner and, eventually, of the Land of Israel. Fifth, ritual impurity can be ameliorated by rites of purification, but that is not the case for moral impurity. Moral purity is achieved by punishment, atonement, or, best of all, refraining from committing morally impure acts in the first place.

Moral and Ritual Impurity

Impurity Type	Source	Effect	Resolution
Ritual	Bodily flows, corpses, etc.	Temporary, contagious defilement of persons and objects	Ritual purification, by means of bathing, waiting, and/or sacrifice
Moral	Sins: idolatry, sexual transgression, bloodshed	Long-lasting defilement of sinners, land, and sanctuary	Atonement or punishment, and ultimately, exile

Sixth, since moral impurity does not produce ritual defilement, sinners—in contrast to those who are ritually impure—are not excluded from the sanctuary. In the case of the suspected adulteress (Numbers 5:11–31), the woman is brought into the sanctuary itself in order to determine her moral status. It also appears that Israelite murderers sought sanctuary in the Temple (Exodus 21:14; cf. 1 Kings 1:50–53 and 2:28–30). Moral impurity does indeed defile the sacred precincts (e.g., Leviticus 20:3). But the effect of moral impurity does not penetrate the holy realm by the entrance of sinners into it. Moral impurity is a potent force unleashed by sinful behavior that affects the sanctuary even from afar, in its own way.

In addition to these phenomenological differences between ritual and moral defilements, there are also terminological distinctions drawn in the texts themselves. Although the term "impure" (*tameh*) is used in both contexts, the terms "abomination" (*to'evah*) and "pollute" (*chanaf*) are used with regard to the sources of moral impurity, but not with regard to the sources of ritual impurity. For all these reasons, it is imperative to distinguish between moral and ritual impurity.

Unfortunately, the last generation of scholarship on both early Judaism and the New Testament did not pay due attention to the biblical distinction between ritual and moral defilements. This means that two fundamental aspects of early Judaism have been overlooked. The first is that early Jews, like their Israelite predecessors, were familiar with not only the notion of ritual impurity but also the notion of moral impurity. The second is that early Jews argued about the relationship between ritual and moral impurity. This latter point proves most helpful in finding a context for the historical Jesus' approach to purity. As we see below, once we begin to understand better the disputes among early Jewish groups regarding the relationship between ritual and moral impurity, we find a credible context for understanding Jesus' approach to these important matters. This reconstruction can, in turn, bolster arguments for the historicity of some of Jesus' purity sayings.

The sections that follow survey the approaches to ritual and moral impurity as taken by the two groups of early Jews about whom we know the most: Rabbinic Judaism, as represented by the Mishnah and other early Rabbinic texts, and the group that lived at Qumran and produced or at least transmitted to us the literature preserved there. This survey also demonstrates that early Jews continued to maintain an interest not only in ritual impurity but also in moral impurity. These sections also sketch out some of the basic disputes among early Jews concerning the approaches to ritual and moral defilement.

RITUAL AND MORAL IMPURITY IN RABBINIC LITERATURE

We begin by looking at some selections from the Mishnah—a Rabbinic law book, which was edited in the Land of Israel, around 200 CE. While much of the Mishnah was composed during the second century CE, a number of its Temple-related traditions could accurately reflect the general practices of the Jerusalem Temple. Even if this proves not to be the case, the Mishnah remains an important source for understanding the practices and the ideologies of the Rabbis in the first two centuries CE.

MISHNAH KELIM 1:1–4

[1]The principle sources of defilement are: a creeping animal, a man who has had a seminal discharge, a person who has had contact with a dead person, a person with a fungus during the days of counting, and purifying water too little in quantity to be sprinkled. All these defile a person or utensils by their touch, and defile clay vessels aerially, but these do not defile by being carried.

[2]Above these are carrion and purifying water in sufficient quantity to be sprinkled, for these substances defile whomever carries them, so as to defile also clothing by contact, although this can be avoided.

[3]Above these is a man who has had intercourse with a menstruating woman, for he defiles the lower layers of bedding (indirectly), just as he defiles the highest layer (directly under him). Above these are fluid from a man suffering an irregular genital flow, his spit, his semen, and his urine, as well as menstrual blood, for these substances defile when they are touched or carried. Above these is a saddle (upon which a person with a defiling genital flow sat), for this defiles a person, even when placed under a large rock. Above this is bedding (upon which the impure person in question slept), which defiles by being touched as by being carried. Above bedding is a man suffering from an irregular flow, for he defiles his bedding, though the bedding does not defile other bedding.

[4]Above a man suffering from an irregular genital discharge is a woman suffering from an irregular genital discharge (of blood), for she defiles her partner through intercourse. Above a woman suffering from an irregular genital discharge is a person suffering from a skin fungus, for such a person defiles what is in a house merely by entering it. Above a person suffering from a skin fun-

gus is a piece of human bone the size of a grain of barley: for this defiles a person for a full seven days. The most severe of all is the human corpse: for this defiles by overhang, while the others do not defile in this manner.

The reader of this selection from the Mishnah may ask a number of questions. At the most basic level, one may ask what this text is even talking about. That question can be answered through careful comparison of the Mishnah's rules with those laid out in the biblical passages, mostly from Leviticus 11–15 and Numbers 19. Clearly, this text is presenting an ordered list of the sources of defilement and their most characteristic defiling effects.

More questions may come to the careful reader, who may be interested to know if these rules apply in all circumstances, or whether a particular severe defilement defiles also in all the ways that a less severe defilement does. Such a reader should keep in mind that the above passage constitutes only the very first paragraphs of the first chapter of the first tractate of the lengthy section of the Mishnah that treats ritual purity rules in great depth. For the curious and unsatisfied reader, there is plenty more where this came from.

Other readers may ask a different question: What interest can such a text have for the study of the New Testament? The answer is: plenty. The first thing to note is how closely the list is tied to the sources of ritual defilement, as laid out in Leviticus 11–15. Every source of ritual defilement listed above is mentioned—however briefly—in these biblical chapters. The text is not, strictly speaking, an exegetical one: no scriptural passage is quoted or explicitly commented upon. Yet the Mishnah here presumes knowledge of the Hebrew Bible, and much exegesis surely lay behind the list, though we cannot be certain exactly what exegetical process led from Leviticus to the Mishnah. Nonetheless, because of its close general ties to the Hebrew Bible, what we said above about biblical purity applies here, too: its sources are natural, unavoidable, and not sinful. Indeed, various obligatory acts, such as burial, sexual relations, and certain sacrificial procedures ("purifying water") are ritually defiling.

A number of other facts emerge from the list: note that the laws are concerned with defilements associated with both men and women. While the genders are not treated equally, it is certainly not the case that men are let off the hook. Note, too, that no exception is made with regard to class: the ritual defilements can affect all persons equally, whether priests or Israelites, rich or poor. Indeed, a good number of the ritual defilements—carrion, corpses, human bones, funguses, and others—defile men and women equally. The careful reader can discern that the ritual purity system of the Rabbis—just like that of the Hebrew Bible—is not primarily about subordinating social classes or even women. A ritual impurity system such as this one, which affects all classes and both genders, is simply not well suited to the subjugation of any particular group or class (Douglas 1999).

A final point emerges from what is absent. We noted above that discussions of ritual impurity in the Hebrew Bible proceed without any assumption that sinful behaviors produce such defilements. This is also certainly the case in Rabbinic Judaism, where the lengthy and detailed rules, of what defiles whom, when, and for how long, do not include a single ruling to the effect that sinful persons simply by virtue of being sinful could ritually defile those around them.

MISHNAH KELIM 1:6–8

[6]There are ten levels of holiness. The Land of Israel is holier than all other lands. And what indicates its sanctity? That the sheaf, the first-fruits, and the two loaves are brought from it, which is not the case with other lands.

[7]Walled cities are holier than the Land of Israel, for those suffering from skin funguses are expelled from them, and a corpse can be carried within them as needed, but once it is taken out, it cannot be brought back in.

[8]The area within the walls (of Jerusalem) is holier than the cities, for holy foods of lesser sanctity and the second tithe are eaten there. The Temple Mount is holier than the city, for men or women suffering from an irregular flow, menstruants, and women who have just given birth may not enter there. The Women's Court (within the Temple complex) is holier than the Temple Mount, for those who have bathed that day (and are not yet fully pure) may not enter it, but a sin-offering is not required of those who have so entered. The Court of Israel is holier than the Women's Court, for those whose purification will be complete upon bringing a sacrifice may not enter there, and those who have so entered are obligated to bring a sin-offering. The Court of the Priests is holier, for lay Israelites may not enter there except when necessary for the laying of hands, the slaughter, or the waving (of sacrifices). Between the hall and the altar is holier, for those (priests) who have a blemish or a shaven head may not enter there. The Sanctuary is holier, for no one may enter there without having washed both hands and feet. The Holy of Holies is holier than all these, for no one enters there except the high priest, on the Day of Atonement, at the time of worship. . . .

Like the previous passage, this one too presents an ordered list. Here we are told of early Judaism's zones of holiness, which are centered on the Temple's inner sanctum, the most sacred spot on earth. The previous passage notes one major ramification of becoming ritually impure: the potential to defile others in the various ways spelled out. In this passage we encounter the second ramification of becoming ritually impure, and indeed the main one altogether: exclusion from the Temple. Depending on how ritually impure one may be at a given time, one would be excluded from entering certain areas of the Temple. These zones of exclusion typically provide the basis for those who describe the early Israelite purity system as exclusivist and hierarchical.

Again, a closer reading of the passage demonstrates otherwise. First, not all exclusions are directly related to the ritual purity system. Some exclusions are based on levels of defilement (so menstruants, for instance, are excluded from the Temple Mount), but women and men, when pure, are admitted. And even ritually impure men and women are not excluded entirely from participation in the Temple service. While sacrifices are performed in the Temple, many of the sacrifices (such as the Passover sacrifice) are consumed anywhere in the city (see 1:8 above). Since not all ritually impure persons are excluded from the city itself, they therefore are not entirely excluded from the participation in these quasi-sacrificial meals either. Presumably, care would have to be taken lest ritually impure people defile holy food or other people who may then wish to return to the Temple. But the people are trusted with this concern, and thus the realms of the sacred and the realms in which impure people are permitted overlap somewhat (see *b. Zevahim* 55a).

It is also important to notice that there is no one-to-one correspondence between purity and class. There are two kinds of exclusions, some based on levels of defilement, and others based on class. If impurity and class status were the same thing, there would be no such distinction: all of the excluded categories would be defiling in some way. For instance, only priests are admitted into the inner parts of the Temple, but this does not mean that all non-priests are inherently impure, for even pure non-priests are not admitted into the inner parts of the Temple. Moreover, impure priests are excluded, just as any other impure person would be. There are statuses of holiness in early Judaism—from the high priest with his special prerogatives on down. But these statuses do not correspond directly and exclusively with the purity system. Even the high priest could become defiled, and if he were, he too would be excluded from the Temple. On the other hand, any Israelite can be just as pure (though not just as holy) as the high priest. Scholars who identify the purity system with the distinctions of status in early Judaism have misread the evidence.

Finally, we must emphasize again what is not mentioned: neither sins nor sinners are excluded from the Temple. The next selection elaborates on this very point.

BABYLONIAN TALMUD, *ERUVIN* 69B

[Commenting on Leviticus 1:2: "When a person from among you brings a sacrifice of cattle . . ."] "*From* among you," and not all of you, thus the apostate is excluded [and is therefore forbidden to bring a sacrifice]. "From *among you*": among *you* I made this distinction, but not among the nations. ". . . of cattle": to include people who make themselves like animals. From here we learn: they accept sacrifices from the sinners of Israel, so that they may repent, with the exception of an apostate, one who pours wine libations, and one who violates the Sabbath in public.

The above selection comes from the Babylonian Talmud, which is a commentary on the Mishnah. While the Babylonian Talmud probably was edited around 600 CE, it contains various traditions, some of which may be significantly earlier, going back to the time of the Mishnah at least. The tradition quoted above confirms what we inferred from our reading of Mishnah *Kelim*: sinners were neither excluded from the Temple nor barred from offering sacrifices. The argument supporting the case is an exegetical one, and typically Rabbinic. In the Rabbis' thinking, every word of the Pentateuch had potential legal meaning. Therefore, where Leviticus states "from among you," with regard to bringing sacrifices, the Rabbis assume that someone was excluded from bringing them—and here they find justification for the exclusion of the apostate. Turning to the very next element, the "among you," the Rabbis limit the exclusion of apostates to Jews—all Gentiles, regardless of their religious allegiances, are permitted to send offerings to the Temple.

This, too, is an important aspect of the Temple service: sacrifices and donations were accepted from non-Jews, even though foreigners were barred from entering as far as Jews were. When a subsequent sentence speaks of offerings "of cattle," the Rabbis more creatively take this as referring not to the animals being offered (which is the plain sense of the verse in question) but to those offering sacrifices. Sacrifices cannot come from cattle directly, but they can come from people who act like cattle, and so sinners are included.

The commentary may seem random or nitpicky. But that is entirely the point: the inclusion of most sinners and the exclusion of only extreme sinners like apostates was not something clearly stated in these verses. The Rabbis could have read these texts to include or exclude practically whomever they had wished. It was their choice to permit the offerings of Gentiles and sinners, and to argue that the permission is grounded not in extrabiblical tradition but in the book of Leviticus itself.

We have seen that in Rabbinic literature, ritual impurity and sin are two distinct issues. Rabbinic literature is, however, familiar with the notion of moral impurity: the idea that certain grave sins bring about a severe defilement that affects the land and sanctuary, even though the sinners themselves are not ritually defiled or ritually defiling. In general, the sources of moral impurity in Rabbinic literature are the same as we find in the Pentateuch: idolatry, sexual transgression, and murder. The effects, too, are the same as found in Scripture: sins bring about a defilement that impacts upon the sanctuary and the land, leading eventually to the departure of the Divine Presence from the sanctuary and the exile of the people from the land.

The levels of Rabbinic interest in the two kinds of defilement are not parallel. Indeed, both the number and the nature of the relevant traditions are quite different. Although perhaps as much as a quarter of the Mishnah deals with ritual impurity, moral defilement is not explicitly discussed even once. There are, however, a number of Rabbinic traditions concerning moral impurity, most of which involve commentary on biblical passages that themselves discuss moral defilement (e.g., Leviticus 18:24–30). Thus the important texts for our concerns include the *Sifra* (an early Rabbinic commentary on Leviticus) and the *Sifre* (on Numbers). These commentaries were composed in the Land of Israel at some time between the publication of the Mishnah and of the Talmud. Again, the possibility that these documents reflect Temple practice cannot be precluded, though our main concern is to discern from them the ideology of the Rabbis themselves.

Remarkably, the Rabbinic treatment of moral impurity (again in contrast to the treatment of ritual impurity) is notably sober and restrained: the biblical verses are taken at their face value, and the notion of moral impurity hardly is developed at all beyond what might be readily inferred from a straightforward reading of the Hebrew Bible. A further characteristic of the Rabbinic approach to the two kinds of impurity is their effort to maintain the strict separation between them. Juxtaposing the sources quoted below with those quotes above reveals that the Rabbis compartmentalized their discussions and applications of ritual and moral impurity. The Tannaim were familiar with both types of impurity, but they rarely discussed the two in tandem. To the contrary, the discussions of moral impurity are devoid of reference to ritual impurity and vice versa.

SIFRA, AHARE MOT PEREK 13:16, 19, ON LEVITICUS 18:24–25, 27–28
(WEISS 1862, 86B–C)

[16]"Do not defile yourselves in these ways" (Leviticus 18:24a): whether in all of them, or a few of them. "For in these ways, the nations were defiled" (v. 24b): these are the Egyptians. "That I am sending out from before you" (v. 24c): these are the Canaanites. "Thus the land became defiled" (v. 25a): this teaches that the land becomes defiled by these things. "And I accounted its iniquity upon it" (v. 25b): as soon as I open the account book, I seize it all. "And the land spewed out its inhabitants" (v. 25c): just like a person who vomits his food.

[19]"For all these abominations were done by the people of the land who were before you (and the land became defiled)" (Leviticus 18:27): this teaches us that the land is defiled by these things. "So do not let the land spew you out just as it spewed out the nation that came before you" (v. 28): this teaches us that the land is subject to exile on account of these things.

SIFRA, AHARE MOT PARASHAH 10:8, ON LEVITICUS 20:1–3
(WEISS 1862, 91C)

"So as to defile My sanctuary and profane My holy Name" (Leviticus 20:3c): this teaches that (Molech worship) defiles the sanctuary, profanes the Name, causes the Divine Presence to depart, brings the sword upon Israel, and exiles them from their land.

SIFRE NUMBERS § 161, ON NUMBERS 35:33–34 (HOROVITZ 1917, 222)

"Do not defile the land in which you live" (Numbers 35:34a): Scripture states that bloodshed defiles the land and causes the Divine Presence to depart; and it was due to bloodshed that the Temple was destroyed.

In addition to idolatry, sexual transgression, and murder, the Rabbis know of only a few other sources of moral defilement, all of them derived exegetically. What is striking is that the few additional sources of moral defilement that the Rabbis identify can also be identified as sources of moral defilement in other early Jewish literature. For instance, the morally defiling force of judicial deceit is known not only from the *Sifra* but also from Qumran's Temple Scroll. The morally defiling force of arrogance is noted not only in the *Mekilta* but also in the Pesher Habakkuk. The passages quoted below therefore testify both to the Rabbinic interest in moral defilement and to the conservative nature of that interest: for the most part, whatever the Rabbis considered to be a source of moral defilement was explicitly identified as such by Scripture or by other earlier Jewish literature. In their treatment of moral defilement, therefore, the Rabbis can be considered to be inheritors of a long tradition more than they were innovators of new ideas.

SIFRA, QEDOSHIM, PEREK 4:1, ON LEVITICUS 19:15
(WEISS 1862, 88D–89A)

"You shall not do evil in judgment" (Leviticus 19:15a): with regard to justice. This teaches that the judge who corrupts justice is called wrongful, hated, shunned, banned, and an abomination, and causes five things: (such a judge) defiles the land, profanes the Name (of God), causes the withdrawal of the Divine Presence, brings the sword down upon Israel, and exiles Israel from its land.

TEMPLE SCROLL LI:11–16

You shall appoint judges and officers in all of your gates, and they shall judge the people with just judgment. They shall not be partial in judgment, they shall not take a bribe, and they shall not twist judgment, for bribery twists judgment, subverts righteous words, blinds the eyes of the wise, causes great guilt, and defiles the house by the sin of transgression. Justice, Justice you shall pursue so that you live, arrive, and take possession of the land which I give you to inherit forever.

MEKILTA DE-RABBI ISHMAEL, YITRO § 9 (LAUTERBACH 1933, 2:274)

All those who are arrogant cause the land to be defiled and the Divine Presence to depart, as it is written, "The haughty and arrogant I will not suffer"

(Psalms 101:5). And the arrogant are called an abomination, as it is written, "Every arrogant person is an abomination to God" (Proverbs 16:5). Idolatry is referred to as an abomination, as it is written: "Do not bring an abomination into your house" (Deuteronomy 7:26). Just as idolatry defiles the land and causes the Divine Presence to depart, so too whoever is arrogant causes the land to be defiled and the Divine Presence to depart.

PESHER HABAKKUK VIII:8–13

The interpretation of it (Habakkuk 2:5–6) concerns the wicked priest who was called by the true name when he first arose, but as he ruled over Israel he became arrogant, left God, violated laws for the sake of wealth, robbed and gathered the wealth of the violent men who rebelled against God. And the wealth of the peoples he took, in order to increase his sinful guilt. And he acted in abominable ways, by every defilement of impurity.

RITUAL AND MORAL IMPURITY COMBINED AT QUMRAN

We have already quoted a few passages from the Dead Sea Scrolls and have seen that the Qumran literature also exhibits an interest in the notion of moral impurity. Various documents from Qumran suggest that the sectarians followed rules of ritual impurity that were in some cases even stricter than those of the Rabbis (see Harrington). When we turn to those documents, we find an approach to purity that is entirely different from what we find in Rabbinic literature. For the Rabbis, as we have seen, ritual and moral impurity were distinct concerns, and their interest in the former was much greater than the latter. At Qumran, we find that the sectarians were interested equally in both concerns. Moreover, they did not so carefully distinguish between the two notions. To the contrary, they seem to have allowed the two notions to absorb into one, so that they considered sinners to be sources of ritual defilement and considered ritual impurity as sinful in some way. We find this approach articulated most clearly in the document known as the Rule of the Community. Generally dated to about 100 BCE, this document describes the laws by which the sect governed itself. Because the Dead Sea sect appears to have consisted primarily of celibate males, we have not employed gender-neutral pronouns when translating rules pertaining to membership in the group.

Stated above is the point that for the Hebrew Bible and Rabbinic Judaism, the sources of ritual impurity were considered natural, unavoidable, even obligatory, and therefore not sinful. These substances could hardly be less natural for the Dead Sea sectarians, but the sectarians seem to have considered them sinful nonetheless. To the degree to which the sectarian system seems removed from its biblical basis, it is at the same time closer to the purity system of Zoroastrianism, the ancient religion of Persia. For Zoroastrianism, ritual impurity—which is connected to practically any substance that exudes from the body—represents evil (see Choksy). It is well known that the theological dualism expressed in a number of the Dead Sea Scrolls is in many ways reminiscent of what we find in Zoroastrianism. The sectarian approach to ritual and moral impurity may well prove to be similarly reminiscent.

RULE OF THE COMMUNITY II:25–III:6

Everyone who refuses to enter [the covenant of God] to go in his own stubborn way, shall not . . . in His true community, for he has abhorred disciplines of knowledge, righteous judgments. He will not prevail to restore his life, and he will not be accounted with the righteous. His knowledge, his strength, and his wealth shall not be brought into the council of the community, these things are polluted, even in his repentance, for when he ploughed he was treading evil. He will not be righteous, for he has stubbornly turned astray. He will see only darkness, even in the direction of light; he shall not be accounted in the sight of the righteous. He shall not be cleared by atonement, nor purified by cleansing waters; he shall not be sanctified in lakes or rivers, nor purified by any bathing. Impure, impure he shall be all the days that he refuses God's judgments, preventing his being disciplined by the council of His community.

RULE OF THE COMMUNITY IV:9–11

And as for the Spirit of Injustice: enlarged desires but hands lazy in righteous service. Evil, falsehood, pride, arrogance, dishonesty, deceit, cruelty, great pollution, short temper, great folly, zeal for presumption, acts of abomination in the spirit of fornication, ways of defilement in impure action, an insulting tongue, blindness of eyes, deafness of ear, a stiff neck and hardened heart—to follow all the ways of darkness, and evil cunning.

RULE OF THE COMMUNITY V:13–14, 18–19

(Those who are not members of the sect) shall not enter the waters in order to touch the pure food of the holy people, for they cannot be purified unless they turn from their evil ways, for one is impure when with those who transgress (God's) word. . . .

A holy person shall not depend on any deeds of those who are nothing, for all who do not know His covenant are nothing and He will destroy from the earth all who despise His words. All their actions are for defilement, and all of their possessions are impure.

RULE OF THE COMMUNITY VI:24–26

And these are the statutes by which they shall judge by the inquiry of the community according to the circumstances. If you shall find among them a man who has knowingly lied with regard to property, he shall be separated from the pure food of the community for one year, and he shall be punished by a fourth of his bread.

RULE OF THE COMMUNITY VIII:16–18

Any man from among the community, the covenant of the community, who shall stray high handedly from all that is commanded, shall not touch the pure food of the holy ones, and he shall not know of their advice, until his deeds are cleared from all injustice so that he walks in the blameless way.

PURIFICATION LITURGY (4Q512) FRAGMENTS 29–32, LINES 8–10

And he shall bless and respond, saying, "Blessed are You [God of Israel, who has saved me from all] my sins and purified me from perverse defilement, to atone (for me) to enter . . . purity."

Each of these passages associates sin with impurity in ways found neither in the Hebrew Bible nor in Rabbinic literature. Indeed, the association is so complete that we cannot speak of either "ritual" or "moral" impurity at Qumran—for them, the distinction does not hold. The first two passages state emphatically that the world outside the community is impure, precisely because it is sinful. Those who sin are incapable of being purified, and all their possessions are impure as well. Because the sect maintains high standards of purity and morality, it must ensure—as we see in the third selection above—that their pure food is kept free of defilement from sinful outsiders. Unlike the Temple (at least according to the Rabbis' rules), the sectarian holy space was closed off to all outsiders and sinners— theirs was truly an exclusive place.

It is not just nonmembers that threaten the purity of the sect: insiders who stray from the true path are to be banned from the pure food for a time, as indicated in the fourth and fifth passages above. The concern here (with a contagious defilement that threatens the status of people and food) is certainly very much like the biblical concept of ritual impurity—except for the key fact that this impurity results from and is directly connected to sinfulness. As implied in these passages—as well as in the first—the process of atonement is intertwined with the process of purification. The sixth and final passage quoted above suggests the other side of this equation. Because the person who is purifying also asks for atonement, it would appear that the process of purification from defilement is intertwined with repentance.

Having examined the Qumranic system, certain aspects of the Rabbinic approach will now be clearer. Noted above is the Rabbinic compartmentalization of ritual and moral impurity, but the point of such compartmentalization becomes clear only by comparison. At Qumran, ritual and moral impurity were fused into a single concept, with the result that the sectarians viewed all outsiders as sinful and defiling. When one believes (1) that one must maintain purity at all times and (2) that sinners are a threatening source of defilement, one has little choice but to remove oneself from the greater society. The sectarian fusion of ritual and moral defilements necessitated, justified, and reinforced their physical separation from other Jews.

Compared with the Qumran sectarians, the Rabbis took an entirely different approach to ritual and moral impurity. By strictly maintaining the distinction between the two sorts of impurity—even though they accepted the importance of both—the Rabbis articulated a distinctively nonsectarian ideology of impurity. The possibility that some early Jews articulated a nonsectarian ideology of impurity is poorly appreciated, especially in certain enclaves of contemporary New Testament scholarship.

Jesus and the Pharisees in Mark 7:1–23

The dispute among early Jews about the relationship between impurity and sin provides a key context for understanding many of the debates about purity that rage in the New Testament. We are told, for instance, that John the Baptist performed a ritually purifying water practice in order to effect atonement (Matthew 3:1–6; Mark 1:2–6; Luke 3:1–6). It also is said, tellingly, that this gave rise to controversies regarding purification (John 3:25). But the most important purity dispute in the Gospels is surely the dispute between Jesus and the Pharisees, recorded in Mark 7:1–23 (cf. Matthew 15:1–20; Luke 11:37–41).

When accused by scribes and Pharisees of disregarding "tradition" by eating with unwashed hands, Jesus utters the famous saying (Mark 7:15): "there is nothing outside a person which by going in can defile but the things that come out of a person are what defile" (cf. Matthew 15:11, 23:25–26; *Gospel of Thomas* 14; Papyrus Oxyrynchus 840). According to the Gospel of Mark, Jesus means by his statement to articulate a rejection of the Jewish food laws (Mark 7:19b). Indeed, a number of scholars follow this line and interpret the entire pericope as Jesus' rejection of the early Jewish approach to purity.

The first step toward understanding these passages is to recognize that the sayings themselves do not constitute a rejection of anything. Many scholars correctly recognize that Mark 7:19b is a later gloss. Many also recognize that the "not . . . but . . ." formulation, when properly understood, implies not a rejection of what follows the "not" but the prioritization of what follows the "but" (cf. Mark 2:17). Once it is recognized that the statement is not a radical rejection of purity, two further observations emerge. First, we cannot say that the statement is too radically anti-Jewish to be considered historically authentic: as we recognize the statement's ambiguity, so too we must recognize its possible historicity. Second, once we recognize that the statement constitutes a prioritization of one thing over another, then it becomes clear that to understand properly the statement as a whole, we must attend to both halves of it. We must explain not only why Jesus gives less importance to the defiling force of what comes into the mouth, but also why he gives more importance to the defiling force of what comes out.

Attention therefore must be paid to Mark 7:21–23, Jesus' list of the things that, by coming out of a person, defile the person (cf. Matthew 15:19): "fornication, theft, murder, adultery, avarice, wickedness, deceit, licentiousness, envy, blasphemy, pride, folly. All these things come from within, and they defile."

What is so striking about the list is the degree of conceptual correspondence between the sins listed here and those that were generally understood to be morally defiling by the Hebrew Bible and the Rabbis—as well as certainly many other early Jews. When Jesus speaks of the defiling force of sexual sins and murder, he is building on explicit biblical precedents concerning moral impurity. When he speaks of the (morally) defiling force of greed, avarice, envy, pride, and deceit, he is making statements that find analogues in Rabbinic literature and other early Jewish texts cited above. Nothing contained in Mark 7:21–22 puts Jesus in radical opposition to first-century Jewish attitudes toward impurity. Nor does anything in these lists necessitate the arguments that they derive from either Diaspora synagogues or Greek philosophical schools. These verses depict Jesus as emphasizing the morally defiling force of what Jews living in the Land of Israel in the first century CE commonly believed to be morally defiling sins.

If we are to accept Mark 7:15 as an authentic Jesus saying—and a number of scholars would agree that we should—then we can assume that Jesus explicitly prioritized the maintenance of moral purity over the maintenance of ritual purity. This thesis indicates that Jesus (or at least his early followers), unlike the later Rabbis, did not compartmentalize these two issues. For Jesus, a discussion of ritual impurity led—inevitably perhaps?—into a discussion of sin. That in and of itself is an important difference between Jesus and the later Rabbis. That Jesus is depicted as downplaying the importance of ritual impurity only serves to widen that gulf.

And this is how we are to understand the unstated Pharisaic side to the Jesus-Pharisee debate in Mark 7:1–23. According to the Pharisees—like the later Rabbis—it is not that attention to ritual impurity is more important than attention to sin. Rather, the issue of the ritually defiling force of unwashed hands has absolutely nothing to do with the issue of the morally defiling force of grave sin. If the two concerns are to be viewed as separate, then the question of their relative importance is irrelevant. In their view, Jesus was wrong to relate them.

In his juxtaposition of ritual and moral defilement, Jesus' approach can be compared to that of Qumran. But there are important differences between Jesus and Qumran as well. While the Qumran sectarians viewed sin as a source of ritual defilement, there is no sense in these passages that Jesus viewed sins as ritually defiling. Jesus' concern was, strictly speaking, with the morally defiling effect that sin can have on individual sinners. Without melding the two differing ideas of impurity, Jesus related the two by explicitly giving priority to one over the other.

There is one way in which Jesus and the Rabbis achieved the same result. Both maintained an interest in the two distinct kinds of defilement without articulating a sectarian ideology of impurity like that espoused by the Qumran texts. The scholars who see Jesus as rejecting an exclusivist, sectarian approach to purity are not entirely wrong: Jesus would have loathed such a system. But Jesus was not alone in his loathing—the later Rabbis, and the earlier Pharisees, too, certainly would have rejected exclusivist purity practices. Such practices were characteristic only of a small group of Jews who withdrew from the defiling multitudes to live by themselves off in the desert, in their own state of exile.

Bibliography

Editions on Which Translations Are Based

Albeck, Hanoch, ed. *The Six Orders of the Mishnah* [Hebrew]. 6 vols. Jerusalem: Bialik Institute, 1952–58.

Charlesworth, James H., ed. *Rule of the Community and Related Documents*. Vol. 1 of *The Dead Sea Scrolls: Hebrew, Aramaic, and Greek Texts with English Translations*. Tübingen: J.C.B. Mohr (Paul Siebeck), 1995.

García Martínez, Florentino, and Eibert J. C. Tigchelaar, eds. *The Dead Sea Scrolls Study Edition*. 2nd ed. 2 vols. Leiden: Brill, 2000.

Horovitz, H. S., ed. *Siphre D'Be Rab, Fasciculus primus: Siphre ad Numeros adjecto Siphre zutta*. Leipzig: Gesellschaft zur Förderung der Wissenschaft des Judentums, 1917.

Lauterbach, Jacob Z., ed. *Mekilta de-Rabbi Ishmael: A Critical Edition on the Basis of the Manuscripts and Early Editions with an English Translation, Introduction and Notes*. 3 vols. Philadelphia: Jewish Publication Society, 1933.

Licht, Jacob. *The Rule Scroll: A Scroll from the Wilderness of Judaea* [Hebrew]. Jerusalem: Bialik Institute, 1965.

Weiss, Isaac H., ed. *Sifra D'Be Rab (Torat Kohanim)* [Hebrew]. Vienna: Jacob Schlossberg, 1862.

Secondary Sources

Booth, Roger P. *Jesus and the Laws of Purity: Tradition History and Legal History in Mark 7*. Sheffield: JSOT Press, 1986.

Borg, Marcus J. *Conflict, Holiness, and Politics in the Teachings of Jesus*. New ed. Harrisburg, PA: Trinity Press International, 1998.

Büchler, Adolph. *Studies in Sin and Atonement in the Rabbinic Literature of the First Century*. London: Oxford University Press, 1928.

Choksy, Jamsheed K. *Purity and Pollution in Zoroastrianism*. Austin: University of Texas Press, 1989.

Douglas, Mary. *Leviticus as Literature*. Oxford: Oxford University Press, 1999.

———. *Purity and Danger: An Analysis of the Concepts of Pollution and Taboo*. London: Routledge and Kegan Paul, 1966.

Eilberg-Schwartz, Howard. *The Savage in Judaism: An Anthropology of Israelite Religion and Ancient Judaism*. Bloomington: Indiana University Press, 1990.

Harrington, Hannah K. *The Impurity Systems of Qumran and the Rabbis*. SBL Dissertation Series. Atlanta, GA: Scholars Press, 1993.

Klawans, Jonathan. *Impurity and Sin in Ancient Judaism*. New York: Oxford University Press, 2000.

———. *Purity, Sacrifice, and the Temple: Symbolism and Supersessionism in the Study of Ancient Judaism*. New York: Oxford University Press, 2006.

———. "Rethinking Leviticus and Rereading *Purity and Danger*: A Review Essay." *Association for Jewish Studies Review* 27.1 (2003a): 89–101.

———. "Ritual Purity, Moral Purity, and Sacrifice in Jacob Milgrom's Leviticus." *Religious Studies Review* 29.1 (2003b): 19–28.

Malina, Bruce J. *The New Testament World: Insights from Cultural Anthropology*. Rev. ed. Louisville, KY: Westminster/John Knox Press, 1993.

Wright, David P. "Unclean and Clean (OT)." Pages 729–41 of *The Anchor Bible Dictionary*, vol. 6. Edited by David Noel Freedman. 6 vols. New York: Doubleday, 1992.

—— 17 ——

Gospel and Talmud

Herbert W. Basser

There are stories in Rabbinic literature of Jesus' arguing certain legal points, the exegesis of which was so good the Rabbis feared they could attract too much appreciation (Basser, 75–77). The Gospels also present material suggesting that Jesus bests his various Jewish opponents in legal argumentation. And while some might have been surprised at his control of the material, we should not be. For had it been otherwise, why would anyone have bothered to pay close attention? Undoubtedly, Jesus spoke the same language and used the same methods current with the other synagogue preachers of his day. We can demonstrate that what we have of his discussions with his interlocutors conforms to the manner now preserved in Rabbinic literature.

Jews have preserved an extensive literature throughout the ages. Their sacred books contain a considerable number of oral and written traditions that stretch back into the periods before Jesus. For instance, Michael Stone (1996) has shown how an eleventh-century Rabbi in Provence copied a document from a source at his disposal, *Testament of Naphtali*, that corresponds almost word for word with a scroll found near the Dead Sea that antedates the first century. (See also I. M. Ta-Shma, *Rabbi Moses Hadarshan and the Apocryphal Literature* [in Hebrew], Jerusalem 2001.)

For our purposes I refer to the methods of this vast literature as found in the Mishnah (m.), which dates to 200 CE, give or take a decade or two, and the Talmuds (one produced in the Galilee, called the Palestinian Talmud, or the *Yerushalmi* [y.], and another produced in Babylonia, called the Babylonian Talmud or *Bavli* [b.]), that discuss the Mishnah. The final date of editing of the Babylonian Talmud is thought to be around the sixth century, whereas that of the Palestinian Talmud is certainly a century or more earlier. I also draw upon sermonic materials based on Hebrew Scriptures: these constitute the midrashim of which we have a number of works. What we use here, *Exodus Rabba* and *Tanhuma*, are closely related and considered to be both edited after the seventh century, but they contain huge chunks of material that are hundreds of years older.

The tractates this chapter cites from the Mishnah and the two Talmuds are as follows: *Yadaim* deals with purity issues concerning hands, *Ketubot* deals with marital obligations of spouses to each other, *Megillah* concerns the laws of the festival of Purim, *Zebahim* details animal sacrifices, *Menahot* deals with flour sacrifices and ritual articles of clothing, *Baba Kamma* addresses laws of civil damages to property and people, and *Baba Batra* deals with laws of real estate. As for the commentaries to scriptures, *Rabba* literatures and *Tanhuma* literatures deal systematically with every verse in the Pentateuch. *Massei* refers to a section at the end of the Book of Numbers.

Rabbinic law has something very touching to say about how we handle, or rather do not handle, the Hebrew Scriptures. Bare hands should not touch sacred writings (*m. Yadaim* 3:5). Holding naked Torah scrolls desecrates the holder (*b. Megillah* 32a). Jewish lore also talks about a touching moment when God delivered the divine laws to Moses. He held a part and Moses held an equal part, and in the intervening space between Moses and God was another equal part held by no one (*Exodus Rabba* 25:1). In the poetry of Jewish law and lore we learn an important lesson that no sociologist of religion can afford to ignore. Between the source of divine instruction and the willing student lies a gulf that humans cannot negotiate directly. So how does the student learn God's Torah? Only by touching the sacred through the medium of a detailed, complex cultural premodern elixir of "logique." Common logic, even that of the postmodernist, is of no use in this exercise of wresting the ineffable word from its secret abode in Scripture. Bare Scripture devoid of its cultural overlays cannot be safely handled.

The texture of the particular fabrics of Rabbinic literature (a literature, likely carried orally for centuries, that defies any positive possibility of dating—even the earliest manuscripts are extremely late) is specific and notable. It would have been unnatural for Jesus and his disciples not to have been saturated with very firm and thoroughly inborn mind-sets to think and understand as other Jews did. In the Gospels, Jesus is shown to teach Scriptures through the rubrics inherent in Rabbinic thought.

Although Rabbinic literature thinks in a particular fashion, it inundates the student with sharp disputes, unexpected pronouncements, and ambiguous teachings. After thousands of years of commentary attempting to unravel the intent of this enchanting land of Rabbis and their methods, the melodic singsong of this literature is still heard in the synagogues and study houses to this day. And does it not make sense that Master Jesus lived in this enchanted land and hummed the same melody and learned the same Torah?

We consider below the evidence from the Gospels that deals with a "literary Jesus." I make no claims regarding the words or actions of the historical Jesus, who may or may not have said the things attributed to him in the Gospels.

LITERAL UNACCEPTABLE: STRETCH APT

We begin our discussion with the method of "literal unacceptable: stretch apt." In this rubric the literal meaning of a biblical verse is rejected on some grounds or other (sometimes on the basis that it is just too obvious to bother stating). Then the words and structure of the verse are reshaped in order to provide a novel sense acceptable to the Rabbinic value system. The outline is (1) verse, (2) face-value meaning and objections to it, and (3) establishing the correct meaning (see below). This redefined meaning is the result of various strategies widely accepted as "Rabbinic license." To see how the method works, we first present examples from the Rabbinic corpus and then from the Gospels:

B. ZEBAHIM 22B

1. The prophet Ezekiel proclaimed: (Ezekiel 44:9) *Thus says the Lord: Any stranger, uncircumcised in heart, and uncircumcised in flesh,—shall not enter into my sanctuary . . . And also etc. (44:7) In that you have brought strangers, uncircumcised in heart, and uncircumcised in flesh, to be in my sanctuary, to profane it, my house. . . .*
   The Rabbis taught:
2. Any stranger—might I think Ezekiel literally means a stranger (a non-Israelite, who obviously cannot officiate in the Temple)? The Scriptures state his disqualification, "uncircumcised in heart." [So we must be talking about a Jewish priest who is uncircumcised in his heart but apart from having impure intentions is otherwise a fit priest. Non-Jews would be disqualified even if they had circumcised hearts and circumcised flesh. If we are not talking of Jewish priests there is no need to mention the other defects since non-priests are forbidden to officiate under any circumstance.]
3. So why call him "stranger"? It means "one whose characteristic behaviors have estranged him to his Father Who is in Heaven."

The Rabbis found here two disqualifications for individuals seeking to enter the Temple, namely, bad character and being uncircumcised, not three (i.e., a non-Israelite plus the others). They used the occasion to teach that even a priest with an impure heart is considered to be as unfit as is an idolater for divine service. That is the point of the verse. The priest with uncircumcised flesh is disqualified by a ritual technicality. Both a circumcised heart and circumcised flesh are required. My dwelling on this passage is not to consider whether it is some kind of anti-Christian polemic or even an early tradition aimed at disqualifying Jewish-Christian priests from officiating in the Temple. That discussion must await another time. As Matthew 6:34, *b. Berakhot* 9b, and *Shemot Rabbah* (the midrash to Exodus) 3s.6 (*Va'era*) would have it, "Each trouble is enough for its own day." In this chapter, my immediate problem is to show how uniformly both the Talmudic Rabbis and the New Testament Jesus use the same select principles to "unpack" biblical and oral law.

The focus of much of Rabbinic legal literature is to stretch Scriptures and oral documents to fit the needs of their organic cultural system. But this "stretching" cannot be said to violate texts, since it is done using the standard forms of argument accepted by the Rabbis' "co-culturists." The literal meanings of many biblical verses are often dismissed as irrelevant on contextual grounds that are intelligible to the community. More novel teachings are derived from special techniques, sometimes establishing a sense opposite to the literal, naked Scripture.

Y. KETUBOT 4:4

1. (Exodus 21:18), *And if men dispute, and one strike the other with a stone, or with the fist, and he die not, but take to [his] bed, (21:19)—if he rise, and walk abroad upon his staff, then shall he that struck [him] be guiltless—*
2. Could you even think that he who struck him could be gallivanting about in the market [guiltless] while the victim [languishing and supported by his staff] eventually expires through his hand.
3. But then what meaning do I establish for "upon his staff"?—"Upon [the staff of] his own strength."

The 1-2-3 form (verse, objection to literalness, reinterpretation) appears again. Indeed, the official Aramaic translation of the Bible (Targum Onqelos) supplies the meaning "his own strength."

B. MENAHOT 99B

1. (Exodus 25:30): *And thou shall set upon the table show bread before me continually.*
   It was taught:
2. Rabbi Yosi said [the literal is impractical], if the old show bread was removed after a part of the morning and the new ones set down during a part of the evening there would be no problem.
3. So what meaning do I establish for the words of Exodus 25:30, "before me continually"?—That the table not rest [for a whole night or day] without bread on it. Said Rabbi Ami, from the words of Rabbi Yosi we can derive that even if one reads a mere chapter of Torah in the morning and a chapter at night he can fulfill Joshua 1:8: *"This book of the Torah shall not depart out of thy mouth; [but you shall meditate in it day and night]."*

Meanings are derived to fit the wider culture and justified by means of set formulas that stretch words beyond their formal contextual sense. The context is not the verse but the wider society and its systems and needs. There is a rationale for doing this. In the case above Rabbi Yosi finds it reasonable to assume bread need not be on the table at all times. New loaves did not have to be balanced on the table edge while the old ones were being removed literally to fulfill the requirement of "continual." It is not totally made clear precisely what his objection to "continual" in its literal sense might be. Nevertheless, his definition of continual is stretched to the limit. On that basis other Rabbis were then willing to find an excuse to shorten the literal times required for Torah study. It should be noted that Rabbi Yosi's interpretation was dismissed long ago, but his intention, as usual, was to alleviate strain and hardship (Basser, 53–56).

Now let us see how Jesus uses these counterintuitive rules of Jewish culture. In the following passages known as "antitheses" we have a juxtaposition of literal understanding and established meaning or personal, pious advice on how to go beyond the measure of the law: a very Rabbinic idea. What is not juxtaposed— what is never even suggested—is "verse" and "its rejection."

MATTHEW 5:43–46

1. (5:43) "You have heard that it was said, '*Love your neighbor*' and [imply] 'hate your enemy.' (5:44) But I tell you:
3. Love your enemies and pray for those who persecute you . . .
2. (5:46) If you love those who love you, what reward will you get? Are not even the tax collectors doing that? And if you greet only your brothers, what are you doing more than others? Do not even pagans do that?"

Since Scripture had no need to talk about loving friends, we posit the point is to talk about a new case—loving your enemy. Matthew 5:46 leads to the conclusion stated in verse 44. Since Scripture commands love of neighbor and so will reward one for fulfilling the commandment, why need it bother to command what is already practiced? It is unnecessary to state, for all people automatically behave this way. Thus we must establish a more congenial meaning for its wording, namely, "Love your enemies." The only difference between the Rabbinic forms we have looked at and Jesus' form is that Jesus stretches the verse first before explaining his objection to taking the verse literally.

The culture of Jewish reading extends a meaning to the divine words that allows for the novel interpretation "love your enemies." The result is intended to serve the greater good of the community and to be consistent with its socioreligious system. The accepted rules of interpretation permit such extensions with little or no question.

What allows the word "neighbor" to be stretched to mean "enemy"? The words "neighbor" and "enemy" share the same Hebrew consonants (*resh ayin*) and differ only in the vowel pronunciation. Both words are written identically. Such word switches are widespread in Rabbinic literature (Kasher 1988). The established meaning stands as the specific accepted sense for that teacher and enters the tradition as a valid proclamation of God's sovereign will.

STRUCTURED LISTS

While we are on the subject of the so-called antitheses, it is important to realize that the Gospels' source materials are not simply raw Scriptures. To the contrary, the sources are established formulations listed in Jewish oral traditions. For example, most of the ordered list found in Matthew 5:38–41 [i.e., (1) eye, (2) cheek, (3) coat] can be found in Rabbinic literature but not in Hebrew Scriptures. Some of the lists, albeit not in the exact words of Scriptures, of both Jesus and Rabbis are evident in the ancient Near Eastern codes (Thomas 1958, 34), showing us that the Jewish lists go back to deep antiquity. In fact, the Rabbis also discuss waiving payments. The Rabbinic materials have much explanatory detail and further categories of damage, but the main examples of damage are eye (physical pain and damage), slapping (pained embarrassment), and garment taking (embarrassment). The chapter in *m. Baba Kamma*, in which this material appears, ends with a discussion of the rules of waiving punishments for blinding eyes, chopping hands, and tearing garments. The Talmud (*b. Baba Kamma* 92a) presents more materials in this regard. For our purposes it is sufficient to look at *m. Baba Kamma* 8:

(8:1) When one injures another he becomes liable to pay for five categories of damage. How so? If he blinded his eye etc. . . . .

(8:6) If he slapped his face he gives him a flat rate of 200 *zuz*, if backhanded [on the right cheek]—400 *zuz*; . . . if he removes his garment from him he gives him 400 *zuz*.

We now turn to the structured list in Matthew 5:

(38) "You have heard that it was said, 'An eye for an eye and a tooth for a tooth.'

(39) But I say to you, Do not oppose evil. But if any one strikes you on the right cheek, turn to him the other also;

(40) and if any one wins a lawsuit against you (so the Syriac translation) to take your coat, let him have your cloak as well;

(41) and if any one forces you to walk one mile, walk with him two miles.

Here we have a list of damages in diminishing severity. The farther down the list an injury occurs, the easier it is to accept it and the easier to suffer an equal indignity. A similar list of items of decreasing severity is found in *m. Baba Kamma* chapter 8 and *b. Baba Kamma* 92a of eye (and hand), cheek, and garment. Although the list is similar in structure, the precise sense of "garment" is not that of a judgment; rather, it concerns a person shaming another by either lifting up or tearing his garment. There is a degree of shame but no physical pain as there is in slapping. Indeed, the Gospel unit breaks the pattern here. The Greek text suggests: "And to the one who desires to judge you and take your shirt, grant him your coat as well." The Syriac I think best gives the import.

However, the unit seems out of place in the list. Losing a court case (or being sued) is hardly in the same category as suffering violence. To be consistent with the supererogatory ethic of the entire list, we should expect "if one grabs your coat, give him your cloak too."

The final item on the list is not found in any Jewish legal codes as an injury; it seems to have been added to the list known to the Rabbis to complete a series of three waivers. Verse 38, which introduces the list, seems to carry with it the notion known to the Rabbis that "physical abuse and embarrassment" requires monetary redress and not physical punishment (see Daube). The assumption then remains that forcing one to walk is also liable to damages.

The upshot of our discussion is that in both style and structure the teachings of Jesus recorded in Matthew's Gospel reflect the methods and oral corpus of his Jewish culture.

RATIONAL ARGUMENTS BASED ON LEGAL EXEGESIS

Rabbinic literature enjoys justifying time-honored laws through exegesis of redundant letters and phrases. It is sometimes feasible, then, to use the interpretation to argue for another practice.

TANHUMA MASSEI 1

[Leviticus 12:3 says—"*He shall be circumcised*" and even on the Sabbath.] Can one not argue: if on the Sabbath one can circumcise, which involves setting right just one of the 248 limbs of a person, then the whole body of a person should certainly be able to be set right!"

The Rabbis proclaim the results of their exegesis, which preceded the above citation, to justify their practice of performing circumcisions on the Sabbath. They then argue from that premise that healing whole bodies must be allowed. A similarly structured argument appears in John 7:

(21) Jesus answered and said to them, I have done one work, and you all wonder at it.

(22) Moses gave you circumcision and you circumcise a person on the Sabbath.

(23) If a man receives circumcision on the Sabbath, that the law of Moses may not be violated, are you angry with me because I have made a person's whole body sound on the Sabbath?

John presents Jesus giving a classic argument in the standard style and form of Rabbinic reasoning. More than that, we have here two variants of the very same teaching.

DEBATE FORMS

We began by talking about rules discouraging people from touching sacred scrolls directly. The Pharisaic practice was the subject of debate. We should now note that a debate form in Rabbinic literature portraying an exchange between members of opposing groups follows a format close to that of Jesus/Pharisee debates.

A—a statement of complaint;

B—a statement of analogous practice (from the opponent's vantage point) to that complained about seeking the opponent's approval;

C—a conclusion—we can now both agree that your complaint is groundless.

Our example, *m. Yadayim* (4,6), provides the following discussions:

A—The Sadducees said: We object to you, Pharisees, when you say, "The sacred scrolls defile the hands but scrolls of *Homoros* (profane works presumably) do not defile the hands."

B—Rabbi Yochanan ben Zakkai said: "And why should this be your only complaint against the Pharisees, after all, they say: the bones of a donkey (Hebrew: *hamor* resonates with *homoros* above) are inherently pure, but the bones of the High Priest Yochanan defile?" They replied to him: "According to their preciousness is their defilement determined, for otherwise a person may make the bones of his father and mother into spoons."

C—He said to them: "It is the very same in the case of the sacred scrolls. According to their preciousness is their defilement determined. And the scrolls of *Homoros* are not precious, so they do not defile the hands."

In short, one would not expect reasonable people to legislate that sacred Scriptures would defile the hands that touched them. Yet the Pharisees did, and they were challenged by their foes, the Sadducees. Rabbi Yochanan ben Zakkai, the chief Pharisee, answered along the Sadducean method of reasoning to demonstrate to them their misunderstanding. He pointed out that the example of the sacred texts is not the only situation in which an esteemed thing causes "defilement." The analogous example that he gave was that of bones. Finally, Rabbi Yochanan then uses the Sadducees' reply to respond to their first claim and says that defilement is also used as a safeguard in the proper handling of books. The sacred scrolls deserve special handling; therefore, they cause defilement of the hands.

We can now look at similar passages in the Gospels which illustrate that Jesus uses the same A-B-C technique:

MATTHEW 12:10–12

A—(10) Looking for a reason to accuse Jesus, they asked him, "Is it lawful to heal on the Sabbath?"

B—(11) He said to them, "If any of you has a sheep and it falls into a pit on the Sabbath, will you not take hold of it and lift it out?

C—(12) How much more valuable is a man than a sheep! Therefore it is lawful to do good on the Sabbath."

MARK 2:23–28

(23) One Sabbath he was going through the grain fields; and as they made their way his disciples began to pluck heads of grain.

A—(24) And the Pharisees said to him, "Look, why are they doing what is not lawful on the Sabbath?"

B—(25) And he said to them, "Have you never read what David did, when he was in need and was hungry, he and those who were with him; (26) how he entered the house of God, when Abiathar was high priest, and ate the show bread, which it is not lawful for any but the priests to eat, and also gave it to those who were with him?"

C—(27) And he said to them, "The Sabbath was made for man, not man for the Sabbath; (28) so the Son of man is lord even of the Sabbath."

LUKE 13:14–16

A—(14) But the ruler of the synagogue, indignant because Jesus had healed on the Sabbath, said to the people, "There are six days on which work ought to be done; come on those days and be healed, and not on the Sabbath day."

B—(15) Then the Lord answered him, "You hypocrites! Does not each of you on the Sabbath untie his ox or his ass from the manger, and lead it away to water it?

C—(16) And ought not this woman, a daughter of Abraham whom Satan bound for eighteen years, be loosed from this bond on the Sabbath day?"

Elsewhere it has been shown that Jesus' specialized vocabulary and reasoning in these passages and his knowledge of technical laws devised by Rabbis to enhance the observance of the Sabbath match the systematic workings peculiar to Rabbinic Sabbath law in minute detail (Basser, 17–33).

The Anti-Jewish Function of Jesus' Teachings

Let us grant that those people who find solid correspondences between the Talmudic teachings of Rabbis and Gospel teachings of Jesus both in form and substance make a persuasive case. Let us even grant the possibility that various traditions in Rabbinic literature might be closer to their Second Temple sources than the variant traditions recorded in the Gospels. It is always possible that long before 70 CE, Hillel the Pharisee thought X and passed that X down to student Rabbi Yochanan ben Zakkai, who passed it to student Rabbi Eliezer, who passed it to student Rabbi Aqiba (died ca. 135 CE), who organized the base of our current Rabbinic literature. Any names of teachers might be used as examples. The above chain of transmission is just what Rabbinic tradition claims, and it could be historically accurate. The tradition we have from the Rabbis could be three transmissions old.

But now we posit another case, which is not the teacher-student case but a popular transmission scenario. Hillel thought X, and someone was there who heard it and passed it on to someone else, who passed it over to someone else. Eventually, seven transmissions later, it got into the Jesus tradition, either from Jesus in the Galilee or from someone else (ca. 30 or 40 CE). Both the Rabbinic and Jesus sayings were redacted in their present forms about fifty to sixty years later. The thirdhand version might well be taken as the more original one even if chronologically later than the seven-transmission one. Chronological dating, although indispensable, is not the only factor in considering the relative dates of materials. How the material reached the writers is a significant factor as well.

Yet, given all the arguments that Jesus' sayings as recorded in the Gospels accurately reflect real teachings of Pharisees and Rabbis, does that mean the intended message of Jesus in the Gospels is concentric with the message of the Rabbis? Not at all! The invective inherent in the Gospels' rhetorical environment and the Evangelists' embedded commentaries on Jesus' motives preclude any such conclusion. Jesus the Jew exhibits in the Gospels a hostility to the Pharisaic, and so Rabbinic, system of learning Torah.

For example, when Jesus protests against one instance of an otherwise faultless Rabbinic ruling, such as that concerning the *Corban* (see Mark 7:11–13)—the special offering vowed to the Deity, which is then unable to be utilized for other purposes—this becomes the occasion for the Gospels to harangue against all Pharisaic rulings. Indeed, the same complaint raised by Jesus about individuals who dedicate their money to the Temple rather than to the upkeep of their parents is addressed by the Rabbis in more detail (Basser, 39 n. 86). Jesus apparently quotes the ancestral tradition verbatim (Basser, 37: "But you say . . .").

When Jesus provides a lesson, in Rabbinic style and structure (Basser, 42–43), of moral purity based on extensions of laws of ritual purity, Mark uses the occasion to dismiss all dietary regulations. The further commentaries of the Church Fathers and subsequent systematic theologians who have debased Rabbinic teachings actually are reading the New Testament in the model of the Gospel writers. While Jewish literatures are replete with Jewish leaders castigating sins of Jews in the hope they will attach themselves to obeying the Torah, the New Testament shifts Jesus' audience from his fellow Jews to the Gospels' Christian readers.

Gospel exegetes must be content to notice how well certain passages in the New Testament satisfy the specifications defining Rabbinic literatures. This observation enables them to explain the unique methods used in Jesus' defense of his or another's behaviors. It appears that we have traces of traditions that intended to highlight his fulfilling the minute details of laws that his interlocutors had overlooked.

Bibliography

Basser, H. W. *Studies in Exegesis: Christian Critiques of Jewish Law and Rabbinic Responses 70–300 C.E.* Leiden: Brill, 2000.

Daube, D. "Matthew v.38f." *Journal of Theological Studies* 45 (1944): 177–87.

Doeve, J. W. *Jewish Hermeneutics in the Synoptic Gospels and Acts.* Assen: Van Gorcum, 1954.

Kasher, R. "The Interpretation of Scripture in Rabbinic Literature." Pages 547–94 in *Mikra: Text, Translation, Reading and Interpretation of the Hebrew Bible in Ancient Judaism and Early Christianity.* Compendia Rerum Iudaicarum ad Novum Testamentum Section II, vol. 1. Edited by M. J. Mulder. Assen: Van Gorcum. Philadelphia: Fortress Press, 1988.

Stone, M. "4QTestament of Naphthali." Pages 73–82 in *Qumran Cave 4, XVII, Parabiblical Texts, Part 3.* Discoveries in the Judean Desert 22. Oxford: Clarendon Press, 1996.

Thomas, D. Winton. *Documents from Old Testament Times.* New York: Harper and Row, 1958.

Zeitlin, I. *Jesus and the Judaism of His Time.* Cambridge: Polity Press, 1988.

—18—

Philo of Alexandria

Gregory E. Sterling

The treatises of Philo of Alexandria are one of the most important sources for our understanding of the exegetical traditions and religious practices of Diaspora Jews in the first century CE. Unfortunately, we know little about Philo's life, although we know more about his family. Eusebius of Caesarea thought that Philo "was inferior to none of the illustrious people in office in Alexandria" (*Hist. Eccl.* 2.4.2). This may be a hyperbolic claim, yet we should not dismiss it too quickly. Philo's brother, Julius Gaius Alexander, moved in elite circles in the empire. He not only held a civic post in Alexandria (Josephus, *Ant.* 18.159, 259; 19.276–77; 20.100) but also had close ties to the Herodian family and through them to the imperial family. It is probable that Berenice, the mother of Agrippa I, was the avenue by which Alexander was appointed the guardian of the Egyptian estates of Antonia (Josephus, *Ant.* 19.276), the daughter of Mark Antony and Octavia and mother of Germanicus and Claudius the emperor (Suetonius, *The Divine Claudius* 1.6; 3.2; 11.2). The basis for such associations was undoubtedly Alexander's wealth. He not only lent Agrippa I 200,000 drachmas on an occasion when the big spender was in financial straits (Josephus, *Ant.* 18.159–60) but also covered nine of the doors of the Jerusalem Temple with gold and silver (Josephus, *War* 5.201–5).

The connections also were possible because Alexander and Philo probably had triple citizenships in the Jewish community of Alexandria, the Greek city of Alexandria, and the Roman Empire. The last is accentuated by the career of Alexander's most famous son, Tiberius Julius Alexander, who is one of the most impressive examples of an individual from the East who worked his way through the *cursus honorum*. He began with a minor post in Egypt (OGIS 663) but quickly assumed more important responsibilities such as the governorship of Judea in 46–48 CE (Josephus, *War* 2.220, 223; *Ant.* 20.100–103), the governorship of Syria (unpublished inscription), a position on Corbulo's staff in 63 CE during the sensitive negotiations with Parthia over Armenia (Tacitus, *Annals* 15.28.3), the governorship of Egypt in 66–70 CE (*Corpus Papyrorum Judicarum* [CPJ] 418b; Josephus, *War* 2.309; Tacitus, *Annals* 11.1), Titus's chief of staff during the first

Jewish War (Josephus, *War* 5.45–46; 6.237; OGIS 586), and finally prefect of the praetorian guard in Rome (CPJ 418b). It is hardly a surprise that the Jewish community selected Philo, Alexander, and the young Tiberius Julius Alexander to represent them before Gaius Caligula after the pogrom in Alexandria in 38 CE (Philo, *Embassy to Gaius* 182, 370; *On Animals* 54; Josephus, *Ant.* 18.257–60).

Apart from his role on the embassy, we know relatively little about Philo. We must reconstruct the evidence based on the autobiographical hints that he provides in his treatises. This is probably due to the fact that he preferred the contemplative life to the active life (*On Special Laws* 3.1–6). Philo received a thorough Greek education (*Prelim. Studies* 74–76). This would have included not only elementary training in a gymnasium and the rite of passage to citizenship in the *ephebeia*, but also tertiary training in rhetoric and, most important, philosophy. He knew a number of Plato's treatises firsthand (e.g., the *Timaeus*) and was fully at home in Hellenistic philosophical thought. The same can be said for his knowledge of the Septuagint: he knew the Pentateuch intimately, a familiarity that suggests that he also received a thorough Jewish education, probably at home and at a "house of prayer" (as Jewish places of worship were called in Alexandria). Jerome was so impressed with his knowledge of Judaism that he thought Philo was a "priest by lineage" (*On Illustrious Men* 11). This appears to be a deduction based on Philo's social status and knowledge of the Scriptures rather than an independent tradition.

Philo put his education to good use by writing extensively. The most likely social setting for his expansive corpus is a private school similar to those of philosophers and physicians such as Philodemus, Epictetus, Plotinus, or Galen. Philo produced three independent commentaries on the Torah that have distinct orientations and different implied audiences: the *Questions and Answers on Genesis and Exodus*, a introductory commentary that poses questions and provides both literal and allegorical answers; the *Allegorical Commentary*, an intricate and elaborate allegorical interpretation of Genesis 2–41; and the *Exposition of the Laws*, a systematic exposition of the entire Pentateuch. Modern scholars divide the remainder of his treatises into two groups: the apologetic treatises, probably composed in connection with the pogrom of 38 and the embassy to Rome that followed it; and the philosophical treatises that employ standard philosophical genres.

Philo's thought proved to be attractive to early Christians, who preserved about two-thirds of his known corpus: thirty-eight treatises and a fragment of another treatise in Greek, plus nine other treatises and two fragmentary works in a rather literal sixth-century Armenian translation. Early Christians found the philosophical, especially the Middle Platonic, readings of Scripture through allegorical exegesis so compelling that they created a Philo Christianus legend. Eusebius reported that Philo went "to Rome at the time of Claudius to converse with Peter who was preaching to those who were there at that time" (*Hist. Eccl.* 2.17.1). The bishop thought that Philo's description of the Therapeutae (a group of monastic Jewish men and women) demonstrated the presence of an early Christian community outside of Alexandria. He considered this proof that Philo "not only knew but welcomed, revered, and held the apostolic men of his age in the highest esteem" (*Hist. Eccl.* 2.17.1–2). Although the Caesarean stopped short of calling Philo a Christian, later Christians did not. The *Acta Johannis* that circulated under the name of Prochurus in the fifth century actually relates his conversion. In some quarters Philo was even elevated to ecclesiastical office: the Byzantine catenae regularly used the lemma "from Philo the bishop" to introduce citations from his works.

Philo and the Historical Jesus

Given Philo's social status and his attraction to early Christians, it is quite natural to ask whether he had any interest in the figures that helped to lay the basis for Christianity. He may have had occasion to learn about them firsthand. At least we know that he made one pilgrimage to the Temple in Jerusalem (*Providence* 2.64) and may well have made other such trips. It is not unreasonable to hypothesize that Philo heard something—however accurate or inaccurate—about Jesus of Nazareth. Whether he did or not, he never mentioned him or any of his followers; later interpretations of such references are only the anachronistic imaginings of early Christians who wanted to lay claim to his writings.

Philo does, however, provide us with a number of statements that help us to understand the historical Jesus or, more precisely, the ways that the Evangelists portray him in the Gospels. I have grouped these passages into three categories. The first deals with statements that find parallels in the Gospel Passion narratives. The three examples come from two of the apologetic treatises that Philo wrote shortly after the pogrom and the failed embassy to Caligula. Eusebius tells us that Philo set out these momentous events in five treatises (*Hist. Eccl.* 2.5.1). Two of these five must be *Against Flaccus* and *The Embassy to Gaius*, the two from which we have taken the texts below. The opening line of *Against Flaccus* assumes a prior treatment of Sejanus's persecution of Jews (*Flacc.* 1). Eusebius tells us that Philo set out not only Sejanus's abuse of the Jews but also Pilate's (*Hist. Eccl.* 2.5.7). This suggests that Philo either had dealt with each in separate treatises or had combined them in a single treatise. I am inclined to think that the former is more reasonable, since he deals with Flaccus and Gaius separately. We know that the latter required special attention, since Philo concluded *The Embassy to Gaius* with a reference to a succeeding treatise that represented the reversal of fortunes that befell the emperor (*Embassy* 373). This means that the five original books were probably a treatment of Pilate, Sejanus, Flaccus, Gaius, and the reversal of Gaius's fortunes. The works likely were intended for those who wondered whether God had abandoned the Jewish people. Philo concluded *Against Flaccus* with these words: "Flaccus suffered such things, and thereby became an incontestable proof that the Jewish nation had not been robbed of the help that comes from God" (§191). He opens the *Embassy to Gaius* with a similar thought (§§1–7).

The three selections from these treatises serve as background to scenes in the Gospel Passion narratives. The first presents the mocking of an insane individual named Karabas whom the Alexandrians used in order to mock Agrippa I when he visited Alexandria in 38 CE. The scene is strikingly similar to the mocking of Jesus in the Gospels (Matthew 27:27–31; Mark 15:16–20; John 19:2–3). The description is typical of such scenes. Plutarch described how pirates made anyone who claimed to be a Roman walk the plank in similar terms (*Pompey* 24.7–8). Dio Cassius narrated the mocking of the deposed Emperor Vitellius along the same lines (64.20–21). The historicity and possible background of the Gospel scene have been extensively debated (see Brown 1:873–77 and 674–75). The text from Philo represents one of the closest parallels that we have. In the first sentence (36), the word I have translated "indefensible" is a *hapex legomenon* (*askeptos*). Liddell-Scott Jones suggest the meaning "that can not be feigned" (257); however, I do not see how that is appropriate in this context. Several have offered conjectures: Cotelier read "unobserved" (*askeptos*), and Matthaei "defenseless" (*askepes*) (see Cohn-Wendlar 6:127).

The second text relates the scourging of the Jewish magistrates by Flaccus. The text is one of many that depict the horrors of scourging, a punishment that the Evangelists suggest Jesus endured (Matthew 27:26; Mark 15:15; John 19:1). Here in 74 where I have translated ". . . as he was about to govern the city on Egypt's border and the surrounding territory . . . ," I am following an emendation suggested by F. Millar instead of the manuscript readings, which appear to be corrupt (for details see Schürer, 393 n. 12).

The third text is a famous description of Pilate, the prefect who tried Jesus. The text is one of the most important *testimonia* that we have about the career of Pilate. The episode is similar enough to an episode that Josephus relates that the relationship between the two accounts has been an occasion for debate (*War* 2.169–74; *Ant.* 18.55–59). Although there are a number of similarities, there are substantial differences. Philo's account occurs in a letter of Agrippa I to Gaius. The Jewish king attempted to dissuade the emperor from setting his statue up in the Jerusalem Temple. In the course of his argumentation, Agrippa related the magnanimous way that Tiberius treated the Jews. He contrasted the emperor with the prefect, Pontius Pilate, whose unyielding character nearly led to a disaster. Pilate set up some golden shields with an inscription on them in Jerusalem. The Jews objected, probably because Tiberius's name must have appeared as *Tiberius Caesar divi Augusti filius* (Fuks, 507). Pilate realized that the emperor would be furious with him if his actions were discovered. Through this account Agrippa urged Gaius to respect the Temple in the same way that Tiberius had. Whether the historical Pilate was as problematic an administrator as Philo presents him to be is questionable; Philo had good rhetorical reasons for presenting Pilate in the worst possible light.

The second set of texts offer parallels to some of the teaching material attributed to Jesus. I have selected three of the most notable examples. The first is Philo's version of the summary of the Law in two major headings, a summary that is broadly similar to the controversy story about the great commandment in the

Gospels (Matthew 22:34–40; Mark 12:28–34; Luke 10:25–28), although Philo gives the division a particular spin. The Philonic summary occurs in *On Special Laws*. The work is part of Philo's systematic *Exposition of the Law*. After his treatment of creation and the ancestors, he devoted a treatise to the Decalogue and then used the Ten Commandments as headings for other laws in the four-volume *On Special Laws*. Our text comes from his exposition of the Fourth Commandment, keeping the Sabbath (2.39–222). In the immediate context, the Alexandrian explained why Jews rest from labor on the Sabbath: they devote themselves to the study of the Laws. They work with the body on six days and with the mind on the seventh day. The text demonstrates that the twofold summary was common in Judaism and was applied in various ways depending on the context.

The second and third texts come from the fragmentary work that we know as the *Hypothetica*. The text is preserved in two fragments in Eusebius's *Praeparatio Evangelica*. It probably was written in preparation for the embassy and reflects the debates that Philo had with his opponents. In the first fragment, Philo offered a summary of the Law that has a significant number of parallels with the wisdom of *Pseudo-Phocylides* and the summary of the Law in Josephus's *Against Apion*. It is likely that the three drew on common ethical teachings in Judaism that clustered specific laws around major topoi. Philo organized these topoi into a fivefold summary of the Law. Our second selection (the first from the *Hypothetica*) illustrates the principle of *Corban* that appears in Matthew 15:4–6 and Mark 7:9–13 (see also Herbert Basser's chapter in this volume). Philo's statements appear to reflect the same practice that we find attested in the Gospels and on an ossuary lid from Jebel Hallet et-Turi that Joseph Fitzmyer translated as "All that a man may find-to-his-profit in this ossuary/(is) an offering to God from him who is within it" (Fitzmyer 96). The third text is a negative form of the Golden Rule (Matthew 7:12). The saying is widely attested in the ancient world (Dihle); Philo and the Gospel accounts simply are illustrations of the ethical principle. It would be a mistake to make too much of the fact that the version in Matthew is positive in its formulation while the version in Philo is negative, since early Christians also knew the negative form, for example, the Western text of Acts 15:20, 29, and *Didache* 1.2. The value of the Philonic material is, once again, to illustrate the presence of the saying in Judaism.

The final two texts represent Philo's messianic vision. Like Josephus, Philo is remarkably reticent to offer a vision of the future and even more reluctant to speak of a messianic figure. The only place in his large corpus where he appears to do so is in his *On Rewards and Punishments*, the final treatise in the *Exposition of the Law*. Philo opens the *Exposition* with *On the Creation of the World* and closes it with a treatise that took up the blessings and curses of Moses' final instructions in Deuteronomy (see §§79–172, which draw heavily from Deuteronomy 28 as well as Leviticus 26 and 28). In this way the *Exposition of the Law* imitated the structure of the Pentateuch. The first selection comes from the treatment of the blessings (§§79–126) in which Philo offered a vision of a messianic age in which peace is a reality (§§85–98). He opened with a description of the cessation of hostility between humans and animals and among the animals themselves (§§85–90), a vision based on Isaiah 11. The peace of animals suggests a peace among humans (§§91–92). This peace may become a reality in several ways: the voluntary surrender of Israel's enemies (§93) or military victory brought about either by a leader or by wasps (§§94–96).

The citation of Numbers 24:7, "a man will come forth," is particularly important. The text was understood as a messianic vision by many, including, it appears, by Philo. However, Philo does not associate the figure with a Davidic king; any hint of identity is studiously avoided. Rather, the text accentuates the personal qualities of the figure, the courage of the soul and the strength of the body, in keeping with Philo's larger interest in the development of virtue and character within the person. This becomes unmistakably clear in the three qualities that belong to the holy: dignity, strictness, and a benevolent disposition. These qualities and their effect on subjects have a parallel in the work of Diotogenes, a Neopythagorean writer (*Stobaeus* 4.267.5). The common presence of these qualities in Philo and Diotogenes suggests that they came from a Hellenistic work on kingship (Winston 57–58).

The second text comes immediately on the heels of the treatment of curses (§§127–61). It offers a vision for Israel if the people will accept God's corrections. The vision includes the return from the Diaspora. The return is based on "a certain vision more divine than is within the reach of human nature." Some think that this refers to a personal Messiah; however, there is no textual indication that this is an individual. Rather, the vision is Philo's hope for the final redemption of the Jewish people. The two selections show that even a writer like Philo who interpreted Judaism principally in ontological categories did not surrender an eschatological vision including a messianic figure.

PARALLELS TO THE TRIAL OF JESUS

THE MOCKING OF A PERSON AS A ROYAL FIGURE

Philo, Against Flaccus 36–40 *(Cohn-Wendland 6:127)*

[36]There was a certain insane man named Karabas whose madness was not of the wild and beastly type—for this is indefensible both to those who have it and to those who come near—but was of the relaxed and more gentle type. He used to spend his days and nights naked in the streets, undeterred by heat or frost, a toy of children and youngsters who were kicking around. [37]The troublemakers forced the wretch to the gymnasium and stood him up high so that he could be seen clearly by all. They spread out a papyrus and set it on his head in place of a diadem, clothed the rest of his body with a rug in place of a cloak, and in place of a scepter someone gave him a short piece of native papyrus that he had spotted discarded in the road. [38]When, just as in theatrical mimes, he had

received the insignia of kingship and been decked out as a king, young men carrying sticks on their shoulders in place of spears stood on each side of him imitating royal bodyguards. Then others approached: some as if they were going to salute him, others as if they were going to plead a case, and others as if they were going to discuss the affairs of the state. [39]Next, from out of the crowd that was standing all around him, an inappropriate cry rang out as they called him "Marin" which is said to be the word for lord among the Syrians. For they knew that Agrippa was both a Syrian by race and controlled a great portion of Syria over which he ruled as king. [40]When Flaccus heard or rather saw these events, he ought to have seized and confined the insane person so that he would not furnish an occasion for those abusive loudmouths to insult their superiors. He ought to have punished those who had dressed him up because they had dared in both deeds and words, both openly and indirectly, to insult a king, a friend of Caesar, one who had been honored by the Roman senate with praetorian honors. Not only did he fail to rebuke them, but he did not even consider it appropriate to restrain them, giving license and a free hand to those who willfully practice wrong and willfully have it in for another. He pretended not to see the things that he saw and not to hear the things that he heard.

SCOURGING

Philo, Against Flaccus 72, 73–77 (Cohn-Wendland 6:133–34)

[72]Those who were doing these things acted like victims, as if they were in theatrical mimes. The friends and family members of those who were truly the victims, simply because they sympathized with the plights of their relatives, were led away, scourged, tortured on the wheel, and after all these abuses—however much their bodies were able to endure—the ultimate and remaining punishment was a cross.

[73]After Flaccus had thoroughly burglarized, plundered, and left no part of the Jewish community free from his outrageous treachery, the great performer and inventor of wrongs devised an extraordinary and unparalleled attack. [74]From our senate, which our savior and benefactor Augustus appointed to take charge of the Jewish community after the death of the genarch through orders to Magius Maximus as he was about to govern the city on Egypt's border and the surrounding territory, he arrested thirty-eight members who were found in their homes. He immediately ordered them to be bound and organized a fine procession through the middle of the agora that consisted of the elders bound with their hands behind their backs, some with leather straps and others with iron chains. He led them into the theater—a pitiable spectacle and completely ill-suited to the occasion. [75]When they stood opposite their enemies who were seated there to make an exhibition of their shame, he ordered them all stripped and tortured with scourges, a punishment that is cus-

tomarily reserved for the most wicked of evildoers. The result was that some were carried out on stretchers and died immediately; others suffered for such a long time that they despaired that recovery would ever come.

[76]The expanse of his plot has been exposed through other proofs, and yet it will be exposed even more clearly through what I am about to relate. Three men from the senate, Euodos, Tryphon, and Andron, had become property-less, robbed in one attack of all that they had in their homes. Flaccus was not ignorant of what they had suffered. He had been informed on an earlier occasion when he had summoned our rulers under the pretense of working out a reconciliation with the rest of the city. [77]Nevertheless, although he knew full well that they had been deprived of their property, he beat them in the presence of those who had robbed them in order to make them endure a double misfortune, poverty at the same time as outrage to their bodies, while the others had a double pleasure, the enjoyment of another's wealth and the occasion to gloat excessively over the dishonor of those who had suffered loss.

PONTIUS PILATE

Philo, Embassy to Gaius 299–305 (Cohn-Wendland 6:210–11)

[299]I can narrate an act of munificence on Tiberius's part, even though I experienced many injuries when he was alive; however, truth is dear and honorable to you. Pilate was one of his governors, appointed prefect of Judaea. He, not so much to honor Tiberius as to irritate the multitude, dedicated gold shields in Herod's palace in the holy city. They had neither an image nor anything forbidden except the requisite inscription that mentioned these two things: the name of the one who dedicated them and the name of the one for whom the dedication was made. [300]When the crowds learned about this—the deed was already notorious—they enlisted the four sons of the king as allies who were not inferior to kings in dignity and station, his other descendants, and some of their own magistrates and urged him to set straight the innovation brought about by the shields and not to alter the ancestral customs that had been preserved throughout all preceding ages and had not been altered by kings or emperors. [301]When he obstinately refused—for he was rigid by nature and remorselessly harsh—they cried out: "Do not create a revolt, do not start a war, do not destroy the peace. The dishonoring of ancient laws is not the honor of the emperor. Do not let Tiberius be a pretext for an insult against the nation; he wishes none of our laws to be dissolved. But if you claim that he does, produce an edict or a letter or something similar so that we may stop annoying you and select ambassadors to appeal to our lord."

[302]This final remark set him on edge since he became alarmed that if, in fact, they sent ambassadors, they would convict him for the rest of his governorship by running through the acceptance of bribes, the acts of insult, the seizures, the

assaults, the acts of abuse, the successive executions of untried people, and his unending and incredibly vexatious cruelty. [303]Since he was a person who held grudges and had a violent temper, he was in an awkward position: he did not have the courage to take down what had been dedicated nor did he want to do anything that would please his subjects; at the same time, he was not unaware of Tiberius's firmness in such matters. When the magistrates saw this and recognized that he regretted what had been done but did not want to appear to have regrets, they wrote Tiberius very earnest letters of petition. [304]When he read them, what he said about Pilate! What he threatened! How angry he became—even though he was not easily subject to anger—is superfluous to relate, the response alone declares it. [305]For he wrote immediately, not delaying a day, reproaching and rebuking him at great length for the shameless innovation that he had introduced. He ordered him to take down the shields immediately and to transfer them from the metropolis to Caesarea by the sea, also named Augusta after his grandfather, where they should be set up in the temple of Augustus—and they were. In this way both concerns were protected: the honor of the emperor and the ancient custom of respecting the city.

PARALLELS TO SAYINGS ATTRIBUTED TO JESUS

THE SUMMARY OF THE LAW IN TWO PARTS

Philo, On Special Laws 2.63–64 (Cohn-Wendland 5:102)

[63]There are—one may say—two main headings of the innumerable individual rules and teachings: our obligation to God through piety and holiness and our obligation to humanity through love of humanity and justice; each of these is divided into many subcategories that are all praiseworthy. [64]From these things it is clear that Moses did not permit those who follow his instructions to be idle at any time. On the contrary, since we consist of soul and body, he assigned to the body the appropriate tasks and to the soul those that pertain to it. He took pains to see that the one served as a reserve for the other so that while the body was at work the soul could be at rest and, conversely, while the body was resting, the soul would work. The best lives, the contemplative and the active, take turns replacing each other. The active has received the number six for the service of the body; the contemplative the number seven for the knowledge and perfection of the mind.

CORBAN

Philo, Hypothetica 8.7.3–5 (Mras 1:430)

[8.7.3]Again there are other laws such as these. Wives should serve their husbands, not as a result of abuse but with a view to voluntary obedience in all things. Parents should rule their children for their well-being and care. Each individual should have control over his own possessions unless he has invoked the name of God over them or given them to God. Even if it turns out that he has only promised them with a statement, it is not lawful for him to touch or handle them, but he must immediately exclude himself from all of them. [8.7.4]He should not carry off things that belong to the gods nor rob the things that others have dedicated, not even his own, as I said, since if some word of dedication happens to slip, even if he is unaware of it, once he has said it, he is deprived of all. If he regrets or amends what he has said, his life should be taken. [8.7.5]The same is true with regard to other persons over whom he has authority. If a man promises that his wife's support is sacred, he must uphold her support. If a father makes this promise for a son, if a ruler makes this promise for a subject, the same principle applies. The most perfect and best release of dedicated items is when a priest rejects them, since he has been given the authority by God to accept them. Next to this is the release by those in higher positions of authority who can declare that God is satisfied with holy things so that it is not necessary to accept the dedication.

THE GOLDEN RULE

Philo, Hypothetica 8.7.6 *(Mras 1:430)*

[8.7.6]There are many other laws in addition to these which either rest on unwritten customs and practices or are in the laws themselves. What someone hates to experience, he should not do.

PHILO'S MESSIANIC VISION

A PERSONAL MESSIAH?

Philo, On Rewards and Punishments 93–97 *(Cohn-Wendland 5.357–58)*

[93]Either then, he says, war will not pass through the land of the pious at all (Leviticus 26:6) but will subside and shatter by itself when the opponents realize that the battle must be joined with those who have an irresistible ally in Justice. For virtue is magnificent, august, and is capable—quietly and all by itself—of making light of the forces of evils however great they are. [94]Or, if certain madmen filled with an uncontrollable and ungovernable lust for making war eagerly approach, they will make enormous claims in their overly confident state until they join in battle. But when they have come to a trial of arms, they will realize that they have made an empty boast since they are unable to conquer. For overcome by a greater force, they will flee headlong: groups of a hundred will be overcome by groups of five, groups of ten thousand by groups

of a hundred (Leviticus 26:8); those who have come on one road will flee by many roads (Deuteronomy 28:7). [95]But some, although no one is pursuing except fear, will turn their backs to their adversaries for clear targets so that it will be easy for all to fall, slain to a man from the youth up. "For a man will come," says the oracle (Numbers 24:7), and leading an army in battles, he will subdue great and populous nations since God has sent him what is fitting for the devout as an auxiliary, that is the undaunted courage of the soul and the enormous bodily strength. Each of these is terrifying to enemies, but if both are joined together, they are utterly irresistible. [96]Some of the enemy, he says, will be unworthy of defeat by men. For these he arranged swarms of wasps (Exodus 23:28; Deuteronomy 7:20) for their shameful destruction and for the defense of the devout. [97]The latter will not only enjoy a bloodless military victory in security, but will also enjoy an uncontested sovereignty that is to the advantage of their subjects, an advantage that springs from the goodwill or fear or respect (that they have for their rulers). For the devout will practice three significant qualities that lead to an indestructible government: dignity, strictness, and a benevolent disposition. From these the feelings mentioned above are brought about. For a dignified disposition produces respect, a strict disposition fear, and a benevolent disposition goodwill. When these are blended together and harmonized in the soul, they make the subjects obedient to rulers.

THE REDEMPTION OF THE JEWISH PEOPLE

Philo, On Rewards and Punishments 165 (Cohn-Wendland 5:374–75)

[165]When they obtain this unexpected freedom, those who just shortly before were scattered in Greece and in the non-Greek world on islands and continents, will arise with a single impulse, some from one locale and others from another locale, and will hurry to the one appointed place, guided by a certain vision more divine than is within the reach of human nature, unseen by others but visible to the saved alone.

Bibliography

Texts

Cohn, L., P. Wendland, S. Reiter, and I. Leisegang, eds. *Philonis Alexandrini opera quae supersunt.* 7 vols. Berlin: George Reimer, 1896–1930, 1962.

Dittenberger, W. *Orientis graeci inscriptiones selectae.* 2 vols. Leipzig, 1903–5.

Mras, K. *Eusebius Werke 8: Die praeparatio evangelica.* 2 vols. Griechischen christlichen Schriftsteller 43.1–2. Berlin: Akademie Verlag, 1954.

Secondary Works

Amir, J. "The Messianic Idea in Hellenistic Judaism." *Immanuel* 2 (1973): 58–60.

Borgen, P. *Philo of Alexandria: An Exegete for His Time*, pp. 261–81. Supplements to Novum Testamentum 86. Leiden: Brill, 1997.

Box, H. *Philonis Alexandrini in Flaccum: Greek Texts and Commentaries.* London: Oxford University Press, 1939.

Brown, R. *The Death of the Messiah: From Gethsemane to the Grave (A Commentary on the Passion Narrative in the Four Gospels).* 2 vols. Anchor Bible Reference Library. New York: Doubleday, 1994, 1:873–77 and 674–75 (for Karabas) and 851–53 (for scourging).

Crossan, John Dominic. *The Historical Jesus: The Life of a Mediterranean Jewish Peasant*, p. 129 (for Karabas); pp. 380–82 (for Pilate). San Francisco: HarperSanFrancisco, 1991.

Davies, P. S. "The Meaning of Philo's Text about the Gilded Shields." *Journal of Theological Studies* 37 (1986): 109–14.

Dihle, A. *Die goldene Rege: Eine Einführung in die Geschichte der antiken und frühchristlichen Vulgärethik.* Studienheft zur Altertumswissenschaft 7. Göttingen: Vandenhoeck & Ruprecht, 1962.

Fitzmyer, Joseph A. "The Aramaic Qorban Inscription from Jebel Hallet et-Turi and Mk 7:11/MT 15:5." *Journal of Biblical Literature* 78 (1959): 60–65; reprinted in Joseph A. Fitzmyer, ed., *Essays on the Semitic Background of the New Testament*, pp. 93–100. Sources for Biblical Study 5. Missoula, MT: Scholars Press, 1974.

Fuks, G. "Again on the Episode of the Gilded Roman Shields at Jerusalem." *Harvard Theological Review* 75 (1982): 503–7.

Giordano, O. "Gesù e Barabbas." *Helikon* 13–14 (1973–74): 141–73.

Hecht, R. D. "Philo and Messiah." Pages 139–68 in *Judaisms and Their Messiahs at the Turn of the Christian Era.* Edited by J. Neusner, W. S. Green, and E. S. Frerichs. Cambridge: Cambridge University Press, 1987.

Krieger, K.-S. "Pontius Pilatus—ein Judenfeind: Zur Problematik einer Pilatusbiographie." *Biblische Notizen* 78 (1995): 63–83.

Lémonon, J. P. *Pilate et le gouvernement de la Judée: Textes et monuments*, pp. 205–30. Études Bibliques. Paris: J. Gabalda, 1981.

Liddell, H. G., and R. Scott. *A Greek-English Lexicon.* Rev. ed. Edited by H. S. Jones and R. McKenzie. Oxford: Oxford University Press, 1968.

Maier, P. L. "The Episode of the Golden Roman Shields at Jerusalem." *Harvard Theological Review* 62 (1969): 109–21.

McGing, B. C. "Pontius Pilate and the Sources." *Catholic Biblical Quarterly* 53 (1991): 416–38.

Schürer, E. *The History of the Jewish People in the Age of Jesus Christ.* 3 vols. Revised by G. Vermes, F. Millar, and M. Goodman. Edinburgh: T & T Clark, 1973–86.

Schwartz, D. R. "Josephus and Philo on Pontius Pilate." *Jerusalem Cathedra* 3 (1983): 26–45.

———. *Studies in the Jewish Background of Christianity*, pp. 214–17. Wissenschaftliche Untersuchungen zum Neuen Testament 60. Tübingen: J.C.B. Mohr (Paul Siebeck), 1992.

Smallwood, E. M. *Philonis Alexandrini Legatio ad Gaium.* Leiden: Brill, 1961, 1970.

Thatcher, T. "Philo on Pilate: Rhetoric or Reality?" *Restoration Quarterly* 37 (1995): 215–18.

van der Horst, P. *Philo's Flaccus: The First Pogrom.* Philo of Alexandria Commentary Series 2. Leiden: Brill, 2003.

Winston, D. *Logos and Mystical Theology in Philo of Alexandria*, pp. 56–58. Cinncinnati, OH: Hebrew Union College Press, 1985.

Wolfson, H. A. *Philo: Foundations of Religious Philosophy in Judaism, Christianity and Islam*, 2 vols. 2:395–426 (on Philo's messianic vision). Cambridge, MA: Harvard University Press, 1947.

—19—

The Law of Roman Divorce in

the Time of Christ

Thomas A. J. McGinn

Getting divorced was, from a legal perspective, easy for a Roman citizen, even by twenty-first-century U.S. standards. It was even easier than getting married in the first place, since divorce could be unilateral. There were no forms, no procedures, no lawyers—all that was really required was the wish of at least one spouse no longer to be married. There was no intervention by the state to regulate or even to make a record of divorce. In large measure, this was because there was relatively little to settle. The law kept spouses' property separate during marriage, at least in theory. Children as a rule remained with their father after dissolution of a marriage. The father might if he wished allow them to be raised by their mother, though they remained under his legally recognized paternal power (*patria potestas*).

Just as marriage itself was mainly a matter of agreement between the husband and wife (and those in whose *potestas* they stood, if applicable), so divorce demanded little by way of formality in principle. Practicality, however, suggested in both situations the desirability of some external manifestation of the wish to marry or divorce, and in the latter case, some of the legal experts known as jurists seem to incline toward a requirement that the spouse wanting a divorce notify the other of this wish, or at least attempt to do so. At stake was not just the existence (or not) of the marriage itself but questions concerning the legitimacy of children and the devolution of property.

The biggest complications in the Roman law of divorce concern the dowry. Though dowries were not just in the possession but in the actual ownership of husbands for the duration of the marriage, they often had to be returned by them upon divorce. Literary sources show that this was not always easy to do—often the capital was tied up in various investments, some of which might have to be relinquished at a loss. The larger the dowry, the bigger the complications, and the greater the leverage. So moralists decry marrying a woman with a large dowry. The threat, implicit or otherwise, of terminating the union in such cases was a potent one. The woman's superior position threatened to undermine a core ideal of Roman marriage, the paradoxical notion that the spouses should be more or less equal in status, but that the husband should be just a bit "more equal" than the wife (McGinn 2002). There were legally recognized circumstances where the husband was permitted to retain portions of the dowry, and the parties could make their own dispositions about this before marriage, in a manner similar to our pre-nuptial agreements (Treggiari 1991b, 357–61).

Even so, Roman freedom to divorce might strike us as extraordinarily broad, and the rules loose to the point of nonexistent. This laxity had one important exception. A freedwoman was by statute not allowed to divorce her former owner without his consent. The law's casualness otherwise raises an interesting question. If divorce was so easy, was it common as well? The tenor of the moralizing literary sources would have us believe that it was indeed common, and what we know of the complex marital histories of some upper-class Romans tends to reinforce this notion. But the honest answer is that we simply do not know.

Roman attitudes about divorce were not favorable overall. Though it was tolerated widely and did not labor under either religious or philosophical objections, it generally was regarded as a regrettable necessity at best. Persons divorcing for what were considered frivolous reasons were liable to criticism. These might include parting from a virtuous, dutiful, and unwilling spouse. Husbands who divorced wives deemed faultless or fruitful particularly were thought to be in the wrong, but wives divorcing their husbands were more likely to be censured (Treggiari 1991a, 40–41; 1991b, 471–73).

There was all the same a practice of bilateral divorce, in which for any one of a set of commonly recognized reasons a marriage might be ended by mutual consent. These include entering a priesthood, childlessness, old age, illness, or military service (Hermogenian, D. 24.1.60.1; Gaius, D. 24.1.61). There is a linguistic distinction to draw between divorce as *repudium*, in which one party (usually the husband) rejects the other, and divorce as *divortium*, a mutually agreed-upon parting of the ways (Treggiari 1991b, 440–41).

Frequency of divorce is an issue that can be raised only with regard to the upper classes, aside from one partial exception. The first thing to note is that the definition of "frequent" is highly subjective. It can vary significantly from culture to culture and is liable to rapid change within a culture. In her monumental study on Roman marriage, Susan Treggiari collects evidence for divorces attested during the Republic and early Principate (Treggiari 1991b, 516–19). In the first instance, she finds hardly more than three dozen, with about thirty-two clustering between 100 and 38 BCE, many of which can be attributed to politicians on the fast track, such as Sulla, Pompey, and Octavian. In the second group, most known divorces are found in the Julio-Claudian imperial family and families closely associated with it. The scarcity of the evidence and the relatively high danger of importing alien cultural assumptions make it difficult to conclude much with confidence, but if we were to take as a standard the contemporary U.S. ratio of marriages to divorces, about two to one, which in historical terms seems rather high, we can say that *only* the most successful politicians of the late

Republic and early Empire may have approached this rate (Treggiari 1991a, 44–45; 1991b, 473–82).

Evidence for divorce practice from the Roman subelite is even more difficult to obtain, with the exception of a unique body of sources, a collection of more than three hundred census declarations from Roman Egypt, which document important aspects of the lives of nearly eleven hundred registered persons, and rather ordinary persons at that. The vast majority, before 212 CE, were not Roman citizens. The census returns show that divorce was not a rare phenomenon for this sector of the population, with at least seventeen attested cases. The best guess is that the leading motive for divorce was spousal incompatibility (Bagnall and Frier, xv–xvi, 123–24).

Acting as a brake against a high divorce rate might have been the very high value Romans put on marriage. This was the primary relationship for adults in that society. Powerful social, economic, and psychological factors in favor of marriage were set against the lack of legal barriers governing divorce. But the lofty marriage ideal can be seen as cutting both ways. A high standard of expectations for wedded satisfaction might have made many a Roman spouse disinclined to settle for less, resulting in, if not an elevated divorce rate itself, at least a set of rules that facilitated an easy exit from any union at any conceivable moment. Roman divorce law evinces a strong individualistic ethic, one that held for women as much as it did for men, though the law itself is far from the whole story.

It is necessary to register a few caveats before proceeding to the texts. Most of the Roman legal sources that survive date from the early third century CE and are preserved in collections of texts that are even later in origin. All the same, with one important exception regarding the ability of a wielder of *patria potestas* to break up a marriage, the law of divorce does not appear to have undergone any fundamental change in the period extending between Christ and Ulpian. The legal and literary sources cited here are all the product of upper-class males whose perspective, unfortunately, is the only one left to us on this subject. The law itself, as in many societies, is designed by and large for the benefit of the upper classes, though it rarely makes this explicit. Further, the Romans knew of two basic marriage statuses for wives. One, called with *manus*, placed the woman in the legal power of her husband, a power that resembles that of a father (or other male ascendant), namely, *patria potestas*. The other, called without *manus*, did not place the woman in her husband's power but left her in that of her father (or other male ascendant) or with her own, independent legal status (*sui iuris*). Most historians believe that the vast majority of marriages in the period under discussion were without *manus*, and that this had been the case for some time. So it is on this type that we focus our discussion, conceding that some of the rules might have been different in our period, for example, hindering the ability of a wife married with *manus* to initiate a divorce (there is no firm evidence she could do so before the second century CE). Finally, fuller discussion of several of these texts is found in Frier and McGinn, which also contains more details on divorce law and references to modern literature.

Text 1 sets forth the principle that Roman divorce was free and unfettered, in the sense that either party can and should be entitled to end the union at any time. The spouses themselves were not permitted to place legally binding constraints in the way of each other's seeking a divorce. All that was required for a divorce was one party's wish to be single again. Intent was not only sufficient but necessary, in that a spouse who became insane could not divorce, though she or he could be divorced, as is clear in text 2, where the jurist Ulpian cites the opinion of his predecessor Julian (see also Ulpian, D. 24.3.22.8). The most striking aspect of this text is the analogy drawn between the insane woman and the person ignorant of the fact of the divorce. There is no clearer evidence of the complete absence of any duty to inform one's spouse that he or she is no longer married. The issue of fault does not enter into the power to divorce, at least in the period we are discussing, though it was relevant to the disposition of the dowry, as we shall see.

In text 3 Cicero, the greatest public speaker in Roman history, lays out, in a work published in 55 BCE (and whose dramatic date is 91 BCE), the facts of an actual legal case that seems to have occurred in the mid–second century. The case goes to the heart of concerns with status and property that are inherent in the casual nature of Roman divorce procedure. It is fairly easy to reconstruct the arguments on both sides. The plaintiff in this civil suit was the child of the second wife (if she was a wife, QED). He was seeking half his biological father's property and recognition as a legitimate, that is, legally recognized, child of his father. Victory on this latter point was essential to securing the first, since illegitimate children received nothing on intestacy from a father under Roman civil law. The defendant was the son from the first marriage, whose position was secure but who wanted to be instituted as sole heir. Cicero elsewhere (*de Oratore* 1.238) mentions that a major dispute broke out among jurists over this lawsuit, which suggests that at least some of them thought that a form of fixed procedure for divorce was a good idea.

One last point: Why is this case not a simple matter of bigamy? Romans were prohibited from marrying more than one person at the same time, and all unions subsequent to the first would be rendered void. There is no evidence, however, that the husband in this case intended two simultaneous marriages. A manifestation of such a design would be the man's shuttling back and forth between Rome and Spain, acting as husband to each woman.

The Romans had a long-standing rule that prohibited gifts of any value between spouses. The purpose was to maintain a strong regime of separate marital property, ultimately to the benefit of any children born in the union. Text 4 shows how the absence of a definite procedure for divorce might complicate application of this rule. The late first- and early second-century CE jurist Javolenus uses a celebrated case, the notoriously bumpy union between Augustus's political adviser and diplomat Maecenas and his wife, Terentia, which appears to have ended (for the last time!) in the years just preceding Maecenas's death in 8 BCE. The early Augustan jurist Trebatius, commenting on this case, holds that the validity of the gift depends solely on the intent behind the divorce, an opinion reported by his student Labeo. The case then becomes a fact-driven issue of proving intent, with the husband arguing that the first divorce was a sham, the wife that it was serious. Javolenus himself inclines toward the opinion of those jurists, evidently concerned with the ease by which the ban on gifts could be evaded, who insist on a concrete manifestation of the genuineness of this intent to divorce, such as a new marriage or the passage of a long interval of time (though we are not told how long this interval had to be). A later jurist claims that divorce is genuine if it is made with the intent of establishing a permanent separation (Paul, D. 24.2.3). For centuries, the jurists continued to have difficulty distinguishing spats that were serious but temporary from final partings: see Marcellus, D. 23.2.33. None of these texts mentions a formal divorce procedure even as a possible alternative solution. Ulpian to be sure makes reference (D. 24.1.35) to a "statutory protocol" for divorce in this connection, but we cannot be certain what he means by this.

It is clear that most people will have wanted to avoid ambiguity when divorcing. Verbal formulas hallowed by custom and a procedure of sending an oral or even written notice through an intermediary seem to have been recognized widely and practiced by the end of the first century BCE (Treggiari 1991a, 35–36).

In text 5, the jurist Gaius begins with a distinction drawn between terminology appropriate to consensual divorce and that suitable for unilateral divorce. The former case is less likely to require any fixed, formal usages. In the latter case, he cites phrases that are long familiar to us from the literary evidence on Roman divorce. He recommends both what language to use and what procedures to follow without insisting that any are absolutely necessary to effect a divorce. Lack of a standard procedure for divorce may have played a role in the notorious difficulties encountered by Messalina, the wife of the emperor Claudius, and her lover Silius, when they attempted marriage to each other in 48 CE (see Treggiari 1991b, 458).

The jurist Paul, on the other hand, refers to what appears to be a relatively elaborate procedure in text 6 and insists, moreover, that no divorce will be valid without this. Despite his generalizing language, most scholars point to the context of his remarks, a commentary on the adultery law of Augustus, and argue that this limited the scope of its application. The adultery statute required a husband who discovered his wife in the act of adultery to divorce her; it was from the time of the divorce that the clock started to run for potential prosecutors (on this statute, see McGinn 1998, chaps. 5 and 6). So a clear, unambiguous procedure perhaps seemed indispensable in these circumstances (see also Ulpian, D. 38.11.1.1).

Just as the consent of a father (or other ascendant male relative) wielding paternal power (*patria potestas*) granted to his daughter's marriage could be assumed unless he expressly demurred, so she seems to have been free to divorce her husband unless her *paterfamilias* explicitly opposed this, and there is in fact no good evidence for such opposition (Treggari 1991b, 445–46). Nor was the wielder of *potestas* expected to break up the harmonious marriages of children in his power, though he had the theoretical ability to do this, until his right was abrogated by the emperor Antoninus Pius (r. 138–61 CE). The last part of text 7 suggests that, even after Pius's ruling, the father might still take action if it was in the child's best interest.

It does not seem safe to conclude that this right to end a happy union had been exercised regularly in the years just before Pius's intervention. For one thing, the legal sources, for reasons of sociology rather than law, focus almost entirely on cases involving daughters, not sons. In part the explanation for this must be sheer demography. Most men, even those from the senatorial order, seem to have lost their fathers by the time of their first marriage. For most married women, the probability of having a living *paterfamilias*, though greater, was still rather low, and, of course, it decreased with every passing year. The median age at first marriage for subelite women was about twenty years, by which time a slim majority already would have lost their fathers. Upper-class women married earlier and saw their fathers perhaps live a bit longer, but the overall picture is very similar. The survival of another male ascendant, such as a grandfather, wielding *potestas* was unlikely (for the demography, see Saller, 12–69). More important, custom seems to have precluded, in most cases, such a radically negative intervention in a daughter's life by her father. This appears to have been even truer for sons.

The generally recognized freedom to divorce met with one serious limitation in the provision of the Augustan marriage legislation that forbade freedwomen to divorce their former owners, or *patroni*, without the consent of the latter. This law, actually two statutes (18 BCE and 9 CE) that the jurists typically treated as one, encouraged nonsenatorial freeborn males to marry their freedwomen, a practice that, while not illegal, was censured severely before the passage of the legislation (on the Augustan marriage legislation, see McGinn 2002 and 1998, chaps. 3 and 4). Evidently part of this encouragement was a rule that a freedwoman could not divorce her patron-husband against his will. Text 8 shows that the jurists had great difficulty with this statutory prohibition and in some respects attempted to restrict its scope of application, though they were not of one mind about the details (see also Ulpian, D. 23.2.45). In general, they do not accept that the woman can remain married to someone whom she does not wish as her husband, and so interpret the law to mean that, while her union with her former owner is ended, she cannot marry anyone else. So Julian and Ulpian refuse her the right to recover her dowry. Julian proceeds even further and denies her the right to enter into concubinage with another man (the jurists tend to treat concubinage as a monogamous union somewhat analogous, but definitely inferior, to proper marriage: see McGinn 1991). Ulpian, at any rate, is ready to accept the slightest indication that the patron no longer regards himself as married to allow the woman to proceed to a new marriage herself, and he is able to cite a rescript of the emperors Severus and Caracalla (joint reign, 197–211 CE) in support of his view.

While the issue of fault was irrelevant to the question of divorce itself, at least in the period under discussion, it does enter into the matter of the dowry, which was in the husband's ownership and management during the marriage but typically had to be returned when the marriage was dissolved through divorce. Upon suit by an ex-wife for its return, the husband could retain a portion or portions of the dowry under any or all of the five headings given in text 9. Fault, as it was conceived under the rubric of deductions for children, was not necessarily ascribed to the party who initiated the divorce. The classical sources generally are silent on what constitutes fault, for which we may derive an idea from postclassical legislation, such as a law of Constantine from 331 that disallows the husband's status as a drunk, a gambler, or a womanizer as a legitimate motive to divorce him, probably signifying that these behaviors did spell "fault" previously (CTh. 3.16.1: see Treggiari 1991b, 464) and another statute, this time of Theodosius II from 449, that gives as justifications for divorce the spouse's conviction of a major crime, adultery, attempted murder of the other, wife beating, and openly consorting with prostitutes (for the husband) and various forms of behavior deemed immoral (for the wife), which perhaps counted as "fault" regarding disposition of the dowry in classical law (C. 5.17.8). Deduction for immoral behavior is separate but would cumulate with those made under the previous category in case of children. When both spouses are at fault, their offenses are offset (Papinian, D. 24.3.39).

As we have seen, the legal rules are presented overall in a fairly gender-neutral fashion, with exceptions mostly regarding the disposition of the dowry. Does this neutrality reflect, more or less accurately, a real equality between the sexes? One might invoke the analogy of social class, in the sense that Roman private law paints a picture of equality and fairness that belies a great measure of unfairness and inequality flourishing beyond the texts (see, e.g., Frier). The law, through its evidently neutral posture, fosters the interests of those with power. Roman divorce law is no different, in that its apparent evenhandedness masks a real imbalance of advantage between the sexes. For example, it was the wife who typically left the matrimonial home in the wake of a divorce (Treggiari 1991b, 437–38). She was more likely to be separated from her children upon divorce than her husband was, and she also might suffer adverse economic consequences in the form of deductions from her dowry (Treggiari 1991b, 466–67). Whether out of recognition of these ill effects, social conditioning in the proper deportment expected of wives in this matter, or a combination of the two, women were less likely to resort to their right to divorce, guaranteed by the law, than were men (see Treggiari 1991a, 46). A woman might be blamed for initiating a divorce, or ascribed some fault if her husband did so (Treggiari 1991a, 41). Older women, even on the level of the upper classes, might experience difficulty finding a new partner despite the fact that remarriage was a social expectation (Treggiari 1991b, 482). One has the sense that if there were winners and losers in Roman divorce, women more often than not found themselves on the losing side. More certain and no less important is the conclusion that the details of the law cannot be assumed to stand as a straightforward reflection of conditions in life.

Rome and Jesus

The extent to which these cultural views and legal rules had an impact upon Jesus or his followers must remain conjectural; we can determine neither whether the Gospel and epistolary statements concerning divorce reflect Roman law or pagan practice or whether the audiences of these texts (especially those connected with Jesus) found themselves divorced from the Roman system or permanently wed to a local Jewish one. Although we cannot make a full distinction between Judaism and Hellenism (all Judaism had become more or less Hellenized in the wake of Alexander the Great), we should not overdraw the connection either. The following comments are not intended to give a full treatment of divorce practices in Jewish society or sources; rather, they provide some additional information by which the Roman material can be understood.

For example, first-century Jewish law, unlike Roman law, permitted polygyny (as the multiply married Herod the Great so well indicates). From the early second century, we have the papyrus remains of a woman named Babatha, who likely was killed in the second revolt against Rome (132–35 CE). Among her legal documents—which attest her appearances before Roman courts—is a notice understood by some scholars to mean that she had sued her co-wife for a share in the deceased husband's estate. Babatha's case also indicates that Jews, a century after Jesus, could avail themselves of Roman courts.

The availability of divorce in both Jewish and Roman contexts provides the setting for the statements attributed to Jesus. The Gospel of Mark (10:2–12), reflecting the instructions in Deuteronomy 24:1–4, records:

> Pharisees came to test [Jesus], asking, "Is it permitted [i.e., lawful] for a man to divorce his wife?" He answered them, "What did Moses command you?" And they said, "Moses permitted a man to write a certificate [*biblion*] of dismissal and to divorce [her]." But Jesus said to them, "For your hardness of heart he wrote for you this commandment. But from the beginning of creation, 'he [i.e., God] made them male and female. For this reason, a man shall leave his father and mother [and be joined to his wife], and the two will become one flesh.' Thus, they are no longer two but one flesh. Therefore, what God has yoked together, let no person separate." Then, in the house the disciples asked him again about this matter. He said to them, "Whoever divorces his wife and marries another commits adultery against her, and if she divorces her husband and marries another, she commits adultery."

In 1 Corinthians 7:10–11, Paul states, "To the married I give this command—not I, but the Lord—that the wife should not separate from her husband. But if she does separate, let her remain unmarried or else be reconciled with her husband, and that the husband should not divorce his wife." Luke 16:18 echoes Mark: "Anyone who divorces his wife and marries another commits adultery, and whoever marries a woman divorced from her husband commits adultery." Finally, Matthew 5:31–32 records Jesus as saying as part of the "antitheses" in the Sermon on the Mount: "It was said, 'Whoever divorces his wife must give her a certificate [of divorce],' but I say to you that every man who divorces his wife—except for a matter of *porneia*— causes her to commit adultery, and whoever marries a divorced woman commits adultery" (see also Matthew 19:3–9, which repeats Mark 10:2–12 but includes the *porneia* clause—usually understood to refer to the wife's unchastity—while not raising the possibility that a woman could divorce her husband).

Most studies of the "historical Jesus," when the subject turns to divorce, ignore the Roman context. Typical are apologetics that insist both that Jewish men were divorcing their wives for the most frivolous of reasons and that Jesus' restrictive pronouncements were designed to protect women financially in cases of divorce. Jewish women, however, had the "certificate," known as a *get*, which was designed precisely to protect them financially in such situations. Rabbi Aqiba is said to have stated that a man could divorce his wife for any reason—"even if he found another prettier than she . . ." [Mishnah, *Gittin* 9:10], and it is to this pronouncement that New Testament scholars compare Jesus' statements. The verse in the Mishnah, however, actually begins with the statement attributed to the School of Shammai: "A man may not divorce his wife unless he has found unchastity in her, for it is written, 'Because he has found in her indecency in anything' [Deuteronomy 24:1]." The Babylonian Talmud (*Sanhedrin* 22a) quotes Rabbi Eliezer in response to Aqiba: "Whoever divorces his first wife, the very altar sheds tears for him" (see also Malachi 2:16).

Most of the evidence about Jewish divorce in the first century involves the elite. Josephus states that Herod's sister Salome sent a certificate of divorce to her husband, Costobarus (*Ant.* 15.259), and he records the separations of Berenice, the daughter of Agrippa I, from Polemo of Cilicia as well as of her sisters Drusilla from Azizus of Emesa and Mariamne from Julius Archelaus (Josephus, *Ant.* 20.143–47). Josephus himself notes that his first wife left him (*Life* 415). According to Ilan (80), the famous Herodias, known best from Gospel stories concerning the execution of John the Baptist, "acted as a fully empowered party in the cancellation of her marriage with Herod the son of Herod and her subsequent marriage to his high-ranking brother, Antipas" (see Josephus, *Ant.* 18.110). Josephus insists that among the Jews, "it is (only) permitted among us to the man" (*Ant.* 15.259) to divorce as a matter of law. Either this statement is not strictly accurate or, at minimum, some female members of the Jewish elite were claiming for themselves a measure of the freedom theoretically conceded Roman women in divorce, though their own law denied them this. Finally, the Gospel of Matthew states that Joseph, "being a righteous man and not wanting to disgrace [Mary], planned to divorce her secretly" (1:19) upon finding her pregnant.

Given the Roman context of the Gospels, several salient points emerge. First, the Gospels must be seen not only in the light of Rabbinic statements (with all the caveats about retrojecting material from these later texts into first-century practices, accounting for limited Rabbinic influence in the Greek-speaking Diaspora, and determining whether the Rabbinic materials are prescriptive or descriptive) but also in light of Rome's relatively liberal rules in the classical period and later official attempts to curtail them. Second, the evidently class-based concerns of Roman marital and divorce practices cannot be overlooked in analyzing the New Testament texts. Third, the Roman materials caution against stereotypes that depict pagan society as at best debauched and that present women as lacking any control over their fate.

Rome and Christianity

In contrast to contemporary Roman and mainstream Jewish practice, Jesus laid down an absolute, or nearly absolute, prohibition of divorce by both sexes, as we have seen. The passages from Matthew contain an exception for a wife's unchastity, while the other texts have a total ban on divorce for men and women. Both positions can be traced in later Christian writings, but there is little doubt that both male and female Christians in antiquity divorced for various reasons (Evans Grubbs 1995, 65, 70, 210). Constantine in 331 was the first emperor to place limits on unilateral divorce, for both sexes but with a bias in favor of males, in a law mentioned above (Codex Theodosianus [CTh.] 3.16.1), but whether he was influenced by Christian teaching in this measure remains controversial (see Evans Grubbs 1995, 225–60; Arjava 1996, 177–89). His law was abrogated three decades later by Julian (Ambrosiaster, *Quaest. Utr. Test.* 115.12 Corpus Scriptorum Ecclesiasticorum Latinorum 50.322) and mitigated (it is unclear if it had ever been explicitly revived) by Honorius and Constantius in 421, again privileging husbands over wives (CTh. 3.16.2; cf. C. 9.9.34[35]). Emperors in the West and East continued to legislate on the subject of unilateral divorce in the fifth century, with the latter taking a less restrictive approach than the former (Evans Grubbs 1995, 232–37; Arjava 1996, 179–82). Finally in the mid–sixth century, Justinian outlawed divorce by mutual consent (Nov. 117.10, in 542), though his successor, Justin II, overturned this measure a few years later, responding, he claims, to popular demand (Nov. 140, in 566).

THE ROMAN SOURCES

For abbreviations of legal sources, see Frier and McGinn, viii–ix.

1. C. 8.38(39).2 (THE EMPEROR ALEXANDER TO MENOPHILUS; 223 CE)

It has for a very long time been a settled point of law that marriages are free. So it is established that agreements forbidding divorce are not valid and stipulations setting a penalty for someone who initiates a divorce are deemed to be without legal force.

2. D. 24.2.4 (ULPIAN IN THE TWENTY-SIXTH BOOK ON SABINUS)

Julian, in the eighteenth book of his *Digests*, raises the issue of whether an insane woman can divorce her husband or be divorced. He writes that such a woman can be divorced, because she is considered to be in the position of a person who does not know of the divorce. Given her mental condition, she cannot, however, divorce her husband, nor can her guardian, though her father can send notice (of divorce). He would not have dealt with divorce in this place, if it were not certain that the marriage would continue. This opinion seems to me correct.

3. CICERO *DE ORATORE* 1.183 (CICERO IN THE FIRST BOOK OF HIS *ON THE PUBLIC SPEAKER*)

In the experience and memory of our fathers' generation it came about that a *paterfamilias*, when he relocated from Spain to Rome, left a pregnant wife back in the province and married another woman in the capital, without sending news (of divorce) back to his first wife. He died without a valid will, leaving a child born from each woman. Was the controversy over a trivial matter, then, when a judicial inquiry was held over the status of two citizens, not only of the boy born from the second woman but also of his mother, who, if the court found that divorce from an earlier wife occurs (only) through some fixed verbal formula and not through the fact of a second marriage, would be reduced to the status of a concubine?

4. D. 24.1.64 (JAVOLENUS IN THE SIXTH BOOK FROM THE *POSTHUMOUS WORKS* BY LABEO)

After a divorce, an (ex-)husband gave his (ex-)wife certain things to persuade her to return to him. The woman returned and then divorced him (again). Labeo: Trebatius gave his opinion in the case of Terentia and Maecenas that if their divorce were a genuine one, the gift was valid, but that if it were feigned, the reverse was true. But the view of Proculus and Caecilius is correct, that a divorce is genuine and a gift made because of it is valid when another marriage has followed or the woman is single for such a long period of time that there would be no doubt that the marriage is <over>. Otherwise, the gift is void.

5. D. 24.2.2 PR.-1, 3 (GAIUS IN THE ELEVENTH BOOK ON THE PROVINCIAL EDICT)

(pr.) The term "(consensual) divorce" arises from a difference in intentions or the fact that those who put an end to their marriage head in different directions. (1) In the case of unilateral divorce, that is, rejection, these phrases are recommended: "Go ahead and take your things," "Go ahead and tend to your business" . . .
(3) It makes no difference if the announcement is made to the spouse personally or through a person who is in his power or in whose power he or she stands.

6. D. 24.2.9 (PAUL IN THE SECOND BOOK *ON ADULTERIES*)

No divorce is valid unless seven adult Roman citizens have been summoned, as well as a freedman of the person initiating the divorce. By "freedman" we will also understand someone manumitted by his father, grandfather, great-grandfather, and other male ascendants or descendants.

7. *PAULI SENTENTIAE* 5.6.15 (PAUL IN THE FIFTH BOOK OF HIS *SENTENCES*)

The deified Emperor Pius prohibited a father from breaking up a happy marriage . . . unless perhaps question should arise as to where the person might with greater advantage reside.

8. D. 24.2.11 PR.-1 (ULPIAN IN THE THIRD BOOK ON THE *LEX IULIA ET PAPIA*)

(pr.) As to where the statute says "let there be no power of accomplishing a divorce for a freedwoman married to her former owner" this is not regarded as rendering the divorce invalid, since marriage tends to be dissolved through the rules of private law. So we cannot state that the marriage continues to exist, because it has come apart. Julian, in fact, writes that the woman is not entitled to sue to recover the dowry. Rightly so, as long as her former owner wants her as his wife, since she has no legal capacity to marry anyone else. For because the lawmaker understood that the marriage would be more or less ended by the freedwoman's act, he removed from her the legal capacity to marry anyone else. So no matter whom she marries, she is regarded as not being married. Julian to be sure goes even further, holding that she cannot even live in concubinage with anyone other than her ex-owner.
(1) The statute says "as long as her former owner wishes her to be his wife." He ought both to want her to be his wife and to retain his legally recognized status as "former owner." So if he loses this status or stops wanting her as wife, the law ceases to apply.
(2) It is settled law, and quite rightly so, that the privilege of this law loses force under any manifestation at all of the ex-owner's intention no longer to keep her as his wife. So if the former owner wants to launch a suit on property wrongly removed against the freedwoman who divorced him against his will, our Emperor, together with his deified father, wrote in a rescript that he no longer wished her to be his wife by virtue of the fact that he raised this suit or any other which usually arises only in connection with a divorce. So if he initiates a prosecution for adultery or accuses her on some other charge, which no one launches against a wife, the marriage is over. For it should be kept in mind that she is deprived of the legal capacity to marry someone else because her ex-owner wants her to be married to him. Therefore whenever there can be even the tiniest perception that he does not want her as wife, it must be held that at this point the freedwoman begins to enjoy the legal capacity to marry someone else. So if the former owner has betrothed himself to another woman, chosen another woman as wife, or pursued marriage with another woman, he

must be deemed not to want the freedwoman as wife. And if he gets a concubine for himself, the same rule must apply.

9. *TITULI EX CORPORE ULPIANI* 6.9–10, 12–13 (*EXCERPTS FROM ULPIAN'S WORK*)

(9) Deductions from a dowry are made either for children, or moral issues, or expenses, or gifts, or wrongful removal of property.

(10) Deduction for children is made if the divorce occurs through the wife's fault or through that of her *paterfamilias*, in which case one-sixth is deducted from the dowry for each child, up to a limit of three, however . . .

(12) Under the heading of more serious moral offenses one-sixth is deducted, while it is one-eighth for lesser ones. Only adultery counts under the first category; everything else falls in the second.

(13) The husband's offenses are punished in the case of a dowry that must be returned on a (specified) day, in the sense that for more serious offenses he returns the dowry immediately, for less serious ones, within six months. In the case of a dowry that should be returned immediately, he is told to return from its fruits as much as the payment made for a dowry returned over three years.

Bibliography

Arjava, Antti. *Women and Law in Late Antiquity.* Oxford: Oxford University Press, 1996.

Bagnall, Roger S., and Bruce W. Frier. *The Demography of Roman Egypt.* Cambridge: Cambridge University Press, 1994.

Collins, Raymond F. *Divorce in the New Testament.* Collegeville, MN: Liturgical Press, 1992.

D'Angelo, Mary Rose. "Remarriage and the Divorce Sayings Attributed to Jesus." Pages 78–106 in *Divorce and Remarriage: Religious and Psychological Perspectives.* Edited by W. P. Roberts. Kansas City, MO: Sheed and Ward, 1990.

Evans Grubbs, Judith. *Law and Family in Late Antiquity: The Emperor Constantine's Marriage Legislation.* Oxford: Oxford University Press, 1995.

Frier, Bruce W. *Landlords and Tenants in Imperial Rome.* Princeton, NJ: Princeton University Press, 1980.

Frier, Bruce W., and T.A.J. McGinn. *A Casebook on Roman Family Law.* New York: Oxford University Press, 2003.

Ilan, Tal. *Jewish Women in Greco-Roman Palestine.* Peabody, MA: Hendrikson, 1996.

McGinn, Thomas A. J. "The Augustan Marriage Legislation and Social Practice: Elite Endogamy versus Male 'Marrying Down.'" Pages 46–93 in *Speculum Iuris: Roman Law as a Reflection of Social and Economic Life in Antiquity.* Edited by J.-J. Aubert and B. Sirks. Ann Arbor: University of Michigan Press, 2002.

———. "Concubinage and the *Lex Iulia* on Adultery." *Transactions of the American Philological Association* 121 (1991): 335–75.

———. *Prostitution, Sexuality, and the Law in Ancient Rome.* New York: Oxford University Press, 1998.

Saller, Richard P. *Patriarchy, Property and Death in the Roman Family.* Cambridge: Cambridge University Press, 1994.

Treggiari, Susan. "Divorce Roman Style: How Easy and How Frequent Was It?" Pages 31–46 in *Marriage, Divorce and Children in Ancient Rome*. Edited by B. Rawson. Oxford: Oxford University Press 1991a.

———. *Roman Marriage: Iusti Coniuges from the Time of Cicero to the Time of Ulpian*. Oxford: Oxford University Press, 1991b.

—20—

Associations in the Ancient World

John S. Kloppenborg

Life in Greek and Roman cities and towns was organized around two centers, the family and the Polis (city). Each had its own structure, each had cultic aspects and religious observances, and each provided its members with senses of identity, honor, and self-determination. But there were restrictions: even during the period of Greek democracy, participation in the civic assembly was restricted to the adult male population. Women, noncitizens, slaves, and former slaves could not participate.

Between the family and Polis there existed a large number of more or less permanent associations or clubs, organized around an extended family, a specific cult, an ethnic group, or a common profession (Poland; Kloppenborg, *Collegia*). Most of these associations had religious dimensions, and most served broadly social goals. Some were extensions of the family, such as the "brotherhoods" (*phratriai*) of many Greek cities, consisting of groups of related families, all worshiping a common ancestor and usually dwelling in the same district. *Phratriai* could own property, including cemeteries, and functioned as corporations, deriving rents from corporate property and disbursing monies to members. While membership in *phratriai* was restricted to the legitimate male descendants of members, in the Roman period we find other family-based (domestic) associations that included most or all of the dependants (slave and free, men and women) of a Roman family. An example of the latter type of Dionysiac association is the 402-member association of Pompeia Agripinnilla, priestess of Dionysos and wife of a Roman senator and ex-consul, M. Gavius Squilla Gallicanus (see McLean).

A second type of association (partly overlapping family-based groups) was formed around a common cult. Religious clubs had been attested in Athens since the time of Solon (early sixth century BCE), who allowed their existence, provided that they did not act against the interests of the state (Gaius, *Digest* 47.22.4). Cultic associations were extremely popular throughout the Hellenistic and Roman periods, with groups dedicated not only to Zeus, Dionysos, Apollo, and other deities of classical Greece but also to a large number of Anatolian, Syrian, and Egyptian gods. In fact, the latter type of associations provided one of the main vehicles by which cults from the East spread into Greece, Macedonia, and Italy.

By the beginning of the Hellenistic period (late fourth century BCE) in the East and slightly later in the West, cities had significant populations of slaves, former slaves, resident aliens, foreign traders and merchants, and other noncitizens. Separated from their families and cities of origin and excluded from the rights of citizens (including participation in the civic assembly), such persons often joined together to form clubs or associations organized either around a common ethnic identity (and normally observing the cult of the gods associated with that identity) or around a common profession or trade. Neighborhood associations also formed, consisting of residents of an *insula* or street. Naturally, there is considerable overlap among these types of associations: ethnic associations also likely observed the cult of national deities, and since resident aliens clustered in one area of a city, their associations also might be neighborhood associations. Similarly, since both trades tended to cluster in a district or on a single street, neighborhood associations sometimes overlapped with trade associations. For example, the association "of the street of the leatherworkers" (e.g., *SEG* XXIX 1183 [no. 6]), which no doubt consisted mainly of leatherworkers, might have had a few non-leatherworker members who happened to live on or near that street. Trade associations were not even restricted to cities and large towns; the synagogue inscription from the small Judaean village of 'En Gedi may attest the existence of a trade association connected with the balsam industry (see Lieberman). Similar associations may have existed in any town in Judah or Galilee where an industry was centered: pottery at Kefar Hananya, stone vessel manufacturing at Reina in Galilee, fishing at Capernaum and Taricheae (Magdala; cf. the first-century CE association of fishermen and fishmongers at Ephesus [*IEphesus* 20]).

What were the benefits of membership? In the late fourth century BCE, associations of resident aliens from Thrace, Egypt, and Cyprus living in Piraeus, the port city of Athens, obtained the right to buy property and to build temples to (respectively) Bendis, Isis, and the Syrian Aphrodite where merchants and other aliens could worship their national deities. But it would be wrong to think that members of such cultic groups (or the other groups discussed in this chapter) participated in these associations for purely "religious" reasons. "Religion" (for which Hebrew, Aramaic, and Greek do not even have special words) was not a separable aspect of culture but was embedded in the two main foci of life: the family and the Polis. Associations, accordingly, did not simply provide cultic "service" but created social obligations, a sense of belonging and purpose, as well as offered very concrete benefits. Since in the ancient world burial was customarily a duty of one's family of origin, resident aliens were at a severe disadvantage. Hence cultic and ethnic associations routinely took on the responsibility of providing burial for deceased members. Some owned cemeteries specifically for this purpose. Associations also provided support for their members, as is explicit in the case of an anonymous Piraean association (*IG* II^2 1275 [no. 1]), which advertised on a stele its commitment to support members financially and otherwise. The same is true of an association of the Great Mother (*IG* II^2 1327 [no. 2]), whose treasurer offered assistance to members. Thus the cultic association combined functions that are now (in the twenty-first century) divided among synagogues and churches, families, social clubs, social service agencies, and perhaps even banks.

Throughout the Hellenistic and Roman periods, we find a plethora of associations formed by resident aliens united in a common trade and pursuing a common cult, for example, a Delian association of "Poseidonist Shippers and Warehousemen from Beirut" (*IDelos* 1774 [no. 3]) or a group of Selgian stonemasons living and working in Rough Cilicia (*TAM* III 197 [no. 4]). It is likely that Jews ("Judaeans") living in the Diaspora and forming *synagogai*, a common term for associations, would be seen as another instance of a group with links to a distant homeland, practicing their ancestral cult (e.g., *MAMA* VI 264 [no. 5]).

Professional or trade associations are attested, covering a wide range of trades, including bakers, bankers, barbers, clothing cleaners, coppersmiths, dyers, fishmongers, fullers, leather tanners, shippers, stonemasons, timber cutters, and wine tasters (see Harland, 28–53). The main function of such trade-related groups was not economic (e.g., to control either the labor market or the commercial markets) but social. Although there are occasional references to political disturbances—for example, a threatened strike by bakers in Ephesus (see Buckler) and riots by silversmiths in Ephesus (Acts 19:24–41)—the main roles of trade associations seem to have been to provide occasions for banqueting and socializing, and to provide burial for deceased members (e.g., *SEG* XXIX 1183 [no. 6]).

The structure of these associations tended to mimic features of the political assembly, with the result that the association was a "city writ small." In Athenian associations, it was common to have a supervisor (*epimeletes*) assisted by a treasurer (*tamias*) and secretary (*grammateus*), and sometimes a priest or priestess, thus imitating the structure of civic government. In Roman associations, the officials usually were called *magistrates*, *curatores*, or *quinquennales*, with funds being managed by *quaestors*, all terms typical of Roman government. Just as civic assemblies regularly voted honors to citizens who had distinguished themselves by acts of benefaction, associations did the same for members who had shown generosity (e.g., *IG* II² 1327 [no. 2]). While associations in general consisted of nonelite persons joined together on the basis of a common cult, ethnicity, profession or locale, they regularly sought highly placed benefactors and patrons, partly to enhance their prestige by association with one of the civic elite, such as Julia Severa (probably a priestess in the imperial cult) (in *MAMA* VI 264 [no. 5]), and partly for protection, since from time to time the activities of associations were viewed by Roman officials with suspicion. Patrons might be actively solicited, honored at banquets, or voted special commemorative plaques or steles with inscriptions advertising their largesse (*CIL* XI 970 [no. 7]; *CIL* XIV 2112 [no. 8]).

The membership profiles of associations varied widely. *Phratriai* consisted, of course, only of male citizens belonging to a group of related families. Professional associations also appear to have been confined mainly to one gender, though persons of various legal statuses (free, former slaves, and slave) might have been members. Thus timber cutters, bankers, and leather-tanning guilds were probably largely or exclusively male. An all-female association of priestesses is known from first-century Egypt (see Kayser, no. 70, pp. 224–26). It has been suggested that Paul's church in Thessalonica might have begun as a gender-exclusive trade association (Ascough, 186–90). Other associations were widely inclusive, consisting of men and women, slave and free (SIG^3 985 [no. 9]), as at least some of Paul's communities were. Patrons might be of either gender as well: the synagogue mentioned above had an influential civic figure, Julia Severa, as a patron (*MAMA* VI 264 [no. 5]); Agrippinilla was the patron of the large Dionysos association; Phoebe is an example of a woman patron of the Pauline assembly at Cenchreae (Romans 16:1–2). Male patrons, of course, are also common (*CIL* XI 970 [no. 7]; *CIL* XIV 2112 [no. 8]).

While a few very large associations are known to have existed, it would appear from extant membership roles that most associations had fewer than sixty members, that is, the number of persons that could comfortably fit into a villa or in the precincts of a Greek or Roman temple. Some domestic associations met in the homes of their patrons and thus are called simply "the freedmen and freedwomen of the home of NN." Others met in the temples of their deities, and some owned buildings of their own.

From time to time, Roman officials expressed concern about associations and several times attempted to suppress them. A *senatusconsultum* from approximately 133 CE quoted in part in *CIL* XIV 2112 (no. 8) limited *collegia* to those devoted only to collecting monies for funerals for their members and restricted the number of meetings to one per month. An examination of the bylaws of this association in Lanuvium indicates, however, that despite the fact that this *collegium* represented itself as complying with the *senatusconsultum*, it also functioned as a banqueting society and met more frequently than once per month. It would appear that many associations could appear to comply with the Senate's restrictions yet continue their association activities as usual. There were also instances of outright suppression. In response to a letter from Pliny, a governor in Bithynia, who requested permission to form an association of firemen (usually a *collegium* dedicated to Silvanus, the god of the woodlands), Trajan replied by forbidding the association, reminding Pliny that associations already had caused disturbances in the area and arguing that "whatever name we give them, and for whatever purpose, people who meet together sooner or later will become a political association" (Pliny, *Letters* 10.33–34).

Groups of the early Jesus movement in Asia Minor caused the same type of alarm among Roman officials (including Pliny), who were concerned about the existence of antisocial and potentially subversive clandestine associations (see Wilken, as well as the contribution in this volume by Bradley Peper and Mark DelCogliano). Pliny, who examined members of one Christian group in Bithynia that met before dawn to chant hymns and later for a meal, assured Trajan that what he had found was merely a "depraved, excessive superstition" (Pliny, *Letters* 10.96–97) rather than a clandestine conspiracy that was genuinely dangerous to the Roman order. But we might expect that in other locales, in other historical situations, the activities of Jesus groups—meetings, private meals, baptism, strong solidarity, and the disruptions to other groups caused by conversion—would have been looked on with far greater concern and might have provoked outright hostility.

In spite of periodic attempts to suppress associations, they are attested widely from Egypt to Roman Britain, and from North Africa to Dacia and the frontiers of the Rhein, and in all historical periods from the early Hellenistic to the late Roman periods. Their appeal derived in part from the fact that they offered nonelite persons some sense of the self-determination, dignity, and honor that they lacked due to their estate and their exclusion from the political process, and in part from the concrete benefits (burial, conviviality, loans, protection) that these associations conferred. For the elite, too, participation in association life afforded opportunities to demonstrate largesse (and therefore gain honor) and to acquire groups of loyal supporters.

Associations and the Jesus Movement

Would Jesus have been familiar with associations? Although we do not have any direct documentation concerning associations in the region of the Kinneret (Sea of Galilee), the fact that it was renowned for its fishing industry raises the strong possibility that there were associations of fishermen, just as are attested at Joppa (*CIJ* II 945; II CE) and Ephesus in a series of inscriptions (*IEphesus* Ia 20; 54–59 CE; *IEphesus* V 1503; II CE). Luke's account of the call of the fishermen (Luke 5:1–11) pictures two boats working together, one with Simon Peter and the other with the son of Zebedee, his "partners" (*metochoi*, v. 7) and cooperative members (*koinonoi*, v. 10), terms used for members of trade associations. The choice of this term might reflect that Luke, who almost certainly did not write his Gospel in Palestine, was aware of trade associations and pictured Jesus' original disciples as belonging to such an association. On the other hand, it is a priori likely that such associations existed on the western shore of the Kinneret, functioning to regulate the trade and especially to collect and pay fishing taxes (as they did in Ephesus).

It is not necessary to conclude that these Galilean fishermen owned their own boats; just as in other industries of the Hellenistic and early Roman periods, equipment and tools might be leased from owners for use by guild members, who in turn hired seasonal labor to assist with various tasks (see Mark's reference [1:20] to the "hired help" in the boat with the Zebedee brothers; see Hanson, as well as Jonathan Reed's chapter in this volume). The supposition that Simon and his partners owned their boats often has been taken to imply that at least the core members of the Jesus movement were persons of means. But this is hardly a secure assumption. They merely may have leased fishing rights from a wealthier agent, along with the tools of their trade.

We should not think of trade associations on the model of modern labor unions. Ancient trade associations held very little power to bargain for working conditions, and strikes were very rare. The main functions were to facilitate the payment of certain taxes and especially to provide social opportunities and a sense of belonging. In this sense, we should not think of Jesus' call in Mark 1:16–20 as a call of four individual laborers, but rather as a call of persons already embedded in an extrafamilial association, invited to join another, rather less secure and stable group, to "fish for humans."

The connections between associations and the groups of the Jesus movement that formed in the cities of Syria, Egypt, Asia, Greece, and Italy are even stronger. These "churches" would no doubt have been seen by others as cultic associations dedicated to an Eastern deity. Like many other cultic and domestic associations, the Jesus groups (at least in Corinth, Philippi, Ephesus, and Rome) included men and women, and the evidence from Corinth indicates that a fairly wide social spectrum was included, from the wealthy, such as Phoebe (Romans 16:1–2) and Erastus (Romans 16:23), to house owners, such as Stephanos (1 Corinthians 16:15), to persons of lower social status, even slaves, and probably freedmen/women (cf. SIG^3 985 [no. 9]). Like other such cultic associations, the Jesus groups met weekly or monthly, and they ate a sacred meal together. It was in fact the wide differences in social status that accounts for some of the internal tensions within the Jesus groups when they ate together, since it was typically at banquets that social inequalities could become most obvious (see 1 Corinthians 11).

Paul's advice in 1 Corinthians 6 that the Corinthian Christians settle legal disputes internally, within the community, reflects a common practice for an association to arbitrate members' disputes rather than allowing them to go to secular courts (e.g., Papyrus London VII 2193; IG II^2 1368). In fact, association members who insisted on going outside the society sometimes were fined (see Kloppenborg, "Egalitarianism"). Although Mediterranean society was in general agonistic and expected conflict (in particular between males), the Jesus groups and other associations tried to foster more cooperative models of social exchange. Matthew's advice to his group in Matthew 18 and Luke's depiction of the ideal behavior of wealthy Christians suggest a model where more privileged members take special care for the "little ones," just as the Piraean association in IG II^2 1275 (no. 1) prided itself in its assistance to members, and just as the association of the Great Mother (IG II^2 1327 [no. 2]) recognized the benefactions of its treasurer to poorer members. Largesse, after all, was one of the ways in which the Mediterranean elite gained honor in the eyes of others.

In some respects the Jesus groups would have resembled domestic associations, which probably met for the most part in the houses of their patrons (e.g., SIG^3 985 [no. 9]). The more established cultic associations of Isis, Bendis, Sarapis, Men, and the Great Mother, which had been in existence in the Eastern empire for generations, even centuries before the Common Era, already had built temples. As the Jesus groups established themselves, they eventually converted domestic residences for exclusively cultic use (as other groups had done earlier) and by the fourth century were erecting their own buildings for cultic purposes. The first-century Jesus groups, because they were still small in membership, also no doubt kept a much lower civic profile than the more established Eastern cultic groups. We have no evidence of the Jesus groups conducting public parades or festivals, as did the older Bendis group in Athens or the Isis devotees of Corinth. The relative civic invisibility of the Jesus groups was probably a strategy of self-protection. In a xenophobic society, it was safer to be inconspicuous, as Paul seems to recommend in 1 Thessalonians 4.

But one feature especially seems to have marked the Jesus groups: the use of fictive kinship language. Although we find occasional use of brother/sister language for members in Mithraic associations and those of Jupiter Dolichenus, Dionysos Liber, and Bellona, and very occasionally in domestic and professional clubs, the density of such language is overwhelming in the Jesus groups: Paul uses *adelphos* (brother) 20 times in 1 Thessalonians and 119 times in the undisputed letters. Moreover, slaves such as Onesimos were includes as "brothers," something that would have been quite unusual even in those societies that referred to other members as brothers or sisters (Kloppenborg, "Egalitarianism"). The effect of the use of fictive family language in the Jesus groups is not to be underestimated. While in the twenty-first century such language is commonly used among persons who are not kin, and kinship bonds are in fact often very weak, in the first century it was the reverse: kinship language was largely restricted to blood (and adoptive) relations, and the obligations imposed by kinship (for defense, support, burial, and other forms of solidarity) were very strong. Thus for the Jesus groups to extend kinship language to themselves implied sharply heightened social obligation. This strong sense of belonging was perhaps one of their appeals.

TEXTS

1. *IG* II² 1275: OBLIGATIONS OF THE MEMBERS OF A *THIASOS*

[Provenance: Piraeus (Attica); date: 325–275 bce; published: Johannes Kirchner et al., eds. 1913–40. Inscriptiones Graecae II, III. Berlin: Walter de Gruyter. No. 1275.]

[. . .] and if a member [. . .] [. . . .] [. . . .] of the members of the association [. . .] and if any of them should die[. . .] or a son or a . . . or a father or whoever is his closest relative in the association, and they shall attend the cortège—both the members and all the friends. And if a member should be wronged, they and all the friends shall come to his assistance, so that everyone might know that we show piety to the gods and to our friends. To those who do these things, (may) many blessings come upon them, their descendants and their ancestors. When the association members have ratified this law, let there be nothing to take precedence over it. And if a member should either speak or act in contravention of the law, an accusation against him may be lodged by any of the members who so wishes; and if he convicts him, let the members assess the penalty, whatever seems appropriate to the association.

2. IG II² 1327: HONORS FOR THE TREASURER OF AN ASSOCIATION OF THE GREAT MOTHER

[Provenance: Piraeus (Attica); Date: 178/77 BCE; published: Johannes Kirchner et al., eds. 1913–40. Inscriptiones Graecae II, III. Berlin: Walter de Gruyter. No. 1327.]

Gods!

During the archonship of Philon, in the month of Mounichion, in sovereign assembly, for good fortune, Euktemos son of Eumaridos, of the Steirian deme, made the motion: Whereas Hermes son of Hermogenes of the Paionidaian deme, having been treasurer for many years has continually acted piously towards the gods and proved himself generous both to the general membership and to the individual members, putting himself at the disposal of each, and (being) both eager that the appropriate sacrifices to the gods be made and paying for these frequently, generously, often from his own resources, and also for some who had died, when the association had no money, he paid for the tomb so that they might be treated decently even in death, and (he) made expenditures for repairs and he was the one who organized the original collection of the common fund, and he continually talks about and advises what is best and in all things shows himself to be high minded. For good fortune, it seemed good to the members to commend Hermes son of Hermogenes of the deme Paionides, and to crown him on account of the excellence which he has shown to the gods and, collectively to the membership, in order that there might be a rivalry among the rest who aspire to honor knowing that they will receive thanks benefiting those who are benefactors of the association of *orgeones* [sacrificing associates]. And let there be set up an image of him with a plaque in the temple and let it be crowned at every sacrifice. And let the supervisors inscribe this decree on a stone stele and set it up in the Metroon [the temple of Cybele in Athens]. And the cost of both the plaque and the stele is to be shared by the fellowship.

While the following were supervisors: Neonos, of the deme Cholargos, Simon, of the deme Porios, Ergasionos, [. . .]

3. *IDELOS* 1774: POSEIDONIASTAI OF BERYTOS

[Provenance: Delos; date: after 88 bce; published: Félix Durrbach et al. 1926–73. Inscriptions de Délos. 7 vols. Paris: Librairie ancienne Honoré Champion. No. 1774.]

The association (*koinon*) of Berytian Poseidoniastai Merchants and Shippers and Warehousemen dedicated (this) headquarters (*oikos*) and its portico and storehouses to the gods of the homeland.

4. *TAM* III 197: TOMB BELONGING TO AN ASSOCIATION OF SELGIAN STONEMASONS IN CILICIA

[Provenance: Direvli Kalesi (Western Rough Cilicia); date: mid–first century CE; published: George E. Bean and Terence Bruce Mitford. 1970. Journeys in Rough Cilicia, 1964–68. Vol. 3 of Tituli Asiae Minoris, Ergänzungsband. Denkschriften der Österreichen Akademie der Wissenschaften, Phil.-hist. Klasse, vol. 102. Wien, Graz, and Köln: Hermann Böhlaus. No. 197, p. 178.] Face A

Kendeas and Kallimachos, both from Selge, made this.

Face B

(The tomb) of Konbeis and Askos son of Alaikos and Teteskas son of Thes, and Gisnes and Narouras son of Kyes and Roundas and Helais and Kdotailis the younger and Oramis. The tomb belongs to the *koinon* (association). Let no one else bury a body in it. If someone does, let them pay to the *koinon* 100 denarii. Let no one sell his share (in the tomb).

5. *MAMA* VI 264: A SYNAGOGUE BUILT BY A ROMAN PRIESTESS AND RESTORED BY TWO SYNAGOGUE PRESIDENTS

[Provenance: Ercis, near Akmonia (Phrygia); date: late first century CE; published: William M. Calder, Ernst Herzfeld, Samuel Guyer, and C.W.M. Cox, eds. 1928–93. Monumenta Asiae Minoris antiqua. American Society for Archaeological Research in Asia Minor Publications. 10 vols. London: Manchester University Press. Vol. 6, no. 264.]

The *oikos* built by Julia Severa was restored by P(ublius) Tyrronius Kladus, *archisynagogos* [synagogue president] for life, and Lucius son of Lucius, *archisynagogos*, and Popilius Zotikos, *archon* [ruler], from their own resources and the money deposited (by the community?). And they had the walls and ceiling decorated and they had shutters made for the windows and (are responsible for) all other ornamentation. For their excellent conduct, goodwill and diligence shown to the congregation, the congregation honors them with a shield overlaid with gold.

6. *SEG* XXIX 1183: TOMB BELONGING TO A NEIGHBORHOOD GUILD OF
LEATHERWORKERS

*[Provenance: Saittai [Içikler] (Lydia); date: 147/48 CE; published: Supplementum
Epigraphicum Graecum XXIX no. 1183.]*

Year 232, 3rd day of Audnaios. The *synodos* of (the street of the) leatherworkers honored Primus son of Mousaios, who lived 57 years.

7. *CIL* XI 970: MOTION OF AN ASSOCIATION ELECTING A PATRON

*[Provenance: Regium Lepidum (Italy); date: 190 CE; published: Corpus Inscriptionum
Latinarum. 1863–1974. Berlin: G. Reimer. Vol. 11, no. 970.]*

During the sixth consulship of the Emperor Caesar Marcus Aurelius Commodus Antoninus Augustus Pius Felix, and when Marcus Petronius Septimi-
anus was also consul, March 23, in the temple of the Association of Laborers
and Rag dealers of Regium; whereas, in accord with the proposal of the treasurers, P(ublius) Saenius Marcellinus and G(aius) Aufidius Dialogus, it has
been stated that Tutilius Julianus, a generous man distinguished for his manner of life, his unassuming conduct, and his natural modesty, should be
adopted by our association as its patron, so that the evidence of our decision
might serve as an example to other [prospective benefactors]. Concerning
what is to be done in this matter, they resolved as follows: We hold, one and
all, that this honorable proposal has been made by the treasurer and masters of
our association with good counsel; that therefore apologies should certainly be
made to the honorable gentleman Julianus for the unavoidable delay in this
consideration of ours; that he should be asked to undertake, if he please, the
function of patron of our society; and that a bronze tablet inscribed with this
resolution should be placed in his house. Adopted.

8. *CIL* XIV 2112: STATUTES OF AN ASSOCIATION IN LANUVIUM

*[Provenance: Lanuvium, Italy; date: 136 ce; published: Corpus Inscriptionum
Latinarum. 1863–1974. Berlin: G. Reimer. Vol. 14, no. 2112.]*

During the consulship of L(ucius) Ceionius Commodus and Sex(tus) Vet-
tulenus Civica Pompeianus, 5 days before the Ides of June [June 9], at Lanuvium in the temple of Antinoüs in which L(ucius) Caesennius Rufus, patron
of the town, had ordered that a meeting be called through L(ucius) Pompeius
[. . .]us, *quinquennalis* [president for a five-year term] of the devotees of Diana
and Antinoüs, he promised that he would give them [. . .] out of his generosity
the interest on 15,000 sesterces, namely, 400 sesterces, on the birthday of Di-

ana on the Ides of August [August 13], and 400 sesterces on the birthday of Antinoüs, 5 days before the Kalends of December [November 27]; and he instructed the bylaws established by them to be inscribed on the inner side of the porch [of the temple] of Antinoüs as recorded below.

During the consulship of Marcus Antonius Hiberus and Publius Mummius Sisenna on the Kalends of January [January 1, 133 CE], the Benevolent Association of Diana [. . .] and Antinoüs was founded, L(ucius) Caesennius Rufus son of Lucius of the Quirine tribe, being the sole magistrate for the third time and also patron.

A Clause from the **Senatusconsultum** *of the Roman People:*

These are permitted to assemble, convene, and maintain a society: those who desire to make monthly contributions for funerals may assemble in such a society, but they may not assemble in the name of such a society except once a month for the sake of making contributions to provide burial for the dead.

May this be propitious, happy and salutary to Emperor Caesar Trajanus Hadrianus Augustus and the entire Augustan house, to us, to ours, and to our association, and may we have made proper and careful arrangements for providing the proper honors for the dead! Therefore we must all agree to contribute faithfully, so that our society may be able to continue in existence a long time. You, who wish to join this association as a new member, should first read the bylaws carefully before entering, so as not to find cause for complaint later or bequeath a lawsuit to your heir.

Bylaws of the Association

[1] It was voted unanimously that whoever wants to enter this society shall pay an initiation fee of 100 sesterces and an amphora of good wine, and shall pay monthly dues of five asses.

[2] It was voted further that if someone has not paid dues for six consecutive months and he should die, his claim to a funeral shall not be considered, even if he has provided for it in his will. It was further voted that at the death of a paid-up member of our corporation there will be due him 300 sesterces from the treasury, from which sum will be deducted a funeral fee of fifty sesterces, to be distributed at the pyre [among those attending]; the honors, furthermore, will be performed on foot.

[3] It was further voted that if a member dies farther than 20 miles from town and the association is notified, three men chosen from our corporation will be required to go there to make arrangements for his funeral; they will be required to render an account in good faith to the membership, and if they are found guilty of any fraud they shall pay a fourfold fine; they will be given money for the funeral expenses, and in addition a return trip travel allowance of 20 sesterces each. But if a member dies farther than 20 miles from town and

notification is impossible, then his funeral expenses, less emoluments and funeral fee, may be claimed from this society, in accordance with the bylaws of the society, by the man who buries him, if he so attests by an affidavit signed with the seals of seven Roman citizens, and the matter is approved, and he gives security against anyone's claiming any further sum. Let there be no ill will. And no patron or patroness, master or mistress, or creditor shall have any right of claim against the society unless he has been named heir in a will. If a member dies intestate, the details of his burial will be decided by the *quiquennalis* and the membership.

[4] It was voted further that if a slave member of this association dies and his master or mistress unreasonably refuses to relinquish the body for burial, and he has not left written instructions, a symbolic funeral ceremony will be held.

[5] It was further voted that if any member takes his own life for any reason whatever, his claim to burial shall not be considered.

[6] It was voted further that if any slave becomes free, he shall be required to contribute one amphora of good wine.

[7] It was voted further that if any president, in the year when it is his turn in the membership list to provide dinner, fails to comply and provide a dinner, he shall pay 30 sesterces to the treasury; the next man on the list shall give the dinner, and he [the delinquent] shall be required to reciprocate when it is the latter's turn.

[8] Schedule of dinners: 8 days before the Ides of March [March 8]: the birthday of Caesennius [. . .] his father; 5 days before the Kalends of December [November 27]: birthday of Antinoüs; Ides of August [August 13]: the birthday of Diana and of the association; 13 days before the Kalends [of September][August 20]: the birthday of Caesennius Silvanus, his brother [. . .]: the birthday of Cornelia Procula, his mother; 19 days before the Kalends of January [December 14]: the birthday of Caesennius Rufus, patron of the town.

[9] Presidents of the dinner in the order of the membership list, appointed four at a time in turn, shall be required to provide one amphora of good wine each, and for as many members as the society has, bread costing two asses, four sardines, a setting, and warm water with service.

[10] It was voted further that any member who becomes *quinquennalis* in this association shall be exempt from such obligations for the term that he is *quinquennalis*, and that he shall receive a double share in all distributions.

[11] It was further voted that the secretary and the messenger shall be exempt from such obligations and shall receive one and one half shares of every distribution.

[12] It was voted further that any member who has administered the office of *quinquennalis* honestly shall [thereafter] receive one and one half shares of everything as a mark of honor, so that other *quinquennales* will also hope for the same by properly discharging their duties.

[13] It was voted further that if any member wants to make any complaint or bring up business, he is to raise it at a business meeting, so that we may banquet in peace and good cheer on festive days.

[14] It was further voted that any member who moves from one place to another so as to cause a disturbance shall be fined four sesterces. Any member, moreover, who speaks abusively of another or causes uproar shall be fined twelve sesterces. Any member who uses any abusive or insolent language to a *quinquennalis* at a banquet shall be fined twenty sesterces.

[15] It was further voted that on the festal days of his term of office each *quinquennalis* is to conduct worship with incense and wine and is to perform his other functions dressed in white, and that on the birthdays of Diana and Antinoüs he is to provide oil for the society in the public bath before the dinner.

9. *SIG*³ 985: PRESCRIPTIONS OF A (HOUSE?) ASSOCIATION OF ZEUS

[Provenance: Philadelphia (Lydia); date: first century BCE; *published: Wilhelm Dittenberger. 1915–24.* Sylloge Inscriptionum Graecarum. *3rd ed. Leipzig: S. Hirzel. No. 985.]*

For good fortune!
For health and common salvation and the finest reputation the ordinances given to Dionysius in his sleep were written up giving access into his house (*oikos*) to men and women, free people and slaves. For in this place have been set up altars of Zeus Eumenes, and of Hestia his coadjutor, and of the other savior gods, and Eudaimonia, Plutus, Arete, Hygeia, Agathe Tyche, Agathos Daimon, Mneme, the Charitae and Nike. To this man Zeus has given ordinances for the performance of the purifications, the cleansings and the mysteries, in accordance with the ancestral custom and as has now been written. When coming into this *oikos* let men and women, free people and slaves, swear by all the gods neither to know nor make use intentionally of any deceit against a man or a woman, neither poison harmful to men nor harmful spells. They are not themselves to make use of a love potion, abortifacient, contraceptive, or any other thing fatal to children; nor are they to recommend it to, nor connive at it with, another. They are not to refrain in any respect from being well intentioned toward this *oikos*. If anyone performs or plots any of these things, they are neither to put up with it nor keep silent, but expose it and defend themselves. Apart from his own wife, a man is not to have relations with

another married woman, whether free or slave, nor with a boy nor a virgin girl; nor shall he recommend it to another. Should he connive at it with someone, they shall expose such a person, both the man and the woman, and not conceal it or keep silent about it. Woman and man, whoever does any of the things written above, let them not enter this *oikos*. For the gods set up in it are great: they watch over these things and will not tolerate those who transgress the ordinances. A free woman is to be chaste and shall not know the bed of, nor have intercourse with, another man except her own husband. But if she does have such knowledge, such a woman is not chaste, but defiled and full of endemic pollution, and unworthy to reverence this god whose holy things these are that have been set up. She is not to be present at the sacrifices, not to strike against (?) the purifications and cleansings (?), nor to see the mysteries being performed. But if she does any of these things from the time the ordinances have come on to this inscription, she shall have evil curses from the gods for disregarding these ordinances. For the god does not desire these things to happen at all, nor does he wish it, but he wants obedience. The gods will be gracious to those who obey, and always give them all good things, whatever gods give to men whom they love. But should any transgress, they shall hate such people and inflict upon them great punishments. These ordinances were placed with Agdistis [i.e., the temple to the Phrygian mother-goddess], the very holy guardian and mistress of this *oikos*. May she create good thoughts in men and women, free people and slaves, in order that they may obey the things written here. At the sacrifices, both the monthly and annual ones, may they—as many men and women who have confidence in themselves—touch this stone on which the ordinances of the god have been written, in order that those who obey these ordinances and those who disobey them may be evident. Savior Zeus, accept the touch of Dionysius mercifully and kindly, and be well disposed toward him and his family. Provide good recompenses, health, salvation, peace, safety on land and sea . . . [————] [—] likewise . . . [—.]

10. *CIL* III 924: NOTICE OF THE DISSOLUTION OF A COLLEGIUM

[Provenance: Albernus Major (Dacia); date: 167 ce; published: **Corpus Inscriptionum Latinarum.** *1863–1974. Berlin: G. Reimer. Vol. 3, no. 1. pp. 924–27.]*

Authenticated copy made from a notice that was posted at Alburnus Maior near the office of Resculum and in which was written the following: Artemidorus son of Apollonius, president of the association of Jupiter Cernenus, and Valerius son of Nico, and Offas son of Menofilus, treasurers of the same association, by the posting of this notification publicly attest that: of the fifty-four members that used to constitute the above-named association, there remain now in Alburnus no more than seventeen; that even Julius son of Julius, the co-president, has not come to Alburnus or to a meeting of the association since his election as (co-)president; that (Artemidorus) has rendered an account to those who were present of what he had of theirs and was returning and (what he had spent) on funerals; that he had recovered the security he had posted for these sums; that now there were insufficient funds for any more funerals, nor did he have a single coffin; that no one had been willing to attend meetings on the days required by the bylaws (of the society) or to contribute funeral services or fees; and that they (the remaining officers) accordingly publicly attest by this notice that no member should suppose that, should he die, he belongs to an association or that he shall be able to make any request of them for a funeral.

Issued at Alburnus Maior, Feburary 9, during the year that Emperor Lucius Aurelius Verus was consul for the third time and that Quadratus was (co-)consul. Issued at Alburnus Maior. (Seals) of Lucius Vasidius Victor, Gaius Secundinus Legitimus, Stertinus Rusticus, Aelius Plator, [. . .]. Geldon, Ulpius Felix, September Plator.

Bibliography

Ascough, Richard S. *Paul's Macedonian Associations: The Social Context of Philippians and 1 Thessalonians*. Wissenschlaftliche Untersuchungen zum Neuen Testament 2/161. Tübingen: J.C.B. Mohr (Paul Siebeck), 2003.

Barton, Stephen, and G.H.R. Horsley. "A Hellenistic Cult Group and the New Testament Churches." *Jahrbuch für Antike und Christentum* 24 (1981): 7–41.

Buckler, William H. "Labour Disputes in the Province of Asia." Pages 27–50 in *Anatolian Studies, Presented to Sir William Mitchell Ramsay*. Edited by W. H. Buckler and W. M. Calder. Manchester: Manchester University Press, 1923.

Hanson, K. C. "The Galilean Fishing Economy and the Jesus Tradition." *Biblical Theology Bulletin* 27 (1997): 99–111.

Harland, Philip. *Associations, Synagogues and Congregations: Claiming a Place in Ancient Mediterranean Society*. Minneapolis, MN: Fortress Press, 2003.

Kayser, François. *Recueil des inscriptions grecques et latines (non funéraires) d'Alexandrie Impériale (Ier-IIIer s. apr. J.-C.)*. Bibliothèque d'etude 108. Cairo: Institut français d'archéologie orientale du Caire, 1994.

Kloppenborg, John S. "Collegia and Thiasoi: Issues in Function, Taxonomy and Membership." Pages 16–30 in *Voluntary Associations in the Graeco-Roman World*. Edited by John S. Kloppenborg and Stephen G. Wilson. London: Routledge, 1996.

———. "Egalitarianism in the Myth and Rhetoric of Pauline Churches." Pages 247–63 in *Reimagining Christian Origins: A Colloquium Honoring Burton L. Mack*. Edited by Elizabeth A. Castelli and Hal Taussig. Valley Forge, PA: Trinity Press International, 1996.

Lieberman, Saul. "A Preliminary Remark to the Inscription of 'En Gedi." *Tarbiz* 40 (1970): 24–26 (in Hebrew).

McLean, Bradley H. "The Agrippinilla Inscription: Religious Associations and Early Christian Formation." Pages 239–70 in *Origins and Method: Towards a New Understanding of Judaism and Christianity: Essays in Honour of John C. Hurd*. Edited by B. H. McLean.

Journal for the Study of the New Testament Supplements 86. Sheffield, England: JSOT Press, 1993.

Poland, Franz. *Geschichte des griechischen Vereinswesens.* Leipzig: B. G. Teubner, 1909.

Wilken, Robert L. *The Christians as the Romans Saw Them.* New Haven, CT: Yale University Press, 1984.

— 21 —

Anointing Traditions

Teresa J. Hornsby

The account of Jesus' anointing is one of the few events recorded by all four Evangelists (Matthew 26:6–13; Mark 14:3–9; Luke 7:36–50; John 12:1–8). Although the Gospels agree in basic details, such as Jesus' being anointed by a woman in the presence of others, they are inconsistent about where, with whom, how, and why the anointing happens. Matthew's, Mark's, and John's anointings take place in Bethany, whereas the Lucan scene appears set somewhere in Galilee. Matthew, Mark, and Luke place the event in the home of Simon, and John tells us it is in the home of Lazarus. John names "Mary" as the anointer, Luke identifies the unnamed woman as "from the city" and as a "sinner"; Matthew and Mark leave her nameless and otherwise unidentified. The host, Simon, is a leper in Matthew's and Mark's versions, but he is a Pharisee according to Luke, and according to John he is Lazarus, a man Jesus recently raised from the dead. According to John and Luke, the woman anointed Jesus' feet; according to Matthew and Mark, she anointed his head. Matthew, Mark, and John all associate the anointing with Jesus' death and burial; Luke uses the story to comment on hospitality and forgiveness.

As we look at other anointings that occur in literature roughly contemporary with the Gospels, it becomes apparent that Jesus' anointing has its familiar circumstances and its unique ones. My concern is here, primarily, with the anointings in Luke and John; to the numerous students who read the Gospels and conclude, "That's what all the women did with their hair things back then," the evidence suggests rather something unexpected has occurred between Jesus and the anointing woman.

Anointing in the LXX and the New Testament

The Septuagint records various types of anointing. It uses the term *christō* (Hebrew: *mashach*) exclusively to denote a ceremonial anointing, such as the ritual installation of kings and priests (see, e.g., Exodus 28:41; 29:36; Judges 9:8; 1 Samuel 9:16; 15:1). I have located no other example where a kiss is a part of the anointing ceremony of a king or priest; Samuel's kiss is not a strong evocation of the woman sinner in Luke 7:38 who kisses Jesus.

> Samuel took a vial of oil and poured it on his head, and kissed him. (1 Samuel 10:1)

> She stood behind him at his feet, weeping, and began to bathe his feet with her tears and to dry them with her hair. Then she continued kissing his feet and anointing them with the ointment. (Luke 7:38)

Of the Evangelists, only Luke uses *christō* for "anoint," but the context is not the woman's ministrations to Jesus. Rather, it is Jesus' quotation from Isaiah in the Nazareth synagogue: "The spirit of the Lord is upon me because he has anointed me to bring good news to the poor" (Luke 4:18).

The words *aleiphō* and *murizo*, which appear in Luke 7, can be used for anointing kings and priests, but they also are used for the anointing that one performs to adorn oneself, to soothe tired feet, to heal, or to mask offensive odors. Such anointing is a gift or favor a host would graciously provide a guest; it is also the responsibility of a slave to his or her master. The action could thus be compared to the washing of feet, such as found in Genesis 18:4 (Abraham), Genesis 19:2 (Lot), 1 Samuel 25:41 (Abigail), and John 13 (Jesus), as well as in the *Odyssey* and throughout Greek and Roman literature.

For example, Naomi tells Ruth to wash and anoint herself (*aleiphō*) for Boaz (Ruth 3:3 LXX; Hebrew *such*). On the other hand, a person mourning eschews being anointed. Daniel is in mourning for three weeks; during this time, he does not eat rich food, eat meat, drink wine, or anoint (*aleiphō*) himself (Daniel 10:3). Likewise, in 2 Samuel 14:2, Joab tells a woman to pretend to be mourning: "Do not anoint yourself with oil, but behave like a woman who has been mourning many days for the dead." However, Matthew 6:17 states that those who fast should anoint (*aleiphō*) themselves with oil. Mark 6:13 and James 4:14 use *aleiphō* to describe the anointing of the sick. Anointing (*aleiphō*) seems to signify good health and happiness, and its lack suggests sickness, sadness, and death.

Murizo is similar to *aleiphō* but emphasizes the use of fragrant oil; it may thus be translated "pour perfume" rather than "anoint." This term is absent from the LXX, and in the New Testament it appears only in Mark 14:8: after the woman "pours" (*katacheō*) expensive oil on Jesus' head, he proclaims that she has "anointed" (*murisai*) his body for the tomb (14:8).

Anointing and Feet in Greek and Roman Writings

Homer

In the *Odyssey* (19.385–402), Odysseus, disguised as a beggar, returns to his home. His wife, Penelope, asks an old servant woman, Eurycleia, to bathe and anoint the man's body with oil. As she washes (*niptō*) him, she discovers a scar that unmistakably identifies the man as Odysseus (see MacDonald). Striking about Homer's anointing account is the theme of recognition, which finds faint echoes in Matthew and Mark, where the woman recognizes Jesus' kingly role and tragic fate (Matthew 26:12; Mark 14:8). The old woman's response to Odysseus is reminiscent of the anointing woman in Luke: overcome with emotion, she weeps. She is also like Thomas, who according to John 20:27 recognizes Jesus because of his scars (see MacDonald).

Petronius

One of the most intriguing details about the Lucan and Johannine accounts is that the woman uses her hair to wipe the excess ointment from Jesus' feet. This detail is without parallel in literature contemporary to or preceding the Gospels. Petronius's *Satyricon* may be the only other attestation combining a banquet, anointing, and long hair. This satire, written by Nero's *arbiter elagantia*—adviser on all things fabulous—was composed in Latin in 61 CE. Only fragments remain. The longest fragment, "The Cena," describes the lead character, Trimalchio, who invites all types of men to an excellent banquet:

> I am ashamed to tell you what followed: in defiance of all convention, some long-haired boys brought ointment in a silver basin, and anointed our feet as we lay, after winding little garlands round our feet and ankles. (69)

We might conclude that the Lucan and Johannine women similarly acted "in defiance of all convention." Whether the Lucan scene is meant to convey, or disrupt, erotic connotations remains debated.

Clement of Alexandria

Clement's reference to anointing suggests a concern about whether or not the anointing was "useful." Clement uses Jesus' praise for the woman to defend limited—that is, not excessive—use of scents and perfumes.

> Yet, let us not develop a fear of perfume. Let the women make use of a little of these perfumes, but not so much as to nauseate their husbands, for too much fragrance suggests a funeral. . . . Since we make no allowance for pleasure not connected with a necessity of life, surely let us also make distinctions here and choose only what is useful. There are perfumes that are neither soporific nor erotic, suggestive neither of sexual relations nor of immodest harlotry, but wholesome and chaste and refreshing to the mind that is tired and invigorating to the appetite.
>
> A luxury without a useful purpose gives grounds for the charge of being sensual in character, and is a drug to excite the passions. But it is entirely different to rub oneself with oil out of necessity [as opposed to being anointed for pleasure]. The one makes a man womanish but to anoint out of necessity is the better.

Clement believes that an anointing that goes beyond necessity invites slander and may lead to sexual arousal. He does not appear to see—or, more to the point, he does not want to see—the anointing of Jesus as excessive, or at least as pleasurable.

Josephus

Flavius Josephus, a first-century Jewish historian, gives numerous accounts of anointings in his *Antiquities of the Jews* and one account in *Jewish Wars*. All save one reference in the *Antiquities* describe the anointing of priests and royalty: Aaron (3.8.3), Saul (6.5.4), Solomon (7.14.5, 10), Jehu (9.6.1, 2), and Esther (11.6.2). For the accounts of kings, priests pour the oil over the head of the designate. Queen Esther is anointed by eunuchs, and whereas Josephus hints that Esther's is a royal anointing, the Septuagint indicates that it is purely cosmetic (Esther 2:9). The singular account of an ordination not involving priests or kings is in reference to Caius, a man who is seeking an alibi for a murder he has committed. Josephus tells us that he has anointed himself so that he appeared to have been with his wife (19.4.1). Concerning the Essenes, the *Jewish Wars* states that members of this group refuse to anoint themselves: "They think to be sweaty is a good thing" (2.8.3).

Bibliography

Brock, Sebastian P., and Susan Ashbrook Harvey, eds. *Holy Women of the Syrian Orient.* Berkeley: University of California Press, 1987.

Hornsby, Teresa J. "The Gendered Sinner: The Appropriation of a Woman's Body in the Interpretations of Luke 7:36–50." Ph.D. diss., Vanderbilt University, 2000.

Josephus, Flavius. *Complete Works.* Translated by William Whiston. Grand Rapids, MI: Kregel Publications, 1960.

MacDonald, D. Ronald. "Renowned Far and Wide: The Women Who Anointed Odysseus and Jesus." Pages 128–35 in *A Feminist Companion to Mark.* Edited by Amy-Jill Levine. Sheffield: Sheffield Academic Press, 2001.

Marrou, Henri-Irénée, ed., and Marguerite Harl, trans. *Le Pédagogue: Texte en grèc et français avec introduction.* 3 Vols. Sources chétiennes. Paris: Éditions du Cerf, 1960–70.

Petronius. *The Satyricon.* Translated by Michael Heseltine. Cambridge, MA: Harvard University Press, 1975.

22

The Passover *Haggadah*

Calum Carmichael

The Passover *Haggadah* is a composition inspired by the biblical story of the Exodus. Some of it is written in Aramaic, the language of Jesus, and the rest in Hebrew. At the Last Supper, which is portrayed as a Passover meal in the Synoptic Gospels, Jesus and his disciples would have used some version of it. The word *Haggadah*, like the word "gospel," means proclamation, story, and interpretation. As with so many ancient documents, it is not possible to provide much information about the dating of the various parts of the *Haggadah* or the oral traditions that may have contributed to them. In fact, it was not until the Middle Ages that the first formal version appeared.

The earliest extant references to the Passover seder (order [of service]), and there are many, are found in the New Testament. Paul's metaphor in 1 Corinthians, "Purge out therefore the old leaven that you may be a new lump" (5:7), refers to the purging of a house of all leavened material the evening before the seder takes place. Jesus instructs a disciple to locate a room for the Passover meal that is "furnished [with cushions]" (Mark 14:16). During the seder meal, participants recline, a posture signifying freedom and so proclaiming a central motif of the celebration, namely, liberation from slavery. Free Romans would lie, not sit, at table; leaning on their left side, they used the right hand for eating and drinking.

The eating of *Matzah* (unleavened bread) and the drinking from the cups of wine play central parts in the Passover celebration. It is on performing the rites associated with the bread and the wine that Jesus is said to have instituted the Eucharist. The cup of wine—Paul (1 Corinthians 10:16) uses its technical designation, "the Cup of Blessing"—that Jesus takes and over which he says a grace (Mark 14:23) corresponds to the third of the four cups at the seder. When Jesus says that he will not drink wine again until the kingdom of God comes (Mark 14:25), he is referring to the fourth cup. The seder liturgy that accompanies the drinking of the fourth cup anticipates God's universal reign. In his refusal, according to Mark's Gospel, to accept the wine offered to him at the cross (Mark 15:36), Jesus observes the rule that, between the third and fourth cups, no nonliturgical drinking (of alcohol) is permitted. The *Hallel* (psalms of thanksgiving) is sung after the Passover meal; the Gospels record, "And when they [Jesus and his disciples] had sung a hymn, they went out into the Mount of Olives" (Mark 14:26).

A custom referred to in the Talmud is how one of the company assembled for the seder, the most distinguished usually, conducts it. This means that he has to distribute the *karpas* and *Matzah*, that he has to say the blessings aloud, and that he has to recite aloud most of the prescribed prayers. Only at certain points does the company become equally active, especially after the meal when all the participants together sing Psalms and other hymns. In the New Testament, Jesus conducts the seder. He distributes *karpas* after dipping each bit in some liquid, he breaks and distributes the *Matzah*, and he says aloud the blessings over the *Matzah* and the wine. Later, "They sang a hymn," is when the whole company together sang the *Hallel*.

By reading the *Haggadah* carefully, we are able to discern how over time, because of a deteriorating relationship between Jews and Christians, its parts developed. Three examples are noteworthy. First, Moses, the hero of the Exodus story in the Bible, lost what would have been a prominent role in the liturgy. Rather, God alone—"not through the word, not through the messenger"—rescued the people Israel. Second, sometime between the third and eighth centuries CE the order of the service underwent a radical change. Originally, several meal customs that characterized the celebration generated questions about their significance (e.g., "Why do we recline?"). Instead of the natural order, strange meal customs inviting questions, the order was reversed: the questions, now fixed in their formulation, coming first and then the meal. Motivating the change may have been the desire to oppose far-reaching discussion that could lead to the kind of meaning New Testament writers imported into the Passover ritual.

Examination of the third change enables us to explain the nature of Jesus' bewildering claim about the bread: "This is my body" (Matthew 26:26; Mark 14:22; Luke 22:19; 1 Corinthians 11:24). During the seder, the host breaks off a piece from the unleavened bread; this piece, called the *Aphikoman*, is set aside and eaten as the last item of food that night. The word's origin (which derives from a Greek verb meaning "to come, arrive") suggests a reference to the Messiah, "He who comes." Jesus claimed that the Messiah is no longer a hidden, mystical figure but himself. Early Jewish texts suggest that the Messiah would arrive on the night of Passover (*Mekhilta* on Exodus 12:42; Targum Exodus 12:42; Targum Exodus 15:18; Targum Ps 118:23–29; see also *Didache* 10:6). Over the centuries, Jewish circles attributed various fanciful meanings to the *Aphikoman*.

Further links between the Passover *Haggadah* and the New Testament may be detectable, particularly when other Jewish sources are taken into account. There is, for example, a tantalizing hint in the *Haggadah* of a divine birth for Moses: Exodus 2:25, "And God saw the children of Israel, and God knew," serves as "proof" that another text, "And he [God] saw our affliction" (Deuteronomy 26:7), means abstention from sexual intercourse. The reasoning is that the Israelites abstained from intercourse because—and this is biblical—Pharaoh sought to kill the male children. Preventing conception would prevent the eventual murder of the children. But why cite Exodus 2:25 to prove that Deuteronomy 26:7 means sexual abstention? Possibly underlying the discussion is the question of how then Moses comes to be born. The answer may be that we should read the verb "knew" in a sexual sense and infer a divine conception for Moses (Daube; also Allison and Crossan).

The topics of divorce and virginity are central aspects of Matthew's virgin birth story (Matthew 1:18–25), and the two topics appear as well in traditions about the parents of Moses (*Ant.* 2:213; Targum Exodus 2:1; *Exodus Rabbah* 1:13, 19; *b. Baba Batra* 120a; *b. Sotah* 12a). Amram divorces his wife, Jochebed, in order to avoid the slaughter of any children they might produce. The Babylonian Talmud suggests that before the birth of Moses, Jochebed miraculously becomes a virgin again, "the tokens of maidenhood" having been restored to her (*b. Baba Batra* 120a; see Allison and Crossan).

Pharaoh's destruction of the Hebrew male children is often understood to underlie the Matthean story about Herod's "slaughter of the innocents." On closer examination, however, the better link to Matthew is the Aramean Laban (father-in-law of Jacob/Israel) who, according to the *Haggadah*, was worse than Pharaoh. Laban sought to kill all Israel's children, male and female, and not just the males. The details, linguistic and substantive, of Matthew 2:13–18 correspond closely to what is recounted about Laban in the *Haggadah* (see also *Genesis Rabbah* on 25:20).

Mark 12 recounts together four incidents involving questions. This series evokes the section of the *Haggadah* wherein three types of sons ask their own question and a fourth son, unable to engage his curiosity, has it aroused for him: a wise son asks about all the detailed rules of Passover; a wicked son asks in such a way as to exclude himself from the Jewish community; a son of plain piety inquires about essentials; and a son unable to ask is initiated into learning what Scripture says about the Exodus story. In Mark, questioners first ask Jesus about a tricky legal requirement concerning the payment of taxes. Next, questioners inquire in such a way as to mock the notion of resurrection and thereby (according to tradition [see the Mishnah, *Sanhedrin* 10]) cut themselves off from the community. Then, a questioner asks about fundamental requirements of the moral life. Finally, Jesus himself, in response to his audience's "not daring to ask him any question" (Mark 12:34), poses a problem about conflicting scriptural verses.

In the Gospels, Jesus sometimes says "I am" without any predicate. For example, in Mark 6:50, where the disciples are in a boat during a storm, Jesus says to them, "I am; be not afraid." "I am" communicates the sense of the presence of God in and through Jesus. In these "I am" sayings, Jesus echoes the "I am" of the burning bush in Exodus 3:6 or the "I am and no other" of the *Passover Haggadah* in the sense of the manifestation of the Divine Presence.

THE *HAGGADAH*

SANCTIFICATION

[The host, taking the first cup of wine that evening, says:]
"Blessed are you, Lord our God, King of the Universe, creator of the fruit of the vine. Blessed are you, King of the Universe, who chose us from every

people, and exalted us above every tongue, and sanctified us by His commandments. You have given us, Lord our God, in love, meeting times for celebrating, festivals and seasons for joy, and this day, the festival of unleavened
bread, the appointed time of our liberation, a holy occasion to remember the
coming out of Egypt. You have chosen us and You have sanctified us out of
all peoples. As our heritage, You have given us meeting times when You sanctify us in gladness and joy. Blessed are You, who sanctifies Israel and the
seasons.

FIRST CUP OF WINE

Blessed are You, Lord our God, King of the Universe, who has preserved us,
and sustained us, and enabled us to attain this season." [The first cup of wine
is drunk.]

WASHING THE HANDS

[Washing of hands by the host, who then distributes a piece of the *karpas* that
has been dipped in water or vinegar.]

KARPAS

Blessed are You, Lord our God, King of the Universe, creator of the fruit of the
earth.

MATZAH

[Division of the middle *Matzah* of three representing, respectively, the priest,
the Levite, and the Israelite, the three divisions of the Jewish people. A
broken-off portion of the middle *Matzah*, the smaller of the two, is kept until
the end of the service, when it is eaten as the last item of food that night. It is
called the *Aphikoman*.]

THE RECITAL

This [*Matzah*] is the bread of affliction that our fathers ate in the land of
Egypt. Let all who are hungry enter and eat, let all who are in want come and
observe the Passover. This year we celebrate it here, but next year we shall
celebrate it in the Land of Israel. This year we are slaves, but next year we
shall be free.

Wherein differs this night from other nights? Because on other nights we
may eat leavened or unleavened bread, but on this night unleavened only. On
other nights we may eat different types of herbs, but on this night bitter only.
On other nights we need not dip herbs even once, but on this night we dip

twice. On other nights we eat either sitting or reclining, but on this night we all recline.

We were Pharaoh's slaves in Egypt and the Lord our God brought us out from there with a mighty hand and an outstretched arm. If the Holy One, blessed be He, had not brought our fathers forth from Egypt, then we and our children and our children's children, would be slaves to Pharaoh in Egypt. So, even were we all wise, all full of understanding, all advanced in years, all knowledgeable in the Law, we are yet under the commandment to tell of the coming out of Egypt. The more one recounts the coming out of Egypt, the more praiseworthy he is.

It is told of Rabbi Eliezer, Rabbi Joshua, Rabbi Eliazar ben Azariah, Rabbi Aqiba, and Rabbi Tarphon that they were once reclining together at Bene Berak and telling about the coming forth from Egypt all night, until their disciples came and said to them, "Our Masters, the time has come to read the morning prayer." Rabbi Eleazar ben Azariah said, "Behold, I am like a man of seventy years, yet I never understood why the coming forth from Egypt should be told at night until Ben Zoma interpreted it." It is said, "That you may remember the day when you came forth from the land of Egypt all the days of your life" (Deuteronomy 16:3). "The days of your life" mean the days only, "All the days of your life" mean the nights also. But other sages say, "The days of your life" mean this world; "All the days of your life" mean the days of the Messiah are included also.

FOUR TYPES OF SONS

Blessed be the Omnipresent, blessed be He; blessed be He who gave the Law to His people Israel, blessed be He.

The Law makes reference to four types of son: a wise, a wicked, a plainly pious, and one who does not know how to inquire.

What does the wise son say? "What is the meaning of the testimonies, statutes, and judgments that the Lord our God has commanded us?" You then instruct him about all the laws of the Passover, (and) that there is no dismissing the *Aphikoman* after the Passover lamb.

What does the wicked son say? "What is the meaning of this service to you?" To you, but not to him. Since he excludes himself from the group and so spurns his religion, you must then set his teeth on edge by saying to him, "It is on account of that which the Lord did for me when I came forth from Egypt." "For me," not for him. For had he been there he would not have been redeemed.

What does the son of plain piety say? "What is this?" You say to him, "By strength of hand the Lord brought us out of Egypt, from the house of bondage."

And for him who does not know how to ask, you yourself open up for him.

As it is said, "And you shall tell your son in that day, saying, 'It is on account of that which the Lord did for me when I came forth out of Egypt.'" . . .

LABAN AND PHARAOH

Come and learn what Laban, the Aramean, sought to do to Jacob our father. While Pharaoh issued a decree [of death] only for the male children, Laban sought to uproot all the children. As it is said, "An Aramean would have destroyed my father, and he went down into Egypt, and sojourned there, few in number; and he became there a nation, great, mighty, and populous" (Deuteronomy 26:5).

"And he [Jacob] went down into Egypt"—compelled by the word of God. "And sojourned there"—teaching that he did not go down to Egypt to settle but to sojourn there. As it is said, "And they said to Pharaoh, 'To sojourn in the land are we come, for your servants have no pasture for their flocks, for the famine is sore in the land of Canaan. Now therefore, we pray you, let your servants dwell in the land of Goshen'" (Genesis 47:4).

"Few in number." As it is said, "Your fathers went down into Egypt with threescore and ten persons; and now the Lord your God has made you as the stars of heaven for multitude" (Deuteronomy 10:22). "And he became there a nation," teaching that Israel was distinguished there.

"Great, mighty." As it is said, "And the children of Israel were fruitful, and increased abundantly, and multiplied, and grew exceedingly mighty; and the land was filled with them" (Exodus 1:7).

"And populous." As it is said, "I caused you to multiply as the bud of the field, and you did increase and grow great, and you attained to excellent ornaments; your breasts were fashioned, and your hair was grown; yet you were naked and bare" (Ezekiel 16:7).

"And the Egyptians evil entreated us, and afflicted us, and laid upon us hard bondage" (Deuteronomy 26:6).

"And the Egyptians evil entreated us." As it is said, "Come, let us deal wisely with them; lest they multiply, and it come to pass that when there befalls us any war, they also join themselves to our enemies, and fight against us, and get them up out of the land" (Exodus 1:10).

"And afflicted us." As it is said, "Therefore they did set over them taskmasters to afflict them with their burdens. And they built for Pharaoh treasure cities, Pithom and Rameses" (Exodus 1:11).

"And laid upon us hard bondage." As it is said, "And the Egyptians made the children of Israel to serve with rigor" (Exodus 1:13).

"And we cried to the Lord, the God of our fathers, and the Lord heard our voice and saw our affliction and our travail and our oppression" (Deuteronomy 26:7).

"And we cried to the Lord, the God of our fathers." As it is said, "And it came to pass in the course of those many days that the king of Egypt died; and the children of Israel sighed by reason of their bondage, and they cried, and their cry came up to God by reason of their bondage" (Exodus 2:24).

"And the Lord heard our voice." As it is said, "And God heard their groaning, and God remembered His covenant with Abraham, with Isaac, and with Jacob" (Exodus 2:24).

"And saw our affliction," meaning abstention from sexual intercourse. As it is said, "And God saw the children of Israel, and God knew" (Exodus 2:25).

"And our travail," referring to the sons. As it is said, "Every son that is born you shall cast into the river, and every daughter you shall save alive" (Exodus 1:22).

"And our oppression," referring to the vexation. As it is said, "Moreover, I have seen the oppression wherewith the Egyptians oppress them" (Exodus 3:9).

"And the Lord brought us out of Egypt with a mighty hand and with an outstretched arm and with great terribleness and with signs and with wonders (Deuteronomy 26:8).

"And the Lord brought us out of Egypt"—not through an angel, and not through a seraph, and not through a Messenger [and not through the Word, and not through the Messenger], but the Holy One, blessed be He, in His glory and Himself. As it is said, "For I will pass through the land of Egypt this night, and I will smite all the firstborn in the land of Egypt, both man and beast, and against all the gods of Egypt I will execute judgment, I am the Lord" (Exodus 12:12).

"For I will pass through the land of Egypt in that night"—I and not an angel.

"And I will smite all the firstborn in the land of Egypt"—I and not a seraph. "And against all the gods of Egypt I will execute judgment"—I and not the Messenger, I the Lord, I am and no other.

"With a mighty hand," referring to the blight. As it is said, "Behold, the hand of the Lord is upon your cattle which are in the field, upon the horses, upon the asses, upon the camels, upon the herds, and upon the flocks; there shall be a very grievous blight" (Exodus 9:3).

"And with an outstretched arm," referring to the sword. As it is said, "And a drawn sword in his hand stretched out over Jerusalem" (1 Chronicles 21:16).

"And with great terribleness," referring to the uncovering of the Divine Presence. As it is said, "Or has God assayed to come to take him a nation from the midst of another nation by temptations, by signs, and by wonders, and by war, and by a mighty hand, and by an outstretched arm and by great terrors, according to all that the Lord your God did for you in Egypt before your eyes?" (Deuteronomy 4:34).

"And with signs," referring to the rod. As it is said, "And you shall take in your hand this rod, by which you shall do the signs" (Exodus 4:17).

"And with wonders," referring to the blood. As it is said, "And I will show wonders in the heavens and in the earth: blood, and fire, and pillars of smoke" (Joel 2:30). . . .

PASCHAL OFFERING, *MATZAH*, AND BITTER HERBS

Rabban Gamaliel used to say: "Anyone who does not make mention of the following three things on Passover has not fulfilled his obligation. These are: the Passover sacrifice, the *Matzah*, and the bitter herb."

The Passover sacrifice that our fathers used to eat at the time when the Temple was standing—on what account? It is on account of the Holy One, blessed be He, passing over the houses of our fathers in Egypt. As it is said, "And you shall say, 'It is the sacrifice of the Lord's Passover, for that He passed over the houses of the children of Israel in Egypt, when He smote the Egyptians, and delivered our houses. And the people bowed the head, and worshiped'" (Exodus 12:27).

The *Matzah* that we eat—on what account? It is on account of the lack of time to leaven the dough of our fathers because the supreme King of Kings, the Holy One, blessed be He, revealed himself to them and redeemed them. As it is said, "And they baked unleavened cakes of the dough which they brought forth out of Egypt, for it was not leavened, because they were thrust out of Egypt, and could not tarry, neither had they prepared for themselves any food" (Exodus 12:39).

The bitter herb that we eat—on what account? It is on account of the Egyptians embittering the lives of our fathers in Egypt. As it is said, "And they made their lives bitter with hard bondage, in mortar and in brick, and in all manner of service in the field, all service wherein they made them serve was with rigor" (Exodus 1:14).

In every generation a man must so regard himself as if he came forth himself out of Egypt. As it is said, "And you shall tell your son in that day, saying, 'It is on account of that which the Lord did for me when I came forth out of Egypt'" (Exodus 13:8). Not our fathers only did the Holy One, blessed be He, redeem, but us also He redeemed with them. As it is said, "And He brought us out from there, that He might bring us in, to give us the land which He swore to our fathers" (Deuteronomy 6:23).

SECOND CUP OF WINE

[The celebrants, raising their (second) cups of wine, say:]

Therefore are we bound to give thanks, praise, laud, glorify, exalt, honor, bless, extol, and adore Him who performed all of these wonders for our fathers and for us. He has brought us forth from slavery to freedom, from anguish to joy, from mourning to a Festival day, from darkness to great light, and from bondage to redemption. Let us recite, therefore, before Him a new song. Hallelujah!

[There follows the singing of the first two Psalms of the *Hallel*:]
"Praise, O you servants of the Lord, praise the Name of the Lord . . ." (Psalm 113)
"When Israel went forth out of Egypt . . ." (Psalm 114)

THE BLESSING OF REDEMPTION

Blessed are You, Lord, King of the Universe, who redeemed us, and redeemed our fathers, from Egypt, and enabled us to attain this night, to eat *Matzah* and bitter herb. Likewise, Lord our God and God of our fathers, do You enable us to attain other meetings and times that come to us in peace, that give joy in the building of Your city and make us exult in Your service. There shall we partake of the sacrifices and of the Passover offerings, the blood of which shall acceptably touch the wall of Your altar. And there shall we give thanks to You with a new song, for our redemption and for the ransom of our soul. Blessed are You, Lord, who has redeemed Israel.

Blessed are You, Lord our God, King of the Universe, creator of the fruit of the vine.

[The second cup of wine is drunk.]

WASHING THE HANDS

[The celebrants, washing their hands, say:]
Blessed are You, Lord our God, King of the Universe, who sanctified us by His commandments, and commanded us concerning the washing of hands.

[The host distributes portions from the upper and middle pieces of unleavened bread.]

THE BLESSING OVER BREAD

Blessed are You, Lord our God, King of the Universe, who brings forth bread out of the earth.

THE BLESSING OVER THE *MATZAH*

Blessed are You, Lord our God, King of the Universe, who sanctified us by His commandments, and commanded us concerning the eating of *Matzah*.

BITTER HERB

[The host distributes the bitter herb in a mixture (*Haroseth*) designed to mod-
ify its bitterness.]

Blessed are You, Lord our God, King of the Universe, who sanctified us by His
commandments, and commanded us concerning the eating of the bitter herb.

[Combining bitter herb and *Matzah* (but no longer lamb since the destruction
of the Temple), the host explains:]

In remembrance of the Temple, according to the custom of Hillel:

Thus did Hillel when the Temple still stood: he used to wrap together the
Passover offering, the *Matzah*, and bitter herb, and eat them as one, to fulfill
that which is said: "They shall eat it with unleavened bread and bitter herbs"
(Numbers 9:11).

[The meal is eaten.]

TSAPHUN (THAT WHICH IS HIDDEN)

[The host distributes the *Aphikoman* among the members of the company.]

BAREKH (BLESSING [AFTER THE MEAL])

[Before the Blessing the third cup of wine, the Cup of Blessing, obligatory for
all celebrants, is filled.]

"When the Lord turned round the captivity of Zion, we were like to them that
dream. Then was our mouth filled with laughter, and our tongue with exulta-
tion. Then said they among the nations, 'The Lord has done great things for
them.' The Lord has done great things for us, at which we rejoiced. Bring release from our captivity, Lord, as streams that return in the south. They that
sow in tears shall reap in joy. Though he goes on his way weeping, bearing the
store of seed, he shall come back with joy, bearing his sheaves" (Psalm 126).

[*Host:*] Masters, let us say the Blessing.
[*Celebrants:*] May the Name of the Lord be blessed from this time forth and
forever.
[*Host:*] Let us bless Him of whose bounty we have eaten.
[*Celebrants:*] Blessed be He of whose bounty we have eaten and through whose
goodness we live.

[Blessing continues and includes the following excerpts:]

Blessed are You, Lord our God, King of the Universe who sustains the entire
world in His goodness, in grace, loving-kindness, and mercy. . . . Let us render

thanks to You, Lord our God, because You did give as an inheritance to our fathers a desirable, goodly, and fulsome land. And because You did bring us forth, Lord our God, from the land of Egypt, and did redeem us from the house of bondage. . . .

Have mercy, Lord our God, on Israel Your people, and on Jerusalem Your city, and on Zion the dwelling place of Your glory, and on the kingdom of the House of David, Your anointed one, and on the great and holy House which is called by Your Name. Our God, our Father, do You shepherd us, sustain us, support us, maintain us, and deliver us. Deliver us, Lord our God, speedily from all our troubles. And we pray You, Lord our God, make us not dependent on gifts at the hands of flesh and blood, nor on their loans, but only on Your full, open, holy, and ample hand that we may never ever be ashamed or disgraced.

Our God, and God of our fathers, may there rise, and come, and arrive, and be seen, and accepted, and heard, and visited, and remembered—the remembrance of us, and the visitation of us, and the remembrance of our fathers, and the remembrance of the Messiah, son of David Your servant, and the remembrance of Jerusalem Your holy city, and the remembrance of all Your people the house of Israel—for deliverance, and for good, and for grace, and for loving-kindness, and for mercy, and for life, and for peace, before You on this day, the Feast of Unleavened Bread. Remember us on it, Lord our God, for good, and visit us on it for a blessing, and save us on it for life. And with message of salvation and mercy, pity us and show us grace, and be merciful to us and save us—for to You are our eyes turned, for You are a gracious and merciful God and King.

And build Jerusalem the holy city speedily in our days. Blessed are You, Lord, who in His mercy builds Jerusalem. Amen. . . .

May the Merciful One reign over us, forever and ever . . .

May the Merciful One send to us Elijah the prophet, may He be remembered for good, to bring us good tidings, saving acts and consolations . . .

May the Merciful One find us worthy of the days of the Messiah and of the life of the world to come . . .

A tower of salvation is He to His king, and shows loving-kindness to His anointed, to David and his descendants for evermore. He who makes peace in His high places, may He make peace for us and for all Israel. And say you, Amen. . . .

Blessed are You, Lord our God, King of the universe, creator of the fruit of the vine.

THIRD CUP OF WINE

[The third cup of wine, the Cup of Blessing, is drunk.]

"Pour out Your wrath upon the nations that know You not and upon the kingdoms that have not called on Your Name. For they have devoured Jacob and laid waste his dwelling place" (Psalm 79:6, 7).

"Pour out Your indignation upon them. And let the fierceness of Your anger overtake them" (Psalm 69:25).

"Pursue them in wrath and destroy them from under the heavens of the Lord" (Lamentations 3:66).

FOURTH CUP OF WINE

[The fourth and last cup of wine, the Cup of Redemption, is filled and the remainder of the *Hallel* (Psalms 115–18) sung:]

"Not to us, Lord, but to Your Name give glory, for Your loving-kindness and for Your truth's sake" (Psalm 115) . . .

"I love that the Lord should hear my voice and my supplications" (Psalm 116) . . .

"Praise the Lord, all you nations. Laud Him, all you peoples" (Psalm 117) . . .

"Give thanks to the Lord, for He is good. For His mercy endures forever. . . . I will give thanks to You, for You have answered me. And You are become my salvation. The stone that the builders rejected is become the headstone of the corner. This was the Lord's doing. It is marvelous in our eyes. This is the day that the Lord has made. We will rejoice and be glad therein. We beseech You, Lord, save now. We beseech You, Lord, save now. We beseech You, Lord, make us now to prosper. We beseech You, Lord, make us now to prosper. Blessed be he that comes in the Name of the Lord. We bless you out of the house of the Lord. The Lord is God, He has given us light. . . . Give thanks to the Lord, for He is good. For His loving-kindness endures forever (Psalm 118).

[The Blessing of the Song follows the recital of the *Hallel*:]

All Your works shall praise You, Lord our God, and Your pious ones, the just who do Your will, and all the house of Israel shall, in song, thank and bless and laud and glorify and exalt and reverence and sanctify and ascribe kingship to Your Name, our King. For it is good to give thanks to You and becoming to sing praises to Your Name, for from everlasting to everlasting You are God.

[The Great *Hallel* is recited:]

"Give thanks to the Lord, for He is good . . ." (Psalm 136)

THE BLESSING OF THE SONG

The breath of all that lives shall praise Your Name, Lord our God, and the spirit of all flesh shall glorify and exalt Your remembrance, our King. Continually, from everlasting to everlasting, You are God, and beside You we have no King who redeems and saves, delivers and protects, sustains and pities in all times of trouble and stress, we have no King but You. You are God of the first and of the last. . . .

Even though our mouths were filled with song as the sea, and our tongues with joy as its multitude of waves, and our lips with praise as the expanse of the firmament, though our eyes were radiant as the sun and the moon, and our hands were outspread as the wings of the eagle of heaven, and our feet were fleet as the hinds, we should yet be inadequate to thank You, Lord our God, and God of our fathers, for one in a thousand of the many thousands of thousands and myriads of myriads of loving-kindnesses that You have bestowed on our fathers and on us. . . .

Your loving-kindnesses have not deserted us; forsake us not, Lord our God, forever. Wherefore, the limbs that You have formed in us, and the breath and spirit that You have blown into our nostrils, and the tongue which You have placed in our mouths—behold! They shall thank, bless, laud, glorify, extol, reverence, hallow, and ascribe kingship to Your Name, Our King. . . .

Blessed are You, Lord God and King, great in praises, God of thanksgivings, Lord of wonders, who delights in songs of praise, King and God, Life of all worlds.

Blessed are You, Lord our God, King of the Universe, creator of the fruit of the vine.

[The fourth and last cup of wine is drunk followed by a Blessing:]

Blessed are You, Lord our God, King of the Universe, for the vine and for the fruit of the vine, and for the pleasant, goodly, and fulsome land, which You did please to give as an inheritance to our fathers, to eat of its fruit and to be satisfied with its goodness. Have mercy, Lord our God, on Israel Your people and on Jerusalem Your city and on Zion the abode of Your glory and on Your altar and on Your shrine. Build again Jerusalem the Holy City speedily in our days; bring us up into its midst and cause us to rejoice in its establishment, so that we may eat of its fruit and be satisfied with its goodness and bless You for it in holiness and purity. And make us to rejoice on this Feast of Unleavened Bread. For You, Lord, are good, and do good to all, and we shall thank You for the Land and for the fruit of the vine. Blessed are You, Lord, for the Land and for the fruit of the vine.

Bibliography

Allison, Dale. *The New Moses: A Matthean Typology*. Minneapolis, MN: Fortress Press, 1993.

Carmichael, Deborah. "David Daube on the Eucharist and the Passover Seder." Pages 89–108 in *New Testament Backgrounds*. Edited by Craig A. Evans and S. E. Porter. Sheffield: Sheffield Academic Press, 1997.

Crossan, John Dominic. "Virgin Mother or Bastard Child?" Pages 37–55 in *A Feminist Companion to Mariology*. Edited by Amy-Jill Levine with Maria Mayo Robbins. London: T & T Clark, 2005.

Daube, David. *New Testament Judaism: Collected Works of David Daube*. Edited by Calum Carmichael. Vol. 2. Berkeley: Robbins Collection, University of California, 2000.

Glatzer, Nahum, ed. *The Passover Haggadah*. New York: Schocken Books, 1969.

Jeremias, Joachim. *The Eucharistic Words of Jesus*. London: SCM Press, 1966.

Petuchowski, Jakob. "'Do This in Remembrance of Me' (1 Cor. 11:24)." *Journal of Biblical Literature* 76 (1957): 293–98

Roth, Cecil, ed. *The Haggadah*. London: Soncino Press, 1934.

Zeitlin, Solomon. "The Liturgy of the First Night of Passover." *Jewish Quarterly Review* 28 (1948): 444–49.

—23—

Joseph and Aseneth: Food as an Identity Marker

Randall D. Chesnutt

Joseph and Aseneth, an apocryphal romance now often included in the Old Testament Pseudepigrapha, recounts the conversion of the Gentile Aseneth to the God of Israel, her marriage to the patriarch Joseph, and the social and religious conflicts surrounding that conversion and marriage. Genesis 41:45, 50–52, and 46:20 provide the biblical point of departure for this tale by referring in passing to Joseph's marriage to Asenath (LXX Aseneth), daughter of the Pagan priest Potiphera (LXX Pentephres). The work was composed in Greek and is extant in sixteen Greek manuscripts and several versions.

The evidence remains compelling that *Joseph and Aseneth* was written by a Jew around the turn of the eras (Chesnutt 1995; Collins) despite a recent revival of the older view that the work may be a much later Christian composition (Kraemer). The very problem in the biblical text for which the story of Aseneth's conversion offers a solution—namely, that the revered patriarch married a Pagan woman—is a problem to the Jewish conscience. The ethnic particularism evidenced in Aseneth's physical profile (1:5: "She bore no resemblance to the virgins of the Egyptians, but was in every way similar to the daughters of the Hebrews; and she was as tall as Sarah and as graceful as Rebecca and as beautiful as Rachel") is even more pronounced when the gap between the hero and heroine is explained in ethnic as well as religious terms: intimacy with anyone outside the tribe and kindred (*phulē* and *suggeneias*) is taboo (8:5–7). This taboo applies not only in the patriarchal setting of the narrative but also to the author's own social world, as discussed further below. Aseneth converts to "the God of Joseph" (6:6), "the God of my [Joseph's] father Israel" (8:9), "the Lord God of the powerful Joseph, the Most High" (11:7), and "the God of the Hebrews" (11:10), and the narrative is as concerned with her incorporation into the family of Jacob as with her acceptance by God (22:3–10). All this suggests Jewish rather than Christian authorship. Alleged affinities with late antique Christian sources are all very general; certainly there is nothing distinctively Christian in the work.

Egypt is the most likely place of composition. The pervasive contrast between Israelite and Egyptian characters and between the God of Israel and the Egyptian gods leaves the impression that the Egyptian setting of the story was dictated not merely by the biblical framework but also by the milieu in which the author and his community actually lived. In addition, Egyptian elements are discernible in various individual motifs, such as the depiction of Joseph in terms reminiscent of the solar deity Re and the portrayal of Aseneth in terms that evoke the image of the Egyptian goddess Neith.

The date of the work is uncertain. Dependence on the Septuagint means that it cannot have been composed prior to approximately 100 BCE. A Hellenistic Jewish work in which Gentile conversion to Judaism is considered a realistic possibility must have been composed before Hadrian's measures against Judaism in 132–35 CE. If an Egyptian provenance is assumed, *Joseph and Aseneth* must have been written before the great Jewish revolt under Trajan (117–19 CE) that resulted in the decimation of Egyptian Jewry. A more specific date within these broad limits is difficult to determine, but the conciliatory attitude toward Gentiles fits better before than after 70 CE, and in Egypt such an outlook fits better before than after the pogrom against Alexandrian Jews in 38 CE. The absence of any allusion to the Romans and the depiction of Egypt as an independent country with rulers favorably disposed toward Jews may reflect the Ptolemaic period in Egypt before the Roman takeover in 30 BCE, but this is by no means certain. Lexical considerations and the relationship between this work and other Greek romances are likewise inconclusive as criteria for dating. The alleged affinities with late antique Christian sources that lead some to date the work to the third or fourth century CE, as noted earlier, are very general and afford no basis for such a late dating of the work. In sum, while a precise date cannot be determined, composition sometime in the first century BCE or CE seems probable. This means that *Joseph and Aseneth* may be cited as evidence of thought and practice in at least some Jewish circles roughly contemporaneous with Jesus and the origins of Christianity.

Opinion varies on the purpose of the work. Some consider it missionary propaganda designed to win Gentile converts to Judaism, while others maintain that it was written for Jewish readers and designed to address such intramural issues as the status of Gentile converts within the Jewish community and the propriety of marriage between a Gentile convert to Judaism and one who is born Jewish (see the survey in Chesnutt 1995, 20–64, 256–65).

The narrative begins with the beautiful virgin Aseneth secluded in luxurious penthouse quarters adjoining the house of her father, Pentephres, priest of Heliopolis and chief of Pharaoh's noblemen, in order to avoid all suitors. Joseph, who is touring Egypt to gather grain, announces plans to dine in Pentephres' house. Aseneth arrogantly refuses her father's suggestion that she be given to Joseph in marriage, but when Joseph arrives, she is awestruck by his beauty, changes her mind, and falls madly in love with him. The ethnic and religious barrier to a relationship between the two characters is explained in the first excerpt translated below (7:1, 5): as a man of God, Joseph cannot sit at table with a foreigner, much less marry one. When at her father's suggestion Aseneth comes forth to kiss Joseph, the patriarch spurns her in the pointed language of 8:5–7, the second excerpt. Here the author uses meal language—specifically, a life-giving bread, cup, and ointment that stand in contrast to the defiling food, drink, and ointment of idolaters—to distinguish the "worshiper of God" from the idolatrous Gentile and to justify the former's separatism from the latter. In the third excerpt, 8:9, Joseph blesses Aseneth and prays that she be brought from darkness to light, from error to truth, from death to life, so that she can be numbered among the people of God. Among the other metaphors, the language of eating the "bread of life" and drinking a "cup of blessing" is again used to describe the exalted status of God's people into which Aseneth's anticipated transformation is to lead.

Promising to return in a week, Joseph departs. Aseneth retires to her penthouse, goes into mourning, repudiates her idols, and penitently turns to the God of Israel. The fourth excerpt, 11:3–14, represents her first soliloquy on how to address the God from whom she is alienated by reason of her idol worship and her defilement from food tainted by idolatry. Following another soliloquy and a lengthy prayer of confession and penitence, Aseneth is visited by a "man from heaven" who provides heavenly acknowledgment of her conversion and describes the blessings that now accrue to her. Foremost among these are life and immortality, in which Aseneth participates symbolically by eating from a mysterious honeycomb that is said to be the same immortal food eaten by the angels in paradise and is equated with the "bread of life," "cup of immortality," and "ointment of incorruption." When Joseph returns and learns that she has renounced idolatry and has received the "bread of life" and "cup of blessing," he embraces and kisses the gloriously transfigured Aseneth. The couple marries amid elaborate festivities, and from their union Manasseh and Ephraim are born.

In the second part of the double novella, Pharaoh's son becomes jealous of the couple and enlists the aid of some of Joseph's brothers to murder Joseph and abduct Aseneth. The plot fails because of support for the couple by some of Joseph's other brothers and timely divine intervention. Pharaoh's son is mortally wounded during the conflict, and when the grief-stricken Pharaoh also dies, Joseph becomes king of Egypt.

The selected excerpts address several issues of Jewish self-identity that permeated the Jewish world of Jesus and early Christianity. The author especially is concerned to represent the people of God as those who avoid the contaminating effect of physical intimacy and intermarriage with Gentiles and who eat apart from idolaters and idol-tainted food. Most expressive of the difference between God's people and idolaters is their respective food, drink, and ointment. According to 8:5, it is improper for the man who worships God to kiss an alien woman because the former blesses with his mouth the living God, eats blessed bread of life, drinks a blessed cup of immortality, and is anointed with blessed ointment of incorruption, whereas the latter blesses with her mouth dead and dumb idols, eats bread of strangling from the table of idols, drinks a cup of deceit from the libation of idols, and is anointed with ointment of destruction. That the ethnic and religious dichotomy expressed here is not merely literary but a real one in the author's community is evidenced by the further interdiction against the woman who worships God kissing an alien man. This interdiction is different from what precedes in that nothing in the story line calls for it; there is no Israelite woman in the story for whom exogamy is a possibility. The generalization from the specific case at hand to a related situation beyond that represented in the narrative betrays a didactic interest in clarifying Jewish identity in a Pagan environment, especially with regard to the polluting effect of intermarriage and of food defiled by idolatry.

The formulaic references to the bread of life, cup of immortality, and ointment of incorruption often have been supposed to reflect some sort of sacred meal, perhaps related to the meals of known groups such as the Qumran sectarians, the Egyptian Therapeutae, the mystery religions (especially the Isis cult), and the early Christians (see the survey of views in Chesnutt 1995, 20–64, 128–35). More likely the reference is not to a special ritual meal but to Jewish scruples about food in general and, by metonymy, to the entire Jewish way of life. Any ritual practice that underlies the language was not primarily initiatory, inasmuch as 8:5 presents Joseph—not Aseneth—as the one who eats bread of life, drinks a cup of immortality, and is anointed with ointment of incorruption. Here the language of eating, drinking, and being anointed clearly refers to the continuing experience of those who worship God rather than to an initiatory act. Aseneth herself never actually receives any bread, cup, or ointment anywhere in the narrative; instead, she eats a piece of honeycomb (itself a symbol of immortality in antiquity) and is then told by the man from heaven that she has eaten bread of life, drunk a cup of immortality, and been anointed with ointment of incorruption. This explicit equation of eating the honeycomb with receiving the bread, cup, and ointment makes it unlikely that either half of the equation refers to a fixed ritual. If *Joseph and Aseneth* echoes an actual ritual meal, the particular form of the ritual is no longer recoverable.

The triad of bread, cup, and ointment is reminiscent of the biblical formula "grain, wine, and oil" (e.g., Deuteronomy 7:13; 12:17; 14:23; 18:4; 28:51; 2 Chronicles 31:5; 32:8; Ezra 3:7; Nehemiah 5:11; Hosea 2:8, 22; Joel 2:19; Haggai 1:11; Psalm 104:14–15; see also Judith 10:5; *Jubilees* 13:26; 32:12; 1QH 10.24; *Testament of Judah* 9:8; *Sibylline Oracles* 3.243, 745; Josephus, *War* 1.15.6; and Revelation 6:6) and, like that formula, summarizes the staples of life. Moreover, these staple items are precisely those regarded in Jewish tradition as most susceptible to defilement (Chesnutt 2005). Whether the triadic formula in *Joseph and Aseneth* echoes some special Jewish ritual that is set over against Pagan rites or simply originated in the peculiarly Jewish use of these staple commodities in contrast to the defiling food, drink, and oil of outsiders, it functions in the narrative as a representative expression for Jewish life in a Gentile environment.

The repeated employment of three staple items to contrast the life-giving diet of the pious with the defiling food of idolaters combines with the explicit concern to avoid defilement at table (7:1) to suggest that meals were very important to the self-identity of the community behind this text, as they were in the Jewish world of the historical Jesus. The importance of meal practices as consummate expressions of

Jewish life is well known. Food, meals, and table fellowship serve as grounds of distinction among various Jewish groups and between Jews and non-Jews throughout our sources on early Judaism (e.g., Daniel 1:1–16; Additions to Esther 4:17; *Jubilees* 22:16; 1 Maccabees 1:62–63; 2 Maccabees 6:18–21; 7:1; 3 Maccabees 3:4–7; *Letter of Aristeas* 128–42; *Sibylline Oracles* 4.24–30; 1QS 6.2–23; 7.15–20; 8.16–19; 1QSa 2.11–22; Galatians 2:11–14; Acts 10–11), including the Gospels and early Rabbinic sources; in the latter no less than two-thirds of the traditions attributed to the Houses of Shammai and Hillel have to do directly or indirectly with table fellowship.

The inclusion of oil of anointing in the triad in *Joseph and Aseneth* alongside the bread and cup has been thought strange, but in fact oil was a staple commodity in Jewish tradition and throughout the Near East, as the widespread occurrence of the triad "grain, wine, and oil" itself attests. Because oil was such a staple commodity, because the lengthy process of production constantly exposed it to contamination, and because Pagan oil often was associated with Pagan rites, many Jews considered oil even more susceptible to impurity than other sources of defilement (Chesnutt 2005). In numerous Jewish texts, including the Qumran scrolls, the writings of Josephus, and the Rabbinic corpus, oil ranks alongside food and drink as one of the basic realities of daily life most threatening to Jewish purity, but also, if used properly, most symbolic of Jewish identity (11QTemple 47.5–14; 49.5–21; CD 12.5–17; 4QOrdinances[b] (=4Q513) frg. 13.4–6; 4Q284a frg. 1; Josephus, *War* 2.8.3; 2.21.2; *Life* 13; *Ant.* 12.3.1; *m. Tohorot* 3.1–4; 9–10; *m. Edduyot* 4.6; *m. Avodah Zarah* 2.6; *b. Berakot* 62a; *b. Hagigah* 25a). Occasionally the three items are combined and their proper use adduced as benchmarks by which to gauge and express Jewish identity, as in the Temple Scroll's insistence on the purity of "wine and oil and all food and all drink" (11QTemple 47.5–14) and the Talmud's ban on the "bread, wine and oil of heathens" (*b. Avodah Zarah* 36a–b; *b. Shabbat* 17b). It is not surprising, therefore, that ointment appears in *Joseph and Aseneth* alongside food and drink in a triadic formula that sets the uniquely Jewish use of these staples over against their usage by idolaters and employs the triad as an expression for a distinctively Jewish way of life.

Numerous other aspects of *Joseph and Aseneth* besides the meal language invite consideration in connection with the study of Jesus and the Gospels. The following questions illustrate the broad range of potentially instructive lines of inquiry. How does Jesus' attitude toward Gentiles compare with the image of Gentiles in *Joseph and Aseneth*, especially this work's placement of the Gentile convert on a par with those who belong to the people of God by birth? How does Jesus' attitude toward women compare with that in *Joseph and Aseneth*? Does the designation of Joseph as "son of God" shed any light on the New Testament usage of that Christological category? Does the language of Aseneth's being "fashioned anew" bear any kinship to the "new birth" imagery of John 3 and other images of conversion in the New Testament? Is the representation of Aseneth's transformation as passage from death to life akin to the Johannine Jesus' statement that the one who believes in him "has passed out of death into life" (John 5:24–25)? Is it significant that

Johannine dualism in general resembles the life-death, knowledge-ignorance, light-darkness, and truth-error antitheses in *Joseph and Aseneth*? Are the warnings attributed to Jesus about familial hostility toward those who follow him (Mark 13:12–13; Matthew 10:21–22; Luke 12:51–53; *Gospel of Thomas* 16) elucidated by the familial and social tensions that Aseneth anticipates as a consequence of her renouncing her religious past and being aggregated into a new religious community? Should the expression "bread of life" in John 6 be seen in connection with *Joseph and Aseneth*—the only roughly contemporaneous Jewish work that uses the exact expression even as it shares with John 6 a decidedly "realized" eschatology and the idea that the one who eats the life-giving food will not die but will live forever? Do the "Lord's Prayer" and other hymns and prayers in the Gospels reflect affinities of thought and language with the extensive soliloquies and prayers in *Joseph and Aseneth*? How do Jesus' ethical teachings relate to the ideal of nonretaliation toward offenders advocated by Aseneth and others in the last part of *Joseph and Aseneth*? Such questions underscore the importance of *Joseph and Aseneth* for anyone interested in the study of the historical Jesus and the Jewish milieu of both Jesus and the Gospels.

Joseph and Aseneth is extant in two major recensions. An English translation of the longer is found in James H. Charlesworth, *The Old Testament Pseudepigrapha*. The other, about one-third shorter, appears in English translation in H.F.D. Sparks, *The Apocryphal Old Testament*. The translation below is based on Christoph Burchard's critical edition of the Greek text (Burchard 2003), which remains our best text base (Burchard 1970, 2005) in spite of recent arguments for the priority of the short recension at some points (Standhartinger; Kraemer).

7:1, 5–6

And Joseph entered the house of Pentephres and sat upon the throne. And they washed his feet and prepared a table for him by itself, for Joseph would not eat with the Egyptians, because this was an abomination to him. . . . And Joseph always kept the face of his father Jacob before him, and he remembered his father's commandments. For Jacob used to say to his son Joseph and all his sons, "My children, be on strong guard against associating with an alien woman, for association with her is destruction and corruption." Therefore Joseph said, "Let that woman leave this house."

8:5–7

It is not proper for a man who worships God, who blesses with his mouth the living God and eats blessed bread of life and drinks a blessed cup of immortality and is anointed with blessed ointment of incorruption, to kiss an alien woman, who blesses with her mouth dead and dumb idols and eats from their table bread of strangling and drinks from their libation a cup of deceit and is anointed with ointment of destruction. Rather, the man who worships God will kiss his mother and the sister born of his mother and the sister from his tribe and kinsfolk and the wife who shares his bed, who bless with their mouths the living God. Likewise, it is not proper for a woman who worships God to kiss an alien man, for this is an abomination before the Lord God.

8:9

Lord God of my father Israel,
the Most High, the Powerful One of Jacob,
who gives life to all things,
and calls them from darkness into light,
and from error into truth,
and from death into life;
you, Lord, bless this virgin,
and renew her with your spirit,
and fashion her anew with your hidden hand,
and make her alive again with your life,
and let her eat your bread of life,
and let her drink your cup of blessing,
and count her among your people,
    whom you chose before all things came into being,
and let her enter your rest,
    which you prepared for your chosen ones,
and let her live in your eternal life forever and ever.

11:3–14

And she said in her heart without opening her mouth,
What shall I do, I the lowly one,
or where shall I go;
with whom shall I take refuge,
or what shall I say,
I, the virgin and an orphan and desolate and abandoned and hated?
For all have come to hate me,
and besides these my father and my mother,
for I have even come to hate their gods, and I destroyed them,
and I gave them up to be trampled under people's feet.
And therefore my father and my mother and all my family have come to
    hate me,
and they have said, "Aseneth is not our daughter

because she destroyed our gods."
And all people hate me,
for I have even come to hate every man
and all who sought to woo me.
And now in this lowly state of mine, all have come to hate me
and rejoice over this distress of mine.
And the Lord God of the powerful Joseph, the Most High,
hates all who worship idols,
for he is a jealous and frightful God toward all who worship alien gods.
Therefore he has come to hate me as well,
because I worshiped dead and dumb idols, and blessed them,
and ate from their sacrifices,
and my mouth is defiled from their table,
and I am not bold enough to appeal to the Lord God of heaven,
the Most High, the Mighty One of the powerful Joseph,
for my mouth is defiled from the sacrifices of the idols.
But I have heard many say
that the God of the Hebrews is a true God and a living God
and a merciful God and compassionate and patient and very forbearing
    and kind
and does not count the sin of a lowly person
nor expose the lawless deeds of a distressed person at the time of his
    distress.
For this reason I will muster courage,
and I will turn to him,
and I will take refuge in him,
and I will confess all my sins to him,
and I will pour out my request before him.
Who knows whether he might see my lowly state and have mercy on me?
Perhaps he will see this desolation of mine and have compassion for me,
or see my orphanage and protect me,
for he is the father of the orphans and protector of the oppressed and
    helper of the distressed.
I will muster courage and cry out to him.

Bibliography

Burchard, Christoph. *Joseph und Aseneth kritische herausgaben.* Pseudepigrapha Veteris Testamenti Graece 5. Leiden: Brill, 2003.

———. "Joseph and Aseneth." Pages 177–247 in *The Old Testament Pseudepigrapha.* 2 vols. Edited by James H. Charlesworth. Garden City, NY: Doubleday, 1983–85.

———. "The Text of *Joseph and Aseneth* Reconsidered." *Journal for the Study of the Pseudepigrapha* 14 (2005): 83–96.

————. *Untersuchungen zu Joseph und Aseneth: Überlieferung-Ortsbestimmung.* Wissenschaftliche Untersuchungen zum Neuen Testament 8. Tübingen: Mohr, 1965.

————. "Zum Text von 'Joseph und Aseneth.'" *Journal for the Study of Judaism* 1 (1970): 3–34.

Chesnutt, Randall D. *From Death to Life: Conversion in Joseph and Aseneth.* Journal for the Study of the Pseudepigrapha. Supplement Series 16. Sheffield: Sheffield Academic Press, 1995.

————. "Perceptions of Oil in Early Judaism and the Meal Formula in *Joseph and Aseneth.*" *Journal for the Study of the Pseudepigrapha* 14 (2005): 113–32.

————. "The Social Setting and Purpose of Joseph and Aseneth." *Journal for the Study of the Pseudepigrapha* 2 (1988): 21–48.

Collins, John J. *"Joseph and Aseneth*: Jewish or Christian?" *Journal for the Study of the Pseudepigrapha* 14 (2005): 97–112.

Humphrey, Edith M. *Joseph and Aseneth.* Guides to Apocrypha and Pseudepigrapha. Sheffield: Sheffield Academic Press, 2000.

Kraemer, Ross S. *When Aseneth Met Joseph: A Late Antique Tale of the Biblical Patriarch and His Egyptian Wife, Reconsidered.* New York: Oxford University Press, 1998.

Philonenko, Marc. *Joseph et Aséneth: Introduction, text critique, traduction et notes.* Studia post biblica 13. Leiden: Brill, 1968.

Sänger, Dieter. *Antikes Judentum und die Mysterien: Religionsgeschichtliche Untersuchungen zu Joseph und Aseneth.* Wissenschaftliche Untersuchungen zum Neuen Testament 2.5. Tübingen: Mohr, 1980.

Sparks, H.F.D. *The Apocryphal Old Testament*, pp. 465–503. Oxford: Clarendon Press, 1984.

Standhartinger, Angela. *Das Frauenbild im Judentum der hellenistischen Zeit: Ein Beitrag anhand von "Joseph und Aseneth."* Arbeiten zur Geschichte des antiken Judentums und des Urchristentums 26. Leiden: Brill, 1995.

—24—

The Pliny and Trajan Correspondence

Bradley M. Peper and Mark DelCogliano

The tenth book of Pliny's letters (*Epistulae* X.1–121) is a collection of his official correspondence with Emperor Trajan. Pliny wrote the majority of these letters (*Epistulae* X.15–121) while he was governor of Bithynia-Pontus, a Roman maritime province bordering the southern coast of the Black Sea. Because Bithynia-Pontus experienced frequent problems after its annexation (66 BCE), Trajan convinced the Senate in 110 to remove the province's longtime public status and allow him to appoint a *legatus Augusti pro praetore*, a position in which the emperor decided both the individual to represent him and his length of term. For this new position, Trajan chose Gaius Plinius Luci filius Caecilius Secundus (61–112), commonly called Pliny the Younger to distinguish him from his famous uncle, the writer-historian Pliny the Elder (23–79). Upon his assumption of gubernatorial duties in the autumn of 110, Pliny spent the first year of his administration touring the western region of Bithynia and visiting such cities as Prusa, Nicaea, and Nicomedia.

It was only at the beginning of his second year in office, in the autumn of 111, that he visited the eastern part of his province, Pontus. From Pontus, he wrote to Trajan about a problem concerning the Christians, most likely from the seacoast city of Amisus, the inland capital of Amastris, or some city in between. The value of their correspondence extends beyond its being the sole surviving example of such communication between an emperor and a provincial governor; it is also among the earliest of the non-Christian references to Jesus and his followers (Tacitus wrote his description of Nero's persecution some five years later [*Annales* XV.44]). Although these letters (*Epistulae* 96 and 97) do not paint a complete portrait of Jesus and the early Christian movement, they do provide an invaluable resource for both assessing the validity of the Christian accounts and reconstructing what they invariably omit. In particular, these letters provide evidence of the continued existence and development of institutions reportedly initiated by Jesus, an imperial perception of Christianity and the person of Jesus, the persecutions that the canonical Gospels portray Jesus as predicting, and how the Roman government dealt with religious movements perceived as a civic threat.

Pliny, who acquired information concerning Christian liturgical assemblies from his examination of Christian apostates, recounts that participants met twice on a fixed day, once before dawn and again later in the day. This "fixed day" was most likely Sunday, the day on which Jesus was reported to have risen from the dead (Matthew 28:1–10; Mark 16:1–8; Luke 24:1–12; John 20:1–10; Acts 20:7; *Didache* 14).

Pliny reports that the Christians at their morning service antiphonally sang a hymn to Christ as if to a god (*carmenque Christo quasi deo dicere secum invicem*). By describing their activities as such, Pliny may have perceived Christian worship to be similar to that of hero cults, which were especially prevalent in the eastern part of the empire. His use of the formula "as if to a god" echoes how the ancients typically described a person worshiped in a hero cult. Yet while hero cult practices included offerings (e.g., sacrifices, libations, and/or incense), altars, images, and processions, Pliny makes no reference to such rituals among Christians. Furthermore, Pliny may also have considered the Christians to be marring the integrity of a true hero cult. Although the individual worshiped in a hero cult was considered to possess divine attributes, the person was not considered to be an actual divinity. The Christian belief that Christ was a divine being, rather than a human possessing divine attributes, may have led Pliny and other Roman elites to regard Christian belief and worship as "a depraved and fanatical superstition" (cf. Tacitus, *Annales* 15.44.4; Suetonius, *Nero* 16.2). Therefore, Pliny's opinion about Christ reflects how an educated Roman official would have viewed Jesus, though it may not correspond to how Christians themselves regarded Jesus.

The services Pliny concisely describes should be understood in terms of the early Christian *synaxis*, Eucharist, and *Agape*. The *synaxis*, or service of the word, was a continuation of a Jewish synagogue practice that consisted of reading and expositing Scripture, singing psalms, and reciting prayers. The Gospels record that Jesus participated in these services on the Jewish Sabbath (see Matthew 13:53–58; Mark 6:1–6; Luke 4:16–30).

As for the Eucharist and *Agape*, these institutions developed from accounts of Jesus' last supper with his disciples (Matthew 26:26–30; Mark 14:22–26; Luke 22:14–23). The Eucharist, also known as the Lord's Supper, was a ritual reenactment of Jesus' last supper in which participants shared a common loaf of bread and a cup of wine (1 Corinthians 10:16–17; 11:23–26). The *Agape*, or love feast, was a communal assembly for an actual meal (Jude 12; Ignatius, *Epistula ad Romanos* 7.3, *Epistula ad Smyrnaeos* 8.2); such fellowship meals were also a common feature of ancient Jewish and Pagan gatherings (see John Kloppenborg's contribution in this volume). Initially, the Eucharist and *Agape* were celebrated conjointly as part of a common service, much as Jesus himself reportedly had done (see 1 Corinthians 11:20–21). At some point, however, the Eucharist and

Agape became separated, and the Eucharist was then attached to the morning *synaxis*, whereas the *Agape* was reserved for the evening (Justin, *Apologia* I.65–67; Tertullian, *De Corona* 3, *Apologeticum* 39). Pliny's description of Christian liturgical practices indicates that this was probably the liturgical arrangement observed by the Pontic Christians until he promulgated Trajan's decree, which prohibited all organized societies not explicitly sanctioned by the state. The prohibition prompted the Pontic Christians, fearing that their ritual too closely resembled the common meals associated with organized societies, to abandon their weekly *Agape*.

Although Pliny investigated the Christians' activities, at no point did he proactively search for Christians in his province; he only tried those who were accused before him. Indeed, Trajan himself explicitly told Pliny regarding the Christians, "These people should not be sought out" (*Epistula* X.97). Thus, Christians were being prosecuted based on the accusations of private citizens (*delatores*), not through an administrative policy. Roman persecution of Christians remained as such until the systematic and sustained persecution during the reign of Decius in 249–51. The Gospels record Jesus predicting that his followers would be dragged before Roman authorities and questioned because of him (Matthew 10:17–20; Mark 13:9–11; Luke 12:10–11; John 15:18–27). Jesus could have predicted these isolated persecutions, but it seems more likely that these predictions are retrojections inserted into the Jesus tradition by the Evangelists, who sought to bolster the resolve of their readers when faced with the individual persecutions such as those experienced by Paul and Silas (Acts 16:19ff.; 18:12ff.; 21:27–26:32).

Pliny's procedure for dealing with the Christians provides an example of how a Roman governor would handle cases brought before him by the local citizenry and councils. While legal actions were instigated chiefly by the public, the provincial governor alone performed the actual trials (*cognitio extra ordinem*). A Roman governor possessed the ability to deny any case, or if he accepted a case and found the accused guilty, to determine the punishment. Like Pliny, Pontius Pilate, the Roman governor of Judea from 26 to 37, exercised such judicial power over Jesus (Matthew 27:1–26; Mark 15:1–15; Luke 23:1–25; John 18:28–19:16).

Given the judicial procedures operative in Roman provinces, certain questions arise concerning Pilate's decision to execute Jesus. Did Pilate perceive Jesus as a political subversive and thereby take a more proactive role in his death? Or did Pilate view Jesus as Pliny viewed the Christians, fanatical yet benign to the empire? If the latter, did Pilate bow to the pressures of local authorities such as the high priest, Caiaphas, something that is conceivable given a governor's primary concern for maintaining the peace of his province? While Pliny's letter cannot answer these questions, it does, however, provide insight into the legal and social issues with which a governor, such as Pontius Pilate, would have to grapple when handling accusations brought before him by local authorities.

PLINY TO TRAJAN

EPISTLE X.XCVI

[1]It is customary for me, my lord, to submit to you all matters in which I am uncertain how to proceed. For who is better able to direct my doubts or inform my ignorance?

Because I have never been present at any judicial investigation concerning the Christians, I do not know the usual type of questions to ask or extent of punishment to inflict. [2]Nor am I sure concerning these points. Should there be some distinction made when dealing with the young, or should they be treated no differently from adults? Should a pardon be given for recanting, or should someone who was known to be a Christian gain anything by ceasing to be one? Should the name "Christian" itself be punished when no crimes have been committed, or should only the crimes associated with the name be punished?

For the time being, I have followed this procedure with those who were accused before me as Christians. [3]First, I asked them if they were Christian. Then, I asked those who admitted to this a second and a third time, while threatening them with punishment. Those who persisted in their admission I ordered to be led away for execution. I did this because I had no doubt that, whatever they were confessing, stubbornness and unyielding obstinacy warrant nothing less than punishment. [4]There were others beset with a similar insanity whom, because they were Roman citizens, I have officially designated to be sent back to the city for trial.

As it so often happens, the accusations quickly became more widespread and varied in nature because I was currently handling the matter. [5]An anonymous pamphlet was published containing the names of many accused persons. For those on the list who denied that they were or had been Christians, if they repeated after me an invocation to the gods and made offerings of incense and wine to your statue (which for this very purpose I had ordered to be brought in with the images of the gods), and also cursed Christ—for it is said that a true Christian cannot be compelled to commit any of these acts—then I concluded that they ought to be released.

[6]Others, who had been named by an informer, said that they were Christian but soon thereafter denied it, claiming that they indeed had been Christian but have ceased to be one: some three years ago, others several years ago, and a few even twenty years ago. All of these individuals venerated both your statue and the images of the gods, and then they cursed Christ. [7]Moreover, they maintained that the sum total of their guilt and error had amounted to nothing more than that they regularly had assembled on a fixed day before dawn to sing antiphonally amongst themselves a hymn to Christ as if to a god and also to bind themselves by an oath, not to some criminal act, but rather not to commit theft, robbery, or adultery, not to deceive the trust of another person, and not to refuse returning

an entrusted deposit when called upon to do so. After they were finished with these things, it was their custom to disperse and then reassemble again to take food that was of a common and harmless nature; they, however, had stopped this practice after my edict that was promulgated following your orders, which forbade the existence of organized societies. [8]I, therefore, considered it all the more necessary to determine from an examination of two slave-women called deaconesses what the truth was, and I even did so by means of torture. What I found was nothing more than a depraved and fanatical superstition.

[9]And so, I have postponed further investigation and now turn to you for advice. This matter seemed to me worthy of your consideration, especially given the number of people being tried; for many persons of every age, of every rank, and even of both sexes are being summoned and will continue to be summoned to stand trial. Furthermore, the infection of this superstition has spread, not only through the towns but also through the villages and countryside; it appears, however, that this disease can be checked and remedied. [10]For it is quite evident that the temples, which until now were nearly abandoned, have once again begun to be thronged, and the sacred rites, which for so long were let to pass, have been resumed, and the flesh of sacrificial animals is now available everywhere, for which until recently few buyers were to be found. From this, it is easy to see that a great many people could reform if they are given an opportunity to recant.

TRAJAN TO PLINY

EPISTLE X.XCVII

[1]You have followed the proper judicial procedure, my dear Secundus, when examining the cases of those formally accused before you as Christians. For, it is impossible to establish something of universal application that has a more-or-less fixed procedural rule. [2]These people should not be sought out. If they are accused and found guilty, then they should be punished—provided, however, that if they deny being Christians and make this evident by their actions (that is by making offerings to our gods), then they should receive a pardon for their recantation, however suspect they were of being Christians in the past. Moreover, anonymously published pamphlets should not be admitted as evidence in any criminal charge; for this not only sets a dangerous precedent but also does not keep with the spirit of our times.

Bibliography

Beard, Mary, John North, and Simon Price. *Religions of Rome.* 2 vols. New York: Cambridge University Press, 1998.

Carter, Warren. *Pontius Pilate: Portraits of a Roman Governor.* Collegeville, MN: Liturgical Press, 2003.

Mynors, Roger A. B., ed. *C. Plini Caecili Secundi Epistularum Libri Decem*. Oxford: Clarendon Press, 1963.

Radice, Betty. *The Letters of the Younger Pliny*. New York: Penguin, 1963.

Sherwin-White, Adrian N. *The Letters of Pliny: A Historical and Social Commentary*. Oxford: Clarendon Press, 1966.

———. *Roman Society and Roman Law in the New Testament*. The Sarum Lectures, 1960–61. Oxford: Clarendon Press, 1963.

Wilken, Robert. *The Christians as the Romans Saw Them*. 2nd ed. New Haven, CT: Yale University Press, 2003.

Williams, Wynne. *Pliny the Younger: Correspondence with Trajan from Bithynia (Epistles X)*. Warminster: Aris and Phillips, 1990.

—25—

Imitations of Greek Epic in the Gospels

Dennis R. MacDonald

Narrative poetry, the oxygen of Greco-Roman culture, is undetectable to most readers of the New Testament. Despite centuries of erudite attention to early Christian literature, the works of Homer (eighth century BCE), Euripides (ca. 485–407 BCE), and other poets are nearly absent from comparative consideration. The prestigious six-volume *Anchor Bible Dictionary* does have an entry on Homer: see "Weights and Measures." A dry measure gets an entry, but the most influential author of antiquity does not. There is no entry for Hesiod (date uncertain but before 675 BCE), Aeschylus (ca. 525–455 BCE), Euripides, or even Vergil (70–19 BCE), the most important Latin author of his time, whose *Aeneid* significantly shaped Roman imperial identity and propaganda. There is, of course, an entry on poetry; it reads, "Poetry, Hebrew. See Psalms, Book of; Parallelism; Budde Hypothesis." There is nothing about "Poetry, Greek."

The standard edition of the Greek New Testament (*Novum Testamentum Graece*) provides an appendix listing citations and allusions to literature outside the New Testament. One will find about three thousand references to the Old Testament and three hundred from other Jewish sources. For all of Pagan Greek literature, there exist five references, only two from poetry: one from Menander (ca. 342–292 BCE) and one from Euripides. Homer, Hesiod, Aeschylus, and Sophocles (ca. 495–406 BCE) are entirely absent. This same silence obtains to virtually all introductions to the New Testament, many commentaries, and even books devoted to locating the New Testament in its ancient literary environment.

This silence has multiple causes, including the absence of classical training among many New Testament scholars. More profound, however, may be the distance of classical Greek poetry from the Gospels and Acts in time, culture, and literary genre. When scholars attempt to locate early Christian narrative in its literary environments, they understandably look to Jewish literature, the Bible above all, or to contemporary Greek literature, or to literature that resembles its genre. Polytheistic poetry written nearly a millennium earlier is hardly the most likely repository of literary models or analogues. Other contributing factors to the absence of classical poetry in New Testament scholarship may be the stereotypical divorce of "Judaism" from "Hellenism" and a reluctance to acknowledge the indebtedness of early Christian narratives to Pagan literature. Philo, a Jewish philosopher (first century CE), frequently quoted Greek poetry, the Jewish historian Josephus (first century CE) imitated Homeric epic frequently, and several Hellenistic Jews composed poetry on biblical themes in emulation of Greek classics (e.g., Theodotus, Philo Epicus, Ezekiel the Tragedian, and "Sosates, the Jewish Homer"). Even the Book of Tobit, originally written in Aramaic, imitates the first four books of the *Odyssey* (see MacDonald, "Tobit and the Odyssey").

This absence of attention to Homer and other poets starkly contrasts with the following statement by an anonymous contemporary to the Evangelists: "From the earliest age, children beginning their studies are nursed on Homer's teaching. One might say that while we were still in swathing bands we sucked from his epics as from fresh milk. He assists the beginner and later the adult in his prime. In no stage of life, from boyhood to old age, do we ever cease to drink from him" (Ps.-Heraclitus *Quaestiones Homericae* 1.5–6). Exceptional students memorized all of the *Iliad* and the *Odyssey* (according to Xenophon *Symposium* 3.5; cf. 4.6 and Plato's *Ion*), but anyone who knew how to write Greek had been exposed to Homeric epic. The standard catalog of manuscripts from Greco-Roman Egypt lists more than six hundred for Homer (see Pack). After Homer the next best preserved authors were Demosthenes (384–322 BCE) with eighty-three, Euripides with seventy-seven, and Hesiod with seventy-two. Of these authors, only Demosthenes was not a poet; he was an orator. Manuscripts of philosophers and historians are even rarer.

Furthermore, literary education in antiquity to a large extent involved imitating poetry, even for writing prose. The beginning student would trace the letters of the names of Homeric characters; later he might create a list of archaic words in the *Iliad*, ask the *grammatikos* (teacher of literature) for definitions, and then paraphrase the model. Greeks called this practice *mimesis* and Romans *imitatio*. Even though imitation was not limited to Homer, his epics were the most popular targets, even for the writing of prose. When the first-century BCE rhetorician Philodemus asked the question, "Who would claim that the writing of prose is not reliant on the Homeric poems?" the answer he expected was "no one" (*On Poetry* 5.30.36–31.2). So familiar were the epics that accomplished authors could cite apposite lines, embed allusions, and twist characterizations or plots confident that their cleverer readers would be pleased when they recognized the transformation of a familiar model (see David B. Gowler's contribution in this volume).

Narrative poetry was a cultural inevitability even for the illiterate. *Homeridae* (members of an ancient guild of Homeric recitation) and *rhapsodes* ("song-stitchers," poetic performers) recited the epics publicly, and Greek cities continued to stage Attic poetry long after the rise of Christianity. The stories of the poets provided ancient visual artists, both Greek and Roman, with many favorite characters and episodes; they appear on temple friezes, wall paintings in private homes, sarcophagi, vases, mosaics, gems, mirrors, jewelry boxes, and even coins. Even

Christians owned such objets d'art. For example, the depiction of Odysseus strapped to the mast and sailing past the Sirens serves in third-century Christian sarcophagi to depict the journey of the soul to heaven.

I am convinced and have tried to demonstrate in a stream of publications that Mark and Luke-Acts are saturated with strategic imitations of classical Greek literature, Homeric poetry above all (see bibliography). To make the case, I have developed and applied six criteria for identifying mimesis: (1) the accessibility and popularity of the proposed model, (2) evidence of analogous imitations of the same story or speech, (3) the volume or number of similarities between two works, (4) the order of the similarities, (5) the presence of distinctive or unusual traits that bind the two works together, and (6) the interpretability of the differences between the two works. I will apply these criteria in an example later in this chapter.

Critics of my work have seldom questioned these six criteria as such; instead, they occasionally object that a name, a phrase, or a motif that I identify as a distinctive trait is insufficiently unusual to link the two works. Others propose biblical stories instead of Greek classics as models. Others understandably argue that the mimetic strategy must have failed insofar as the vast majority of early Christian interpreters, not to mention modern scholars, seem to have been unaware of the classical antecedents.

Usually, these objections issue from a desire to protect the hegemony of form criticism, which characteristically views the development of early Christian narrative diachronically from historical memory, to the creation of Christian oral tradition and written sources from various Jewish and Gentile Christian environments, to the appropriation, or redaction, of these materials into the New Testament texts as we have them. Some form critics view the Evangelists as tinkering editors and not as authors of literature. Form criticism continues to illumine many early Christian texts, but it alone cannot account for the enormous success of the Gospels and Acts as works of narrative art.

To say that Mark and Luke imitated classical poetry by no means implies that they plagiarized or mindlessly aped their models. They had little interest in showing that Jesus or the apostles were Christian clones of Odysseus, Hector, or Dionysus; instead, these two Evangelists transvalued or otherwise spun their mimetic targets to show that Jesus and his followers were wiser, more courageous and moral, less violent and vengeful than their Pagan counterparts. The God of the Christians was more just and compassionate than the gods of Olympus. One might say that reading the Gospel passages as imitations of Greek poetry makes them truly evangelical; they present their good news in stories designed to transform their culture by superseding it.

But the Gospels and Acts are not primarily evangelical works; they were written for those who already believed that Jesus was the Son of God, the Jewish Messiah. Mark and Luke wrote not to convert their readers but to provide the burgeoning Christian movement a literary narrative to shape its identity, much as classical Greek poetry—Homeric epic above all—had shaped Greek culture, including religion. In this respect, Mark and Luke-Acts are similar to the *Aeneid*, which was composed about a century earlier. In this Latin epic, Vergil transformed Homeric epic and other literature into a lavish and powerful mythology that profoundly shaped Roman politics, society, and culture.

For the purposes of this volume, I have chosen to present my translations of passages on the death and burial of Hector in books 22 and 24 of Homer's *Iliad*. As we shall see, Vergil used the death of Hector as his primary model for the death of Turnus at the end of the *Aeneid*. I then will present the death of Jesus in Mark as yet another imitation of Homer's famous story. Among the scores of other examples I might have chosen are comparisons of the death of Agamemnon and the death of John the Baptist (*Odyssey* 11.385–434 and Mark 6:17–29); Polyphemus and the Gerasene Demoniac (*Odyssey* 9.105–542 and Mark 5:1–20); Nestor's feast for forty-five hundred men and Jesus' feeding the five thousand (*Odyssey* 3.1–67 and Mark 6:32–44); Hermes' walking on water and Jesus' performance of the same feat (*Iliad* 24.322–442 and Mark 6:45–52); blind Tiresias and blind Bartimaeus (*Odyssey* 11.90–151 and Mark 10:46–52); the recognition of Odysseus by Laertes and the recognition of the risen Jesus by two disciples on the way to Emmaus (*Odyssey* 24.205–411 and Luke 24:13–53); the lying dream to Agamemnon and the vision of Cornelius (*Iliad* 2.1–41 and Acts 10:1–8); Priam's escape from the hut of Achilles and Peter's escape from the prison of Agrippa (*Iliad* 24.677–718 and Acts 12:1–17); Dionysus's prison break and that of Paul and Silas (*Bacchae* 576–795 and Acts 16:13–34); Hector's farewell to Andromache and Paul's farewell to the Ephesian elders (*Iliad* 6.369–502 and Acts 20:18–38); and the shipwrecks of Odysseus and Paul (*Odyssey* 5.451–93 and Acts 27:1–28:11).

The first two criteria for detecting mimesis have to do with the status of the proposed model. The death and burial of Hector satisfies the first criterion, accessibility, magnificently. No educated Greek would have been ignorant of the famous ending of the most famous of all Greek books. The ending of the *Iliad* also satisfies the second criterion, analogy, insofar as many authors imitated the death of Hector when narrating the deaths of other heroes. Here I present one of the most obvious.

The Death and Burial of Hector (selections from *Iliad* 22 and 24)

Already in *Iliad* 6, Hector had said his final farewells to his family. His mother Hecuba offered him wine to soften the pain of battle, but the hero refused it:

> "Stay while I can bring you honey-sweet wine so that you can pour a libation to father Zeus and the other immortals first and then you yourself benefit from it as well, if you drink it. Wine greatly enhances strength for an exhausted man, just as you are exhausted from defending your friends." Great flashing-helmeted Hector then answered her, "Royal mother, do not bring me honey-sweet wine lest you weaken me and I forget my might and courage." (6.256–65)

According to *Iliad* 7 to 17, Hector enjoyed a string of military successes until Achilles rejoined the fight to vindicate the death of his friend Patroclus. Single-handedly the Myrmidon captain routed the Trojans back to their city. Despite the pleadings of his father, Priam, and his mother, Hecuba, Hector decided to face Achilles man to man in hopes that his god Apollo once again would give him victory. He told himself, "It is better to charge each other in strife as soon as possible; then we will know to which of us the Olympian [i.e., Zeus] will extend the glory" (22.129–30).

At first Hector turned bravely to face his foe, but when he saw Achilles in the glorious armor that Hephaestus had made him, he panicked:

> A valorous man fled in the lead, but one far greater swiftly pursued. They were not contending for prizes awarded men for swiftness of foot—a sacrificial animal or an ox hide—they ran for the life of horse-taming Hector. . . . All the gods looked on, and the Father of men and gods began a discussion with them, . . . "Come, you gods, consider and decide whether we should save him from death or—noble though he be—subdue him to Peleides Achilles." Then the goddess, owl-eyed Athena, spoke to him, "O Father, god of the dazzling bolt and dark cloud, what a thing you have said! Do you now want to free from grievous death a mere mortal long ago doomed by fate?" (158–61, 166–67, 174–80)

Zeus yielded to his daughter, and she "darted down from the peaks of Olympus" to assist Achilles (186–87).

The Greek champion continued chasing the Trojan around the city, while Apollo urged Hector on. "Then the Father extended the golden scales and placed in them two fates of crippling death: one for Achilles and the other for horse-taming Hector. Gripping it in the middle, he raised it up, and Hector's day of doom sank down and went to the house of Hades. Then Phoebus Apollo left him" (208–13). Without Apollo's help, Hector was doomed.

Athena came to Achilles and told him to catch his breath while she tricked Hector into fighting. Disguising herself as Deïphobus, Hector's brother, she told him that she would join him in the fight.

As is often the case in duels in the *Iliad*, the fight began with trading taunts. When Achilles cast an errant spear, Hector again taunted him: "You missed, god-like Achilles! You do not know my fate from Zeus! . . . You will not be able to plant your spear in my back as I run, but if a god allows it, drive yours through my chest as I charge you! Now then, dodge my bronze spear! O that you might receive the entire shaft with your flesh!" (279–80, 284–86).

Hector then let fly his spear, but it, too, missed. So he turned to Deïphobus for another, but he was not there. Then Hector knew in his mind and said:

> "Alas! Surely the gods have summoned me to death, for I thought that the hero Deïphobus was next to me, but he is inside the wall; Athena has deceived me! Now indeed wicked death is at hand, no longer far off—no escape! For this was a long-standing inclination of Zeus and far-shooting son of Zeus [Apollo] who in the past gladly rescued me. But now at last my doom has arrived!" (295–303)

Hector fought bravely but fell to Achilles's spear. "The end of death engulfed him, and his soul, flying from his limbs, went to the house of Hades, lamenting her fate" (361–63).

After Hector died, Achilles and his comrades stood over the corpse and gloated. "'Surely Hector is softer to handle now than when he burned our ships with blazing fire!' Thus some soldier would speak and stab him as he stood over him.". . . . Achilles himself boasted, "We have won great fame, for we have killed noble Hector, whom the Trojans in the city prayed to as to a god" (373–75, 393–94).

The Trojans watched in horror as Achilles slew their champion and desecrated his corpse by dragging it behind his chariot. Priam was overwhelmed with grief and lamented his loss. It seemed to him and to the Trojans that "majestic Ilium as a whole was burning with fire from top to bottom" (410, cf. 24.727–28). Hecuba cried out, "O my child, I am crushed! . . . Night and day you were my boast throughout the city and relief to Trojan men and Trojan women throughout the town who prayed to you as a god" (431–35).

> Andromache heard the wailing and lamenting from the tower; her joints quivered, and her shuttle fell to the ground. . . . [S]he rushed through the hall like a mad-woman, her heart pounding, and her maidservants went with her. When she got to the tower and the crowd of men, she stopped at the wall to take a look and saw him being dragged around the city. Fast horses were dragging him mercilessly to the hol-low ships of the Achaeans. Black night engulfed her eyes; she fell backward and gasped out her spirit. (447–48, 460–67)

Despite Achilles' dragging of the corpse, the gods protected it from mutilation, decay, and defilement by birds and dogs.

The final book of the *Iliad* narrates the return of Hector's corpse to Troy for a fitting burial. Encouraged by divine visitations, Hector's father, King Priam, set out at night for the Greek camp; he was attended only by his herald Idaeus, who drove a wagon full of an enormous ransom. As they made their way across the plain, Hermes in the form of a Myrmidonian soldier met them and agreed to es-cort them to Achilles' bivouac:

> When they arrived at the walls and the ditch protecting the ships where the guards were beginning to prepare their supper, the messenger Argeïphontes shed sleep over all of them, instantly opened the gates, thrust aside the bolts, and brought Priam in-side together with the glorious gifts on the wagon. . . . [At Achilles' hut] only one bar of pine secured the door, but one that three Achaeans used to drive home, and three used to draw back the great bolt of the doors—three of the others, though Achilles would drive it home on his own. Then Hermes the Helper opened it for the old man and brought in the marvelous gifts for the swift-footed son of Peleus. He dismounted from behind the horses to the ground and said: "Old man, I who have come to you am an immortal god, Hermes; for my father sent me to escort you. But now I am go-

ing back. . . ." When he had said this, Hermes went off to high Olympus. (443–48, 453–62, 468–69)

Priam went to Achilles, knelt, and "kissed his terrible, murderous hands that had slain his many sons" (478–79). Achilles was astonished: "I know in my mind—nor has it escaped my attention—that one of the gods brought you to the swift ships of the Achaeans. For no mortal would dare come into the camp—not even one in his prime. And no mortal could escape the notice of the guards or easily shove back the bar of our doors" (563–67). Achilles agreed to relinquish the corpse, and he told the grieving father to stop weeping: "You will not raise him back to life" (551). Achilles ordered two soldiers to unload the ransom and maidservants to prepare the body. "Then the maidservants washed and anointed the body with oil and wrapped it in a beautiful cape and tunic, and Achilles himself lifted it and placed it upon a bier" (587–89).

> Priam dined with Achilles and went to sleep, intending to return to Troy in the morning. The others—both gods and men, chariot-fighters—slept throughout the night, subdued by soft sleep. But sleep did not overtake Hermes the Helper, who debated in his mind how to escort King Priam from the ships unnoticed by the powerful gatekeepers. He stood over his head and spoke to him, saying: "Old man, you have no concern for harm—the way you are still sleeping among your enemies—since Achilles has spared you. Now you have ransomed your dear son and have given much for him. But your sons whom you left behind might have to give three times such a ransom for your life, if Agamemnon, son of Atreus, learns of you, or if all the Achaeans learn of you."
>
> So he spoke, and the old man was terrified and awoke his herald. Hermes yoked the horses and mules for them, and he himself swiftly drove them through the camp. No one knew about them. (677–91)

Priam escaped because the guards were still asleep and the doors and gates were still open. (This passage seems to have been Luke's model for Peter's prison escape past sleeping guards and automatic doors in Acts 12:1–17.)

Priam and Idaeus later drove the corpse back to Troy, where three women led in the lamentations: Hecuba, Helen, and Andromache, who predicted that her son by Hector "will never reach his prime before the city is destroyed from top to bottom" (727–29). The Trojans burned his body and then "took the bones, placed them in a golden chest, and covered it with soft purple robes. Immediately they then placed it in a hollow ditch and heaped large stones over it" (795–98).

The Death of Turnus in Vergil's *Aeneid*

Vergil's epic ends with the death of Turnus, the Rutulian champion, who plays the role of Homer's Hector; Aeneas, on the other hand, resembles victorious Achilles. Latinus and Amata tried to convince Turnus not to face Aeneas one-on-one, but he insisted on doing so (12.18–63). The scene recalls the futile appeals of Paris and Hecuba to Hector at the beginning of *Iliad* 22. Just as Achilles slew Hector in armor made by Hephaestus at the request of his mother, Thetis, Aeneas, a new Achilles, wore armor made by Vulcan at the request of his mother, Venus. Turnus struck Aeneas, but when his sword snapped on the divinely forged armor, he ran; Aeneas pursued. "They do not seek a trivial prize for sport; they contend for the life and blood of Turnus" (12.764–65; cf. *Iliad* 22.158–61). Rutulian women and men watched helplessly from the walls of Ardea, like the Trojans in the *Iliad* who watched Achilles chasing Hector (107–9, 131–33).

As in Homer, Vergil's gods involve themselves in the action. Juno looked down on the battlefield and summoned Turnus's sister, the immortal nymph Juturna, to assist him. She sent a portent, an eagle slaying a swan, that the Rutulians took to be propitious (154–60, 244–65). She also disguised herself as Turnus's charioteer to keep her brother from danger and to goad him on. Juturna clearly plays a role similar to that given to Apollo in the *Iliad*. Venus, on the other hand, came to the rescue of her smitten son, removed the arrow, and healed the wound (411–24). Juturna and Venus both retrieved weapons for their favorites (781–90), just as Athena had retrieved a spear for Achilles in Homer.

Then "Jupiter himself holds up a scale with dishes of equal weight and places in them the different fates of the two men—whom the fighting dooms and whose death tilts the balance" (725–27; cf. *Iliad* 22.208–13). When he asked Juno to stop supporting Turnus, she agreed: "Now I yield and leave the fighting—in horror" (818). He then sent a messenger to Juturna, who darted down from Olympus in the form of a small bird, but she recognized the sign: she would have to withdraw. "With a great groan the goddess plunged into the depths of the river" (886). The death of Turnus, like the death of Hector, played itself out as a spectacle before the gods.

The fight between Aeneas and Turnus, like the fight between Achilles and Hector, begins with a taunt by the Trojan: "Change your shape any way at all! Gather whatever courage or skill you can! If you wish, fly on wings to the lofty stars or hide yourself in the ground, a hollow prison!" (891–94). The Rutulian responded by "wagging his head" and saying: "Brave one, your raging speech does not frighten me! The gods terrify me—Jupiter's enmity" (894–95).

Turnus was entirely unaware that Juno and Juturna had agreed to abandon him. As he battled Aeneas, it went badly for him, and the truth suddenly dawned on him. "Then various thoughts spin in his mind. He looks at the Rutulians and the city. He freezes with fear and trembles before impending death. He sees nowhere to escape, nowhere to thrust against his foe, nowhere a chariot or his sister, the charioteer" (914–18). This passage obviously imitates the moment of Hector's discovery that his brother, Deïphobus (Athena in disguise), had vanished: "no escape!" After Aeneas disabled him with a spear, Turnus asked him to return his body to his loved ones (931–38). Aeneas finishes him with a sword. Homer had written that Hector's "soul went to Hades, flying from his limbs and bewailing her fate." The last line of the *Aeneid* reads: "And with a groan his life fled indignant to Shades below" (952). Because the epic ends here, Aeneas cannot gloat over Turnus, as Achilles had gloated over Hector, but Vergil used Achilles' gloat as his model for that of Mezentius over fallen Orodes (8.736–46). Vergil clearly modeled a section of the mourning for the Trojan warrior Euryalus after Andromache's collapse at the wall (9.475–502).

Vergil's imitation of the death of Hector satisfies mimetic criteria 3, 4, and 5: a high density of parallels, a similar sequence of presentation, and the presence of unusual motifs in both. Experts thus agree: Vergil imitated the death of Hector when composing his account of the death of Turnus. These parallels also satisfy criterion 6, interpretability; Aeneas plays the role of the victorious Achilles in slaying his Hector, but without Achilles' irrational savagery, gloating, and mutilation of a corpse.

The Death and Burial of Jesus in the Gospel of Mark

At first glance it might appear that Mark's Passion narrative and the death of Hector have little in common. There is no chase, no lifting of divine scales, and no duel. Furthermore, Mark's story bears traces of biblical influence, especially Psalms 22 and 69, and perhaps Zechariah 9–14, Isaiah 53, Amos 8:9, and Wisdom 2. On the other hand, the death and burial of Jesus in many respects echoes the death and burial of Hector.

Criteria 3, 4, and 5 assess similar texts to judge the likelihood of a literary connection between them. The potential parallels between the death of Hector and the death of Jesus are not only dense (criterion 3) but for the most part follow the same sequence (criterion 4). Furthermore, many of the parallels between them are unusual (criterion 5), such as the refusal to drink wine, the recognition of divine abandonment, the call for an ally (or the perceived call for an ally in Mark) who never appeared, a gloat that mocked the supposed divinity of the victim, three women watching and mourning from a distance, and the dangerous, nocturnal rescue of the corpse.

The implications of Mark's imitations are enormous. The accounts of the death of Jesus in the Gospels of Matthew and Luke clearly rely primarily—if not exclusively—on Mark. The same probably is the case also for the Gospel of John. In other words, one can trace all stories in the New Testament concerning Jesus' demise to Mark's literary creativity. What is more, the earliest Evangelist seems not to have incorporated a preexisting Passion narrative and need not have known a coherent oral narrative of Jesus' death. Virtually all of Mark 15:22–46 seems to have been generated from biblical texts and *Iliad* 22 and 24.

On the other hand, one must not use Mark's literary originality to deny the historicity of Jesus' death. The Epistles of Paul, written much earlier than Mark, refer to Jesus' last meal with his followers, his Crucifixion, his burial, and his Resurrection (though not to an empty tomb; Romans 8:34; 1 Corinthians 1:18 and 23, 11:23–25, and 15:4–7; Philippians 2:9; 1 Thessalonians 1:10). Mark surely received at least this much information from tradition.

It is also important to recognize that Mark did not merely copy Homeric episodes; he strategically transformed them and by so doing satisfies criterion 6, interpretability. Unlike Hector, Jesus was no warrior but an innocent victim of violence. Whereas Zeus and Apollo had indeed abandoned Hector, Jesus' God would vindicate him. Most significant, Hector stayed in his tomb; no amount of Priam's tears could raise him back to life (*Iliad* 24.551). After three days, however, Jesus' tomb was empty.

Mark repeatedly imitated Homeric epic throughout his Gospel, and another anonymous Evangelist did so often in Luke-Acts. There are scores of such imitations. Indeed, classical Greek poetry may well be the most ignored, misunderstood, and fruitful literary reservoir for gaining a new appreciation of early Christian narratives.

MARK 15:22–23

And they brought him to the place called Golgotha (which may be translated as the Place of a Skull). They gave him wine mixed with myrrh, but he did not take it.

Hecuba offered Hector wine, but he refused it; he wanted a clear head for the fighting.

MARK 15:29–32

Those who passed by derided him, wagged their heads, and said, "Aha! Destroyer of the Temple and builder of it in three days, rescue yourself by coming down from the cross!" So too the high priests with the scribes were saying, "He rescued others, but he cannot rescue himself! Let the Messiah, the King of Israel, now come down from the cross, so we may see it and believe!" Those who were crucified with him also reviled him.

Jesus made no response to the taunts. In *Iliad* 22, Achilles and Hector traded taunts; Hector addressed his foe as "god-like" and invited him to drive his spear through his chest, "if a god allows it."

MARK 15:33–34

It was the sixth hour [viz., noon] and darkness came over the whole earth until the ninth hour [3:00 P.M.]. And in the ninth hour, Jesus cried in a loud voice, "Eloi, eloi, lema sabachthani," which interpreted means "My God, my God, why have you forsaken me?"

Hector recognized that his gods had deserted him when he turned to Deïphobus for a spear and did not find him there. Jesus interpreted darkness at noon as God's desertion of him. Even though Jesus cites the beginning of Psalm 22, the quotation functions much like Hector's lament. By having Jesus utter the psalm in Aramaic, the earliest Evangelist permits a clever pun. Greek speakers mistook "Eloi, Eloi!" to be a cry for Elijah to come and rescue him, as Hector had vainly called for Deïphobus.

MARK 15:35–36

When some of the bystanders heard this, they began saying, "Look! He is calling Elijah!" Someone ran off, filled a sponge with sour wine, fixed it to a reed, offered it to him to drink, and said, "Wait, let's see if Elijah comes to take him down!"

Neither Deïphobus nor Elijah arrived to help.

MARK 15:37–38

Jesus gave a loud cry and sent out his spirit. The veil of the sanctuary was ripped in two, from top to bottom.

According to Homer, Hector's "soul, flying from his limbs, went to the house of Hades, bewailing her fate." When Priam saw Hector die, he grieved as though "majestic Ilium as a whole was burning with fire from top to bottom."

MARK 15:39

Now when the centurion who stood facing him saw that in this way he breathed his last, he said, "Oh sure, this man was God's son!"

There is nothing in Mark to suggest that this utterance by the centurion was anything other than a gloat; ironically, of course, Jesus was God's Son. Similarly in *Iliad* 22, Achilles stood over Hector's corpse and gloated, "We have killed noble Hector, whom the Trojans in the city prayed to as to a god."

MARK 15:40–41

Women were watching from a distance, among them were Mary Magdalene, Mary the mother of James the younger and Joses, and Salome, who had followed him and served him when he was in Galilee. Many other women, too, had come up with him to Jerusalem.

In the *Iliad*, the Trojans watched from the walls as Achilles slew Hector. Hecuba, Helen, and Andromache led the laments.

MARK 15:42–43

When it was late, and since it was the day of Preparation, that is, the day before the Sabbath, Joseph of Arimathea, a distinguished member of the council, who was also himself waiting expectantly for the kingdom of God, dared to go to Pilate and asked for the body of Jesus.

According to *Iliad* 24, Priam, king of Troy, set out at night on a dangerous journey to rescue the body of his son from his murderer. When he entered Achilles' abode, he begged for the corpse.

MARK 15:44–45

Then Pilate was amazed that he [Jesus] might already be dead; and summoning the centurion, he asked him whether he had been dead for some time. When he learned from the centurion that he was dead, he granted the body to Joseph.

Jesus' quick death allowed burial before the body could be desecrated; the gods preserved Hector's body from desecration.

MARK 15:46

And having bought a linen shroud and taken him down, he wrapped him in the linen shroud and placed him in a tomb that had been cut out of rock, and he rolled a stone at the door of the tomb.

The women in the *Iliad* "wrapped the body in a beautiful cape and tunic, and Achilles himself lifted it and placed it upon a bier." Later, the Trojans heaped stones over Hector's mound.

Bibliography

Bonz, Marianne Palmer. *The Past as Legacy: Luke-Acts and Ancient Epic.* Minneapolis, MN: Fortress Press, 2000.

Hinds, Stephen. *Allusion and Intertext: Dynamics of Appropriation in Roman Poetry.* New York: Cambridge University Press, 1998.

Knauer, Georg Nicolaus. "Vergil's Aeneid and Homer." Pages 390–412 in *Oxford Readings in Vergil's Aeneid*. Edited by S. J. Harrison. Oxford: Oxford University Press, 1990.

MacDonald, Dennis R. *Christianizing Homer: "The Odyssey," Plato, and "The Acts of Andrew."* New York: Oxford University Press, 1994.

———. *Does the New Testament Imitate Homer? Four Cases from the Acts of the Apostles*. New Haven, CT: Yale University Press, 2003.

———. "The Ending of Luke and the Ending of the *Odyssey*." Pages 161–68 in *For a Later Generation: The Transformation of Tradition in Israel, Early Judaism and Early Christianity*. Edited by Randal A. Argall, Beverly A. Bow, and Rodney A. Werline. Harrisburg, PA: Trinity Press International, 2000.

———. *The Homeric Epics and the Gospel of Mark*. New Haven, CT: Yale University Press, 2000.

———. "Luke's Eutychus and Homer's Elpenor: Acts 20:7–12 and *Odyssey* 10–12." *Journal of Higher Criticism* 1 (1994): 5–24.

———. "Renowned Far and Wide: The Women Who Anointed Odysseus and Jesus." Pages 128–35 in *A Feminist Companion to Mark*. Edited by Amy-Jill Levine with Marianne Blickenstaff. Sheffield: Sheffield Academic Press, 2001.

———. "The Shipwrecks of Odysseus and Paul." *New Testament Studies* 45 (1999): 88–107.

———. "The Soporific Angel in Acts 12:1–17 and Hermes' Visit to Priam in *Iliad* 24: Luke's Emulation of the Epic." *Forum*, n.s., 2.2 (1999): 179–87.

———. "Tobit and the Odyssey." Pages 11–40 in *Mimesis and Intertextuality in Antiquity and Christianity*. Edited by Dennis R. MacDonald. Studies in Antiquity and Christianity. Harrisburg, PA: Trinity Press International, 2001.

Morgan, Teresa. *Literate Education in the Hellenistic and Roman Worlds*. New York: Cambridge University Press, 1998.

Pack, Roger A. *The Greek and Latin Literary Texts from Greco-Roman Egypt*. 2nd ed. Ann Arbor: University of Michigan Press, 1965.

Snodgrass, Anthony M. *Homer and the Artists: Text and Picture in Early Greek Art*. New York: Cambridge University Press, 1998.

—26—

Narratives of Noble Death

Robert Doran

We all have to die, but few of us are given the express choice, as was Achilles, of either living a long but inglorious life or a short, glory-filled one. How one faces death, and for what causes one will die, powerfully mark one's identity, one's sense of who one is. The most precious thing one possesses is one's life, and to give away one's life is to give away one's treasure. The noble death, then, is to spend what one owns, one's life, for something other. In this chapter, I have chosen seven stories about such noble deaths. The first three deal with individuals giving their lives for the safety of their people. The second four discuss more philosophic choices for undergoing death.

"Better to Have One Man Die for the People" (John 11:50)

In the first group, I have placed stories from Pompeius Trogus, Livy, and 2 Maccabees. The work of Pompeius Trogus, who wrote at the time of Augustus, is preserved in the faithful epitome made by Marcus Junianus Justinus in the third century CE. The story concerns Codrus, allegedly king of Athens in the eleventh century BCE. Livy, who also wrote at the time of Augustus, reproduces traditions about the history of Rome. The narrative here presented recounts the action of Publius Decius Mus, Roman consul, during a war with the Latins in 340 BCE. These first two stories are drawn from traditional material—Decius may not even have been present at the battle—but their appearance and propagation by these Augustan historians evidences their enduring value as examples of public-mindedness. The final selection in this group consists of the stories told in 2 Maccabees of the Judean martyrs. These martyrs endured persecution during the Hasmonean revolt of the mid–second century BCE. Written down in 2 Maccabees in the late second century BCE, these stories are elaborately told and were very influential in later Christian writers.

Philosophic Deaths

The second group comprises excerpts from Plutarch, Diogenes Laertius, Philostratus, and 4 Maccabees. Plutarch, who died early in the second century CE, wrote a letter to his friend, Paccius, to advise him how to remain composed during his busy life. The letter is now called "On Composure." In this excerpt, Plutarch points to Stilpon (ca. 380–300 BCE), third head of the Megarian school of philosophy, and to Socrates to stress that human identity lies in each person's power and cannot be taken away, even by torture. Diogenes Laertius, who dates probably from the first half of the third century CE, reports in his *Lives of the Philosophers* about the fourth century BCE philosopher Anaxarchus of Abdera. When tortured, Anaxarchus claimed that the real Anaxarchus was untouched by the torture being applied to the body. The piece from Flavius Philostratus is from his *Life of Apollonius of Tyana*, a Neopythagorean philosopher of the first century CE, and tells of his trial before the emperor Domitian. The final piece is from 4 Maccabees, a philosophical reflection on the martyrdoms told in 2 Maccabees, which dates from the late first or early second century CE. The composer of this possible funeral oration argues that reason as informed by the Mosaic Law can control the passions.

NOBLE DEATH AND THE GOSPELS

The death of Jesus was a traumatic event for his early followers. How were they to interpret it, and in what framework were they to narrate it? Stories had often been told of heroes who died (see also Dennis MacDonald's contribution in this volume), and the motifs these stories contained resonate in the Gospel narratives.

The most obvious motif is that of individuals who gave their lives for the salvation of their people. Here the saying attributed to Jesus at Mark 10:45 ("The Son of Man came . . . to give his life as a ransom for many") as well as the thanksgiving over the cup at the Last Supper reflect this sense of Jesus' death being for the salvation of those who follow him. The unconscious prophecy of the high priest Caiaphas at John 11:50 betrays the same notion.

The sense of fate that overshadows so many epic heroes, from Achilles and Hector in Homer's *Iliad* to Turnus at the hands of Aeneas in Vergil's *Aeneid* (see again MacDonald's contribution) also surrounds Jesus as he goes to Jerusalem, for it is there that a prophet must die (Luke 13:34). The risen Jesus in Luke's Gospel will detail how his death was necessary according to the scriptures (Luke 24:26–27, 45). The prayer of Jesus in Gethsemane that he will do his Father's will whatever the cost resonates with stories of Jewish heroes and heroines who died in obedience to the Law.

The difference between the Synoptic Gospels' Gethsemane scene and the incident in John's Gospel at 12:27, where Jesus refuses to ask his Father to save him from this hour, leads us to note the difference between the death of Jesus on the cross in the Gospels of Matthew and Mark and that in the Gospel of John. Where Jesus in the two former Gospels cries out, "My God, my God, why have you forsaken me?" John's Jesus makes sure that the Scriptures have been fulfilled and then dies. Jesus' sense of certitude in going back to the Father which pervades John's narrative might be compared to that of the philosophers who know that a part of them cannot be touched by death.

JUSTINUS, *EPITOMA POMPEI TROGI* 2.6.16–21

Between the Athenians and the Dorians there existed old grudge enmities that the Dorians were about to avenge by war, and they consulted oracles about the outcome of the combat. The answer was that they would have the upper hand unless they killed the Athenian king. Should it come to war, before all else care for the (Athenian) king was commanded to the (Dorian) soldiers.

At that time, Codrus was the Athenian king. When the god's answer as well as the enemy's commands became known, Codrus changed from his royal attire and entered the enemy's camp in tattered clothes, carrying brushwood on his shoulders. There, amidst the turmoil of those obstructing his way, he was killed by a soldier whom he had severely wounded with a sickle. When the body of the king was recognized, the Dorians left without a battle. So the Athenians, by the power of a leader offering himself to death for the salvation of the fatherland, were freed from war.

LIVY, *HISTORY OF THE ROMAN PEOPLE* 8.9.1–8.10

Before they led out to battle, the Roman consuls Decius and Manlius offered sacrifices. The diviner is said to have shown to Decius that the upper part of the liver had been cut off from the section pertaining to the one sacrificing; otherwise the sacrifice was acceptable to the gods. Manlius had obtained remarkably favorable omens. Decius said, "Nevertheless, all is well if favorable omens have been obtained by my colleague."

With the ranks drawn up in the way described above (8.8.3–19), they moved forward. Manlius was in charge of the right wing, Decius of the left. At first the action was waged on both sides with equal strength and ardor, but then the Roman spear-soldiers on the left, not sustaining the assault of the Latins, withdrew toward the second line of soldiers.

Amidst this confusion, the consul Decius called out in a loud voice to Marcus Valerius, "We need the help of the gods, Marcus Valerius. Therefore, state pontiff of the Roman people, come and perform the words by which I will devote myself to the infernal gods on behalf of the legions." The pontiff ordered him to put on the purple-bordered toga and, with his head covered and his hand stretched under the toga toward his chin, to stand on a spear placed under his foot. He said, "Janus, Jupiter, Father Mars, Quirinus, Bellona, Lares, divine Novensiles, the Indigites gods, the gods in whose power are we and our enemies, and the spirits of the dead, I implore and supplicate you, I seek your favor and plead that you help forward might and victory for the Roman people of the Quirites, and cause the enemies of the Roman people of the Quirites to be affected by terror, awe, and death. As I have formally declared by words, on behalf of the commonwealth of the Roman people of the Quirites, of the army, the legions and the auxiliaries of the Roman people of the Quirites, I devote the legions and the auxiliaries of the enemy together with myself to the spirits of the dead and to Earth."

Once he had implored in this way, he ordered the lictors to go to Titus Manlius and quickly inform his colleague that he had devoted himself on behalf of the army. Girded in the Gabinian way and armed, he leapt onto his horse and thrust himself into the midst of the enemy, noticed by both armies and having an appearance much more majestic than that of humans, as though sent from heaven as an expiatory offering for all the wrath of the gods who would avert the disaster from his own troops and take it to the enemy. So all the terror and fear carried by his presence disturbed the front lines of the Latins and then spread throughout the whole army. This was most clearly seen in that, wherever he was carried by his horse, there they feared as if struck by a disaster-bringing star. When he fell down covered with spears, at that moment the Latin cohorts were clearly thrown into confusion, fled, and were widely ravaged. At the same time, the Romans, their spirits freed from supernatural restraint, sprang to attack as if for the first time the signal for battle had been given, and they started a fresh assault. The skirmishers were running in and out of the first two lines of battle, and were joining their forces to the spearmen and the second line, while the third line, leaning on their right knee, were awaiting the consul's signal to enter the fray.

As the struggle continued since the number of Latins in some areas were prevailing, the consul Manlius heard of the end of his colleague. After he had honored such a memorable death, as justice and purity required, with tears no less than with praise, he hesitated for a moment whether it was time to have the third line enter the fray. Then, determining that it was better to keep them fresh for the final confrontation, he commanded the least experienced unit of the third line to come up from the rear in front of the standards. As soon as they moved up, the Latins at once roused their own third line, as if their adversaries had done the same. For some time they fought fiercely. Although they were themselves tired and had broken or blunted their spears, the Latins had pushed back the enemy and thought it already subdued and down to the last line. At that moment, the consul said to his third line, "Enter the fray now fresh against weary foes, mindful of your fatherland, and your parents, wives and children, mindful of the consul who lies dead for the sake of your victory." When the third line rose up fresh with brightly shining armaments, a new line appearing unexpectedly, they drew in the first two lines. Raising a shout, they threw into disorder the front ranks of the Latins and pierced their fronts with spears.

With the prime power of fighters fallen, the Romans, almost untouched, passed through the other Latin units as if they were unarmed. They hewed the enemy's formation with such slaughter that they left behind scarcely a quarter of the enemy. The Samnites also, drawn up a short distance away at the foot of the mountains, caused fear to the Latins.

For the rest, among all the citizens and allies especial commendation belonged to the consuls, one of whom turned onto himself alone all the threats and perils from the upper and the lower gods, and the other took part in the battle with such bravery and level-headedness that, as those among both the Roman and Latins who transmitted to later generations a record of the battle readily agree, whichever side Titus Manlius had led would have without a doubt been victorious. The Latins regrouped from the flight at Minturnae. The camp was the second spoil taken, and many destined to die were caught there alive, especially Campanians. The body of Decius was not found on that day, as night fell upon the searchers. On the next day, it was found covered with spears among a great many slaughtered enemies. Funeral rites appropriate to his death took place, with his colleague celebrating with praise.

2 MACCABEES 6:18–7:42

Eleazar was one of the leading officials, a man at that time advanced in age and, in personal appearance, most honorable. He was being pressed to open his mouth to eat pig meat. However, he accepted death with honor rather than life with defilement, and went by free choice toward the instrument of torture. He spat out the meat, approaching the torture instrument as one should if one stands firm to guard oneself from what it is not lawful to take because of affection for life.

Those in charge of the unlawful sacrificial repast took him aside privately because of their long-standing acquaintance with the man. They urged him to pretend by eating meat that he could legally use and that would be supplied and prepared by him, as if he were eating what had been ordered by the king from the meats coming from the sacrifice. By eating this way, he would be released from the sentence of death and obtain favorable treatment because of his previous friendship with them.

However, he took up again the high-principled position, one worthy of his time of life, his distinguished family, his acquired and remarkable way of life, and his honorable behavior since he was a child, one especially in accord with the holy and God-founded code of laws. He promptly declared that they should conduct him into Hades. "It is beneath the dignity of my time of life to pretend, so that many youths, when they think that ninety-year-old Eleazar has crossed over to foreign ways, will themselves through me be deceived by means of my pretense for the sake of this brief and fleeting life, and that I myself incur defilement and ignominy for my old age. If for now I remove from myself punishment from humans, neither alive nor dead shall I escape the hand of the Almighty. Therefore, I will courageously leave this life. I will show myself worthy of my old age and leave for the youth a noble example to die willingly and nobly for the august and holy laws."

Having said this, he straightaway went to the instrument of torture. Those leading him changed their recent good-will to ill-will because of the aforesaid words, as they thought them to be foolishness. About to die under the blows, he groaned aloud and said, "To the Lord who possesses knowledge, it is clear that, though I could have been released from death, I endure these harsh sufferings in my body as I am flogged, but suffer them content in soul because of the fear of Him." So in this way, he exchanged this life for another; he left behind his own death as an example of nobility and a memorial of excellence not only to the youth but also to the bulk of the nation.

Also, seven brothers along with their mother were seized. Tortured with whips and cords, they were being constrained by the king to eat of the unlawful pig's flesh. Their spokesperson said, "Why should you question and learn from us? For we are ready to die rather than transgress the ancestral laws." Enraged, the king ordered that frying pans and cauldrons be heated. When they were straightaway heated, he ordered that the spokesperson's tongue be cut out, that he be scalped and that his hands and feet be cut off while the other brothers and his mother looked on. The king commanded that the completely disabled man be brought to the fire and, still breathing, be fried. As the fumes from the frying pan amply spread abroad, the brothers with their mother encouraged each other to die nobly, saying, "The Lord God watches and truly he relents upon us, just as Moses made clear in the song where he confronted and witnessed against the community, 'The Lord will relent upon his servants.'"

After the first had died in this fashion, they led the second along, mocking him. They tore the skin with its hairs off his head and asked whether he would eat rather than have his body punished limb by limb. He used his ancestral speech to say, "No!" Thereupon he received the next torment like the first brother. At his last gasp he said, "You wretch! You remove us from this present life, but the king of the universe will raise us up to return to eternal life since we die in defense of his laws."

After this person, the third was being mocked. Asked to speak, he boldly stretched forth his hands and said nobly, "I acquired these from the heavenly one and I take no notice of them on account of his laws. From him, I hope to gain them again." He was regarding the sufferings as naught so that the king himself and his companions were astonished at the spirit of the young man.

When he was put to death, they tormented and tortured the fourth likewise. On the point of death he said, "As for those being put to death by men, they have chosen to await what is hoped for from God, namely to be raised again by him. As for you, there will be no resurrection into life."

Next they brought forward the fifth and were torturing him. But he looked at the king and said, "You do what you want as you have authority among humans, although you are mortal. But do not suppose that our race has been abandoned by God. Be obstinate, and see his magnificent power as he will torment you and your seed."

After this brother, they brought the sixth. About to die, he said, "Do not be falsely misled. For we are suffering these things because of our own fault as we sinned against our own God. But do not think that you will get off scot-free, because you have tried to fight against God."

The mother was extraordinarily marvelous and worthy to be singled out for mention. She had seen seven sons perishing in one day, yet she bore it with a strong heart because of her hope in the Lord. Filled with noble resolution, she was encouraging each in the ancestral language. She stirred up her womanly way of reckoning with manly ardor as she said to them, "I do not know how you came into my womb: I did not bestow breath and life to you, nor did I organize the components of each. So, the creator of the world, he who arranged human production and invented the production of all things, will mercifully give back to you breath and life, as you now take no notice of yourselves on account of the laws."

Antiochus, however, thought that he was being despised and suspected the language as disparaging. He not only appealed to the still-surviving youngster with words, but he guaranteed on oath that, if he would change from his ancestral traditions, he would enrich him and make him envied, hold him as friend, and entrust him with royal service. When the young man showed not the slightest interest, the king recommended to the mother that she act as adviser to the lad for his safety. As he kept on recommending, she undertook to persuade her son. Leaning toward him, she scoffed at the cruel tyrant and spoke in the ancestral language, "Son, pity me who carried you around in my womb for nine months and suckled you three years. I brought you up and led you to this age, and nurtured you. I beseech you, child, to look toward heaven and earth and, on seeing all that is in them, to know that God did not make these things from what existed and the human race came into existence in the same way. Do not fear this public executioner, but be worthy of your brothers. Embrace death, so that I may get you back along with your brothers in God's mercy."

As soon as she stopped, the young man said, "For whom are you waiting? I do not obey the king's ordinance, but I obey the ordinance of the law given to our ancestors through Moses. You are the originator of all damage to the Hebrews, but you shall certainly not escape God's grasp. For we suffer because of our own sins. If our living Lord has been angry for a little while for punishment and instruction, he will again also be reconciled with his own servants. As for you, unholy and most polluted of all humans, do not in insolence be falsely buoyed up with uncertain hopes because you raised your grasp upon the servants of heaven. For you have not yet escaped the judgment of the all-powerful God, the overseer. For our brothers have fallen, having endured under divine compact brief pain for everlasting life, but you will obtain by God's sentence the proper penalties for arrogance. I, like my brothers, surrender both body and soul for the sake of the ancestral laws. I call upon God soon to deal propitiously with the nation, and so you, by means of afflictions and whippings, acknowledge that He alone is God and the wrath of the Almighty, which rightly was applied upon our whole nation, come to a halt in me and my brothers."

Enraged, the king engaged him more severely than the others, vindictive because of the taunting. So he left life undefiled, trusting completely in the Lord.

After her sons, the mother died.

2 MACCABEES 14:37–46

Rhazis, one of the elders from Jerusalem, was informed against to Nicanor as a man who loved his fellow citizens, who was exceedingly well spoken of and called on account of his good-will a father of the Jews. For, during the former periods of separation, he had pronounced judgment for Judaism, and had risked body and soul in defense of Judaism with all zeal. As Nicanor wished to show plainly the ill-will which he felt toward the Jews, he sent over five hundred soldiers to seize him. For he thought that, by seizing him, he would bring misfortune to the Jews. With the mob about to lay hold of the tower, as they were breaking through the outer door and ordering to bring forward fire and set the doors on fire, Rhazis was hemmed in on all sides. He enjoined on himself the sword, willing to die nobly rather than be in the power of offenders and maltreated in a manner unworthy of his own nobility. Not hitting the right spot with the thrust because of the haste of the action and with the crowds coming through the doorways, he nobly ran onto the wall and courageously threw himself headlong into the crowd. As the crowd quickly stepped back and a space opened up, he landed in the middle of the empty space. Still breathing and emotionally at fever pitch, he stood up. With blood gushing forth and his injuries hard to endure, he went through the crowd at a run. Completely drained of blood, he stood on a steep rock. He exposed his guts, took them in both his hands and hurled them into the crowd. Calling on him who is master of life and death to give them back to him again, he left life in this way.

PLUTARCH, *ON COMPOSURE*

When Demetrius captured the city of the Megarians, he asked Stilpon that surely nothing belonging to Stilpon had been carried away. Stilpon said that he did not see anyone carrying "what belonged to me." So, although Fortune should plunder or take away everything else, we have ourselves such a thing "which even the Achaeans could not carry or drive off."

Therefore, one ought not disparage or put Nature down, as if Nature possessed nothing strong and lasting, nothing beyond the reach of Fortune. On the contrary, if we know that the weak and perishable part of the human, which waits for Fortune, is a petty part of the human, but that we ourselves master the better portion, in which the greatest of goods—worthwhile opinions, knowledge, and discourse leading to virtue—once established have an existence which does not diminish or perish, we ought to be undaunted and confident as regards the future. We should say to Fortune what Socrates, appearing to speak to his accusers, said to the jurors, namely, that Anytus and Meletus are able to kill but they are not able to hurt. For Fortune indeed is able to encompass with sickness, to take away possessions, to calumniate one to the assembly or tyrant, but it is not able to make a good, courageous and great-souled person evil, cowardly, mean-spirited, base, and envious. Fortune is not able to take away that attitude whose constant presence is a greater help for glory than a pilot is for seafaring.

DIOGENES LAERTIUS, *LIVES OF THE PHILOSOPHERS* 9.58–59

Anaxarchus accompanied Alexander the Great and flourished in the 110th Olympiad. He had as an enemy Nicocreon, the tyrant of Cyprus. Once, at a banquet, Alexander asked him what he thought of the meal. Aiming at Nicocreon, Anaxarchus said, "O king, everything is lavishly presented. For the rest, the head of some satrap ought to be served." For that, Nicocreon bore a grudge. After the death of the king, when Anaxarchus on a sea voyage put in unwillingly in Cyprus, Nicocreon seized him. He threw him into a mill and ordered him to be pounded with iron grinders. Anaxarchus, however, paid no attention to the vengeance, and uttered that well-known saying, "Pound the sack of Anaxarchus, but Anaxarchus you do not pound." When Nicocreon ordered his tongue to be cut off, the word is that he bit it off and spat it forth to him.

PHILOSTRATUS, *LIFE OF APOLLONIUS OF TYANA* 7.14–8.12

Apollonius responded, ". . . a wise man will die certainly for the sake of the causes you noted, but anyone, even someone not wise, would die for the sake of these. For to die for the sake of liberty is enjoined by law, and nature determines one to die for the sake of kin, friends, and youthful lovers. But nature and law are served by all humans; nature is served by them willingly, law unwillingly. But it is especially befitting for the wise to die for the sake of those things they pursue. For law does not enjoin these, nor does nature produce them, but those the wise man exercises himself in out of resolute strength. If anyone were to outlaw these, let fire come on the wise man, let an axe come on him, since none of these will conquer him nor drive him to any lie, but he will hold onto whatever he knows no less than to the mystery rites into which he had been initiated . . ."

[Apollonius and his companion Damis journeyed to Rome, and were arrested. Various encounters with opponents and fellow prisoners are recorded. Finally, Apollonius was led before the emperor Domitian:]

7 [31]About to enter, Apollonius said, "Damis, you seem, as far as I can tell, to think that Aecus is the watchman of these gates, as he is said to be of Hades, for you look like a dead man." Damis said, "Not yet dead, but about to die." Apollonius said, "Damis, you appear to me to have an unnatural view about death, although you have been with me for some time, studying philosophy from your youth. I thought both that you had prepared yourself for it and also knew my overall plan (for dealing with it). For, just as heavily armed fighters need not only courage but also a plan of attack which lets them know the opportune moments that arise in the fight, so philosophers must be careful about the opportune moments in which to die, so that they come to them not without a plan, not resigning themselves to die but with the best choice. Because I have chosen well and in accordance with an opportune moment which was appropriate to philosophy, if someone wished to kill me, I defended myself against others in your presence, and, in order to teach you, I spoke plainly."

[The emperor Domitian tried to get Apollonius to denounce Nerva as a traitor but, failing, imprisoned Apollonius. Again, Apollonius is shown interacting with his jailors, other inmates, and some who try to entrap him. At one point, in the presence of Damis, he miraculously took the chains off his legs and then put them back on to show that he is there of his own free will. Then comes the trial:]

8 [4]Such skirmishes took place before the trial, but the following took place during it. The courtroom was set up as if at a meeting for a panegyric: all the distinguished persons were present for the trial, as the emperor was making an effort to convict him before as many as possible on the same charge as that of Nerva and his friends. However, Apollonius was simply disregarding anything to do with the emperor, so that he did not even look at him. When his accuser insulted him for his disregard, and ordered him to look at the god of all humans, Apollonius lifted up his eyes to the ceiling, showing that he looked toward Zeus, and held that the one impiously flattered to be worse than the flatterer. The accuser cried out, "Emperor, time is running on. If you allow him a big block of time to speak, he will stuff our throats. I have this scroll on which are written the charges he must answer. Let him defend himself against them one by one."

The emperor praised the accuser as if he had advised the best procedure, and commanded the man to defend himself according to the procedure advised by the accuser. However, the emperor passed over the other charges as not worthy for someone to bring into account, but questioned him about four charges that he considered difficult and hard to answer.

He said, "Apollonius, why do you not wear the clothing everybody does, but have picked out a peculiar kind?" He answered, "Because the earth which feeds me also clothes me, and I don't trouble the poor animals."

He asked again, "Why do people call you a god?" He said, "Because a person recognized as good is honored by the title of god." (I showed in my narrative about the Indians whence this saying came into the man's philosophy.)

Third, he questioned him about the plague in Ephesus. He said, "From where were you urged or by whom advised that you foretold that those in Ephesus would fall diseased?" He said, "Emperor, I perceived the danger first because I lead a more sensitive life. If you wish, I will speak about the nature of plagues." (I think the emperor feared that he would list the injustice, the unclean marriages, and whatever he had not rightfully done with their corresponding diseases.) He said, "I don't need such an answer."

When he brought in the fourth question against Nerva and his friends, he did not immediately rush in but, after stopping for a long time and pondering much, like someone feeling dizzy, he questioned not as everyone expected. For they thought that he would throw away the pretense and not keep himself from naming Nerva and his friends and shouting savage threats about the sacrifice. But he did not act in this way, but sneakily approached the question. He said, "Tell me. When you left your house on such and such a day and went into the country, to whom did you sacrifice the child?" Apollonius, as if rebuking a child, said, "Be quiet! For *if* I left the house, I was in the country. *If* this was so, then I sacrificed. *If* I sacrificed, then I ate of it. But let trustworthy people say this." When the man said this and the approval aroused was greater than was appropriate to an imperial courthouse, the emperor thought the audience in agreement with Apollonius, and, affected somewhat by the answers, for they were strong and intelligent, he said, "I acquit you of the charges, but stay until we can talk privately."

Emboldening himself, Apollonius said, "Thank you, emperor. However, because of these offenders, the cities have fallen to ruin, the islands are full of refugees, the mainland full of lamentation, the armies full of cowardice and the senate full of suspicion. If you wish, give me an opportunity to speak, but, if you don't want me to, send someone to take my body, but my soul cannot be taken. Indeed, you cannot even take my body, 'for you will not kill me, for I am not destined to die.'"

On saying this, he disappeared from the courtroom. He selected the present moment well as he foresaw that the tyrant was clearly not going to question him sincerely about anything essential—for the tyrant was somehow proud of not having killed Apollonius—and [Apollonius] did not want to be drawn into such a discussion. Rather, he thought he would best attain his goal if his nature were not to be unknown, and it were to be known that he was never to be captured against his will. Also, he no longer had fear for his friends, for the tyrant had not started to say anything about them. How, then, could he possibly kill them upon charges not relied upon in the courtroom? Such are the facts I found in the trial proceedings.

[Philostratus then provides the speech Apollonius would have given in his defense if allowed the time:]

8 [8]When he left the courtroom in such a godlike and ineffable manner, the tyrant was not affected the way many thought he would be. For they thought he would shout savage threats over this, pursue the man, and proclaim to the whole world that no place could accept him. Yet he did nothing like this, but, as if struggling against the general opinion or rather, as if understanding that humans alone could do nothing against the man. But let us reckon if he paid no attention to it from what happened next, for he will be seen to have been thrown into utter confusion rather than scornful.

For he was hearing another case after this one, where a city was contending against someone over a will. But not only did the names of the disputants escape him, but the very meaning of the case, for his questions were meaningless, and his answers not pertinent to the case at hand. Such behavior strongly argues how the tyrant had been driven out of his senses and at a loss—especially since flatterers had persuaded him that nothing escaped him.

In such a state Apollonius put the tyrant, making him who was the terror of the Greeks and barbarians appear a toy of the philosophy of Apollonius. Apollonius himself left the courtroom before noon, and he appeared in the late afternoon to Demetrius and Damis in Dicaearchia, for this is why he had commanded Damis not to wait for his defense but to walk to Dicaearchia. He did not say what he had in mind beforehand, but he commanded the one most well-disposed toward him to do what followed on what he had planned.

Damis had arrived on the previous day and talked with Demetrius about what happened before the trial. From what he heard, Demetrius felt more concerned than someone who is hearing about Apollonius, and questioned him again on the next day about the same things as he was in distress with him down by the sea (the one that figures in the stories about Calypso). For they despaired of his coming, since the harshness of tyranny applied to everyone. However, because of the man's nature, they were honoring his orders. Tired, they sat down in the temple of the Nymphs in which there is a jar, made of white stone, containing a spring of water which neither overflows the mouth nor dips below it even if someone draws off some. After discussing the nature of the water, not very earnestly because of their despondency over the man, they came back to speak about what happened before the trial.

Damis broke into wailing, and said something like this, "Shall we ever see, O gods, our excellent companion?" On hearing this, Apollonius, who was already standing in the temple, said, "You will see him or rather you have already seen him." "Alive?" said Demetrius. "If dead, we have not yet ceased to lament you." Stretching out his hand, Apollonius said, "Take hold of me. If I escape you, I am a specter who has come from the realm of Persephone such as the underworld gods make appear to those very despondent through mourning. But if, when touched, I stand firm, persuade Damis that I live and have not thrown off my body." No longer could they disbelieve, but they rose up and clung to the man and kissed him.

4 MACCABEES 1:1–17

About to present a most philosophic discourse whether reverent reason is absolute master of the passions, I would straightforwardly advise you actively to pay attention to this philosophy. For this discourse is altogether necessary for knowledge, and contains moreover praise of the greatest virtue, namely, of prudence. If, therefore, reason is observed to control the passions that prevent temperance, namely, gluttony and lust, and also is again observed to rule the passions that hinder justice, such as malice, and those that hinder fortitude, namely anger and fear and pain, how then, some might possibly say, is reason not master of forgetfulness and ignorance if it controls the passions? Whoever attempts to say this is altogether absurd. For reason does not control its own passions, but those opposed to justice, fortitude and prudence—not so as to make them impotent, but so as not to yield to them. On many and various grounds, therefore, I could present to you that reason is in absolute control of the passions, but I would point this out far better by the bravery of those who died for the sake of virtue, namely Eleazar and the seven brothers and their mother. All these, by disregarding the pain until death, showed that reason controls the passions. For their virtue, it is incumbent on me to praise those men with their mother who died about this time for the sake of nobility, but I would rather congratulate them for their honors. Since they were marveled at for their fortitude and endurance not only by all humans but also by those who tortured them, they became responsible for the tyranny against their nation being destroyed as they conquered the tyrant by their endurance. So through them the fatherland was cleansed. To talk about reason first of all, as I am in the habit of doing, is allowable as I begin the proposed topic, and thereafter I will turn toward the discourse about the martyrs, as I glorify God most wise.

We are investigating, therefore, if reason is in absolute control of the passions. We determine then what is reason and what is passion, and all the kinds of passions, and if reason controls all of them. Reason, then, is a mind with correct calculation preferring the life of wisdom. Wisdom is knowledge of divine and human affairs and of their causes. Such knowledge is the education acquired through the Law, through which we learn about the divine affairs in a reverent way and about human affairs usefully. Prudence, justice, fortitude and temperance constitute the kinds of wisdom. The most important of all is prudence by means of which reason controls the passions. As regards the natures of the passions, the most comprehensive are two, namely pleasure and pain. Each of these is naturally both in the body and in the soul.

[The author continues with an exposition of various passions, then speaks of Mosaic Law in controlling passions. He gives an example from the life of David of reason's control, before starting to retell the incidents from 2 Maccabees, particularly the story of Eleazar and the seven brothers and their mother. At the death of the seventh son, the author begins to extol reason again:]

4 MACCABEES 13:23–14:20

So then, as brotherly love excites sympathy, the seven brothers were most sympathetic toward each other. For, educated by the same Law, and practicing the same virtues and brought up together in a just way of life, they loved each other exceedingly. For the common zeal for nobility heightened their goodwill and concord toward each other. Along with piety they established brotherly love as most desirable. However, although nature, close acquaintanceship and excellent mores increased brotherly affection among them, the ones remaining were sustained through their piety, as they saw their brothers maltreated and tortured to death. Even more, they urged them toward the torture so that they not only despised the pains but even conquered the emotions of brotherly love.

O reasonings more kingly than kings, freer than the free! O reasonings from the holy and harmonious concord of the seven brothers concerning piety! Not one of the seven blessed ones feared or hesitated to die, but all hastened to death through torture as if they were running on the road to deathlessness. Just as hands and feet move in concord with the directions of the soul, so those holy youths moved as by the deathless soul of piety toward a death concordant to the defense of piety. O all-holy seven of brothers in concord! Just as the seven days of the world's creation encircle piety, so the youths dance encircling seven, as they dismiss the fear of tortures. At present we shiver as we hear of the affliction of those youths, but they were not only seeing, not only were hearing the pronouncement of the immediate threat, but they also suffered and steadfastly endured. They did this even under the pains of fire, than which there is nothing more painful. For the power of fire is sharp and cutting and swiftly dissolves bodies.

Do not think it wonderful if reasoning controlled those men in the tortures, since a mind even of a woman despised more diverse pains. For the mother of the seven youths endured the mangling of each one of her children. See how entwined is the love of a parent as it involves everything in a deep-seated compassion. Even animals without reason have a compassion and love toward their offspring which is similar to that found in humans. For as regards birds, the tame variety shield their young by nesting under the roofs of houses, while those who make their nests on mountaintops, in clefts of rocks, in tree openings or treetops give birth and prevent anything from approaching. If they cannot prevent, they circle around their young and suffer in their love, calling out in their own language and helping their young as much as they can. Why is it necessary to give from the world of animals without reason further examples of the compassion toward their young when even the bees, at the time for making the honeycomb, ward off whatever approaches and stab with a sting like a sword whatever approaches and repulse it till death. But not even compassion for her children moved the mother of the young men, she who had a soul like Abraham's!

Bibliography

Barton, Carlin A. *Roman Honor: The Fire in the Bones*. Berkeley: University of California Press, 2001.

Hengel, Martin. *The Atonement: A Study of the Origins of the Doctrine in the New Testament*. Philadelphia: Fortress Press, 1981.

Rajak, Tessa. "Dying for the Law: The Martyr's Portrait in Jewish-Greek Literature." Pages 39–67 in *Portraits: Biographical Representation in the Greek and Latin Literature of the Roman Empire*. Edited by M. J. Edwards and Susan Swain. Oxford: Clarendon Press, 1997.

Seeley, David. *The Noble Death: Graeco-Roman Martyrology and Paul's Concept of Salvation*. Sheffield: JSOT Press, 1990.

Sterling, Gregory. "Mors Philosophi: The Death of Jesus in Luke." *Harvard Theological Review* 94 (2001): 383–402.

van Henten, Jan Willem. *The Maccabean Martyrs as Saviours of the Jewish People: A Study of 2 and 4 Maccabees*. Leiden: Brill, 1997.

van Henten, Jan Willem, B.A.G.M. Dehandschutter, and M.J.W. van der Klaauw. *Die Entstehung der jüdischen Martyrologie*. Leiden: Brill, 1989.

van Henten, Jan Willem, B.A.G.M. Dehandschutter, M.J.W. van der Klaauw, and Friedrich Avemarie. *Martyrdom and Noble Death: Selected Texts from Graeco-Roman, Jewish and Christian Identity*. London: Routledge, 2002.

Williams, S. K. *Jesus' Death as Saving Event: The Background and Origin of a Concept*. Missoula, MT: Scholars Press, 1975.

— 27 —

Isaiah 53:1–12 (Septuagint)

Ben Witherington III

Isaiah 53, certainly one of the most challenging texts from the Hebrew Scriptures to be translated into Greek in several versions (LXX, Aquila, Symmachus, and possibly by one or more early Christians), was used rather heavily in early Christian circles; on the textual issues raised by the Hebrew text, which are not a few, see Oswalt (373–410). It seems likely that the Hebrew version was more influential for Jesus and his earliest Aramaic-speaking followers, but it seems clear enough that in Acts 8:32–33 Luke is following the LXX, and in general this seems to be the case in the New Testament when the author was writing in Greek. For better or worse, the LXX was the Bible for Greek-speaking Christians, particularly in congregations dominated by Gentiles. Because of the importance of both dominant versions, this chapter offers a parallel-column translation so that the differences can be seen. It does not attempt to present the text in a form that suggests it is a lyric or poem, but the Hebrew text lends itself to that sort of rendering more than the Greek text.

On the history of the interpretation of this text, see Janowski and Stuhlmacher; on the exegesis and interpretation of the Hebrew texts, besides Oswalt one also should consult Childs and Westermann. I am basically in agreement with the translation of Jobes and Silva (218–26), though I have chosen to go a slightly different way on some minor issues.

Hebrew Version	*LXX*
Who has believed what we have heard?	Lord, who has believed our report?
And to whom has the arm of the Lord been revealed?	And to whom has the arm of the Lord been revealed?
For he grew up before him like a young plant, and like a root out of dry ground; he had no form or majesty that we should look at him, nothing in his appearance that we should desire him	He grew up before him like a child, like a root in a dry land. There is no form to him or glory: when we saw him, he had no form or beauty.

Hebrew Version	*LXX*

He was despised and rejected by others; a man of suffering and acquainted with infirmity; and as one from whom others hid their faces he was despised, and we held him no account.

Surely he has borne our infirmities and carried our diseases; yet we accounted him stricken, struck down by God, and afflicted. But he was wounded for our transgressions, crushed for our iniquities; upon him was the punishment that made us whole, and by his bruises we are healed.

All like sheep have gone astray; we have all turned to our own way, and the Lord has laid on him the iniquity of us all. He was oppressed, and he was afflicted, yet he did not open his mouth; like a lamb that is led to the slaughter, and like a sheep that before its shearers is silent, so he did not open his mouth.

By a perversion of justice he was taken away. Who could have imagined his future? For he was cut off from the land of the living, stricken for the transgression of my people.

They made his grave with the wicked, and his tomb with the rich, although he had done no violence, and there was no deceit in his mouth. Yet it was the will of the Lord to crush him with pain.

When you make his life an offering for sin, he shall see his offspring, and shall prolong his days; through him the will of the Lord shall prosper. Out of his anguish he shall see light; he shall find satisfaction through his knowledge. The righteous one, my servant, shall make many righteous, and he shall bear their iniquities. Therefore I will allot him a portion with the great, and he shall divide the spoil with the strong; because he poured out himself to death, and was numbered with the transgressors; yet he bore the sin of many, and made intercession for the transgressors.

But his form was without honor. Failing in comparison to all humans; a man in calamity and knowing how to carry weakness, because his face was turned away, he was without honor and not esteemed.

This one carries our sins, and suffers pain for us, and we recognized him to be in trouble, in blow(s) and in ill-treatment. But he was wounded because of our lawlessness and has been weakened because of our sins; the discipline of our peace was upon him; by his bruise we were healed.

We have all wandered like sheep, each one has wandered in his own way; and the Lord handed him over to our sins. And because of his affliction he does not open his mouth; like a sheep he was led to slaughter, and as a lamb is silent before the one shearing it, so he does not open his mouth.

In humiliation, his judgment was taken away. Who will describe his generation? Because his life is taken from the earth; he was led to death because of the lawlessness of my people.

And I will give the wicked for his burial, and the rich for his death, because he did not commit lawlessness, nor was deceit found in his mouth. And the Lord desires to cleanse him from the blow.

If you give [an offering] for sin, your soul will see a long-lived seed. Moreover the Lord desires to take away from the distress of his soul, to show him light, and to mold him with understanding—to justify a righteous man who is serving many well; and he himself will bear their sins. Therefore he shall make many inherit, and he will distribute the spoils of the powerful, because his soul was handed over to death, and he was reckoned among the transgressors. And he himself bore the sins of many, and because of their sins he was handed over.

The most noticeable and basic difference between the Greek and the Hebrew versions of Isaiah 53 is that the Greek translation focuses more on the honor and shame dimensions of the text. Notice the stress on the servant being without honor, and even his form was without honor and glory. He did not have "face" and would not show his "face." The preoccupation with his outward form or beauty or "face" probably reflects how some of the Greek virtues are in the mind of the translator and so affect his rendering of the text. The servant's humiliation also is spoken of in the Greek text. Second, notice how in the Greek version the issue is not just sin but also lawlessness. Third, there is also in the Greek a focus on the sufferer being justified as a righteous person, rather than him making many righteous, as the Hebrew text says. Both texts stress the person being a sin-bearer for others, but this idea certainly is stressed more in the Hebrew than in the Greek text.

What "I will give the wicked for his burial" in the Greek rendering is meant to convey remains obscure. Does the phrase mean God will prompt a wicked person to provide for the sufferer's burial?

The Greek version places more emphasis on the speaker having observed the distress and suffering of the servant. Moreover, the Greek version says that because of the servant's own affliction he did not open his mouth. It is not certain, in the last paragraph of the Greek text, whether the translator is speaking about the servant's causing others to inherit, or whether the sufferer's inheritance is in view.

The relevance of this material for the study of the historical Jesus depends in part on whether one thinks Jesus both knew and used the Hebrew Scriptures in his teaching, and if he did, it affected the way he evaluated and presented his own role. Most scholars are convinced that Jesus both knew and used the Hebrew Scriptures, as we find evidence of this in all our primary source material—in Mark, Q, special M, special L, and John. We also find it in the editorial work of all four Evangelists. There is then multiple confirmation that Jesus drew on the Hebrew Scriptures. The more delicate and difficult question to answer is how Jesus applied those Scriptures to himself. First, is there evidence he did so; second, if he did, in what way did he apply such evidence; and, finally, did Jesus use Isaiah 53 to help conceptualize the way he viewed his ministry? In regard to this last question, M. Hooker in her seminal study has said no, and H. Wolff followed by O. Betz and many others, in equally detailed studies have said yes.

The case that Jesus was influenced by the Servant Songs found in Isaiah 40–55 is based not simply on one text or another (e.g., Mark 10:45) but on a nexus of interrelated motifs, themes, and texts. For example, the use of the concept and phrase "Good News" on the lips of Jesus crops up in various texts and places. Concerning the anointing story found in Mark, Matthew, and John (see Teresa Hornsby's contribution in this volume), the earliest form of that story includes Mark 14:9, where Jesus speaks of the proclamation of the Good News, a clear echo from Isaiah, probably Isaiah 52:14 and perhaps Isaiah 53:1. This same sort of usage is found in Luke 4:18–19 in a direct quotation of Isaiah 61:1–2. In more developed form, we find this very same use of Isaiah 52:14–53:1 in John 12:32–38. Notice how John 12:38 quotes Isaiah 53:1. At the very least, this evidence means that three different Evangelists, using different materials, all agreed that Jesus drew on Isaiah 53 to conceptualize some of what he was doing and what was happening to him. Since Matthew simply takes over the material from Mark 14 in his account of the anointing in Matthew 26, we may assume the first Evangelist also believes that Jesus drew on such materials. In fact, we have direct confirmation of this in the quotation of Isaiah 53:4 in Matthew 8:17, which refers to taking our infirmities and bearing our iniquities. The important point about the verse is that it relies on the Hebrew, not the Greek, version of Isaiah 53:4. This must be taken as primitive evidence connected to the ministry of Jesus at the very latest by Jewish Christians who knew the Hebrew Scriptures (i.e., likely the earliest Jerusalem-based Jewish Christians).

The two texts usually presented to demonstrate that Jesus saw himself as the suffering servant in Isaiah 53 are Mark 10:38, 45 and Mark 14:22–24. Found in our earliest Gospel, both these texts go beyond the Passion predictions found in Mark 8–10 in which Jesus states that the Son of Man must suffer many things, be killed, and on the third day arise. But it needs to be borne in mind that it is not just Isaiah 53 that is influencing the diction of these Markan texts. It is also, for instance, another Servant Song found in Isaiah 43:3–4 that speaks of God providing a ransom for Israel. The ransom concept is not found in Isaiah 53, but since early Jews read these Servant Songs as a whole and did not atomize and compartmentalize the text the way we do today, we must look more widely. When early Jews read Isaiah 53, they did not read or interpret the chapter in isolation from the previous Servant Songs. It is therefore not a very telling critique to say that because the ransom concept is not found in Isaiah 53, therefore Jesus was not shaped by this Servant Song. The concept of "the many" is quite prominent in Isaiah 53, as is the concept of substitutionary atonement or sin-bearing. These concepts are also found in Mark 10:45. The concept of ransom as well as the promise to serve rather than be served (see Isaiah 43:23–24) is found in Isaiah 43. We rightly may conclude that Mark 10:45 reflects a combination of ideas found in Isaiah 43 and 53. Mark 10:38 in addition seems to reflect Isaiah 53:10 in the concept of a cleansing death, which Jesus calls a baptism. Mark 14:24 also seems to reflect Isaiah 53 in the phrase "blood of the new covenant poured out for the many," and since we find part of this phrase also in Paul (cf. 1 Corinthians 11:25), it must go back before the time of the writing of Mark's Gospel.

The historical likelihood that Jesus spoke of shedding his blood in the place of many seems high, not least because Maccabean martyrs had conceptualized their roles like this before Jesus (see Robert Doran's contribution to this volume). That Jesus went further and read such an act in light of the Servant Songs in Isaiah is probable in light of the evidence above (see the more detailed discussion of Mark 10:45 and other relevant texts in Witherington). This in turn means when we find indisputable echoes, quotes, or allusions to the Servant Songs (particularly of Isaiah 52–53) in places as diverse as Acts 8, Romans 10 and 15, and 1 Peter, it seems likely, especially since early Jews in non-Jesus contexts did not apply Isaiah 53 to a messianic figure (on the Jewish interpretation of this text, see Driver and Neubauer), that these later Christian texts are developing further a trend that Jesus himself set in motion when he drew on the Servant Songs to conceptualize and explain his mission and ministry, and in particular his coming violent death. This conclusion, perhaps, is partially confirmed by the fact that several of the echoes or allusions to Isaiah 53 in the Gospels reflect the Hebrew text, whereas texts like Acts 8 draw upon the LXX.

Bibliography

Betz, O. "Jesus and Isaiah 53." Pages 70–87 in *Jesus and the Suffering Servant*. Edited by William H. Bellinger Jr. and William R. Farmer. Harrisburg, PA: Trinity Press International, 1998

Childs, Brevard. *Isaiah*. Louisville, KY: Westminster/John Knox Press, 2001.

Driver, S. R., and A. Neubauer. *The Fifty-third Chapter of Isaiah According to the Jewish Interpreters*. New York: KTAV, 1969.

Hooker, Morna. *Jesus and the Servant*. London: SPCK, 1959.

Janowski, Bernd, and Peter Stuhlmacher, eds. *Der Leidende Gottesknecht*. Tübingen: Mohr, 1996.

Jobes, Karen, and Moisés Silva. *Invitation to the Septuagint*. Grand Rapids, MI: Baker, 2000.

Litwak, Kenneth. "The Use of Quotations from Isaiah 52.13–53.12 in the New Testament." *Journal of the Evangelical Theological Society* 26 (1983): 385–94.

Oswalt, John N. *The Book of Isaiah, Chapters 40–66*. Grand Rapids, MI: Eerdmans, 1998.

Westermann, Claus. *Isaiah 40–66*. Philadelphia: Westminster Press, 1969.

Witherington, Ben. *The Christology of Jesus*. Minneapolis, MN: Fortress Press, 1990.

Wolff, Hans Walter. *Jesaja 53 im Urchristentum*. Giessen: Brunnen Verlag, 1984.

—28—

Thallus on the Crucifixion

Dale C. Allison Jr.

Thallus was a Pagan or Samaritan historian who wrote a history of the eastern Mediterranean world from before the Trojan War to his own day, which was the middle or latter part of the first century CE. His work, written in Greek, has perished and is known only through mention in later writers. Among these is the ninth-century Byzantine historian George Syncellus, who, in a quotation from another lost history—that of the early third-century Julius Africanus—refers to Thallus's words about the darkness that accompanied the death of Jesus (cf. Matthew 27:45; Mark 15:33; Luke 23:44). According to Julius Africanus, Thallus attributed that darkness to an eclipse.

We, unfortunately, do not have Thallus's own words about the matter, only Julius Africanus's summary of their import. Yet the fact that the latter states his disagreement with Thallus's interpretation—"This, it seems to me, is contrary to reason"—strongly implies that Thallus was offering a mundane explanation for what happened when Jesus died. If so, and if Thallus, as so many have thought, wrote in the 50s of the first century, then he would be both the earliest non-Christian witness to Jesus and the earliest witness to the tradition (oral or written we do not know) that a darkness coincided with the Crucifixion. Although this hardly entails the historicity of such an event, it would establish a pre-Markan origin for the story.

TRANSLATION: FRAGMENT FROM JULIUS SEXTUS AFRICANUS, QUOTING THALLUS

There fell upon the whole world a most fearful darkness; and, with an earthquake, the rocks were rent and many places in Judaea and the rest of the earth were thrown down. In the third book of his *Histories*, Thallus calls this darkness an eclipse of the sun. This, it seems to me, is contrary to reason. For the Hebrews celebrate the Passover on the fourteenth day of the moon [when it is full], and what happened to our savior happened one day before Passover. Yet an eclipse takes place only when the moon comes under the sun [i.e., when the moon is not full].

Bibliography

Holladay, Carl R. *Fragments from Hellenistic Jewish Authors.* Vol. 1, *Historians*, pp. 343–69. Chico, CA: Scholars Press, 1983.

Theissen, Gerd, and Annette Merz. *The Historical Jesus: A Comprehensive Guide*, pp. 84–85. Minneapolis, MN: Fortress Press, 1998.

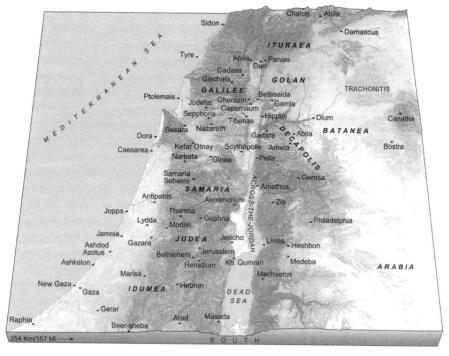

Map 1. Palestine at the time of Jesus. Map created by J. Monson.

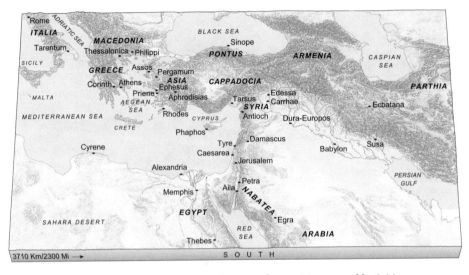

Map 2. The Roman Mediterranean at the time of Jesus. Map created by J. Monson.

GLOSSARY

Abba — An Aramaic term literally meaning "the father"; it appears in the New Testament at Mark 14:36 (Jesus' address to God), Romans 8:15, and Galatians 4:6.

AD — *Anno Domini*, Latin for "year of our Lord"; a system of dating established ca. 526 by the monk Dionysius Exiguus (Dennis the Short), based on his estimate of when Jesus was born. See CE.

agape — A Greek term meaning "love"; used in the New Testament with the connotation of self-giving or divine love (in distinction to *philos* [brotherly love, friendship] and *eros* [sexual love]); the designation for the "love feast."

Amora (pl. Amoraim) — Aramaic for "speaker"; the Amoraim were Rabbinic teachers ca. 200–400 CE (the generation after the Tannaim) who compiled the Babylonian and Palestinian Talmuds.

antitheses — The literary form "You have heard . . . but I say"; most famously recorded in the Sermon on the Mount (Matthew 6:21–48).

apocalyptic — From the Greek for "revelation" or "uncovering"; a type of literature, often ascribed to an ancient worthy, that speaks of heavenly secrets, is highly symbolic, and frequently has an eschatological focus (e.g., the Book of Revelation).

Apocrypha (New Testament) — Early Christian works (e.g., *Acts of Paul and Thecla*, *Infancy Gospel of Thomas*) consisting of Gospels, Acts, Letters, Apocalypses, and other genres usually ascribed to New Testament figures.

Apocrypha (Old Testament) — From the Greek for "hidden"; a term designating the books (e.g., 1 Maccabees, Judith, Wisdom of Solomon) written by Jews during Hellenistic and Roman times (ca. 200 BCE–100 CE), included in the LXX, and which became canonical for Catholic and Orthodox Christianity. See also Deuterocanonical Texts.

apostle — From the Greek for "sent out"; used by the church to designate Jesus' twelve select disciples (so Luke), as well as others (e.g., Paul, Junia) who proclaimed the Christian message.

Apostles' Creed — A formal statement consisting of twelve articles of Christian belief traditionally ascribed to the Twelve Apostles although a product of the second- and third-century church; the title first appears in the writings of Ambrose (ca. 390).

apotheosis — From the Greek for "from" (*apo*) and "god" (*theos*); the elevation of a human being into a deity.

Aqedah (sometimes *Akedah*) — Hebrew for "binding" (of Isaac); the account in Genesis 22 of the divine command to Abraham that he sacrifice his son Isaac.

Aramaic—A Semitic language closely related to Hebrew and Syriac; parts of the Books of Daniel and Ezra are in Aramaic, as are the Targumim.

baptism—From the Greek for "to immerse in water" or "to wash with water"; the term signifies ritual immersion. See miqvah.

Bar Kokhba Revolt—the Second Revolt against Rome by the Jews of Israel (132–35 CE); named after the Jewish leader Bar Kokhba (Aramaic: "Son of the Star") proclaimed Messiah by Rabbi Aqiva.

Bavli—See Talmud.

BC—Before Christ; the period before the birth of Jesus as dated by Dionysius Exiguus (see AD).

BCE—Before the Common Era or Before the Christian Era; a nonconfessional expression for BC.

canon—From the Greek for "reed, measuring stick, plumb line"; the list of books considered inspired or official; the foundation documents of a community.

CE—Common Era or Christian Era; a nonconfessional expression for AD.

Christ—Greek for "anointed one"; it translates the Hebrew *meshiach*, or "messiah."

Christology—Teachings about the nature of the Christ.

Church Fathers—Early Christian teachers of the second century onward, such as Tertullian, Origen, Jerome, and Eusebius; the writers of the Patristic ("of the fathers") texts.

corban—Hebrew term for an offering dedicated to God (see Leviticus 1:2; Numbers 7:13).

criteria of authenticity—Techniques by which scholars propose to sift authentic Jesus material from the additions made by the early church or the Evangelists.

Dead Sea Scrolls—Jewish documents found in 1948 and subsequently in caves near the Dead Sea (see Qumran), including numerous copies of biblical books (except for Esther) and commentaries on them.

Deuterocanonical Texts—The "second part" of the canon of the Old Testament; an alternative designation by Catholic and Orthodox churches for (Old Testament) Apocrypha.

diadochi—From the Greek for "successors"; Macedonian generals who succeeded Alexander the Great (d. 323 BCE), including Ptolemy and Seleucus.

Diaspora—Greek for "dispersion" or "scattering"; the location of Jews outside of Israel.

eschatology—From the Greek for "words concerning the end" (*eschaton* means "end-time"); material describing the end of an age or of time and often involving the in-breaking of divine rule.

Essenes—A Jewish movement, mentioned by both Josephus and Philo, generally associated with the writing and preservation of the Dead Sea Scrolls.

Eucharist—From the Greek for "thanksgiving" or "gratitude" (*eu* means "good"; *charis* "grace"); the sacrament of the Lord's Supper.

Evangelists—From the Greek for "good news"; a technical term for the authors of the canonical Gospels.

exegesis—From the Greek for "to lead out"; critical interpretation of biblical material.

first triumvirate—From the Latin for "group of three men"; the term refers to Julius Caesar, Marcus Licinius Crassus, and Gnaeus Pompey (Pompey the Great), who, in 60 BCE, agreed to share rule of the Roman Empire.

form criticism—The analysis of literary types or conventions (forms), such as the report of an exorcism or a prayer and variations on them.

Gehenna—From the Hebrew for "Hinnom Valley"; a garbage dump southwest of Jerusalem where in ancient times children were sacrificed to Molech; a place of punishment by fire of the damned (see Mark 9:43ff. and Matthew 10:28).

genizah—From the Hebrew for "hiding"; a storeroom (i.e., "hiding place"), usually of a synagogue, where no longer usable sacred books and ritual objects are kept.

Gentile—a person who is not Hebrew, Israelite, Jew, or Samaritan (Hebrew: *goy*).

Gnosticism—From the Greek for "knowledge"; a diverse belief system promoting a dualistic worldview; many Gnostics viewed the deity of Genesis as a "demiurge," an inept being who seeks to withhold knowledge (*gnosis*) from humanity.

Gospel—From the Old English for "good tale" or "good story" (see Evangelists); the term usually refers to a written account of the life of Jesus.

Haggadah—Hebrew for "narration"; the term refers both to nonlegal (non-*Halakhic*) Rabbinic material and, when used with the article, to the formal text read at the Passover seder.

Halakhah—From the Hebrew for "to walk," "to go"; the term indicates both an individual Jewish law or practice and the entire system of orthopraxy.

Hallel—From the Hebrew for "praise"; the collection of Psalms 113–18 sung at three pilgrimage festivals (Passover, Shavuot [Pentecost], and Sukkot [Booths]), as well as Hannukah and Rosh Hodesh (the start of a new month).

hapax legomenon—From the Greek for "once" and "spoken" or "recorded"; a word recorded only once in the work of an author or in the whole of a language.

Hasmoneans—From Hasmon (or Hashmon), the grandfather of Judah Maccabee; another name for the Maccabees, usually employed in reference to their dynastic rule (142–63 BCE).

havurah (haburah) **groups**—From the Hebrew for "companionship" or "fellowship"; groups (perhaps connected to the Pharisees) that had probationary periods, ate together in ritual purity, and practiced proper tithing.

Hellenism—Greek thought and culture brought to the East by the conquests of Alexander the Great (beginning in 333 BCE).

hippodrome—From the Greek for "horse" (*hippos*) and "race course" (*dromos*); a stadium for horse and chariot races.

incarnation—From the Latin for "flesh" (*carne*); the taking on of physical form by a divine being.

jubilee—From the Hebrew for "ram's horn" (*yovel*); the emancipation of slaves, forgiveness of debt, and restoration of land to its original owners that is to take place every fifty years (see Leviticus 25, 27).

Ketuvim—Hebrew for "writings"; the third section of the Tanakh that includes books such as Esther and Ruth.

Levites—Members of the tribe of Levi; Levites are a priestly group of Temple functionaries (see Numbers 18; Deuteronomy 17–18; 2 Kings 23; Ezekiel 44; and 1, 2 Chronicles [passim]) distinguished from the Kohanim, who are descendants of Aaron.

Logos—Greek for "word"; the Stoic principle of reason that provided coherence to the world; for Hellenistic Jews such as Philo, the mediating entity between God and the world; for the Gospel of John, the preexistent Christ.

LXX—See Septuagint.

Maccabees—Jewish family who led the rebellion against Antiochus IV Epiphanes in 167 BCE (see Hasmoneans).

mashal—From the Hebrew for "to be like"; a general term for parable as well as allegory or fable.

Masoretic Text (MT)—The received form of the Tanakh; edited and standardized by the Masoretes, ca. seventh through ninth centuries CE.

Mekhilta—Rabbinic commentary on the Book of Exodus.

Messiah—Hebrew for "anointed" (Greek: *Christos*); the term comes to indicate one with a divine commission and/or a savior figure.

midrash (pl. midrashim)—From the Hebrew for "inquire" (*darash*); with the connotation of an interpretation, an expansion, and/or explanation of biblical texts (a type of Haggadah).

miqvah (or mikveh)—Jewish ritual bath.

Mishnah—From the Hebrew for "teaching"; a collection of Jewish laws (Oral Torah) consisting of six major units codified ca. 200; the first part of the Talmud.

Nag Hammadi—Egyptian village where in 1945 a collection of Gnostic writings was discovered.

nativity—The story of the circumstances surrounding the birth of a (famous) person.

Nazirite—An individual consecrated to God, usually for a set period, who avoids wine and alcohol, corpses, and haircuts.

Nevi'im—Hebrew for "prophets"; the second division of the Tanakh.

Nicene Creed—Statement of faith developed at the Council of Nicea (325 CE) and designed to unify Christianity under Constantine's rule.

nimshal—The moral or point of a mashal.

Noachide Laws—Seven laws given to Noah to provide Gentile nations a moral code.

Oral Torah (or Oral Law)—Jewish legal material traditionally seen as delivered to Moses on Mount Sinai (along with the Written Torah); the Oral Law was eventually written down in the Mishnah/Talmud.

ossuary—A container or receptacle for human bones.

Pagan—From Latin for (village) peasant; for the purposes of this volume, refers to belief systems other than those typically identified as Jewish, Samaritan, or Christian and those who hold them.

Parousia — From the Greek for "presence" or "coming"; the arrival of a great figure; the term comes to refer to the Second Coming of Jesus.

Passion narrative — From the Latin for "suffering"; the account of Jesus' suffering and death.

Passover — Eight-day Jewish holiday (spring pilgrimage festival during the times of the Jerusalem Temple) commemorating the Exodus from Egypt (Exodus 12–13) and celebrated by the seder meal along with abstention from leavened products.

Patristic — See Church Fathers.

Pax Romana — Literally "Roman peace" (Latin); the "peace" enforced on the empire by Roman military strength.

Pentateuch — From the Greek for "five scrolls," the first five books of the Bible: Genesis, Exodus, Leviticus, Numbers, and Deuteronomy; one definition of **Torah**.

pericope — From the Greek for "to cut around"; a narrative unit that can be analyzed apart from its literary context (e.g., story, poem, saying).

pesher — Hebrew for "interpretation"; a scriptural commentary associated with the Dead Sea Scrolls and used to show, often cryptically, how the biblical material relates to the interpretive community.

Peshitta — From the Syriac for "simple"; the Syriac translation of the Bible (both Old Testament/Tanakh and New Testament).

prefect — Roman agent having administrative, juridical, and financial authority (along with auxiliary troops) over the provinces, including the governors of Judea 6–41 CE.

procurator — Roman agent who replaced the prefects in Judea, 44–66 CE.

Pseudepigrapha — From the Greek for "false/deceitful" (*pseudos*) and "writing" (*epigraphē*); a collection of Jewish writings, most dating ca. 200 BCE–100 CE; many are attributed to ancient worthies such as Ezra and even Adam.

pseudonymity — The practice of writing under the name of an ancient worthy.

Q — A (hypothetical) document believed to have provided material to Matthew and Luke (e.g., the Lord's Prayer, the Beatitudes).

Qumran — A site on the West Bank, near the northwest corner of the Dead Sea, where the majority of the Dead Sea Scrolls were found.

Rabbi — Hebrew for "my master"; the term comes to refer to recognized teachers of Halakhah and Haggadah following the destruction of the Temple in 70 CE; Rabbinic texts include the Talmud and Midrash collections.

redaction criticism — Analysis of how the editor (redactor) of a text collects, modifies, and presents received material.

Sanhedrin — From the Greek for "assembly" (of persons seated together); a Jewish legislative and judicial body.

Second Temple period — Judaism from the beginning of Persian rule (538 BCE) to the destruction of the Temple by Rome in 70 CE.

seder — From the Hebrew for "order"; the ritualized meal celebrating the festival of Passover (see Haggadah).

Septuagint (abbreviated LXX) — Initially the Greek translation of the Pentateuch, the term (from the Greek for "seventy": the designation is based on the legend that the text was translated by seventy scholars) eventually refers to the Greek translation of the entire Tanakh.

Shekinah — From the Hebrew for "dwelling"; the presence or manifestation of God at creation and in human life.

Sicarii — From the Latin for "daggermen"; a Jewish anti-Roman band known for assassinating collaborators.

Sifra — Rabbinic commentary on the book of Leviticus.

Sitz im Leben — German for "setting in life"; the sociohistorical context of a document.

Son of Man — A human being (Ezekiel, Psalms); in Daniel 7:13, the symbol of the covenant community who appears in the heavenly throne room and who is given earthly rule; Jesus' preferred self-designation; in *1 Enoch*, a redeemer; in the New Testament Gospels, Jesus' preferred self-designation.

source criticism — Analysis of a particular text to determine the sources used by the author (redactor).

sukkah — Hebrew for "booth"; a temporary dwelling place; Leviticus 23:42–43 commands the people to live in such booths for seven days to commemorate the Exodus and its aftermath (the holiday is Sukkot).

synagogue — From the Greek for "to gather together"; a place where Jews assemble for prayer, worship, and other community activities.

Synoptic Gospels — The Gospels ascribed to Matthew, Mark, and Luke, which "together" (*syn*) "see" (*optic*) in that they tell what is in general the same story (in distinction from John's Gospel).

Talmud — From the Hebrew for "study" or "learning"; a compendium of Jewish law and lore consisting of the Mishnah and the Gemara (commentary on the Mishnah); the Babylonian Talmud (*Bavli*) was codified ca. 700 CE, the Palestinian (*Yerushalmi*) ca. 400 CE.

Tanakh (Tanak, Tanach) — Acronym for "Torah, Nevi'im, Ketuvim"; the canon of the synagogue.

Tanna (pl. Tannaim) — From the Hebrew for "repeater"; the Tannaim were the Rabbis from ca. late first century BCE to 200 CE who compiled the Mishnah.

Targum (pl. Targumim) — From the Hebrew for "translation"; designates Aramaic translations (most containing also interpretive glosses) of the Tanakh.

Teacher of Righteousness (or Righteous Teacher) — Founder and leader of the group associated with the Dead Sea Scrolls/community at Qumran.

Therapeutae (m); Therapeutrides (f.) — From the Greek for "healers"; male and female ascetics devoted to prayer and study of Scripture and who meet for common meals and liturgical worship (described by Philo in *De vita contemplativa*).

Torah — Hebrew for "instruction" or "law"; the first five books of the Bible (the Books of Moses; Pentateuch); the term can also refer to the interpretation of this material (see Oral Law).

typology—The drawing of connections between earlier (prefigurations) and later (fulfillments) texts.

Yerushalmi—See Talmud.

Zealot—From the Greek for "enthusiasm"; a first-century CE Jewish group advocating independence from Roman rule and promoting messianic expectations.

INDEX OF ANCIENT WORKS

OLD TESTAMENT

Genesis

1.26	216
1.28	268
2–41	297
4.8	240–41
5.18–24	87
6–9	92
6.1–4	92
9.7	268
14	27
14.10	113
14.18–20	92, 121
18	27
18.4	340
19.2	340
21	27
21.21	241
22	409
34.5	269
39.4	217
41.45, 50–52	357
46.20	357
47.4	348
49.27	215

Exodus

1.7, 10–13	348
1.14	350
2.22, 24	349
2.25	344, 349
3.6	345
3.9	349
4.17	349
9.3	349
12–13	413
12.12	349
12.27	350
12.39	350
12.42	344
13.8	350

14.15	213–14
14.19	214
14.21, 22	58, 214
15.18	248
16.4	214
17.1–7	59
18.25	116
21.14	270
21.18, 19	288
23.28	306
25.30	288
28.41	339
29.36	339

Leviticus

1.2	274, 412
7.19–21	269
10.10	269
11	25
11–15	268, 272
12.3	291
13–16	268–69
18.21	239
18.24–30	269, 276
18.28	213, 269, 276
19	125
19.15	277
19.17–18	126
19.18	245
19.20, 31	269
19.34	245
20.1–3	269–70, 276
21.1–4	268–69
21.10–15	268
21.17	18
22.3–7	269
22.28	244–45
23.42–43	414
24.14	20
24.16	224

Leviticus (*continued*)

25	411
25.8–55	13, 122
25.13	122
26	300
26.6	305
26.8	306
26.12	213
27	411
28	300

Numbers

5.11–31	270
7.13	412
9.11	352
10.29	215
12.10	269
15.37–41	13
18	412
19	268–69, 272
20.1–13	59
24.7	301, 306
24.14	163
35.33–34	269, 277

Deuteronomy

4.30	220
6.23	350
7.13	360
7.20	306
7.26	278
10.22	348
12.17	360
14.23	360
15.2	123
16.3	347
17–18	412
18.4	360
18.15–18	79
18.15–19	58
18.17–19	113
21.23	128
24.1–4	33, 269, 316–17
26.5–8	348–49
26.7	344
27.4	56
28	300
28.7	306
28.15–68	88
28.51	360
33.12	215

Joshua

1.8	288
3.14–17	58
4.2–23	56
6.20	58

Judges

7.25	113
9.7–15	206
9.8	339
13	27
13.5	92
14.14	206

Ruth

3.3	340

1 Samuel

1–2	27
1.1	217
1.1–2.26	92
1.11	218
9.16	339
10.1	340
15.1	339
17	11
25.41	340

2 Samuel

5.8	250
12.1–14	206
14.1–20	206, 211
14.2	340
21.19	11

1 Kings

1.50–53	270
2.28–30	270
6–7	48
14.24	269
17–19	13
17.3–5	56
18.31	56
21	13

2 Kings

1–6	13
1.8	56
2.8, 14	56
4–5	27
4.19–37	149
5	149

5.10–14	56	**Proverbs**	
8–9	13	8	90
13	13	16.5	278
16.3	247	23.25	153
21.6	247	24.17	32
23	412		
23.10	247	**Ecclesiastes**	
		9.8	218
1 Chronicles			
20.5	11	**Song of Songs (Canticles)**	
21.16	349	4.15	214
2 Chronicles		**Isaiah**	
31.5	360	1.5–6	206
32.8	360	2.22	217
		5	247
Ezra		5.1–7	206, 211–12,
3.7	360		243
		5.8–25	87
Nehemiah		6	246
5.11	360	10.34–11.1	129–30
		11	256, 301
Esther		11.1	129
2.9	342	11.1–5	90
		11.4b	129
Psalms		11.15	58
2	90, 256	24.23	248
7.7b–8a	123	30.27–28	59
22	8, 37, 380,	31.4	248
	382	35.6	250
68.28	214–15	38	27
69	37, 380	38.21	149
69.25	354	40–55	402
78.15	214	40.3	56, 59, 117
79.6, 7	353	40.9	248
82.1, 2	123	42	249
101.5	277–78	42.1–4	90
104.14–15	360	43.3–4	403
105.39	214	43.16	58
106.34–40	269	43.23–34	403
107	7	49.1–6	90
110	27	50.11	219
110.4	121	51.4–8	90
113	351	51.10	58
113–118	411	52–53	403
114	351	52.7	123, 248
115–18	354	52.13–53.12	90–91
126	352	52.14–53.1	402–3
126.1	155–56	53	37, 127, 380,
128.6	156		400–404
136	354	53.2	223
146.7–8	119	58.6	119

Isaiah (*continued*)
61 — 249
61.1–2 — 119, 122–23, 402
63.11 — 58
66.23 — 247
66.24 — 246, 252

Jeremiah
2.7 — 269
2.23 — 269
3.1 — 269
3.12 — 220
3.25 — 220
22.13–19 — 87
25.11 — 156
29.10 — 156
31.9 — 221

Lamentations
3.66 — 354

Ezekiel
5.11 — 269
7.7 — 248
8.1–11.25 — 269
9.4 — 116
9.9 — 218
16.7 — 348
17.3–10 — 206
19.2–14 — 206
22.21 — 117
23.2–21 — 206
24.3–5 — 206
36.17, 19 — 269
44 — 412
44.7, 9 — 287
44.23 — 269

Daniel
1.1–16 — 361
2.45 — 120–21
5.29 — 215
7 — 30, 90–91
7–12 — 87
7.13 — 414
7.13–14 — 180
7.14, 23, 27 — 120–21
9.25–26 — 123

10.3 — 340
12.3 — 88

Hosea
2.2–15 — 206
2.8, 22 — 360
5.6 — 269
6.10 — 269
11.3 — 214

Joel
2.19 — 360
2.30 — 350

Amos
8.9 — 37, 380

Obadiah
21 — 248

Micah
4.6–8 — 250
7.6 — 13

Nahum
1.2 — 126
2.13–14 — 128

Habakkuk
2.4 — 219
2.5–6 — 278

Zephaniah
3.19 — 250

Haggai
1.11 — 360

Zechariah
9–14 — 37, 380
11.11 — 116
13.6 — 71
13.7 — 116
14.9 — 248

Malachi
2.16 — 59, 317
3.2–3 — 59
4.5–6 — 59

APOCRYPHA/DEUTEROCANONICAL LITERATURE

Judith
10.5　　360

Additions to Esther
4.17　　361

Wisdom of Solomon
2　　37, 380

Sirach
24　　90

Baruch
49–51　　88

1 Maccabees
1.60–61　　15
1.62–63　　361
4.45–46　　58

9.27　　58
14.41　　58

2 Maccabees
6.18–21　　361
6.18–7.42　　389–92
7.1　　361
14.37–46　　392

3 Maccabees
2.21　　68
3.4–7　　361
5.7　　68
6.2–3　　68

4 Maccabees
1.1–17　　397–98
13.23–14.20　　398–99

NEW TESTAMENT

Matthew
1　　93
1–2　　28, 92
1–5　　8
1.1–17　　5
1.18–25　　345
1.19　　317
1.20　　79
1.21　　92
2.13–18　　345
2.15　　250
2.16–18　　19
2.23　　92
3.1–6　　281
3.3　　117
3.9　　56
3.12　　250
3.15　　10
3.17　　249
5　　32, 124, 290
5–7　　79
5.1–12　　31
5.3　　5
5.6　　250
5.17　　5
5.17–18　　12
5.21–22　　12
5.31–32　　33, 251, 316
5.32　　4

5.38–46　　289–90
5.39–42　　13
5.44　　32
5.48　　7
6.9　　26
6.12　　13, 250
6.17　　340
6.19–20　　136
6.34　　12, 287
7.2　　248, 252
7.12　　245, 300
7.24–27　　221
8　　4
8.11　　30, 248
8.17　　403
8.28–34　　5
9.9　　4
9.20–22　　147–48
10　　79
10.6　　5, 13
10.17–20　　36, 368
10.21–22　　362
10.32–33　　91
10.34–35　　13
11.2–5　　119
12.1–8　　140–41
12.10–12　　33, 292–93
12.38–42　　91
12.39　　250

Matthew (*continued*)

13	79
13.17	249
13.24–30	91
13.30	250
13.33	12
13.36–43	91
13.53–58	367
13.55	19, 50
14	19
15	13, 17, 33
15.1–20	281
15.4–6	300
15.19	282
15.24	5
16.4	250
16.19–20	136
18	79, 328
18.10–14	216
18.14	249
18.15–17	34, 125
18.23–35	250
19.3–9	251, 316
19.7–9	33
19.10–12	13
19.12	10
19.16–30	248
19.28	91
20.1–15	50
20.1–16	220
21	4, 19, 31
21.12–14	257
21.12–16	144–45
21.14–15	250
21.23–27	142
21.33	247
21.33–46	243
22.1–14	217
22.30	89
22.34–40	34, 299–300
23	26, 31, 257
23.25–26	281
24–25	79
24.26–27	91
24.30	180
24.37–39	91
24.43–44	91
24.47–51	50
25	12
25.31–46	90
26	403
26.3	53
26.6–13	34, 339

26.12	341
26.17–19	4
26.26	344
26.26–30	367
26.52	246, 252
26.57	53
26.64	180
27.1–26	368
27.3–10	250
27.26–31	21, 36, 299
27.45	405
27.46	8
27.51	37
28.1–10	367

Mark

1.2–6	281
1.3	117
1.4	10
1.4–8	56–57
1.11	249
1.16–20	328
1.19–20	51
1.20	327
1.29–31	137
1.32	6
1.43–44	6
2.4	4, 51
2.14	4
2.17	281
2.23–28	33, 293
3.2	194
3.12	6
3.14–19	57
3.22	194
3.35	34
4.11–12	13, 245–46, 252
4.24	248, 252
4.38	7
5	4, 53
5.1–20	5, 375
5.25–34	147–48
5.41	13, 182
5.43	6
6	19, 52
6.1–6	367
6.3	50
6.7	57
6.13	340
6.16–18	56
6.17–29	375
6.27–28	56

6.32–52	375	14.16	343
6.50	345	14.22	344
7	17, 32, 33	14.22–26	367
7.1–13	257	14.23	343
7.1–23	281–83	14.25–26	343–44
7.9–13	300	14.35–36	64
7.11–13	294	14.36	26
7.18–20	12	14.50	8
7.19	6	14.61	196
7.21–22	182	14.62	90, 180
7.21–23	282	14.64	224
7.24–8.10	6	15.1–15	368
7.33–34	13	15.15–20	21, 36, 299
8	13	15.22–46	380–83
8–10	403	15.29–32	381
8.17–18	246	15.33	37, 405
8.21	246	15.34	8
8.38	91, 250	15.36	343
9.1	34	15. 40–41	8
9.11–13	57	16.1–8	367
9.12	246	16.9–20	5
9.44, 46	246		
9.48	246, 252	**Luke**	
10.1–12	4	1–2	92
10.2–12	33, 251, 316	1.1	5
10.11–12	13	1.1–4	4
10.38	403	1.30–35	120
10.45	386, 402–3	1.32–35	30
10.46–52	375	1.34–35	79
11	4, 19, 31	2.1	18
11.15–17	144–145, 257	3	19
11.27–33	142	3.1–6	281
12	224, 345	3.3, 4	117–18
12.1	247	3.8	57
12.1–9	223	3.9	117
12.1–11	50	3.10–14	56
12.1–12	243, 247	3.17	250
12.13–17	42	3.22	249
12.25	89	4.16–21	119
12.28–34	33, 299–300	4.16–30	252, 367
12.34	345	4.18	340
13	36	4.18–19	249, 402
13.1	48–49	4.21	14
13.9–11	368	5.1–11	327
13.12–13	362	5.19	51
13.24–27	30, 89	5.27	4
13.26	180	6	124
13.26–27	91	6.1–5	140
14	403	6.15	13
14.3–9	34, 339	6.20	5
14.8	340, 341	6.20–23	124
14.9	402	6.20–49	31
14.12–16	4	6.21	250

Luke (*continued*)

6.22		24.5	249
6.31, 36	90	24.13–53	375
7.20–22	7, 245	24.26–27, 45	386
7.24	119		
7.34	49	**John**	
7.36–50	13	1	14
	13, 34,	1.1	10, 21
	339–40	1.23	117
8.26–39	5	1.29	4
8.43–48	147–48	1.30	10
9	19	1.38	24
10.18	13, 89	2	5, 8, 19, 25,
10.24	249		31, 52
10.25–28	33, 299–300	2.13–16	257
11.4	50	2.14–16	137
11.29–32	91	2.16	251
12.8–9	91	3	361
12.10–11	36, 368	3.25	281
12.39–40	91	3.32	250
12.51–53	362	4	13, 16, 26
12.58–59	50	4.20, 25	58
13.1–2	35	5	15
13.10–17	257	5.24–25	361
13.14–16	33, 293	5.25–29	91
13.28–29	248	6	9, 13, 35, 362
13.34	386	6.1, 23	49
14.15–24	217	6.25–59	8
15.3–7	216	7	33, 291
15.11–32	213, 220	8	224
16.9	249, 252	10.33	224
16.18	251, 316	11.50	36, 386–87
17.3–4	34, 125	12	34
17.22–18.8	91	12.1–8	339
19	4, 19, 31	12.24–25	181
19.45–46	144–45, 257	12.27	386–87
20.1–8	142	12.32–38	403
20.9–19	243, 247	13	340
20.36	89	13.1, 23	4
21.1–4	136	14.2	249
21.27	180	15	13
22	30	15.18–27	36, 368
22.7–13	4	18.28	4
22.14–23	367	18.28–19.16	368
22.16, 18	114	18.33–37	196
22.19	345	18.36	12
22.28–30	91, 248	19.1	299
22.29–30	114	19.2–3	21, 36, 299
22.35–38	13	19.31	4
23	20	19.37	251
23.1–25	368	20.1–10	367
23.44	405	20.27	341
24.1–12	367	21.1	49

Acts

1	18–19
5.36	58
5.36–37	26
8	37, 403–4
8.26–40	127
8.32–33	400
10	28
10–11	361
10.1–8	375
12	22
12.1–17	375
13.13–52	253
15.20, 29	300
16	36, 368
16.13–34	375
18	36, 368
19.24–41	325
20.7	367
20.18–38	375
21	10
21–26	36
21.27–26.32	368
21.38	58
24.24	22
25.12	22
27.1–28.11	375

Romans

7.2–3	251
8.12–15	72
8.15	26, 64
8.34	380
10, 15	403
16.1–2	326, 328
16.23	328

1 Corinthians

1.18, 23	380
5.7	343
6	328
7	10
7.10–11	251, 316
7.10–16	33
10.16	343
10.16–17	367
11	328
11.17–22	114
11.20–21	367
11.23–25	380
11.23–26	367
11.24	344

12.2	193
15.4–7	380
15.20	22
15.36–37	181
15.42–54	89
16.15	328

Galatians

2.11–14	361
2.15–16	85
3.1–5	85
3.26–4.6	72
4.6	26, 64

Philippians

2.9	380
3	17
3.20–21	89

1 Thessalonians

1.10	380
4	329

1 Timothy

2	10

2 Timothy

3.13	58

Hebrews

2.3	59
2.12–13	128
3.7–4.13	59
6.19–7.10	27, 121
7.1–3	93
7.4–10	122

James

3.6	247
4.14	340

1 John

1.6	250

Jude

12	367

Revelation

1.7	180, 251
6.6	360
14	10
19	30
19.6–9	114

PSEUDEPIGRAPHA

1 Enoch
1–36	87
1.2–3	89
6–11	92
9	90
37–71	89, 91
46–49	89–92, 95–98
51	89–92, 98–99
52.4–5	90
62–63	89–92, 99–101
81.1–4	87
92–105	87–89
93.1, 3	89
94.6–100.9	87
102.4–103.15	88
103.9–104.6	93–95
104.7–8	88
106–7	92–93, 102–4

2 Enoch
71–72	92, 104–8

2 Esdras
13.1–3	180

Joseph and Aseneth
1.5	357
6.6	357
7.1, 5–6	358, 360, 362
8.5–7	357–60, 362–63

8.9	357, 359, 363
11.3–14	357, 359, 363–64
12.8–11	69–70
22.3–10	357

Jubilees
13.26	360
32.12	360

Letter of Aristeas
128–42	361

Lives of the Prophets
10.2–4	137

Psalms of Solomon
1	257–58
2	256–58
4	257, 258–60
8	256–57
8.1–13	260
17	256, 261–63
17–18	31, 257
18.1–9	263–64

Sibylline Oracles
3.243, 745	360
4.24–30	361

Testament of the Twelve Patriarchs
T. Judah 9.8	360

DEAD SEA SCROLLS

1QH
	67
10.24	360

1QM
	23
17.5–8	122

1QpHab
8.8–13	278

1QS
2.25–3.6	279
2.25–3.9	118
4.9–11	279
5.13–14, 18–19	279
5.24–6.1	125–26
6.2–23	361

6.24–26	279–80
7.15–20	361
8.12–16	117
8.16–18	280
8.16–19	361
11.5–11	114

1QSa (1Q28A)
2.11–12	114
2.11–22	115, 361
12, 14, 19–20	114

4Q14
	129

4Q169
1.5–9	128

4Q246		4Q525	124–25
1–2	120–21		
		11QMelchizedek (11Q13)	
4Q284a		2.2–25	122–23
frg. 1	361	2.13	113
4Q285		11QTemple	19
frg. 4–7	129–30	47.5–14	361
		49.5–21	361
4Q460	68	51.11–16	277
4Q477	126	CD (Cairo-Damascus Document)	
		9.2–8	126
4Q512	280–81	12.22–13.7	116
		14.18–19	116
4Q513	361	19.7–13	116
		19.33–35	117
4Q521	118–19	20.1–3	116–17

GREEK AND ROMAN LITERATURE

Aeschylus		47.3	195
Prometheus		55	196
848–52	83	57–60	196
Suppliants		63	196
17–19	83	64	196–97, 203–4
		82.6	195
Aesop		90	195, 204
Fables		*De deo Socratis*	
11	225	15.153	168
21	225–26	*Metamorphoses*	
40	226	1.1	194
70	226	4.28–6.24	193
77	226	11	194
82	226	11.5–6	197–99
149	226	11.7–15	199
		11.21	199–200
Apthonius		11.23	200
2–4	133	11.24–25	201
		11.27	193–94
Apuleius of Madauros			
Apologia pro se de Magia		**Arrian**	
5	196	*Anabasis*	
9.3	196	7.30	84
13.5–6	196		
25	202	**Augustus**	
26	196–97, 202	*Res Gestae*	
28.2	196	34–45	74–75
30.1	196		
42	202	**Aulus Gellius**	
42–48	196	*Attic Nights*	
43	195, 202–3	13.4.1–3	82, 84

Calpurnius Siculus
Ecologue   176

Cicero
De Oratore
  1.183   319
  1.238   312
De Res Publica
  1.36.56   72–73
  1.41   80, 85
  2.2   80, 85
  39.64   72–73

Dio Cassius
Roman History
  53.16.6–8   76–77
  53.18.2–3   76–77
  64.20–21   299

Dio Chrysostom
Discourses
  1.22–25, 39–40   75

Diodorus of Sicily
Library of History
  4   80, 83, 84

Diogenes Laertius
Lives of Eminent Philosophers
  3.1–2   81
  3.45   81, 85
  5.80   222
  6.32   137
  6.42   133
  9.58–59   393

Dionysius of Halicarnassus
Roman Antiquities
  1.76.3–4   80
  1.77.1   81
  1.77.2   81, 84
  8.59   173
  8.60–62   172–73

Diotogenes
Stobaeus
  4.267.5   301

Epictetus
Discourses
  1.9.4–7   75–76
  3   33

Euripides
Bacchae
  576–795   375

Gaius
Digest
  24.1.61   310
  24.2.2   319
  47.22.4   323

Herodotus
Histories
  2.134   222

Hermogenes of Tarsus
  3–4   27, 132–3
  6.13–15   136
  10–11   136
  30–64   139–40

Hermogenian
Digest
  24.1.60.1   310

Homer
Iliad
  2.1–41   375
  2.819–22   79
  5.247–48   79
  5.385   191
  6–17   375–76
  8.424   191–92
  10.193   192
  10.521, 564, 572   191
  14.315–28   80
  20.199–209   79, 80
  22   375–78,
                                    379–82
  24   375–78, 380,
                                    383
  24.59   79
  24.551   381
Odyssey
  3.1–67   375
  5.116–28, 451–93   80
  9.105–542   375
  11.90–151, 285–434   375
  19.385–402   340–41
  24.205–411   375

Horace
Odes
  1.2   73
  3.24.26–30   73–74

Iamblichus
Life of Pythagoras 172

Justinian
Novellae 318

Justinus
Epitoma Pompei Trogi
2.6.16–21 387

Labeo
Digest 319

Life of Aesop
1–142 227–37
125–26 224
132 224

Livy
History of the Roman People
8.9.1–8.10 387–89

Lucan
Pharsalia 175–76

Marcellus
Digest 313

Mithras Liturgy 182–92

Ovid
Fasti
2.127–33 74
Metamorphoses
14.581–608 85
14.588 80

Papinian
Digest 315

Paul
Digest
24.2.3 313
24.2.9 319–20

Pauli Sententiae
5.6.15 320

Petronius
Satyricon
69 341

Philodemus
On Poetry
5.30.36–31.2 373

Philostratus
Life of Apollonius of Tyana
1.4.5–9 81–84
1.6 81
3.39.1–10 174
4.20 173–74
4.45 175
6.43 174–75
7.14–8.12 393–97
Lives of the Sophists
587 195
590 195

Plato
Alcibiades
121e–122a 202
Phaedo
60d 222
Phaedrus
247b–d 203
Seventh Epistle
2.312e 203

Pliny-Trajan Correspondence
10.1–121 366
10.33–34 326
10.96 369–70
10.96–97 326, 366, 368, 370

Plutarch
On Composure 392–93
Moralia
III.208C 136
IX.114–19 83
179D 145
190E 141
229C 141
331B 145–46
Parallel Lives
"Alexander"
2.4 82
3.1–4 82–83
4.9–10 145–46
"Cato the Younger"
19.5 143
"Lucullus"
40.3 143

Plutarch (*continued*)
 "Lysander"
  22.1   141
 "Numa"
  4.1–4   83–84
 "Pompey"
  24.7–8   299
 "Romulus"
  2–4   80–81
  7.3–4   84

Porphyry
 Life of Pythagoras
  2   81
  27   172

Ps.-Heraclitus
 Quaestiones Homericae
  1.5–6   373

Quintillian   136

Suetonius
 Lives of the Twelve Caesars
  "Augustus"
   94.4   83
   101   74
  "Claudius"
   1.6, 3.2, 11.2   296
   25.4   22
  "Nero"
   16.2   367

Tacitus
 Annals
  11.1, 15.28.3   296
  15.44   366–67

Histories
  4.81   176–77

Theon
  3–4   132
  5–18   133
  25–26   133
  31–35, 39–40   136
  100–102   136
  111–13   137
  190–400   138–39
  314–17   143
  318–33   143

Ulpian
 Digest
  23.2.33   313
  23.2.45   314
  24.1.35   313
  24.2.4   318–19
  24.2.11   320–21
  24.3.22.8   312
  38.11.1.1   313
 Excerpts from Ulpian's Work
  6.9–10, 12–13   321

Vergil
 Aeneid
  8, 9, 12   378–80

Xenophon
 Symposium
  3.5, 4.6   373

FLAVIUS JOSEPHUS

Antiquities of the Jews
 2.347–48   167
 3.8.3   342
 6.5.4   342
 7.14.5, 10   342
 9.6.1, 2   342
 11.6.2   342
 12.3.1   361
 13   17
 13.171–73   16
 13.256   56
 14.22–30   152
 15.259   317

 18   21, 23, 35
 18–20   22
 18.5.4   56
 18.36–37   50
 18.55–59   299
 18.63–64   20, 55
 18.85–87   56, 60
 18.110   317
 18.116–19   60
 18.118–19   19
 18.136   56, 60
 18.159–60   296
 18.257–60   296–97

19	22	2.21.2	361
19.4.1	342	2.169–74	299
19.276–77	296	2.220, 223	296
20	23	2.259–60	61
20.9.1	19	2.261–63	58, 61
20.97–98	58, 61	2.309	296
20.100–103	296	5.45–46	297
20.143–47	317	5.201–5	296
20.167–70	61–62	6.237	297
20.188	59, 62	7.437–38	59
20.200–201	55	7.437–40	62

Jewish War

		Life	
1.15.6	360	12	16
1.439–42	59	13	361
2	21–22, 35	415	317
2.8.3	361	424–25	59, 62

PHILO OF ALEXANDRIA

On Animals

		On Illustrious Men	
54	297	11	297

On the Embassy to Gaius

		Preliminary Studies	
1–7	298	74–76	297
114–15	69		
144–45	177	*Providence*	
182	297	2.64	298
292–93	69		
299–305	303–4	*On Rewards and Punishments*	
370	297	79–172	300
373	298	85–98	300–301
		91–93, 94–96	301

Against Flaccus

1	298	93–97	305–6
36–40	299, 301–2	127–61	301
72, 73–77	302–3	165	306
74	299		
191	298	*On Special Laws*	
		1.315	58

Hypothetica

		2.39–222	300
8	21	2.63–64	304
8.7.3–6	304–5	3.1–6	297

EARLY CHRISTIAN LITERATURE

Acts of Peter

		Clement of Alexandria	
24	223	*Exhortation to the Greeks*	
		12.120	182

Ambrosiaster

		The Instructor	
Quaestiones Veteris et Novi Testamenti		3.1	223
115.12	318		

Didache

1.2	300
1.2b	7
10.6	344
14	367

Eusebius

Church History

2.4.2	296
2.5.7	298
2.17.1	297
2.17.1–2	297–98
3.39.15	138

Gospel of Thomas

2.1	136
14	281
16	362
96	12
100	136

Ignatius of Antioch

Romans

7.3	367

Smyrnaeans

8.2	367

Infancy Gospel of Thomas

2.1	136

Irenaeus

Against Heresies

1.26	85–86

Justin Martyr

First Apology

65–67	368
66.4	179

Origen

Against Celsus

1.37	82, 84–85

Tertullian

Apologeticum

39	368

On Baptism

5	179

On the Crown

3	368
15	179

Prescription against Heretics

40	179

Theodosius II

Codex Theodosianus

3.13.1	315
3.16.2	318

EARLY JEWISH LITERATURE

Mishnah

Berakhot

5.1, 5	158–59

Yoma

8.9	70–71

Sukkah

2.9	212

Ta'anit

3.8	152–53

Megillah

4.4–10	239

Gittin

9.10	317

Baba Qama

8.1, 6	290

Sanhedrin

10	345

'Eduyoth

2.10	247
4.6	361

Avodah Zarah

2.6	361

'Avot

1	17
1.1	12
3.9–10	157–58

Kelim

1.1–4, 6–8	271–73, 275

Oholoth

5.5	52

Parah

8.5–7	52

Tohorot

3.1–4, 9–10	361

Yadaim

3.5	286
4.6	292

Tosefta

Berakhot

3.20	159

Babylonian Talmud
  Berakhot
    9b   287
    31b   218
    33a   159–60
    34b   160
    62a   361
  Shabbat
    14b   52
    17b   361
    31a   17
    115a   240
    153a   218
  'Erubin
    69b   274
  Pesahim
    68a   242
  Ta'anit
    23a   155–56
    24–25   161
    25b   71
  Megillah
    3a   242
    23b–25a 239
    32a   286
  Hagigah
    25a   361
  Ketubot
    50a   156
  Sotah
    8b   248
    12a   345
  Gittin
    20a   34
    56b   23
  Baba Qama
    79b   218
    92a   290
  Baba Batra
    120a   345
  Sanhedrin
    22a   317
    43a   19, 194
  Avodah Zarah
    36a–b   361
  Zebahim
    22b   287
    55a   274
  Menahot
    29b   156
    99b   288

Jerusalem Talmud
  Berakhot
    2.8 [5c] 220
  Ketubot
    4.4   288

Avot de Rabbi Natan
  A.4   23
  A.24   221
  B.31   163

Mek[h]ilta de-Rabbi Ishmael
  Pisha
    14   344
  Beshalah
    3   214
    4   214
    5   214–15
  Bahodesh
    6. 136–43 71
  Yitro
    9   277–78

Sifra
  3.3   213
  4.1   277
  10.8   276
  11.14   213
  13.16, 19 276

Sifre
  84   215–16
  161   277

Genesis Rabbah
  8.27   216–17
  25.20 345
  86.2   217

Exodus Rabbah
  1.13, 19 345
  3.6   287
  25.1   286

Deuteronomy Rabbah
  2.24   220–21

Lamentations Rabbah
  2.4   163

Ecclesiastes Rabbah
  3.11   219

Midrash Tanhuma
  Massei 1   291

Targum Onqelos
  Ex 15.18   248

Targum Neophyti I
  Gen 4.8   241

Targum Pseudo-Jonathan
  Gen 21.21   241
  Gen 38.25   248
  Lev 19.18, 34   245
  Lev 19.21   239
  Lev 22.28   244–45
  2 Sam 5.8   250
  2 Sam 23.4   250
  Isa 24.23   248
  Isa 31.4   248
  Isa 35.6   250
  Isa 40.9   248
  Isa 52.7   248
  Ezek 7.7   248
  Oba 21   248
  Mic 4.6–8   250
  Zeph 3.19   250
  Zech 14.9   248

Targum Exodus
  2.1   345
  12.42   344
  15.18   344

Targum 1 Samuel
  8.3   249
  12.3   249

Targum 2 Samuel
  14.14   249

Targum Isaiah
  5.1–7   247
  5.17b   242
  5.23   249
  6.9–10   245
  8.19   249
  24.23   248
  25.6–8   248
  27.8   248
  31.4   248
  32.6   250
  33.15   249
  41.8–9   249
  42.3, 7   249
  43.10, 20   249
  44.1   249
  48.6a   250
  50.11   246, 252
  53.3–9   243
  57.3   250
  66.24   246

Targum Jeremiah
  2.2   250
  23.28b   250
  33.25   250

Targum Hosea
  11.1   250
  13.3   250

Targum Zephaniah
  1.12   249
  2.2   250

Targum Zechariah
  11.12–13   250
  12.10   251
  14.21   251

Targum Job
  36.7   248

Targum Psalms
  118.23–29   344

SAMARITAN LITERATURE

Memar Marqah
  4.12   58

INDEX OF ANCIENT PERSONS

Aaron, 113–17, 342
Abiathar, 293
Abigail, 340
Abraham, 5, 14, 57, 69, 72, 121–22, 225, 238, 248, 264, 293, 340, 347, 349, 399
Achilles, 26, 79–80, 375–83, 386
Adam, 14, 106–8, 216–17
Aelian, 144
Aemilianus, 202–4
Aeneas, 26, 79–80, 85, 378–80, 385–86
Aeschylus, 83, 372
Aesop, 2, 29, 222–37
Agamemnon, 375, 378
Agathe Tyche, 335
Agathos Daimon, 335
Agrippinilla, 323, 326
Ahikar, 225
Aion, 180, 184–86
Albinus, 22
Alcmene, 80, 83–84
Alexander Jannaeus, 16–17, 127
Alexander Severus, 318
Alexander the Great, 14–15, 26, 46–47, 82–84, 92, 145–46, 167, 316, 393
Amata, 378
Ami, Rabbi, 288
Amphictione, 81–82
Amram, 345
Amulius, 81
Ananus, 22
Anaxarchus of Abdera, 386, 393
Anaxilaides, 81
Anchises, 79–80
Andromache, 375, 377–78, 380, 383
Antho, 81
Antigonus, 18
Antinoüs, 332–35
Antiochus IV Epiphanes, 15, 390–92
Antipater, 17–18
Antonia, 296
Antoninus Pius, 313–14, 320
Aphrodite, 26, 44, 79–80, 324. *See also* Venus

Apis, 83
Apollo, 26, 80–85, 168, 223, 228–29, 233–34, 236, 323, 376–77, 379, 381
Apollonius of Tyana, 2, 8, 26–28, 81–84, 169–70, 173–75, 386, 393–97
Apthonius, 132
Apuleius of Madauros, 2, 181, 193–205, 224
Aqiba (Akiva), Rabbi, 71, 163, 247, 294, 317, 347
Aquila, 400
Aretas IV, 56
Arete, 335
Aristaeus, 26, 80
Aristobulus, 17–18
Ariston, 81–83
Arrian, 84
Artapanus, 225
Asclepius, 26, 28, 44, 80, 83, 85, 166–78, 196
Athanaeus, 252
Athena, 376, 379
Attis, 181
Augustus Caesar, 18, 26, 41–45, 47, 49, 66–67, 73–76, 82–83, 170, 177, 302, 304, 310, 312–13, 385
Aulus Gellius, 82, 84
Avtolas the Elder, Rabbi, 214
Azizus of Emesa, 317

Babatha, 316
Bacchus, 195–96
Bartimaeus, 375
Bathsheba, 210
Belial, 113, 122–23
Bellona, 329, 388
Ben Zoma, Rabbi, 347
Bendis, 324, 328–29
Berenice (daughter of Herod Agrippa I), 317
Berenice (mother of Herod Agrippa I), 296
Bitenosh, 92
Boaz, 340
Bun bar Hiyya, Rabbi, 219–20

Cadmus, 80
Caecilius, 319
Caiaphas, 40, 53, 55, 57, 368, 386
Cain and Abel, 107, 240–42
Caius, 342
Calpurnius Siculus, 170, 176
Caracalla, 314
Cato, 143
Catullus, 59, 62
Cerinthus, 85
Chavion of Megalopolis, 82
Chedorlaomer, 121
Cicero, 72–73, 80, 85, 312, 319
Claudius, 22–23, 36, 45–46, 296–97, 313
Clearchus, 81
Clement of Alexandria, 182, 223, 341
Cleopatra, 18, 66
Codrus, 385, 387
Constantine, 315, 318
Constantius, 318
Corbulo, 296
Cornelius, 375
Coronis, 80, 168
Costobarus, 317
Cumanus, 22
Cyrene, 80

Damis, 394, 396–97
Danae, 80
Daniel, 2, 14, 87–92, 215, 340
David, 5, 11, 14, 16, 31, 91–92, 113–14, 123,
    129–30, 140, 145, 210–11, 254, 256,
    261–62, 293, 301, 353, 397–98
Decius (Emperor), 368
Decius (Publius Decius Mus), 385, 387, 389
Deïphobus, 376, 379, 381–82
Demeter, 80, 181
Demetrius, 392, 396–97
Demetrius of Phalerum, 222
Demetrius III of Syria, 127
Demosthenes, 139, 373
Diana, 332–35
Dio Cassius, 36, 76, 252, 299
Dio Chrysostom, 16, 75–76
Diocles of Peparethus, 81
Diodorus of Sicily, 80, 83–84
Diogenes Laertius, 37, 81, 85, 133, 136–37,
    143–44, 169, 172–73, 222, 386, 393
Dionysius of Halicarnassus, 80–81, 84
Dionysus (Dionysos), 8, 26, 80, 323, 326, 329,
    374–75. See also Bacchus; Liber
Diotogenes, 301

Domitian, 24, 76, 386, 394
Domna Julia, 169
Drusilla, 22, 317

Eleazar, Rabbi, 217–18
Eliazar ben Azariah, Rabbi, 347
Eliezar (Hasmonean), 15
Eliezar ben Simeon, Rabbi, 23
Eliezer (martyr in 2 Maccabees), 389–90, 397–98
Eliezer (priest in 3 Maccabees), 68
Eliezer, Rabbi, 293–94, 317, 347
Elijah, 2, 13, 57, 59, 353, 382
Elisha, 2, 13, 27, 57, 149, 253
Elisha ben Abuyah, Rabbi, 221
Empedocles, 169, 172–73
Ennius, 85
Enoch, 92, 102–4
Epameinondas, 143
Epaphus, 83
Ephraim, 359
Epictetus, 33, 75–76, 297
Erastus, 328
Eratostheues, 82
Essenes, 16, 25, 110–11, 121, 128, 257, 342
Esther, 110, 225, 242, 342
Ethiopian official, 126
Euripides, 138, 372–73
Europa, 80
Euryalus, 380
Eurycleia, 340
Eusebius, 138, 252, 296–98, 300
Eve, 14
Ezekiel, 116, 287
Ezekiel the Tragedian, 373

Fabius Pictor, 81
Fadus, 22, 58, 61
Felix, 22, 58, 61–62
Festus, 22, 59, 62
Flaccus, 21, 298–99, 301–3
Florus, 23, 83

Gaius (jurist), 310, 313, 319
Gaius Caligula, 19, 21–22, 43–44, 69,
    297–99, 303
Galen, 297
Gamaliel (Gamliel) I, Rabbi, 217–18, 240, 350
Gamaliel II, Rabbi, 24
Gavius Squilla Gallicanus, 323
George Syncellus, 37, 405
Germanicus, 296
Great Mother, 324, 328, 330. See also Kybele

Hadrian, 47, 333, 358
Hadrian of Tyre, 195
Hanina ben Dosa, Rabbi, 13, 28, 151–52, 157–65
Hannah, 217–18
Harmonia, 80
Hector, 374–83, 386
Hecuba, 375–79, 381, 383
Helen, 378, 383
Hephaestus, 376, 379
Hera, 80, 82. See also Juno
Hercules, 26, 80, 175
Hermes, 80, 375, 377–78. See also Mercury
Hermogenes of Tarsus, 27, 132–33, 136–40
Herod Agrippa I, 21–22, 36, 296, 299, 302, 317, 375, 378–80
Herod Agrippa II, 18, 22–23
Herod Antipas, 19–21, 24–25, 49–50, 54, 56, 60, 254, 317
Herod Archelaus, 19
Herod Philip, 21, 56, 60
Herod the Great, 8, 18, 21, 25, 47–49, 52, 60, 256, 316–17, 345
Herodias, 19, 21, 26, 56, 60, 317
Herodotus, 222
Hesiod, 139, 225, 372–73
Hestia, 335
Hezekiah, 149
Hilaria, 181
Hillel, Rabbi, 17, 52, 242, 293–94, 352, 361
Hippolytus, 114, 170
Homer, 2, 36, 73, 79–80, 138, 191–92, 225, 340–41, 372–78, 381–82, 386
Honi the Circle-Drawer, Rabbi, 2, 28, 150–58, 161–65
Honorius, 318
Horace, 73–74
Hoshiya, Rabbi, 216
Hygeia, 335
Hypseus, 80
Hyrcanus II, 17–18

Iamblichus, 169, 172
Iasion, 80
Idaeus, 377–78
Io, 83
Irenaeus, 85
Isaac, 27, 92, 248, 349
Isaiah, 2, 14, 59, 127, 129–30, 149, 210, 220–21, 243, 400–404
Isis, 28, 181, 193, 195, 197–99, 223, 227–28, 324, 328–29, 360

Jacob, 68–69, 248–49, 345, 348–49, 353, 357, 362–63
James, brother of Jesus, 20, 22–23, 40, 53, 55
Jannes, 204
Janus, 388
Jason (High Priest), 15
Javolenus, 312–13, 319
Jehu, 342
Jeremiah, 14
Jerome, 297
Joab, 340
Jochebed, 345
John (brother of James), 51
John Hyrcanus, 57
John of Gischala, 23
John the Baptist, 6, 9, 17, 19, 25–26, 49, 53, 55–63, 112–13, 117–18, 195, 204, 250, 253–54, 281, 317, 375
Jonah, 14, 137, 206
Jonathan (Maccabee), 16
Jonathan ben Uzziel, Rabbi, 242
Joseph (husband of Mary), 40, 50, 53, 79, 85, 93, 254, 317
Joseph (son of Caiaphas), 53
Joseph (son of Jacob), 35, 64, 67–69, 216–17, 225, 357–65
Joseph bar Chiyya, Rabbi, 242
Joseph of Arimathea, 383
Josephus, 10–11, 15–17, 20–26, 35, 50, 55–63, 75, 110, 127, 149, 152, 164, 167, 247, 299–300, 317, 342, 361, 373
Joshua, 57–59
Joshua, Rabbi, 347
Judah Maccabee, 15
Judah the Patriarch, Rabbi, 163, 207, 214
Julia Severa, 325–26, 331
Julian (jurist), 312, 314, 318, 320
Julian the Apostate, 318
Julius Africanus, 37, 405–6
Julius Archelaus, 317
Julius Caesar, 18, 28, 42, 73, 170, 175–76
Julius Gaius Alexander, 296–97
Juno, 379. See also Hera
Jupiter, 83, 84–85, 170, 329, 336, 379, 388. See also Zeus
Justin Martyr, 179, 252
Justin of Tiberius, 15
Justin II, 318
Justinian, 318
Justinus, 385, 387
Juturna, 379

Karabas, 299, 301–2
Kore, 181
Kybele, 181. *See also* Great Mother

Laban, 345, 348
Labeo, 312, 319
Laertes, 375
Lamech, 92, 102–4
Latinus, 378
Lazarus, 34, 339
Liber, 195–96. *See also* Dionysus
Livy, 37, 385, 387–89
Lot, 340
Lucan, 175
Lucius, 181, 193, 197, 199, 200
Lycurgos, 232–33
Lysander, 141–42

Maecenas, 312, 319
Magius Maximus, 302
Manasseh, 359
Manlius, 387–89
Marcellus, 313
Marcus Valerius, 387
Mariamne (Mariamme), 19, 21, 60, 317
Marc Antony, 18, 66, 296
Mars, 26, 80–81, 84–85, 388
Mary (mother of Jesus), 4, 10, 79, 85, 93, 317
Mary and Martha, 9, 34, 339
Meir, Rabbi, 217–18, 220
Melchizedek (Melkisedek), 27, 93, 104–8, 113, 120–23
Men, 328
Menander, 372
Menelaus, 15
Menophilus, 318
Mercury, 196, 203. *See also* Hermes
Messalina, 313
Methuselah, 92, 102, 104, 106
Mezentius, 379
Michael, 106–8, 120, 122
Moses, 8, 11, 14, 17, 19, 35, 58–59, 60, 79, 111, 113, 117, 156, 167, 195, 204, 213, 215, 225, 286, 291, 300, 304, 344–45, 390–91

Naaman, 253
Naomi, 340
Nathan, 210–11
Nathan, Rabbi, 71–72, 221
Nectanebo, 232–33
Neith, 358
Nero, 23, 36, 44–45, 75, 176, 341, 366
Nerva, 394–95

Nestor, 375
Nicocreon, 393
Nike, 335
Nir, 93, 104–8
Noah (Noe), 27, 92–93, 102–7
Novensiles, 388
Numa, 83
Numitor, 84

Octavia, 296
Odysseus, 173, 340–41, 374–75
Olympias, 82, 84
Onesimus, 329
Onias III, 15
Origen, 82, 84–85
Orodes, 379
Osiris, 83, 181
Ovid, 74, 80, 85

Paccius, 386
Papias, 138
Papinian, 315
Paris, 378
Patroclus, 376
Paul (jurist), 313, 316, 319–20
Paul of Tarsus, 4, 9–10, 17, 22, 26, 35, 36, 58, 64, 72, 86, 89, 91, 180, 193, 326, 328–29, 343, 368
Paulus Fabius Maximus, 43
Peleus, 79–80, 377
Peneius, 80
Penelope, 340
Pentephres (Potiphera), 357–58, 362
Perictione, 81
Persephone, 80, 396
Perseus, 80
Peter, 4, 40, 51, 138, 146–47, 327, 375
Petronius, 35, 224, 341
Pharisees, 10, 16–19, 21, 23–25, 31, 35–36, 52, 55, 127, 257, 267, 281–83, 291–94, 297–99, 303–4, 339
Philip II of Macedon, 82, 145–46
Philo Epicus, 373
Philo of Alexandria, 10–11, 21–22, 31, 33, 35–36, 58, 69, 110, 170, 177, 225, 247, 296–308, 373
Philodemus, 297, 373
Philostratus, 27–28, 37, 81–84, 169, 173–75, 195, 252, 386, 393–97
Phineas, Rabbi, 219
Phoebe, 326, 328
Plato, 26, 81–85, 196–97, 202–3, 222, 224, 297

Plautus, 224
Pliny the Elder, 16, 110, 366
Pliny the Younger, 36, 195, 326, 366–71
Plotinus, 297
Plutarch, 27, 36–37, 80–84, 136, 141, 143,
    145–46, 299, 386, 392–93
Polemo of Cilicia, 317
Polyphemus, 375
Pompeius Trogus, 37, 385, 387
Pompey, 17–18, 31, 67, 256, 310
Pontius Pilate, 4, 14, 19–20, 22, 24–26,
    35–36, 40, 47, 55, 57, 60–61, 298–99,
    303–4, 368, 383
Porphyry, 81, 169, 172
Poseidon, 44
Priam, 375–78, 381–83
Prochurus, 298
Proculus, 318
Promathion, 81
Prometheus, 83
Proteus, 27, 81–84
Ptolemy, 15
Pythagoras, 16, 28, 81, 136, 167, 166–78
Pythias, 81

Quintillian, 136
Quirinus, 388

Rachel, 357
Re, 358
Rebecca, 357
Remus, 81, 84
Reuben, Rabbi, 219
Rhea, 80–81, 84
Romulus, 26, 80–81, 84–85
Ruth, 206, 340

Sabinus, 318
Sadducees, 16–19, 25, 55, 111, 127, 292
Salome (sister of Herod the Great), 317
Salome Alexandra, 17, 60
Samson, 27, 92
Samuel, 27, 92, 340
Samuel Pargarita, Rabbi, 220
Sarah, 357
Sarapis, 328
Satan, 13, 27, 89, 293
Saul, 211, 342
Scipio Africanus, 72–73
Sejanus, 298
Semele, 80, 83
Seneca, 143–44
Severus, 314

Shammai, Rabbi, 17, 52, 317, 361·
Sicarii, 23, 59, 62
Silas, 36, 368, 375
Silius, 313
Silvanus, 326
Simeon b. Shatah, Rabbi, 153–54, 163
Simeon bar Kochba (Kokba), 27, 71, 150,
    162–63
Simon (Jesus' host), 339
Simon (Maccabee), 16
Simon bar Giora, 23
Socrates, 8, 222, 224, 386, 393
Solomon, 14, 342
Solon, 323
Sopanim, 93, 104–6
Sophocles, 372
Sosates, 373
Speusippus, 81
Stephanos, 328
Stilpon, 386, 392
Suetonius, 4, 26, 74, 83, 296
Sulla, 310
Symmachus, 400

Tacitus, 176–77, 252
Tarchetius, 81
Tarphon, Rabbi, 347
Teacher of Righteousness, 16, 67, 111–12,
    117, 127–28
Teratius, 81
Terentia, 312, 319
Tertullian, 140, 179
Thallus, 20, 37, 405–6
Theodosius II, 315
Theodotus, 373
Theon, 132–33, 136–39, 141, 143
Therapeutae/Therapeutrides, 10, 21,
    297–98, 360
Thetis, 26, 79–80, 379
Theudas, 22, 26, 58, 61
Thomas, 341
Tiberius, 24, 41, 47, 49, 299, 303–4
Tiberius Julius Alexander, 22, 24,
    296–97
Tiresias, 375
Titus, 23–24, 296
Trajan, 47, 75, 195, 326, 358, 366–71
Trebatius, 312, 319
Turnus, 375, 378–80, 386
Tyndares, 83

Ulpian, 311–14, 318, 321
Uriah the Hittite, 210–11

Venus, 85, 379. *See also* Aphrodite
Vergil (Virgil), 73, 372, 375, 378–80, 386
Vespasian, 23–24, 28, 176–77
Vitellius, 299

Xanthos, 228–32

Yochanan ben Torta, Rabbi, 163
Yochanan ben Zakkai (Jochanan ben Zakkai),
   Rabbi, 23–24, 70, 155, 157, 160, 163,
   217–18, 292–93

Yosi, Rabbi, 288–89
Yudan, Rabbi, 216–17

Zealot(s), 13, 23, 25
Zechariah, 116
Zeira, Rabbi, 220
Zeus, 26, 28, 44, 66, 75, 80–81, 83–84,
   168, 170, 191–92, 228–29, 235–37, 323,
   335–36, 375–76, 381, 394. *See also*
   Jupiter
Zoroaster, 202, 204, 278–79